5

THE BOOK OF

Great

Conversations

EDITED, FROM HISTORICAL SOURCES,

IN DRAMATIC FORM AND WITH

BIOGRAPHICAL SKETCHES, BY

Louis Biancolli

SIMON AND SCHUSTER, NEW YORK

ACKNOWLEDGMENTS

Frederick the Great (1) (2) from *Frederick the Great* by Henri de Catt, translated by F. S. Flint; published by Constable & Co. Ltd., London.

Ancien Régime dialogue and Jean-Jacques Rousseau (1) (2) from *Memoirs of Madame d'Epinay*, translated by E. G. Allingham; published by Routledge and Kegan Paul Ltd., London.

Jean-Jacques Rousseau (3) from *Dialogue with Rousseau*, from the manuscript versions in the Malahide Papers, first published and copyrighted in 1928 by Ralph H. Isham; by permission of The Viking Press, Inc.

Casanova-Voltaire dialogue from *Casanova's Memoirs*, translated by Arthur Machen; by permission of Alfred A. Knopf, Inc.

Napoleon (3) from *With Napoleon in Russia* by General de Caulaincourt, edited by George Libaire, copyright 1935 by William Morrow and Company, Inc.; by permission of William Morrow and Company, Inc.

Napoleon (7) from *A Diary of St. Helena* by Lady Malcolm, edited by Sir Arthur Wilson, K.C.I.E.; published by George Allen & Unwin Ltd., London.

Wagner-Rossini dialogue from *La Visite de R. Wagner à Rossini* by E. Michotte; published by Librairie Fischbacher, Paris.

Lincoln dialogue from *Lincoln Talks*, edited by Emanuel Hertz; by permission of The Viking Press, Inc.

Bismarck dialogue from *Bismarck's Table Talk*, edited by Charles Lowe; published by Grevel & Company, Ltd., London.

The Goncourt Brothers dialogues from *The Goncourt Journals* by Edmond and Jules Goncourt, translated by Lewis Galantiere, copyright 1937, Doubleday & Company, Inc.

Alfred Lord Tennyson dialogue from *William Allingham: A Diary*, edited by H. Allingham and D. Radford, published by Macmillan & Co. Ltd., London; by permission of Henry W. Allingham.

Oscar Wilde dialogue from *Echo de Paris* by Laurence Housman; published by Jonathan Cape Ltd., London.

Thomas Hardy dialogue from *Real Conversations* by William Archer; published by William Heinemann Ltd., London.

Anatole France-Auguste Rodin dialogue from *Rambles with Anatole France* by Sandor Kemeri, translated by Emil Lengyel, published by J. B. Lippincott Company; by permission of Emil Lengyel.

George Bernard Shaw dialogue from *Thinking It Over* by Hesketh Pearson, published by Harper & Brothers; originally printed in *The Adelphi* magazine, London; by permission of Hesketh Pearson.

Thomas Masaryk (1) from *Conversations with Masaryk* by Emil Ludwig; published by Robert M. McBride and Company.

Thomas Masaryk (2) from *Masaryk on Thought and Life* by Karel Capek, translated by M. R. Weatherall; by permission of The Macmillan Company and George Allen & Unwin Ltd., London.

Clemenceau dialogue from *Georges Clemenceau* by Jean Martet, translated by Milton Waldman, copyright 1930, Longmans, Green & Co., Inc.

MANUFACTURED IN THE UNITED STATES OF AMERICA
AMERICAN BOOK—STRATFORD PRESS, INC., NEW YORK

To
my beloved wife
EDITH

In Praise of Conversation

The best of life is conversation. EMERSON

Discussion: The anvil on which the spark of truth is struck forth.
WEBSTER

It is good to rub and polish our brain against that of others.
MONTAIGNE

Conversation is the image of the mind. As the man is, so is his talk. PUBLILIUS SYRUS

A great thing is a great book, but greater than all is the talk of a great man. EARL OF BEACONSFIELD

The free conversation of a friend is what I would prefer to any entertainment. HUME

The world is best enjoyed and most immediately while we converse blessedly and wisely with men. THOMAS TRAHERNE

"Let me not live," saith Aretine's Antonia, "if I had not rather hear thy discourse than see a play." ROBERT BURTON

A single conversation across the table with a wise man is better than ten years' study of books. LONGFELLOW

There is no arena in which vanity displays itself under such a variety of forms as in conversation. PASCAL

There studious let me sit
And hold high converse with the mighty dead.

JAMES THOMSON

That is the happiest conversation where there is no competition, no vanity, but a calm, quiet interchange of sentiments.

DR. JOHNSON

If it were not for respect for human opinions, I would not open my window to see the Bay of Naples for the first time, whilst I would go five hundred leagues to talk with a man of genius whom I had not seen.

MME. DE STAEL

The tone of good conversation is brilliant and natural; it is neither tedious nor frivolous; it is instructive without pedantry, gay without tumultuousness, polished without affectation, gallant without insipidity, waggish without equivocation.

ROUSSEAU

Intellectual conversation, whether grave or humorous, is only fit for intellectual society; it is downright abhorrent to ordinary people, to please whom it is absolutely necessary to be commonplace and dull.

SCHOPENHAUER

There is a sort of knowledge beyond the power of learning to bestow, and this is to be had in conversation; so necessary is this to understanding the characters of men that none are more ignorant of them than those learned pedants whose lives have been entirely consumed in colleges and among books.

FIELDING

Wise, cultivated, genial conversation is the last flower of civilization, and the best result which life has to offer us,—a cup for gods, which has no repentance.   EMERSON

If the minds of men were laid open, we should see but little difference between that of the wise man and that of the fool. The great difference is that the first knows how to pick and cull his thoughts for conversation, by suppressing some and communicating others; whereas the other lets them all indifferently fly out in words.   ADDISON

I praise God for you, Sir; your reasons at dinner have been sharp and sententious; pleasant without scurrility, witty without affectation, audacious without impudency, learned without opinion, and strange without heresy.   SHAKESPEARE

Conversation is the music of the mind, an intellectual orchestra where all the instruments should bear a part but where none should play together.   COLTON

Macaulay is like a book in breeches . . . He has occasional flashes of silence that make his conversation perfectly delightful.   SYDNEY SMITH

Solitary reading will enable a man to stuff himself with information; but, without conversation, his mind will become like a pond without an outlet—a mass of unhealthy stagnature. It is not enough to harvest knowledge by study; the wind of talk must winnow it and blow away the chaff; then will the clear, bright grains of wisdom be garnered, for our own use or that of others.   WILLIAM MATTHEWS

On the Ethics of
Publishing Private Conversations

GONCOURT: The conversations which I have reported are a kind of stenographic record. They reproduce not only the ideas of the speakers but most often their very expressions. I am convinced that any open-minded reader gifted with some insight will recognize that my desire, my ambition, was to make the men I portrayed real. Nothing in the world would have induced me to attribute words to them which they did not speak.

HURET: No doubt what they said was still very fresh in your mind when you wrote it down?

GONCOURT: Why, I wrote everything down the same evening, or, at the very latest, the following morning. There was absolutely no danger of confusion.

HURET: Monsieur Renan's objection is not only against the alleged inaccuracy of your "phonography" but also against the fact that you divulged matters discussed in confidence.

GONCOURT: Yes, I know. Monsieur Renan regards me as an indiscreet person. I acknowledge the reproach. Yet I am not at all sorry for what I did. My indiscretions are not revelations of private life, but in every sense revelations of the thoughts and ideas of my contemporaries—documents for the intellectual history of the period. Yes, I repeat . . . I am not at all sorry for what I did, for since the world began the only interesting memoirs have been written by indiscreet people. My only crime is that, at their date of publication, twenty years after I wrote them down, I am still alive—for which, to be perfectly frank, I am not very remorseful.

—EDMOND DE GONCOURT to JULES HURET (*Echo de Paris*, 1890)

TABLE OF CONTENTS

INTRODUCTION   xxi

Socrates

HE CHIDES HIS DISCIPLES FOR BEHAVING LIKE WOMEN AS   3
    HE PREPARES TO TAKE THE HEMLOCK. "I sent away the
    women, for I have heard that a man should die in peace."

Michelangelo

1. WHILE COMPARING FLEMISH AND ITALIAN PAINTING HE   8
    PAUSES TO EXPLAIN WHY ARTISTS ARE UNSOCIABLE.
    "His Holiness embarrasses me when he asks me why I don't come to
    see him more often."

2. WAS DANTE RIGHT TO CONSIGN BRUTUS AND CASSIUS TO   23
    HELL FOR MURDERING CAESAR? "Whoever kills a tyrant
    kills not a man but a beast disguised as a man."

Frederick the Great

1. JUST BEFORE THE BATTLE A GERMAN CONQUEROR ANA-   32
    LYZES A FRENCH TRAGEDIAN'S VERSES. "When you have
    been accustomed for a long time, as I have been, to all this brawl of
    battle, you will not think it strange that, on the eve of the day on
    which a battle is to be fought, anyone should amuse himself as I am
    doing."

2. DURING THE BATTLE HE TWITS AN AIDE FOR BELIEVING   38
    IN A LIFE AFTER DEATH. "In following your system you have,
    I agree, no risk to run, whether you are mistaken or are not mis-
    taken."

Table of Contents

Ancien Régime

A GROUP OF FRENCH WITS DELIGHT THEMSELVES BY DISCUSSING THE IMPROPRIETIES. "Madame, one is bound to admit that one can never speak up for innocence without being slightly improper."   44

Jean Jacques Rousseau

PORTRAIT IN DIALOGUE I

1. MME. D'ÉPINAY REPROVES HER BOORISH PROTÉGÉ FOR RIDICULING THE COMPANY SHE KEEPS. "I should cut a poor figure among a lot of artificial persons walking tiptoe in their Sunday best—that's not my style at all."   53

2. MME. D'ÉPINAY REVILES ROUSSEAU FOR UNGALLANT SUSPICIONS AND SHOWS HIM THE DOOR. "Monsieur, go! Your presence makes me sick."   64

3. THE OLD REBEL ENJOYS COLD PORK, PICKLED TROUT, AND THE IMPUDENCE OF YOUNG BOSWELL. "Suppose her passion is still lively, and she threatens to tell her husband what has happened unless I agree to continue our intrigue?"   67

Casanova-Voltaire

THE GREAT AMORIST INTERRUPTS HIS MAJOR OCCUPATION TO ARGUE FOR THE NECESSITY OF SUPERSTITION AMONG THE MASSES. "The essence of freedom consists in thinking you have it."   81

Benjamin Franklin

A SKIRMISH IN LONDON WITH BRITAIN'S SECRETARY OF STATE FOR AMERICA. "I must set you right there, Mr. Franklin."   100

Dr. Samuel Johnson

PORTRAIT IN DIALOGUE II

1. AN EXPLOSION AT MR. DILLY'S THE BOOKSELLER.   "I hate   109
   all impudence; but the impudence of a chit's apostasy I nauseate!"

2. WITH PONDEROUS GIBES, HE DENIES THAT MEN HAVE   113
   MORE LIBERTY THAN WOMEN.   "We have all the labor and
   the danger, and the women all the advantages."

3. HE IS CALLENGED TO EXPRESS HIMSELF ON THE ISSUE OF   116
   DEATH AND SALVATION.   "No rational man can die without uneasy apprehension."

4. A DISSENTING MINISTER BRAVES A STORM ON THE RIGHT   118
   OF MINORITIES TO PREACH WHAT THEY BELIEVE.   "But,
   sir, is it not very hard that I should not be allowed to teach my children?"

5. THE ABSTEMIOUS DOCTOR IS NOMINATED TO WRITE TO A   124
   FRIEND OF "THE CLUB" FOR A HOGSHEAD OF CLARET.
   "As I drink none, I am no more than humble scribe."

6. THE SOCIAL WISDOM VERSUS THE PERSONAL FOLLY OF   130
   DRINKING WINE.   "Sir, there is no more reason for your drinking
   with *him*, than for his being sober with you."

7. GOOD FRIDAY THOUGHTS ON GARDENS, PARK WALLS,   134
   CHERRIES, AND ORANGE PEEL.   "In an orchard there should
   be enough to eat, enough to lay up, enough to be stolen, and enough
   to rot upon the ground."

8. WHILE EATING MUTTON AT MRS. THRALE'S, HE FLIRTS IN-   137
   NOCUOUSLY WITH HIS NEIGHBOR FANNY BURNEY.   "Are
   you making mischief between the young lady and me already?"

9. HE PREPARES THE BASHFUL MISS BURNEY FOR AN ENCOUN-   142
   TER WITH THE FORMIDABLE BLUESTOCKING, MRS.
   MONTAGU.   "So, at her, Burney—at her, and down with her!"

10. A BEAUTIFUL HOSTESS REPROACHES HIM ON THE INFRE-   150
    QUENCY OF HIS COMPLIMENTS.   "It constantly moves my in-
    dignation to be applied to, to speak well of a thing which I think con-
    temptible."

11. SIR JOSHUA REYNOLDS FAILS IN HIS DEFENSE OF DAVID   152
    GARRICK.   "Besides, besides, sir, besides—do you not know,—are
    you so ignorant as not to know that it is the highest degree of rudeness
    to quote a man against himself?"

Goethe

PORTRAIT IN DIALOGUE III

1. THE WORLDLY AUTHOR OF *THE SORROWS OF WERTHER* 158
   REBUKES A TIMID UNIVERSITY GRADUATE ON THE SO-
   CIAL TABOOS. "Have you ever been in love yourself?"

2. HE SHOCKS A YOUNG PROFESSOR OF HISTORY BY DISMISS- 163
   ING THE WHOLE RECORD OF THE PAST AS A TISSUE OF
   LIES. "Not everything in history actually happened."

3. A MUSICAL GATHERING AT WEIMAR FEATURING A 176
   TWELVE-YEAR-OLD UNKNOWN—FELIX MENDELSSOHN-
   BARTHOLDY. "Go down into the garden and cool off! You are
   burning like fire!"

4. AN OLYMPIAN OF WORLD LITERATURE TURNS HIS GAZE 180
   ON HIS OWN COUNTRYMEN, AND ON THREE GREAT
   POETS—VOLTAIRE, BYRON, AND HIMSELF. "The Germans
   cannot stop being Philistines!"

5. HE TELLS AN ENGLISH MUNITIONS MANUFACTURER THAT 187
   ROCKETS WOULD HAVE PROVED USEFUL TO SATAN IN
   PARADISE LOST. "In any case, it would have been more poetic."

6. AFTERNOON THOUGHTS ON BISHOPS, ENGLISHMEN, MAD- 190
   HOUSES, AND DANGEROUS BOOKS. "I am ready to follow
   Your Highness into hell, but I am determined not to follow you into a
   madhouse."

Napoleon

PORTRAIT IN DIALOGUE IV

1. FAMILY REUNION IN THE TUILERIES ON THE EVE OF A 199
   CORONATION. "Have you a throne to give me, my dear brother?"

2. NAPOLEON AND GOETHE: A CONQUEROR OF MEN INTER- 204
   RUPTS HIS BREAKFAST TO QUESTION A POET. "Sire, I observe that when Your Majesty travels he does not neglect to take notice
   of even the smallest objects."

3. A FORMER FRENCH AMBASSADOR TO RUSSIA HEARS AN EM- 210
   PEROR PREPARING FOR WAR AMID PROTESTATIONS OF
   PEACE. "I repeat, I do not want war."

4. MOSCOW AND THE ROAD BACK. "Can you picture to yourself, 218
Caulaincourt, the figure you would cut in an iron cage, in the main
square of London?"

5. NAPOLEON AND METTERNICH: AN IMPERIAL TANTRUM 222
OVER THE PROSPECT OF AUSTRIAN NEUTRALITY. "I was
brought up on the battlefield, and a man like me does not concern himself much about the lives of a million men."

6. EPILOGUE TO WATERLOO: A DEFEATED CONQUEROR CON- 230
SIDERS THE SHAPE OF THINGS TO COME. "I shall go to
the United States. They will give me some land. . . . I shall exist on the
products of my fields."

7. FINALE ON ST. HELENA: AN IRATE CAPTIVE LECTURES A 235
BRITISH GOVERNOR ON THE PROPER BEHAVIOR TO-
WARD A FORMER EMPEROR. "I am an emperor in my own
circle, and will be so as long as I live."

Shelley-Trelawny

A POET AND AN ADVENTURER EXCHANGE THOUGHTS ON 243
WOMEN, BOOKS, AND CLIPPERS DURING A TRIP TO LEG-
HORN. "We are indebted to the poets for having transformed
women from what they were to what they are."

Byron-Trelawny

A BITTER EXILE SOUNDS OUT A COUNTRYMAN ON THE SITU- 254
ATION AT HOME AND TOASTS A "ROYAL PERSONAGE."
"If I met the Devil at your table I should treat him as a friend of yours."

Byron-Kennedy

AN ERRANT POET DISCUSSES THE STATE OF HIS SOUL WITH 259
AN ANXIOUS BRITISH MINISTER. "What, then, you think me
in a very bad way?"

Charles Lamb

SOME LONDON WITS GATHER TO CONSIDER WHICH OF THE 274
CELEBRATED DEAD THEY WOULD MOST HAVE LIKED
TO MEET. "Yet, I would rather have seen Chaucer in company with
the author of the *Decameron*, and have heard them exchange their best
stories together."

Hazlitt-Northcote

1. AN ESSAYIST AND A PAINTER EXCHANGE THOUGHTS ON 287
PRUDERY AND NUDITY. "I have seen pictures muffled up to the
chin that had twenty times as much vice in them."

2. APOLOGIA PRO VITA SUA. "You certainly have not spared others. 293
Why should you expect nothing but the milk of human kindness?"

Alexandre Dumas

AN ASPIRING YOUNG WRITER SPURNS A SUGGESTION MADE 298
BY AN OFFICE COLLEAGUE. "Dumas: What *is* France waiting
for? Lassagne: The historical novel. Dumas: But the history of
France is so boring! Lassagne: What!"

Stendhal

A FIERY ADVOCATE OF FREE THOUGHT FINDS HIMSELF IN A 307
LAIR OF ADVERSARIES. "You see, we have no way of understanding one another. I am a rat and you are a cat."

Victor Hugo

AUTHOR MEETS ACTRESS: A YOUNG PLAYWRIGHT SPARS VER- 315
BALLY WITH HIS LEADING LADY OVER THE LINE, "MY
SUPERB AND GENEROUS LION." "The fact is that it seems
awfully funny to me to be calling Monsieur Firmin 'my lion.'"

Heinrich Heine

PORTRAIT IN DIALOGUE V

1. A GERMAN EXPATRIATE PULLS THE LEG OF A REPRESENTA-　324
   TIVE OF THE FRENCH PRESS.　"There's nothing so amusing as
   to mystify your contemporaries, but, taking everything into account,
   there's nothing so difficult."

2. THE BIG THREE: HEINE, BALZAC, AND EUGÈNE SUE CLASH　327
   AT BREAKFAST OVER A SHEAF OF "ISMS," PAUSING LONG
   ENOUGH TO CONSIDER A MARITAL PROBLEM.　"I can't
   understand why fidelity is more strongly demanded of a man than of a
   woman. We lose nothing by a woman's infidelity."

3. A BRITISH VISITOR HEARS A GLOWING TRIBUTE TO HIS　337
   COUNTRYMEN, THE INMATES OF BEDLAM.　"I found Eng-
   lish madmen infinitely saner than my own Germans or than these Parisians—indeed, much saner than myself."

Thomas Carlyle

A GLOOMY DEAN OF ENGLISH LETTERS BEMOANS THE STATE　344
OF ENGLISH MORALS AND POLITICS.　"I see no hope for these
times—they must go to perdition their own way."

Wagner-Rossini

REUNION IN PARIS: A RETIRED COMPOSER OF THE OLD　362
SCHOOL INVITES A FELLOW EXPATRIATE TO EXPOUND
THE MUSIC OF THE FUTURE.　"Ah! Monsieur Wagner—like a
new Orpheus you have no fear of crossing the redoubtable threshold!"

Lincoln

WASHINGTON, D.C., 1864

A NEW ENGLAND MOTHER PLEADS WITH A PRESIDENT FOR　384
THE LIFE OF HER SON OVER A WAR SECRETARY'S PRO-
TEST.　"Don't be in such a hurry, Stanton; listen to any woman
speaking for her son's life."

Bismarck

AT VERSAILLES

THE IRON CHANCELLOR IS OUTSMARTED BY A BOGUS SPAN- 393
ISH GRANDEE DURING THE SIEGE OF PARIS. "No one will
ever make me believe that Paris is a heroic city; but, be that as it may,
we shall soon be in it."

Meanwhile in Paris

ERNEST RENAN PRECIPITATES A LITERARY STORM BY CALL- 400
ING THE BESIEGERS "A SUPERIOR RACE." "The Germans
have very few pleasures, and of these the greatest are hatred, meditation,
and vengeance."

The Goncourt Brothers

RECORDED FRAGMENTS OF INTIMATE COLLOQUIES AMONG 404
FLAUBERT, GAUTIER, DAUDET, ZOLA, TURGENIEFF, AND
OTHERS. "I never go near a woman without a feeling of respect and
surprise at my good luck."

Alfred Lord Tennyson

A POET-LAUREATE REMINISCES ABOUT SOME EARLY LITERARY 415
ENTHUSIASMS AND PUZZLES OVER THE CASE OF JOHN
KEATS. "He was a livery-stable-keeper's son. I don't know where he
got it from . . . unless from heaven."

Leo Tolstoy

AN AMERICAN REFORMER STOUTLY RESISTS THE DOCTRINE 419
OF NON-RESISTANCE IN THE COUNTRY PLACE OF A
GREAT PACIFIST. "KENNAN: Suppose that this bleeding, defenseless, half-naked girl had appealed to you for protection and had thrown
herself into your arms; suppose it had been your daughter—would you
still have refused to interfere by an act of violence? TOLSTOY (silent
for a few moments; his eyes filled with tears): Do you know absolutely
that that thing was done?"

Walt Whitman

A PATRIARCH OF AMERICAN POETRY CELEBRATES HIS SEV-   428
ENTY-SECOND BIRTHDAY WITH CHAMPAGNE AND TES-
TIMONIALS.   "I must say to my friends further along the table that
I am about half blind and I cannot see more than ten feet ahead and
hardly that—else I am sure I should specify them."

Oscar Wilde

THE LAST PHASE: AN EXILE ENTERTAINS SOME FRIENDS IN A   454
PARIS CAFÉ.   "The world will not listen to me now."

Thomas Hardy

WILLIAM ARCHER FEELS OUT HIS HOST ON THE CHANCES OF   475
A MIDNIGHT VISITATION FROM THE SPIRIT WORLD.   "I
seriously assure you that I would give ten years of my life—well, perhaps
that offer is rather beyond my means—to see a ghost."

Anatole France-Auguste Rodin

REUNION AT VILLA SAÏD: A BROKEN FRIENDSHIP IS REPAIRED   490
AT THE SHRINE OF AN ANCIENT STATUE OF APHRODITE.
"A Greek girl with a body like a flower ..."

Shaw-Chesterton

TWO MASTERS OF WIT AND PARADOX BREAK A LANCE OVER   498
THE ABSORPTION OF ALCOHOL.   "There is only one form of
drunkenness I acknowledge—the drunkenness of sobriety."

Thomas Masaryk

1. HOW AN AMIABLE ACADEMIC RECLUSE BECAME A REVO-   507
LUTIONARY AND FOUNDED A COUNTRY.   "It was no use; I
had to bring about the necessary reform by revolutionary means."

2. KAREL CAPEK SOUNDS OUT THE FATHER OF HIS COUNTRY 516
ON HIS RELIGIOUS AND PHILOSOPHICAL BELIEFS. "They
told me that this year the nightingales were singing because they had
plenty of mosquitoes. And a thought passed through my mind: do those
nightingales sing their praises to the Good Lord for those mosquitoes?
And those mosquitoes—that buzzing of theirs, is that also a song of
praise because the nightingales are swallowing them as they fly?"

Clemenceau

AN AGING TIGER BEWAILS THE SOFTNESS OF HIS CONTEMPO- 527
RARIES AND NOSTALGICALLY SURVEYS HIS OWN CA-
REER. "The truth is that all of you are just waiting for an excuse to
twiddle your thumbs."

H. G. Wells-Joseph Stalin

LIBERALISM VERSUS MARXISM. "I am more to the left than you, Mr. 551
Stalin."

INDEX 567

INTRODUCTION

THIS IS a book of recorded talk. Perhaps in these days of dictaphones and sound tracks, "recorded talk" may sound misleading. For the recorders here are only diarists and letter-writers, biographers and autobiographers, not machines. What they record is the talk of statesmen, musicians, artists, and writers of many centuries. As a rule they are not themselves literary artists, these faithful chroniclers. Strictly speaking, only a scant few are men and women of letters. Mostly, they are the friends, secretaries, and associates of people whose words were memorable enough to invite perpetuation in a midnight diary entry or some chatty, gossipy note to a distant correspondent. Much of this recorded conversation was caught in mid-flight, sur le vif, as the French say. Perhaps some diligent scribe has jotted down notes as fast as the social amenities permitted, and often these notes are the sole document of a crucial dialogue in the life of a celebrated man. Frequently, the recording hand has awaited the first moment of solitude to recapture the detail and flavor of the colloquy. And sometimes weeks and months have passed before the remembered talk has entered the annals of time.

We owe them much, these Mmes. d'Épinays and Bölönis, these Eckermanns and Michottes and Henri de Catts. Often they have handed down the only vivid glimpse of a great personality in action, of a giant thinker in a train of thought. Where the biographers have probed and dissected at book-length, these lowlier scribes—always excepting Boswell—have contented themselves with a few flashes of revealing dialogue. For while the great biography joins the portrait gallery of history, the dialogue remains a breath of real life, the candid close-up of the subject, snapped during the greatest sport of all—Talk. Nor should we look for the artist's tell-tale hand in the wording or development of the dialogue. That might mar the effect of realism. For the only effects here are the effects of life itself, erratic, rambling, but natural and spontaneous—in a word, unplanned. Luckily for us, the control and direction of art are usually missing. The slightest hint of design would invite the suspicion of editing, of tampering with the raw material. Thus, these dialogues are not orderly drama directed toward a projected climax. Rarely do they settle an issue or even round out a complete cycle of reasoning. In short, they are not "imaginary conversations," in which the author, using actual or fictitious personages, steers the exchange of ideas into convenient channels of agreement or disagreement.

Yet, in a larger sense they are drama, perhaps the greatest spoken drama of all, that of actual human discourse mirroring the odd, unpredictable ways of man as a creature of reason and impulse. The dramatis personae may not be the Hamlets and Macbeths and Lears, uttering sublime lines and living out their tragic turmoil in brief imitations of life. They are, instead, the Wagners, Rodins, Byrons, Bismarcks, Napoleons and Dr. Johnsons—each called upon to speak some passing thought or pronounce some quick judgment, without hope of recall. We may feel cheated when their discourse is abruptly snapped off at some crucial turn in the conversation. We grow furious at the sudden drift of the talk into some idle current of chit-chat. We are even tempted to revile the chronicler for lapsing into direct discourse and noting blandly that the "fascinating conversation continued in this vein for several hours." Repeatedly, we are reminded of the many hours of magic talk irretrievably lost for want of a recording hand or for sheer indolence and fatigue in the hand scrawling the speedy memorandum.

We are powerless before this laxity. Much as we should desire, we cannot discipline the pen that scribbled a final line at the point of greatest interest. We are in no position to order the material revamped or the dialogue brightened. The interlocutor can never be taken to task for an awkward silence at an exciting juncture. We cannot ask Lady Malcolm to supply further details of an imperial skirmish on St. Helena. We may chide Eckermann for not veering the Olympian Goethe into worldlier channels and for lingering needlessly over details of outmoded scholarship. And soon a more glaring omission confronts us. It dawns on us that very little indeed has survived of the great talk of the past. At the many turning-points in history, around the tables of peace and negotiation, on the eve of battle, our recording angel is conspicuous by his absence. The peace parley or council of war is then handed down in the cold detachment of indirect discourse. The Caesar or Washington or Jefferson is made to utter some terse comment of fulfillment, and the rest is silence, or, at best, a war dispatch.

Chance, we now realize, is our only ally. Design and plan brought the Frenchman De Catt to the side of Frederick the Great to read Racine and Corneille with that warrior-dilettante amid the smoke and smell of dynastic warfare. But pure chance has given us the record of those midnight musings on Alexandrines, hemorrhoids, and the immortal soul. Sheer luck is responsible for the precious report of the reunion of Anatole France and Rodin, Lady Luck, actually, in the shape of the Hungarian

Mme. Bölöni, who not only esteemed these two men but was a trained writer, besides. Without the chance impulse of an obscure Monsieur Michotte, where would we look for an extended and scrupulously detailed account of the historic meeting between Wagner and Rossini? Again, we owe this record to the purest chance, for had this M. Michotte died before transcribing the notes he had jotted down years earlier, our only source would be the few meager lines in Wagner's autobiography.

Yet, all things considered, chance has been fairly generous. Admittedly the best of the world's talk has literally vanished into thin air, with nothing but a scant footnote in history to mark its passing. But the salvage from this Babel of time is large enough to give us the true savor of much that was said. The world, to be sure, has had but one Boswell, the undiscourageable busybody who by sheer persistence and impudence of note-taking bestowed the breath of living speech on the greatest of biographies; the same Boswell, indeed, who braved the ill-temper of Rousseau for some priceless bequest of words to the waiting world. For to this prying meddler we owe not only the survival of Samuel Johnson as The Great Talker, but vivid verbal flashes, too, of the French apostle of Liberty, preserved in a series of lifelike interviews. There is, then, only one Boswell, and it is even possible that the company of great men is safer without the shadowing menace of a second. But there are many smaller Boswells, men and women who have saved the reverberating echo of Dr. Johnson's talk from the arid makeshift of indirect discourse. There is Anna Seward, for instance, confiding in a letter to a friend the best account of that Aetna of rhetoric in eruption. There is Sir Joshua Reynolds, remembering with some admitted liberties his own fumbling futility before this same avalanche of certainty. There are Mrs. Thrale and the indefatigable Miss Burney, all spurred to reminiscent note-taking by the grand pontifications of perhaps the most massive ego in world literature.

We have called this material the heritage of chance. None of these men and women was duty-bound to record the overheard dialogue. Only the inner compulsion to preserve something worth saving prodded them on. Some natural indolence, a growing drowsiness over the midnight diary entry and the final silence would have shrouded the talk of a few hours earlier. For the best of these dialogues were written down the same night, while the words still rang in the diarist's ears. No great effort is needed to discern the passage of time in those dialogues put in writing months and years after the event. Some of the freshness has gone; the sparkle of naturalness is dimmed, and perhaps that welcome crudeness of unedited discourse is lost forever. To the Burneys, the Henri de Catts, the Eckermanns, and Lady Malcolms is due some special citation for sacrificing an hour's sleep to jot down the good talk still fresh in their memory. One envisions them in candlelight, bent over paper and quill, straining to recall in precise wording the give-and-take of the recent colloquy. Theirs was no easy task, for the human impulse to alter and improve and add must often have been strong. While the playwright putting words into the mouths of created characters could do as he pleased, these chroniclers had to abide by the stern edict of accuracy. They were journalists, in a way, with no right to mold the material to suit themselves. Reporters, they were bound, in self-imposed assignment, to transmit the bare facts and to quote the words as spoken. They could have simplified their job and strained their memory less by giving brief résumés of the talk, without the line-by-line sequence of a scene out of a play. The Saint-Simons and Pepyses and Horace Walpoles were journalists, too, magnificent ones in their way; but one misses in their pages the life-like glow of the meticulously itemized and sustained dialogue.

Then, many devoted keepers of journals and diaries affect an irritating modesty. Their subject, the Napoleon or Lord Byron, takes the center of the stage and engages in one long, unbroken monologue after another. Occasionally the gaping listener shyly interposes the pale semblance of a query to remind us that he is there. Most of the memoirs of members of Napoleon's entourage are of this kind, the worshipful record of a long series of operatic solos. Las Cases is such an offender and so are Bourrienne and Montholon. Metternich and Caulaincourt at least speak up. With Lord Byron it is much the same: Lady Blessington extensively reports her "conversations" with the "pilgrim of eternity," but again we have soliloquy rather than colloquy, and a good deal of it in the dully doctored rendering of that glamorous chronicler. We go, instead, to Trelawny for a few pages of sustained duet; just as we consult this fabulous swashbuckler for the best glimpse, in spoken actuality, of the wraithlike Shelley. Perhaps even better than Trelawny, as recorder of Byron's talk, is the Reverend James Kennedy, who visited the poet in Cephalonia on the eve of his departure for death and apotheosis in the malarial marshlands of Missolonghi. This sanguine man of God, a dedicated savior of lost souls, sought him out as an errant genius worth rescuing from the quicksands of sin. The Reverend argued at great length with Byron and the record of their long discourse is extant in Dr. Kennedy's posthumous volume, now some 110 years out of print. A real exchange of opinion marks the playlike dialogue reported, and nowhere else has Byron so frankly unbosomed himself in recorded discourse. Our aim, thus, is dialogue, not monologue, and for that reason even Horace Traubel's fascinating memoirs of Walt Whitman fail to qualify for insertion here. Again it is the beloved vagabond overheard in one unaccompanied aria after another. We appeal, instead, to a long-forgotten report, made by Traubel and a public stenographer, of a birthday "round-table" at Whitman's house in Camden, New Jersey.

Perhaps, after all, these diligent amanuenses are playwrights of a sort—certainly not the manipulators of great action or of startling shifts in the pageant of human psychology—but dramatists none the less. Like the playwrights, they are rendering spoken lines. If the playwrights have art on their side, they, in turn, have history on theirs. They have, moreover, an advantage that is the despair of all writers of historical drama—they possess either the actual words of the character, or a close approximation. They need rarely risk the anachronism of word or value. They are eaves-droppers, not imitators, of life. Naturally, we must exercise caution in distinguishing the actual from the merely veracious. A degree of poetic reconstruction is sometimes inevitable; the swing from the real to the imaginary is always tempting. Plato was probably the great example of this; but his aim, except in a few instances, went beyond literal presentation. What concerned him was the truthful picture of the cross-currents of thought in talkative Athens. In the end we are impressed by the man's prodigious artistic and intellectual powers rather than by the gallery of true-to-life portraits in dialogue. Nevertheless, in the death chamber of Socrates we have no right to suspect Plato of tampering with the facts. There is little poetic adornment in this scene of valiant resignation and there are too many harsh details of reality to suggest more than a hint of creative intervention. In the Phaedo, at any rate, Plato is the man for our book.

With the diaries of Mme. d'Épinay we enter the realm of controversy because of the unsavory glimpses of Rousseau. There we may brush aside the charges and counter-charges of Rousseauans and anti-Rousseauans and weigh the reports of the conversations on their merits. We find that many present this churlish darling of French high society in a highly flattering light, that as a rule there is little discrepancy between the entries in these journals of dialogue and the revealing pages of the Confessions. For the truth of the final clash between Mme. d'Épinay and her lionized pet our guess is as good as that of the scholars. In any event, we are indebted to this urbane and cultivated little woman for some priceless talking pictures of the leisured ranks of the ancien régime. Then, Mme. d'Épinay has this advantage over Rousseau: that she faithfully entered the day's happenings, complete with the spoken word, in her midnight journal. Whatever else Rousseau has bequeathed us, and it is a massive legacy, he did not leave a diary of the day's conversations.

Moreover, we must tread circumspectly through the pages of Laurence

Housman's sustained record of the conversation with Oscar Wilde.* We
do so, however, with the author's own warning that much of it is recon-
structed from the memory of an episode of twenty years before. Yet, the
talk had a basis in fact, and throughout the dialogue Housman has scattered actual words and anecdotes. We begin to suspect he is over-modest
about how much he recalled in precise detail. We even find ourselves
hoping, ironically, that he is a better stenographer than artist. We conclude that if Wilde had not said just that, he probably would have, or
should have. So sound a biographer of Wilde as Hesketh Pearson was
convinced, after close scrutiny and research, that Housman had preserved
far more of what was said than he cared to acknowledge. The same reservation does not apply to Michotte's record of the conversation between
Rossini and Wagner, also published many years after the event. Michotte
had asked permission of the speakers to sit by with a pencil and pad,
promising not to print his transcript till both were dead. Having introduced the two to one another, he retired to a corner of Rossini's study and
assumed a strictly stenographic role.

I must now ask a little sympathy for the few liberties I have taken with
the material. Substantially it remains as the books and magazines have
handed it down. Often the original exists in the dialogue form of the
theater. In many instances, the talk is all there in the form of spoken
dialogue in a work of fiction. In such cases I have merely removed the
quotation marks, eliminated the "he saids" and "she replied" and affixed
the speakers' names in dramatic sequence. Where the chronicler has in-
jected some descriptive word or phrase, I have given it in parentheses, with
little or no change, as a playwright's directions. In some instances I have
rendered a few words of indirect discourse in spoken dialogue, my purpose
being to save the dramatic continuity. Where any such alteration of form
has been made, an admission to that effect will be found in a footnote or
in the brief preface to the dialogue. I was tempted to take greater liberties,
such as linking two or three of Eckermann's conversations into one con-
tinuous unit; but I abstained in the interests of historical accuracy. Where
I have used more than one dialogue from the same source I have indicated

---

* In two other cases I have adopted a more liberal canon of qualification for inclusion
in this book. The first is Sir Joshua Reynolds' sketch of Dr. Johnson on the subject of
David Garrick, though there we have an example of clever reconstruction within the
framework of actuality, both of substance and occasion. The second instance is Baron
Langon's grapevine record of the family council in the Tuileries on the eve of Napoleon's coronation. My reasons for including that obviously doctored account are given
in the preface to my translation of Langon's dialogue. The Baron, at any rate, insisted
he obtained the record from a lady in Napoleon's entourage and gave it to the world as
a plausible report of a known episode. I use it merely as curtain-raiser on the more fully
authenticated drama that follows.

the time intervening between them. Henri de Catt's talks with Frederick the Great offered possibilities of facile patchwork, for in many instances nothing betrayed the break in the resumed conversation. But my judgment rebelled against the use of a synthetic text, especially since this occasional practice might reflect on the integrity of the other dialogues.

I have explained why the straight monologue was omitted, despite the promising title of "Conversation" on the book containing it. I rejected it to preserve some uniformity, just as I had decided that the use of the character-by-character device of theatrical dialogue would provide added consistency. I am prepared to grant that, for verbatim accuracy, few of the dialogues measure up to the Wells-Stalin interview. There a third man was present whose double duty it was to interpret and carefully take down every word uttered; besides which, the transcribed text was later pronounced authentic by both speakers. Still, the remaining dialogues have qualities of their own. Many boast the spontaneity of informal encounter; some have the special charm of chance survival through unofficial hands. Most often they lack the self-consciousness that cannot be avoided where the speakers know that their words will be printed and quoted.

Perhaps I should relate how this idea of a book of actual conversations came to me. One day I was strolling along East 59th Street, New York— a bookhunter's paradise second only to the happy-hunting-grounds of lower Fourth Avenue. For the exorbitant sum of ten cents I purchased an old volume entitled Lives of Celebrated Women, published many years ago by John W. Lovell Company in New York, at "150 Worth Street, Corner Mission Place," as the title page revealed. The three celebrities were Joan of Arc (in the essay of Michelet, misspelled "Mitchelet"), Mary, Queen of Scots (in the brief narrative of Lamartine), and Vittoria Colonna (in the seventy-five-page biography of Thomas Adolphus Trollope, brother of the novelist).

I must confess that my reason for making the extravagant purchase was Vittoria Colonna. This great Italian sonneteer and friend of Michelangelo has always fascinated me. Trollope's biography proved disappointing as a whole, though it was refreshing to find this Victorian writer so genuinely excited over the sonnets of the sixteenth-century Italian poet. Moreover, the quotations and renderings showed a sympathetic insight into the poetry of the period. That much was gratifying to one long enamored of Italian literature in general and of the memory of this fabulous recluse in particular. But the writing was involved and rambling, and I was about to abandon my reading when I came upon what was to me an astounding disclosure. I knew that Vittoria Colonna was idolized by the great painter and sculptor, that her memory was enshrined for all time in some of Michelangelo's own beautiful sonnets. I knew, too, that these two had met and conversed on several occasions. What I did not know was that in the government archives of Lisbon there reposed a manuscript of the Portuguese painter Francesco de Hollanda, containing the report of four actual dialogues with Michelangelo, three of them with Vittoria participating. Of course, my first move was to rush to the library to hunt for the source volume named by Trollope. This was a book by Count A. Raczynski entitled Les Arts en Portugal, published in Paris in 1846, and containing the four dialogues in a French translation commissioned by the author. Trollope himself had located this book by an elaborate chain of references leading to a volume printed in 1857 as part of the Archivio Storico Italiano series of the city of Florence.

Then, with mingled feelings of relief and disappointment, I discovered through the files of the Art Department of the New York Public Library that some years ago the manuscript had been released for publication in Portugal, and that from the Portuguese original of de Hollanda both a German and an English rendering had been made. What I was already excitedly telling myself was a "find" had proved nothing of the sort. Someone had been there before me, and the actual work of salvage was done. The English translation—the work of Aubrey F. G. Bell—had been printed in 1928 in a small volume by the Oxford University Press. I now proceeded to read the four dialogues in the French of Raczynski's unnamed translator, the Portuguese of de Hollanda, and the scholarly and scrupulously accurate version of Bell. Each time I found these dialogues fascinating for some fresh reason. At first, it was merely the thrill of coming upon something new and unsuspected. Then came the thrill of confronting Vittoria Colonna and Michelangelo face to face, as it were. Finally, I noted with sharpening attention the wealth of revealing detail embedded in the talk itself. When I told people of the existence of these dialogues with Michelangelo they were frankly skeptical, but also considerably interested.

I then found myself wondering if a great deal more of this material was not being threatened with ultimate interment in forgotten books. It was an easy next step to resolve on a way of rescuing some of it from oblivion. The answer seemed to be an anthology or treasury of such salvaged talk. Then it came to me that the literary genre of the "imaginary conversation" had almost obscured the existence of a closely allied genre, this "actual conversation." We all knew of Eckermann and Boswell; but once we had named them we had almost exhausted the genre, if genre it was. The great critics had written long essays on Plato, Lucian, Landor, Bishop Berkeley

—the classics of this "imaginary" shelf—but none, as far as I could tell, had dwelt on the real dialogue as anything deserving classification. True, there was small scope here for creative activity, little, perhaps, to warrant a place in literature for this form of writing, except in the case of Boswell. If any literary scholar ever thought about it at all, it was to view such conversations as a branch of reporting or merely as one of the many devices of the memoir form of biography and autobiography.

I do not insist that these dialogues are all literature or that their preservation reveals anything more in the chronicler than a painstaking ideal of honest reporting or approximate reconstruction. I do feel they are documents of unusual human interest. Some, no doubt, are of more specific accuracy than others, but each unquestionably contributes some measure of truth to the final picture of the central figure involved. It may be that these dialogues can best be grouped with letters and diaries as material out of which history and biography are molded. My feeling is that they live in their own right as spoken memorials, casual or crucial, of some actual encounter between two or more people who have shaped human thought and made history. It was with the assurance that they were readable and rewarding in themselves that I resolved to bring several of them together in a single volume.

A final word of explanation about the translations used in this volume. Where an available rendering has been borrowed, I have made due acknowledgment in my prefatory remarks to the conversation. In a few instances I have made my own rendering despite existing translations, and my reasons for doing so will also be found in the respective prefaces. To the best of my knowledge, several of the dialogues are appearing in English for the first time. These include the second of the Michelangelo conversations, the Wagner-Rossini, the Stendhal, two of the Heine dialogues, the Napoleon-Fleury (as well as Baron Langon's jeu d'esprit of the pre-Coronation reunion at the Tuileries), the Goethe-Luden, and the Goncourt sequel to the Bismarck episode of the Siege of Paris. Diligent investigation in several public and university libraries has revealed no translation of these dialogues previous to mine. However, I am prepared to stand corrected on this point. In any case, wherever possible, I have made my own translation directly from the printed text of the original edition.

LOUIS BIANCOLLI

THE BOOK OF

Great
Conversations

Socrates

HE CHIDES HIS DISCIPLES FOR BEHAVING
LIKE WOMEN AS HE PREPARES TO
TAKE THE HEMLOCK.

*I sent away the women, for I have heard
that a man should die in peace.*

IT SEEMED only fitting that a treasury of the world's recorded talk should
begin with the brave farewell prison colloquy of history's most celebrated talker. Fitting, for one thing, because this dauntless old man of
seventy was put to death in an Athenian dungeon in 399 B.C. for defending the right of free speech. Socrates, the self-styled gadfly of the
Greek institutions, died that men might speak out their minds on all
subjects. Fitting, too, because these are the last poignant words of a man
who had loved human discourse with an undying passion. For this Socrates
was the talker par excellence—a magnificent listener no less than a sublime
speaker. It was that gifted and irresponsible god of a man, Alcibiades, who
avowed of Socrates: "He has only to speak and my tears flow." And he
spoke to all who would listen: to politicians and poets, to freemen and
slaves, to prostitutes and ladies of high birth. For several decades a huddle
of young men, locked in deep discourse with this squat, brutish-featured
man, was a daily sight on the streets of Athens. Hundreds of Athenian
youths became better men for listening. Wits were sharpened in the company of this man, sham was unmasked, and truth, or, at any rate, a search
for truth, for the moment replaced a smug, unquestioning way of thinking.
There were many who never forgave Socrates his exposure of fraud and
hypocrisy, many in high office or priestly officialdom who feared his sharp
vision. So they plotted to rid Athens of this apostle of pitiless self-study.
The government indicted him as a public offender. Enemies charged him
with corrupting the youth of Athens and preaching the worship of false
gods. A poet, a tanner, and an orator, shamed for all time, gave the evidence, and this beloved idler, after the most moving and valiant self-defense in history, was found guilty and condemned to death.

It is here in the death chamber, awaiting the fatal cup of hemlock, that
we find this noble warrior of the mind. A stranger knowing nothing of

3

the man would scarcely be impressed by his appearance. Nature has not been very kind to this grotesque, gnomish figure with bulging eyes, broad, stub nose, and coarse, thick lips. One recalls that beside the godly Alcibiades he had been a strange sight indeed. Ironically, perhaps, none has hymned masculine beauty more warmly than this cruelly ill-favored mockery of a man. Perhaps it is best this way, for the unsullied beauty and purity of this man's mind stand out in sharper relief. Out of the great love we instinctively feel for the friendly and ennobling soul beneath, we learn to cherish the very ugliness of this rugged face. We have only to hear a few words to know we are in the presence of a hero. It is but a few days since Socrates has stoutly rejected his friend Crito's facile plan of escape from the death cell. Socrates in flight, he has told the grieving Crito, would be only Socrates the coward playing into his judges' hands. Official Athens would have asked for no better weapon with which to combat his memory. No, he has chosen to die innocent, "a victim not of the laws but of men." And not long before that, in court, Socrates had flung his final taunt to an angry jury: "We go our ways—I to die, and you to live. Which is better only God knows."

Gathered about him in this bleak cell are a group of faithful followers. Of native Athenians we find Antisthenes, Apollodorus, Critobulus and the same Crito. Of those from other lands there are Simmias the Theban and Euclid and Terpsion from Megara. One must not forget Echecrates of Phlius to whom the devoted Phaedo narrates the events in Plato's famous dialogue. By a tragic twist of fate, Plato, who will fashion a lasting memorial to his beloved teacher, is not himself present, being ill at home. . . .

The narrative that follows, though handed down by a man who was not an eyewitness, "has the air of accuracy and truth" in all its painful details. The episode was too deeply lodged in the memory of men for Plato to alter it. It is very possible that in the earlier part of the Phaedo dialogue, Socrates is what we suspect him to be in many of the other dialogues, the mouthpiece of Plato's own magnificent language. But the artist in Plato could only abstain before the simple pathos and realism of this final glimpse of Socrates—Socrates, in the sensitive words of Irwin Edman, "facing the unknown, and comforting his young friends who feel and fear for him in the shadow of his death, urging them to be of good cheer, and persuading them by argument and poetical fable to the 'sweet hope' of immortality." The portion of the Phaedo used below is from the standard translation of Professor Benjamin Jowett, which first appeared in 1871.

SOCRATES: Wherefore, Simmias, seeing all these things, what ought not we to do in order to obtain virtue and wisdom in this life? Fair is the prize, and the hope great. I do not mean to affirm that the description which I have given of the soul and her mansions is exactly true—a man of sense ought hardly to say that. But I do say that inasmuch as the soul is shown to be immortal, he may venture to think, not improperly or unworthily, that something of the kind is true. The venture is a glorious one, and he ought to comfort himself with words like these, which is the reason why I lengthen out the tale. Wherefore, I say, let a man be of good cheer about his soul, who has cast away the pleasures and ornaments of the body as alien to him, and rather hurtful in their effects, and has followed after the pleasures of knowledge in this life, who has adorned the soul in her own proper jewels, which are temperance, and justice, and courage, and nobility, and truth—in these arrayed she is ready to go on her journey to the world below, when her time comes. You, Simmias and Cebes, and all other men, will depart at some time or other. Me already, as the tragic poet would say, the voice of fate calls. Soon I must drink the poison; and I think I had better repair to the bath first, in order that the women may not have the trouble of washing my body after I am dead.

CRITO: And have you any commands for us, Socrates—anything to say about your children, or any other matter in which we can serve you?

SOCRATES: Nothing particular, only, as I have always told you, I would have you look to yourselves. That is a service which you may always be doing to me and mine as well as to yourselves. And you need not make professions. For if you take no thought for yourselves, and walk not according to the precepts which I have given you, not now for the first time, the warmth of your professions will be of no avail.

CRITO: We will do our best. But in what way would you have us bury you?

SOCRATES: In any way that you like; only you must get hold of me, and take care that I do not walk away from you. (*Turning to the others, with a smile.*) I cannot make Crito believe that I am the same Socrates who has been talking and conducting the argument. He fancies that I am the other Socrates whom he will soon see, a deady body—and he asks, How shall he bury me? And though I have spoken many words in the endeavor to show that when I have drunk the poison I shall leave you and go to the joys of the blessed—these words of mine, with which I comforted you and myself, have had, as I perceive, no effect upon Crito. And therefore I want you to be surety for me now, as he was surety for me at the trial: but let the promise be of another sort; for he was my surety to the judges that I would remain, but you must be my surety to him that I shall not remain, but go away and depart. And then he will suffer less at my death, and not be grieved when he sees my body being burned or buried. I would not have him sorrow at my hard lot, or say at the burial, Thus we lay out Socrates, or, Thus we follow him to the grave or bury him. For false words are not only evil in themselves, but they infect the soul with evil. Be of good cheer then, my dear Crito, and say that you are burying my body only, and do with that as is usual, and as you think best.

(*Rises and goes into the bathchamber with Crito, who bids the others wait. Socrates' children are brought into the prison cell after he has taken the bath. The women of the family also enter and Socrates talks with them, giving them a few directions in the presence of Crito. Then Socrates dismisses them and returns to the others. The hour of sunset is near. Socrates sits down again with his friends, but not much is said.*)

(*Jailer enters.*)

JAILER (*standing by Socrates*): To you, Socrates, whom I know to be the noblest and gentlest and best of all who ever came to this place, I will not impute the angry feelings of other men, who rage and swear at me when, in obedience to the authorities, I bid them drink the poison. Indeed I am sure that you will not be angry with me, for others, as you are aware, and not I are the guilty cause. And so fare you well, and try to bear lightly what must needs be. You know my errand.

SOCRATES: I return your good wishes, and will do as you bid.

(*Jailer bursts into tears, turns away, and leaves.*)

SOCRATES (*turning to the others*): How charming the man is. Since I have been in prison he has always been coming to see me, and at times he would talk to me, and was as good as could be to me, and now see how generously he sorrows for me. But we must do as he says, Crito. Let the cup be brought, if the poison is prepared; if not, let the attendant prepare it now.

CRITO: Yet, the sun is still upon the hilltops and many a one has taken the draught late, and after the announcement has been made to him, he has eaten and drunk, and indulged in sensual delights. Do not hasten then; there is still time.

SOCRATES: Yes, Crito, and they of whom you speak are right in doing thus, for they think that they will gain by the delay. But I am right in not doing thus, for I do not think that I should gain anything by drinking the poison a little later; I should be sparing and saving a life which is already gone: I could only laugh at myself for this. Please, then, to do as I say, and not to refuse me.

(*Crito makes a sign to the servant, who goes in and returns shortly, accompanied by the jailer, carrying the cup of poison.*)

SOCRATES: You, my good friend, who are experienced in these matters, shall give me directions how I am to proceed.

JAILER: You have only to walk about until your legs are heavy, and then to lie down, and the poison will act. (*Hands the cup to Socrates.*)

SOCRATES (*taking the cup in the easiest and gentlest manner, without the least fear or change of color or feature, and looking at the man with all his eyes*): What do you say about making a libation out of this cup to any god? May I, or not?

JAILER: We only prepare, Socrates, just so much as we deem enough.

SOCRATES: I understand; yet I may and must pray to the gods to prosper my journey from this to that other world. May this then, which is my prayer, be granted to me. (*Holds the cup to his lips and readily and cheerfully drinks of the poison. As Phaedo watches him drinking he bursts into tears and covers his face. Crito, also unable to restrain his tears, gets up and moves away, followed by Phaedo. Apollodorus breaks out into a loud cry. Socrates alone remains calm.*)

SOCRATES: What is this strange outcry? I sent away the women mainly in order that they might not offend in this way, for I have heard that a man should die in peace. Be quiet then, and have patience.

(*Walks about until his legs begin to fail; then lies on his back, as directed; the jailer looks at his feet and legs and after a while presses his foot hard.*)

JAILER: Can you feel?

SOCRATES: No. (*Feeling his legs, which have grown cold and stiff.*) When the poison reaches the heart, that will be the end. (*Begins to grow cold about the groin; uncovers his face.*) Crito, I owe a cock to Asclepius. Will you remember to pay the debt?

CRITO: The debt shall be paid. Is there anything else?

(*There is no answer; in a minute or two a movement is heard. The attendants uncover him. The eyes are set. Crito closes Socrates' eyes and mouth.*)

Michelangelo

1.

WHILE COMPARING FLEMISH AND ITALIAN
PAINTING HE PAUSES TO EXPLAIN WHY
ARTISTS ARE UNSOCIABLE.

*His Holiness embarrasses me when he asks me
why I don't come to see him more often.*

For three decades—from 1534 to 1564—there was no man in Rome
whose company was more eagerly sought than that of Michelangelo
Buonarroti. At the same time, there was no man in all Italy, not excepting
the Pope, whose company was so hard to obtain. Absorbed in his gigantic
labors of art, Michelangelo preferred to be left alone. He resisted intru-
sions on his time and work like an animal at bay. The approaches of
Roman society he curtly rebuffed, and few dared to engage him in idle
chatter as he daily strode through the streets of Rome on his way to the
Sistine Chapel. Rome's proudest name, this surly and morose recluse was
revered at a distance. Yet, the princes and poets and painters who passed
through Rome continued to seek ways to pay personal homage to this
artist of artists who was called "the divine." Many implored the Pope to
intercede. Yet even His Holiness, much as he chided him on his unsocial
ways, saw little of the lone genius who for seven years worked daily in
the Sistine Chapel on his stupendous fresco of "The Last Judgment."
To his very face Michelangelo had told Pope Paul III that he could serve
him better while at work than in his venerable company. No one else in
Rome would have taken the liberty. The Pope had understood. Michelangelo was given a free hand to glorify in art the faith they both shared,
and his exalted employer strictly forbade others to invade the privacy
the artist craved.

More and more, as he worked at his huge conception of the final wrath,
Michelangelo shut out the world. All his life he had worked unremittingly,
and several cities carried memorials in marble and canvas of his giant
labors. In 1539, at sixty-four, he had glory and adulation enough for a dozen
men. Still, as he looked back on his life his soul darkened. He had seen

treachery and intrigue, known the transience of love, watched men destroy themselves in their mad gropings for power. This first of Roman citizens had loved one city above all others—Florence—had once defended her as engineer-in-chief of her fortifications, only to see her fall prey to the tyrants. A heavy weariness of spirit was upon Michelangelo as he worked at his colossal fresco in the Sistine Chapel. "The Last Judgment" suited his mood perfectly.

It was in 1539, in the midst of his deepening gloom, that Vittoria Colonna stepped into the life of Michelangelo. This gifted poet and patroness of the arts had come to Rome from Ferrara to be close to the official world of her faith. Though a widow for fourteen years, she still mourned her beloved Marquis of Pescara, mourned him and commemorated him in a never-ending stream of sonnets and acts of devotion. Only the Pope's refusal had prevented this most accomplished of Renaissance women from taking the veil. Vittoria was the friend of many of Italy's greatest poets and scholars, and Michelangelo had been among her countless correspondents. Now, in Rome, they met for the first time and a great friendship sprang up that was to last till Vittoria's death in 1547. Fascinated by the keen mind and broad culture of this woman, the painter became a changed man. In the company of Vittoria, life offered new vistas for this aging solitary. Where there had been a sullen bitterness, there was now tenderness. Michelangelo, at sixty-four, became a lover, writing impassioned sonnets to this woman who was herself one of Italy's foremost sonneteers. A platonic lover, to be sure, for Vittoria, though denied her wish to enter a convent, had remained a nun in body and spirit since the death of her husband. Yet, when she died Michelangelo grieved her as if she had been his wife, mistress, and friend combined. "On her, in all his loyalty and reverence," wrote Sidney Colvin, "he poured out all the treasures of his mind and all his imprisoned powers of tenderness and devotion." Together these two discussed poetry and painting, Platonic ideals, and God. At long last this sad and lonely Titan had come out of his shell. In her presence the grim and stern-visaged Michelangelo even learned to laugh! This new friendship was good for Vittoria, too. Endless brooding over the death of her husband had made her an old woman at forty-nine. If anyone in Italy could, for a moment, replace the Marquis in her mind and heart, it was this sublimely endowed artist. There was something of the mother in Vittoria's tenderness, too. For Michelangelo, with his churlish, unsociable ways, often struck her as a shy, unhappy child.

Like Pope Paul before her, Vittoria learned never to intrude on Michelangelo's work. She, too, guarded him from an inquisitive world. But, being a soft-hearted woman, she sometimes yielded to the appeals of those who longed to meet the great painter. In such cases, an ambassador or cardinal would apply some tactful pressure, and Vittoria would adroitly arrange for Michelangelo to be present at a specified place on a specified day. In 1539 this specified place was almost inevitably her semi-cloistral abode at Monte Cavallo, which she had chosen as residence because close by was the Church of San Silvestro, where her friend Fra Ambrogio of Siena frequently preached on Biblical themes. Outside she kept a little garden, which provided a cool shelter during the hot weather. Here many of Italy's great artists and writers came to pay chaste court to this gracious queen of literary and social Rome.

It was doubtless in this cloistered retreat that the Siennese ambassador Lattantio Tolomei one day presented to Vittoria Colonna his young friend, the Portuguese painter Francesco d'Ollanda. And it was probably there that d'Ollanda first met Michelangelo. D'Ollanda was only twenty years old at the time and something of a cheeky and persistent lad, for which, of course, we must be thankful, as we shall see later. Having met Michelangelo, Francesco now wondered how he could meet the great man again. The double wall of work and temperament surrounding Michelangelo seemed impenetrable. As luck would have it, the Portuguese youth called on his friend Lattantio one Sunday afternoon. The servants informed him that Lattantio had gone to the Church of San Silvestro with the Marchioness of Pescara to hear Fra Ambrogio lecture on the Epistles of St. Paul. Spurred by the prospect of an edifying afternoon, Francesco lost no time in following his friend to Monte Cavallo. It is thanks to his decision to do so that we have the Four Dialogues on Painting which Francesco d'Ollanda wrote down as the record of a series of talks with Michelangelo and Vittoria Colonna in the shady garden of San Silvestro.

For reasons unknown, these Quatro Dialogos sobre a Pintura remained buried in the Lisbon archives for three centuries before they were exhumed and given to the world. They are by no means the work of a practiced literary artist, yet, if we may trust Francesco's memory, they tell us much about the literary and artistic preoccupations of Renaissance Rome, and they offer some insight into the character of Michelangelo. The painter's deference to Vittoria is a beautiful thing to watch, and whether or not the presumptuous young Portuguese was able to fathom Vittoria's attitude to the great Florentine, the text at any rate yields some helpful clues. Tested by the style of the letters and sonnets exchanged by these friends, neither of which Francesco could possibly have seen, many passages in the Dialogues ring absolutely true. To be sure, they are wordy talkers, these Italians of Renaissance Rome. Perhaps it is the fault of Francesco's prolix pen, or perhaps it was the habit of the day to burden the conversation with an enormous array of facts and axioms. Certainly we have moved far from those erudite exchanges. In any case, Francesco's dialogues—and Donato Giannotti's—are all the conversational record we have of sixteenth-century Rome and its almost legendary first citizen. "It is but rarely that we are permitted to approach a great genius in the highest moments of his inspiration," writes F. G. Bell in the searching preface to his own rendering from the Portuguese text.* "The brief Dialogues of d'Ollanda give us such an opportunity. . . ." We may be amused at the great man's artistic chauvinism, but few can fail to thrill to his eloquent statement of the artist's creed.

Before we return to Francesco at the Church of San Silvestro let us try to visualize the course of Michelangelo's own strollings at that moment. With his color-grinder Urbino as company, the painter has left his house, which occupies a site between the Quirinal and the Capitol, and is advancing along the Via Esquilina. The two men are probably discussing details of the following day's work in the Sistine Chapel. Suddenly they are stopped by a messenger of Vittoria's. The Marchesa, Michelangelo is told, requests his company at Monte Cavallo. The two men turn in that direction.

At San Silvestro, Francesco has been waiting for Fra Ambrogio to finish his intricate sermon on the meaning of St. Paul's Epistles. The afternoon is warm, and the young Portuguese is thinking of the cool garden adjoining the church. Fra Ambrogio has now ended his discourse. The Marchesa invites Francesco and the others to join her in the garden. Shrewdly she suspects what is on this young painter's mind—that he had expected to find Michelangelo as well among Fra Ambrogio's listeners. Vittoria sits down on one of the garden benches and graciously invites Francesco and Lattantio to sit beside her. . . .

VITTORIA: If I'm not mistaken, I believe Francesco d'Ollanda would rather hear Michelangelo talk about painting than listen to Brother Ambrogio preach on the Epistles of St. Paul.

FRANCESCO (*somewhat piqued*): Your Excellency seems to think that my only interest is in painting and that I understand nothing else. Frankly

---

* Professor Bell contrives to convey a consistently archaic note in his version. While ingenious, the device would have clashed with the style of my rendering of the Donato dialogue that follows. To preserve a certain uniformity, I therefore decided to translate d'Ollanda's Portuguese afresh. L. B.

I should always like to listen to Michelangelo. But when it comes to the Epistles of St. Paul I prefer to hear Brother Ambrogio.

LATTANTIO: Don't be so sensitive, Francesco. The Signora doesn't mean that a man who paints is incapable of doing anything else. We Italians have a much higher idea of painting than that. Perhaps all that she implied was that in addition to enjoying what you have just heard, you would also have the pleasure of hearing Michelangelo today.

FRANCESCO: If such is the case, Her Excellency would only be doing what has always been her gracious habit—to accord far more than one would dare ask or expect.

VITTORIA (*smiling*): One must know how to give to one who knows how to be grateful ... (*calls one of her attendants*). Please take this message to Michelangelo. Tell him that Signor Lattantio and I are in this cool chapel and that the church is closed and very pleasant. Ask him if he will be kind enough to come and spend a few hours with us, hours that will be a loss to him but a gain to us. Don't say anything about the Portuguese Francesco d'Ollanda's being here.

(*Francesco, in a whisper, remarks to Lattantio on Vittoria's tact and delicacy "in the smallest matters."*)

VITTORIA: What are you two saying? *

LATTANTIO: He was marvelling at the great tact you show in everything, even in sending someone on an errand of this kind. It so happens that Michelangelo does his best to avoid meeting Signor Francesco d'Ollanda, because he knows that once he begins talking with him he can never break away.

VITTORIA: I suspected that, knowing Michelangelo the way I do. . . . I scarcely know how to get him to talk about painting.

BROTHER AMBROGIO: I very much doubt whether Michelangelo will consent to talk about painting at all, knowing that the Portuguese here is himself a painter. My advice is that he should conceal himself when Michelangelo arrives. Then he will hear him on the subject.

FRANCESCO (*with some bitterness*): It isn't as easy as you think to conceal the Portuguese from Michelangelo's eyes. He would detect my presence, even though I were hidden, better than you would if I were standing right here before you and you wore glasses in the bargain. You'll see when he comes whether he notices me or not.

(*Vittoria and Lattantio laugh. . . . After some moments of silence there is a knock on the gate. It is Michelangelo, whom Vittoria's attendant has encountered by chance walking along the Via Esquilina*

---

* Indirect discourse in original.

deep in conversation with his color-grinder Urbino.* Michelangelo enters. Vittoria rises to greet him and remains standing some time before asking him to sit between her and Lattantio. Francesco takes a seat some distance away. After a short silence Vittoria begins to talk about various subjects, never mentioning painting until she feels confident that Michelangelo is in the right mood.)

VITTORIA: It is a well-known fact that anyone is thoroughly beaten who engages Michelangelo in a contest of wit and intellect, which is his special element. The only way to gain an advantage over him and reduce him to silence is to discuss lawsuits and . . . painting.

FRANCESCO (*stepping forward*): I know no better way to accomplish that than to let him know that I am here, for he hasn't noticed me yet. (*To Michelangelo.*) I was certain that the only way of preventing you from seeing some trivial object was to place it right before your eyes.

MICHELANGELO (*turning to Francesco with amazement*): Please forgive me, Signor Francesco, for not having seen you. I had eyes only for the Signora. But since you are here you must help me as a colleague.

FRANCESCO: You have given me a most excellent reason for excusing you. But it seems to me that the Signora produces contradictory effects with the light she radiates, much as the sun melts and hardens with the same rays. In short, her presence has made you blind to everything else, whereas I am unable to see and hear you unless she is there. I am well aware that a man of intelligence will be so profitably occupied in the company of Her Excellency that he will scarcely have time to think of his neighbor.

(*Brother Ambrogio rises, takes his leave of the Marchesa, bids the others good-by, and departs.*)

VITTORIA: His Holiness has been kind enough to authorize me to build a new convent on the slope of Monte Cavallo, not far from here; at the very place, in fact, where the ruined portico stands from which it is said Nero watched Rome burn. Perhaps the vestiges of such an evil man may be thus effaced by the tread of proud women. I don't know, Michelangelo, what size and shape to give the building, nor where to put the entrance. Do you think it would be possible to salvage some of the old structure in building the new one?

MICHELANGELO: By all means! The ruined portico might serve as belfry. . . . In any case I'm certain the convent can be built without any trouble. When we leave here, we might look over the site, if Your Excellency is agreeable, and I might make some suggestions.

---

* D'Ollanda does not tell us whether Urbino accompanied his master to Vittoria's or returned home alone.

VITTORIA: I hardly dared ask you; but I see that the words of our Lord, *"Deposuit potentes et exaltavit humiles,"* * never fail. You, Michelangelo, have the merit of being wisely generous, not thoughtlessly prodigal, which explains why your friends place your character even higher than your works. Those who only know you by the work of your hands know the least perfect thing about you. For me your way of isolating yourself, of escaping our idle conversations, and your refusal to paint the portraits of many princes who ask you is no less worthy of high praise than the way you have made one great masterpiece of the work of your whole life.

MICHELANGELO: Perhaps you give me credit for more than I deserve, Signora. But since you have brought up the subject, permit me to express some grievances against the public on behalf of myself, certain other painters of my character, and of Master Francesco here. Of the hundreds of slanders circulating about eminent painters, the most persistent is that they are eccentric and unapproachable. Actually, Signora, painters are very human people. But, no, the fools persist in regarding them as fantastic and capricious eccentrics. Yet this is so false to the true character of the artist. To be sure, painters take on certain peculiarities, especially here in Italy, where painting has achieved such perfection. Yet isn't it asking too much to expect such artists, absorbed in their work, to waste their time in making themselves socially agreeable? As it is, there are very few artists who practice their art conscientiously enough. People are very unfair when they condemn as proud and unsociable any sincere artist whose one desire is to be left alone to do his work. If such a man appears surly and discourteous, it is not from arrogance. As a rule, he finds few people who know enough to discuss his art with him. He accordingly resents any futile conversations that might divert him from the profound concentration required by his work. I must admit to Your Excellency that even His Holiness embarrasses me when he asks me why I don't come to see him more often. To be perfectly frank, I believe I am of much greater use to him in my own home than in his company. I even told His Holiness that I preferred working for him in my own way to standing a whole day in his presence, as so many others do.

FRANCESCO: You're a lucky man, Michelangelo! Among all the princes of the world only the Pope would pardon such an offense!

MICHELANGELO: That is precisely the kind of offense all rulers should be disposed to overlook. Oddly enough, these important commissions I

---

* "He humbled the proud and raised the meek."

am working on have given me a great sense of independence. At times, while conversing with the Pope, I forget myself so completely that I put on this fur cap of mine and talk away with the greatest freedom. He hasn't condemned me to death for it. On the contrary, he allows me full liberty, and it is then that my mind can serve him best. . . . Of course, one occasionally comes upon a fool who prefers solitude for its own sake, who is prepared to sacrifice his friends and turn the world against him out of a purposeless desire to be left alone. You would be right in condemning such an eccentric. But if a man's work or the circumstances of his life require him to live by himself, and if such a man asks nothing of the world but to leave him in peace, then I think it a grave injustice to intrude upon him. What do you want of him? What right have you to ask him to while away his time in idle chatter when all he asks is peace and quiet? Don't you realize there are certain kinds of work requiring such complete absorption of a man's faculties that nothing is left over for the enjoyment of your social pastimes? If, however, such a man has the same leisure you have and fails to observe your rules of etiquette, I am quite willing to regard his behavior as a capital offense. But as a rule you only seek the society of such a man and shower him with praise because it reflects honor on yourselves. It is sufficient for you to know that a pope or an emperor deigns to talk to him. I say to you in all frankness that an artist who is more interested in satisfying the ignorant than in serving his art cannot possibly be a superior person. And the same is true of an artist who has nothing strange and peculiar about him, or, at any rate, what is commonly thought to be strange and peculiar. As for the crude and uninspired dullards, one doesn't need a lantern to find them. They are in all the public places of the world.

VITTORIA (*after a short silence*): Of course, if an artist's friends were like those good men of antiquity. . . . Archesilas, for instance. One day he went to see his friend Apelles, who was sick and in need. Archesilas raised his friend's head, and while pretending to adjust the pillow put some money under it. Later Apelles' old servant-woman discovered the money and cried out in surprise. The sick man smiled and said, "There's nothing to be surprised at. Archesilas put it there."

LATTANTIO: My experience has been that the great painters would not change places with anyone. And no matter how great they are, they seem content with the meager pay that their art brings them. I should be the first to wish them better fortune, if they did not already regard themselves as the most fortunate of men. The genius who is destined for great painting sees the emptiness of the lives and pleasures of the self-styled mighty of the earth, the mighty whose names die with them, who never in their lives suspected that the best things had passed them by. Such men never really lived, despite the treasures they accumulated; whereas a genius, through his masterpieces, lives forever. The genius learns to deny himself the ordinary pleasures of the world and his own self-esteem grows as he finds himself striving toward a kind of glory that has never attracted mediocre minds. An emperor is less proud of his empire than a painter is of his representation of a single work of God. It was never quite as important to the emperor to acquire a new province as it is to the painter to achieve a satisfactory perfection in matters far more difficult and uncertain than the conquest of colonies from the Pillars of Hercules to the Ganges River. It is no more difficult for the emperor to vanquish his strongest enemies than it is for a painter to produce a work that completely carries out the idea in his mind. Finally, the emperor is no happier drinking out of his golden goblet than the painter is drinking out of his clay cup. The Emperor Maximilian once pardoned a painter who had been condemned to death. "I can create a duke or a count," were his memorable words, "but only God can make a painter."

VITTORIA: I should like your advice, Signor Lattantio. Shall I ask Michelangelo to enlighten me on some points of painting? I have a feeling that to prove his thesis that great men are reasonable and not eccentric, he will not respond in his usual way.

LATTANTIO: Michelangelo could scarcely refuse to make an exception in favor of Your Excellency, by divulging some secrets which he rightly withholds from the world.

MICHELANGELO (*to Vittoria*): Your Excellency need only ask for something that is worthy of being offered to her, and it shall be hers.

VITTORIA (*smiling*): Well, now that we have made a beginning, I should like very much to know what you think of Flemish painting. My own feeling is that it is more devout in mood than Italian painting.

MICHELANGELO (*slowly*): Generally speaking, Flemish painting will satisfy pious people more than any being produced in Italy. Flemish painting will make such people weep, whereas Italian painting doesn't always have that effect. That is due not so much to the vigor and merit of Flemish painting as to the susceptibility of very devout people. Flemish painting will seem beautiful to women, especially to very old and very young women, not to mention nuns and other religious devotees, besides some members of the nobility who are deaf to the true harmony of a work of art. In Flanders they paint, preferably, to beguile the sense of sight. They select objects which are charming in them-

selves, or subjects of which no one can say anything bad—like saints
and prophets. . . . They are fond of painting rivers, bridges and very
green fields covered with shady trees—what are called landscapes—with
great numbers of people scattered on all sides. Though it all may strike
some people as highly effective, actually such painting is neither artistic
nor thoughtful. There is no symmetry, no proportion, no selectivity,
no grandeur. In short, such painting is without body or strength, and
yet there are places where they paint worse than in Flanders. If I am so
critical of Flemish painting, it is not because it is wholly bad, but because by trying to depict so many objects with equal perfection, when
a single outstanding one would suffice, it depicts none of them satisfactorily. The term "true painting" can only be applied to the work that
is done here in Italy. That is why good painting is called "Italian." If
it were equally good in any other country, it would take the name of
that country. Good painting is in a sense an act of devotion, for nothing ennobles the soul and invites piety so much as the achievement of
perfection. And perfection, of course, approaches God and unites with
him. Now, good painting is nothing but a copy of God's perfections, a
mere shadow of his own brushstrokes, a piece of music, perhaps. Only
the liveliest and rarest intelligence can sense how vast and difficult is
this perfection. Very few have reached it and known how to reproduce
it. I would even go so far as to say that Italy offers the only climate in
the world where one can paint well. Even if it were possible for other
countries to have greater geniuses than our own, they would still not
produce painting as good as ours. Let me tell you why. Pick out any
good painter of some other country and tell him to paint whatever he
likes and does best. Then call in some third-rate Italian apprentice and
have him paint anything you like. When they both finish, compare
their work. You will see that the painting done by the Italian student is
artistically superior to that of the other. This is so true that if Albrecht
Dürer himself, a man of delicacy and skill in his own style, wanted to
fool me . . . or Francesco d'Ollanda here . . . by trying to palm off an
imitative work of his as genuinely Italian, he would fail. Whether it was
a good, mediocre, or bad painting, I would know at once that it was not
painted in Italy and that it was not the work of an Italian. So I repeat,
no nation or people, with the exception of one or two Spaniards, can
hope to copy or imitate the Italian style of painting, which is that of
ancient Greece, without betraying itself as foreign, whatever pains it
may take. If by a miracle some foreign painter should learn to paint
well, one might say of him, even if he were not imitating the Italians,
that he paints like an Italian. So what is known as "Italian painting" is

not only the painting that is done in Italy but any painting whatsoever
that is good and true. I repeat, since it is here that the greatest masterpieces are produced, greater and nobler than those of any other country, it is customary to give the name "Italian" to good painting, even
when it is done in Flanders and Spain. Of course, painting, in a larger
sense, comes not from Italy or any other country, but from heaven. Yet
its oldest and most numerous vestiges of antiquity are in Italy, and I
think it is here, too, that true painting will finally end.

FRANCESCO: What you are saying, actually, is that painting is the exclusive
property of the Italians. Well, why should that surprise anyone? It is
common knowledge why the Italians paint well and the others do not.
To begin with, the Italian is very studious by nature. Then, if he is talented, he comes into the world with a taste and love for the things that
enrich his talent. Moreover, once he has adopted an art or technique,
the Italian is not content with remaining a mere craftsman. He studies
ways of becoming unique in his field. His one desire is to establish himself as a model of perfection. Mediocrity will never satisfy him, for this
word "mediocrity" is held in contempt in Italy. All aspire to be eagles,
soaring far above the others, into the very sun. There is a great advantage in being born in Italy. You Italians find yourselves in a country
that is the mother and custodian of the arts and sciences. What magnificent models your ancestors have left you! No other country has anything like it. From your very infancy, whatever your inclination may
be, beauty and instruction meet your gaze on every street. During your
first years of life you grow accustomed to splendid sights that even the
old of other lands never behold. As you grow older, your eyes become
so used to the power and recognition of ancient art that no matter how
uneducated you may be, you cannot resist the impulse to copy and imitate it. Another reason is the great number of men of superior taste and
talent which Italy boasts. You Italians have great masters to model
yourselves upon. Your cities are covered with their masterpieces, and
with the great works of art that are being continually unearthed. Compare yourselves with my people, the Portuguese. Though some have
shown talent and understanding, we have done very little in the arts.
We are inclined, on the whole, to disdain painting, and are almost
ashamed to admit any knowledge of it. The consequence is that Portuguese painting is imperfect. For Italians—I can't say the same for the
Germans and French—the greatest and most flattering distinction is to
be inimitable as a painter or in the possession of some rare faculty.
From among Italy's nobles and princes, captains and scholars, cardinals and popes, only he is glorified who has profoundly and uniquely

mastered his profession. Many of Italy's great rulers are now wrapped in oblivion. Today it is only Michelangelo, a painter, who is called "the divine." It also occurs to me that another reason why Italians paint better than anyone else is that they are paid better than anyone else. Here in Italy a portrait often brings as much as a thousand *crusados*. And you know better than I do that other types of painting also bring better prices here than anywhere else. (*To Vittoria.*) So you see, Your Excellency, what a vast difference of circumstance there is between your country and mine as regards painting.

VITTORIA: And, yet, in spite of all those disadvantages, it strikes me that you talk and act more like a good Italian than like someone from the other side of the mountains. In any case, however culture may differ, the same virtue, the same good, and the same evil prevail everywhere.

FRANCESCO: People in my country would certainly be surprised to hear you praise me that way, making the distinction between Italians and those who, as you say, come from the other side of the mountains. On the other hand, Signora, we have some old and beautiful cities in Portugal, especially Lisbon, where I was born. We have good customs, a brilliant court and brave fighting men. We have princes who are equally great in war and peace. And best of all, we have a powerful king who rules over us with the greatest tranquillity, who governs distant colonies of primitive people whom he has converted to the faith, a king who is feared throughout the East, a king, moreover, who patronizes the fine arts. It was this same king who, fooled by my feeble talent, sent me to Italy to study art and learn from Master Michelangelo here. It is only too true that we do not possess magnificent buildings and paintings like yours. Yet, gradually, we are losing the traits of barbarism which the Goths and the Moors left behind them in Spain and Portugal. I very much hope that when I return to my country I shall be able to do something to raise the level of painting and architecture closer to yours. Unfortunately, these are almost lost arts in Portugal. They are without splendor or glory there, and they have fallen into such complete disuse that very few people value or understand them. Notable exceptions are our king, who encourages merit of every kind, the Infante Dom Luis, and his highly cultivated brother, who combines excellent taste with great knowledge in matters of art. The others understand nothing about painting and do nothing for it. •

MICHELANGELO: Your king and your princes are to be congratulated.

LATTANTIO: We Italians have this great advantage over every other nation in the world: we have learned to master and honor the noblest arts and sciences. But bear this in mind, Master Francesco—if anyone lacks knowledge and esteem of painting, it is his own fault, certainly not the fault of this great and illustrious art. Only a person completely destitute of judgment would maintain otherwise. Let me prove my point by citing a number of ancient and contemporary examples. Powerful emperors and kings, sages and philosophers, men to whom nothing was unknown—all have venerated painting. They have felt proud of understanding it; they have eulogized it; they have been magnanimous in their patronage. Look at the high esteem in which our holy Mother the Church, through her popes and cardinals, her great princes and prelates, holds the art of painting. And you will find that all through history nothing has excited the admiration of people like painting. They often thought of it as a miracle. Celebrated kings like Alexander the Great, Demetrius, and Ptolemy prided themselves on knowing a good deal about painting. Think of the many Caesars who thought well of it! The great Caesar himself, Augustus, Agrippa, Claudius, Caligula, even Nero, who was perhaps virtuous only in that respect. And Vespasian and Titus, who had the famous paintings made for the Temple of Peace after he defeated the Jews and destroyed Jerusalem! What about the great Emperors Trajan and Hadrian, who himself wielded a delicate brush, according to Dion the Greek? And Marcus Aurelius, of whom Julius Capitolinus reports that he once studied painting and that his master was Diogenitus himself? Helius Lampridius tells us that the Emperor Alexander Severus painted a whole genealogical gallery to prove that he was descended from the Metellus family. Plutarch relates that at Mitylene the great Pompey designed the plan and structure of the theater that was later reproduced in Rome. Of course, the noble art of painting is worthy of veneration in itself. It needs no defense other than its own merit. My sole purpose in citing these examples is to prove to anyone who may think of this art as beneath him that there have been others, greater than himself, who have judged it worthy of their esteem. Who would dare to compare himself with the Alexanders? Who will ever surpass Caesar in great deeds? Who can hope to match the glory of the Pompeys and the Trajans? And yet these same Alexanders and Caesars not only loved the sublime art of painting and rewarded it well but they practiced it with their own hands. Who could be so presumptuous as to disdain this art? Who, indeed, does not feel humble before its power?

VITTORIA: Is there one wise and virtuous man—unless he be a saint in complete retirement—whose heart is not filled with veneration before the devout contemplations of this sacred art? One could sing its praises endlessly, if one had the time. Painting recalls melancholy man to gaiety. Saints and sinners are alike reminded of human misery. It awakens compunction among the cruel and the hardened. It brings penitence to the worldly and prompts the contemplative mind to meditation. It arouses fear and repentance. It shows us the threats and torments of Hell, and as far as possible it pictures the glory and peace of the blessed and the inscrutable face of God. Better than anything else it shows us the humility of saints, the constancy of martyrs, the chastity of virgins, the beauty of angels, and the love and charity that kindle the breasts of the seraphim. Painting lifts our spirit above the stars and brings us face to face with the Kingdom of the eternal. It evokes the presence of celebrated men whose very bones have long since vanished from the earth. It inspires us with emulation of their deeds, as we contemplate the spectacle of their hopes and thoughts, their dangers in battle, their piety, their habits of life, and their great actions. Painting reveals to warriors the military science of other times and stirs their emulation of the glory of famous captains. Scipio Africanus himself testified to this. This art preserves the memory of the living for those who follow. It shows us strange and ancient customs, varieties of distant nations; it shows us all kinds of buildings, animals, and monsters. It would take countless words to describe these things in writing, and then they would be imperfectly understood. This noble art of painting goes even further. It gives us the living likeness of any great man whose actions arouse our desire to see him before our very eyes. It brings close the beauty of a fair unknown of some distant place, a fact which made Pliny ponder deeply. By preserving a painted image, it adds many years to the life of one who dies. It consoles the grieving widow who has the likeness of her dead husband constantly before her. And the sons left fatherless so young, once they are men delight in treasuring the likeness of their beloved father. They are less likely to shame his memory.

(*Vittoria pauses, moved almost to tears; Lattantio, to take her mind off her own memories, continues the discourse.*)

LATTANTIO: Apart from all these great attributes of painting, is there another art that can so ennoble and embellish temples and palaces, weapons and fortresses—or anything else susceptible of order and beauty? That is why many great minds have asserted that painting is man's only surety against mortality and the envy of time. Pythagoras had this very thing in mind when he said that men were like immortal God in three things only—in knowledge, in painting, and in music.

MICHELANGELO (*turning to Francesco*): I am certain, Signor Francesco, that if your countrymen in Portugal could see the beautiful paintings that hang in many Italian homes, they would not be so deaf to the music of this art. They would at once esteem it and strongly desire to emulate it. However, it is not surprising that they should neither understand nor value what they have never seen and what is not theirs.

(*Michelangelo rises, remarking that it is time for him to go. As Vittoria also rises, Francesco, ever the presumptuous one, begs her to invite the little group back to Monte Cavallo the following day. She assents, and Michelangelo gives his word to be present. The men accompany Vittoria to the gate, and Lattantio accompanies Michelangelo back to his house. Francesco escorts Vittoria to her cloistral dwelling nearby. There he leaves her in the company of a group of religious devotees and returns home.*)

Michelangelo

2.

WAS DANTE RIGHT TO CONSIGN BRUTUS AND CASSIUS TO HELL FOR MURDERING JULIUS CAESAR?

*Whoever kills a tyrant kills not a man
but a beast disguised as a man.*

Surly and inaccessible as Michelangelo was, we have seen how under the benign influence of the Marchioness of Pescara he could be drawn out of his shell and even made to laugh. There were one or two others who could count on the painter's occasional company for a stroll through the streets of Rome. Urbino, the color-grinder, was one of them. The others used the magic formula of being, like Michelangelo, Florentine exiles. A patriotic Florentine, Michelangelo long brooded over the fate of the beloved city he had for years adorned with his genius. The Medicis had been his patrons and his sponsors, yet when these despots were expelled, Michelangelo had joined the republican rebels. When the Medicis, reinforced, returned to besiege Florence, Michelangelo was put in charge of the fortifications. The city fell and in the bloodbath of revenge that followed Michelangelo was spared only because he was Michelangelo. The city was no longer his. He remained to finish what work he was doing and in 1534 settled in Rome for good. Yet the memory of Florence hung over his thoughts for thirty years. He had watched this beautiful city win freedom for one magnificent respite from bondage and then bow down again to tyranny.

Other Florentines in Rome also remembered the good fight, men like the writer Antonio Petreo; the scholar, grammarian and printer Francesco Priscianese; the bank agent Luigi del Riccio; the political theorist and historian, Donato Giannotti. These few had ready access to Michelangelo's heart, and often they gathered together to recall the heroic days of the short-lived republic.

Of these men Donato was perhaps closest to Michelangelo. They had both served Florence in public capacities—the painter as engineer-in-chief

23

of defense and officer of the Militia, Donato as Secretary of the Council of Ten. Donato had now entered the service of Cardinal Ridolfi, another Florentine exile. To his death he nursed one hope—the return of liberty to Florence—and he expressed his ideals in a lengthy Trattato della repubblica fiorentina. No man in Italy hated despotism so much as the fiery Donato Giannotti, and even Michelangelo was appalled by his open advocacy of tyrannicide. Donato loved this dour fellow Florentine, was proud to share banishment with such a man, but, as we shall see, did not hesitate to berate the older man for his moral and political qualms. Certainly Donato's challenging tirade is in sharp contrast with the casuistic apologia doggedly maintained by Michelangelo.

Donato was a versatile man of letters. Besides his political writings he left a mass of biographies of famous condottieri, two comedies (one in prose, the other in verse), and an imaginary Dialogue on the Republic of Venice. But it is for another little work of his, composed perhaps only as a personal record and not printed till three centuries later, that we cherish his memory. The manuscript was found in the Vatican Library early in the nineteenth century, published in 1859, and first edited and persuasively authenticated in 1939 by the Italian scholar Deoclecio de Campos for a reprint by the Florentine publisher Sansoni. So far as I know, my translation is the first to appear in English. The title reveals little of the booklet's exciting content: Dialoghi—Dei Giorni che Dante consumò nel cercare l'Inferno e il Purgatorio—dialogues on the number of days it took Dante to complete his tour of Hell and Purgatory. The shock of surprise comes when we discover that Michelangelo is the chief speaker. To be sure, some of the thrill evaporates as we advance into the chapter-and-verse involvements of the first dialogue. Presently, as the second dialogue opens, the mood changes and our first excitement returns. The dreary detail of calculation has ended, and the speakers are passionately discussing political assassination. Was Dante right in consigning Brutus and Cassius to hell for murdering Caesar? Suddenly we are in the company of exiles from a despot-ridden city. There is a terrible immediacy to their thoughts on the violent removal of tyrants. This is Donato's favorite theme, and Michelangelo, for all his love of Florence, bristles as Donato casts aspersions on Dante's judgment. But, first, let us set the scene of the conversation as Donato himself gives it to us.

It is the afternoon of a spring day in 1546. The Florentines Luigi del Riccio, Antonio Petreo, Francesco Priscianese, and Donato Giannotti are accompanying their great fellow exile on a stroll outside the gates of Rome. They are deep in the second part of a conversation that had started that morning on the streets of Rome. Luigi and Antonio were strolling along

amiably discussing Dante's allegorical travels. Whom should they meet
at the Campodoglio but Michelangelo and Donato. Together the friends
had continued their walk toward the Laterano, Michelangelo now becoming the main speaker. At San Giovanni the friends had parted company. Michelangelo had turned down Luigi's invitation to lunch with the
curious remark, "Io non mi voglio tanto rallegrare" ("I don't want to
amuse myself too much"), but had agreed to rejoin the group and resume
the discussion that afternoon. It is now after lunch. The Florentines have
re-assembled at Priscianese's printing shop. They begin their walk at the
Porta del Popolo, advance some distance beyond the gate, and ultimately
reach the Molle Bridge. Up to this point Luigi, Antonio and Michelangelo have done all the talking. Donato, doubtless nursing his own
thoughts, has been waiting for a chance to expound his favorite thesis.
And now, as the strollers pause at the bridge, the chance has come.

ANTONIO: While talking we have come as far as the Molle Bridge. It would
be wise to turn back now, because if we cross the bridge the walk back
will be too long. And if we still have time before we reach the outskirts
of Rome, we can stroll through one of those gardens that we shall find
along the way.

LUIGI: Let's do as you say. And since there's no reason to remain silent during the walk back, let someone suggest a topic for discussion that will
occupy us at least till we reach Rome. Surely this is the time for Signor
Donato to speak up. He has been very quiet all morning and afternoon.

DONATO: I have been quiet as you say, and I am not sorry, for I have profited a great deal more by listening than I would have done by talking.
But since there must be no doubt about my being among you, I should
like now to discuss a point with Signor Michelangelo in the little time
that remains before it grows dark. Whether I shall agree with him I
very much doubt, because he is so fond of Dante that he regards everything he wrote as having been dictated by Truth herself. . . . It is true
Dante was a very learned man, and a man of great distinction in human
affairs, so it may be presumed that what he said was either the truth or,
at any rate, very close to it. But with all that, Dante was only a man,
and if he was ever wrong about anything, that's no reason to be astonished.

MICHELANGELO: As you must have observed, I have read this poet very
diligently. Up to now I have found nothing in his writings which I am
convinced was not expressed with full deliberation and good reason.

And if you will point out one single passage in which this is not so, I shall admit having made a great mistake.

DONATO: That will not be so difficult for me to do.

MICHELANGELO: Please proceed.

DONATO: Doesn't it strike you as wrong that Dante should put Brutus and Cassius in the mouths of Lucifer?

MICHELANGELO: If you have nothing more to add, I shall cling to my judgment about Dante. This is an old argument, and others have refuted it.

DONATO: It has been refuted by others, as you say, but if you don't refute it better than they did, I shall not change my opinion. I shall always say that Dante committed a very grave error in putting Brutus and Cassius in hell and in the mouths of Lucifer for killing Julius Caesar.

MICHELANGELO: Just what are you trying to say?

DONATO: I am saying that Dante blundered grievously because he did not know his history and because he did not realize that to these two men Caesar was the ruling tyrant of their country. If he had known that, Dante would never have inflicted such punishment upon Caesar's assassins. In the second place, it shows how little he knew of the consensus of men of all countries, men who, with one voice, have always revered, commemorated, and exalted those who to free their countries have assassinated the tyrants. Moreover, Dante betrays his ignorance of the fact that the laws of the world all promise the highest rewards, and not the vilest penalties, to those who remove such despots. He showed, too, that he knew nothing of the great honors bestowed by the Roman people upon the first Brutus and Valerius Publicola for having driven the Tarquins from Rome and restored freedom to the country—or, on the other hand, with what loathing Mallius Capitolinus was hurled to his death from the Tarpeian Rock, not, mind you, for having been a tyrant, but for having shown an inclination to become one. I leave aside Aratus Sicionius, Timoleonus, Dion of Syracuse, Trasibulus, all valorous men, all destroyers of tyranny, all remembered by the world with honor and reverence. If Dante had known these things, he would never have blundered into such a shameful treatment of Brutus and Cassius, two men whom the world has always found and will always find worthy of veneration. And if you tell me that Dante knew only too well who Julius Caesar was, and who Brutus and Cassius were, and that wise and good men have always honored tyrannicides, and, finally, that he thoroughly understood what he was writing, I will answer that you have refuted the charge of ignorance against Dante, but that in doing so you have imputed to him a much graver and more contemptible offense. For you make him a wicked and malicious monster by assuming that he deliberately denounced and punished those who he knew should be praised and rewarded. . . . I might mention many other things, but I have no intention at present of delivering an invective against Dante. I think my position is sufficiently clear from what I have said. And I shall continue maintaining it unless Signor Michelangelo persuades me it is false. That, I feel certain, will be none too easy.

MICHELANGELO: It will not be very difficult for me to prove the falsity of the shameful conception of Dante which you have invented. I see quite clearly now that when you told us earlier today that you did not understand Dante you were speaking the truth. For the fact is, you do not understand him.

DONATO: I understand this much: he has placed Brutus and Cassius in hell, and I would place them in the best part of heaven.

MICHELANGELO: I quite agree with you that Brutus and Cassius deserve the praise which the whole world has given them. But that is no reason why you should talk of Dante the way you have, accusing him of so much.

DONATO: You contradict yourself. You admit that Brutus and Cassius should be praised and honored, yet you do not want me to attack Dante for having condemned them!

MICHELANGELO: If you listen to me for a moment, I shall convince you that I am not contradicting myself. I shall prove that Dante knew all those things quite well, and that he was not a scoundrel but a good man, and that he always denounced evil and always defended the good and pursued it. Then I shall tell you why he put Brutus and Cassius in the mouths of Lucifer.

DONATO: Speak—I shall listen gladly.

MICHELANGELO: If you had read the first canto carefully, you would have seen how well Dante understood the nature of tyrants and what severe punishments were in store for them both from God and from man. For he puts them among those who commit violent crimes against their neighbors. These he desires punished in the first ring of the Seventh Circle, punished in a pool of boiling blood, each tormented according to the degree of guilt involved. . . . And if any tyrant escapes death, by the grace of God, and amid the many crimes typical of tyranny manages to do some little good, then Dante consigns him to Purgatory to atone his sins through some terrible penance. These men he puts among the insolent, who must repent their sin on the First Terrace of Purgatory by carrying such enormous weights that their backs are bent till they seem to crawl along the ground. . . . Accordingly, since it is clear that Dante, by condemning tyrants to both Hell and Purgatory, fully understood the nature of tyranny, it is unreasonable to suppose that he did not know that Caesar was a tyrant and that Brutus and Cassius were justified in slaying him. Moreover, whoever kills a tyrant kills not a man but a beast disguised as a man. For, being deprived of all natural love for their fellow creatures, it follows that tyrants are without human sympathies, and hence are not men but wild animals. That tyrants bear no love to their neighbors is self-evident. They would not otherwise appropriate what is not theirs. But please note that I am speaking only of despots, not of those princes who either rule their states from legitimate succession or have been freely elected and govern their cities with the consent of the governed. And I say this to prevent your placing any malicious interpretation on my words. Thus, it is clear that whoever kills a tyrant is not committing homicide, since he kills a monster and not a man. I repeat, therefore, that Brutus and Cassius did not sin when they slew Caesar. First, because they killed a man whom the Roman law made it obligatory upon every Roman citizen to kill. Second, because they did not kill a man, but a beast in human form. Dante knew all this as well as anyone else. Tell me, have you read Dante's noble tribute to Cato in the "Convivio"? If Dante had condemned the assassination of Caesar, would he have spoken so reverently of Cato, who was Caesar's enemy and who preferred suicide to seeing his country enslaved? What further proof do you want of Dante's attitude than the words about Cato in the first Canto of the "Purgatorio"? . . . In those words Dante says that Cato died for the freedom of Rome, which he had defended against Caesar. It follows that if Cato fought on the side of liberty and Caesar opposed him, by Dante's definition, Caesar was a tyrant, and that being a tyrant it follows that his assassination was justified and that Brutus and Cassius for performing the deed should be rewarded and glorified. Therefore Dante understood the nature of tyrants and saw with what justice they were slain. He speaks with honor of those who have been compelled to destroy them. Consequently we must assume that such tyrannicides as Brutus and Cassius deserved the highest rewards and not the vilest punishment.

DONATO: Your conclusion, in short, is this: that Dante was not ignorant and that he knew quite well what he was writing. That is, he recognized that Brutus and Cassius were fine, courageous citizens. And, to reward them for their noble conduct, he placed them in the mouths of Lucifer! So that if Dante was not ignorant, then he was a mean and wicked man!

MICHELANGELO: You are not as patient with me as I am with you. Try to listen for a few moments and then perhaps you will calm down. As you must know, Dante punishes the worst sins in the Circles closest to the center. Thus, in the very last Circle, which is frozen, he punishes the traitors. These he divides into four species, since this crime is committed against four distinct classes of persons—against one's family, against one's country, against one's friends, and against imperial and divine majesty. This final species of treachery is punished in the last sphere of Frost, the one, namely, which encircles the center and is called "Giudecca." * And since Dante, following Christian opinion, accepts the world dominion of the Roman Emperors as a special act of Providence, it follows that he regards anyone who betrays Roman majesty as a traitor to be condemned to the same place and the same punishment as the traitor who betrays divine majesty. Finding it necessary, therefore, to offer examples of treachery against the Roman Empire, he chose Brutus and Cassius, who slew Caesar and in his person betrayed the Roman Empire.

DONATO: Couldn't he have chosen others? So many Roman emperors were assassinated that Dante did not lack for candidates to place in Lucifer's mouths!

MICHELANGELO: Dante needed the most famous examples in history. He found none of greater fame than Brutus and Cassius, and he did not think he was being unfair to them, since he was placing them in Hell not as Brutus and Cassius but as men who were guilty of betraying imperial majesty. And, by the same token, while he saw this imperial majesty vested in Caesar, he did not acquit Caesar of the infamy of becoming a tyrant and reducing his country to slavery.

DONATO: Will you kindly tell me something? Dante says he saw Caesar in Limbo, amid a group of excellent men, describing him as,

> *"Cesare armato con gli occhi grifagni."* †

Why does Dante put him in Limbo? Does he put him there as Caesar or as His Imperial Majesty?

MICHELANGELO: In a moment I'll be good and angry.

DONATO: Become as angry as you wish. I shall still cling to my opinion. I grant you all you say, but if you don't advance any further proof to the contrary I shall continue to believe—whatever the others may feel—that Dante showed very poor judgment!

MICHELANGELO: It is such a simple matter and yet you refuse to understand it.

DONATO: I understood quite well what you said. I quite agree that Dante

---

* Named from Judas Iscariot.
† "Caesar armed with fierce eyes."

signifies by Brutus and Cassius not the actual Brutus and Cassius but those who betray imperial majesty, and that in Caesar he does not mean to depict Caesar, but imperial majesty. But I frankly dislike seeing Caesar in Limbo and Brutus and Cassius in the mouths of Lucifer. In fact, I feel so strongly about it that I would gladly put Dante there myself, if he is not there already. He does not deserve anything better for that one sin!

MICHELANGELO: I see that I am wearing myself out for nothing. You are so stubborn that nothing I can say will help. Nevertheless, I shall add a few words. How do you know Dante did not feel that Brutus and Cassius did wrong in killing Caesar? Don't you know how much ruin and misery came into the world as a result of his death? Don't you see what a calamitous succession of emperors followed him? Would it not have been better if he had lived and carried out his ideas?

DONATO: The one idea he had was to be called "King."

MICHELANGELO: I grant you that. But wasn't that a lesser evil than what followed? How do you know that Caesar would not in time have tired of ruling and like Sulla restored freedom to the country and reconstituted the Republic? Now, if by continuing to live, he had done that, would not Brutus and Cassius have committed a great wrong in killing him? It is an act of great presumption to set out to kill the head of a state, whether he be just or unjust, for no one knows for certain what good can come of his death, and there is always the hope that some good can come of his remaining alive. For that reason I am considerably annoyed by people who believe that there can be no good unless it begins with some act of evil—that is, with a few deaths. They don't understand that times change, that unforeseen developments may arise, and that men get tired and change their minds. Out of all that it often happens—without anybody ardently hoping and striving and risking his life for it—that the very good will come about which many have thought desirable. Don't you think there were many people in the time of Sulla who longed to see Rome free and would gladly have seen him assassinated? But when they saw Sulla voluntarily renounce the dictatorship and restore liberty, don't you think they felt relieved that the Republic should be reconstituted peacefully and remorseful that they had desired Sulla's assassination? And, so, assuming that Caesar had lived and had also acted like Sulla, it would follow that whoever had thought of killing him would have done a great wrong. It is very possible that Dante believed Caesar would have done the same as Sulla, and for that reason judged that Brutus and Cassius were at fault and therefore deserved the sentence he imposed upon them.

DONATO: Well, have you finished your speech? Certainly it was a beautiful one and should be inscribed in letters of gold. And don't doubt it for a moment, I shall make a little book out of today's discussion. Now, suppose we all go home. We've reached the outer gate and it's already growing dark. I don't think I care to answer this nonsense of yours about Brutus and Cassius and Caesar any further, particularly since the others are laughing at us.

ANTONIO: As a matter of fact, we have enjoyed watching you both get excited over your difference of opinion.

DONATO: I was not aware of it, and besides, I was not especially eager to prolong the argument. . . . Well, Signor Antonio, you go along with Signor Luigi. I'll accompany Signor Michelangelo as far as his house. He is no longer a young man and he needs someone to look after him. And even if he has become quite furious with me, I'll make my peace with him on the way.

LUIGI: We have talked all day about Dante. Let our very last words be about him too. Suppose, Signor Michelangelo, you recite to us now the sonnet which you wrote a few days ago in praise of Dante.

MICHELANGELO: I am quite willing, though the sonnet is hardly worthy of your ears:

> *From heaven his spirit came, and robed in clay*
> *The realms of justice and of mercy trod,*
> *Then rose a living man to gaze on God,*
> *That he might make the truth as clear as day.*
> *For that pure star that brightened with his ray*
> *The undeserving nest where I was born,*
> *The whole wide world would be a prize to scorn;*
> *None but his maker can due guerdon pay.*
> *I speak of Dante, whose high work remains*
> *Unknown, unhonored by that thankless brood,*
> *Who only to just men deny their wage.*
> *Were I but he! Born for like lingering pains,*
> *Against his exile coupled with his good*
> *I'd gladly change the world's best heritage.**

---

* Translated by John Addington Symonds (*The Sonnets of Michael Angelo Buonarroti and Tommasso Campanella*, Smith, Elder & Co., London, 1878).

Frederick the Great

1.

JUST BEFORE THE BATTLE A GERMAN
CONQUEROR ANALYZES A FRENCH
TRAGEDIAN'S VERSES.

*When you have been accustomed for a long time,
as I have been, to all this brawl of battle, you will
not think it strange that, on the eve of the day on
which a battle is to be fought, anyone should amuse
himself as I am doing.*

IN THE conversations that follow we make our single visit to a battlefield.
There, during a lull in the bloody fighting, we eavesdrop on the cynical
musings of one of history's most complex characters—Frederick II, called
The Great. The picture of this arch-militarist and ruthless empire builder
composing French verses amid war's carnage would seem too preposterous
to be true. Yet of such contradictory elements was this warrior-king's
character made. One hour he is ordering thousands of men to certain,
needless death; the next he is rewriting a passage from a French play. A
short respite of sleep and he has again plunged into the prolonged horror
of the Seven Years' War. No ruler was ever involved in such vast intrigue,
and yet no man can shed such facile tears over a few lines of Racine. With
equal application he might compose a symphony or pilfer a province from
an unwary neighbor. This man has finally brought almost the whole of
Europe against his one grim little kingdom of Prussia. And yet, facing a
giant massing of foes, he can call for his flute and play a new sonata by his
court composer Quantz. A strategist of bold genius, he yearns rather to
be recognized as a French poet, and the one man he worships and envies
and flatters and resents is the fickle Frenchman Voltaire. To possess the
mind of Voltaire this absolute monarch would forfeit empire and wealth.
For he has crossed swords with this nimblest of wits, has corresponded
with him in mounds of letters, has fêted him sumptuously in the glittering salons of the Sans Souci palace at Potsdam . . . only to have the
Frenchman maliciously lampoon him for his pains. They had been friends,

32

these two, and though Frederick still smarts from the memory of Voltaire's banter, he misses the man. To be sure, there is no earthly use for a Voltaire in the thick of the day's battle. But in these few hours of rest from the giant ordeal of holding back the combined armies of Austria, France, Russia, Sweden, and Saxony, the discourse of a Voltaire would be good.

Instead, it is Frederick now who talks, and in place of a Voltaire to tease and excite him he has a Henri de Catt to listen and applaud. Doubtless it is just as well that we have this obscure, hero-worshipping Swiss teacher to keep Frederick company. He will at least record these nocturnal colloquies with the meticulous devotion of a private secretary. Actually Henri de Catt was engaged by Frederick as a reader. The king's passion for French was such that he wrote only in French, spoke French on any pretext, and by comparison, regarded his own native German as a barbarian tongue. For Frederick there was only one literature—French literature—and one poet—Racine. That France was now his enemy was a matter of little consequence to this German who adored her speech and her poets. It is merely one of the many ironies of these talks between battles that their language is French. It is the man's major obsession, so much so that De Catt soon loses his function as "reader" and becomes, to all intents and purposes, "listener." One begins to suspect that Frederick is more concerned with impressing this Swiss schoolteacher with his fluent French than with crushing the gathering foe. Perhaps the language itself stimulates this spate of confidences, and perhaps, too, Frederick knows that De Catt will repair to his own tent to jot down his priceless notes. Certainly they make a strange pair—De Catt, devout, naïve, sycophantic, the exact opposite of the regretted Voltaire; and Frederick, cynical, agnostic, yet almost laughably sentimental. They talk of all things— of Racine and science, of the immortality of the soul. By sheer accretion of detail the chats become a psychological study of a massive egotist with a restless brain, a neurotic and hypochondriac forever talking of colic and hemorrhoids, of headaches and enemas.

All of it—the poetry, the flute-playing, the weeping, the petty complaining—finds its way into De Catt's carefully kept diary. Says Lytton Strachey of this journal: "It is like one of those photographs—old-fashioned and faded, perhaps, but still taken sur le vif—which one turns to with an eager curiosity, of some remarkable and celebrated man." Today we would say "candid" of such a photograph, and such it is. "Nobody can help believing in the bland acceptance of Catt's photographic plate." It was Lord Rosebery, who, hailing the release of the manuscript from the Prussian State Archives in 1884, remarked that if Johnson had his Boswell, Goethe his Eckermann, Byron his Moore—Frederick the Great had his Henri de Catt. To that rigorous British historian De Catt's narrative was "one of the most faithful portraits of that monarch that we possess." De Catt's account covers only two years—1758–1760—of the Seven Years' War; but they were suspenseful years that were making or breaking this Prussian conqueror. The coalition was closing in; Berlin had fallen, and Frederick, in deep fits of gloom, even thought of suicide. "It is against this lurid background of frenzied struggle and accumulating horror that De Catt shows us his portrait of his master," says Strachey. "Clearly enough, these evening tête-à-têtes were the one vestige left to him in his terrible surroundings of the pleasures of private life, of the life of intellectual cultivation and unofficial intercourse: and the spectacle of this grim old conqueror seeking out the company of a mediocre young man from Switzerland with whom to solace himself in rhymes and rhapsodies would be pathetic if such a word were not so totally inapplicable to such a character . . . for what Catt shows us is a man for whom literature was not merely a pastime but a passion. . . ."

A word about this "mediocre young man from Switzerland." De Catt was living a tranquil, humdrum life as a Swiss teacher when he decided to spend his summer vacation in Holland in 1754. One day he took a trip on a canal boat from Amsterdam to Utrecht. A fellow-passenger on that boat was a rather grumpy gentleman in a black wig who rudely introduced himself to De Catt as first musician to the King of Poland. Soon, however, they were chatting amicably about religion, literature . . . and kings. The stranger asked him if he played the flute and was sorry to learn De Catt did not, for they might have tried a duet together. Presently the man began a fiery attack on all kings. De Catt, fearful that others might be listening, hurriedly replied: "I have not the honor to be acquainted with kings." At Utrecht the two men parted. A few weeks later a letter reached De Catt from Berlin inviting him to join the king as official reader. The man in the black wig had been Frederick the Great. Overnight the timid Swiss pedagogue was catapulted into a life of battles, courts, and high affairs of state. De Catt remained with Frederick till his death, becoming one of the few men in the king's confidence. The memoirs were first published in Leipzig in 1884. The following conversations are selected from the rendering of F. S. Flint, published by Constable & Co. Ltd. as *Frederick the Great*.

The date of the conversation that immediately follows is August 24, 1758. The setting is a partially demolished mill at Neudammer-Mühle which Frederick is using as headquarters. Henri de Catt tells us exactly what has been going on that day and we can only share his astonishment as he enters Frederick's room later that night:

"At three o'clock in the afternoon, the King marched in two columns, and toward eight o'clock in the evening, he entered the camp between Nabern and Dermietzel. He posted the advance-guard himself at the canal of Mietzel; this advance-guard with a portion of the artillery had crossed the bridge of Dammühle and thereby had the said canal at its back. While on the march we could see a portion of the enemy camp on the hill at Zicher; we even saw his cavalry form up in battle order at our approach, but there was no engagement. As we had arrived so late at the camp and we were on the eve of a battle, and I had already seen the King before setting out, I certainly did not think that I should be called. I was, however, at about nine o'clock in the evening. I found the King in a very small room of the mill, occupied in writing. I thought that the King was making his dispositions for the battle, but not at all; he was writing verses."

DE CATT: Verses, Sire? And tomorrow Your Majesty will give battle!

FREDERICK: Well, what is there so extraordinary in that? Can I not, like anybody else, employ myself on verses and amuse myself by making some, perhaps pretty bad ones? I have given my mind the whole day to the capital affair, which I have turned about in all ways. My plan is made, my decision taken. I may well be permitted, it seems to me, to scribble and rhyme just like anybody else.

DE CATT: Nobody, Sire, will dispute that permission. I say merely that in so critical a moment as must be the moment of giving battle, it is very difficult to find any inclination to versify.

FREDERICK: When you have been accustomed for a long time, as I have been, to all this brawl of battle, you will not think it so strange that, on the eve of the day on which a battle is to be fought, anyone should amuse himself as I am doing. Besides, sir, I am not composing; I am endeavoring to correct an author and to do better than he, if it is possible. When you left me today, I wished to read Rousseau's "Ode to Fortune," and, in opening my book, I fell on the Ode to Count de Sinzendorff, two strophes of which seemed to me rather ill-written. A moment's patience, sir. I have the last strophe to look over and rewrite. I shall soon be done, and I will show you my fine work. (*Frederick writes.*) ... Here it is; perhaps, for a day of fatigue as this has been, you will find that the poet has again come off well with his great work.

DE CATT: Yes, Sire, Your Majesty has come off well in such a moment. I doubt whether the generals whom you have and will have to combat ever write verses on the eve of a battle.

FREDERICK: I have a better opinion of them than you have. They would write verses just as I do, if they knew how. This little exercise refreshes your head and your ideas, and I have great need for both my head and my ideas to be fresh.

DE CATT: As this "little exercise," as Your Majesty calls it, seems to me a very singular thing, may I venture to ask you for this sheet which you have just written. It will always recall to me a remarkable and interesting circumstance.

FREDERICK: Certainly; if it will give you any pleasure, and if you attach a value to it which it assuredly does not deserve. Keep it and do what you like with it. The ode is a rather difficult form. Malherbe brought to it a great correctness of poetic harmony and style. If poets are generally unsuccessful with odes, especially with odes of praise, it is because they exaggerate too much. By carrying the praise too far, it becomes cruelly insipid. My beloved Racine, in his odes, is at an immense distance from his tragedies. I require a commentary for the first; I need none for the latter, and, with these, although he says in verse almost what I might say in prose, yet there is nothing to equal the magic and harmony of his verses.

DE CATT: I think, Sire, that it would be very difficult to rewrite passably a passage from Racine, for example:

Celui qui met un frein à la fureur des flots.

FREDERICK: You are right, that would be very difficult, but, my dear sir, suppose I try what I can do with it?

(*Picks up his pen.*)

(*Generals are announced.*)

(*To De Catt.*) Wait a moment here. I will go out and give them the dispositions; each one must know perfectly what he has to do. If my plans are followed, I hope all will go well.

(*Frederick goes out to instruct the generals.*)

(*A half hour later.*)

FREDERICK: Well, everything has been said. Let us see now what I shall have to say about *"Celui qui met un frein."*

(*Writes for fifteen minutes and gives the imitation to De Catt.*)

FREDERICK: Now, my friend, here are some grapes. Let us eat them, for who knows who will eat grapes tomorrow. We shall start at the break of day. I shall attack the Russians with my left wing; I shall refuse the right, and it is here that I advise you to remain. You will be less exposed here than anywhere else. Cling to the regiment of my poor brother, the Prince of Prussia. I hope that you will only have cannon fire to suffer. Good evening; I am going to bed, where I shall certainly need no one to lull me to sleep. Try, my friend, to find a spot on which to rest your head. If you hear the fire receding, remember that this means that things are going well with us. Good evening. Pray for me, for my army, and do not forget yourself.

(*De Catt passes the rest of the evening, wrapped in a cloak at the foot of a tree outside the mill. Shortly after midnight he notes a light in a nearby tent and enters to copy down the conversation with Frederick. Then he passes into Frederick's quarters and finds the King already taking his coffee. De Catt approaches the lackey who had been on duty outside Frederick's door.*)

DE CATT: Has His Majesty rested a little?

LACKEY: Rested, sir? He slept so soundly that I had some difficulty in awakening him.

(*The following day, August 25, De Catt notes: "The battle being unquestionably won, the King, at a quarter past eight in the evening, wrote a letter on a drum to the queen, and one to the ministry about the victory."*)

Frederick the Great

2.

DURING THE BATTLE HE TWITS AN AIDE FOR BELIEVING IN A LIFE AFTER DEATH.

*In following your system you have, I agree,
no risk to run, whether you are mistaken
or are not mistaken.*

DURING the summer of 1758 the Prussian King, who was facing one of the greatest coalitions of powers ever assembled against one state, also numbered among his enemies a rather commonplace vexation—hemorrhoids. Attacks would be brought on by over-indulgence in macaroni. "It was necessary," we learn, "to have recourse to the usual remedies." These consisted of enemas and "antispasmodic powders." During such seizures Frederick was inclined to grow apologetic about his enfeebled mental powers: "When I suffer from this complaint, my intellectual faculties do not perform their operations with the ease which I should desire. Good or bad health forms our ideas and all our philosophy." Perhaps it was only natural that during his worst spells Frederick should muse gloomily on the prospects of a Hereafter. It is during one of these neurasthenic and physiological seizures unbecoming to majesty that De Catt marches into the King's quarters one day at the redolently named town of Schmirsitz. There he finds his unpredictable master sketching the stately palace of Sans Souci, with its magnificent gardens, colonnades, and Chinese pagodas. De Catt soon realizes what is on Frederick's mind. . . .

FREDERICK: See the fine work I am on here.
DE CATT (*looking at the sketch and noting a kind of mausoleum at the end of the terrace, near a small grove*): Is this a work of antiquity, Your Majesty?
FREDERICK: No, my dear sir, that is a vault. I will have it surrounded by

38

cypresses, and it is there that I shall rest. Don't you think that I shall be comfortable there?

DE CATT: Your Majesty puts before me a very distressing idea.

FREDERICK: And why should we not come to an end one day? And should we not prepare for this end, and prepare with a tranquil mind, and I more than others? I, to quote Chaulieu, "who feel that old age is advancing with great strides, and who by a thousand changes know already the decay which the multitude of years brings on." * And then, after all, my friend, what is death? To quote Chaulieu once more: "Death is simply the end of life; it is followed by no pains or benefits; it is a sure asylum, and the end of our evils; it is the beginning of an eternal rest. And, to imagine it in a pleasanter guise, it is but a peaceful sleep that by a wise care the law of the universe persuades never to have an awakening. We leave the bosom of nature without effort, and return on our steps along the same road. Ah! why make a dreadful picture of an evil which assuredly is not felt on the other side?" † That, sir, is a good philosopher, who excels, as regards reasoning, all these philosophers in *us*. Is that not so? Chaulieu appears to me a philosopher who says to himself: "I wish to make myself happy in this world, and, to attain my end, I will endeavor to free myself from all constraint, to throw off every inconvenient yoke; I will refuse myself no pleasure, which alone will be the unique object of my life; I will combat with all my forces everything that runs counter to my views, which seem to me very wise." It is thus that I figure the philosophy of M. de Chaulieu, "regarding Charon and his bark with contempt."

DE CATT (*turning aside a conversation which appeared to serve no pur-*

---

* Moi qui sense qu'à grands pas la vieillesse s'avance,
  Et qui par mille changements
  Connais déjà la décadence
  Qu'apporte le nombre des ans.
      (Epistle No. 26, to the Abbé Courtin)
† La mort est simplement le terme de la vie,
  De peines, ni de biens, elle n'est point suivie,
  C'est un asile sûr, c'est la fin de nos maux,
  C'est le commencement d'un éternel repos.
  Et, pour s'en faire encore une plus douce image,
  Ce n'est qu'un paisible sommeil
  Que par une conduite sage
  La loi de l'univers engage
  A n'avoir jamais de réveil.
  Nous sortons sans efforts du sein de la nature
  Par le même chemin retournons sur nos pas.
  Eh! pourquoi s'aller faire une affreuse peinture
  D'un mal qu'assurément on ne sent point là—bas?
      (Epistle 27, to Madame la Duchesse de Bouillon)

pose): Your Majesty has a very tenacious memory. It is astonishing how much you have been able to learn by heart, and with what accuracy you remember it all.

FREDERICK: It is because I have exercised my memory a good deal. . . . But this is not the point. You condemn, I suppose, the ideas of my divine Abbé, and, like the orthodox person you are, you throw yourself headlong on the immateriality and the immortality of the soul.

DE CATT: I do not know, Sire, that I throw myself headlong, without reflection, as your phrase would convey. But—I agree, I believe in its immateriality and its immortality.

FREDERICK: How is it possible, my friend, that you can believe these things? Do you not see that the soul is only a modification of the body, and that, consequently, it is absurd to maintain that it can subsist and be preserved after our body is destroyed? They depend so much the one on the other that the one cannot subsist without the other. And tell me in good faith, can you in any way at all form an idea of an immaterial being, depict it, as I have depicted my Sans Souci? If you can, depict for me, I beg you, this immaterial being.

DE CATT: I could not do so, Sire, because an immaterial substance has neither form nor qualities perceptible to the senses, but I can very easily convince myself that what thinks in me has no parts. Can one logically deny the possibility of an immaterial substance because it cannot be represented in a material form? And, in supposing once more, Sire, that mutual dependence between the body and spirit, which is very true, may I legitimately conclude, from the dependence of these two things, that these two things are the same and identical? The taking of Olmütz, let me suppose, is announced at this moment to Your Majesty. Your joy is all the greater because you were not expecting, at this moment, this success. What connection, I venture to ask, is there between the effect and that which causes it? An articulated sound has struck and vibrated in your ear and your brain. That is a physical effect. But this vibration is followed by the feeling of joy, and this feeling is followed by the idea that the plans which Your Majesty has conceived will now be proceeded with. Is there in this feeling and in this idea any resemblance to the vibration of the acoustic nerves? Do you find a mechanical connection between this vibration which you have experienced and the ideas which have followed it?

FREDERICK: Sir, sir, your imagination leads you astray. You have a holy horror of the materiality of your soul, and it is your imagination which is behind what you say.

DE CATT: I think rather, Sire, that it is my understanding which rises up against that materiality, and which dictates my language. (*Wishing to cut short a conversation which distresses him because he perceives a little acrimony in Frederick.*) But, Sire, at Klein-Latein, you did me the honor to quote to me two instances which you had hit upon, that of the gunpowder and of Quantz,* saying at the same time that these instances seem to hint that there might be a real difference between our body and that which thinks in us.

FREDERICK: That is true, but these instances do not prove the immortality of the soul, with which you were imbued in your tender childhood, and you would not dare to cast a philosophical eye at this assertion of immortality, which you would fear to see overthrown. Your philosophy, like mine, would see no necessary connection between the immateriality of your soul and its immortality.

DE CATT: I confess frankly to Your Majesty that, in fact, I do not see this necessary connection. I do not know the nature of my soul well enough to conclude decisively that after death it will remember its former state, or that it will be able to continue to exercise its faculties. The idea and hope of the immortality of my soul are founded not on what I know of its nature, not on what I believe about germs and fecundation, but on what I know of God and his perfections. I am well aware that I cannot cite this as proof against philosophers who would deny the existence of a God and of his attributes. But these philosophers will never prove to me that man really dies.

FREDERICK: Eh, who is denying the existence of a God? Not I! He must be admitted, when we see in this universe both evident purposes and very simple and often striking means of attaining them. This world cannot be the effect of chance; there is too much order in it. I do not know God, but, as I have told you, I always worship him sincerely. Believe me, at bottom, there are uncertainties everywhere, but I have my system. I save myself by saying that everything we see is eternal, that everything is finished at death, and, if I am mistaken, my dear sir, I shall have both the pleasure of the surprise, and that of talking with you again above or below, as you will; but let this be as late as possible. Perhaps I should have been as good a believer as yourself, if in my youth especially, and in the following years of my life, I had seen the good believers follow and practice the duties which their belief prescribed.

---

* The argument was that since the force of gunpowder depends on the dryness of the weather and the playing of Quantz, Frederick's flute-player, on the condition of the flute, this proved that "one thing has a property contradictory of the other,"—an argument first used by De Catt on May 24 and then turned against him by Frederick on June 7. It is hard to see exactly what either the gunpowder or Quantz's flute-playing establishes one way or the other.

For example, my father was certainly a very good believer and very good Protestant. Being very ill, he was advised and exhorted even by the priests to be reconciled with his brother-in-law of Hanover, who had upset his bile: "You must write to him, Sire, and tell him that you have forgiven all his faults."—"Well, then, we shall write, but at any rate, if I recover, do not send my letter; send it only if I should die." And yet, I should have said to my father, your resentments, hatreds, angers, desires for vengeance must be sacrificed to the religion which you believe. We must pardon seventy times seven the brother who offends us, without which there is no pardon for our offenses. Ah, my dear sir, how the bad examples of parents, in all cases, lead youth astray and corrupt it, and how much should fathers and mothers endeavor to present but good examples to their children, who model themselves always on what they hear and on what they see done! . . . Do not laugh at my erudition and my doctrine; nothing is truer than what I tell you. Permit me to add one thing, and that is to wish you a good night, an immaterial and immortal soul, and that, if one day you have children, you may constantly set before them, with your better half, good and salutary examples. You see that, without thinking altogether in your Calvinistic manner, I yet think in a good fashion. But good evening; or otherwise, I shall keep you here for another hour. I think it is very nearly eight o'clock?

DE CATT: Nearly ten, Sire.

FREDERICK: Ten? Why, this is beyond a joke!

(*De Catt then observes that he was occupied until midnight in writing down this singular conversation.*)

(*The following evening.*)

FREDERICK: Do you know, sir, that I shall become annoyed with you if you keep me another time until ten o'clock, I who am usually up at three!

DE CATT: We must not then debate any more those questions on which I have not the good fortune to agree with Your Majesty.

FREDERICK: Ah, I see, I see! You are afraid that I shall sink your religious system.

DE CATT: I do not fear so at all, Sire.

FREDERICK: But confess to me, you would think it a great pity if Catt were not immortal. You are pleased at the idea of immortality. It tickles you, and so you believe your soul to be immortal.

DE CATT: It is not at all, Sire, because I desire it that I believe it immortal, but because this is founded on proofs which will never be destroyed.

And suppose even that I believe it because I desire it, would Your Majesty wish to tear from me this pleasant hope, to annihilate this mainspring of my actions, and to take away from me what is a consolation when I am being attacked by those evils to which we are so much exposed in this life?

FREDERICK: Ah, my dear sir, since you speak in this tone, I will take good care not to take away from you an illusion that pleases you, or to destroy your hopes and reduce you to despair. If it is a barbarous thing to warn a man of the unfaithfulness of his dear spouse, it is a hundred times more barbarous to put before him a system that will destroy all his hopes. And, then, too, in following your system, you have, I agree, no risk to run, whether you are mistaken or are not mistaken. . . . When I spoke to you yesterday of my father, you must not imagine that he gave us bad examples. He only gave us good ones. The faults which his children may have committed are their own faults. My father did not occasion them. He was really in all respects a good man. He was literally a philosopher-king in all the force of the term. Perhaps he went too far in expecting too much of humanity, and in desiring that his subjects and all those about him should have the austere morals which he had himself. . . . (*Takes up his flute.*) Now, if you would like to hear a new solo by Quantz, I will play it, and this music will not keep you until ten o'clock. . . . I tried it after dinner. It appeared to me to be superior to what I have had of him in this kind. This man does not grow old.

(*"This solo lasted an hour, and this time I had a pleasant evening which left me time to sup."—De Catt*)

[*The following day they returned to one of Frederick's favorite subjects, Racine—the King declaiming several scenes from* Mithridate *by heart.*]

Ancien Régime

A GROUP OF FRENCH WITS DELIGHT THEMSELVES
BY DISCUSSING THE IMPROPRIETIES.

*Madame, one is bound to admit that one can
never speak up for innocence without being
slightly improper.*

F ROM the field headquarters of a Prussian conqueror to the urbane atmosphere of a Paris dinner party of the year 1750 would seem a long leap indeed. Actually they have much in common. For Frederick II is as much a child of this 18th century as the saloniers whom we shall soon overhear at the dinner table of Mlle. Quinault of the Théâtre-Français. They are all creatures of this same so-called "Enlightenment"; they play with the same ideas of Diderot, Rousseau, and Voltaire; in fact, they even speak the same language. To be sure, Frederick's is a strange kind of "enlightenment." Arch-aggressor and absolute ruler, he seems scarcely a votary of the Cult of Reason. He has plunged Europe into the extended holocaust of the Seven Years' War. Yet this Frederick prides himself on being a rationalist, a man of science, a pupil of Voltaire; in short, a man above dogma and superstition. Later it will be said of him, as of one or two fellow autocrats, that he tempered his despotism with "benevolence," that if he ruled with an iron fist, he at least refrained from sanctioning torture and human furnaces.

In any case, we may be certain of one thing—this Prussian is a frustrated Frenchman. To take part in the conversation we shall hear he would possibly barter the next day's victory. Frederick has long relished this suavely adroit give-and-take, with its naughty overtones of refined candor. He would himself have much to say about Voltaire and modesty at Mlle. Quinault's table. He remembers the gatherings of Europe's great minds in his own Sans Souci palace, remembers the same Voltaire whom he had housed and fêted only to become another butt of his scathing satire. Yes, this evening at Mlle. Quinault's would bring nostalgic twinges to Frederick the Great. It is the sort of thing that makes him look upon his own Germans as barbarians and his own language as anathema.

One would scarcely blame Frederick. For the company we now meet

44

*belongs to what has been called "the most seductive society in Europe."
It is a world of idle, carefree talk and easy refinement. An air of sophisticated bonhomie hovers about these princes and writers and ladies of
leisure. For this is a class with time on its hands and the money to make
this time count in a ceaseless game of pleasure; a class blithely oblivious
that its decades are numbered. This is the Paris of Louis XV, and as likely
as not some new jest is making the rounds about Mme. de Pompadour
or Mme. du Barry. It is a day of lavish spending, of châteaux and battalions of servants. If a grim auditor waits at the end of this trail of
squandering, no one seems very much perturbed. "Après moi le déluge!"
cries a nonchalant king, and a whole leisured class adopts it as its motto.
Meanwhile, for those within the pale it is good while it lasts, this old
regime of velvety manners and easy badinage. The morals are easy, and
no ménage is complete without lover and mistress. An elaborate game of
mutual blindness governs the wanderings of husbands and wives. The
one impropriety is to be dull; the one indiscretion to arrange a poor party,
and the one infidelity to betray not a husband but a lover.*

"In this indolent, self-indulgent life, all declaimed against outworn
morality and puritanic precepts," writes E. G. Allingham in the shrewd
preface to his translation of Mme. d'Épinay's Mémoires (Routledge &
Kegan Paul Ltd., London, 1930). They declaimed so strongly that many
openly patronized the very men whose inflammatory words would one day
demolish their world. Into their salons they brought the same Condillacs
and Diderots who lashed in print at their wasteful and leisured para-
sitism. Proudly they paraded their pet "bears" from the ranks below.
Remember, they boasted of being "enlightened." Allingham has pictured
the scene for us: "A young married woman would have her 'set' of
friends, some of whom she met daily at her house or theirs. Dinner was
at one o'clock. The afternoon was spent in amusing themselves—they
read, had a concert among themselves. Sometimes a party of friends would
act a play written by one of them. The men would draw or paint, the
ladies would sew. There was conversation on every possible topic. In the
evening there would be little intimate suppers, or a party would go to
the theater or a ball."

Such a "young married woman" with such a "set" was Louise Florence
Pétronille Tardieu d'Esclavelles d'Épinay. Like other wealthy aristocrats
of the day, Mme. d'Épinay commuted between a château in the country
and a house in Paris. Her "set" was one of the most brilliant of the day.
In her Paris salon or at "La Chevrette" in the valley of Montmorency
one might meet the "encyclopédistes" Diderot, Condillac, and d'Alembert; the clever Duclos, gossipy chronicler of the times; the Marquis de

Saint-Lambert, skeptic, poet, and soldier; the Baron von Grimm, chatty literary historian; and, if one's luck were good, the mighty Voltaire himself. And in 1748, Mme. d'Épinay added her most prized exhibit of all, a shabby, neurasthenic, but fiery-tongued young writer by the name of Jean Jacques Rousseau. We shall hear a great deal more of this favorite "bear" of Mme. d'Épinay when later we visit the château of "La Chevrette."

For the present our interest in this little lady is the fact that she keeps a diary in which each day's happenings, however trivial, are faithfully recorded. It is a diary of her soul, as well as of her salon. In time, as we shall see, these same Mémoires et Correspondence will become a battlefield of rabid wrangling between the foes and friends of Rousseau. Meanwhile, on this spring day in Paris of 1750 Mme. d'Épinay has been to visit her gifted friend of the Théâtre-Français. This Mlle. Quinault, of a famous theatrical family, is a salonière in her own right. Her particular crowd meets twice a week, either at her house or that of the Comte de Caylus. For the moment we surrender the narrative to Mme. d'Épinay, who sets the scene at Mlle. Quinault's dinner table:

("Yesterday Mlle. Quinault paid me a visit. She pestered me to go and dine with her and I could not very well refuse. There were five of us: M. le Prince de . . ., * the Marquis de Saint-Lambert, M. Duclos, and I. The Marquis is exceedingly clever, and not only is he a powerful thinker but there is delicacy and taste in his thought as well. He writes verse, and not amateur stuff either, for he is a true poet. One can see plainly enough from the freedom and confidence pervading this circle that they think a great deal of and are sure of one another. One hour's conversation in that house gives one a wider outlook and more satisfaction than almost any book I have read so far. Until dessert conversation was noisy, and general—desultory talk about the ballet and the new taxes and nothing much else. At dessert Mlle. Quinault signed to her niece to leave the table. She retired and so did the servants. She is a young girl, about twelve or thirteen. I asked her aunt why we were not to have the pleasure of seeing more of her, for she did not, as a matter of fact, put in an appearance till just at dinner time."—Mme. d'Épinay)

---

* Never identified with certainty, though assumed to have been the Prince de Beauvau.

MLLE. QUINAULT: She must keep in the background.

MME. D'ÉPINAY: Your niece bids fair to be very attractive . . . (*about to call the niece back.*)

MLLE. QUINAULT: Ah, no, if you please. Quite enough that we should restrain ourselves up to dessert for that baby. Now, when we can put our elbows on the table and say just what comes into our heads, we don't want servants and children about. Eh—enough—enough—it won't be so easy to make the tender Arbassan * keep his tongue in check before us. We couldn't talk freely before the child.

DUCLOS: Faith, Madame, you know nothing about it. I should show her things in their true light, right away. Just let me try.

MLLE. QUINAULT: Oh, I've no doubt. But the days are gone when a spade was called a spade, and one must pick up the language of one's own period and country while one is young.

DUCLOS: And that's not Nature's, which is the only right language.

MLLE. QUINAULT: Yes, when it has not been twisted, for language or no language, Nature has been working away at what we call modesty for many a long day.

DUCLOS: Not on our so-called modesty of today: take savage countries, for instance, where women go naked till the age of puberty and are unashamed.

MLLE. QUINAULT: As you will, but I believe that the germ of modesty was inherent in man.

SAINT-LAMBERT: I think so too. Time, purity of morals, the itch of jealousy, and the interests of pleasure have all combined to foster it.

DUCLOS: And education has done a lot to bolster up the sublime virtues designated as "the proprieties."

THE PRINCE: But at one time not only savages but everyone went naked.

DUCLOS: Yes, indeed, all mixed up together, fat, plump, chubby-cheeked, innocent and gay: let's have a drink!

MLLE. QUINAULT (*singing as she pours him a glass*):

> *Il t'en revient encore une image agréable*
> *Qui te plait plus que tu ne veux.*†

True—this garment that fits so beautifully is the only one with which Nature has provided us.

DUCLOS: Cursed be he who first thought of putting another on top of it.

MLLE. QUINAULT: He must have been some humpbacked, skinny, de-

---

* An unexplained reference to M. Duclos.

† "There keeps coming back to you an agreeable image which pleases you more than you wish."

formed little dwarf, for no one good to look at ever wants to conceal himself.

SAINT-LAMBERT: But whether one is good or bad to look at, one has no sense of modesty when one is by oneself.

MME. D'ÉPINAY: But is that really so, Monsieur? I seem to have the feeling just the same when I am by myself.

SAINT-LAMBERT: It is because we are in the habit of being modest before others that we still continue to be modest when by ourselves, Madame, but you must allow that it is not much use to take the feeling home, for it gradually wears off, and becomes less sensitive.

DUCLOS: That's sure. I swear to you that when there's no one to see me, I hardly blush at all.

MLLE. QUINAULT: And never when anyone does see you. A fine comparison! the modesty of Duclos!

DUCLOS: Faith, it's as good as anyone else's. I bet that you, all of you, when it's hot, kick your sheets to the foot of the bed. Then good-by modesty, fine virtue, that we fix on ourselves in the morning—with pins.

MLLE. QUINAULT: Ah, there's many a virtue like that in the world!

SAINT-LAMBERT: How many vices and virtues are there which were never included in Nature's code nor inscribed in the regulations of universal morality?

THE PRINCE: There are a multitude of purely conventional vices and virtues, according to country, customs, and even climate: but the evil which was inscribed in the code of universal morality is evil always. It was evil ten thousand years ago; it is evil today.

SAINT-LAMBERT: The only morality that is inviolable and sacred is universal morality.

DUCLOS: In other words—Law and Order—Reason, in fact.

SAINT-LAMBERT: The Will of all humanity.

DUCLOS: Or in two words, Monsieur, the immutable decree of pleasure, need or pain.

MLLE. QUINAULT: That's very fine—what he's said: he talks like an oracle. Let's drink to the oracle. (*They all drink.*)

DUCLOS: If I were to go back to the very beginning . . .

MME. D'ÉPINAY: To the beginning?

DUCLOS: I should see the human species scattered stark naked on the face of the earth.

MLLE. QUINAULT: You seem to like that idea from the way you keep returning to it.

DUCLOS: Yes, but I was going to remark that if anyone at that time did cover himself with an animal's pelt he did so because he was cold.

MME. D'ÉPINAY: And why not from shame?

DUCLOS: What for? Because of being what he was?

THE PRINCE: And yet there comes a time when Nature herself seems abashed and contrives a veil with which to cast a shade.

MLLE. QUINAULT: Fine, Messieurs, this is becoming scientific.

SAINT-LAMBERT: If that were Nature's intention, she would not take so long about it: besides she casts her veil where there is nothing to hide.

DUCLOS: Ah, were we all uncovered, what beautiful arms, what tumbled heads, to say nothing of all the rest, should we not see!

MLLE. QUINAULT: And it might cost less to be more beautiful—and may be better.

MME. D'ÉPINAY: I think that whatever one's idea of modesty may be, one cannot separate it from the sense of shame.

THE PRINCE: But, Madame, what is shame?

MME. D'ÉPINAY: I can only explain what I mean by shame by saying that I feel a dislike of myself every time I am ashamed. I have at such times, as it were, a desire for solitude, and a feeling of wanting to hide myself.

SAINT-LAMBERT: Very well put, Madame, but the dissatisfaction with yourself would not exist were it not that you were conscious of some imperfection, that is certain. If the imperfection for which you blush is known only to yourself, the feeling of shame is swift, slight, and transitory. On the other hand, it is prolonged and bitter if the censure of others is added to that of your own conscience.

MME. D'ÉPINAY: If that be so, why then am I relieved when I own the reason of my shame?

SAINT-LAMBERT: Because mere confession is to your credit, which is proved by the fact that you probably would not have had the courage to look anyone who had guessed it in the face.

DUCLOS: That's precisely why I always acknowledge my faults.

MLLE. QUINAULT: When you see that it's no good to try and hide them.

THE PRINCE: Then there are faults and faults. Those that we own are next door to virtues. There is more to be gained than lost by admitting them.

MME. D'ÉPINAY: Once you say that man can go naked unashamed, you will admit a good deal more.

DUCLOS: Ah, no doubt. But for the precepts and example of your mother, and your nurse's lectures, you would have dared to do so.

THE PRINCE: It is a funny thing, but it is only among human beings that one finds this shame in obeying natural impulses.

SAINT-LAMBERT: Yet Nature is not only respectable, viewed merely as in her broad and general aspect: whenever she is in command she becomes the fount of a mutual sympathy, affectionate friendliness, and active kindliness that permeate all other feelings.

MLLE. QUINAULT: It remains to be seen whether those objects which, simply because they are concealed from our eyes, so powerfully affect us for good or ill would not leave us cold and unmoved could we always behold them: there are instances of this.

DUCLOS: Do you think that tact would also dwindle to insignificance?

SAINT-LAMBERT (*enthusiastically, presenting a glass to Mlle. Quinault*): Mademoiselle, I beg you give me a glass of champagne. Messieurs, I will write you an ode, and you shall see that the most delightful of all human alliances is the one that should have been the most solemn. Legislation has missed the mark. Why do not youth and maid present themselves? . . . (*Blank in M.S.*) Why does not the . . . (*blank in M.S.*) lead the wedded pair thither and why is not the sacrifice consummated under a vast veil? Around them loveliest perfumes should have risen and sweetest music drowned the young bride's cries and sighs; noble, voluptuous hymns should have been chanted in honor of the gods, invocations on behalf of the child to be which would have invested the ceremony with solemn importance. The bride, instead of indulging in petty, shrinking timidity and foolish tears, would have feared lest she should avert the blessing of the gods upon their union, and their favors from the child to be conceived in her womb.

MLLE. QUINAULT: There's a sublime thought worthy of Pindar or Anacreon. There's your true poet!

DUCLOS: Ah, my word, I'd go to a wedding every day, if they were all like that.

THE PRINCE: But how comes it, now, that so natural and necessary and general an act should be done under cover?

SAINT-LAMBERT: And so delightful!

DUCLOS: Because desire implies seizure. The man inflamed by passion carries off the woman for himself, just as a dog who seizes a bone carries it in his mouth until he finds a corner wherein to devour it; and even as he eats it he glances round and growls, for fear lest it be snatched from him. I have already said to him who can hear that jealousy is the germ of modesty.

SAINT-LAMBERT: If Nature is very enlightened, she is sometimes very foolish.

MLLE. QUINAULT: Ah, very true. Drink, gentlemen, drink.

(*Each takes another glass of champagne. Duclos tosses off three glasses, and the two bottles they have opened are drained in a minute.*)

THE PRINCE: Now, let us go back to where we were. We were talking of a dog and seizure. What the devil was Duclos saying?

DUCLOS: Faith, Prince, I'm sure I don't know. But no matter. I can easily say something else, no trouble to me.

MME. D'ÉPINAY: Monsieur was saying that jealousy was the germ of modesty.

THE PRINCE: But—just one moment, gentlemen. There are other natural actions which we conceal, and which have nothing to do with jealousy.

DUCLOS: Ah, by God! I should think so. He would indeed be shameless who was too lazy for self-respect. Faith! All said and done, it's as well to be private sometimes. The accompaniments of passion's transport. . . .

MLLE. QUINAULT: Shut up. Duclos, you go too far—

DUCLOS: But, by God, I don't see. What I said was very mild.

SAINT-LAMBERT: Madame, one is bound to admit that one can never speak up for innocence without being slightly improper.

DUCLOS: Nor for modesty without being impudent.

MLLE. QUINAULT: That's why you speak so well. But change the subject, or use language fit to listen to.

SAINT-LAMBERT: Certainly. 'Tis a fair mirror that one fears to sully with one's breath.

(*"However, the dissertation was soon brought to a full stop by a man who brought in a new poem by Voltaire; to Mme. d'Épinay it seemed charming, and she thought the others criticized it too severely. The Prince and M. de Saint-Lambert were the only ones who stood up for the verses and the author. After it had been read the Prince turned to Mlle. Quinault."*—Allingham)

THE PRINCE: Well, what do you think of it, Madame?

DUCLOS: He's a ruffian.

MLLE. QUINAULT: I don't know whether to regard the satire as offensive, but one cannot attach any importance to his praise.

SAINT-LAMBERT: Why not? No eulogy could have been put more neatly and more gracefully.

MLLE. QUINAULT: Oh, yes, but he does it from no motive of justice. It's only to annoy one man that he speaks well of another.

THE PRINCE: He has a fine wit.

MLLE. QUINAULT: Yes, but very ill-natured.

DUCLOS: He is not to be trusted, and one of these days he will go a bit too far, and then some filibuster who has nothing to lose by it will set fire to his fine goods and chattels—and a good thing too.

SAINT-LAMBERT: They'll never ease him of a kindly heart.

MLLE. QUINAULT: Oh, yes, that's the special virtue of the heartless.

SAINT-LAMBERT: It's the one virtue without which there are pretty few others. Oh, happy he who can examine his own life and find that the good and evil in it are fairly balanced. Oh, undoubtedly the real good Voltaire has done far outweighs the harm attributed to him, and when you add to that an outstanding genius absolutely indisputable, you will feel a good deal more than mere toleration for him, that is, unless you make up your mind to throw your Poussins, Raphaels, and Guidos into the fire, because you have discovered some tiny imperfection in the corner of a picture.

MLLE. QUINAULT: Oh, oh, enough of that, and let's simply say that it's best to avoid this sort of folk altogether.

Jean Jacques Rousseau

PORTRAIT IN DIALOGUE I

1.

MME. D'ÉPINAY REPROVES HER BOORISH PROTÉGÉ FOR RIDICULING THE COMPANY SHE KEEPS.

*I should cut a poor figure among a lot of
artificial persons walking tiptoe in their
Sunday best—that's not my style at all.*

S O FAR we have met this Mme. d'Épinay as the humble diarist of the proceedings around the dinner table of her friend Mlle. Quinault. Her part in the discussion on modesty has been modest indeed, and one or two of her remarks would argue a prudish nature. She is by no means a prude, however. The wife of a philandering husband, she has in turn taken a lover, a M. de Francueil, whose duties at her château in Montmorency also include teaching her young son music and drawing. Later M. Francueil will be replaced by the Baron von Grimm, who will dominate her life, inherit the voluminous manuscript of the Mémoires, and play a part in the gathering drama of Rousseau. It is Rousseau who concerns us now. For when we next confront Mme. d'Épinay she is in the company of this erratic apostle of the "natural man." The relation between these two is strange. Mme. d'Épinay has become a kind of protectress of the erudite boor. She has introduced him to the "encyclopédistes," and they have commissioned articles from him. One of her friends has even secured him a job. Though on terms of the warmest confidence, they are not lovers; indeed, the all-revealing Rousseau himself tells us that she is not his type, being rather "emaciated" for his taste. Later Mme. d'Épinay will provide a charming cottage, the "Hermitage," in which this brilliant "bear" of hers may compose novels and articles. Quite properly Rousseau accepts this patronage as the rightful reward of genius. If Mme. d'Épinay provides for him handsomely, he in turn stimulates her mind and dazzles and titillates her titled guests. For ten years this friendship continues. Rousseau flourishes as writer and thinker, is lavishly lionized by the Montmorency set, and honestly worships this little woman who has made him her protégé.

Then the whole thing bursts like a bubble. Mme. d'Épinay grows indignant over an unsavory account of Rousseau's lovemaking with her sister-in-law, the Comtesse d'Houdetot. Moreover, they quarrel over the Baron von Grimm, whom Rousseau has come to resent as her lover and counsellor. A sharp exchange of letters begins between Rousseau and the man whom he suspects of undermining him at Montmorency. Diderot enters the quarrel, and for a time it is hard to say which side he is on. Finally, Mme. d'Épinay falls sick and prepares to depart for Geneva. Diderot urges Rousseau to accompany his benefactress. Rousseau suspects that Mme. d'Épinay is pregnant by the Baron von Grimm and that her friends are conspiring to entangle Rousseau in the scandal. Such is Rousseau's version of the story; Mme. d'Épinay's is different. She presents herself as an innocent and maligned victim of it all. The episode is highly complicated, and the testimony on both sides becomes suspect the more we read of it. Devotees of Rousseau accepted his defense and gallantly acquitted him of any caddish betrayal of Mme. d'Épinay. The latter part of the Mémoires, which portray Rousseau as a devious and ungrateful scoundrel, have been dismissed as a fabrication of the Baron von Grimm, into whose skillful hands the manuscript fell. The partisanship has continued from 1818, the year of the publication of the Mémoires, down to this day. That Rousseau was a flighty and suspicious man no one can doubt. Nor can there be much doubt that Diderot and Grimm played a fiendish little game of their own in winning Mme. d'Épinay away from her pet beneficiary. One hesitates to take sides, but to berate the generous-minded and freedom-loving Rousseau as a "monster of ingratitude" seems excessive. In any case, it would seem prudent to tread cautiously through those portions of Mme. d'Épinay's Mémoires in which Rousseau assumes the guise of villain. There is no reason, however, to question the veracity of her earlier reports of encounters with the unpredictable genius whom she had taken under her wing.

On this September afternoon of 1751 we find Rousseau and Mme. d'Épinay on the very best of terms. Mme. d'Épinay is sport enough to accept in friendly fashion Rousseau's strictures about the company she keeps, and she even invites and is given a frank appraisal of her mental and physical attributes. Before long, the conversation drifts into the familiar channel of religion. . . . Mme. d'Épinay had witnessed and duly recorded a clash between Rousseau and Saint-Lambert at Mlle. Quinault's some days earlier. Saint-Lambert had been denouncing all faiths, when Rousseau, in a surge of anger, blurted out: "If it is cowardly to speak ill of an absent friend, it is a crime to speak ill of one's God who is present! And I, gentlemen, believe in God! I shall leave you if you say another word!" . . . And now, in this lovely park of "La Chevrette" at Mont- morency, Mme. d'Épinay reverts to that discussion, eliciting from Rous- seau an impassioned retort. Angrily he avows a belief in hell for the "Great and the Rich" for whose "vexations and atrocities . . . there is no justice in this world." Mme. d'Épinay has just left her lover Francueil, who is teaching her son how to read music. She invites Rousseau to a walk in the park. An hour later she will be back in her room, writing in her diary: "I have just had an original conversation with M. Rousseau, which is worth noting." The conversation follows:

MADAME: Now why is it that I have not seen you at my house for such an age, nor during my stay in Paris?

ROUSSEAU: Because when I want to see you, Madame, I like to have you all to myself.

MADAME: Do you?

ROUSSEAU: Of course, I do—where should I come in, in your own set? I should cut a poor figure among a lot of artificial persons walking tiptoe in their Sunday best—that's not my style at all.

MADAME: What nonsense—when have you seen such people at my house?

ROUSSEAU: Eh, but I have, Madame: your sister-in-law—to go no further— with her die-away eyes and her smile of voluptuous disdain; Maure- paire, with his raillery; Madame de Versel, bowing like a devotee to dis- play her fine neck; Duclos, despotic, cutting, and traitorously brusque; Jelyotte, honeyed and bumptious; all of them with a high sense of pro- priety and without any morals.

MADAME: You are very severe, but even more unjust, Monsieur. I should think it quite natural if you took it upon yourself to criticize me, for you have known me for some years and have seen me in the country where I am so informal that it does not take long to get to know me. But, with the exception of Duclos, you have hardly seen the ladies and gentlemen you have mentioned.

ROUSSEAU: I am only expressing, Madame, the general opinion of them, and certainly what I have seen of them has given me no desire to in- vent excuses for them.

MADAME: Do you know—you make me trouble? I hardly dare ask your opinion of me, though I am longing to know it.

ROUSSEAU: You can have it, Madame, if it will give you any pleasure. I promise you an equal frankness; and if you are not quite satisfied with yourself as you are, you will be with what I say you can be, if only these ladies and gentlemen will leave you alone. But I can tell you that they would degrade the fairest nature Heaven ever formed.

MADAME: Oh, Rousseau, you are talking twaddle! But let us see what you think of me. We'll dismiss my face—I'm not pretty, I know.

ROUSSEAU: You vary according to your mood. When one catches you full-face, when you are looking down, looking inwardly, you are better than pretty; in the usual way, you have many faces. I gather from those that I know that you have one which I do not know and which may not be the least interesting, but of those I have seen I like the reflective one best.

MADAME: That is strange, I should never have thought it; but go on to character, that is what I want to know.

ROUSSEAU: Perhaps, Madame, I ought to start by telling you what other people think of you, as then you will be better able to judge of the worth of my opinion.

MADAME: Certainly—certainly.

ROUSSEAU: They say you lack character, are good-natured, but insincere, inclined to intrigue, inconstant, fickle, quick-witted, and that you pose as intellectual though you are really only superficial.

MADAME: Monsieur, Monsieur, is that what they say of me? It is not possible!

ROUSSEAU: Yes, Madame, and although possibly not a word of it is true and I do not believe half of it, it does not surprise me.

MADAME: What! You don't believe half of it, Monsieur? If you only knew how different I am from that. To think that they could say such things!

ROUSSEAU (*laughing*): So you think that you are the first woman to whom injustice has been done? What does it point to? I can tell you. You are good-natured and often taken in; you do not suspect ill-will or deception until you have proof positive: you are always wavering as to what you ought or ought not to do, and what with being hesitating and contradictory in all you do and say, and what with your mortal dread of offending or wounding others, you appear insincere and lacking in character.

MADAME: But what am I to do to avoid giving this impression, for what you have just said is true.

ROUSSEAU: Ah, that's not so easy, and I am reminded of a remark once made to me by a friend of mine, whose character in point of weakness is rather like your own. He is—apart from that—a man of most distinguished merit, a transcendent genius, who has not his match in this century. He is Diderot. I said to him one day, "But how is it that you, with your easy-going temperament, which induces you to spend half your life making blunders, and carefully keeping them dark, and the other half in patching them up, do not frequently appear insincere?" "Simply because I am neither true nor false," said he, "but transparent." He is open, and you, Madame, are true but not open.

MADAME: Yes, and again, that is true. But, Monsieur, intriguing, now! Surely not?

ROUSSEAU: All the same, from over-anxiety to do what is right, and often from a desire to avoid taking credit for it, or rather from fear of failing in your good intentions, you take a roundabout course, instead of making straight for your aim.

MADAME: That is very odd.

ROUSSEAU: As for pose and superficiality, there they misjudge you. On the contrary, there is a good deal of simplicity about you. In spite of having read a lot, and learned a lot, you are ignorant, because you have read in the wrong way without method or selection. Your thoughts are the fruit of your own good brains rather than of your reading. You have no clear-cut ideas or principles in your head: but how could you have acquired any, living in a world that has none?

MADAME: I have formed them for myself: it seems to me that they exist independently of education, in the heart of every decent person, and from them he never departs.

ROUSSEAU: Madame, you are fortunate in being able to think so.

MADAME: As for my brains, I think they are good, but my mind is slow, reflective, and disconnected.

ROUSSEAU: That statement is not incorrect but hardly, I think, quite true. You are, for instance, a good mother, but so far you have loved your friends for themselves and your children for yourself. But your feeling for the latter is in proportion to the pleasure they give you: still, that will not last. You are courageous, high-minded, virtuous in a way, and if you will only surround yourself with decent people, I can tell you that you will some day be a very fine woman: but I am not going to tell you that people will speak any better of you for that.

MADAME: As long as my friends do me justice, and my heart knows itself not unworthy of their esteem, all will be well.

ROUSSEAU: Quite right.

MADAME: But you, in your turn, are you not going to ask me what I think of you?

ROUSSEAU: Perhaps, Madame, I do not care to know.

MADAME: Oh well, I do not mind your indifference. But, by the way, do you know I also rather liked the way you went for Saint-Lambert the other day. All the same, I was very much puzzled for the rest of the day.

ROUSSEAU: I expect you were: there are some prejudices imbibed so early and so enrooted in our souls that it is difficult to get rid of them. They are so universally accepted, and proclaimed so constantly and so effectively, not only by men but by the wonders of Nature, ceaselessly renewed before our eyes, that one can hardly refuse credence to such an array of proof, the animal world, plants, fruits of the earth, rain, the seasons.

MADAME: Still it worried me, yet I think Saint-Lambert had the best of it. . . .

ROUSSEAU: Madame, sometimes in the corner of my little room, sitting with my head in my hands, or in the deep darkness of night, I think as he does. But see yonder (*pointing with one hand toward the sky, his head uplifted, his face inspired*), when sunrise disperses the mists that curtain the earth, and unfolds before me the sparkling and wonderful panorama of Nature, the mists of my mind are dispelled as well: I recover my faith in God, my belief in Him. I marvel before Him, I adore Him, I am prostrate in His presence.

MADAME: But, Monsieur, if you, who have so great a leaning toward belief, have your moments of doubt, others must certainly have theirs also. And that being so, I should feel, if I may say so, more confidence in your intellectual conviction than in that which resulted from the evidence of your eyes. Tell me truly, you who have meditated often on this matter, you who have all manner of knowledge that I can never hope to attain, tell me where you would look for the most direct proof.

ROUSSEAU: Madame, our lights are so limited it is hardly possible to say. Shall I tell you a story?

MADAME: Ah! You are going to answer me with a story! All right, please tell it to me!

ROUSSEAU (*reflecting a moment*): Once upon a time a man was cast ashore on a strange land—a land peopled with men and women of every cast of countenance, and of all ages. He gazed upon the different objects that attracted his attention and looked amid the throng for someone who could inform him as to the laws and customs of the land, for he liked the place and desired to abide there. Seeing three long-bearded men who were sitting apart, talking, he went up to them and said, 'Messieurs, be so kind as to tell me where I am and to whom this land belongs. If the manners and customs of the inhabitants are on a par with the wisdom and method that I observe even in the village of the land, your ruler must be one of the greatest and best of princes.'

" 'Nothing is easier than to gratify your curiosity,' replied one of the old men to the stranger. 'You are in the Kingdom of the Benevolent Genius, who dwells yonder on the opposite coast. You were cast on this shore willy-nilly, and by his command, for he has a passion for making people happy, and to this end he causes strangers to be shipwrecked. Those who are not drowned he takes under his protection, and shuts them up for a certain period in this country that you so rightly admire. These gentlemen and I are his ministers, commissioned by him to instruct his subjects in his will and see that they observe the laws he imposes, under pain of penalty or hope of award.'

" 'But, Messieurs, since this country is so beautiful, why does he not dwell among his subjects, and what is he doing yonder?'

" 'He is relieved from the necessity of showing himself as we are his deputies,' answered the old man; 'we are directly inspired by the Genius. But you must be told the conditions.'

" 'Conditions!' said the stranger. 'Did you not say that I am here by the will of the Genius, and that I had no say in the matter?'

" 'True,' said the old man.

" 'Then it is absurd to talk to me of conditions,' replied the stranger, 'since I am not at liberty to accept or refuse them.'

" 'Not at liberty!' returned the old man. 'What blasphemy! Disabuse yourself of that mistaken idea, and quickly!'

" 'Let him talk,' interposed his companion in a low voice, 'and beware of believing in liberty yourself, or you will offend the great kindness of the Spirit.'

" 'Moreover, Monsieur,' continued the first speaker, in a modest, caressing manner, 'before proceeding further, let me tell you that I should be addressed as Monseigneur, for such is the will of the Benevolent Genius who has appointed me to see that his orders are carried out. There is but one man in the whole country above us three.'

"The stranger knew not what to think of three apparently sensible men—to judge from their bearing, age and respect shown them—calmly talking such wild nonsense.

"While they were talking they heard a great noise, in which cries of both pain and joy were intermingled: the stranger, surprised and curious, asked what the matter was. 'From time to time,' replied the third old man, 'the Genius, to test his subjects' fortitude, permits them to be done to death, while they, with dying lips, extol his goodness, mercy, and justice. This honor is reserved for those he loves best. Of course all his subjects are equally bound to believe him perfect, for they are pledged to that in their first sleep.'

" 'What, Monseigneur! You take oaths in your country in your sleep?' cried the stranger.

" 'It is the rule,' replied the old man, 'and you yourself took the oath when you were cast on this shore.'

" 'I—took the oath! I'll be hanged if I can make head or tail of this,' returned the stranger.

" 'You are none the less pledged,' returned the Minister, 'and this is how the ceremony, without which you could not be regarded as a citizen of the island, was carried out. As soon as we hear that a stranger has arrived in our country, we go to receive him: then we pick out two of our citizens, all of whom are expected to be thoroughly versed in our laws, our manners and customs, and they are made to stand on either side of the stranger, who, as he lies asleep upon the ground, is questioned and told the conditions on which he may become a citizen of the island: the two sponsors take the oath for him by which he promises to conform all his days to the beliefs and law of the land.'

" 'You are making game of me,' replied the stranger wrathfully. 'And to what, if you please, do you make me out to be pledged?'

" 'Well,' said the old man, 'among other things to believe that the Genius is full of justice and kindness, for he loves his subjects and only causes them to be unhappy for their good, or through their own fault or someone else's; to believe that his heart is closed to passion and that the wrath he manifests is not really wrath at all, and his sorrow and his seeming joy are also non-existent, for his soul has attained to such perfection that it can only be perturbed in semblance or figuratively speaking. An abridged list of the rest of your obligations is contained in the twelve folio volumes with which I now present you, and which you must learn by heart at your leisure. But know that if you misinterpret a single word, you are lost beyond all hope of mercy.'

"The seriousness with which all this was told him made the stranger think for an instant that either the brains of the old men or his own brain had turned. He left them, went about the town, and received the same information from various other persons.

"As it was impossible to get away from the island, he decided to do pretty much as others did, though at heart he could not bring himself to believe a word of what he had been told to believe. One day, fatigued after a long walk, he sat down in a little boat on the shore, and letting his mind drift, said to himself, 'It's all a myth—there's no opposite coast—this vast expanse of water is bounded by the sky-line—I can see it!' As he gazed and mused, he fell asleep, and while he slept a fresh wind arose, which, stirring sea and boat, bore him insensibly to the opposite shore. He did not wake till he had got there.

" 'Goodness!' said he, 'now at least I shall see this weird Genius!' And he set about looking for him.

"He scoured the island from end to end, and finally found him, or maybe he did not find him, for I'm bound to admit that versed as I am in tales of travel, I would not like to vouch for their entire veracity; anyway, if he found him, he doubtless said to him: 'Monsieur Genius, if you only know what they say of you on the other side I think you would laugh heartily over it, and indeed I am not to blame in that I have been unable to credit a word of what I have been told you have done for me, and that I even doubted your very existence, for all I was told was so absurd that it was impossible to believe it.' The Spirit probably smiled at the stranger's frankness, and in majestic, mocking accents replied, 'Little it matters, my friend, whether you, or the likes of you, believe or do not believe in my existence. Be easy. Besides, neither for your good nor for your ill have you dwelt in and explored these lands, for once a person finds himself on the road on which you were, he is bound to pass through them, for the way leads nowhere else. For the same reason the current carried you hither. Apropos of this I could,' he probably added, 'give you some very illuminating information, but you must know, my child, that I have something better to do than teach a young scaramouch like you. Go, and settle in some corner, and leave me in peace, till time and need dispose of you afresh. Good evening.'

"The stranger as he retired must have said to himself, 'I knew quite well that if there was a Genius on that shore he would be good and kind, and easy to deal with. Anyhow, there is nothing like being honest with oneself, if one would avoid self-deception."

MADAME: That does indeed seem to me very essential. But it is equally important, I think, to be in harmony with oneself.

ROUSSEAU: You are right, Madame, but that one never can be: the great point is to know one's own inconsistencies, and to keep those which are the most conducive to happiness. That is the royal road to the acquirement of a well-balanced mind and a contented heart. But what I have told you is only a story. Don't attach more importance to it than it deserves.

MADAME: But why? I did like it so very much.

ROUSSEAU: Generally speaking, Madame, when an idea or notion is vague and when one cannot quite prove that it is false, one had better stick to it, especially if it helps one to do what is right and proper.

MADAME: But, Monsieur, that is exactly what the idea in question does not do at all, as was, for instance, so very clearly proved the other day.

ROUSSEAU: Anyway, you won't deny that it consoles the afflictions that are so common in this world.

MADAME: What! But you are going far beyond the existence of God and Natural Religion. You are going back on what you said the other day. Now you are admitting punishment and reward, and revealed religion in all its forms.

ROUSSEAU: Madame, it's one of those inconsistencies so conducive to happiness.

MADAME: I have no more to say. I see you only make use of religion as one of a series of illusions, but I think there are others of a more cheerful and pleasing character.

ROUSSEAU: If I knew of one more comforting, I should adopt it. But where can I turn for one that would provide us, as this does, with just and true testimony of our good deeds? It gives us length of days in its promise of a better and infinite existence; it inspires pity for the wicked and for the fate he lays up for himself.

MADAME: Yes, and makes us cruel toward the good man for whom it appoints a hell in this world.

ROUSSEAU: Does it not promise him an eternal reward for his good deeds? It lessens the horror of the tomb: it detaches us from life which we are bound to lose—often—at the very time when, but for that, it were most dear to keep. It gives us the promise of seeing once more the friends we have lost.   .

MADAME: A most attractive hope, were it well founded.

ROUSSEAU: Above all, it enables us to endure the irksome and abominable inflictions of the great of the earth who, in cold blood, without a qualm, for a freak or frivolity, will bring despair and want upon many thousands of men, men whom it is their duty to render happy. Mine is not a ferocious nature, but when I see no justice in the world for these monsters, I like to think there is a hell for them. And who knows how far they would go if they did not believe in a hell? For such as they this fear is needful, not for the people, as you were saying the other day. True or false, it awaits them at the last. Having lived as scoundrels, it is well they should die despairing. Let us not deny ourselves this vengeance—little enough, but all we shall get out of them. For the rest, Madame, I must confess that I do not care for public discussions of this kind. I utterly disliked that dinner of Mlle. Quinault's. Of all who brayed there, the Marquis was the only one who said what he really thought. There was more of mannerism than of conviction in what was said. Eh, why the devil proclaim a disbelief when you are not quite sure of being able to support your theory. I would like to peer into the depths of the souls of the obstinately godless when they come to die, and I am sure that I should very often see there a trouble, distress, fear, that their outward calm cannot quite disguise. I wish to live as a good man and a good Christian because I wish to die in peace, and also because this desire in no way upsets the tenor of my life and soothes me with hope against the time when I shall be no more. Faith, 'tis an ill service you render a man who has suffered from stone in the bladder all his days, to tell him that he need look for no compensation for a misfortune, chronic and undeserved.

MADAME: That is all quite right, but I like your story best of all.

Jean Jacques Rousseau

2.

MME. D'ÉPINAY REVILES ROUSSEAU FOR UNGALLANT SUSPICIONS AND SHOWS HIM THE DOOR.

Monsieur, go! Your presence makes me sick.

FOR *the scene of the final break between Mme. d'Épinay and Rousseau we have two versions, hers and his. Madame's may be found in her* Mémoires, *Rousseau's in his famous* Confessions. *That astute biographer Matthew Josephson has compared them with care and concluded that Mme. d'Épinay's is either the prejudiced account of a jealous woman or, as already suggested, the subtly contrived fabrication of the Baron von Grimm. Mr. Josephson feels that with the growing friction at Montmorency over Grimm and the episode of the Comtesse de Houdetot, the tone of the Mémoires changes. The cool, objective observer has become the woman scorned. The picture of Rousseau on his knees and of Mme. d'Épinay showing him the door is certainly not a pleasant one for his admirers to behold. It is reprinted here with the admonition that it be read cautiously, with Rousseau's own version in mind.*

Diderot, Rousseau tells us, had become increasingly meddlesome about his personal affairs. At the "Hermitage," one day, Rousseau received the letter from Diderot which we shall find Mme. d'Épinay reading out loud in the dialogue that follows. The letter threw him into a rage, and as Josephson puts it, "his mind saw darkly Diderot, Grimm, and Mme. d'Épinay all plotting his ruin." To make matters worse, Diderot had addressed the letter "Care of Madame d'Épinay." This roundabout way only confirmed Rousseau's suspicions of foul play. Promptly Rousseau wrote back to his officious friend: "Admit that in prescribing for me so dogmatically what I should do, without being in a position to judge, you are being perfectly idiotic." Insinuatingly, he adds:– "And what is worse, I see that your advice does not come from you." Rousseau now rushed to "La Chevrette" to face Grimm and Mme. d'Épinay with an embarrassing exposé of their plotting. "I read to them," he recounts, "in a loud and clear voice, my two letters with an intrepidity of which I should not have believed myself capable. . . . They did not answer a word. Above all, I saw that arrogant man cast down his eyes, not venturing to meet the angry flashes from my own. But at the same instant, in the bottom of his heart, he was vowing destruction, and I am positive that they agreed upon it before they parted."

In the version appearing in the Mémoires, Rousseau and Mme. d'Épinay are alone at that crucial moment. The "arrogant" Grimm is not present to "cast down his eyes" in acknowledged guilt. It is the evening of a late September day in 1757. Madame's servant has just brought in a sheaf of letters, among which is one addressed to Rousseau. Mme. d'Épinay gives it to him. As he reads the letter, Rousseau becomes furious, bangs his head with his fists, and begins to swear. . . .

MME. D'ÉPINAY: What is the matter? Whatever has upset you like this?

ROUSSEAU: Dash it! (*Tearing the letter with his teeth and throwing it down on the floor.*) They're no friends, they're tyrants! The imperious tone this Diderot takes! I don't want their advice!

MME. D'ÉPINAY (*Picking up the letter and reading*): "I heard that Madame d'Épinay is going to Geneva, but I do not hear that you are accompanying her. Do you not see that if she has behaved as badly to you as you suppose, you have now the one opportunity of paying back your debt to her, and then breaking decently with her. If you do not do this, and let her go in the state you see her to be in, she will, seeing how ill-disposed she is toward you, make a grievance against you out of it, and you'll never be rid of it. Besides, are you not afraid that your conduct may be misconstrued, and that you will be thought ungrateful, or something or other? I know, of course, that your conscience is perfectly clear, but is that, in itself, enough, and can we afford to disregard the opinion of others?" (*Turning to Rousseau.*) What is this supposition of yours? And what reason has M. Diderot for thinking that I am ill-disposed toward you? What wrong have I done you, please?

ROUSSEAU (*recovering himself as if from a dream, stands dumbfounded. Snatches the letter from her hand*): It's all because of my former doubts, but you told me there was nothing in them, and I've never given the matter a thought since, as you very well know. Would you really like it if I went to Geneva?

MME. D'ÉPINAY: And you have actually spoken against me to M. Diderot?

ROUSSEAU: I ask your pardon. He came to see me when my heart was sore and I could not resist telling him my trouble. How can one be reserved with a person one is fond of?

MME. D'ÉPINAY: You don't find it so difficult, Monsieur, to suspect a friend, and bring a groundless charge against her?

ROUSSEAU: If I had been certain, Madame, that you were guilty, I should have carefully avoided saying so. I should have felt too humiliated and unhappy about it.

MME. D'ÉPINAY: And was that your reason for not enlightening M. Diderot, since?

ROUSSEAU: Of course—you had not done it—no occasion arose for telling him, and I thought no more about it.

MME. D'ÉPINAY (*grows indignant, and is about to order him out of the room when Rousseau falls at her feet, begging her pardon and assuring her that he would write at once to Diderot and clear her*): Just as you like. In the future, your doings will be nothing to me. You are content to wrong me most cruelly. You swear daily to me that life will not be long enough to make up for it, and at the same time you make me out to your friend as an abominable creature. You allow him to go on thinking of me in this way and you think that as long as you tell me today that you made a mistake, all is well.

ROUSSEAU: I know Diderot, and the powerful effect of first impressions upon him. I was waiting for some proof of your innocence.

MME. D'ÉPINAY: Monsieur, go! Your presence makes me sick. I am only too glad to be going away. I could not bring myself to see you again. You can tell all whom it may concern that I did not want to have you with me, as we are unsuitable travelling companions, seeing the state of health we are both in. Go! And do not let me see you again.

(*Rousseau leaves in a fury.*)

Jean Jacques Rousseau

3.

THE OLD REBEL ENJOYS COLD PORK, PICKLED TROUT, AND THE IMPUDENCE OF YOUNG BOSWELL.

*Suppose her passion is still lively, and she threatens
to tell her husband what has happened unless I
agree to continue our intrigue?*

Five years after his explosive break with Mme. d'Épinay, Rousseau found himself involved in a far more serious conflict—with the authorities this time. The storm had been slowly gathering with the publication of his Nouvelle Héloise, Le Contrat Social, and Emile. The first of these was regarded as immoral, the second as anti-monarchist, and the third as heretical. Suddenly, in July 1762, with one concerted blow, the enemy cracked down on the offender. Warrants were issued for Rousseau's arrest. Luckily, friends informed him in time of the impending action, and the ailing philosopher slipped across the border to find refuge in Motiers at Neufchatel, then belonging to Prussia. There, thanks to the official sanction of Frederick II, Rousseau found the quiet he needed to continue his work unmolested. To Frederick he gave his promise to write "nothing scabrous or exciting" that might arouse the good burghers of Motiers against him. And in the Governor of Neufchatel, the Scottish-born Lord-Marshal George Keith, he found a friend of "unswerving loyalty." In a few weeks Rousseau's mistress and nurse, the illiterate servant girl Thérèse Levasseur, joined him at Motiers. The happiness of this "excellent savage," as the hearty Lord-Marshal called him, would thus seem complete.

Yet the world does not forget a Jean Jacques Rousseau for long. Soon a stream of pilgrims began to make its way to this charming white cottage with the thatched roof and balcony windows that opened on a wide span of Swiss valley. Motiers speedily became a Mecca for princes and preachers and philosophers. Political exiles came for advice. Edward Gibbon came for a heart-to-heart talk, and charlatans and curiosity-seekers besieged this sage of Motiers by the dozen. Access to this celebrated hermit had become a rare privilege indeed. Yet, we are scarcely surprised to learn that one day early in December of 1764 there stood in the doorway of the cottage at Motiers, garbed resplendently in buckskin breeches, scarlet coat and gold-laced waistcoat, a young gentleman from Scotland named James Boswell.

Inveterate pursuer of illustrious names, this restless Scotch barrister had turned off from the main route of his "grand tour" to stalk the two greatest quarries in Europe—Rousseau and his not-too-distant fellow exile at Ferney, Voltaire. A four-word entry in Boswell's voluminous journal reveals the state of his mind:– "Voltaire, Rousseau—immortal names!" Back in London, the year before, this roving reporter and votary of genius had already added to his catalogue of names one that would make even his own "immortal"—Dr. Samuel Johnson. His last glimpse of the man whose inseparable shadow he would soon become was on Harwich Beach —"rolling his majestic frame in his usual manner."

Boswell's appearance at Rousseau's cottage was by no means unheralded. Indeed, the visit was the result of very thorough planning and strategy. First, he had tactfully availed himself of his Scottish origin by securing a letter of introduction from the Lord-Marshal. Then he had written a typically flamboyant note from his room at the inn of Motiers, the kind of erratic document that would arouse the interest of a Jean Jacques Rousseau. Boswell now waited. To give himself, as he puts it, a "vigorous and solemn tone" for the approaching encounter, he next took a long and pensive stroll over the beautiful countryside. When he returned to the inn, a maid was waiting with Rousseau's reply: "I am ill and in pain, unable to receive visits. However, I cannot refuse that of Monsieur Boswell, provided that, in view of my condition, he would kindly make it short."

Excitedly Boswell dons his picturesque raiment and rushes out to the cottage. There he is met at the door by Mlle. Levasseur—"a little, lively, neat French girl"—who shows him upstairs to Rousseau's room. "At length," Boswell recounts, "his door opened and I beheld him, a genteel, black man in the dress of an Armenian." With Rousseau in his girdled caftan and bonnet and Boswell in his buckskin breeches and scarlet coat, the two must have looked like some incongruous creatures out of a wildly scrambled opera libretto. "Many, many thanks," says Boswell. "Will you be seated?" returns Rousseau. How quickly the two hit it off may be gathered from Boswell's remark: "I seized his hand and thumped him on the shoulder."

Thus began a series of conversations that extended from December 3 to December 15. Rousseau's mood fluctuated from day to day. He might chuckle gleefully over young Boswell's candid self-analysis, or he might become his old petulant self. "You are irksome to me," he bellows at the end of the second interview. "It is my nature. I cannot help it." BOSWELL: "Do not stand on ceremony with me." ROUSSEAU: "Go away!" And Boswell, not a whit hurt, goes away only to return in the same high spirits the following morning. Why Rousseau put up with this arrant intruder from Scotland is explained by Mr. Josephson: "Boswell's native bent for serious propositions, his fantastic spirit, his indifference to snubs, his passion to confess himself, all suited Rousseau perfectly." Perhaps, these very qualities commended Boswell to that still more exacting companion, Dr. Johnson, and made him the supreme journalist that he was. In his room at the Motiers hostelry Boswell wrote down memoranda of each conversation, never letting more than a day elapse after the event. Many of these notes have been preserved, and the full narrative appears in Boswell's Journal.

This brings us to the question of why this remarkable non-Johnsonian example of Boswell's powers as reporter was not given to the world till 1927. That sensitive student of the 18th century, Louis Kronenberger, has briefly told the story: "The interviews with Rousseau are taken from the eighteen volumes of Boswell's Private Papers. That these papers existed was not known until a generation ago; and for a time their owner, Lord Talbot de Malahide (Boswell's great-great-grandson), refused to release them. But in 1927 he sold the entire collection, amounting to more than a million words, to Lt. Col. Ralph H. Isham. Colonel Isham turned them over to the late Geoffrey Scott, and subsequently to Professor Frederick Pottle of Yale, to be edited for private publication. The task involved a great amount of deciphering, annotating and fitting together; and the eighteen volumes were published, in a limited edition, over a period of years." Mr. Kronenberger used the Rousseau dialogues in his excellent Portable Johnson & Boswell, issued by the Viking Press in New York in 1947. Few would dispute his judgment that "beyond the great vividness of the interviews, they reveal, more than anything in the 'Life' does, Boswell's ability to portray himself in the frankest and most foolish light."

The dialogues that follow are the last two which Boswell held with Rousseau. The previous one, occurring on December 5, had ended with Boswell promising—or threatening—"to come back to you." To this Rousseau had rejoined: "I don't promise to see you. I am ill. I need a chamberpot every minute." BOSWELL: "Yes, you will see me." ROUSSEAU: "Be off;

and a good journey to you." On Friday the 14th we find Boswell returning
to his inn at Motiers after an arduous trip. He tells us:

Friday 14 December.
("At eight I got on horseback and had for my guide a smith called
Dupuis. I said, 'Since when (depuis quand) have you had that name?'
I passed the Mountain Lapidosa, which is monstrously steep and in a
great measure covered with snow. I was going to Rousseau, which con-
sideration levelled the roughest mountains. I arrived at Motiers before
noon. I alighted at Rousseau's door. Up and I went and found Made-
moiselle Vasseur, who told me, 'He is very ill.' 'But can I see him for a
moment?' 'I will find out. Step in, sir.' I found him sitting in great
pain."—Boswell)

ROUSSEAU: I am overcome with ailments, disappointments, and sorrow. I
have my bellyful; everyone thinks it my duty to attend to him.

BOSWELL: That is most natural; and is it not a source of satisfaction to you
to find you can be of so much help to others?

("He gave a deprecatory shrug. I had left with him when I was last
here what I called a sketch of my life, in which I gave him the impor-
tant incidents of my history and my melancholy apprehensions, and
begged his advice and friendship. It was an interesting piece."—
Boswell)

ROUSSEAU: I have read your memoir. You have been gulled. You ought
never to see a priest.

BOSWELL: But can I yet hope to make something of myself?

ROUSSEAU: Why, yes. Your great difficulty is that you think it so difficult
a matter. Come back in the afternoon. But put your watch on the table.

BOSWELL: For how long?

ROUSSEAU: A quarter of an hour, and no longer.

BOSWELL: Twenty minutes.

ROUSSEAU: Be off with you!—Ha! Ha!

("Notwithstanding the pain he was in, he was touched with my sin-
gular sally, and laughed most really. He had a gay look immediately. I
dined in my old room with the two boarders. After dinner I walked
out. There had fallen much rain, and the Vallon was all overflowed.
Nature looked somewhat different from the time that I was first here.
I was sorry that such a scene was subject to any change. At four I went
to Monsieur Rousseau."—Boswell)

BOSWELL: I have but a moment allowed me; I must use it well. Is it possible to live amongst other men, and to retain singularity?

ROUSSEAU: Yes, I have done it.

BOSWELL: But to remain on good terms with them?

ROUSSEAU: Oh, if you want to be a wolf, you must howl. I attach very little importance to books.

BOSWELL: Even to your own books?

ROUSSEAU: Oh, they are just rigmarole.

BOSWELL: Now you are howling.

ROUSSEAU: When I put my trust in books I was tossed about, as you are, though it is rather by talking that you have been tossed. I had nothing stable here (*striking his head*) before I began to meditate.

BOSWELL: But you would not have meditated to such good purpose if you had not read.

ROUSSEAU: No. I should have meditated to better purpose if I had begun sooner.

BOSWELL: But I, for example, would never have had the agreeable ideas I possess of the Christian religion, had I not read the Savoyard's Creed. To tell the truth, I can find no certain system. Morality appears to me an uncertain thing. For instance, I would like to have thirty women. Could I not satisfy that desire?

ROUSSEAU: No!

BOSWELL: Why?

ROUSSEAU: Ha! Ha! If Mademoiselle were not here, I would give you a most ample reason why.

BOSWELL: But consider, if I am rich, I can take a number of girls; I get them with child; propagation is thus increased. I give them dowries, and I marry them off to good peasants who are very happy to have them. Thus they become wives at the same age as would have been the case if they had remained virgins, and I, on my side, have had the benefit of enjoying a great variety of women.

ROUSSEAU: Ah! You will be landed in jealousies, betrayals, and treachery.

BOSWELL: But cannot I follow the Oriental usage?

ROUSSEAU: In the Orient, the women are kept shut up; it means keeping slaves; and, mark you, their women do nothing but harm, whereas ours do much good since they do a great deal of work.

BOSWELL: I should like to follow the example of the old patriarchs, worthy men whose memory I hold in respect.

ROUSSEAU: But are you not a citizen? You must not pick and choose one law here and another law there; you must take the laws of your own society. Fulfill your duties as a citizen, and if you hold fast, you will win respect.

BOSWELL: I should not tell what I was doing; but I'd do it.

ROUSSEAU (*continuing*): And as for your lady, when you go back to Scotland you will say, "Madam, such conduct is against my conscience, and there shall be no more of it." She will applaud you; if not, she is to be despised.

BOSWELL: Suppose her passion is still lively, and she threatens to tell her husband what has happened unless I agree to continue our intrigue?

ROUSSEAU: In the first place, she will not tell him. In the second, you have no right to do harm for the sake of good.

BOSWELL: True. Nonetheless, I can picture some very embarrassing situations. And pray explain how I can expiate the evil I have already done?

ROUSSEAU: Ah, sir, there is no expiation for evil, except good.

("*A beautiful thought this. Nevertheless I maintained my doctrine of satisfaction by punishment. Yes, I must ever think that immutable justice requires atonement to be made for transgressions, and this atonement is to be made by suffering. This is the universal idea of all nations, and seems to be a leading principle of Christianity. I gave myself full scope; for since I left England I have not had anybody to whom I could lay open entirely my mind till I found Monsieur Rousseau.*"—Boswell)

BOSWELL: When I get to France and Italy, may I not indulge in the gallantries, usual to those countries, where the husbands do not resent your making love to their wives? Nay, should I not be happier as the citizen of such a nation?

ROUSSEAU: They are corpses. Do you want to be a corpse?

BOSWELL: But pray tell me, has a virtuous man any true advantages? Is he really better off than a man given up to sensuality?

ROUSSEAU: We cannot doubt that we are spiritual beings; and when the soul escapes from this prison, from this flesh, the virtuous man will find things to his liking. He will enjoy the contemplation of happy souls, nobly employed. He will say, "I have already lived a life like that." Whereas those who experience nothing but the vile passions which have their origin in the body will be dissatisfied by the spectacle of pleasures which they have no means of enjoying.

BOSWELL: Upon my word, I am at a loss how to act in this world; I cannot determine whether or not I should adopt some profession.

ROUSSEAU: One must have a great plan.

BOSWELL: What about those studies, on which so much stress is laid? Such as history, for instance.

ROUSSEAU: They are just amusements.

BOSWELL: My father desires me to be called to the Scottish bar; I am certainly doing right in satisfying my father; I have no such certainty if I follow my light inclinations. It follows that I must give my mind to the study of the laws of Scotland.

ROUSSEAU: To be sure; they are your tools. If you mean to be a carpenter, you must have a plane.

BOSWELL: I do not get on well with my father. I am not at my ease with him.

ROUSSEAU: To be at ease you need to share some amusement.

BOSWELL: We look after the planting together.

ROUSSEAU: That's too serious a business. You should have some amusement that puts you on an equal footing: shooting, for example. A shot is missed and a joke is made of it, without any infringement of respect; you enjoy a freedom which you take for granted. Once you are involved in a profession, you must keep on with it even though another, and apparently better, should present itself. If you keep changing, you can achieve nothing. . . . Are you greedy?

BOSWELL: Yes.

ROUSSEAU: I am sorry to hear it.

BOSWELL: Ha! Ha! I was joking; for in your books, you write in favor of greed. I know what you are about to say, and it is just what I was hoping to hear. I wanted to solicit your soup. I had a great desire to share a meal with you.

ROUSSEAU: Well, if you are not greedy, will you dine here tomorrow? But I give you fair warning, you will find yourself badly off.

BOSWELL: No, I shall not be badly off; I am above all such considerations.

ROUSSEAU: Come then at noon; it will give us time to talk.

BOSWELL: All my thanks.

ROUSSEAU: Good evening.

("*Mademoiselle carried me to the house of a poor woman with a great many children whom M. Rousseau aids with his charity. I contributed my part. I was not pleased to hear Mademoiselle repeat to the poor woman just the common consolatory sayings. She should have said something singular.*"—Boswell)

Saturday 15 December
("*At seven in the morning I got on horseback and rode about a league to St. Sulpice where I saw the source of the Ruse, the river which runs thro' the Vallée de Travers. It is a prodigious romantic place. I could not determine whether the water gushes in an immediate spring*

from the rock, or only issues out here having pierced the mountain upon which is a lake. The water comes forth with great violence. All around here I saw mountains and rocks as at Hartfell in Annandale. Some of the rocks were in great courses like huge stone walls along which grew the towering pines which we call pitch firs, and which are much handsomer than the firs of Scotland. I was full of fine spirits. Gods! Am I now then really the friend of Rousseau? What a rich assemblage of ideas! I relish my felicity truly in such a scene as this. Shall I not truly relish it at Auchinleck? I was quite gay, my fancy was youthful, and vented its gladness in sportive sallies. I supposed myself in the rude world. I supposed a parcel of young fellows saying, 'Come, Boswell, you'll dine with us today?' 'No, gentlemen, excuse me; I'm engaged. I dine today with Rousseau.' My tone, my air, my native pride when I pronounced this! Temple! You would have given half a guinea to see me at that moment. I returned to my inn, where I found the Court of Justice of the Vallon assembled. I entered and was amused to hear a justice of peace and honest farmers and a country minister all talking French. I then went to M. Rousseau."—Boswell)

BOSWELL: I hope your health is better today.

ROUSSEAU: Oh, don't speak of it.

(*"He seemed unusually gay. Before dinner we are all so, if not made to wait too long. A keen appetite gives a vivacity to the whole frame."* —Boswell)

BOSWELL: You say nothing in regard to a child's duties toward his parents. You tell us nothing of your Emile's father.

ROUSSEAU: Oh, he hadn't got one. He didn't exist.

(*"It is, however, a real pity that M. Rousseau has not treated of the duties between parents and children. It is an important and a delicate subject and deserves to be illustrated by a sage of so clear a judgment and so elegant a soul. He praised* The Spectator.*"*—Boswell)

ROUSSEAU: One comes across allegories in it. I have no taste for allegories; though your nation shows a great liking for them.

(*"I gave him very fully the character of Mr. Johnson."*—Boswell)

ROUSSEAU (*with force*): I would like that man. I would respect him. I would refrain from shattering his principles, were I to find I could do so. I should like to see him but from far off, for fear he might deal me a blow.

(*"I told him how averse Mr. Johnson was to write, and how he had his levee."*—Boswell)

ROUSSEAU: Ah, I understand. He is a man who enjoys holding forth.

("I told him Mr. Johnson's bon mot upon the innovators: That truth is a cow which will yield them no more milk, and so they are gone to milk the bull."—Boswell)

ROUSSEAU: He would detest me. He would say, "Here is a corruptor: a man who comes here to milk the bull."

("I had diverted myself by pretending to help Mademoiselle Vasseur to make the soup. We dined in the kitchen, which was neat and cheerful. There was something singularly agreeable in this scene. Here was Rousseau in all his simplicity, with his Armenian dress which I have surely mentioned before now. His long coat and nightcap made him look easy and well. Our dinner was as follows: 1. A dish of excellent soup. 2. A bouilli of beef and veal. 3. Cabbage, turnip and carrot. 4. Cold pork. 5. Pickled trout which he jestingly called tongue. 6. Some little dish which I forget. The dessert consisted of stoned pears and of chestnuts. We had red and white wines. It was a simple good repast. We were quite at our ease. I sometimes forgot myself and became ceremonious."—Boswell)

BOSWELL: May I help you to some of this dish?

ROUSSEAU: No, sir. I can help myself to it.

BOSWELL: Might I help myself to some more of that?

ROUSSEAU: Is your arm long enough? A man does the honors of his house from a motive of vanity. He does not want it forgotten who is the master. I would like everyone to be his own master, and that no one should play the part of host. Let each one ask for what he wants; if it is there to give, let him be given it; otherwise, he must be satisfied without. Here you see true hospitality.

BOSWELL: In England, it is quite another matter. They do not want to be at ease; they are stiff and silent, in order to win respect.

ROUSSEAU: In France, you find no such gloom among folk of distinction. There is even an affectation of the utmost liberty, as though they would have you understand, "We stand in no fear of losing our dignity." That is a more refined form of self-esteem.

BOSWELL: Well, and do you not share that yourself?

ROUSSEAU: Yes, I allow that I like to be respected; but only in matters of importance.

BOSWELL: You are so simple. I expected to find you quite different to this: the great Rousseau. But you do not see yourself in the same light as others see you. I counted on finding you enthroned and talking with a grave authority.

ROUSSEAU: I? Uttering oracles? Ha! Ha! Ha!

BOSWELL: Yes, and I should be much in awe of you. And, in truth, your simplicity might be open to criticism; it might be said, "M. Rousseau does not make himself sufficiently respected." In Scotland, I can assure you, a very different tone must be taken to escape from the shocking familiarity which is prevalent in that country. Upon my word, I would not put up with it. Should I not be justified in forestalling it by fighting a duel with the first man who should treat me that way, and thus live at peace for the rest of my life?

ROUSSEAU: No. That is not allowable. It is not right to stake one's life on such follies. Life is given us for objects of importance. Pay no heed to what such men say. They will get tired of talking to a man who does not answer them.

BOSWELL: If you were in Scotland, they would start off by calling you "Rousseau, Jean Jacques, how goes it?" with the utmost familiarity.

ROUSSEAU: That is perhaps a good thing.

BOSWELL: But they would say, "Poh! Jean Jacques, why do you allow yourself all these fantasies? You're a pretty man to put forward such claims. Come, come, settle down in society like other people"; and this they will say to you with a sourness which, for my part, I am quite unable to imitate for you.

ROUSSEAU: Ah, that's bad.

("*There he felt the thistle, when it was applied to himself on the tender part. It was just as if I had said, 'Howt Johnie Rousseau man, what for hae ye sae mony figmagairies? Ye're a bonny man indeed to mauk sicana wark; set ye up. Canna ye just live like ither fowk?' It was the best idea that could be given in the polite French language of the rude Scots' sarcastical vivacity.*"—Boswell)

BOSWELL: I have leanings toward despotism, let me tell you. On our estates, I am like an ancient lord, and I insist on respect from the tenants.

ROUSSEAU: But when you see an old man with white hair do you, as a young man, have no feelings at all? Have you no respect for age?

BOSWELL: Yes. I have even, on many occasions, been very affable. I have talked quite freely with the tenants.

ROUSSEAU: Yes, you forgot yourself, and became a man.

BOSWELL: But I was sorry for it afterwards. I used to think, "I have lowered myself."

ROUSSEAU: Ha! Ha! Ha!

BOSWELL: Yesterday I had in mind to ask a favor of you, to give me credentials as your ambassador to the Corsicans. Will you make me His Excellency? Are you in need of an ambassador? I offer you my services: Mr. Boswell, Ambassador Extraordinary of M. Rousseau to the Isle of Corsica.

ROUSSEAU: Would you care to be King of Corsica?

BOSWELL: By my word! Ha! Ha! Not I. It is beyond my powers (*with a low bow*); all the same, I can say, "I have refused to be a King."

ROUSSEAU: Do you like cats?

BOSWELL: No.

ROUSSEAU: I was sure of that. It is my test of character. There you have the despotic instinct of men. They do not like cats because the cat is free, and will never consent to become a slave. He will do nothing to your order, as the other animals do.

BOSWELL: Nor a chicken, either.

ROUSSEAU: A chicken would obey your orders if you could make them intelligible to it. But a cat will understand you perfectly, and not obey them.

BOSWELL: But a cat is ungrateful and treacherous.

ROUSSEAU: No. That's all untrue. A cat is an animal that can be very attached to you; he will do anything you please out of friendship. I have a cat here. He has been brought up with my dog; they play together. The cat will give the dog a blow with his tail, and the dog will offer him his paw. (*"He described the playing of his dog and cat with exquisite eloquence, as a fine painter draws a small piece. He put some victuals on a trencher, and made his dog dance round it. He sung to him a lively air with a sweet voice and great taste."*) You see the ballet. It is not a gala performance, but a pretty one all the same. (*"I think the dog's name was Sultan. He stroked him and fed him, and with an arch air said, 'He is not much respected, but he gets well looked after.'"*—Boswell)

BOSWELL: Suppose you were to walk in upon a drinking party of young folk who should treat you with ridicule, would you be above minding it?

ROUSSEAU: It would put me out of countenance. I am shy by nature. I have often, for example, been overcome by the raillery of women. A party such as you describe would be disagreeable to me. I would leave it.

(*"I was comforted to find that my sensibility is not despicable weakness."*—Boswell)

BOSWELL: The Anglican Church is the one for me.

ROUSSEAU: Yes. It is no doubt an excellent religion; but it is not the Gospel, which is all simplicity. It is another kind of religion.

BOSWELL: The Gospel, at the outset, was simple and rigid equally; as when Paul says it is better not to marry than to marry.

ROUSSEAU: Paul? But that is not the Gospel.

BOSWELL: Then you have no liking for Paul?

ROUSSEAU: I respect him, but I think he is partly responsible for muddling your head. He would have been an Anglican clergyman.

BOSWELL: Mr. Johnson is a Jacobite, but he has a pension of £300 sterling from the King.

ROUSSEAU: He ought not to have accepted a pension.

BOSWELL: He says that he does not drink the health of King James with the wine given him by King George.

ROUSSEAU: But you should not employ the substance given you by this wine in attacking King George.

MLLE. LEVASSEUR: Shall you, sir, see M. de Voltaire?

BOSWELL: Most certainly. (*To Rousseau*) M. de Voltaire has no liking for you. That is natural enough.

ROUSSEAU: Yes. One does not like those whom one has greatly injured. His talk is most enjoyable; it is even better than his books.

BOSWELL: Have you looked at the *Philosophical Dictionary*?

ROUSSEAU: Yes.

BOSWELL: And what of it?

ROUSSEAU: I don't like it. I am not intolerant, but he deserves . . .* It is very well to argue against men's opinion; but to show contempt, and to say, "You are idiots to believe this," is to be personally offensive. Now go away.

BOSWELL: Not yet. I will leave at three o'clock. I have still five and twenty minutes.

ROUSSEAU: But I can't give you five and twenty minutes.

BOSWELL: I will give you even more than that.

ROUSSEAU: What! Of my own time? All the kings on earth cannot give me my own time.

BOSWELL: But if I had stayed till tomorrow I should have had five and twenty minutes, and next day another twenty-five. I am not taking these minutes. I am making you a present of them.

ROUSSEAU: Ah! Since you don't steal my money, you are giving it to me. (*"He then repeated part of a French satire ending with, 'and whatever they leave you, they count as a gift.'"*—Boswell)

BOSWELL: Pray speak for me, Mademoiselle. (*To Rousseau*) I have an excellent friend here.

ROUSSEAU: Nay, but this is a league.

BOSWELL: No league at all.

MLLE. LEVASSEUR: Gentlemen, I will tell you the moment the clock strikes.

ROUSSEAU: Come; I need to take the air after eating.

---

* "*I forget his expression here.*"—Boswell

(*"We walked out to a gallery pendent upon his wall."*—Boswell)

BOSWELL: In the old days I was a great mimic. I could imitate everyone I saw. But I do it no longer.

ROUSSEAU: It is a bad quality; for it compels one to seize upon all that is small in a character.

BOSWELL: True; but I assure you there was a nobleness about my art; I carried mimicry to such a point of perfection. I was a kind of virtuoso. When I espied any singular character I would say, "It must be added to my collection." (*"He laughed with all his nerves."*—Boswell)

ROUSSEAU: You are an oddity.

BOSWELL: I am a physiognomist, believe me. I have studied that art very attentively, I assure you, and I can rely on my conclusions.

ROUSSEAU: Yet I think the features of the face vary between one nation and another, as do accent and tone of voice; and these signify different feelings among different peoples.

BOSWELL: But, in time, one learns to understand them.

ROUSSEAU: The roads are bad. You will be late.

BOSWELL: I take the bad parts on foot; the last league of the way is good. Do you realize that I shall make a good barrister before a Court of Justice?

ROUSSEAU: Yes. But I regret you have the talents necessary for defending a bad case.

BOSWELL: Have you any commands for Italy?

ROUSSEAU: I will send a letter to Geneva for you to carry to Parma.

BOSWELL: Can I send you anything back?

ROUSSEAU: A few pretty tunes from the opera.

BOSWELL: By all means. Oh, I have had so much to say that I have neglected to beg you to play me a tune.

ROUSSEAU: It's too late.

MLLE. LEVASSEUR: Sir, your man is calling for you to start.

(*"M. Rousseau embraced me. He was quite the tender St. Preux. He kissed me several times, and held me in his arms with elegant cordiality. Oh, I shall never forget that I have been thus."*—Boswell)

ROUSSEAU: Good-by. You are a fine fellow.

BOSWELL: You have shown me great goodness, but I deserved it.

ROUSSEAU: Yes. You are malicious; but 'tis a pleasant malice, a malice I don't dislike. Write and tell me how you are.

BOSWELL: And you will write to me?

ROUSSEAU: I know not how to reach you.

BOSWELL: Yes, you shall write to me in Scotland.

ROUSSEAU: Certainly; and even at Paris.

BOSWELL: Bravo! If I live twenty years, you will write to me for twenty years?

ROUSSEAU: Yes.

BOSWELL: Good-by. If you live for seven years, I shall return to Switzerland from Scotland to see you.

ROUSSEAU: Do so. We shall be old acquaintances.

BOSWELL: One word more. Can I feel sure that I am held to you by the slenderest thread? By a hair?

ROUSSEAU (*seizing a hair of Boswell's head*): Yes. Remember always that there are points where our souls are linked.

BOSWELL: It is enough. I, with my melancholy, I, who often look on myself as a despicable being, as a good-for-nothing creature who should make his escape from life—I shall be upheld forever by the thought that I am linked to M. Rousseau. Good-by. Bravo! I will live to the end of my days.

ROUSSEAU: That is undoubtedly a thing one must do. Good-by.

("Mademoiselle accompanied me to the outer door. Before dinner she told me, 'M. Rousseau has a high regard for you. The first time you came, I said to him, "That gentleman has an honest face. I am sure you will like him."' I said, 'Mademoiselle is a good judge.' 'Yes,' said she, 'I have seen strangers enough in the twenty-two years that I have lived with M. Rousseau, and believe me, I have sent many away simply because I did not fancy their way of talking.' I said, 'You have promised to let me have your news from time to time.' 'Yes, sir.' 'And tell me what I can send you from Geneva. Make no ceremony.' 'Well, if you will, a garnet necklace.' We shook hands cordially, and away I went to my inn. My eldest landlady looked at me and said, 'Sir, I think you are crying.' This I retain as a true eulogium of my humanity. I replied, 'I may well be unhappy to leave M. Rousseau. I will see you again in seven years.' I got a-horseback and rode by the house of M. Rousseau. Mademoiselle waited for me at the door, and cried, 'Bon voyage; write to us.' Good creature. I rode gravely to Yverdun contemplating how this day will appear to my mind some years hence. I was received cordially by my gallant Baron and my amiable Madame de Brackel: Yet did my spirits sink pretty low. No wonder after such a high flow."—Boswell)

Casanova-Voltaire

THE GREAT AMORIST INTERRUPTS HIS MAJOR OCCUPATION TO ARGUE FOR THE NECESSITY OF SUPERSTITION AMONG THE MASSES.

The essence of freedom consists in thinking you have it.

IN THE Hôtel de l'Epée of Zurich early in August, 1760, a strange melancholy seized a Venetian gentleman of thirty-five who flauntingly gave his name as Jacques Casanova de Seingalt. A man with a vast aptitude for pleasure, he suddenly found life unappetizing. . . . The mood had been descending upon him since he had quitted Paris earlier that year. The boredom of directing the state lotteries in Paris had precipitated another of those periods of wandering so frequent in his restless career. Perhaps a short stay in Germany had added to his gloom. Moreover, the most exciting event of his life—the escape from the notorious Venetian dungeon, "The Leads"—was now four years old and there was no one in this prim Swiss hostelry to whom he cared to recite its thrills. And, strangest of all, even the book of romance happened to be temporarily closed. For Casanova this was a bleak state indeed.

• Suddenly, in an access of despair, Casanova determined to find refuge from the world's tedium in a monastery. The abbot whom he consulted shrewdly advised him to wait. Casanova waited, and sure enough the prospect slowly brightened again. To begin with, a Mlle. Dubois, who knew "à merveille les choses de la table et du lit," slipped into his life as the thoughtful gift of a M. de Chavigny, the French ambassador at Soleure. Mlle. Dubois's charm alone would perhaps have dispelled the monastic reverie. But there was something far more exciting now. Casanova discovered that with a little effort he could satisfy the ambition of his lifetime—to visit Voltaire, the Titan of world letters, and add him to his growing collection of personally interviewed celebrities.

Not far from Geneva, in a huge mansion which he had named "Les Délices," the great foe of tyranny and dogma now lived in magnificent banishment. The place had become the Mecca of the writers, crusaders,

81

and curiosity-seekers of all Europe. Voltaire held intellectual court at "Les Délices," and it was only fitting that Casanova, whose worship of genius was only second to his main preoccupation, should desire to pay his respects. Again M. Chavigny proved of service. At Soleure the obliging ambassador was staging a performance of Voltaire's farce-lampoon, L'Écossaise. Now, Voltaire was particularly fond of that play because it pilloried in devastating style the court critic Fréron, who had become a special bête-noir of his. Casanova volunteered to play the part of Murray in M. Chavigny's production of L'Écossaise. The performance was a huge success, and Casanova was now provided with the best possible introduction to the exiled philosopher.

And as he gravitated toward Geneva, Casanova put a finishing touch to his preparations. He visited the Swiss savant, Albert de Haller, at Roche. Haller's erudition in all fields was rivalled only by that of Voltaire, whose heretical opinions he was far from sharing. A touch of venom—and no doubt jealousy—crept into his parting words to Casanova: "M. de Voltaire is a man whom one should meet, although many people seem to find him greater at a distance than near." As it turned out, the visit to Haller provided Casanova with just what he needed to elicit from Voltaire a retort that was to become one of the most quoted "mots" of history. Casanova now wound up his affair with Mlle. Dubois with a characteristic "tender farewell," and the stage was set for the eagerly awaited encounter with Voltaire. On the 22nd of August, 1760, armed with his credentials as actor, Casanova set out after supper for "Les Délices" in the company of a M. Villars-Chandieu of Geneva, who was to make the formal introduction. . . .

Voltaire had purchased this magnificent châlet in 1755, not long after the French authorities exiled him for publishing tracts charged with being a pernicious and subversive threat to law and order. To the visitors who streamed from all corners of Europe to pay homage, the châlet offered other attractions besides the wit and wisdom of Europe's keenest mind. The estate commanded a majestic view of Lake Geneva and the Alps surmounting it. Fifteen windows of the mansion opened on this regal panorama. A vista of endless gardens stretched far around. "There is not a more beautiful view in the world," was Voltaire's own opinion. And within this view lay a portion of the beloved France which had shown him the door.

Voltaire had much to be thankful for at "Les Délices." There were printers close at hand in Geneva for his bristling pamphlets. His great wealth allowed him to run his house on a seigneurial scale. A battalion of servants, gardeners, and secretaries moved about the place. A French chef reigned over the kitchen, and on the enormous payroll were a postillion and a fireworks expert. A private theater was erected for the performance of the master's plays, and Voltaire often acted in them himself. To and from "Les Délices" poured a correspondence fantastic in volume and scope. All the great and near-great of Europe exchanged letters with this venerable exile. Voltaire always kept open house and at the nearby Ferney estate which he acquired later. His home was constantly overrun with guests. If one were lucky one might chance upon a Gibbon, a d'Alembert, a Charles James Fox, a Marmontel, even an inquisitive young man from England named James Boswell. Mostly, they came to honor the man whose intellectual valor had given all freethinking men fresh hope in the good fight against repression and superstition. Others came for the entertainment and to view the oddities of the place. Voltaire even kept a pet monkey and bear. Presiding over the whole establishment as a combined hostess and housekeeper was the niece of Voltaire, known to all as "Mlle. Denis"—a woman of simple, homespun ways in this Swiss mansion of wisdom, who sighed daily for her beloved Paris.

It was at this attractive house outside of Geneva that Casanova began a series of five visits on August 22, 1760. Each night this fabulous Venetian would note down as much of the conversation as he remembered. We have his word for it that the talks as given in his Mémoires * represent

---

* The conversations used below have been rendered in dialogue form, with scarcely more omitted than the usual "I saids" and "he replieds." All of Casanova's pertinent interpolations have been retained where they occur in the original. The translation used is that of Arthur Machen. This first appeared in London in 1894 in a now rare and unabridged edition which for the first time contained a few chapters discovered by Arthur Symons. Only 330 sets of twelve volumes each were printed of that edition. In 1926 a new edition of Machen's scholarly translation was brought out "for subscribers only" by the Venetian Society (New York and London). It is from Chapter IX of Volume VI of that edition, which bore an "appreciation" by Havelock Ellis, that the following extracts have been made. The story of Casanova's manuscript and its many textual and linguistic adventures is a devious and fantastic one. Ernest Boyd has told it very succinctly in his introduction to the "Modern Library" abridgement of the Mémoires first issued in 1929. Boyd's account follows:

"Giacomo Casanova, who liked to be known as Jacques Casanova de Seingalt, was born in Venice, on April 2, 1725, and died at the Château of Dux in Bohemia, on June 4, 1798. The last fourteen years of his life were spent as Count Waldstein's librarian at Dux, and it was in that retreat that he wrote the Mémoires which were to make him famous, in spite of himself, for he seems to have written chiefly to beguile his premature old age rather than with any thought of posterity. The curious and complicated history of the manuscript shows this. . . .

"In 1820 a certain Carlo Angiolini, who was the son-in-law of Casanova's younger sister, brought a manuscript entitled, 'The Story of My Life to the Year 1797,' to the

only a small portion of the extensive notes he made. Naturally he presents himself in as advantageous a light as possible. We have no way of checking his boast that his recitation from Ariosto's Orlando Furioso brought tears to the eyes of Europe's most caustic cynic. Still, few scholars have seriously questioned the genuineness of Casanova's report. In his preface to a recently printed Entretiens avec Voltaire, Henri de Regnier, of the French Academy, speaks of the episode as "one of the most vivid chapters of the Mémoires." And to explain the note of resentment and pique that crept into Casanova's reminiscences of Voltaire, M. de Regnier offers a highly tenable theory. In the course of the five conversations with his exuberant guest, Voltaire committed the grievous affront of never once asking him to narrate his celebrated escape from "The Leads," a two-hour recital, as a rule, at which Casanova had become a virtuoso. Observes M. de Regnier: "A host should allow his guests to exhibit themselves to best advantage. Voltaire was found wanting in that respect, and no doubt Casanova never forgave him for it."

Those even casually acquainted with the Mémoires will scarcely be surprised to learn that Casanova the amorist was far from idle in the intervals between his talks with Voltaire. Ernest Boyd hardly exaggerated when he wrote that "the sequel to his conversations with Voltaire is like a chapter from Boccaccio." After all, Casanova himself has warned us in advance that his autobiography "is that of a bachelor whose chief business in life was to cultivate the pleasures of the senses." And now we return to M. Villars-Chandieu and his Venetian friend as they advance into the magnificent reception hall of "Les Délices." Voltaire was just leaving the table as they appeared. "He was in the middle of a court of gentlemen and ladies," Casanova recalls, "which made my introduction a solemn one; but with this great man solemnity could not fail to be in my favor."

---

firm of Brockhaus in Leipzig. The work was in twelve volumes and ended abruptly with the year 1774. Nobody seems to know how it came into Angiolini's possession, nor what happened to the concluding portion. Even the manuscript as left by Casanova has never been printed. It was first translated from the original faulty French into German and was published, with many omissions and alterations, from 1822 to 1828.

"At the same time, Herr Brockhaus had the French text revised by a French professor in Dresden named Jean Laforgue, who polished Casanova's undoubtedly shaky French, but who also made various suppressions and alterations. In this form, the work also appeared in twelve volumes between 1826 and 1837. Meanwhile other editions began to appear, some of them pirated, all presenting variants upon the German and the French editions of Brockhaus, which were and are the nearest thing we have to the authentic Memoirs of Jacques Casanova.

"The original manuscript still reposes in the safe of the Brockhaus firm and there is little chance of its being published in its entirety. Casanova used the crudest language in describing his amorous adventures . . ."

CASANOVA: M. de Voltaire, this is the happiest moment of my life. I have been your pupil for twenty years, and my heart is full of joy to see my master.

VOLTAIRE: Honor me with your attendance on my course for twenty years more, and promise me that you will bring me my fees at the end of that time.

CASANOVA: Certainly, if you promise to wait for me.

(*"This Voltairean sally made all present laugh, as was to be expected, for those who laugh keep one party in countenance at the other's expense, and the side which has the laughter is sure to win; this is the rule of good society; I was not taken by surprise; I had expected this and hoped to have my revenge."—Casanova*)

(*Enter two Englishmen, who are presented by Voltaire to Casanova.*)

VOLTAIRE: These gentlemen are English. I wish I were.

(*"I thought the compliment false and out of place; for the gentlemen were obliged to reply out of politeness that they wished they had been French, or if they did not care to tell a lie, they would be embarrassed to tell the truth. I believe every man of honor should put his own nation first."—Casanova*)

VOLTAIRE (*turning again to Casanova*): Since you are Venetian you must know Count Algarotti.

CASANOVA: I know him, but not because I am a Venetian, as seven-eighths of my dear countrymen are not even aware of his existence.

VOLTAIRE: I should have said, "as a man of letters."

CASANOVA: I know him from having spent two months with him at Padua, seven years ago, and what particularly attracted my attention was the admiration he professed for M. de Voltaire.

VOLTAIRE: That is flattering for me, but he has no need of admiring anyone.

CASANOVA: If Algarotti had not begun by admiring others, he would never have made a name for himself. As an admirer of Newton he endeavored to teach the ladies to discuss the theory of light.

VOLTAIRE: Did he succeed?

CASANOVA: Not as well as M. de Fontenelle in his *Plurality of Worlds*. However, one may say he has succeeded.

VOLTAIRE: True. If you see him at Bologna, tell him I am expecting to hear from him about Russia. He can address the letters to my banker, Bianchi, at Milan, and they will be sent to me.

CASANOVA: I will not fail to do so if I see him.

VOLTAIRE: I have heard that the Italians do not care for his style.

CASANOVA: No; all that he writes is full of French idioms. His style is wretched.

VOLTAIRE: But do not these French turns increase the beauty of your language?

CASANOVA: They make it insufferable, as French would be, mixed with Italian or German, even though it were written by M. de Voltaire.

VOLTAIRE: You are right; every language should preserve its purity. Livy has been criticized on this account; his Latin is said to be tainted with patavinity.*

CASANOVA: When I began to learn Latin, the Abbé Lazzarini told me he preferred Livy to Sallust.

VOLTAIRE: The Abbé Lazzarini, author of the tragedy *Ulisse il giovane?* You must have been very young. I wish I had known him. But I knew the Abbé Conti well; the same Conti that was Newton's friend, and whose four tragedies contain the whole of Roman history.

CASANOVA: I also knew and admired him. I was young, but I congratulated myself on being admitted into the society of these great men. It seems as if it were yesterday, though it is many years ago; and now in your presence my inferiority does not humiliate me. I wish to be the younger son of all humanity.

VOLTAIRE: Better so than to be the chief and eldest. . . . May I ask you to what branch of literature you have devoted yourself?

CASANOVA: To none; but that, perhaps will come later. In the meanwhile I read as much as I can, and try to study character on my travels.

VOLTAIRE: That is the way to become learned, but the book of humanity is too vast. Reading history is the easier way.

CASANOVA: Yes, if history did not lie. One is not sure of the truth of the facts. It is tiring, while the study of the world is amusing. Horace, whom I know by heart, is my guide-book.

VOLTAIRE: Algarotti, too, has all Horace in his head. Of course, you are fond of poetry?

CASANOVA: It is my passion.

VOLTAIRE: Have you made many sonnets?

CASANOVA: Ten or twelve I like, and two or three thousand which in all probability I have not read twice.

VOLTAIRE: The Italians are mad about sonnets.

CASANOVA: Yes; if one can call it a madness to desire to put thought into measured harmony. The sonnet is difficult because the thought has to be fitted exactly into the fourteen lines.

---

* Provincial characteristics of certain Latin writing; from the ancient word for Padua, "Patavium."

VOLTAIRE: It is Procrustes' bed, and that's the reason you have so few good ones. As for us, we have not one; but that is the fault of our language.

CASANOVA: And of the French genius, which considers that a thought when extended loses all its force.

VOLTAIRE: And you do not think so?

CASANOVA: Pardon me, it depends on the kind of thought. A witty saying, for example, will not make a sonnet; in French or Italian it belongs to the domain of the epigram.

VOLTAIRE: What Italian poet do you like best?

CASANOVA: Ariosto; but I cannot say I love him better than the others, for he is my only love.

VOLTAIRE: You know the others, though?

CASANOVA: I think I have read them all, but all their lights pale before Ariosto's. Fifteen years ago I read all you had written against him, and I said that you would retract when you had read his works.

VOLTAIRE: I am obliged to you for thinking that I had not read them. As a matter of fact I had done so, but I was young. I knew Italian very imperfectly, and being prejudiced by the learned Italians who adore Tasso I was unfortunate enough to publish a criticism on Ariosto which I thought my own, while it was only the echo of those who had prejudiced me. I adore your Ariosto.

CASANOVA: Ah! M. de Voltaire, I breathe again. But be good enough to have the work in which you turned this great man into ridicule excommunicated.

VOLTAIRE: What use would that be? All my books are excommunicated. . . . But I will give you a good proof of my retraction.

("*I was astonished! The great man began to recite the two fine passages from the thirty-fourth and thirty-fifth cantos, in which the divine poet speaks of the conversation of Astolpho and St. John, and he did it without missing a single line or committing the slightest fault against the laws of prosody! He then pointed out the beauties of the passages with his natural insight and with a great man's genius. I could not have had anything better from the lips of the most skilled commentators in Italy. I listened to him with the greatest attention, hardly daring to breathe, and waiting for him to make a mistake, but I had my trouble for nothing.*"—Casanova)

(*Applause.*)

CASANOVA (*turning to the company*): I am more than astonished! All Italy should know what I have seen!

VOLTAIRE: And I, sir, will let all Europe know of the amends I owe to the greatest genius our continent has produced.

("Greedy of the praise which he deserved so well, Voltaire gave me the next day his translation of the stanza which Ariosto begins thus: 'Quindi avvien che tra principi e signori.' ") *

MME. DENIS (*to Casanova*): Do you think the passage my uncle has just recited one of the finest Ariosto wrote?

CASANOVA: Yes, but not the finest.

VOLTAIRE: It ought to be; for without it Signor Lodovico † would not have gained his apotheosis.

CASANOVA: He has been canonized, then? I was not aware of that.

("Everybody laughed except myself, and I continued to look perfectly serious.")

VOLTAIRE (*vexed at not seeing Casanova laugh like the rest*): Why aren't you laughing? Are you thinking of some more than human passage?

CASANOVA: Yes.

VOLTAIRE: What passage is that?

CASANOVA: The last thirty-six stanzas of the twenty-third canto, where the poet describes in detail how Orlando became mad. Since the world has existed no one has discovered the springs of madness, unless Ariosto himself, who became mad in his old age. These stanzas inspire horror, M. de Voltaire, and I am sure they must have made you tremble.

VOLTAIRE: Yes, I remember they render love dreadful. I long to read them again.

MME. DENIS (*with a side glance at Voltaire*): Perhaps the gentleman will be good enough to recite them.

CASANOVA: Willingly, if you will have the goodness to listen to me.

VOLTAIRE: You have learned them by heart, then, have you?

CASANOVA: Yes, it was a pleasure and no trouble. Since I was sixteen, I have read over Ariosto two or three times every year. It is my passion, and the lines have naturally become linked in my memory without my having given myself any pains to learn them. I know it all, except his long genealogies and his historical tirades, which fatigue the mind and do not touch the heart. It is only Horace that I know throughout, in spite of the often prosaic style of the epistles, which are certainly far from equalling Boileau's.

---

* "Les papes, les Césars, apaisant leur querelle,
Jurent sur l'Evangile une paix éternelle;
Vous les voyez l'un de l'autre ennemis;
C'était pour se tromper qu'ils s'étaient réunis.
Nul serment n'est gardé, nul accord n'est sincère;
Quand la bouche a parlé, le coeur dit le contraire.
Du ciel qu'ils attestaient, ils bravaient le courroux;
L'intérêt est le dieu qui les gouverne tous."

† Ariosto.

VOLTAIRE: Boileau is often too lengthy. I admire Horace, but as for Ariosto, with his forty long cantos, there is too much of him.

CASANOVA: It is fifty-one cantos, M. de Voltaire.

MME. DENIS: Come, come, let us hear the thirty-six stanzas which earned the author the title of divine, and which are to make us tremble.

("*I then began, in an assured voice, but not in that monotonous tone adopted by the Italians, with which the French so justly reproach us. The French would be the best reciters if they were not constrained by the rhyme, for they say what they feel better than any other people. They have neither the passionate, monotonous tone of my fellow-countrymen, nor the sentimentality of the Germans, nor the fatiguing mannerisms of the English. To every period they give its proper expression, but the recurrence of the same sounds partly spoils their recitation. I recited the fine verse of Ariosto as if it had been rhythmic prose, animating it by the sound of my voice and the movements of my eyes, and by modulating my intonation according to the sentiments with which I wished to inspire my audience. They saw how I hardly could restrain my tears, and every eye was wet; but when I came to the stanzas:*"

> Poiche allargare il freno al dolor puote,
> Che resta sola senza altrui rispetto,
> Giù dagli occhi rigando per le gote
> Sparge un fiume di lacrime sul petto, . . .

the tears coursed down my cheeks to such an extent that everyone began to sob. M. de Voltaire and Mme. Denis threw their arms round my neck, but their embraces could not stop me, for Orlando, to become mad, had to notice that he was in the same bed in which Angelica had lately been found in the arms of the fortunate Medor, and I had to reach the next stanza. For my voice of sorrow and wailing I substituted the expression of that terror which arose naturally from the contemplation of this fury, which was in its effects like a tempest, a volcano, or an earthquake. When I had finished I received with a sad air the congratulations of the audience."—Casanova)

VOLTAIRE: I always said so! The secret of drawing tears is to weep one's self, but they must be real tears, and to shed them the heart must be stirred to its depths. I am obliged to you, sir (*embracing Casanova*), and I promise to recite the same stanzas myself tomorrow, and to weep like you.*

---

* "He kept his word."—Casanova.

MME. DENIS: It is astonishing that intolerant Rome should not have condemned "Orlando Furioso."

VOLTAIRE: Far from it. Leo X excommunicated whoever should dare to condemn it. The two great families of Este and Medici interested themselves in the poet's favor. Without that protection it is probable that the one line on the donation of Rome by Constantine to Silvester, where the poet speaks of *puzza forte,** would have sufficed to put the whole poem under an interdict.

CASANOVA: I believe that the line which has excited the most talk is that in which Ariosto throws doubt on the general resurrection. Ariosto, in speaking of the hermit who would have hindered Rhodomonte from getting possession of Isabella, widow of Zerbin, paints the African, who, wearied of the hermit's sermons, seizes him and throws him so far that he dashes him against a rock, against which he remains in a dead swoon, so that *al novissimo di forse fia desto*.† This *forse*,‡ which may possibly have been placed there only as a flower of rhetoric or as a word to complete the verse, raised a great uproar, which would doubtless have greatly amused the poet if he had had time!

MME. DENIS: It is a pity that Ariosto was not more careful in these hyperbolical expressions.

VOLTAIRE: Be quiet, niece, they are full of wit! They are all golden grains, which are dispersed throughout the work in the best taste.

(*"The conversation was then directed toward various topics, and at last we got to L'Écossaise, which we had played at Soleure. They knew all about it."*—Casanova)

VOLTAIRE: If you like to play it at my house, I will write to M. de Chavigne to send you Lindane, and I myself shall play Montrose.

CASANOVA: I am obliged to go on my journey tomorrow. Madame M. is at Basle. . . .

VOLTAIRE (*exclaiming loudly and "arousing the whole company against me"*): I shall consider your visit an insult unless you spare me a week, at least, of your society.

CASANOVA: Sir, I have come to Geneva only to have the honor of seeing you, and now that I have obtained that favor I have nothing more to do.

VOLTAIRE: Have you come to speak to me, or for me to speak to you?

CASANOVA: In a measure, of course, to speak to you, but much more for you to speak to me.

---

* Italian for "smells strongly."
† "to be perhaps awakened on the judgment day."
‡ "perhaps."

VOLTAIRE: Then stay here three days at least. Come to dinner every day, and we will have some conversation.

(*"The invitation was so flattering and pressing that I could not refuse it with a good grace. I therefore accepted, and I then left to go and write."*—Casanova)

(The following day Casanova went again to Délices. "I was silent during the repast, but at dessert, M. de Voltaire, knowing that I had reasons for not liking the Venetian Government, introduced the subject; but I disappointed him, as I maintained that in no country could a man enjoy more perfect liberty than in Venice. 'Yes,' said he, 'provided he resigns himself to play the part of a dumb man.' And seeing that I did not care for the subject, he took me by the arm to his garden, of which, he said, he was the creator. The principal walk led to a pretty running stream. ' 'Tis the Rhône,' said he, 'which I send into France.' 'It does not cost you much in carriage, at all events,' said I. He smiled pleasantly and showed me the principal street of Geneva, and Mont Blanc, which is the highest point of the Alps. Bringing back the conversation to Italian literature, he began to talk nonsense with much wit and learning but always concluding with a false judgment. I let him talk on. He spoke of Homer, Dante, and Petrarch, and everybody knows what he thought of those great geniuses, but he did himself wrong in writing what he thought. ... I accompanied M. de Voltaire to his bedroom, where he changed his wig and put on another cap, for he always wore one on account of the rheumatism to which he was subject. I saw on the table the '*Summa*' of St. Thomas, and among other Italian poets the '*Secchia Rapita*' of Tassoni."—Casanova)

VOLTAIRE: This is the only tragi-comic poem which Italy has. Tassoni was a monk, a wit, and a genius as well as a poet.

CASANOVA: I will grant his poetical ability but not his learning, for he ridiculed the system of Copernicus, and said that if his theories were followed astronomers would not be able to calculate lunations or eclipses.

VOLTAIRE: Where does he make that ridiculous remark?

CASANOVA: In his academical discourses.

VOLTAIRE: I have not read them, but I will get them. (*Taking a pen and noting the name down.*) But Tassoni criticized Petrarch very ingeniously.

CASANOVA: Yes, but he dishonored his taste and literature thereby, as did Muratori.

VOLTAIRE: Here he is. You must allow that his learning is immense.

CASANOVA: *Est ubi peccat.**

VOLTAIRE (*opening a door, showing a "hundred great files full of papers"*):
That's my correspondence. You see before you nearly fifty thousand
letters, to which I have replied.

CASANOVA: Have you a copy of your answers?

VOLTAIRE: Of a good many of them. That's the business of a servant of
mine, who has nothing else to do.

CASANOVA: I know plenty of booksellers who would give a good deal to get
hold of your answers.

VOLTAIRE: Yes; but look out for the booksellers when you publish anything, if you have not yet begun. They are greater robbers than
Barabbas.

CASANOVA: I shall not have anything to do with these gentlemen till I am
an old man.

VOLTAIRE: Then they will be the scourge of your old age.

(*Casanova quotes a macaronic verse by Merlin Coccaius.*)

VOLTAIRE: Where's that from?

CASANOVA: It's a line from a celebrated poem in twenty-four cantos.

VOLTAIRE: Celebrated?

CASANOVA: Yes; and, what is more, worthy of being celebrated. But to
appreciate it one must understand the Mantuan dialect.

VOLTAIRE: I could make it out, if you could get me a copy.

CASANOVA: I shall have the honor of presenting you with one tomorrow.

VOLTAIRE: You will oblige me extremely.

("We had to leave his room and spend two hours in the company,
talking over all sorts of things. Voltaire displayed all the resources of
his brilliant and fertile wit, and charmed everyone in spite of his sarcastic observations which did not even spare those present, but he had an
inimitable manner of launching a sarcasm without wounding a person's feelings. When the great man accompanied his witticisms with a
graceful smile he could always get a laugh. He kept up a notable establishment and an excellent table, a rare circumstance with his poetic
brothers, who are rarely favorites of Plutus as he was. He was then sixty
years old, and had a hundred and twenty thousand francs a year."—
Casanova)

(*Between these literary sessions with Voltaire, Casanova managed
to gather material of another kind for his later reminiscences. A syndic
of the town invited him to a series of late suppers with some Genevan
young ladies of high birth. Moreover, he found time for another favor-*

---

* "That is where he sins."

ite indulgence—gambling, admitting that he lost a small fortune at
cards to a couple of Englishmen.)

("After a good night's sleep I awoke in an active mood, and began
to write a letter to Voltaire in blank verse, which cost me four times the
pains that rhymed verses would have done. I sent it to him with the
poem of Teofilo Folengo, but I made a mistake in doing so, as I might
have known he would not care for it. One cannot appreciate what one
does not understand. I then went to Mr. Fox [a fellow traveller], where
I found the two Englishmen, who offered me my revenge. I lost a hundred louis, and was glad to see them set out for Lausanne. . . . At noon
I went to M. de Voltaire's. He was not to be seen, but Madame Denis
consoled me for his absence. She had wit, learning without pretension,
taste, and a great hatred for the King of Prussia, whom she called a
villain. She asked about my beautiful housekeeper, and congratulated
me on having married her to a respectable man. Although I feel now
that she was quite right, I was far from thinking so then; the impression
was too fresh on my mind. Madame Denis begged me to tell her how
I had escaped from The Leads, but as the story was rather a long one I
promised to satisfy her another time. M. de Voltaire did not dine with
us; he appeared, however, at five o'clock, holding a letter in his hand."
—Casanova)

VOLTAIRE: Do you know the Marquis Albergati Capacelli, senator of
Bologna, and Count Paradisi?

CASANOVA: I do not know Paradisi, but I know Albergati by sight and by
reputation; he is not a senator, but one of the "Forty," which at
Bologna are fifty.

VOLTAIRE: Dear me! That seems rather a riddle!

CASANOVA: Do you know him?

VOLTAIRE: No, but he has sent me Goldoni's plays, the translation of my
"Tancred," and some Bologna sausages, and he says he will come and
see me.

CASANOVA: He will not come; he is not such a fool.

VOLTAIRE: How a fool? Would there be anything foolish in coming to
see me?

CASANOVA: Certainly not as far as you are concerned; but very much so for
his own sake.

VOLTAIRE: Would you mind telling me why?

CASANOVA: He knows what he would lose; for he enjoys the idea you seem
to have of him, and if he came you would see his nothingness, and
good-by to the illusion. He is a worthy man with six thousand sequins

a year, and a craze for the theater. He is a good enough actor, and has written several comedies in prose, but they are fit neither for the study nor for the stage.

VOLTAIRE: You certainly give him a coat which does not make him look any bigger.

CASANOVA: I assure you it is not quite small enough.

VOLTAIRE: But tell me how it is with this forty and this fifty of Bologna.

CASANOVA: Just as at Basle noon is at eleven.

VOLTAIRE: I understand; just as your Council of Ten is composed of seventeen members.

CASANOVA: Exactly; but the cursed "Forty" of Bologna are men of another kind.

VOLTAIRE: Why cursed?

CASANOVA: Because they are not subject to the fisc, and are thus enabled to commit whatever crimes they like with perfect impunity. All they have got to do is to live outside the state borders on their revenues.

VOLTAIRE: That is a blessing, and not a curse. But let me return to our subject. I suppose the Marquis Albergati is a man of letters?

CASANOVA: He writes well enough, but he is fond of the sound of his own voice, his style is prolix, and I don't think he has much brains.

VOLTAIRE: He is an actor, I think you said?

CASANOVA: Yes, and a very good one, above all, when he plays the lover's part in one of his own plays.

VOLTAIRE: Is he a handsome man?

CASANOVA: Yes, on the stage, but not elsewhere; his face lacks expression.

VOLTAIRE: But his plays give satisfaction?

CASANOVA: Not to persons who understand play-writing; they would be hissed if they were intelligible.

VOLTAIRE: And what do you think of Goldoni?

CASANOVA: I have the highest opinion of him. Goldoni is the Italian Molière.

VOLTAIRE: Why does he call himself poet to the Duke of Parma?

CASANOVA: No doubt to prove that a wit as well as a fool has his weak points. In all probability the duke knows nothing about it. He also calls himself a barrister, though he is such only in his own imagination. Goldoni is a good playwright, and nothing more. Everybody in Venice knows me for his friend, and I can therefore speak of him with authority. He does not shine in society, and in spite of the fine satire of his works he is a man of an extremely gentle disposition.

VOLTAIRE: So I have been told. He is poor, and wants to leave Venice. The managers of the theaters where they play his pieces will not like that.

CASANOVA: People talked about getting him a pension, but the project has been relegated to the Greek Kalends, as they said that if he had a pension he would write no more.

VOLTAIRE: Cumae refused to give a pension to Homer, for fear that all the blind men would ask for a pension.

("We spent a pleasant day, and he thanked me heartily for the copy of the *Macaronicon*, which he promised to read." Casanova then joined the syndic in paying another visit to the hospitable Genevan ladies. . . . "After a calm and refreshing sleep of ten hours, I felt myself able to enjoy and appreciate the delightful society of M. de Voltaire. I went to his house, but I was disappointed in my hopes, as it pleased the great man to be in a fault-finding and sarcastic mood the whole day. He knew I had to leave on the morrow.")

(*At dinner.*)

VOLTAIRE: Thank you for the present of the "Merlin Coccaius." You certainly gave it to me with good intentions, but I owe you no thanks for praising it so highly, as you made me waste four hours in reading nonsense.

CASANOVA (*feeling his hair stand on end, but mastering his emotions; quietly*): One day, perhaps, you will find yourself obliged to praise the poem more highly than I have done. (*Cites instances of the insufficiency of a first perusal.*)

VOLTAIRE: That's true, but as for your Merlin, I will read him no more. I have put him beside Chapelain's *Pucelle*.

CASANOVA: Which pleases all the critics, in spite of its bad versification, for it is a good poem, and Chapelain was a real poet though he wrote bad verses. I cannot overlook his genius. . . . Chapelain has the merit of having rendered his subject-matter agreeable, without pandering to the tastes of his readers by saying things shocking to modesty and piety. So thinks my master, Crébillon.

VOLTAIRE: Crébillon! You cite a weighty authority! But how is my friend Crébillon your master, may I ask?

CASANOVA: He taught me to speak French in less than two years, and as a mark of my gratitude I translated his *Rhadamiste* into Italian Alexandrines. I am the first Italian who has dared to use this meter in our language.

VOLTAIRE: The first? I beg your pardon, as that honor belongs to my friend Pierre-Jacques Martelli.

CASANOVA: I am sorry to be obliged to tell you that you are making a mistake.

VOLTAIRE: Why, I have his works, printed at Bologna, in my room!

CASANOVA: I don't deny that, I am only talking about the meter used by Martelli. What you are thinking of must be verses of fourteen syllables, without alternative masculine and feminine rhymes. However, I confess that he thinks he has imitated the French Alexandrines, and his preface made me explode with laughter. Did you read it?

VOLTAIRE: Read it? I always read prefaces, and Martelli proves there that his verses have the same effect in Italian as our Alexandrine verses have in French.

CASANOVA: Exactly, that's what's so amusing. The worthy man is quite mistaken, and I only ask you to listen to what I have to say on the subject. Your masculine verse has only twelve poetic syllables, and the feminine thirteen. All Martelli's lines have fourteen syllables, except those that finish with a long vowel, which at the end of a line always counts as two syllables. You will observe that the first hemistich in Martelli always consists of seven syllables, while in French it has only six. Your friend Pierre-Jacques was either stone deaf or very hard of hearing.

VOLTAIRE: Then you have followed our theory of versification rigorously.

CASANOVA: Just so, in spite of the difficulty, as nearly all our words end with a short syllable.

VOLTAIRE: What reception was accorded to your innovation?

CASANOVA: It was not found pleasing, because nobody knows how to recite my verses; but I hope to triumph when I deliver them myself before our literary clubs.

VOLTAIRE: Do you remember any of your version of the *Rhadamiste?*

CASANOVA: I remember it all.

VOLTAIRE: You have a wonderful memory. I should be glad to hear it.

(*"I began to recite the same scene that I had recited to Crébillon ten years before, and I thought M. de Voltaire listened with pleasure."*— Casanova)

VOLTAIRE: It doesn't strike me as at all harsh.

(*"This was the highest praise he would give me. In his turn the great man recited a passage from* Tancred, *which had not as yet been published, and which was afterwards considered, and rightly, a masterpiece. We should have got on very well if we had kept to that, but on my quoting a line of Horace to praise one of his pieces, he said. . . ."*— Casanova)

VOLTAIRE: Horace was a great master who gave precepts which will never be out of date.

CASANOVA: Yet you yourself have violated one of them, but you have violated it grandly.

VOLTAIRE: Which is that?

CASANOVA: You do not write *"contentus paucis lectoribus."* *

VOLTAIRE: If Horace had had to combat the hydra-headed monster of superstition, he would have written as I have written—for all the world.

CASANOVA: It seems to me that you might spare yourself the trouble of combating what you will never destroy.

VOLTAIRE: That which I cannot finish others will, and I shall always have the glory of having been the first in the field.

CASANOVA: Very good; but supposing you succeed in destroying superstition, what are you going to put in its place?

VOLTAIRE: I like that! If I deliver the race of man from a wild beast which is devouring it, am I to be asked what I intend to put in its place?

CASANOVA: It does not devour it; on the contrary, it is necessary to its existence.

VOLTAIRE: Necessary to its existence! That is a horrible blasphemy, the falsity of which will be seen in the future. I love the human race. I would fain see men free and happy, like myself, and superstition and freedom cannot go together. Where do you find an enslaved and yet a happy people?

CASANOVA: You wish, then, to see the people sovereign?

VOLTAIRE: God forbid! There must be a sovereign to govern the masses!

CASANOVA: In that case you must have superstition, for without it the masses will never obey a mere man decked with the name of monarch.

VOLTAIRE: I will have no monarch; the word expresses despotism, which I hate as I do slavery.

CASANOVA: What do you mean, then? If you wish to put the government in the hands of one man, such a man, I maintain, will be a monarch.

VOLTAIRE: I would have a sovereign ruler of a free people, of which he is the chief by an agreement which binds them both, which would prevent him from becoming a tyrant.

CASANOVA: Addison will tell you that such a sovereign is a sheer impossibility. I agree with Hobbes—of two evils choose the lesser. A nation without superstition would be a nation of philosophers, and philosophers would never obey. The people will be happy only when they are crushed and downtrodden, and bound in chains.

VOLTAIRE: This is horrible; and you are of the people yourself. If you have

---

* satisfied with a few readers.

read my works you must have seen how I show that superstition is the enemy of kings.

CASANOVA: Read your works? I have read and re-read them, especially in places where I have differed from you. Your ruling passion is the love of humanity. *Est ubi peccas.** This blinds you. Love humanity, but love it as it is. It is not fit to receive the blessings you would lavish on it, and which would only make it more wretched and perverse. Leave men their devouring monster; it is dear to them. I have never laughed so heartily as at Don Quixote assailed by the galley-slaves whom his generosity had set free.

VOLTAIRE: I am sorry that you have such a bad opinion of your fellow-creatures. And, by the way, tell me whether there is freedom in Venice.

CASANOVA: As much as can be expected under an aristocracy. Our liberty is not so great as that which the English enjoy, but we are content.

VOLTAIRE: Even under The Leads?

CASANOVA: My imprisonment was certainly despotic; but as I had knowingly abused my liberty I am satisfied that the government was within its rights in shutting me up without the usual formalities.

VOLTAIRE: All the same, you made your escape.

CASANOVA: I used my rights, as they used theirs.

VOLTAIRE: Very good! But as far as I can see, no one in Venice is really free.

CASANOVA: That may be; but you must agree that the essence of freedom consists in thinking you have it.

VOLTAIRE: I shall not agree to that so easily. You and I see liberty from very different points of view. The aristocrats, the members of the government even, are not free in Venice. For example, they cannot travel without permission.

CASANOVA: True, but that is a restriction of their own making to preserve their power. Would you say that a Bernese is not free, because he is subject to the sumptuary laws, which he himself has made?

VOLTAIRE: Well, well, I wish the people made the laws everywhere. (*Abruptly*) What part do you come from?

CASANOVA: From Roche. I should have been very sorry to leave Switzerland without seeing the famous Haller. In my travels I render homage to my learned contemporaries, and you come the last and best.

VOLTAIRE: You must have liked Haller.

CASANOVA: I spent three of the happiest days of my life with him.

VOLTAIRE: I congratulate you. He is a great man and worthy of all honor.

---

* "That's where you sin."

CASANOVA: I think as you do, and I am glad to hear you doing him justice; I am sorry he was not so just toward you.

VOLTAIRE: Well, you see we may both of us be mistaken.

("No more was said of literature and I became a silent actor till M. de Voltaire retired, when I approached Madame Denis, and asked her if she had any commands for me at Rome. I went home well pleased at having compelled the giant of intellect to listen to reason, as I then thought foolishly enough; but there was a rankling feeling left in my heart against him which made me for the next ten years criticize all that he wrote. I am sorry now for having done so, though on reading my censures over again I find that in many places I was right. I should have done better, however, to have kept silence, to have respected his genius, and to have suspected my own opinions. I should have considered that if it had not been for those quips and cranks which made me hate him on the third day, I should have thought him wholly sublime. This thought alone should have silenced me, but an angry man always thinks himself right. . . . If we meet in the halls of Pluto, the more peccant parts of our mortal nature purged away, all will be made up. He will receive my heartiest apologies, and he will be my friend, I his sincere admirer. . . . I spent part of the night and the whole of the following day in writing down my conversations with Voltaire, and they amounted nearly to a volume, of which I have only given a mere abridgment. Toward the evening my Epicurean syndic called on me, and we went to sup with the three nymphs, and for five hours we indulged in every species of wantonness, in which I had a somewhat fertile imagination. . . ."—Casanova)

Benjamin Franklin

A SKIRMISH IN LONDON WITH BRITAIN'S SECRETARY
OF STATE FOR AMERICA.

I must set you right, there, Mr. Franklin.

Envoy extraordinary of the grumbling American colonies, Benjamin Franklin had first been to London in 1757 as agent for Pennsylvania. In subsequent years both Georgia and New Jersey also engaged the astute advocate to argue their claims and present their grievances in England, and Massachusetts followed in 1770. Franklin proved an eloquent spokesman for his mistreated land. As special pleader for the colonies he aided strongly in bringing about the repeal of the notorious "Stamp Act," which he later termed "the mother of mischief." Watching him present the case in Parliament, Edmund Burke remarked that Franklin was like a master being examined by a parcel of apprentices. In the rising tide of bitterness, Franklin tried at first to act as conciliator, one result being that he was accused in America "of being too much an Englishman and in England of being too much an American." This was especially so when he preached moderation after the imposition of the Townshend Acts. These acts, with their exorbitant duties on imports, were in line with Britain's policy of stifling native American trade and industry. Actually, Franklin was playing a shrewd waiting game. And meanwhile he could reach the ears of the British people.

For a time English officialdom treated this bland diplomat from overseas handsomely. Franklin found English society courteous and attentive, and he was permitted to pamphleteer unhampered. And if at home Harvard, Yale, and William and Mary had honored him with degrees, Oxford now went them one better by bestowing upon him the degree of Doctor of Civil Laws. However, as the clouds gathered and activities at home sharpened to a crisis, Franklin could feel a change in the social climate of England. And perhaps best representative of this change was the attitude of the Earl of Hillsborough.

This arrogant Briton had been made Secretary of State for America in 1768. On taking up his duties Hillsborough immediately contracted a violent dislike of all agents from the colonial assemblies, maintaining that all business should be transacted with the colonies through their governors. Such governors, Hillsborough knew, were "not likely to insist on colonial self-government," as Carl Van Doren points out. Franklin's designation as agent of Massachusetts came in 1770. The Earl had had two years in which to consolidate his antiassembly position. It was natural that he would clash with any man presenting credentials as the delegate of the colonial assembly. Legality, of course, was on Franklin's side, for the colonial governor, as an appointee of the British King, could not infringe the right of the assembly to send its own agent to the King. However, Massachusetts had already been rallying the other colonies for concerted action against the Townshend Acts, and there was talk in England about trying the leaders for treason.

Thus, Franklin was undoubtedly prepared for the insolent reception accorded him at his first interview with Hillsborough on January 16, 1771. That same day he sat down and recorded the episode as fully and accurately as he could. The following February 5 Franklin forwarded the detailed account to Samuel Cooper of the Massachusetts House of Representatives. With one very minor change to direct discourse in the opening, the conversation is rendered here exactly as Franklin reproduced it, dialogue form and all. After reading the report, Cooper must have fully endorsed Franklin's comments about the Earl's "conceit, wrongheadedness, obstinacy, and passion."

To Mr. Van Doren, Franklin's masterly biographer, we owe these added details of the visit to the Earl of Hillsborough:— "The Governor Bernard whom Franklin found with Hillsborough was Sir Francis Bernard, with whom as governor the people of Massachusetts had been so dissatisfied that he had been recalled; and the Secretary Pownall was John Pownall, Secretary of the Board of Trade, who seemed to Franklin to have a 'strong bias' against the Americans." We now turn to Franklin's own chronicle of that prerevolutionary skirmish with imperial insolence:

"Wednesday, January 16, 1771
"I went this morning to wait on Lord Hillsborough. The porter at first denied his Lordship, on which I left my name and drove off. But before the coach got out of the square the coachman heard a call, turned, and went back to the door, when the porter came and said: 'His Lordship will see you, sir.' I was shown into the levee room, where I found Governor Bernard, who I understand attends there constantly. Several other gentlemen were there attending, with whom I sat down

a few minutes, when Secretary Pownall came out to us, and said his Lordship desired I would come in.

"*I was pleased with this ready admission and preference, having sometimes waited three or four hours for my turn; and, being pleased, I could more easily put on the open, cheerful countenance that my friends advised me to wear. His Lordship came toward me, and said:—*

HILLSBOROUGH: I was dressing in order to go to Court; but hearing that you were at the door, who are a man of business, I determined to see you immediately.

FRANKLIN: Thank you, your Lordship. My business at present is not much. It is only to pay my respects to your Lordship and to acquaint your Lordship with my appointment by the House of Representatives of Massachusetts Bay to be their agent here, in which station if I could be of any service— *

HILLSBOROUGH (*his countenance changing at the naming of the province, cutting him short "with something between a smile and a sneer"*): I must set you right, there, Mr. Franklin. You are not an agent.

FRANKLIN: Why, my Lord?

HILLSBOROUGH: You are not appointed.

FRANKLIN: I do not understand your Lordship; I have the appointment in my pocket.

HILLSBOROUGH: You are mistaken; I have later and better advices. I have a letter from Governor Hutchinson; he would not give his assent to the bill.

FRANKLIN: There was no bill, my Lord; it was a vote of the House.

HILLSBOROUGH: There was a bill presented to the governor for the purpose of appointing you and another, one Dr. Lee, I think he is called, to which the governor refused his assent.

FRANKLIN: I cannot understand this, my Lord; I think there must be some mistake in it. Is your Lordship quite sure that you have such a letter?

HILLSBOROUGH: I will convince you of it directly. (*Rings the bell.*) Mr. Pownall will come in and satisfy you.

FRANKLIN: It is not necessary that I should now detain your Lordship from dressing. You are going to Court. I will wait on your Lordship another time.

HILLSBOROUGH: No, stay; he will come immediately. (*To the servant*) Tell Mr. Pownall I want him.

(*Mr. Pownall comes in.*)

---

* Franklin meant to add: "to the public I should be very happy."

HILLSBOROUGH: Have not you at hand Governor Hutchinson's letter mentioning his refusing his assent to the bill for appointing Mr. Franklin agent?

POWNALL: My Lord?

HILLSBOROUGH: Is there not such a letter?

POWNALL: No, my Lord; there is a letter relating to some bill for the payment of a salary to Mr. De Berdt, and I think to some other agent, to which the governor had refused his assent.

HILLSBOROUGH: And is there nothing in the letter to the purpose I mention?

POWNALL: No, my Lord.

FRANKLIN: I thought it could not well be, my Lord; as my letters are by the last ships, and they mention no such thing. Here is the authentic copy of the vote of the House, appointing me, in which there is no mention of any act intended. Will your Lordship please to look at it?

HILLSBOROUGH (*with seeming unwillingness takes the paper, but he does not look at it*): An information of this kind is not properly brought to me as Secretary of State. The Board of Trade is the proper place.

FRANKLIN: I will leave the paper then with Mr. Pownall to be—

HILLSBOROUGH (*hastily*): To what end would you leave it with him?

FRANKLIN: To be entered on the minutes of that Board, as usual.

HILLSBOROUGH (*angrily*): It shall not be entered there. No such paper shall be entered there while I have anything to do with the business of that Board. The House of Representatives has no right to appoint an agent. We shall take no notice of any agents but such as are appointed by acts of Assembly, to which the governor gives his assent. We have had confusion enough already. Here is one agent appointed by the Council, another by the House of Representatives. Which of these is agent for the province? Who are we to hear in provincial affairs? An agent appointed by act of Assembly we can understand. No other will be attended to for the future, I can assure you.

FRANKLIN: I cannot conceive, my Lord, why the consent of the governor should be thought necessary to the appointment of an agent for the people. It seems to me that—

HILLSBOROUGH (*with a mixed look of anger and contempt*): I shall not enter into a dispute with *you*, sir, upon this subject.

FRANKLIN: I beg your Lordship's pardon; I do not presume to dispute with your Lordship. I would only say that it seems to me that every body of men who cannot appear in person where business relating to them may be transacted should have a right to appear by an agent. The concurrence of the governor does not seem to be necessary. It is the business of the people that is to be done; he is not one of them; he is himself an agent.

HILLSBOROUGH (*hastily*): Whose agent is he?

FRANKLIN: The King's, my Lord.

HILLSBOROUGH: No such matter. He is one of the corporation by the province charter. No agent can be appointed but by an act, nor any act pass without his assent. Besides, this proceeding is directly contrary to express instructions.

FRANKLIN: I did not know there had been such instructions. I am not concerned in any offense against them, and—

HILLSBOROUGH: Yes, your offering such a paper to be entered is an offense against them. (*Folding it up again without having read a word of it.*) No such appointment shall be entered. When I came into the administration of American affairs I found them in great disorder. By *my* firmness they are now somewhat mended; and while I have the honor to hold the seals I shall continue the same conduct, the same *firmness*. I think my duty to the master I serve, and to the government of this nation, requires it of me. If that conduct is not approved, *they* may take my office from me when they please. I shall make them a bow, and thank them; I shall resign with pleasure. That gentleman knows it (*pointing to Pownall*); but while I continue in it I shall resolutely persevere in the same *firmness*.

FRANKLIN (*reaching out for the paper, which Hillsborough returns to him*): I beg your Lordship's pardon for taking up so much of your time. It is, I believe, of no great importance whether the appointment is acknowledged or not, for I have not the least conception that an agent can *at present* be of any use to any of the Colonies. I shall therefore give your Lordship no further trouble. (*Withdraws.*)

In the months that followed Hillsborough modified his tactics. Sporadic efforts at conciliation designed to improve his own position were now made. Franklin quickly saw through the Earl's hypocrisy and duplicity and refused to be trapped, the result being that "he threw me away as an orange that would yield no juice and therefore not worth more squeezing." Once more the Earl became surly and uncivil. Franklin exposed Hillsborough's trickery when he pretended to encourage Massachusetts' request for a large tract of untaxed land. In the end Franklin won. Hillsborough was forced to resign on August 1, 1772, and Lord Dartmouth, recommended by Franklin himself, was appointed by the King to replace him. To his son Franklin wrote: "He has served us by the very means he meant to destroy us, and tripped up his own heels into the bargain." Hillsborough neither forgot nor forgave. He never tired of branding Franklin as "one of the most mischievous men in England." When the Revolution finally broke out Hillsborough shouted in the House of Lords that Newgate Prison was the place for Benjamin Franklin. From where he stood on his pedestal of privilege, the Earl was probably right.

Dr. Samuel Johnson

PORTRAIT IN DIALOGUE II

IN THE long history of conversation one reaches Dr. Johnson with the feeling that all things lead up to him and lead away from him. And in his devoted shadow, James Boswell, one soon recognizes the very model of what the earthly recording angel should be. These two have become forever linked in the minds of men who read. In the permanent temple of letters one needs the other as much as the other needs him. No one has worded this unique duality so aptly as Louis Kronenberger: "Unwearied and inseparable, Johnson and Boswell move from one generation to another—the greatest social talker whose talk has been recorded, and the greatest biographer the world has ever known."

It is impossible—and futile—to say whether alone either Johnson or Boswell would have survived among the enduring names that have molded men's habits of speech and thought. That Johnson would have remained a revered name in the close and musty sancta of scholarship is likely. But the rest of the world would soon have passed him by. He lives by the good grace of a nosy, pushing, impudent, but wondrously worshipful young man who early attached himself to him. As for this same James Boswell, oblivion would even more certainly have overtaken him if the great Dr. Johnson had flatly and consistently refused him his company. Only the young Scotsman's pertinacity kept them together. Yet, for all his stinging gibes at this fawning celebrity-seeker, Johnson had nothing to complain of. In time he even came to cherish this dog-like devotion, and in the blackest moments of physical and mental anguish he found Boswell an anxious and helpful friend. And to a man of Johnson's irrepressible sarcasm, young Boswell, with what seemed an oafish naïveté and fatuous imperviousness to snubs, was a heaven-sent butt.

Even less could Johnson complain of the posthumous benefits of this friendship. For in relaying the power and charm of this incorrigible talker, Boswell gave to the world the most perishable, yet the most salient quality of the late Samuel Johnson. Thus, in life and in death James Boswell was to be his most thoughtful friend. His most thoughtful friend and his most unsparing portraitist, too, for Boswell the meticulous artist was to overlook nothing in painting his prodigious subject, "wart and all."

Applying the word "artist" to Boswell inevitably brings up the question

106

of his final place in the scale of literary values, besides the corollary question of the accuracy of his records of Johnson's conversations. Generations of critics have tended to dismiss Boswell as a mere stenographer. It was felt that if we had any reason to thank Boswell it was for having provided the world with a verbatim report of the talk of England's undisputed king of conversationalists. A meddlesome and conceited fool, he had at least had the good practical sense to jot down what he had heard. No one seemed to question Boswell's stenographic precision. More recent criticism has altered this picture—so much so that in some quarters the figure of Boswell now bulks as large as Johnson's and promises even to outgrow him. For the conversations are no longer regarded as word-for-word reports taken down by an expert speed-writer, but as the conscious reconstructions of an amply equipped intellect. Far from being a mere shorthand reporter, Boswell is now presented as a man of vast imaginative resource. Nothing short of an artist, gifted with marked creative power, it is contended, could have so masterfully evoked the living immediacy of these scenes and recaptured Johnson's weighty pronouncements in all their rolling splendor. In the words of that stalwart American Boswellian, Frederick A. Pottle, the riddle of Boswell may be simply solved "by assuming that he had a mind that stretched parallel to Johnson's throughout the whole range of the topics discussed." Or, to revert to Professor Pottle's fellow-advocate Kronenberger: "Boswell was far more an artist than an ape. An ape might have caught Johnson's single statements, but only a man of great capacities could have written up, as Boswell wrote them, many-voiced and rounded scenes. Here, in the pauses, the changes of pace, the build of the argument and the sting of the rejoinders, there exists an expert dramatic sense for controlling dialogue."

From all this some might suppose that in rescuing Boswell as artist we had lost him as trustworthy stenographer, a role that previous literary history had patronizingly—and gratefully—assigned him. This would be wrong. Boswell was never a stenographer in the sense that he "took down" the conversations on the spot. Actually, most of his scantily scribbled notes were jotted down in his own room after the conversations had taken place. "Very little rote memory was involved in the process," writes Professor Pottle. "For the conversations elaborated long after the events, he had merely written cues containing a good deal of circumstantial detail, a fading memory of a few more details, and a mental organism unparalleled among biographers and historians for its power to reconstruct the past selectively and vividly within the strict limits of historical fact." To Mr. Kronenberger the conversations were "in the final sense the product of Boswell's artistic 'ear,' of his unerring sense of what constituted the Johnsonian statement and the Johnsonian style."

In the company that Dr. Johnson kept such an "ear" was by no means an uncommon phenomenon. Records of his talk were faithfully made by a quartet of brilliant ladies who at one time or another came within earshot of this fabulous talker. One thinks of the widow Thrale, Fanny Burney, Anna Seward, and Miss Laetitia Matilda Hawkins, whose morose and tight-fisted father Dr. Johnson pilloried for all time as "a most unclubable man." They, too, committed their memories to writing—Miss Burney with the lavish hand of an adoring friend and inveterate diarist, the Misses Seward and Hawkins spurred only, perhaps, by some catty random impulses. There are those admirers of Miss Burney who go so far as to place the Johnsonian entries in her voluminous diaries above Boswell's reports. Certainly they have a vivid pace of their own, and unquestionably the plethora of domestic commonplace adds a special note of reality. Miss Burney spent weeks on end at Mrs. Thrale's Streatham mansion, where Johnson was provided with his own private room. So the sprightly little minx who secretly wrote the day's best-seller, Evelina, had a chance to behold the formidable man in an atmosphere of homely routine. In the ensuing "portrait in dialogue"* we shall reserve this domesticated Johnson—as distinct from the "clubable" Johnson—for the last. As for Miss Seward, it is to her that we owe a priceless glimpse of this enveloping personality in a moment of wrathful explosion. To Miss Hawkins we are indebted for the preservation of Sir Joshua Reynolds' reconstruction of Dr. Johnson on the delicate subject of his former elocution pupil, David Garrick. The rest is Boswell.

---

* Because of the variety of hands contributing to this many-sided "portrait," I thought it advisable to depart somewhat from chronological order.—L. B.

Dr. Samuel Johnson

1.

AN EXPLOSION AT MR. DILLY'S
THE BOOKSELLER.

I hate all impudence; but the impudence
of a chit's apostasy I nauseate!

IN HIS seventieth year, Dr. Johnson dominated the literary world of
London with unabated power. Talk had become the major indulgence
of this rumbling tower of learning. Writers, ministers, painters, statesmen
sought him out for a session of deep discourse on some knotty theme. In
the heat of argument reason might be on the side of the adversary, but
even reason quailed before the pontifical edicts of this ponderous man.

The center of every home and club he frequented, Dr. Johnson, while
soft and generous in many ways, was a formidable combatant indeed in
the area of dispute. On matters of linguistics there might be some
yielding; on topics of literature and history there was none at all; on
matters of church and king there was only iron-clad bigotry. If there were
two things Dr. Johnson flailed unsparingly, they were republicanism and
religious conversion. These were the unpardonable sins, threatening civilization itself. All else might be understood, perhaps forgiven; but republicanism was rebellion against law and order, and conversion was apostasy.
It was, accordingly, with some trepidation that Mrs. Knowles, known as
"The Quaker Lady," approached this roaring lion on a point of great risk.
The good woman had been asked to intercede on behalf of a young girl
named Jenny Harry. For Dr. Johnson, Jenny had committed the sin of
sins—conversion from the English church to Quakerism. The gentle eloquence of Mrs. Knowles had won this new proselyte.

Before making the change, Jenny had been befriended by Dr. Johnson
at the home of her guardian, a Mrs. Spry. Her conversion struck him like
a thunderbolt. The girl's father disowned her, an act causing her great
emotional distress, besides the loss of one hundred thousand pounds.
Several Anglican clergymen were delegated to reason with the girl—to no

avail. Jenny Harry had seen the light and followed it. Nothing could now deflect her from what she saw as her path of duty.

Most painful of all, perhaps, was the reaction of Dr. Johnson. At the house of Mrs. Knowles, where the girl boarded after leaving her guardian, he would now slight her cruelly. One April day in 1778 Jenny came home in tears: Dr. Johnson had snubbed her on the street. In desperation, she implored Mrs. Knowles to intercede. "You are to meet him soon at Mr. Dilly's," she said; "plead for me!" In Mrs. Knowles Jenny had a valiant advocate, for this woman was accustomed to being rallied on her Quakerism without flinching. Theologians and the blustering potentates of London wit had never frightened her. Soft-spoken and graceful, she met all raillery with calm and reasoned conviction.

In the literary party "at Mr. Dilly's, the bookseller" on that afternoon of April 15, 1778, were Dr. Johnson, Boswell, Dr. Mayo, Mrs. Knowles, and Anna Seward, the so-called "Swan of Lichfield." It is to Miss Seward that we owe this unparalleled picture of the redoubtable doctor in a rage, preserved for us in the girl's letter to a Mrs. Monpessan (Letters of Anna Seward, Six Volumes, London, 1811). Besides a natural penchant for gossip, Miss Seward had a pique of her own to indulge. It was Sir Walter Scott who suggested that the girl resented Johnson on social grounds. Both were natives of Lichfield, but from different strata—Johnson being the son of a local tradesman and the girl a member of the town's best society. As a poet in London the lovely socialite never amounted to much, whereas the tradesman's son now ruled England's literary scene. Whatever truth there is in Scott's implication, we can only applaud the girl for giving her vote to Mrs. Knowles in the contest with the explosive bigot over the soul of Miss Jenny Harry. And we owe her our thanks for allowing this encounter to enter the annals of history in all its impromptu detail.

MRS. KNOWLES: I am to ask thy indulgence, Doctor, toward a gentle female to whom thou usedst to be kind, and who is uneasy at the loss of that kindness. Jenny Harry weeps at the consciousness that thou wilt not speak to her.

JOHNSON: Madam, I hate the odious wench, and desire you will not talk to me about her.

MRS. KNOWLES: Yet what is her crime, Doctor?

JOHNSON: Apostasy, madam; apostasy from the community in which she was educated.

MRS. KNOWLES: Surely the quitting one community for another cannot be a crime, if it is done from motives of conscience. Hadst thou been educated in the Romish church, I must suppose thou wouldst have abjured its errors, and that there would have been merit in the abjuration.

JOHNSON: Madam, if I had been educated in the Roman Catholic faith, I believe I should have questioned my right to quit the religion of my fathers; therefore, well may I hate the arrogance of a young wench who sets herself up for a judge on theological points and deserts the religion in whose bosom she was nurtured.

MRS. KNOWLES: She has not done so; the name and the faith of Christians are not denied to the secretaries.

JOHNSON: If the name is not, the common sense is.

MRS. KNOWLES: I will not dispute this point with thee, Doctor, at least at present; it would carry us too far. Suppose it granted that, in the mind of a young girl, the weaker arguments appeared the strongest, her want of better judgment should excite thy pity, not thy resentment.

JOHNSON: Madam, it has my anger and my contempt, and always will have them.

MRS. KNOWLES: Consider, Doctor, she must be sincere. Consider what a noble fortune she has sacrificed.

JOHNSON: Madam, madam, I have never taught myself to consider that the association of folly can extenuate guilt.

MRS. KNOWLES: Ah! Doctor, we cannot rationally suppose that the Deity will not pardon a defect in judgment, supposing it should prove one, in that breast where the consideration of serving him, according to its idea, in spirit and truth, has been a preferable inducement to that of worldly interest.

JOHNSON: Madam, I pretend not to set bounds to the mercy of the Deity; but I hate the wench, and shall ever hate her. I hate all impudence; but the impudence of a chit's apostasy I *nauseate*.

MRS. KNOWLES: Jenny is a very gentle creature. She trembles to have offended her parent, though far removed from his presence. She grieves to have offended her guardian, and she is sorry to have offended Dr. Johnson, whom she loved, admired, and honored.

JOHNSON: Why, then, madam, did she not consult the man whom she pretends to have loved, admired, and honored, upon her newfangled scruples? If she had looked up to that man with any degree of the respect she professes, she would have supposed his ability to judge of fit and right at least equal to that of a raw wench just out of her primer.

MRS. KNOWLES: Ah! Doctor, remember it was not from amongst the witty and the learned that Christ selected his disciples, and constituted the teachers of his precepts. Jenny thinks Dr. Johnson great and good; but she also thinks the gospel demands and enjoins a simpler form of worship than that of the established church; and that it is not in wit and eloquence to supersede the force of what appears to her a plain and regular system, which cancels all typical and mysterious ceremonies, as fruitless and even idolatrous; and asks only obedience to its injunctions, and the ingenuous homage of a devout heart.

JOHNSON: The home of a fool's-head, madam, you should say, if you will pester me about the ridiculous wench.

MRS. KNOWLES: If thou choosest to suppose her ridiculous, thou canst not deny that she had been religious, sincere, disinterested. Canst thou believe that the gate of Heaven will be shut to the tender and pious mind, whose *first* consideration has been that of apprehended duty?

JOHNSON: Pho, pho, madam, who says it will?

MRS. KNOWLES: Then if Heaven shuts not its gate, shall man shut his heart? If the Deity accepts the homage of such as sincerely serve Him under every form of worship, Dr. Johnson and this humble girl will, it is to be hoped, meet in a blessed eternity, whither human animosity must *not* be carried.

JOHNSON: Madam, I am not fond of meeting fools anywhere; they are detestable company, and while it is in my power to avoid conversing with them, I certainly shall exert that power; and so you may tell the odious wench whom you have persuaded to think herself a saint, and of whom you will, I suppose, make a preacher; but I shall take care she does not preach to *me*.

BOSWELL (*whispering to Miss Seward*): I never saw this mighty lion so chafed before.

(*Miss Seward adds that "the loud and angry tone in which he thundered out these replies to his calm and able antagonist frightened us all, except Mrs. Knowles, who gently, not sarcastically, smiled at his injustice."*)

Dr. Samuel Johnson

2.

WITH PONDEROUS GIBES, HE DENIES THAT MEN HAVE MORE LIBERTY THAN WOMEN.

We have all the labor and the danger, and the women all the advantage.

W E HAVE not quite finished with this literary party "at Mr. Dilly's the bookseller." For although Miss Seward has furnished us with a vivid account of it, let us remember that the observant Boswell was there, too. True, he makes but a belated entrance into the dialogue, and then only in a cautious whisper about "the mighty lion" to Miss Seward. But we may be sure that Boswell's memory was not idle. Oddly enough, when Mrs. Knowles sent him her own version of the dialogue about Miss Harry, Boswell refrained from using it because his notes did not sustain her in every detail. When the version appeared in "The Gentleman's Magazine" of June, 1791, Boswell's comment was: "No doubt the lady appears to have greatly the advantage of Dr. Johnson in argument as well as expression."

In any case, we have Boswell's confirmation of the substance of the quarrel, of Johnson's reference to the blameless young convert as "an odious wench" who "knew no more of the Church which she left and that which she embraced than she did of the difference between the Copernican and the Ptolemaic systems." Of the final access of Johnsonian rage, Boswell merely reports: "He then rose again into passion, and attacked the young proselyte in the severest terms of reproach, so that both ladies seemed to be much shocked." It is possible Boswell was remiss here, or merely devoutly discreet. In any case, he handsomely repairs the omission by supplying running dialogue on two further topics discussed that day at Mr. Dilly's—one on the comparative liberty of men and women, the other on death. In the second of these Boswell allots himself an inconspicuous role, feeling no doubt that he had allowed himself ample compensation by quoting Dr. Johnson as saying to Mrs. Knowles: "You, madam, have been flattering me all the evening. I wish you would *give Boswell a little now. If you knew his merit as well as I do, you would say a great deal. He is the best travelling companion in the world." In Boswell's account, it is again Mrs. Knowles who "affected to complain that men had much more liberty allowed them than women." And it is again Dr. Johnson who takes up the cudgels. . . .*

JOHNSON: Why, madam, women have all the liberty they should wish to have. We have all the labor and the danger, and the women all the advantage. We go to sea, we build houses, we do everything, in short, to pay our court to the women.

MRS. KNOWLES: The Doctor reasons very wittily, but not convincingly. Now, take the instance of building. The mason's wife, if she is ever seen in liquor, is ruined. The mason may get himself drunk as often as he pleases, with little loss of character; nay, may let his wife and children starve.

JOHNSON: Madam, you must consider, if the mason does get himself drunk, and let his wife and children starve, the parish will oblige him to find security for their maintenance. We have different modes of restraining evil. Stocks for the men, a ducking-stool for women, and a pound for beasts. If we require more perfection from women than from ourselves, it is doing them honor. And women have not the same temptations that we have. They may always live in a virtuous company. Men must live in the world indiscriminately. If a woman has no inclination to do what is wrong, being secured from it is no restraint to her. I am at liberty to walk into the Thames, but if I were to try it my friends would restrain me in Bedlam, and I should be obliged to them.

MRS. KNOWLES: Still, Doctor, I cannot help thinking it a hardship that more indulgence is allowed to men than to women. It gives a superiority to men to which I do not see how they are entitled.

JOHNSON: It is plain, madam, one or the other must have the superiority. As Shakespeare says, "If two men ride on a horse, one must ride behind."

DILLY: I suppose, sir, Mrs. Knowles would have them ride in panniers, one on each side.

JOHNSON: Then, sir, the horse would throw them both.

MRS. KNOWLES: Well, I hope that in another world the sexes will be equal.

BOSWELL: That is being too ambitious, madam. We might as well desire to be equal with the angels. We shall all, I hope, be happy in a future state, but we must not expect to be all happy in the same degree. It is enough, if we be happy according to our several capacities. A worthy car-man will get to heaven as well as Sir Isaac Newton. Yet, though equally good, they will not have the same degrees of happiness.

JOHNSON: Probably not.

Dr. Samuel Johnson

3.

HE IS CHALLENGED TO EXPRESS HIMSELF ON THE ISSUE OF DEATH AND SALVATION.

No rational man can die without uneasy apprehension.

("*I expressed a horror at the thought of death.*"—Boswell)

MRS. KNOWLES: Nay, thou should'st not have a horror for what is the gate of life.

JOHNSON (*standing upon the hearth, rolling about, with a serious, solemn, and somewhat gloomy air*): No rational man can die without uneasy apprehension.

MRS. KNOWLES: The Scriptures tell us, "The righteous shall have *hope* in his death."

JOHNSON: Yes, madam. That is, he shall not have despair. But, consider, his hope of salvation must be founded on the terms on which it is promised that the mediation of our Saviour shall be applied to us—namely obedience. And where obedience has failed, then, as supplementary to it, repentance. But what man can say that his obedience has been such as he would approve of in another, or even in himself upon close examination, or that his repentance has not been such as to require being repented of? No man can be sure that his obedience and repentance will obtain salvation.

MRS. KNOWLES: But divine intimation of acceptance may be made to the soul.

JOHNSON: Madam, it may. But I should not think the better of a man who would tell me on his deathbed he was sure of salvation. A man cannot be sure himself that he has divine intimation of acceptance. Much less can he make others sure that he has it.

BOSWELL: Then, sir, we must be contented to acknowledge that death is a terrible thing.

JOHNSON: Yes, sir, I have made no approaches to a state which can look on it as not terrible.

MRS. KNOWLES (*seeming to enjoy a pleasing serenity in the persuasion of benignant divine light*): Does not St. Paul say, "I have fought the good fight of faith, I have finished my course; henceforth is laid for me a crown of life"?

JOHNSON: Yes, madam. But here was a man inspired, a man who had been converted by supernatural interposition.

BOSWELL: In prospect death is dreadful, but in fact we find that people die easy.

JOHNSON: Why, sir, most people have not *thought* much of the matter, so cannot *say* much, and it is supposed they die easy. Few believe it certain they are then to die, and those who do, set themselves to behave with resolution, as a man does who is going to be hanged. He is not the less unwilling to be hanged.

MISS SEWARD: There is one mode of the fear of death which is certainly absurd, and that is the dread of annihilation, which is only a pleasing sleep without a dream.

JOHNSON: It is neither pleasing nor sleep; it is nothing. Now mere existence is so much better than nothing that one would rather exist even in pain, than not exist.

BOSWELL: If annihilation be nothing, then existing in pain is not a comparative state, but is a positive evil, which I cannot think we should choose. I must be allowed to differ here, and it would lessen the hope of a future state founded on the argument that the Supreme Being, who is good as He is great, will hereafter compensate for our present sufferings in this life. For if existence such as we have it here be comparatively a good, we have no reason to complain, though no more of it should be given to us. But if our only state of existence were in this world, then we might with some reason complain that we are so dissatisfied with our enjoyments compared with our desires.

JOHNSON: The lady confounds annihilation, which is nothing, with the apprehension of it, which is dreadful. It is in the apprehension of it that the horror of annihilation consists.

Dr. Samuel Johnson

4.

A DISSENTING MINISTER BRAVES A STORM ON THE RIGHT OF MINORITIES TO PREACH WHAT THEY BELIEVE.

*But, sir, is it not very hard that I should
not be allowed to teach my children?*

ON THE subject of conversation Dr. Johnson once said to Boswell: "There must, in the first place, be knowledge, there must be materials; in the second place, there must be a command of words; in the third place, there must be imagination, to place things in such views as they are not commonly seen in; and in the fourth place, there must be presence of mind, and a resolution that is not to be overcome by failures; this last is an essential requisite; for want of it many people do not excel in conversation. Now I want it; I throw up the game upon losing a trick." Boswell, astonished to find his idol making such an admission, replied: "I don't know, sir, how this may be; but I am sure you beat other people's cards out of their hands." Johnson, evidently not hearing the remark, went on talking so "triumphantly" that the spellbound Boswell exclaimed to his neighbor Mrs. Thrale: "Oh, for shorthand to take this down!" Shrewdly and prophetically, she assured the enraptured Scotsman, "You'll carry it all in your head—a long head is as good as shorthand."

How well Boswell could carry sustained conversation in his head is best borne out by a full reading of the "Life." The following selections are merely a taste of the banquet of talk that awaits the reader who comes upon that massive biography for the first time. They have been chosen for their range of subject and because they offer sustained dialogue. There are admittedly far more priceless gems of wit and wisdom throughout the "Life" than any offered here. Some of those have become proverbial, part of the very fiber of the English language. But they are scattered treasures, set in brief fragments of talk. Our aim in this volume has been the more leisurely dialogue, rather than the uproarious anecdote or the memorable epigram. We leave the meticulous Boswell to set his own scenes.

(Friday, May 7, 1773 ... "I dined with him this day at the house of my friends, Messieurs Edward and Charles Dilly, booksellers in the Poultry. There were present, their elder brother Mr. Dilly of Bedfordshire, Dr. Goldsmith, Mr. Langton, Mr. Claxton, Reverend Dr. Mayo,* a dissenting minister, the Reverend Mr. Toplady, and my friend the Reverend Mr. Temple. . . . I introduced the subject of toleration."—Boswell)

JOHNSON: Every society has a right to preserve public peace and order, and therefore has a good right to prohibit the propagation of opinions which have a dangerous tendency. To say the magistrate has this right is using an inadequate word. It is the society for which the magistrate is agent. He may be morally or theologically wrong in restraining the propagation of opinions which he thinks dangerous, but he is politically right.

DR. MAYO: I am of the opinion, sir, that every man is entitled to liberty of conscience in religion, and that the magistrate cannot restrain that right.

JOHNSON: Sir, I agree with you. Every man has a right to liberty of conscience, and with that the magistrate cannot interfere. People confound liberty of thinking with liberty of talking—nay, with liberty of preaching. Every man has a physical right to think as he pleases, for it cannot be discovered how he thinks. He has not a moral right, for he ought to inform himself and think justly. But, sir, no member of a society has a right to teach any doctrine contrary to what the society holds to be true. The magistrate, I say, may be wrong in what he thinks, but while he thinks himself right he may and ought to enforce what he thinks.

DR. MAYO: Then, sir, we are to remain always in error, and truth never can prevail, and the magistrate was right in persecuting the first Christians.

JOHNSON: Sir, the only method by which religious truth can be established is by martyrdom. The magistrate has a right to enforce what he thinks, and he who is conscious of the truth has a right to suffer. I am afraid

---

* Dr. Mayo's calm temper and steady perseverance rendered him an admirable subject for the exercise of Dr. Johnson's powerful abilities. He never flinched: but, after reiterated blows, remained seemingly unmoved as at the first. The scintillations of Johnson's genius flashed every time he struck, without his receiving any injury. Hence he obtained the epithet of THE LITERARY ANVIL."—Boswell.

there is no other way of ascertaining the truth but by persecution on the one hand and enduring it on the other.

GOLDSMITH: But how is a man to act, sir? Though firmly convinced of the truth of his doctrine, may he not think it wrong to expose himself to persecution? Has he a right to do so? Is it not, as it were, committing voluntary suicide?

JOHNSON: Sir, as to voluntary suicide, as you call it, there are twenty thousand men in an army who will go without scruple to be shot at and mount a breach for five-pence a day.

GOLDSMITH: But have they a moral right to do this?

JOHNSON: Nay, sir, if you will not take the universal opinion of mankind, I have nothing to say. If mankind cannot defend their own way of thinking, I cannot defend it. Sir, if a man is in doubt whether it would be better for him to expose himself to martyrdom or not, he should not do it. He must be convinced that he has a delegation from heaven.

GOLDSMITH: I would consider whether there is the greater chance of good or evil upon the whole. If I see a man who has fallen into a well, I would wish to help him out. But if there is a greater probability that he will pull me in than that I shall pull him out, I would not attempt it. So were I to go to Turkey, I might wish to convert the grand Signor to the Christian faith. But when I considered that I should probably be put to death without effectuating my purpose in any degree, I should keep myself quiet.

JOHNSON: Sir, you must consider that we have perfect and imperfect obligations. Perfect obligations, which are generally not to do something, are clear and positive; as, "Thou shalt not kill." But charity, for instance, is not definable by limits. It is a duty to give to the poor, but no man can say how much another should give to the poor or when a man has given too little to save his soul. In the same manner it is a duty to instruct the ignorant, and of consequence to convert infidels to Christianity. But no man in the common course of things is obliged to carry this to such a degree as to incur the danger of martyrdom, as no man is obliged to strip himself to the shirt in order to give charity. I have said that a man must be persuaded that he has a particular delegation from heaven.

GOLDSMITH: How is this to be known? Our first reformers, who were burned for not believing bread and wine to be Christ . . . ?

JOHNSON (*interrupting*): Sir, they were not burned for not believing bread and wine to be Christ, but for insulting those who did believe it. And, sir, when the first reformers began they did not intend to be martyred. As many of them ran away as could.

BOSWELL: But, sir, there was your countryman Elwal, who you told me challenged King George with his black guards and his red guards.

JOHNSON: My countryman Elwal, sir, should have been put in the stocks —a proper pulpit for him, and he'd have had a numerous audience. A man who preaches in the stocks will always have hearers enough.

BOSWELL: But Elwal thought himself in the right.

JOHNSON: We are not providing for mad people. There are places for them in the neighborhood.*

DR. MAYO: But, sir, is it not very hard that I should not be allowed to teach my children what I really believe to be the truth?

JOHNSON: Why, sir, you might contrive to teach your children *extra scandalum*, but, sir, the magistrate, if he knows it, has a right to restrain you. Suppose you teach your children to be thieves?

DR. MAYO: This is making a joke of the subject.

JOHNSON: Nay, sir, take it thus: that you teach them the community of goods, for which there are as many plausible arguments as for most erroneous doctrines. You teach them that all things at first were in common, and that no man had a right to anything but as he laid his hands upon it, and that this still is, or ought to be, the rule amongst mankind. Here, sir, you sap a great principle in society—property. And don't you think the magistrate would have a right to prevent you? Or, suppose you should teach your children the notion of the Adamites and they should run naked into the streets, would not the magistrate have a right to flog 'em into their doublets?

DR. MAYO: I think the magistrate has no right to interfere till there is some overt act.

BOSWELL: So, sir, though he sees an enemy to the state charging a blunderbuss, he is not to interfere till it is fired off!

DR. MAYO: He must be sure of its direction against the state.

JOHNSON: The magistrate is to judge of that. He has no right to restrain your thinking, because the evil centers in yourself. If a man were sitting at this table and chopping off his fingers, the magistrate, as guardian of the community, has no authority to restrain him, however he might do it from kindness as a parent. Though, indeed, upon more consideration, I think he may, as it is probable that he who is chopping off his own fingers may soon proceed to chop off those of other people. If I think it right to steal Mr. Dilly's plate, I am a bad man. But he can say nothing to me. If I make an open declaration that I think so, he will keep me out of his house. If I put forth my hand, I shall be sent to New-

---

* "Meaning Moorfields."—Boswell.

gate. This is the gradation of thinking, preaching, and acting. If a man thinks erroneously he may keep his thoughts to himself, and nobody will trouble him. If he preaches erroneous doctrine, society may expel him. If he acts in consequence of it, the law takes place, and he is hanged.

DR. MAYO: But, sir, ought not Christians to have liberty of conscience?

JOHNSON: I have already told you so, sir. You are coming back to where we were.

BOSWELL: Dr. Mayo is always taking a return postchaise, and going the stage over again. He has it at half-price.

JOHNSON: Dr. Mayo, like other champions for unlimited toleration, has got a set of words. Sir, it is no matter, politically, whether the magistrate be right or wrong. Suppose a club were to be formed to drink confusion to King George the Third and a happy restoration to Charles the Third. This would be very bad with respect to the State. But every member of that club must either conform to its rules or be turned out of it. Old Baxter, I remember, maintains that the magistrate should "tolerate all things that are tolerable." This is no good definition of toleration upon any principle, but it shows that he thought some things were not tolerable.

GOLDSMITH (*noticing that the Reverend Mr. Toplady is about to speak and that Johnson seems to be on the point of stopping him*): Sir, the gentleman has heard you patiently for an hour! Pray allow us now to hear him!

JOHNSON (*sternly*): Sir, I was not interrupting the gentleman. I was only giving him a signal of my attention.* Sir, you are impertinent.

TOPLADY (*to Johnson*): Sir, you have untwisted this difficult subject with great dexterity.

(*After the conversation at Dilly's, Boswell accompanied Dr. Johnson and Bennett Langton, the Greek scholar, to the famous literary club which had been established in 1764 as a meeting-place for London's nimblest wits. In short order, the club had become a kind of high tribunal of letters where reputations were made and unmade. Its empire over the commonwealth of books was undisputed. One can see why in a mere list of its distinguished members. This included Burke, the orator and philosopher; Gibbon, the historian; Reynolds, the painter and esthetic theorist; Garrick, the actor-playwright; Goldsmith, the poet,*

---

* One is forced to draw one's own conclusions about the nature of this "signal." Boswell merely notes that "Johnson uttered some sound, which led Goldsmith to think that he was beginning again."

essayist, novelist, and playwright, and the pontifex maximus *himself,*
Dr. Johnson. When the three friends arrived that day they found
Burke, Garrick, and the hapless Goldsmith, who had been cut down
by the irate Johnson at Dilly's. Goldsmith sat brooding silently over
Johnson's rebuke. Boswell then tells us what happened: "Johnson perceived this, and said aside to some of us, 'I'll make Goldsmith forgive
me,' and then called to him in a loud voice, 'Dr. Goldsmith, something
passed today where you and I dined. I ask your pardon.' Goldsmith answered placidly, 'It must be much from you, sir, that I take ill.' And so
at once the difference was over, and they were on easy terms as ever,
and Goldsmith rattled away as usual." Though these sharp exchanges
were quite frequent between Goldsmith and Johnson, the two were
really extremely fond of one another. Only a year after the episode at
Dilly's, Goldsmith died suddenly. Burke burst into tears when he heard
the news, and Johnson, his foremost baiter, mourned him as he might
have mourned a son.)

Dr. Samuel Johnson

5.

THE ABSTEMIOUS DOCTOR IS NOMINATED TO WRITE TO A FRIEND OF "THE CLUB" FOR A HOGSHEAD OF CLARET.

As I drink none, I am no more than humble scribe.

(*Friday, April 3, 1778. "I dined with him in London, in a company where were present several eminent men, whom I shall not name, but distinguish their parts in the conversation by different letters."—* Boswell)

F: I have been looking at this famous antique marble dog of Mr. Jennings, valued at a thousand guineas, said to be Alcibiades's dog.

JOHNSON: His tail then must be docked. That was the mark of Alcibiades's dog.

E: * A thousand guineas! The representation of no animal whatever is worth so much! At this rate a dead dog would indeed be better than a living lion.

JOHNSON: Sir, it is not the worth of the thing but of the skill in forming it which is so highly estimated. Everything that enlarges the sphere of human powers, that shows man he can do what he thought he could not do, is valuable. The first man who balanced a straw upon his nose; Johnson who rode upon three horses at a time; in short, all such men deserved the applause of mankind, not on account of the use of what they did but of the dexterity which they exhibited.

BOSWELL: Yet a misapplication of time and assiduity is not to be encouraged. Addison, in one of his *Spectators*, commends the judgment of a King who, as a suitable reward to a man that by long perseverance had attained to the art of throwing a barleycorn through the eye of a needle, gave him a bushel of barley.

---

* Probably Edmund Burke; "J" has been identified as Sir Joshua Reynolds. The other initials have baffled investigators. It is known, however, that Gibbon, Sheridan, and George Fordyce were present at the "Club" that night.

JOHNSON: He must have been a King of Scotland, where barley is scarce.

F: One of the most remarkable antique figures of an animal is the boar of Florence.

JOHNSON: The first boar that is well made in marble should be preserved as a wonder. When men arrive at a facility of making boars well, then the workmanship is not of such value, but they should however be preserved as examples, and as a greater security for the restoration of the art, should it be lost.

E: We hear prodigious complaints at present of emigration. I am convinced that emigration makes a country more populous.

J: That sounds very much like a paradox.

E: Exportation of men, like exportation of all other commodities, makes more be produced.

JOHNSON: But there would be more people were there not emigration, provided there were food for more.

E: No; leave a few breeders, and you'll have more people than if there were no emigration.

JOHNSON: Nay, sir, it is plain there will be more people, if there are more breeders. Thirty cows in good pasture will produce more calves than ten cows, provided they have good bulls.

E: There are bulls enough in Ireland.

JOHNSON (smiling): So, sir, I should think from your argument.

BOSWELL: You said exportation of men, like exportation of other commodities, makes more be produced. But a bounty is given to encourage the exportation of corn, and no bounty is given for the exportation of men, though, indeed, those who go gain by it.

R: But the bounty on the exportation of corn is paid at home.

E: That is the same thing.

JOHNSON: No, sir.

R: A man who stays at home gains nothing by his neighbor's emigrating.

BOSWELL: I can understand that emigration may be the cause that more people may be produced in a country, but the country will not therefore be the more populous; for the people issue from it. It can only be said that there is a flow of people. It is an encouragement to have children, to know that they can get a living by emigration.

R: Yes, if there were an emigration of children under six years of age. But they don't emigrate till they could earn their livelihood in some way at home.

C: It is remarkable that the most unhealthy countries, where there are the most destructive diseases, such as Egypt and Bengal, are the most populous.

JOHNSON: Countries which are the most populous have the most destructive diseases. *That* is the true state of the proposition.

C: Holland is very unhealthy, yet it is exceedingly populous.

JOHNSON: I know not that Holland is unhealthy. But its populousness is owing to an influx of people from all other countries. Disease cannot be the cause of populousness, for it not only carries off a great proportion of the people; but those who are left are weakened, and unfit for the purpose of increase.

R: Mr. E., I don't mean to flatter, but when posterity reads one of your speeches in Parliament, it will be difficult to believe that you took so much pains, knowing with certainty that it could produce no effect, that not one vote would be gained by it.

E: Waiving your compliment to me, I shall say in general that it is very well worth while for a man to take pains to speak well in Parliament. A man who has vanity speaks to display his talents; and if a man speaks well he gradually establishes a certain reputation and consequence in the general opinion, which sooner or later will have its political reward. Besides, though not one vote is gained, a good speech has its effect. Though an act which has been ably opposed passed into a law, yet in its progress it is modelled, it is softened in such a manner, that we see plainly the Minister has been told that the members attached to him are so sensible of its injustice or absurdity from what they have heard that it must be altered.

JOHNSON: And, sir, there is a gratification of pride. Though we cannot out-vote them we will out-argue them. They shall not do wrong without its being shown both to themselves and to the world.

E: The House of Commons is a mixed body. I except the minority, which I hold to be pure (*smiling*) but I take the whole House. It is a mass by no means pure; but neither is it wholly corrupt, though there is a large proportion of corruption in it. There are many members who generally go with the Minister, who will not go all lengths. There are many honest well-meaning country gentlemen who are in Parliament only to keep up the consequence of their families. Upon most of these a good speech will have influence.

JOHNSON: We are all more or less governed by interest. But interest will not make us do everything. In a case which admits of doubt, we try to think on the side which is for our interest, and generally bring ourselves to act accordingly. But the subject must admit of diversity of coloring; it must receive a color on that side. In the House of Commons there are members enough who will not vote what is grossly unjust or absurd.

No, sir, there must always be right enough, or appearance of right, to keep wrong in countenance.

BOSWELL: There is surely always a majority in Parliament who have places or who want to have them, and who therefore will be generally ready to support government without requiring any pretext.

E: True, sir; that majority will always follow

*Quo clamor vocat et turba faventium.**

BOSWELL: Well now, let us take the common phrase, placehunters. I thought they had hunted without regard to anything just as their huntsman, the Minister, leads, looking only to the prey.

J: But taking your metaphor, you know that in hunting there are few so desperately keen as to follow without reserve. Some do not choose to leap ditches and hedges and risk their necks, or gallop over steeps, or even to dirty themselves in bogs and mire.

BOSWELL: I am glad there are some good, quiet, moderate political hunters.

E: I believe in any body of men in England I should have been in the Minority.

P: The House of Commons resembles a private company. How seldom is any man convinced by another's argument; passion and pride rise against it.

R: What would be the consequence if a Minister, sure of a majority in the House of Commons, should resolve that there should be no speaking at all upon his side?

E: He must soon go out. That has been tried; but it was found it would not do.

(*The conversation shifts first to linguistics, then to books on travel.*)

JOHNSON: . . . There has been, of late, a strange turn in travellers to be displeased.

E: From the experience which I have had, and I have had a great deal—I have learned to think *better* of mankind.

JOHNSON: From my experience I have found them worse in commercial dealings, more disposed to cheat, than I had any notion of; but more disposed to do one another good than I had conceived.

J: Less just and more beneficent.

JOHNSON: And really it is wonderful, considering how much attention is necessary for men to take care of themselves, and ward off immediate evils which press upon them, it is wonderful how much they do for others. As it is said of the greatest liar that he tells more truth than

---

* Horace, Odes, Bk. III, 24:26—"Summoned by the clamor of applauding throngs."

falsehood, so it may be said of the worst man that he does more good than evil.

BOSWELL: Perhaps from experience men may be found *happier* than we suppose.

JOHNSON: No, sir. The more we inquire we shall find men the less happy.

P: As to thinking better or worse of mankind from experience, some cunning people will not be satisfied unless they have put men to the test, as they think. There is a very good story told of Sir Godfrey Kneller, in his character of a justice of the peace. A gentleman brought his servant before him, upon an accusation of having stolen some money from him; but it having come out that he had laid it purposely in the servant's way, in order to try his honesty, Sir Godfrey sent the master to prison.

JOHNSON: To resist temptation once is not a sufficient proof of honesty. If a servant, indeed, were to resist the continued temptation of silver lying in a window, as some people let it lie, when he is sure his master does not know how much there is of it, he could give a strong proof of honesty. But this is a proof to which you have no right to put a man. You know, humanly speaking, there is a certain degree of temptation which will overcome any virtue. Now, insofar as you approach temptation to a man you do him an injury, and, if he is overcome, you share his guilt.

P: And, when once overcome, it is easier for him to be got the better of again.

BOSWELL: Yes, you are his seducer; you have debauched him. I have known a man resolve to put friendship to the test, by asking a man to lend him money, merely with that view, when he did not want it.

JOHNSON: That is very wrong, sir. Your friend may be a narrow man, and yet have many good qualities. Narrowness may be his only fault. Now you are trying his general character as a friend by one particular singly, in which he happens to be defective, when, in truth, his character is composed of many particulars.

E: I understand the hogshead of claret, which this society was favored with by our friend the Dean, is nearly out. I think he should be written to to send another of the same kind. Let the request be made with a happy ambiguity of expression, so that we may have the chance of his sending *it* also as a present.

JOHNSON: I am willing to offer my services as secretary on this occasion.

P: As many as are for Dr. Johnson being secretary hold up your hands. . . . Carried unanimously!

BOSWELL: He will be our dictator.

JOHNSON: No, the company is to dictate to me. I am only to write for wine, and I am quite disinterested, as I drink none. I shall not be suspected of having forged the application. I am no more than humble *scribe*.
E: Then you shall *pre*scribe.
BOSWELL: Very well. The first play of words today.
J: No, no—the *bulls* of Ireland.
JOHNSON: Were I your dictator, you should have no wine. It would be my business *cavere ne quid detrimenti Respublica caperet,** and wine is dangerous. (*Smiling*) Rome was ruined by luxury.

* "To see that no harm came to the republic."

Dr. Samuel Johnson

6.

THE SOCIAL WISDOM VERSUS THE PERSONAL FOLLY OF DRINKING WINE.

Sir, there is no more reason for your drinking with him than for his being sober with you.

("*On Tuesday, April 28, (1778), he was engaged to dine at General Paoli's,* where, as I have already observed, I was still entertained in elegant hospitality, and with all the ease and comfort of a home.... At General Paoli's were Sir Joshua Reynolds, Mrs. Langton, Marchese Gherardi of Lombardy, and Mr. John Spottiswoode, of Spottiswoode, the solicitor.... We talked of drinking wine.*"—Boswell)

JOHNSON: I require wine only when I am alone. I have then often wished for it, and often taken it.

SPOTTISWOODE: What, by way of a companion, sir?

JOHNSON: To get rid of myself, to send myself away. Wine gives great pleasure; and every pleasure is of itself a good. It is a good, unless counterbalanced by evil. A man may have a strong reason not to drink wine; and that may be greater than the pleasure. Wine makes a man better pleased with himself. I do not say that it makes him more pleasing to others. Sometimes it does. But the danger is that while a man grows better pleased with himself, he may be growing less pleasing to others. Wine gives a man nothing. It neither gives him knowledge nor wit; it only animates a man and enables him to bring out what a dread of the company has repressed. It only puts in motion what has been locked up in frost. But this may be good, or it may be bad.

SPOTTISWOODE: So, sir, wine is a key which opens a box; but this box may be either full or empty?

JOHNSON: Nay, sir, conversation is the key: wine is a pick-lock, which forces open the box, and injures it. A man should cultivate his mind so as to have that confidence and readiness without wine which wine gives.

---

* Pasquale Paoli, exiled revolutionary leader from Corsica.

BOSWELL: The great difficulty of resisting wine is from benevolence. For instance, a good worthy man asks you to taste his wine, which he has had twenty years in his cellar.

JOHNSON: Sir, all this notion about benevolence arises from a man's imagining himself to be of more importance to others than he really is. They don't care a farthing whether he drinks wine or not.

REYNOLDS: Yes, they do for the time.

JOHNSON: For the time! If they care this minute, they forget it the next. And as for the good worthy man; how do you know he is good and worthy? No good and worthy man will insist upon another man's drinking wine. As to the wine twenty years in the cellar—of ten men three say this merely because they must say something; three are telling a lie when they say they have had the wine twenty years; three would rather save the wine; one, perhaps, cares. I allow it is something to please one's company; and people are always pleased with those who partake pleasure with them. But after a man has brought himself to relinquish the great personal pleasure which arises from drinking wine, any other consideration is a trifle. To please others by drinking wine is something only if there be nothing against it. I should, however, be sorry to offend worthy men:

> Cursed be the verse, how well so e'er it flow,
> That tends to make one worthy man my foe.

BOSWELL: Cursed be the *spring*, the water.*

JOHNSON: But let us consider what a sad thing it would be if we were obliged to drink or do anything else that may happen to be agreeable to the company where we are.

LANGTON: By the same rule you must join with a gang of cut-purses.

JOHNSON: Yes, sir. But yet we must do justice to wine; we must allow it the power it possesses. To make a man pleased with himself, let me tell you, is doing a very great thing:

> Si patriae volumus si nobis *vivere cari*.†

Boswell is a bolder combatant than Sir Joshua: he argues for wine without the help of wine; but Sir Joshua with it.

REYNOLDS: But to please one's company is a strong motive.

JOHNSON: I won't argue any more with you, sir. You are too far gone.‡

---

* Boswell remarks, "I was at this time myself a water-drinker, upon trial, by Johnson's recommendation."

† Horace, Epistle I, iii, 29: "If we wish to live dear to ourselves and to our country."

‡ "Johnson, from drinking only water, supposed everybody who drank wine to be elevated."—Boswell.

REYNOLDS: I should have thought so indeed, sir, had I made such a speech as you have now done.

JOHNSON (*drawing himself in and blushing*): Nay, don't be angry. I did not mean to offend you.

REYNOLDS: At first the taste of wine was disagreeable to me; but I brought myself to drink it that I might be like other people. The pleasure of drinking wine is so connected with pleasing your company that altogether there is something of social goodness in it.

JOHNSON: Sir, this is only saying the same thing over again.

REYNOLDS: No, this is new.

JOHNSON: You put it in new words, but it is an old thought. This is one of the disadvantages of wine: it makes a man mistake words for thoughts.

BOSWELL: I think it is a new thought; at least, it is in a new *attitude*.

JOHNSON: Nay, sir, it is only in a new coat; or an old coat with a new facing. (*Laughing heartily.*) It is the old dog in a new doublet. . . . An extraordinary instance, however, may occur where a man's patron will do nothing for him unless he will drink. *There* may be a good reason for drinking.

(*Boswell mentions a nobleman who, he believes, "was really uneasy if his company would not drink hard."*)

JOHNSON: That is from having had people about him whom he has been accustomed to command.

BOSWELL: Supposing I should be tête-à-tête with him at table.

JOHNSON: Sir, there is no more reason for your drinking with *him* than his being sober with *you*.

BOSWELL: Why, that is true; for it would do him less hurt to be sober than it would do me to get drunk.

JOHNSON: Yes, sir; and from what I have heard of him, one would not wish to sacrifice himself to such a man. If he must always have somebody to drink with him, he should buy a slave, and then he would be sure to have it. They who submit to drink as another pleases make themselves his slaves.

BOSWELL: But, sir, you will surely make allowance for the duty of hospitality. A gentleman who loves drinking, comes to visit me. . . .

JOHNSON: Sir, a man knows whom he visits; he comes to the table of a sober man.

BOSWELL: But, sir, you and I should not have been so well received in the Highlands and Hebrides, if I had not drunk with our worthy friends. Had I drunk water only as you did, they would not have been so cordial.

JOHNSON: Sir William Temple mentions that in his travels through the

Netherlands he had two or three gentlemen with him, and when a bumper was necessary, he put it on *them*. Were I to travel again through the islands, I would have Sir Joshua with me to take the bumpers.

BOSWELL: But, sir, let me put a case. Suppose Sir Joshua should take a jaunt into Scotland; he does me the honor to pay me a visit at my house in the country. I am overjoyed at seeing him. We are quite by ourselves. Shall I unsociably and churlishly let him sit drinking by himself? No, no, my dear Sir Joshua, you shall not be treated so. I *will* take a bottle with you!

Dr. Samuel Johnson

7.

GOOD FRIDAY THOUGHTS ON GARDENS, PARK WALLS, CHERRIES, AND ORANGE PEEL.

In an orchard there should be enough to eat,
enough to lay up, enough to be stolen, and
enough to rot upon the ground.

(*April 18 (Good Friday), 1783 . . . "I found him at breakfast, in his usual manner upon that day, drinking tea without milk, and eating a cross-bun to prevent faintness. We went to St. Clement's church, as formerly. When we came home from church, he placed himself on one of the stone-seats at his garden-door, and I took the other, and thus in the open air, and in a placid frame of mind, he talked away very easily. . . . I record this minute detail, which some may think trifling, in order to show clearly how this great man, whose mind could grasp such large and extensive subjects, as he has shown in his literary labors, was yet well-informed in the common affairs of life, and loved to illustrate them."—Boswell*)

JOHNSON: Were I a country gentleman, I should not be very hospitable. I should not have crowds in my house.

BOSWELL: Sir Alexander Dick tells me that he remembers having a thousand people in a year to dine at his house—that is, reckoning each person as one, each time that he dined there.

JOHNSON: That, sir, is about three a day.

BOSWELL: How your statement lessens the idea!

JOHNSON: That, sir, is the good of counting. It brings everything to a certainty, which before floated in the mind indefinitely.

BOSWELL: But *omne ignotum pro magnifico est* *—one is sorry to have this diminished.

JOHNSON: Sir, you should not allow yourself to be delighted with error.

BOSWELL: Three a day seem but few.

---

* "Whatever is unknown seems magnificent."—Tacitus (*Agricola*, XXX.)

JOHNSON: Nay, sir, he who entertains three a day does very liberally. And if there is a large family the poor entertain those three, for they eat what the poor would get. There must be superfluous meat. It must be given to the poor or thrown out.

BOSWELL: I observe in London that the poor go about and gather bones, which I understand are manufactured.

JOHNSON: Yes, sir. They boil them and extract a grease from them for greasing wheels and other purposes. Of the best pieces they make a mock ivory, which is used for hafts to knives and various other things. The coarse pieces they burn and pound, and sell the ashes.

BOSWELL: For what purpose, sir?

JOHNSON: Why, sir, for making a furnace for the chemists for melting iron. A paste made of burned bones will stand a stronger heat than anything else. Consider, sir: if you are to melt iron you cannot line your pot with brass because it is softer than iron and would melt sooner, nor with iron, for though malleable iron is harder than cast iron, yet it would not do. But a paste of burned bones will not melt.

BOSWELL: Do you know, sir, I have discovered a manufacture to a great extent of what you only piddle at—scraping and drying the peel of oranges.* At a place in Newgate Street there is a prodigious quantity prepared, which they sell to the distillers.

JOHNSON: Sir, I believe they make a higher thing out of them than a spirit. They make what is called orange-butter, the oil of the orange inspissated, which they mix perhaps with common pomatum, and make it fragrant. The oil does not fly off in the drying.

BOSWELL: I wish to have a good walled garden.

JOHNSON: I don't think it would be worth the expense to you. We compute, in England, a park-wall at a thousand pounds a mile. Now a garden-wall must cost at least as much. You intend your trees should grow higher than a deer will leap. Now let us see. For a hundred pounds you could only have forty-four square yards, which is very little. For two hundred pounds you may have eighty-four square yards, which is very well. But when will you get the value of two hundred pounds of walls, in fruit, in your climate? No, sir, such contention with Nature is not worth while. I would plant an orchard, and have plenty of such fruit as ripen well in your country. My friend Dr. Madden, of Ireland, said that "in an orchard there should be enough to eat, enough to lay up, enough to be stolen, and enough to rot upon the ground." Cherries are an early

---

* Johnson supposedly collected the peel of squeezed oranges to prepare a medicine. He once recommended "dried orange peel, finely powdered."

fruit. You may have them. And you may have the early apples and pears.

BOSWELL: We cannot have nonpareils.

JOHNSON: Sir, you can no more have nonpareils than you can have grapes.

BOSWELL: We have them, sir, but they are very bad.

JOHNSON: Nay, sir, never try to have a thing merely to show that you *cannot* have it. From ground that would let for forty shillings you may have a large orchard, and you see it costs you only forty shillings. Nay, you may graze the ground when the trees are grown up. You cannot while they are young.

BOSWELL: Is not a good garden a very common thing in England, sir?

JOHNSON: Not so common, sir, as you imagine. In Lincolnshire there is hardly an orchard. In Staffordshire very little fruit.

BOSWELL: Has Langton no orchard?

JOHNSON: No, sir.

BOSWELL: How so, sir?

JOHNSON: Why, sir, from the general negligence of the county. He has it not because nobody else has it.

BOSWELL: A hothouse is a certain thing. I may have that.

JOHNSON: A hothouse is pretty certain. But you must first build it, then you must keep fires in it, and you must have a gardener to take care of it.

BOSWELL: But if I have a gardener at any rate?

JOHNSON: Why, yes.

BOSWELL: I'd have it near my house. There is no need to have it in the orchard.

JOHNSON: Yes, I'd have it near my house. I would plant a great many currants. The fruit is good, and they make a pretty sweetmeat.

Dr. Samuel Johnson

8.

WHILE EATING MUTTON AT MRS. THRALE'S, HE FLIRTS INNOCUOUSLY WITH HIS NEIGHBOR FANNY BURNEY.

*Are you making mischief between the
young lady and me already?*

"LITTLE BURNEY" was Johnson's affectionate way of calling her. She was small, shy, and unobtrusive, blushed and stammered in conversation. To the bulky and bearish Johnson she was some frail and inconspicuous doll to pet and fondle paternally. Perhaps the veneration he felt for her father, the classical scholar and musicologist, had something to do with it, but only at first. In his last years, she was like a daughter, and there was no woman, not even Mrs. Thrale, whose company he sought more eagerly than that of this bashful and retiring slip of a girl. Nor was Johnson alone in his attachment to "Little Burney." Others like Garrick, Reynolds, or the redoubtable Burke himself might be seen hovering about her in protective fondness. All seemed to cherish the sweet simplicity and meekness of the girl. Yet it was this same "Little Burney" who in 1778 gave them the surprise of their lives. Early that year an anonymous novel was printed in London that speedily outsold every other book on the market. Its title was Evelina. Critics praised it lavishly. Burke and Reynolds confessed sitting up all night to read it, and one and all speculated on the identity of its author. Then one day a timid little girl confided her secret to Mrs. Thrale, and before long all London knew that "Little Burney" was the vivacious and shrewdly observant author of Evelina. Towering above the vast chorus of praise was the thunderous voice of Dr. Samuel Johnson. The man was indeed proud of his gifted protégée. It was that same year of the spectacular success of Evelina that Miss Burney was first invited to Mrs. Thrale's magnificent country house at Streatham.

Before we follow Miss Burney to that pleasant retreat from the dirt and bustle of London another secret of hers must be divulged, a secret that

in turn explains the secret of her success as a novelist. Fanny Burney kept
a diary. For seventy-two years, from the time she was fifteen to her death,
she faithfully recorded every happening she witnessed and every scrap of
conversation she overheard. Thus, the natural sparkle and verve of her
dialogue as novelist were those of a practiced hand. Miss Burney's memory
was phenomenal, and if she lacked the power and sweep of Boswell, she
at least had a flair for precision of detail and setting, however commonplace. A six-volume edition of this Diary was issued by Macmillan and
Company in 1904, with the brilliant preface and notes of Austin Dobson.
It is from that edition, based on the earlier one of 1842–46 (edited by Miss
Burney's niece Charlotte Francis Barrett), that the dialogues quoted here
have been taken. One browses through this voluminous Diary and Letters
fascinated by the tang of reality, the crisp sense of talk caught in the very
flight. Even the most trivial tittle-tattle assumes the wondrous glow of a
living world rescued from the mists of time. "Little Burney," with her
chattery bedtime jottings, gives us back the late eighteenth and early
nineteenth centuries in an intimacy that no other chronicler even re-
motely approaches. In this massive book of Fanny Burney's life, Streatham
opens a fresh chapter in August, 1778. Dr. Johnson now looms as the
central character of her diary.

In the conversations given below we discover Dr. Johnson in rather
fortunate circumstances. He is almost exclusively in the company of ladies,
particularly of three: Mrs. Thrale, Mrs. Montagu, and Miss Burney. Miss
Burney we have already been introduced to. Mrs. Montagu was that redoubtable bluestocking and ruler of London society who, in an uneman-
cipated age, was prepared to match her erudition with any man's. As for
Mrs. Thrale, hers was a more complicated role in the drama of Dr. Johnson. Mrs. Thrale was at first married to an affluent brewer who maintained
a house in town and a suburban mansion on the south side of the common
between Streatham and Tooting. In 1765 Dr. Johnson and he became
close friends, and the brewer, relishing his daily draught of Johnsonian
wisdom, set up a private apartment for the great man at both houses.
Johnson became a permanent fixture in the lives of the Thrales, and no
doubt much of the attraction was the gracious and cultured Hester Thrale,
who conducted one of the best salons of the day. In this congenial atmosphere Johnson flourished happily till 1781, when his friend Henry Thrale
died. Johnson comforted the widow and aided her in disposing of the
brewery. There were those who, knowing Johnson's great fondness for
Mrs. Thrale, supposed that in due time the two might even marry. Perhaps
Johnson himself entertained the thought. In any case, it came as a harsh
blow when Mrs. Thrale's engagement to the Italian musician Gabriele

Piozzi was announced in 1783. Streatham was sold, and Johnson, stricken with anguish of mind and body, hobbled back to his own dismal quarters in London. What letters he found of Mrs. Thrale's—presently Mrs. Piozzi —he now consigned to the flames as memorials of a cruel betrayal.

But that is looking ahead into the dark future of Johnson's last years. For the moment we are in Streatham, a magnificent white house "very pleasantly situated in a fine paddock." A midsummer peace and beauty are on the surrounding sweep of lawn. Mrs. Thrale, ever the welcoming hostess, meets two guests at the door: "Ah, I hear Dr. Burney's voice! And you have brought your daughter? Well, now you are good!" Father and daughter are immediately made to feel at home, and soon the table is spread for dinner. Mrs. Thrale bids Fanny and her father sit on each side of her. Politely, Fanny "hopes" she is not taking the place of Dr. Johnson, who has not yet made his entrance. "No," replies Mrs. Thrale sweetly, "he will sit by you, which I am sure will give him pleasure." Miss Burney now takes up the narrative, carrying it through that August dinner to the September visit of Mrs. Montagu to Streatham, and the postcript on Dr. Johnson's compliments. . . .

("*Soon after we were seated this great man entered. I have so true a veneration for him that the very sight of him inspires me with delight and reverence, notwithstanding the cruel infirmities to which he is subject; for he has almost perpetual convulsive movements, either of his hands, lips, feet, or knees, and sometimes of all together. Mrs. Thrale introduced me to him, and he took his place. We had a noble dinner and a most elegant dessert. Dr. Johnson, in the middle of dinner, asked Mrs. Thrale what was in some little pies that were near him.*"—Fanny Burney)

MRS. THRALE: Mutton, so I don't ask you to eat any, because I know you despise it.

JOHNSON: No, madam, no. I despise nothing that is good of its sort; but I am too proud now to eat of it. Sitting by Miss Burney makes me very proud today!

MRS. THRALE (*laughing*): Miss Burney, you must take care of your heart if Dr. Johnson attacks it; for I assure you he is not often successless.

JOHNSON: What's that you say, madam? Are you making mischief between the young lady and me already? (*Drinks Mrs. Thrale's and Miss Burney's health.*) 'Tis a terrible thing that we cannot wish young ladies well, without wishing them to become old women!

SEWARD: * But some people are old and young at the same time, for they wear so well that they never look old.

JOHNSON (*laughing*): No, sir, no; that never yet was; you might as well say they are at the same time tall and short. I remember an epitaph to that purpose:—

> ... *lies buried here;*
> *So early wise, so lasting fair,*
> *That none, unless her years you told,*
> *Thought her a child, or thought her old.*

(*"Mrs. Thrale repeats some lines in French, and Dr. Johnson some more in Latin. An epilogue of Mr. Garrick's to Bonduca † is mentioned, and Dr. Johnson says it is a miserable performance, and everybody agrees it is the worst he has ever made."*)

SEWARD: And yet it has been very much admired; but it is in praise of English valor, and so I suppose the subject made it popular.

JOHNSON: I don't know, sir, anything about the subject, for I could not read on till I came to it; I got through half a dozen lines, but I could observe no other subject than eternal dullness. I don't know what is the matter with David; I am afraid he is grown superannuated, for his prologues and epilogues used to be incomparable.

MRS. THRALE: Nothing is so fatiguing as the life of a wit: he and Wilkes ‡ are the two oldest men of their ages I know; for they have both worn themselves out by being eternally on the rack to give entertainment to others.

JOHNSON: David, madam, looks much older than he is; for his face has had double the business of any other man's; it is never at rest; when he speaks one minute, he has quite a different countenance to what he assumes the next; I don't believe he ever kept the same look for half an hour together, in the whole course of his life; and such an eternal, restless, fatiguing play of the muscles must certainly wear out a man's face before its real time.

MRS. THRALE: Oh, yes, we must certainly make some allowance for such wear and tear of a man's face. ... (*Someone mentions the name of Sir John Hawkins.§*) Why, now, Dr. Johnson, he is another of those whom

---

* William Seward, author of *Anecdotes of Some Distinguished Persons.* In a letter to Boswell, Johnson calls him "a great favorite at Streatham." Not to be confused with the Reverend Seward of Lichfield, father of Anna Seward.

† A play by George Colman adapted from Beaumont and Fletcher.

‡ John Wilkes, 1727–97, writer, reformer, and political figure.

§ Author of *A History of Music*, 1776; noted for his irascible temper and tight-fistedness.

you suffer nobody to abuse but yourself; Garrick is one, too; for if any other person speaks against him, you browbeat him in a minute!

JOHNSON: Why, madam, they must know when to abuse him, and when to praise him; I will allow no man to speak ill of David that he does not deserve; and as to Sir John, why really I believe him to be an honest man at the bottom; but to be sure he is penurious, and he is mean, and it must be owned he has a degree of brutality, and a tendency to savageness, that cannot easily be defended.

("*We all laughed, as he meant we should, at this curious manner of speaking in his favor, and he then related an anecdote that he said he knew to be true in regard to his meanness. He said that Sir John and he once belonged to the same club, but that as he ate no supper after the first night of his admission, he desired to be excused paying his share.*"
—Miss Burney)

ALL: And was he excused?

JOHNSON: Oh yes; for no man is angry at another for being inferior to himself! We all scorned him, and admitted his plea. For my part I was such a fool as to pay my share for wine, though I never tasted any. But Sir John was a most *unclubable* man! And this reminds me of a gentleman and lady with whom I travelled once; I suppose I must call them gentleman and lady, according to form, because they travelled in their own coach and four horses. But at the first inn where we stopped, the lady called for—a pint of ale! and when it came, quarrelled with the waiter for not giving full measure!

Dr. Samuel Johnson

9.

HE PREPARES THE BASHFUL MISS BURNEY FOR AN ENCOUNTER WITH THE FORMIDABLE BLUESTOCKING, MRS. MONTAGU.

So, at her, Burney—at her, and down with her!

Streatham, September, 1778—Tuesday

("At tea-time the subject turned upon the domestic economy of Dr. Johnson's own household. Mrs. Thrale has often acquainted me that his house is quite filled and overrun with all sorts of strange creatures, whom he admits for mere charity, and because nobody else will admit them—for his charity is unbounded,—or, rather, bounded only by his circumstances. The account he gave of the adventures and absurdities of the set was highly diverting, but too diffused for writing, though one or two speeches I must give. I think I shall occasionally theatricalize my dialogues.")—Miss Burney)

MRS. THRALE: Pray, sir, how does Mrs. Williams like all this tribe?

JOHNSON: Madam, she does not like them at all; but their fondness for her is not greater. She and Desmoulins * quarrel incessantly; but as they can both be occasionally of service to each other, and as neither of them have any other place to go to, their animosity does not force them to separate.

MRS. THRALE: And pray, sir, what is Mr. Macbean? †

JOHNSON: Madam, he is a Scotchman: he is a man of great learning, and for his learning I respect him, and I wish to serve him. He knows many languages, and knows them well; but he knows nothing of life. I advised him to write a geographical dictionary; but I have lost all hopes of his ever doing anything properly, since I found he gave as much labor to Capua as to Rome.

MR. THRALE: And pray who is clerk of your kitchen, sir?

JOHNSON: Why, sir, I am afraid there is none; a general anarchy prevails

* A daughter of Dr. Johnson's godfather.
† Wrote a *Dictionary of Ancient Geography*, 1773, for which Johnson furnished a preface.

in my kitchen, as I am told by Mr. Levat,* who says it is not now what it used to be!

MRS. THRALE: Mr. Levat, I suppose, sir, has the office of keeping the hospital in health, for he is an apothecary.

JOHNSON: Levat, madam, is a brutal fellow, but I have a good regard for him; for his brutality is in his manners, not his mind.

MR. THRALE: But how do you get your dinners dressed?

JOHNSON: Why, De Mullin has the chief management of the kitchen; but our roasting is not magnificent, for we have no jack.

MR. THRALE: No jack? Why, how do they manage without?

JOHNSON: Small joints, I believe, they manage with a string, and larger are done at the tavern. (*Gravely*) I have some thoughts of buying a jack, because I think a jack is some credit to a house.

MR. THRALE: Well, but you'll have a spit, too?

JOHNSON: No, sir, no; that would be superfluous; for we shall never use it; and if a jack is seen, a spit will be presumed!

MRS. THRALE: But pray, sir, who is the Poll † you talk of? She that you used to abet in her quarrels with Mrs. Williams, and call out, "At her again, Poll! Never flinch, Poll!"?

JOHNSON: Why, I took to Poll very well at first, but she won't do upon a nearer examination.

MRS. THRALE: How came she among you, sir?

JOHNSON: Why, I don't rightly remember, but we could spare her very well from us. Poll is a stupid slut; I had some hopes of her at first; but when I talked to her tightly and closely, I could make nothing of her; she was wigglewaggle, and I could never persuade her to be categorical. I wish Miss Burney would come among us; if she would only give us a week, we should furnish her with ample materials for a new scene in her next work.

(*Johnson asks Mrs. Thrale, who has been reading her copy of* Evelina *during his absence from Streatham.*)

MRS. THRALE: Why, Burke!—Burke sat up all night to finish it; and Sir Joshua Reynolds is mad about it, and said he would give fifty pounds to know the author. But our fun was with his nieces—we made them believe I wrote the book, and the girls gave me the credit of it at once.

JOHNSON (*angrily*): I am sorry for it, madam. You were much to blame; deceits of that kind ought never to be practiced; they have a worse tendency than you are aware of.

MRS. THRALE: Why, don't frighten yourself, sir; Miss Burney will have all

---

* Robert Levett, (1701–82), a surgeon who lived in Johnson's house since 1763.
† Miss Carmichael, another pensioner of Johnson's.

the credit she has a right to, for I told them whose it was before they went.

JOHNSON: But you were very wrong for misleading them a moment; such jests are extremely blamable; they are foolish in the very act, and they are wrong, because they always leave a doubt upon the mind. What first passed will be always recollected by those girls, and they will never feel clearly convinced which wrote the book, Mrs. Thrale or Miss Burney.

MRS. THRALE: Well, well, I am ready to take my Bible oath it was not me; and if that won't do, Miss Burney must take hers too.

JOHNSON (*to Miss Burney, whom he observes reading his* Life of Cowley): Do put that away now, and prattle with us; I can't make this little Burney prattle, and I am sure she prattles well; but I shall teach her another lesson than to sit thus silent before I have done with her.

MISS BURNEY: To talk is the only lesson I shall be backward to learn from you, sir.

JOHNSON: You shall give me a discourse upon the passions. Come, begin! Tell us the necessity of regulating them, watching over and curbing them! Did you ever read Norris's *Theory of Love?*

MISS BURNEY (*laughing and starting a little*): No, sir.

JOHNSON: Well, it is worth your reading. He will make you see that inordinate love is the root of all evil. Inordinate love of wealth brings on avarice; of wine, brings on intemperance; of power, brings on cruelty; and so on. He deduces from inordinate love all human frailty.

MRS. THRALE: Tomorrow, sir, Mrs. Montagu dines here, and then you will have talk enough.

(*Johnson begins to see-saw, with a countenance strongly expressive of inward fun, and after enjoying it some time in silence, he suddenly, and with great animation, turns to Miss Burney.*)

JOHNSON: Down with her, Burney! Down with her! Spare her not! Attack her, fight her, and down with her at once! You are a rising wit, and she is at the top. When I was beginning in the world, and was nothing and nobody, the joy of my life was to fire at all the established wits, and then everybody loved to halloo me on. There is no game now; everybody would be glad to see me conquered. But then, when I was new, to vanquish the great ones was all the delight of my poor little dear soul! So, at her, Burney—at her, and down with her! Mark now, if I contradict her tomorrow, I am determined, let her say what she will, that I will not contradict her.

MRS. THRALE: Why, to be sure, sir, you did put her a little out of countenance last time she came. Yet you were neither rough, nor cruel, nor ill-natured; but still, when a lady changes color, we imagine her feelings are not quite composed.

JOHNSON: Why, madam, I won't answer that I shan't contradict her again, if she provokes me as she did then; but a less provocation I will withstand. I believe I am not high in her good graces already; and I begin (*laughing heartily*) to tremble for my admission into her new house. I doubt I shall never see the inside of it.

MRS. THRALE: Oh, I warrant you, she fears you, indeed; but that, you know, is nothing uncommon: and dearly I love to hear your disquisitions; for certainly she is the first woman for literary knowledge in England, and if in England, I hope I may say in the world.

JOHNSON: I believe you may, madam. She diffuses more knowledge in her conversation than any woman I know, or, indeed, almost any man.

MRS. THRALE: I declare I know no man equal to her, take away yourself and Burke, for that art. And you who love magnificence, won't quarrel with her, as everybody else does, for her love of finery.

JOHNSON: No, I shall not quarrel with her upon that topic. (*Looking very intently at Miss Burney*) Nay, it's very handsome.

MISS BURNEY (*amazed*): What, sir?

JOHNSON: Why, your cap. I have looked at it some time, and I like it very much. It has not that vile bandeau across it, which I have so often cursed.

MRS. THRALE: Well, sir, that bandeau you quarrelled with was worn by every woman at court at last birthday, and I observed that all the men found fault with it.

JOHNSON: The truth is, women, take them in general, have no idea of grace. Fashion is all they think of. I don't mean Mrs. Thrale and Miss Burney, when I talk of women! They are goddesses! And therefore I except them.

MRS. THRALE: Lady Ladd never wore the bandeau, and said she never would, because it is unbecoming.

JOHNSON (*laughing*): Did not she? Then is Lady Ladd a charming woman, and I have yet hopes of entering into engagements with her.

MRS. THRALE: Well, as to that I can't say; but to be sure, the only similitude I have yet discovered in you is in size. There you agree mighty well.

JOHNSON: Why, if anybody could have worn the bandeau, it must have been Lady Ladd; for there is enough of her to carry it off; but you are too little for anything ridiculous; that which seems nothing upon a Patagonian will become very conspicuous upon a Lilliputian, and of you there is so little in all that one single absurdity would swallow up half of you. . . . (*After a silence, turning to Miss Burney*) Come, Burney, shall you and I study our parts against Mrs. Montagu comes?

MRS. THRALE: Miss Burney, you must get up your courage for this encounter! I think you should begin with Miss Gregory; * and down with her first!

JOHNSON: No, no, always fly at the eagle! Down with Mrs. Montagu herself! I hope she will come full of *Evelina!*

(*The great bout, alas, did not come off, for Mrs. Montagu proved very civil to the meek little authoress urged by Johnson to such combative gallantry. Miss Gregory our tireless diariest found "a fine young woman" who seemed "gentle and well-bred." As for her redoubtable companion, Miss Burney describes her as "middle-sized, very thin," and as looking "infirm." She credited her with "a sensible and penetrating countenance and the air and manner of a woman accustomed to being distinguished, and of great parts." With only the faintest trace of cattiness, she recalled Dr. Johnson's quoting a certain Mrs. Hervey, who remembered Mrs. Montagu "trying for this same air and manner." When she arrived Mrs. Montagu began by apologizing for the loss of a book about politics by S. N. H. Linguet which she had borrowed from Dr. Burney. "But my ease and tranquillity were soon disturbed," Miss Burney confides, "for she had not been in the room more than ten minutes, ere, turning to Mrs. Thrale . . ."*)

MRS. MONTAGU: Oh, ma'am—but your *Evelina*—I have not got it—I sent for it, but the bookseller had it not. However, I will certainly have it.

MRS. THRALE: Ay, I hope so, and I hope you will like it too; for 'tis a book to be liked.

(*Miss Burney begins "a vehement nose-blowing, for the benefit of handkerchiefing my face."*)

MRS. MONTAGU (*drily*): I hope, though, it is not in verse? I can read anything in prose, but I have a great dread of a long story in verse.

MRS. THRALE: No, ma'am, no; 'tis all in prose, I assure you. 'Tis a novel; and an exceeding. . . . But it does nothing good to be praised too much, so I will say nothing more about it; only this, that Mr. Burke sat up all night to read it.

MRS. MONTAGU: Indeed? Well, I propose myself great pleasure from it; and I am gratified by hearing it is written by a woman.

MRS. THRALE: And Sir Joshua Reynolds has been offering fifty pounds to know the author.

---

* Daughter of John Gregory, a doctor, whose letters, *A Father's Legacy to His Daughters*, were published in 1774. She lived with the formidable Mrs. Montagu and was also invited to Streatham by Mrs. Thrale.

MRS. MONTAGU: Well, I will have it read on my journey; I am going to Berkshire, and it shall be my travelling book.

MRS. THRALE: No, ma'am, if you please, you shall have it now. Queeny, do look for it for Mrs. Montagu, and let it be put in her carriage, and go to town with her.

("*Miss Thrale rose to look for it, and involuntarily I rose too, intending to walk off, for my situation was inexpressibly awkward; but then I recollected that if I went away, it might seem like giving Mrs. Thrale leave and opportunity to tell my tale, and therefore I stopped at a distant window, where I buried myself in contemplating the country.*"—Miss Burney)

MRS. THRALE: And Dr. Johnson, ma'am, says Fielding never wrote so well —never wrote equal to this book; he says it is a better picture of life and manners than is to be found anywhere in Fielding.

MRS. MONTAGU (*surprised*): Indeed? That I did not expect, for I have been informed it is the work of a young lady, and therefore, though I expected a very pretty book, I supposed it to be a work of mere imagination, and the name I thought attractive; but life and manners I never dreamed of finding.

MRS. THRALE: Well, ma'am, what I tell you is literally true; and for my part, I am never better pleased than when good girls write clever books —and that this is clever. . . . But all this time we are killing Miss Burney, who wrote the book herself!

(*Miss Burney abruptly takes to her heels, running out of the room "with the utmost trepidation, amidst astonished exclamations from Mrs. Montagu and Miss Gregory.*")

LATER AT DINNER. DR. JOHNSON HAS RETURNED.

("*The conversation was not brilliant, nor do I remember much of it; but Mrs. Montagu behaved to me just as I could have wished, since she spoke to me very little, but spoke that little with the utmost politeness. But Miss Gregory, though herself a very modest girl, quite stared me out of countenance, and never took her eyes off my face. When Mrs. Montagu's new house was talked of, Dr. Johnson, in a jocose manner, desired to know if he should be invited to see it.*"—Miss Burney)

MRS. MONTAGU (*looking well pleased*): Ay, sure; or else I shan't like it: but I invite you all to a housewarming; I shall hope for the honor of seeing all this company at my new house next Easter day: I fix the day now that it may be remembered.

JOHNSON (*clapping a hand on Miss Burney's shoulder, and calling out*

aloud to make certain that she would be included in the invitation):
Little Burney, you and I will go together!

MRS. MONTAGU: Yes, surely; I shall hope for the pleasure of seeing *Evelina*.

JOHNSON: *Evelina?* Has Mrs. Montagu then found out *Evelina?*

MRS. MONTAGU: Yes, and I am proud of it: I am proud that a work so commended should be a woman's.

JOHNSON: Has Mrs. Montagu read *Evelina?*

MRS. MONTAGU: No, sir, not yet; but I shall immediately, for I feel the greatest eagerness to read it.

JOHNSON: I am very sorry, madam, that you have not read it already, because you cannot speak of it with a full conviction of its merit: which, I believe, when you have read it, you will find great pleasure in acknowledging.

(*Miss Burney prepares tea, and later Mrs. Montagu and Miss Gregory seat themselves on each side of her.*)

MRS. MONTAGU: I can see that Miss Burney is very like her father, and that is a good thing, for everybody would wish to be like Dr. Burney. Pray, when you see him, give my best respects to him; I am afraid he thinks me a thief with his Linguet; but I assure you I am a very honest woman, and I spent full three hours in looking for it.

MRS. THRALE: I am sure Dr. Burney would much rather you should have employed that time about some other book.

(*Mrs. Montagu and Miss Gregory leave.*)

JOHNSON (*after remarking what an ugly cap Miss Gregory had on, takes both of Miss Burney's hands and looks at her "with an expression of much kindness"*): Well, Miss Burney, Mrs. Montagu now will read *Evelina*.

MISS BURNEY: You were very kind, sir, to speak of it with so much favor and indulgence at dinner; yet I hardly knew how to sit it then, though I shall be always proud to remember it hereafter.

JOHNSON (*kindly*): Why, it is true that such things are disagreeable to sit, nor do I wonder you were distressed; yet sometimes they are necessary.

MISS BURNEY: Well, sir, I don't think I shall mind Mrs. Montagu herself now; after what you have said, I believe I should not mind even abuse from any one.

JOHNSON: No, no, never mind them! Resolve not to mind them! They can do you no serious hurt.

MRS. THRALE: Mrs. Montagu inquired very particularly what kind of book it was.* I told her that it was a picture of life, manners, and characters. "But won't she go on?" says she. "Surely she won't stop here?" "Why,"

---

* Indirect discourse in original.

said I, "I want her to go on in a new path—I want her to write a comedy." "But," said Mrs. Montagu, "one thing must be considered; Fielding, who was so admirable in novel-writing, never succeeded when he wrote for the stage."

JOHNSON: Very well said. That was an answer which showed she considered her subject.

MRS. THRALE: "Well, but *a propos*," said Mrs. Montagu, "if Miss Burney does write a play, I beg I may know of it; or, if she thinks proper, see it; and all my influence is at her service. We shall all be glad to assist in spreading the fame of Miss Burney." ...

(*Dr. Johnson evidently departed at this point.*)

MRS. THRALE (*to Miss Burney*): Oh, *a propos*; now you have a new edition coming out, why should you not put your name to it?

MISS BURNEY: Oh, ma'am, I would not for the world!

MRS. THRALE: And why not? Come, let us have done now with all this diddle-daddle.

MISS BURNEY: No, indeed, ma'am; so long as I live I never can consent to that.

MRS. THRALE: Well, but seriously, Miss Burney, why should you not? I advise it with all my heart, and I'll tell you why; you want hardening, and how can you get it better than by putting your name to this book, to begin with, which everybody likes, and against which I have heard nobody offer any objection? You can never write what will please more universally.

MISS BURNEY: But why, ma'am, should I be hardened?

MRS. THRALE: To enable you to bear a little abuse by and by.

MISS BURNEY: Oh, Heaven forbid I should be tried in that way!

MRS. THRALE: Oh, you must not talk so; I hope to live to see you trimmed very handsomely.

MISS BURNEY: Heaven forbid! I am sure I should hang or drown myself in such a case!

MRS. THRALE: You grieve me to hear you talk so; is not everybody abused that meets with success? You must prepare yourself not to mind a few squibs. How is Dr. Johnson abused! And who thinks the worse of him?

("*This comparison made me grin, and so our discourse ended. But pray Heaven may spare me the horror irrecoverable of personal abuse! Let them criticize, cut, slash without mercy my book, but let them neglect me; but may God avert my becoming a public theme of ridicule! In such a case how should I wish* Evelina *had followed her humble predecessors to the all-devouring flames, which, in consuming her, would have preserved her creatress.*"—Fanny Burney)

Dr. Samuel Johnson

10.

A BEAUTIFUL HOSTESS REPROACHES HIM
ON THE INFREQUENCY OF HIS
COMPLIMENTS.

*It constantly moves my indignation to
be applied to, to speak well of a thing
which I think contemptible.*

(*Monday, September 21, 1778*
*"Last night, when we were talking of compliments and of gross
speeches, Mrs. Thrale most justly said that nobody could make either
like Dr. Johnson. . . ."*—Fanny Burney)

MRS. THRALE: Your compliments, sir, are made seldom, but when they are
made they have an elegance unequalled; but when you are angry, who
dares make speeches so bitter and so cruel?

JOHNSON: Madam, I am always sorry when I make bitter speeches, and I
never do it but when I am insufferably vexed.

MRS. THRALE: Yes, sir; but you suffer things to vex you that nobody else
would vex at. I am sure I have had my share of scolding from you!

JOHNSON: It is true, you have; but you have borne it like an angel, and you
have been the better for it.

MRS. THRALE: That I believe, sir; for I have received more instruction from
you than from any man, or any book, and the vanity that you should
think me worth instructing always overcame the vanity of being found
fault with. And so you had the scolding, and I the improvement.

MISS BURNEY: And I am sure both make for the honor of both!

JOHNSON: I think so too. But Mrs. Thrale is a sweet creature, and never
angry; she has a temper the most delightful of any woman I ever knew.

MRS. THRALE: This I can tell you, sir, and without any flattery—I not only
bear your reproofs when present, but in almost everything I do in your
absence, I ask myself whether you would like it, and what you would
say to it. Yet I believe there is nobody you dispute with oftener than
me.

MISS BURNEY: But you two are so well established with one another that you can bear rebuff that would kill a stranger.

JOHNSON: Yes; but we disputed the same before we were so well established with one another.

MRS. THRALE: Oh, sometimes I think I shall die no other death than hearing the bitter things he says to others. What he says to myself I can bear, because I know how sincerely he is my friend and that he means to mend me; but to others it is cruel.

JOHNSON: Why, madam, you often provoke me to say severe things, by unreasonable commendation. If you would not call for my praise, I would not give you my censure; but it constantly moves my indignation to be applied to, to speak well of a thing which I think contemptible.

MISS BURNEY: Well, this I know, whoever I may hear complain of Dr. Johnson's severity, I shall always vouch for his kindness, as far as regards myself, and his indulgence.

MRS. THRALE: Ay, but I hope he will trim you yet, too!

JOHNSON: I hope not: I should be very sorry to say anything that should vex my dear little Burney.

MISS BURNEY: If you did, sir, it would vex me more than you can imagine. I should sink in a minute.

MRS. THRALE: I remember, sir, when we were travelling in Wales how you called me to account for my civility to the people. "Madam," you said, "let me have no more of this idle commendation of nothing. Why is it that whatever you see, and whoever you see, you are to be so indiscriminately lavish of praise?" "Why, I'll tell you, sir," said I, "when I am with you, and Mr. Thrale, and Queeny, I am obliged to be civil for four!"

(*Adds Miss Burney: "There was a cutter for you! But this I must say, for the honor of both—Mrs. Thrale speaks to Dr. Johnson with as much sincerity [though with greater softness], as he does to her."*)

Dr. Samuel Johnson

11.

SIR JOSHUA REYNOLDS FAILS IN HIS DEFENSE
OF DAVID GARRICK.

*Besides, besides, sir, besides,—do you not
know,—are you so ignorant as not to know,
that it is the highest degree of rudeness to
quote a man against himself?*

As a farewell glimpse of Dr. Johnson in verbal action, we offer the following "reconstruction" by Sir Joshua Reynolds. The theme is again
David Garrick, of whom Mrs. Thrale has charged Dr. Johnson with suffering "nobody to abuse" but himself. Boswell had discovered the doctor's
touchiness on the subject at their very first encounter in Tom Davies'
bookshop at 8 Russell Street, Covent Garden, on that crucial May day
of 1763 that first brought them together. To make conversation, Boswell
had ventured to find fault with the great actor. The eruption was prompt:
"Sir, I have known David Garrick longer than you have done; I know of
no right you have to talk to me on the subject." Actually, Garrick had
been one of his three pupils in the "academy" he had set up in 1735 at
Edial, near his native Lichfield. Garrick had accompanied Johnson to
London in 1737, and the two remained friends and associates, meeting
frequently at "The Club."

Johnson knew Garrick's merit, but he bristled over the spectacle of
fawning adulation before a man who, after all, was merely the mouthpiece
of other men's genius. And it was only poetic justice that Johnson should
occasionally cut down his former pupil to his rightful size. For Garrick,
richly gifted in the art of mimicry, could be quite merciless in his side-
splitting caricatures of the burly and bellowing Dr. Johnson. It would
seem only fitting that another portraitist—working, to be sure, in another
medium—should supply the picture of Johnson in a spasm of "brow-
beating" on the subject of David Garrick. To what extent Johnson considered Garrick his exclusive property as a theme for conversation is well
brought out in this dialogue.

Sir Joshua's amusing "skit" first appeared in Miss Hawkins' three-

volume collection of Anecdotes, published in London in 1822–24. Miss
Hawkins was herself a qualified judge of Johnson's style, having heard
him repeatedly at Mrs. Thrale's house. The dialogue reached this gossipy
lady by a devious path, if we are to accept her account: "A lad whose uncle
was one of Johnson's friends and who lived in great intimacy with Sir
Joshua Reynolds' family has allowed me to reproduce the following jeu
d'esprit which in my humble judgment is a very vivid imitation of Johnson's language and manner. It was thrown off by Sir Joshua without any
idea of publication to illustrate a remark which he had made that 'Johnson
considered Garrick as his own property and would not suffer anyone to
praise or blame him but himself.' " In reading the "skit" let us bear in mind
that what we have here is in no sense a strictly factual or stenographic
record, but an imaginative reconstruction "within the strict limits of
historical fact."

Of Johnson's talk Reynolds elsewhere had this to say: "In arguing he
did not trouble himself with much circumlocution, but opposed, directly
and abruptly, his antagonist. He fought with all sorts of weapons; with
ludicrous comparisons and similes; if all failed, with rudeness and overbearing. He thought it necessary never to be worsted in argument. He had
one virtue which I hold one of the most difficult to practice. After the
heat of contest was over, if he had been informed that his antagonist
resented his rudeness, he was the first to seek after a reconciliation; and
of his virtues the most distinguished was his love of truth."

REYNOLDS: Let me alone, I'll bring him out. (*Aside*) I have been thinking,
 Dr. Johnson, this morning, on a matter that has puzzled me very much;
 it is a subject that I dare say has often passed in your thoughts, and
 though I cannot, I dare say *you* have made up your mind upon it.
JOHNSON: Tilly fally! what is all this preparation? What is all this mighty
 matter?
REYNOLDS: Why, it is a very weighty matter. The subject I have been
 thinking upon is predestination and free will, two things I cannot reconcile together for the life of me. In my opinion, Dr. Johnson, free will
 and foreknowledge cannot be reconciled.
JOHNSON: Sir, it is not of very great importance what your opinion is upon
 such a question.
REYNOLDS: But I meant only, Dr. Johnson, to know your opinion.
JOHNSON: No, sir, you meant no such thing; you meant only to show these
 gentlemen that you are not the man they took you to be, but that you

think of high matters sometimes, and that you may have the credit of having it said that you held an argument with Sam Johnson on predestination and free will; a subject of that magnitude as to have engaged the attention of the world, to have perplexed the wisdom of man for these two thousand years; a subject on which the fallen angels, who *had yet not lost their original brightness,* found themselves *in wandering mazes lost.* That such a subject could be discussed in the levity of convivial conversation is a degree of absurdity beyond what is easily conceivable.

REYNOLDS: It is so, as you say, to be sure; I talked once to our friend Garrick upon this subject, but I remember we could make nothing of it.

JOHNSON: O noble pair!

REYNOLDS: Garrick was a clever fellow, Dr. Johnson; Garrick, take him altogether, was certainly a very great man.

JOHNSON: Garrick, sir, may be a great man in your opinion, as far as I know, but he was not so in mine; little things are great to little men.

REYNOLDS: I have heard you say, Dr. Johnson—

JOHNSON: Sir, you never heard me say that David Garrick was a great man; you may have heard me say that Garrick was a good repeater—of other men's words—words put into his mouth by other men; this makes but a faint approach toward being a great man.

REYNOLDS: But take Garrick upon the whole, now, in regard to conversation—

JOHNSON: Well, sir, in regard to conversation, I never discovered in the conversation of David Garrick any intellectual energy, any wide grasp of thought, any extensive comprehension of mind, or that he possessed any of those powers to which *great* could, with any degree of propriety, be applied.

REYNOLDS: But still—

JOHNSON: Hold, sir, I have not done—there are, to be sure, in the laxity of colloquial speech, various kinds of greatness; a man may be a great painter, he may be likewise a great mimic; now you may be the one, and Garrick the other, and yet neither of you be great men.

REYNOLDS: But, Dr. Johnson—

JOHNSON: Hold, sir, I have often lamented how dangerous it is to investigate and to discriminate character, to men who have no discriminative powers.

REYNOLDS: But Garrick, as a companion, I heard you say—no longer ago than last Wednesday, at Mr. Thrale's table—

JOHNSON: You tease me, sir. Whatever you may have heard me say, no longer ago than last Wednesday, at Mr. Thrale's table, I tell you I do

·not say so now: besides, as I said before, you may not have understood me, you misapprehended me, you may not have heard me.

REYNOLDS: I am very sure I heard you.

JOHNSON: Besides, besides, sir, besides,—do you not know,—are you so ignorant as not to know, that it is the highest degree of rudeness to quote a man against himself?

REYNOLDS: But if you differ from yourself, and give one opinion today—

JOHNSON: Have done, sir. The company, you see, are tired, as well as myself.

Goethe

W HEN Napoleon remarked after parting with Goethe, "Voilà un homme!" he made perhaps the wisest observation of his career. This was indeed a man, in the Renaissance sense of world outlook and complete absorption in life. Mentally and physically this man lived a full life. A supreme humanist, he could echo Landor's line, "Nature I loved and next to nature art," and add that he too had warmed both hands before the fire of life. It is not surprising that a scholar should call Goethe's life his greatest masterpiece, a work of rounded unity and steadiness of vision. And there were many Goethes in this "masterpiece": Goethe the eternal student; Goethe the perennial lover; Goethe the supreme lyrist and epic poet; Goethe the playwright and novelist; Goethe the philosopher; Goethe the scientist; Goethe the state chancellor of Weimar. Measured by ordinary accomplishment, each one of them seems the work of a lifetime. Yet, these many aspects appear together at all times, like some complex human polyphony moving on several planes of activity.

In this unique composite one misses only one aspect, the man of political action. There Goethe was a mere spectator when he was not a thorough-going fatalist. Revolutionary action disturbed his Olympian calm, and his political thinking, such as it was, oriented itself toward one man—Napoleon. If he misplaced his faith, he could at least be pardoned the one great blunder of his life. We shall later find Goethe meeting this architect of chaos at Erfurt and remembering him as an "equal in genius." Yet, one should not be too unfair. Goethe, a patrician by nature, remained politically aloof as a master of temperament. One sympathizes with Professor Heinrich Luden, who, at Weimar in December, 1813, urged Goethe to join the fight for a free Germany, only to be sent away crying when the great man shook his head and replied: "Ich denke an meine Ruhe"— Goethe was always thinking of his tranquillity. Still, these ardent young nationalists and revolutionaries who came to see him made generous allowances. They came to recognize that Goethe's mission was on another level, and that in any case he had helped to create the mental climate within which forceful new ideas, if properly applied, became explosive.

There was one other side to Goethe that deserves special attention— the conversationalist. In quantity of talk recorded by friends, disciples, and associates, only Napoleon rivals him. But, whereas much of the Corsican's preserved talk is either spurious or liberally doctored, that of Goethe is almost all authentic, some of it more so than the rest. With Napoleon we are often faced with the record of partisans. If we search long enough we are likely to find that each of his Boswells had some ax of his own to grind. In the case of Goethe, perhaps the sole vitiating element is the vanity of the interlocutor. The students and professors who report their meetings so word the dialogue as not to appear meek nonentities in the presence of greatness. It is very possible that Professor Luden developed and polished a few of his own remarks in the record of his conversation with Goethe in Jena in 1806. It is obvious that Eckermann stylized his dialogues and further weakened them—for us—by showing some of them to Goethe. In any case, there is a rich variety of theme in this legacy of Goethe's "Gespräche." To be sure, a great deal is fragmentary, mere flashes of interspersed dialogue, unsuitable for the purposes of this book. Much is trivial and dated; much heavy with long-winded platitudes. Yet here and there one comes upon several revealing pages—perhaps only the self-revelation of Goethe's visitor and the impression made upon him. We have, at such moments, the thrilling sense of being in the company of one of the most amazingly many-sided personalities of history.

And if Professor Biedermann accomplished one purpose with his ten-volume labor of love, it was to prove to the world that Eckermann's Gespräche mit Goethe by no means exhausted the subject. In sustained continuity, Eckermann's contribution is unique. But for the great single dialogue, one must consult Professor Luden. Moreover, Eckermann's narrative is limited to the last decade of Goethe's long life. Needless to say, Goethe did not begin to talk for posterity at seventy-four. In the brief "Portrait in Dialogue" that follows it may be well to read—or reread—Talleyrand's report of the meeting between Goethe and Napoleon at Erfurt in 1808 (see page 204). As a matter of chronology, and perhaps irony, that amiable talk belongs after Professor Luden's own colloquy with Goethe in 1806 at Jena, the Jena which was presently the scene of one of Prussia's most crushing defeats at the hands of the "genius" whom Goethe revered as his equal.

Goethe

1.

THE WORLDLY AUTHOR OF *THE SORROWS OF WERTHER* REBUKES A TIMID UNIVERSITY GRADUATE ON THE SOCIAL TABOOS.

Have you ever been in love yourself?

CHARLES AUGUSTUS, hereditary prince of Weimar, first invited Goethe to that cultural center in December, 1774. Goethe politely refused. The following year, after a trip to Switzerland, Goethe accepted a second invitation and the twenty-six-year-old poet arrived at the capital of the duchy of Saxe-Weimar on November 7. It remained his home till the end of his life—a period of fifty-seven years. In Weimar Goethe was given wide scope for his multiple gifts. The Duke, who became a close friend, promptly assigned him a place in the cabinet and gave him every facility for his scientific researches. Mining, agriculture, and horticulture speedily benefited from Goethe's unique opportunity to combine theory and practice. Naturally the poet flourished, too, in this meeting-place of Germany's leading men of letters. And here in Weimar Goethe soon founded a theater that for a time was to surpass every other in Europe. In Weimar, too, the beautiful friendship and fruitful artistic association with Friedrich Schiller developed.

In time students, scholars, poets flocked from everywhere to visit this versatile genius. They came to talk literature, science, and, when indiscreet, politics. They even came for vocational guidance and emotional counsel. By 1786, when Goethe was a mere thirty-seven, he had already become a kind of father-confessor to a whole new generation of restless young men. In part this was a natural outgrowth of his novel, The Sorrows of Werther, written several years before. Werther, the romantic suicide, had made all Europe weep, and a whole cult of life and literature had grown up about the novel's high-pitched emotionalism. These starry-eyed young men who came to Weimar saw something more in Goethe. He was the Bohemian par excellence, preaching and practicing a free code of love— a man of innumerable liaisons, completely unshackled by convention, and

158

at the moment the lover of the brilliant Charlotte von Stein. This was emphatically a man to visit. . . .

In 1854 there appeared in Berlin a volume entitled, Berühmte Schriftsteller. This contained Professor Dietmar's record of a conversation he had held with Goethe in Weimar in July, 1786, shortly after completing his university studies. The conversation was later reprinted by Professor Biedermann in his monumental Gespräche, from which I have made all the translations that follow. We must compliment Professor Dietmar posthumously for not attempting to mask his youthful naïveté and clumsiness. The picture is rather amusing and typical. Dietmar is eager to meet Goethe; when he meets him he is even more eager to impress him, first as an observant young man, second as a man of the world. The little episode begins early in July, while Dietmar is waiting for his degree.

One afternoon, in a part of the ducal garden known as "The Star," Councillor Wieland, the so-called "German Voltaire," introduces Dietmar to Duke Charles Augustus. Later we find Dietmar doing a curious thing. Observing Goethe in a group, he climbs up a linden tree, and thus perched, begins unceremoniously to study the great man's behavior in company. Someone spots him there and the ducal garden is swept by gales of laughter. The following day Dietmar is commissioned by the Duke to bring him a report on the Educational Institute at nearby Schnepfenthal. When he returns from Schnepfenthal he makes his report to the Duke in the same corner of the garden. Also present on this occasion is Johann Karl Musäus, a noted writer of fairy tales, at the time a Weimar professor. As Dietmar prepares to leave, he tells Musäus how much he regrets not having met Goethe that day in the garden. What follows is Dietmar's own record. . . .

MUSÄUS: That can be remedied very easily. If you go to his house about six o'clock this evening, I'll accompany you. Just announce yourself as the student whom he spotted eight days ago on the linden tree in the Duke's garden. He will certainly receive you after such an introduction. We all laughed good and loud over your elevated position!

(*At six o'clock Dietmar goes to the address given him by Musäus, who evidently left him at the door after hearing him announce himself as the tree-sitter of the ducal garden.*)

GOETHE: So you've come back from your trip to Schnepfenthal? Did you satisfy your intellectual curiosity?

("*I told him everything that interested me at the Salzmann Educational Institute. He especially liked the proposal I made to Professor Salzmann that natural history should be taught the children during evening hours with a magic lantern.*"—Dietmar)

GOETHE: He has a brother in Erfurt who does excellent paintings of animals. He might paint the animal world on glass for him and he could use it for that purpose. While it's a fine thing to teach geography to youngsters as early as possible, I am of the opinion that one should begin with the immediate surroundings of nature. Whatever makes an impression on their eyes and ears sharpens their attention. Sun, moon, and stars, fire, water, snow, ice, clouds, thunderstorms, animals, plants, and stones make the most forceful impressions on a child's mind. Children have trouble differentiating created forms from natural objects. One shouldn't be surprised when a child asks its father: "How do you make a tree?" . . . Did you also see the sights of Erfurt?

DIETMAR: I was in the cathedral. They showed me the remarkable choir vault which doesn't rest on any pillars, and also a dreadful painting showing Saint Christopher in massive size. In the belfry I spent some time inspecting the huge bell which Gerhard de Campis cast in the year 1497. It must weigh all of fourteen tons.

GOETHE: It grumbles in a deep, solemn bass and is only heard on holidays. The church is old and was built during the time of Boniface. The little bells, I've been told, are almost two hundred years older. . . . Nothing about Luther?

DIETMAR: I visited the little hill—Steiger—where Luther's boyhood friend Alexis was struck dead by lightning at his side.

GOETHE: That same stroke of lightning cast a great light over Germany, for it drove Luther, who wanted to study law, into the monastery and led him to the discovery of a spark of Truth. Did you see the cell he occupied while he lived in Erfurt?

DIETMAR: I looked over the narrow little room and then copied down Luther's biography which is written in red letters on the white partition board. On a round tablet over the door there was a Latin inscription which read:

"*Cellula divino magnoque habitata Luthero . . .*" *

GOETHE: I know it. The Augustine church in which Luther preached was recently renovated. Did you see Lavater † in Gotha?

---

* The cell inhabited by the great and divine Luther.
† A famous divine and writer on religious subjects (1741–1801); Lavater, who saw Goethe that summer at Weimar, remarks that he found him "older, colder, wiser, firmer, more reserved, and more practical."

DIETMAR: I spoke with him.

GOETHE: He is no great friend of mine. It is ridiculous the way he thinks about me. I'm told that in a copper-plate engraving showing Satan tempting Christ in the wilderness he let them put my face on the Tempter. That's the kind of fantasy that often leads him to exaggerated ideas. Our friend Musäus has explained him rather well. . . . What have you read of my books?

DIETMAR: *The Sorrows of Werther.*

GOETHE: What effect did the story of his passion have on you?

DIETMAR: I found his feelings for Lotte so purely human that I forgave him everything he felt, said, and did.

GOETHE: Have you ever been in love yourself?

DIETMAR: I won't deny it. When I was twenty-one I found myself in the company of a beautiful widow who aroused my warmest feelings. But circumstances prevented me from letting her know how I felt. I worshipped her and I only felt good in her presence. But I realized how impossible it was to declare my love.

GOETHE: Was she very beautiful?

DIETMAR: I thought so, and people told me that before she married she was the most beautiful girl in the neighborhood.

GOETHE: Do you know that the heart has secrets about which the mind knows nothing?

DIETMAR: I've often sensed that without being able to put it into words.

GOETHE: Do you know that *le paradis est pour les âmes tendres, et condamnés sont ceux qui n'aiment rien.**

DIETMAR: I'm convinced of that. Still, though love makes people happy, it also brings a great deal of pain and suffering with it. . . . I've memorized a beautiful passage in *Werther* which is my favorite.

GOETHE: And which passage is that?

DIETMAR: "Who would cast the first stone at a maiden who in a moment of rapture forgot herself in the irresistible joy of love? Even the lawgivers themselves, these cold-blooded pedants, are moved to withhold their punishment."

GOETHE: The whole theory of social restraint rests on a flimsy premise of prejudice. There are situations in love in which the heart is eloquent and the tongue silent. Yes, the heart is even afraid to betray its small but violent actions. And so, not to endanger itself, this fearful heart chooses silence, or tries to turn the conversation to trifling and irrelevant matters. . . . I've never yet talked so seriously with a young man who had just finished college.

---

* Paradise is for tender souls, and hell for those who love nothing.

DIETMAR: Forgive me—I'm twenty-seven years old. I began my university studies at Halle rather late.

GOETHE: People passing through Weimar often torture me with long boring visits, and since I'm now working on osteology * I sometimes drag out all my bone specimens to show them. My visitors suddenly become bored with me and respectfully make their departure. . . . I forgot all about my specimens while talking to you.

---

* This was one of his most serious pursuits at the time, leading to the significant discovery of the intermaxillary bone of man and its place in Goethe's pre-Darwinian picture of the common origin of species.

Goethe

2.

HE SHOCKS A YOUNG PROFESSOR OF HISTORY BY DISMISSING THE WHOLE RECORD OF THE PAST AS A TISSUE OF LIES.

Not everything that history offers us has actually happened. And what has actually happened has not happened the way it is presented, and what we know to have happened is only a very small part of what actually happened.

THE SUMMER of 1806 finds Goethe in the university town of Jena, fêted by friends and besieged by admirers. In the record of parties and visits entered in his Tagebuch there seems little foreboding of the bloody catastrophe that will overwhelm the city in two short months. The shadow of Napoleon is drawing closer, and soon Goethe, as aloof from the struggle as ever, will be treating French officers billeted in his home at Weimar with the utmost courtesy. The collapse of Prussia means nothing to him, and Germany remains a myth, at best a "geographical expression." In the talk that follows with Professor Heinrich Luden, Goethe's remarks about history become doubly ironic and significant. One senses the fatalism that is laying hold of Goethe even before the Napoleonic disaster of October. He is retreating more and more into the cynical, supra-mundane realm of Faust, the complete first part of which he is soon to publish.

It is a Goethe contemptuous of recorded history whom we meet in his temporary residence at Jena. And, ironically, it is a young historian-to-be, and an ardent nationalist to boot, who confronts him. Professor Luden's report of the conversation first appeared in his Rückblicke in mein Leben, published in Jena in 1847. Flodoard von Biedermann incorporated it later in the first volume of his collection of Goethe's Gespräche.

Luden was only twenty-six at the time of the interview. He was bubbling over with excitement at the prospect of teaching history at the University of Jena, and perhaps writing it. Goethe, the thinker and author of the already published fragment of Faust—the so-called Urfaust—bulked as the one man in all Germany worthy of his confidence. Like that other young exalté, Dietmar, Luden somewhat bungled the preliminaries out of sheer excess of ardor. On August 10 Luden was invited to meet Goethe at a party in the house of the scholar Karl Ludwig von Knebel. In his elation, as the hour of the meeting approached, the young professor took a long walk to collect his thoughts. The result was that he arrived late and was politely rebuked. Luden then arranged to see Goethe alone, and a second meeting was set for August 19. Confirmation of this meeting is found in the entry for that date in Goethe's own Tagebuch. In my translation of Luden's record of the dialogue I have omitted the earlier portions, devoted largely to a detailed textual analysis of the Urfaust.

I might add that the conversation is the single specimen in Biedermann's ten volumes of Gespräche that measures up to an ideal dialogue in sustained give-and-take. To what extent Luden embellished it for his published memoirs there is no way of determining. Goethe's share certainly rings true when checked against his writings and correspondence and the conversations of others. And in the light of Luden's subsequent patriotic activities, there seems little point in discounting his courage and presumption in standing up to this great adversary. Goethe, in any case, was never the one to stifle frankness, especially in enthusiastic young men.

August 19, 1806—Jena

("Goethe received me with great friendliness, praised my punctuality, and referred to the party of an earlier evening with pleasure. Then he went to the window. 'It's a beautiful day,' he said. 'I think we'll go into the garden.' We went, and strolled up and down and across, and sat down from time to time. . . . Shortly after the conversation began, it occurred to me that Goethe was putting me to the test by adopting a tone of banter. I sensed that from the drift of his questions and objections, which hurt me somewhat since I was then a young man full of enthusiasm for my new profession and hopeful of a brilliant academic future. . . ."—Luden)

GOETHE: So you want to teach history? want to become . . . a historian, or perhaps already are . . . a historian?

LUDEN: My intention is . . . to make an attempt to teach history. Whether I will succeed in awakening any interest is another matter. Moreover, it would be unpardonable arrogance on my part to say that I am a historian. Still, I don't deny it is my dearest wish to deserve that title some day. Certainly I shall not lack perseverance and exertion. Success will be in God's hands.

GOETHE: Why shouldn't you succeed at teaching history? You have a pure, clear-sounding voice. You have good gestures. You will tell a story well. That isn't hard. And who doesn't like to listen to a good story? Children love it, and old men have the same liking or weakness for it. And why should you begrudge yourself the lofty name of historian? Anybody who occupies himself with *historia* is a *historicus*.

LUDEN: Your Excellency's words are not very encouraging for a young man who has resolved to dedicate his life to history as research, as teaching, and as description.

GOETHE: And why aren't they? I thought I was endowing this Holy Trinity of yours with a dazzling brilliance.

LUDEN: A story which makes young and old lend an ear—say the telling of an anecdote—may be a simple affair. Even so, there aren't many people who know how to tell a good story. On the other hand, knowing how to narrate the great and complicated events of history, like those in the lives of whole nations and peoples, is far more difficult and far less common. I am convinced the study of history, because its scope is immeasurable, is the most difficult of all pursuits.

GOETHE: That's your opinion largely because you are devoting so much time to it now. If Mephistopheles were here, he would doubtless, with great pathos, declaim some sort of doggerel like this:—

> *"In my time, too, they bragged and boasted,*
> *And set themselves up high.*
> *When asked whose work was most important,*
> *'My own,' each would reply.*
> *You say the burden that you bear*
> *Requires all your might,*
> *And though the next man sigh and groan,*
> *His load is always light."* *

---

* Luden admits the verses were not quite the way he remembered them. Only the rhymes and the thought were positively Goethe's. I realize the arrogance of putting my own pitiful rendering in Goethe's mouth.—L. B.

> "So war es schon in meinen Tagen:
> Ein jeder schlägt gar hoch sich an,
> Und würdest du sie alle fragen:
> Das Wichtigste hat er getan.
> Es lastet schwer die schwere Last,
> Die selber du zu tragen hast,
> Und ob ein andrer ächzt und keucht,
> Für dich ist seine Bürde leicht."

Certainly the sentiment isn't wholly wrong. And perhaps every philosopher holds his thoughts as the most valid and his system as the only true one for the simple reason that he has gone to such trouble to master and expound them. As regards history, I am frankly of Wagner's * opinion that it is by no means an easy matter to penetrate to original sources, and the number of such sources which must be reached is by no means small. Still, a great deal of preparation has been done and much accomplished. Most of the sources have been probed for some time. What clear water those springs offered has been drained off by now, and only a muddy deposit remains.

LUDEN: Yet it is possible that investigators themselves have muddied the waters, and that once cleared again, they might offer fresh discoveries. Besides there must be many sources still untapped and unexploited.

GOETHE: And if you finally cleared up and thoroughly investigated all possible sources—what would you find? Nothing but a great truth first discovered a long time ago, and the confirmation of which is near at hand. The truth, namely, that at all times and in all places people have been miserable. Men have always suffered and despaired. They have always tortured and martyred one another. They have embittered each other's tiny fragment of life. And they have neither noticed nor enjoyed the beauty of the world about them or the sweetness of life that this magnificent world offered them. A scant few have been happy and comfortable. Most of them, after dragging along for some years, if offered the chance to start again, would have preferred an immediate farewell. Indeed, what has given them and still gives them any attachment to life is merely the fear of death. So it is, and so it has been, and so it will probably continue. That, in short, is man's fate. What further evidence do we need?

LUDEN (*studying Goethe's grave face for a moment, then, half-laughing*): I find it impossible to believe that this is Your Excellency's own opinion. It strikes me that Mephistopheles has said pretty much the same thing. (*Goethe smiles.*) Even if many people have lived that way in past ages and in our own time, that is no proof that men are condemned to such a fate, and the fate of individual men is certainly not the same thing as the fate of mankind.

GOETHE: Mankind? That's an abstraction. From the very beginning there have only been people and there will only be people.

LUDEN: The word signifies, I think, the Spirit of Man as manifested in the collective life of men. And this collective spirit of all the nations and nationalities of the earth is Mankind.

---

* Gottlieb Heinrich Adolf Wagner (1774–1835), philologist and historian.

GOETHE: It is the same thing with nations as with people. Nations consist of people. They come into life, struggle a little longer, to be sure, but in much the same eccentric fashion, and die much the same way, either from some form of violence or from old age and decrepitude. The common distress and mutual torment of men are equally the distress and mutual torment of nations.

LUDEN: But just as men leave later men something of themselves, so nations leave later nations something of themselves that does not die.

GOETHE: They leave something behind? Granted. Mephistopheles would probably express it, after his own fashion, something like this:

> *"What dying nations leave behind*
> *Is but the merest shadowplay;*
> *And even this eludes your grasp,*
> *Though you pursue it night and day." ***

And the rogue might even add good-naturedly:

> *"Whoever tries to catch a shadow*
> *Grasps nothing but the empty air;*
> *He finds himself hemmed in by night*
> *Who raises shadows everywhere." †*

LUDEN: The shadow which a nation throws, whether it flourishes or dies, falls backward, not forward. It falls on earlier nations and not on us, its descendants. What a nation leaves behind, when it does not pass away completely without legacy, is the spirit of its life. We must take pains to appraise this heritage properly and to make good use of it, and not to be satisfied with a mere inventory of our possession. We must study the history of nations and apply its lessons. For the history of a nation is the life of that nation.

GOETHE: The history of a nation—the life of a nation! That *is* bold! Yet how little is contained in the most detailed history of a nation as against its actual life! And of that little how little is true! And of that little that

---

* "Was Völker sterbend hinterlassen,
    Das ist ein bleicher Schattenschlag;
  Du siehst ihn wohl; ihn zu erfassen,
    Läufst du vergeblich Nacht und Tag."
Again I ask the reader's indulgence for allowing Goethe to recite my English rendering.—L. B.

† "Wer immerdar nach Schatten greift,
    Kann stets nur leere Luft erlangen;
  Wer Schatten stets auf Schatten häuft,
    Sieht endlich sich von düstrer Nacht umfangen."

is true, is there not still some shadow of a doubt? Doesn't it all remain uncertain, rather—the large as well as the small? It would seem to bear out Faust's words: "The periods of the past are like a book of seven seals to us." *

LUDEN: Unquestionably, Your Excellency, the poet is quite right, as far as he goes. He would have been wrong, however, if he had added that only one of those seals is breakable.

GOETHE: Perhaps they are breakable, but to break them open we need the right tool, and that we lack.

LUDEN: I prefer to believe that this instrument is not lacking. In fact, we can apply a triple lever to every historical work and every tradition—the knowledge of the period which preceded the period of the particular tradition; the knowledge of the period which follows the period in question and of which it was a product; and finally the truth which every tradition contains in itself, partly from its very existence and partly from its peculiarities of outlook and interpretation. The fulcrum for each of these levers is human nature, while the power is the investigator's own intelligence.

GOETHE: Your expression reminds me that you were singled out by Thibaut † for honors in mathematics. Did you devote much time to this science?

LUDEN: A good many years, considering the circumstances. I've even written a book about mathematics, which I hope soon to send forth into the world, like a lost son.

GOETHE: It makes me marvel still more that you abandoned this first of all sciences, in which all is certainty and truth, to strike out on the high-road of history, where you can stumble at every step, and to work at discovering something which might still remain controversial, despite your three levers. Johannes Müller ‡ must have prevailed on you to make this change.

LUDEN: To be sure, he did exert a great influence on me. He helped me make my decision sooner. Yet, even without him, I would have decided in favor of history. And then my circumstances did not permit me to enjoy or to be edified by the contemplation of the wonders of creation, or to rejoice in applying my theoretical knowledge solely to earthly matters. Finally, I must confess that this constant association with numbers, letters, and figures, brought about what Mephistopheles prophe-

---

* "Die Zeiten der Vergangenheit
  Sind uns ein Buch von sieben Siegeln."
† B. F. Thibaut, mathematician.
‡ Historian and state official (1752–1809).

sied to the student in his godlike striving: I was seized with a terror of all truth and certainty.

GOETHE: So history, with all its uncertainty, gives you more satisfaction than the truth of mathematics?

LUDEN: Exactly! History is equally satisfying to the mind and heart, to the understanding and the emotions, and awakens the imagination. It is a stimulus to thought and no less a stimulus to creative activity. Frankly I no longer know why a historical truth is less true than a mathematical truth.

GOETHE: Granted that the only condition is to establish the truth. If historical truth could be demonstrated like mathematical truth, all differences would disappear. As long as that cannot be done, the differences will remain, not between two actual truths, but between that which is demonstrably true and that which is true only by assumption.

LUDEN: Actual history is actual truth.

GOETHE: But not everything that history offers us has actually happened. And what has actually happened has not happened the way it is presented, and what we know to have happened is only a very small part of what actually happened. No doubt you know why Sir Walter Raleigh never finished his history, but threw the manuscript into the fire.

LUDEN: I do, Your Excellency. He did, as the anecdote says....

GOETHE: He said so himself.

LUDEN: That I did not know. For I must confess that I have read nothing of Sir Walter's. In any case, he threw the manuscript into the fire because some people who had witnessed the same event he had differed so widely from him in giving an account of it.

GOETHE: That same thing has often happened to many of us, and it will be no different in the future.

LUDEN: The only thing that surprises me is that Sir Walter required a special experience to make the discovery that any object will be differently described by different men. The old proverb: *Duo, quum faciunt idem,* which applies as much to observing and reporting as to acting, should have taught him this great truth. Reading several historians who had described the same event would have also confirmed it. So, I feel he should either have continued his history or never have begun it.

GOETHE: Sir Walter knew for a long time what we all know. He had been doubtless following the same humdrum route. But the day he witnessed that occurrence in front of his house with his own eyes and then heard all the other untrue versions of it, the thought suddenly struck him that there was no such thing as truth in history. Angry and depressed, he resolved at once to stop aiding the spread and continuance of this fraud and refused to give his contemporaries a false and mendacious picture of the world of the past.

LUDEN: He must have had a strange conception of the truth of history. For it goes without saying that the historian can have no more information about past events than has been handed down. So long as he honestly examines this information and honestly passes it on, he is innocent of any deception.

GOETHE: But the deception remains. He is not the originator of the lie but its perpetuator, not the thief, but the receiver of stolen goods. The lie only falls on the writers of your so-called source-material.

LUDEN: Yet if those same writers have honestly reported what they witnessed or what came to their knowledge, they are no less innocent of deceit and lying. They could not give more than they had to give.

GOETHE: The lie still remains. It is merely thrown back one more step—thrown back to the event itself, and this always reaches us in a distorted, untrue, false, and oblique picture of the past. It would be better not to concern ourselves with history at all than to carry about with us such a false and therefore useless and confusing conception of it. This could only lead to our misunderstanding even of the world of our own time and, thus perverted, exert our influence upon it.

LUDEN: If that were so, it would be bad indeed. Yet it would still be in keeping with the destiny of man, and we would have to endure it. But it is not so. The divergences we find in accounts of the same event cannot be hastily dismissed as false testimony. They stem, rather, from the fact that someone has understood an event differently from someone else. The historian must first sift the various accounts of the circumstances surrounding the event in question and apply a critical technique in assessing their true worth. He must compare them with one another and in relation to available facts. He must test them by his knowledge of the condition and nature of the country, of the relation of nations and peoples to one another, of previous and subsequent history, of the internal political situation, and of the character and opinions of the main actors of the drama. Then all uncertainty will vanish, and the truth will reveal itself as a mass of nerves, fibers, muscles, marrow, and skin found to fit the given skeleton of fact. And to this his creative spirit and artistic hand will now give living shape.

GOETHE: That would certainly be quite an operation! But what the historian, after such agony, would call the truth, is that only for him, in other words, is merely subjective truth. Objective truth does not exist.

LUDEN: Fichte once answered Pilate's question "What is truth?" with these words: the truth is what is necessarily thought to be the truth because it is so thought, and what simply could not be thought otherwise.

GOETHE: Thought, namely, by Fichte or by me. So each of us has his own special truth. Mathematical truth, however, is the same for everyone.

LUDEN: Fichte illustrates his statement with mathematical examples. Two times two is four, because it is impossible to think of the matter otherwise, so long as we know what is meant by "two" and "four." Fichte says he could not help laughing when it was first demonstrated to him that four units, no longer thought of as separated, but united, also made four. For that, he reasoned, is self-evident and could not be thought otherwise. And so everything which cannot be thought otherwise inevitably becomes generally accepted as the truth the moment it becomes generally understood.

GOETHE: That only bears out my point. For there is this difference: mathematics forces everyone to acknowledge that all right angles are equal, whereas in historical matters you can never force me to be of your opinion.

LUDEN: No, but I still believe that I can convince anyone of the truth who has not already resolved not to be convinced. That seems preferable to me. The mathematician compels men to accept the truth of his statements. He subjects men's minds to a positive fatalism in which no freedom of decision is possible. The historian leaves the mind free. He appeals to the whole man—to the understanding, the heart, the emotions—and desires only that the conviction of his audiences be free.

GOETHE: One does not necessarily oppose that principle by believing that the march of history is not quite what some historian has represented it to be or as it could ever be represented. And so long as this is the case, it is our privilege to accuse history of error and regard its traditions as false.

LUDEN: There is no doubt that even the most learned, sincerest, most keen-minded and gifted historian may fall into error, because he too must bear his share of the common destiny of man. In any case, what I seek in historical writing is not dead, bare, and precise reality, but a living and colorful world which offers indubitable facts without alteration or distortion, yet facts creatively interpreted and artistically treated.

GOETHE: You regard the historian as a poet, then.

LUDEN: Since I have not accomplished anything yet as a historian, I think I may express myself freely. For I am not speaking *pro domo sua.** I firmly believe that good history cannot be written without a true sense of poetry, and that no one can be a historian, in the best sense of the

---

* "For my own cause" (literally "house").

word, who lacks creative or poetic power. For he must bring before his eyes the world of the past in which the events he proposes to describe occurred. Only in the contemplation of that world can he describe such events and give them true and full significance. That world, however, is not offered for his contemplation. He must create it himself in order to contemplate it.

GOETHE: Even if one were to grant that, there would still be a great differ-ence between the poet and the historian. The poet creates his world freely, after his own idea, and for that reason he can present it as com-plete and perfect. The historian is shackled, for he must so construct his world that all the pieces which history leaves behind fit. He can never really give us a perfect work, for the strain of searching and gath-ering, of patching and gluing together, is always apparent.

LUDEN: The greater the task a historian sets himself and the more difficult his work, the more a successful history deserves gratitude, honor and appreciation and a less successful one leniency and indulgence. Then it should not be overlooked that while the poet only expresses his own ideas in all the depth and scope of his own genius, the historian has to express the idea of God as manifested in the life of man.

GOETHE: You therefore put the historian above the poet. . . .

LUDEN: Certainly not, Your Excellency! I have never subscribed to the habit of placing geniuses on a step-ladder, one higher than the other. I prefer to believe that genius moves on one level rather than on several. In any case, I feel that no one should begrudge high rank to a historian who achieves excellence in his field.

GOETHE: If I am to draw any conclusions from your remarks about his-torical writing and research, it would seem to me Faust was right when he said:

"What we have named the spirit of the times,
Is but the spirit of the lords and masters
In which the times are mirrored." *

LUDEN: I agree with that classical dictum wholly. Yet, if the lords and mas-ters hand down this spirit, even if it is only their own, and if they reveal the times to us in this same mirror of the spirit, we have some cause for satisfaction.

GOETHE: Perhaps—but one more question. What do you finally hope to accomplish with all these historical truths and errors and creative com-

---

* "Was man den Geist der Zeiten heisst,
 Das ist im Grund der Herren eigner Geist,
 In dem die Zeiten sich bespiegeln."

positions? What is the ultimate goal of your studies and your exertions?

LUDEN: That's a big question, Your Excellency, one that would require a long and detailed reply. To answer it briefly, however, I can think of nothing better than the words of Faust:—

> *"Within my inner self shall I perceive*
> *Whatever has been granted to mankind."* *

GOETHE: You mean "enjoy," rather than "perceive."

LUDEN: If you will be so kind, Your Excellency—I insist on the word "perceive," and will rest content with whatever enjoyment such perception might yield. But I should then want to impart this "perception" to others by teaching and writing. Needless to say, I have been speaking only of my own hopes and wishes. Only a very small part of fulfillment lies in man's hands. But, then, *in magnis et voluisse sat est.*†

GOETHE: Yes, yes. We have material for many more conversations. But it is rather late. I'm afraid we must stop for now.

LUDEN: I can't tell you with what feelings I leave, Your Excellency. Our first meeting that evening filled me with the greatest joy, and in this same spirit I came to you this morning. During the conversation, however, a shadow began to fall on my happy mood. I could not dispel it, and now that I am leaving Your Excellency it is beginning to embarrass me dreadfully.

GOETHE: My dear boy, just what do you mean?

LUDEN: When I accepted the appointment to Jena, the thought naturally occurred to me that a happiness would now be mine which I had long yearned for—the happiness of being near you, of seeing you, and of speaking to you. And yet I could not escape a certain dread in thinking of the fulfillment of my hope. Mixed with my desire and my veneration of the first of poets was a frightful timidity. I was afraid that the moment I was introduced, I would act like a drunkard in your presence—confused, helpless, clumsy, and idiotic. But the other evening all my embarrassment vanished in a flash. So quickly, in fact, that I fear I went to the other extreme. And I fear the same thing now—that I have spoken today as I should not have spoken. I don't know how it happened, but I found myself becoming very talkative. I began to feel that it was very wrong and that once having begun I would never know how to stop. I feel certain Your Excellency did not mind whatever I said that was merely erroneous. But I implore you with all my heart and

---

* "Was der ganzen Menschheit zugeteilt ist,
   Will ich in meinem innern Selbst erkennen."
† "In great things even to have had the will is sufficient."—Propertius.

humility to forgive me for saying anything that was improper and offensive.

GOETHE: My dear professor, you can rest assured on that point. We spoke quite frankly with one another, in earnest and in jest. I don't know what either of us should reproach the other for. Our conversation interested me, and entertained me, too; otherwise it would not have lasted so long. In you I found a young man who wishes to see clearly, who does not let himself be confused by hallowed words, nor misled by delusions. You are striving eagerly for the truth, without being insensible to poetry, for you seem able to endure even its illusory images. That is praiseworthy and good. In your scientific pursuits you seem also to be on the right path. Go on with your work, living in history and boldly examining the past undisturbed by the confusions of the present. Search relentlessly through the Yearbooks of the Nations. Communicate honestly and straightforwardly, without any prejudice, what you have found in your researches and believe to be true. In your descriptions follow no set model and resist any temptation to adopt that strained and hammer-blow style which might remind people of Johannes Müller, who is himself only an imitator of Tacitus. Above all, don't become a victim of the tastelessness of the time, and for the would-be wisdom precociously expounded in the so-called literary journals have nothing but contempt. Write, rather, clearly and simply. Don't shy away from poetic fancy, and prefer an easy-going style to that cramped brevity which people are in the habit of calling *schlagend"* * and which is so highly admired. Generations to come will like you if you have to bear the slurs of your contemporaries. In any event, I expect great good to come from your appointment to Jena—for yourself and for the University. And·now (*offering his hand*) my very best wishes and *Auf Wiedersehen!*

(*Professor Luden leaves. He has not gone more than a few steps when Goethe calls out to him. The professor turns sharply about and approaches Goethe, inquiringly.*)

GOETHE: When I asked you to visit me in Weimar, I forgot to add, don't go to an inn but stop at my house. There will always be a place at the table for you, and whenever you can or want to stay overnight in Weimar, you will also find a bed. And so, once again, my very best wishes!

(*An impassioned sequel to the above conversation occurs seven years later in Weimar. For the Luden who comes to pay his respects on December 13, 1813, is a changed and still more forceful man, a revolu-*

---

* "Striking" in the literal sense of delivering blows.

tionary and pamphleteer against Napoleon. Contrastingly, the intervening years have made Goethe even more fatalistic. He turns a deaf ear to Luden's pleas for political action, disapproves of the anti-French journal which Luden is planning and urges him to go back to teaching history—advice that strikes us as ironic after overhearing the Goethe of 1806 rebuking Luden for giving up mathematics for the tissue of lies that was history. "Ich denke nur an meine Ruhe und Ihr Wohl," * Goethe remarks. Yet he convinces Luden of one thing—that, for all his despair and fatalism, he loves Germany deeply. Completely shaken by the encounter, Luden leaves Goethe in tears. Since Luden's record of the later meeting in Weimar is largely a monologue, it disqualifies itself for inclusion in this book.)

---

* "I'm thinking only of my peace of mind and your welfare."

Goethe

3.

A MUSICAL GATHERING AT WEIMAR FEATURING
A TWELVE-YEAR-OLD UNKNOWN—FELIX
MENDELSSOHN-BARTHOLDY.

Go down into the garden and cool off!
You are burning like fire!

W E PAUSE here for a short musical interlude. The date is November 8, 1821; the place is again Weimar, specifically the drawing-room of Privy Councillor Goethe. Early in the afternoon three members of the string section of the Weimar Court Orchestra, among them the violinist Johann Christian Lobe, are admitted by a servant and led upstairs to the drawing-room. Rather mysteriously they have been invited by Goethe to take part in the performance of a piano quartet. The name of the composer, who will himself play the piano part, has not been mentioned.

In the drawing-room the musicians find three music-desks, and beside them an open piano, ready for use. On the piano lies a roll of music manuscript which Lobe, more inquisitive than his two colleagues, proceeds to leaf through. He finds, first, a set of "Studies in Double Counterpoint"; then a set of "Fugues," next a sheaf of "Canons," and finally a Piano Quartet. Lobe lingers over the name appearing on the first page of each of these manuscripts—Felix Mendelssohn-Bartholdy. Neither he nor any of his colleagues has ever seen or heard the name before. Yet a quick glance through the Quartet, written in a "dainty but firm" hand, convinces Lobe that this is the workmanship of a soundly trained artist.[*]

As the musicians begin tuning their instruments, the door opens and a tall man in his middle sixties enters. It is Professor Carl Friedrich Zelter, composer and director of the famous Singing Academy of Berlin. As young Felix's teacher, Zelter has arranged the boy's visit to Weimar.

---

[*] As we do not know even the key of this early work of Mendelssohn's, there is no way of telling whether it is one of the many juvenilia which were destroyed. It is interesting to note, however, that Opus 1, 2, and 3—the first published works of Mendelssohn—are all piano quartets and that Opus 2 is dedicated to Professor Zelter and Opus 3 to Goethe.

What follows is a translation of Lobe's recollection of the session, which first appeared as "Ein Quartet bei Goethe" in 1867 and was later reprinted by Biedermann in Goethe's Gespräche (1889–1896).

Confirmation of the Weimar visit is found in a highly precocious letter of Mendelssohn's of November 10. In it we see quite clearly that the twelve-year-old prodigy and the seventy-two-year-old Titan hit it off beautifully, with Goethe continually kissing the boy, stroking his hair, and pointing to the piano with the words: "I have not yet heard you today— now make a little noise for me." It is a pity that in Lobe's little drama Mendelssohn's part is all dumb-show. We should have preferred a few words from him about his quartet before he obeyed Goethe and ran back into the garden to "cool off." But the humble court violinist has done his best to recapture a moment in the briefly linked lives of a budding genius of music and an aging colossus of thought. Who are we to chastise Lobe for his sins of omission? He could very well have left no record at all of the afternoon musicale in Goethe's drawing-room.

We return to Professor Zelter. . . .

ZELTER (*greeting the three musicians like old friends*): Gentlemen, before we begin, I should like to make a request. You are going to meet a twelve-year-old boy, my pupil Felix Mendelssohn-Bartholdy. His skill as pianist and even more his talent as composer will probably arouse your enthusiasm. Now this boy has a very peculiar nature. The loud cheering of dilettantes leaves him cold. But he listens very eagerly to the statements of musicians and takes them all literally. For children are naturally too unsophisticated to distinguish at all times between well-meant encouragement and deserved recognition. So, gentlemen, if you feel prompted to sing his praises—which is something I always wish and fear at the same time—do so in *tempo moderato* in the least colored key of C major, and not too noisily orchestrated. Until now I have kept him from vanity and self-importance, those accursed enemies of all artistic progress.

(*Before the musicians can answer, Goethe and Mendelssohn enter the room.*)

GOETHE (*returning the bow of his visitors*): My friend (*pointing to Zelter*) has brought a young Berliner * with him. Today he astonished us greatly as a virtuoso. Now we are going to become acquainted with him

---

* Mendelssohn was a native of Hamburg; his family moved to Berlin when he was three years old.

as composer, for which I ask your co-operation. So, now,, my son, let's hear what your young head has produced. (*Goethe strokes Mendelssohn's long locks.*)

(*"Felix dashes over to his roll of notebooks, places the string parts on the music stands and his own principal part on the piano, and then quickly takes his place at the keyboard. Zelter stands behind Felix, ready to turn pages. Goethe remains a few steps to one side, his hand on his hip. The little composer gives us a fiery look, we ready our bows, and at a signal from him, the playing begins. Goethe listens to each movement with the most excited attention, without making any special comments, other than a "Good!" after the first movement, and a "Bravo!," accompanied by a friendly nod, after the second movement. Keeping Zelter's warning in mind, we too confined our reactions to the delighted expressions on our faces. During the performance the boy's face grew redder and redder. When the last movement ended, he sprang from his seat and gave us all a questioning look. He seemed to be eager to hear something about his music."*—Lobe)

GOETHE: Excellent, my son! Bravo! The expressions on the faces of these gentlemen (*pointing to the musicians*) indicate quite clearly that they like your composition. Now go down into the garden—they are waiting for you—and cool off. You are burning like fire!

(*Without further ado Felix rushes out of the room. The musicians make a motion to leave.*)

GOETHE: Please don't go yet, gentlemen! My friend Zelter and I would like your opinion of this boy's composition. I'm sorry you could only hear him in a quartet today. . . . Child prodigies are no longer a rarity nowadays, at least in technical facility. But the ability of this little man in sight-reading and improvisation borders on the miraculous. I would have never thought it possible in one so young.

ZELTER: And yet you heard Mozart in Frankfurt when he was only seven years old.

GOETHE: That's true. I was then twelve years old myself. Like everyone else I was completely amazed by his extraordinary skill. But what your pupil can do, compared to what Mozart could then do, is like the cultivated speech of a grown-up beside the babbling of a child.

ZELTER (*laughing*): To be sure, when it comes to quickness of finger. . . . Take those concertos with which Mozart used to astonish the people of his day. Felix runs them off at sight as the simplest playthings, without ever missing a single note. Still, there are many others who can do that today. What I'm interested in is the boy's creative ability. (*Turn-*

ing to the three musicians) Well, gentlemen, what did you think of the quartet?

(*"We all expressed our sincere conviction that Felix showed more individual thinking than Mozart at the same age, and that Mozart's music of the time was little more than a clever imitation of existing models. We agreed that in this boy the world might one day behold a second Mozart, in an enlarged edition—the more so because he enjoyed such wonderful health and all the outside circumstances were so favorable."*—Lobe)

GOETHE: I sincerely hope it will be that way! But who can predict how a gift will develop? We have seen so many highly promising talents strike out on false paths. Our greatest expectations have brought only disappointment. In the meantime, this young genius is in good hands.

ZELTER: I am going about it very seriously with this boy. With all his freedom of outside composition, I still insist on a rigorous study of counterpoint. But how long can that last? Soon he will outgrow my discipline. Actually, there is very little I can still teach him. And once he is free, we shall know for sure what his real direction is.

GOETHE: Yes. After all, the influence of a teacher is always problematical. What makes an artist great and individual must be created out of himself. To which teachers did Raphael, Michelangelo, Haydn, Mozart, and all the great masters, owe their immortal creations?

ZELTER: You're absolutely right. Many have begun like Mozart but no one has yet caught up with him.

Goethe

4.

AN OLYMPIAN OF WORLD LITERATURE TURNS HIS GAZE ON HIS OWN COUNTRYMEN, AND ON THREE GREAT POETS—VOLTAIRE, BYRON, AND HIMSELF.

The Germans cannot stop being Philistines!

It is very likely that if a sickly, impecunious young man named Johann Peter Eckermann had not walked from Göttingen to Weimar at the end of May, 1823, he would barely have earned a footnote in German literature. A few poems, some essays, one unsuccessful play, and a degree at the University of Jena would scarcely have rescued him from a speedy oblivion. But this lowly son of a yarn-vendor of Hamburg made the journey to Weimar and his name entered the annals of world literature. Out of this visit were to come several lucrative appointments in the ducal court, and something far more important—a book that in a few decades would become one of the most widely translated classics of the nineteenth century. This was the Gespräche mit Goethe, the Conversations with Goethe, that will forever link the name of this obscure student to that of Germany's greatest writer.

Only one thought drew Eckermann to Weimar: to be near the great man and to serve him in whatever capacity he might be useful. Perhaps he came in time. For Goethe had begun to sink into a deep gloom. His friends of many years were dying off. His health had begun to suffer, and a last spurt of romantic passion had met with a humiliating rebuff from a twenty-one-year-old girl named Ulrike von Levetzow. Goethe was seventy-four and all the mature wisdom and cynicism of his years were now finding their way into the second part of Faust. "The gods had doomed him for the time being to intensified loneliness," wrote Brandes, "and to increased mental activity, not in communion with men who were approximately his equals and from whom he could learn, but with his spiritual inferiors; with those who, faithfully receiving, seized with avidity and preserved the thoughts and ideas that come to him as a result of conversation. The gods doomed him, in other words, to conversation with Eckermann."

These are harsh words. An "inferior" Eckermann undoubtedly was; yet who was not in Goethe's presence? Moreover, this young disciple proved to be precisely the man Goethe needed. He was a careful secretary and editor; he was widely read; and best of all, he was a magnificent listener with a magnificent memory. And Eckermann had the goodness—which, according to Brandes, "somewhat vitiates the impression for us"—to submit his conversational jottings to Goethe for approval. Heine was only half right in calling him a parrot, for, like Boswell, Eckermann used some artistic selectivity in preparing the dialogues for publication. And like Boswell he often let the material ferment for days before writing down the essence that remained in his mind.

Eckermann was with Goethe from 1823 to his death in 1832; for long periods almost daily. "Wherever I went, wherever I remained, in my walks and in my daily affairs he was in my thoughts," Eckermann tells us of those years. "Even at night he entered into my dreams." One can only agree with Havelock Ellis that this enchanted young man "was sensitively alive to Goethe." In another personal avowal Eckermann touchingly states that his relation to Goethe was "very peculiar, and of a very intimate kind: it was that of the scholar to the master; of the son to the father; of the poor in culture to the rich in culture." Of these conversations with Goethe, Eckermann printed three volumes, the first two in 1836 (having given his word not to publish the material in Goethe's lifetime) and the third in 1848. It was not easy to make a choice from Eckermann. His best "conversations" are really soliloquies and many of the sustained dialogues are crammed with material about archery, the theory of colors, and German researches in Greek drama that has either lost interest for us or has been superseded by later findings. The following dialogue seemed to be the best—or at least one of the best—for the purposes of this book.

The date is December 16, 1828. Eckermann has been dining with Goethe alone, in his workroom. They have been discussing "various literary matters" and the talk now turns to the Xenien,* a collection of stinging distichs which Goethe and Schiller had brought out together in 1796 as a series of thrusts at the literary Philistines of the time. Each of the satiric couplets had carried their joint authorship, so the scholarly game was on to tell Schiller's share apart from Goethe's—a game that,

---

* A term borrowed from the Latin epigrammatist Martial, meaning, in Greek, "presents given to guests."

despite Goethe's scornful remarks, has never ceased. But let us hear Goethe himself on the subject.

GOETHE: The Germans cannot stop being Philistines. They are now grumbling and quarreling about some verses which are printed both in Schiller's works and mine. They regard it as highly important to determine which really belong to Schiller and which to me. As if anything could be gained from that. As if the existence of such things were not enough. Friends like Schiller and myself, intimate for years, with the same interests, in daily contact and mutual indebtedness, live so completely *into* one another that it is hardly possible to decide to which of the two any particular thoughts belong. We collaborated on many verses. Sometimes I supplied the thought, and Schiller the verse. Sometimes it was the other way around. Sometimes he wrote one verse, and I the next. What does it matter now, all this business of this is mine and this is yours? One must be a thorough-going Philistine, indeed, to attach the slightest importance to clearing up such doubts.

ECKERMANN: Something similar often happens in the literary world, when people, for instance, doubt the originality of this or that well-known writer, and try to trace the sources of his inspiration.

GOETHE: That's all quite ridiculous. We might as well question a well-nourished man about the oxen, sheep, and swine he has eaten to determine the sources of his strength. We come into the world with certain faculties. But we owe our development to the thousand influences of a great world. Of these we assimilate what we can and what suits us. I owe much to the Greek and the French. I am endlessly indebted to Shakespeare, Sterne, and Goldsmith. Yet I have by no means indicated the sources of my inspiration. That would lead us into a boundless realm and would hardly be necessary. The main thing is to have a soul that loves truth and accepts it wherever it finds it. Besides, the world is now so old, and so many eminent men have lived and thought for thousands of years, that there is very little to find and say that is new. Even my theory of colors is not entirely new. Plato, Leonardo da Vinci, and many other excellent men found and said the same thing in separate details long before me. But that I too found it, that I said it again, and that I strove to bring the truth once more into a confused world—that was my contribution. The truth must be repeated over and over again, because error is always being preached around us, indeed not by individuals but by large groups. In periodicals and cyclopedias, in schools and universities, everywhere, in fact, error has the upper hand and is quite comfortable in the feeling that the majority is on its side. Often, too, people teach truth and error together, and cling to the latter. A short time ago I read in an English encyclopedia the doctrine of the origin of Blue. First came the correct view of Leonardo da Vinci. But then followed, with the calmest assurance, the Newtonian error, accompanied, moreover, by the remark that this was the doctrine to adhere to because it was the generally accepted view.

ECKERMANN (*laughing*): Every wax candle, every illuminated cloud of kitchen-smoke that has anything dark behind it, every morning mist when it lies before a shady spot, convinces me daily of the origin of the color blue and teaches me to grasp the blueness of the sky. What the Newtonians mean when they say that the air has the power to absorb all other colors, and of repelling blue alone, is completely beyond me. And I can't see what possible use or pleasure is to be derived from a doctrine in which every thought remains static and every healthy perception vanishes completely.

GOETHE: Innocent soul that you are! These people do not bother about thoughts and perceptions. They are satisfied so long as they have the words at their disposal. Even Mephistopheles knew this and did not express it so badly:—

> "*Above all else rely on words;*
> *Then you can pass through the safe gate*
> *Into the temple of all certainty,*
> *Where even when ideas are wanting,*
> *A timely word will serve as well.*" *

(*laughing*) It is a good thing that all of it is already in print. And I shall go on printing as long as I have anything to say against false doctrines and those who propound them. (*After a long pause*) Excellent men are emerging in the natural sciences, and I observe them with joy. Others begin well, but soon lose out. Their powerful subjective drive leads them astray. Others, again, bank too much on facts, collect a vast number of them and prove nothing. On the whole, the theorizing spirit to probe basic phenomena and to master particular appearances is lacking.

---

* "Vor allem haltet euch an Worte!
  Dann geht ihr durch die sichre Pforte
  Zum Tempel der Gewissheit ein;
  Denn eben wo Begriffe fehlen,
  Da stellt ein Wort zur rechten Zeit sich ein . . ."

("A short visit interrupted our conversation. When we were alone again the talk turned to poetry. I told Goethe I was again reading his shorter poems, and had lingered over two of them in particular: the ballad * about the children and the old man, and 'The Happy Couple.' " † —Eckermann)

GOETHE: I am myself rather fond of these two poems, though the German public has not yet been able to make much out of them.

ECKERMANN: In the ballad a very rich subject is compressed into a narrow compass, by means of all sorts of poetic forms and devices. I especially like the way the old man is made to tell the children the story down to the moment of the poem, allowing the rest to unfold before our eyes.

GOETHE: I carried the ballad around with me a long time before I wrote it down. Years of reflection went into it, and I made three or four trials before I succeeded in making it what it is.

ECKERMANN: The poem of "The Happy Couple" is also rich in *motifs*. Whole landscapes and spans of human life appear in it, warmed through by the sunlight of a charming spring sky, spreading itself over the whole.

GOETHE: I have always liked that poem, and I am happy to see you showing special interest in it. Ending the joke with a double christening is pretty enough, I daresay.

ECKERMANN: I was reading the *Citizen General* ‡ with an Englishman recently and we both felt the strongest desire to see it on the stage. Nothing has aged in the spirit of the work, and in the details of dramatic development there is not a touch that was not designed for the stage.

GOETHE: It was a very good play in its time, and it provided us with many a pleasant evening. To be sure, it was excellently cast, and was so well rehearsed that the dialogue moved along in liveliest fashion. Malcolmi played the part of Märten. You never saw anything more perfect.

ECKERMANN: The part of Schnaps seems equally good to me. I should think the whole repertory offers few better and more thankful roles. There is a clearness, an actual presence, to this character, as in the whole play, highly desirable in the theater. The scene where he comes in with the knapsack and produces the things one after another, and then puts the mustache on Märten and decks himself with the liberty-cap, uniform, and sword, is among the best.

GOETHE: That scene used to be very successful on our stage. It so happens that the knapsack with the articles in it actually had a history. I found

---

* Entitled "Ballade," and begins *"Herein, O du Guter! du Alter herein!"*
† *"Die Glücklichen Gatten."*
‡ *Der Bürgergeneral.*

it during the Revolution, on my travels along the French border, then overrun with emigrants. One such emigrant might have lost it or thrown it away. The articles it contained were the same as those shown in the play. I wrote the scene around it, and the actual knapsack, with all appurtenances, always played its little part, to the delight of our actors, whenever the play was given. (*After a pause*) ... Tell me, now, how are your studies in French literature progressing?

ECKERMANN: I still take up Voltaire from time to time. His great talent gives me endless pleasure. I still know very little of his works. I'm confining myself to the small circle of his short poems addressed to various persons. I read them over and over again, and I can't break away from them.

GOETHE: To be sure, anything a great genius like Voltaire writes is good, though I cannot excuse all the liberties he takes. But you are quite right in lingering over those little poems addressed to persons. They are among the most charming things he ever wrote. There is not a line that is not full of wit, clarity, good cheer, and grace.

ECKERMANN: And one notes his relations to the great and mighty of the earth and is pleased to watch him take his rightful position among them. He seems to feel equal to the highest, and the presence of majesty never overawes his free mind for a moment.

GOETHE: Yes, he was an extraordinary man. With all his freedom and audacity he always kept within the limits of decency, which is perhaps saying still more. I may cite the Empress of Austria as an authority in such matters. She has repeatedly assured me that in those poems of Voltaire's there is not the slightest hint that he ever overstepped the bounds of good taste.

ECKERMANN: Does Your Excellency remember the short poem in which he makes to the Princess of Prussia, afterwards Queen of Sweden, a charming declaration of love, by saying that he dreamed of being raised to royal rank?

GOETHE: It is one of his very best (*reciting the lines*):

> "*Je vous aimais, princesse, et j'osais vous le dire;*
> *Les Dieux à mon réveil ne m'ont pas tout ôté,*
> *Je n'ai perdu que mon empire.*" *

How exquisite that is! And no poet ever had his talent so completely at his command at all times as Voltaire. I remember an anecdote of his

---

* "I loved you, princess, and I was bold enough to tell you;
 When I awoke the gods did not take everything away.
 I only lost my empire."

visit to Madame du Châtelet. Just as he was going away, and the carriage was standing at the door, he received a letter from some young girls in a neighboring convent. They wished to play the *Death of Julius Caesar* on the birthday of their abbess, and begged Voltaire to write a prologue for them. The situation was too delicate for a refusal. So Voltaire at once called for pen and paper, and standing, wrote the desired prologue on the edge of a mantelpiece. It is a poem of some twenty lines, thoroughly thought out and complete, and perfectly suited to the occasion. In short, of the very best.

ECKERMANN: I am very eager to read it.

GOETHE: I doubt whether it is in your collection. It only recently turned up. Indeed, Voltaire wrote hundreds of such poems, of which many may be still hidden away among private possessions.

ECKERMANN: A few days ago I found a passage in Lord Byron in which I was pleased to see that even he had an extraordinary esteem for Voltaire. His works show how much he likes to read, study, and make use of Voltaire.

GOETHE: Byron knew too well where anything was to be had and was too clever not to draw from this universal source of light.

ECKERMANN (*referring to Goethe's repeated expressions of admiration*): I agree wholeheartedly with what Your Excellency says of Byron. But, however great and significant he may be as a talent, I doubt very much whether any decided gain for *pure human culture* results from his writings.

GOETHE: There I must contradict you. The audacity and grandeur of Byron—don't they make for culture? We should take care not to be forever seeking culture in the absolutely pure and moral. Everything that is great promotes culture the moment we become aware of its greatness.

Goethe

5.

HE TELLS AN ENGLISH MUNITIONS MANUFACTURER THAT ROCKETS WOULD HAVE PROVED USEFUL TO SATAN IN *PARADISE LOST.*

In any case, it would have been more poetic.

N‌O ACCOUNT of Eckermann's famous conversations with Goethe can be complete without a few words about Frédéric Soret. Some three years Eckermann's junior, this young Swiss painter and teacher joined the Weimar circle in 1824 as private tutor of the Crown Prince Charles Alexander. Like Eckermann, Soret came to know Goethe intimately, and the three of them often engaged in long conversations in Goethe's home. Perhaps in partial emulation of Eckermann, Soret began keeping a record of these dialogues in his native French. Though a mere handful, they are often superior to Eckermann's in frankness: unlike Eckermann, Soret did not show his notes to Goethe. Later, the obliging Swiss turned over all his material to Eckermann, who not only checked it against his but graciously allowed Soret to appear as partial collaborator in the third volume of the conversations, which was issued in 1848. Eckermann, of course, translated Soret's conversations into German, a neat little reverse process of restoring them to their original language. Biedermann, always the scrupulously exact scholar, quotes them in French from the manuscript of Soret's journal, *Conversations avec Goethe,* in the Weimar archives. It is from Biedermann's ten-volume *Gespräche* that the following selections have been translated.

On April 28, 1825 two Englishmen arrived in Weimar with the idea of paying their respects to Goethe. Being scientists and inventors, they naturally knew of Goethe's brilliant achievements in optics, metallurgy, and other fields. One of these Englishmen was Sir William Congreve, ballistics expert whose invention of the "Congreve rocket" during the Napoleonic wars made him famous. The other was the equally gifted John Frederic Daniell, a chemist and physicist, whose name survives in the "Daniell cell" in telegraphy and as the inventor of an instrument for gauging humidity in the atmosphere. It is probably this "Daniell hygrometer" that Congreve alludes to, in the course of the conversation, as having been useful to Goethe. For meteorology was another of Goethe's innumerable scientific pursuits. In any case, science proves only an opening for the brief dialogue that follows. The Englishmen obviously prefer to hear Goethe on the subject of Lord Byron, and Goethe, a great admirer of the English poet, is only too eager to oblige. The interview occurs in Goethe's house. Soret, who has brought the visitors over to be introduced, has left us the following record. . . .

CONGREVE: You doubtless know Mr. Daniell better than you know me. At least you've made use of his apparatus. But of what use could my rockets be to you?

GOETHE: They don't interest me any the less because I have no use for them in my particular profession.

CONGREVE: Walter Scott once told me that if Milton had known about them, he would have put them into the hands of the devils for the siege of heaven.

GOETHE: That would have been just the weapon for them. Perhaps these gentlemen might have succeeded better in their undertaking.

CONGREVE: In any case, it would have been more poetic. . . . Byron seems to have been a good deal on your mind. You must admit, however, that though he died quite young, he still died too old for his fame.

GOETHE: I don't share your opinion at all. Even his last works, where he let his ardor carry him away, show the imprint of his genius. It is quite obvious he wrote out of the heat of the moment—with extreme speed. They are, if you will, extravagances, but sublime extravagances.

CONGREVE: You're quite right about his always being in a great hurry.

GOETHE: Not always. His *Doge of Venice* must have entailed long study and preparation. He spent three years in that city. Clearly he went to the trouble of making a deep and thorough study of the place. *Sardanapalus* is full of thoughtful beauty, and I could cite other works in which reflection has provided real body to imaginative fantasy. You see, we Germans are greatly interested in Byron's poetry. Byron is one of our favorites, and we see only the poet in him. We leave England the job of finding grievances against him. That is none of our affair.

CONGREVE: Yet you unquestionably like Walter Scott as well?

GOETHE: We like him, too. Our women, who make the fame of an author, are divided into Scottists and Byronists. The Byronists are those with strong hearts and fiery heads—the others prefer Scott.

CONGREVE: I still insist that Byron lost more than he gained by writing too much. The tragedy of great people is that they exert all their power once or twice and then accomplish nothing more that is new.

GOETHE: You appear to reproach Byron for never having rested. He did write without a break, and naturally he ran the risk of either repeating himself or enfeebling his powers. If he had relaxed occasionally—for the intellect requires relaxation as much as the body—he would have been greater than ever, and more truly sublime. What makes him even more admirable in my eyes is that with a genius of that order, his judgment was yet so sure and his eye so penetrating. His *English Bards and Scotch Reviewers* * proves that at his very first attempts he had fully grasped the secrets of art. All his brushstrokes were the strokes of truth.

CONGREVE (*digressing*): You were here during the great war, were you not? Have you never used your pen to describe those scenes?

GOETHE: No! They were the kind of realities that are too terrible and too close. They were too poetic for the imagination of the poet to be able to add anything to them—and then it was no longer my affair.

SORET: They might have been admitted to the domain of poetry by a process different from that adopted by poets. That is, by toning down the harshness and softening the points. For history was then a frightful mass of exaggerations that had come true.†

---

* Mistitled in Soret's French original as *bardes écossais*, an error we may pardonably refrain from imputing to so idolatrous a "Byronist" as Goethe.

† Soret ends the dialogue here, leaving us with the curious impression that his sole contribution to the conversation had thrown Goethe and General Congreve into an awed silence.

Goethe

6.

AFTERNOON THOUGHTS ON BISHOPS, ENGLISHMEN, MADHOUSES, AND DANGEROUS BOOKS.

*I am ready to follow Your Highness into
hell, but I am determined not to follow
you into a madhouse.*

B Y A mere nine years Soret's conversations missed being included in
Margaret Fuller's translation of Eckermann's Conversations, which
has been the partial basis of all subsequent translations in English. Miss
Fuller's version appeared in Boston in 1839, whereas the third volume of
Eckermann's Gespräche, containing Soret's material, did not appear till
1848. Soret's conversations were first made known to the English-speaking
world in the translation made by John Oxenford in 1859. That rendering
became standard through the famous "Bohn Classics." Using the Fuller
translation as a base, Oxenford filled in the gaps and mended some of
the injuries to the German text. However, in rendering the new material
for the first time, he introduced some gaps of his own. This is particularly
noticeable in his censored version of the dialogue that follows. Anyone
acquainted with Soret's original will look in vain, in the standard English
version, for the whole "Lord Bristol" episode. Editorial squeamishness
explains itself in Oxenford's footnote to the effect that some passages of
the conversation "border on the profane." Certainly the Bishop of Derby
is given a rather severe drubbing in the deleted passage, and one realizes
how mid-Victorian England might have recoiled in horror from the
humiliating spectacle. But the conspiracy to keep "Lord Bristol" out of
Goethe's translated conversations has continued. Sedulous hunting has
uncovered no edition in English which reproduces Soret's dialogue in
full. The "Everyman Library" edition (J. M. Dent, 1930) skirts the
difficulty by omitting Soret entirely, but making partial amends with an
appreciative preface by Havelock Ellis. That edition, in turn, is based on
Oxenford's translation, with many, though by no means all, "errors and
infelicities" duly corrected.

We now join Frédéric Soret, this obliging Swiss Huguenot, at Goethe's house on March 17, 1830. The "Riemer" who enters shortly after is Friedrich Wilhelm Riemer, at the moment engaged in editing and collating the huge mass of Goethe's published writings and manuscript. A few years after Goethe's death we find Riemer collaborating with Eckermann on a forty-volume edition of the master's works.

Soret sets the scene for us:

("This evening I spent one or two hours at Goethe's house, first alone, and then with Riemer. The conversation was characteristic in many ways, yet one of the most singular which I have recorded. It was rich in paradoxes. On instructions of the Grand Duchess I returned to Goethe the copy of Gemma von Art, expressing my high opinion of this play to him. He was glad to see something new that showed the imprint of talent."—Soret)

GOETHE (grasping the volume with both hands and glancing at it sideways): But I am always a little opposed to playwrights who offer the theater plays that are far too long to be staged as written. Because of that defect, they rob me of half the pleasure I might derive from them. Look at what a fat volume this *Gemma* makes!

SORET: Schiller wrote them just as long, yet that did not prevent him from being a great dramatist.

GOETHE: That's true. His first plays were especially interminable. He had an exuberance and surplus of ideas and words which he could not control. I admit he took great pains, but despite study and hard work, he never quite corrected himself. One feels it even in his last works. The essential thing is to concentrate.

(Riemer enters, "his presence completely altering the nature of the conversation. . . . I thought of leaving because I knew this was the hour the two of them worked together and I knew he wasn't in the habit of resuming a thread of discourse once it was broken. But he asked me to stay, and the things that were said effaced the memory of what I had earlier heard that evening. The following is the record of our conversation."—Soret):

GOETHE: So Sömmering is dead—and only seventy-five years old! Men are idiots not to have the courage to live longer than that! Bentham is the man for me—that great fool of a radical! He still keeps fit and yet he's my senior by several weeks.

SORET: You might add, Excellency, that he resembles you in still another respect—he goes on working with all the enthusiasm of youth.

GOETHE: True enough—but we happen to be at opposite ends of the chain. He wants to destroy and I want to preserve. To be radical at his age is the height of folly.

SORET: Leaving Bentham aside, I think we ought to make a distinction between two kinds of radicalism. One kind, at the risk of demolishing everything, seeks to destroy in order to rebuild. The other recognizes the weak points of a government, exposes the abuses, proposes ways of remedying them, and in short looks to improve conditions without resorting to violent measures. Your Excellence would scarcely have escaped this second kind of radicalism if you had been an *Englishman*.

GOETHE (*"Adopting from now on the ironic and paradoxical tone of his own Mephistopheles, gives a fresh turn to the conversation, no doubt to avoid political discussion, which he dislikes."*—Soret): Do you take me for an idiot? I hunt down abuses and denounce them!—I who in England would have flourished upon the very products of such abuses! If I had been born in England—and thank God I was not!—I would have been a millionaire Duke, or perhaps a bishop with an income of thirty thousand pounds.

SORET: My congratulations! But suppose by ill luck you did not draw the prize-winning ticket—suppose you drew a blank instead . . . ? There are countless blanks, you know.

GOETHE: I quite agree. But everybody isn't cut out for the grand prize. You don't suppose I would have been imbecile enough to draw a blank? I would have gallantly defended the Thirty-nine Articles. I would have defended them under any guise, especially Article Thirteen. That particular one would have been the object of my very special and tender attention. In a word, I would have lied so much in prose and poetry that the thirty thousand pounds would never have escaped me. One must place himself above everything in order not to be crushed. And then from this great height, one must assume that those below are nothing but madmen and imbeciles. It would merely be adding one more fool to the crowd that allows itself to be abused not to exploit such abuses for one's own good. For we may be sure others would turn such abuses to good profit if we neglected to do so.

SORET: No one could object to those like yourself who would reach such heights through sheer right of conquest. But that isn't the case in England. The majority of those enjoying wealth and position are the least capable and the most stupid. Patronage, luck, and above all, birth, have given them the best share of the booty.

GOETHE: It doesn't matter much whether one has acquired or inherited his worldly goods. True, the one who acquires it himself is a man of genius,

a superior kind of person, who owes his special privileges to the submission of fools. You can readily see that the world is full of small souls
and softheaded fools. I don't have to go looking for madmen in insane
asylums. . . . That reminds me that the Grand Duke once tried to persuade me to visit a madhouse with him. Knowing my great repugnance
for such places, he resorted to trickery. But I discovered the ruse in
time and assured him I had seen enough madmen without visiting
those who were confined. "I am ready to follow Your Highness into
hell," I said, "but I am determined not to follow you into a madhouse."
. . . God, what pleasure I would have in observing the Thirty-nine Articles in my own way—just to make those stupid multitudes marvel!

SORET: That's a pleasure that could be all yours without aspiring to become a bishop. We seem to be here on Mephistopheles' own ground.
Your Excellency has begun marvellously. Why shouldn't you go still
further in that direction?

GOETHE: No. . . . One must be paid well to tell such lies. I would not do it
for less than a bishop's miter and a salary of thirty thousand pounds.
Besides, I have already met the preliminary requirements. Do you
know what one of my very first poems was? A grand dithyramb on the
descent of Jesus Christ into hell! It was even printed, but it isn't well-
known and I haven't spoken of it in my autobiography, for which I am
reserving unpublished matters of another kind. I have just come upon
that poem again. It will serve me as a passport to heaven. You knew
nothing about that, did you, Riemer . . . ?

RIEMER: No, but that reminds me that about a year before I came here I
believe you fell seriously ill and that your life was in danger. During
your delirium you were suddenly heard to recite some very beautiful
verses on the same subject. You were no doubt reciting the poem you
had written as a boy.

GOETHE: That's more than likely. I know the case of an old man who when
he was about to die began declaiming the most beautiful Greek sentences one can imagine. It was Hellenism of the highest order. Every
fool and imbecile began to shout "Miracle!" and the wise men, the
men of genius were already trading on the credulity of these idiots,
when alas! the truth came out! As a child the dying man had been compelled to memorize some Greek themes, without having the faintest
notion what they meant. This had occurred in the presence of a child
of noble birth of the same age, who it was hoped would be encouraged
by the other's example. Fifty years later this inert mass of words stirred
again and began unrolling mechanically in his memory.

(*"Returning to the subject of English bishops in the same tone of malice and irony," Goethe relates his adventure with an actual bishop.*)

GOETHE: While stopping at Jena, Lord Bristol sent word that he wished to see me. I accepted his invitation. He began by being quite vulgar with me. When I saw what his attitude was, I replied by being still more vulgar. This seemed to surprise him. My tactic succeeded, for he promptly became more polite. I outdid myself in rudeness till I was sure I had him in my power. Then I tried to appear somewhat more amiable to him, but always with a certain detached air of independence which prevented any harsh words from being spoken that might have upset the equilibrium of our talk. The good bishop wanted to give me a sermon about *Werther*. His purpose was to arouse my conscience for having led men into the temptation of suicide and even for having caused many to commit it, adding, "It's a criminal and immoral book! . . ." "Stop right there!" I shouted. "What tone do you take with the rulers of this earth, who with one stroke of the pen and in the interests of the literary productions of their diplomats send a hundred thousand men into battle, cause the killing of eighty thousand of them, and incite their own subjects to pillage, rape, and murder? You sing a *Te Deum* about that. How do you dare heap praise upon yourselves when some poor, weak-minded simpletons, terrified by the beautiful sermons on hell that you pronounce from your high pulpit, lose the last shred of sanity remaining to them, and end their wretched lives in insane asylums? And what about those who kill themselves to get to heaven sooner or to escape their religious terrors? What do you do then? You chant your praises to God! So, what right have you, since you raise the point, to prevent a writer of genius from producing a work, which because it happens to be misunderstood by some limited minds, relieves the world of a dozen real morons or monomaniacs who have nothing better to do than to blow out their brains? This is a service to humanity. Why do you come to reproach me for such a trifling matter of firearms, when you priests and princes permit yourselves much worse? Am I not morally certain that those who commit suicide after reading *Werther* are utterly incapable of playing any rational role in the world? Can you say as much for your victims?" After this tirade Monseigneur the Bishop, coarse as he was by nature, became as meek as a lamb. I had found the way to his heart. From that moment he continued to show me the greatest courtesy. When I left, he accompanied me as far as the door and instructed his abbot to see me further. When we were outside, the latter said to me: "You spoke very well, Mr. Goethe! And how quickly you found the secret of pleasing Milord! If you had shown less energy you would have felt very unhappy about your visit."

SORET: You have certainly had your share of annoyances over *Werther*. Which reminds me of your discussion with Napoleon on the same subject. Was Talleyrand present?

GOETHE: Yes, he was there. Unlike Lord Bristol, Napoleon gave me no cause for complaint. He behaved with the utmost courtesy and criticized the book like a man.

(*The conversation turns to novels and plays, Soret suggesting that their power over the public, for good or evil, is enormous.*)

GOETHE: It certainly is a very bad thing when a book has a more profound immoral effect on the public than this daily life about us which crams our ears, if not our eyes, with an abundance of scandalous scenes. Even in the case of children, no one need be alarmed over the effect of a book or play. Daily life, let me repeat, teaches far more than the most powerful book.

SORET: Yet we are all careful not to say things in the presence of children which we think it is bad for them to hear.

GOETHE: That's praiseworthy enough, and I never violate that rule myself. However, I regard the precaution as utterly useless. Children are like dogs in that they possess a fine, sharp sense of smell, especially in detecting anything bad. They always seem to know exactly how some friend of the family stands with their parents. Since they don't know how to be hypocrites, they serve us as excellent barometers when we wish to know just what degree of favor or disfavor we enjoy with the parents. I remember how once someone spoke badly of me in company. The matter seemed so important that I could not rest till I found out who had struck this blow behind my back. In general, everybody here was well-disposed toward me. I thought and thought about it and was unable to decide who could have said these hateful things about me. Then it came to me in a flash. On the street one day I met some little boys whom I knew and who were in the habit of greeting me. This time they did not give me the usual greeting. That was enough for me. Following the clue, I soon discovered that it was the beloved parents of these boys who had been wagging their nasty tongues about me.

Napoleon

O NE approaches the literature about Napoleon as if it were some forbidding jungle in which dangers lurk on all sides. The books and articles about him in all languages would fill a three-story library, and his portrait, shaped by friend and foe alike, is actually a whole bewildering picture gallery. There seems to be not one Napoleon, but as many Napoleons as there are historians and biographers. And the political fortunes of Napoleon did not end with his death; they shifted with every changing regime of nineteenth-century France. This, literally, was a man for the ages. No figure of history ever released such a flood of reminiscences and memoirs as this so-called Man of Destiny. Seventy years after his death secret diaries containing entries about him were still being unearthed and printed for the first time. Few, indeed, were the men and women who, having once moved within talking radius of this man, did not sooner or later commit their recollections to writing. The shelves are loaded with pen-portraits and candid close-ups. No man's public and private life was ever so sedulously subjected to the bifocal microscope of gossip and history. At every stage of his incredible career, from the "whiff of grapeshot" that smashed the French Revolution to his last agony on St. Helena, some watchful witness was on hand to tell the world about him.

We would thus seem to have him complete—Napoleon in battle, Napoleon in love, Napoleon in a tantrum, Napoleon with Metternich, Napoleon with Goethe, Napoleon with Josephine. Through the welter of diaries and reminiscences we soon find ourselves on the most intimate terms with the soldier, the general, the first consul, the emperor, the lover. We accompany him on his vast conquests, trudge back with him from a Moscow in flames, overhear him contemplate flight to America after the rout at Waterloo. Through the eyes and ears of kings and queens, nobles, cabinet ministers, soldiers and generals, secretaries and chambermaids, we come to know this man as few men have ever been known. Yet we remain baffled by the final mystery—the driving force behind it all. Was it love of power, of France, the gigantic compensation of an upstart's ego? Or was this pudgy little Corsican who won and lost an empire merely the pawn in a game of reaction—the Frankenstein monster created by the counter-revolution only to be destroyed in panic by its creators?

About one thing there can be little doubt. No man ever felt such a strong compulsion for self-revelation. However overmastering the passion for conquest and power, the urge to talk about himself was still stronger. Seldom was Europe flooded with such an endless spate of words. If Napoleon does not quite explain himself in the end, it was not for want of trying. History knows no monologist like this bilingual Frenchman of Italian origin. And yet he could listen with an equally passionate interest, listen and remember with a dogged unforgetfulness. The talk was warm, forceful, rich in invective. Often it was the talk of a simple man thinking out loud; just as often it could be the fiendishly contrived talk of an arch-schemer. It could be the overpowering, torrid, persuasive hyperbole of a demagogue asking a nation to gamble away its destiny at his word; it could be the proud impudence of a conqueror at bay. He could spout revolutionary doctrine like the most unswerving of Jacobins, and erupt in high dudgeon over any hint of a royal affront. One senses the parvenu forever assuring himself—and the world—of his right to be where he is. Nothing, not even exile, could silence this tongue in life.

Of the massive library that grew about Napoleon, a tidy portion is occupied by the countless volumes of his recorded talk. For the most part it is the ceaseless talk of soliloquy. One pictures Bourrienne, Montholon, Gourgaud, Las Cases in an attitude of gaping adoration as the great man unburdens himself. Page after page of self-vindication, sometimes without the meekest interruption, this monologue flows on through hundreds of volumes. But here and there we come upon a real conversation. Some superior dramatic sense has prompted the writer to record both sides of a colloquy. We are, of course, on treacherous ground. Whom are we to trust and who are the charlatans? For many years following the death of Napoleon the market was good for such revelations. Some of these have fared better than others in the hands of Napoleonic scholars. Many were discarded as pure fabrications, others were discounted as the memoirs of fanatic partisans or sworn foes, and a great number were found to be imaginative expansions of factual trifles. Yet, in one way or another, each has added to the vast unfinished portrait that is Napoleon Bonaparte. One German historian, Friedrich Kircheisen, collected enough of such Gespräche mit Napoleon to fill ten huge tomes. With a more liberal canon of accuracy, he might easily have filled ten more.

For the "Portrait in Dialogue" that follows a mere handful of such talks has been selected. That they add up to a real "portrait" of Napoleon would, of course, be a preposterous claim. The purpose has been rather to overhear Napoleon during a few of the significant crises in his crowded career. To what degree the dialogues are "real" and factual is a matter for endless and fruitless dispute. Their authenticity would appear to grow with each succeeding selection. That is, we are right in taking Baron Langon's report of the family council on the eve of Napoleon's coronation with a generous pinch of salt. The material travelled too elaborate a circuit before reaching the Baron. Fleury de Chaboulon, whose record of the Waterloo debacle is famous, is far more trustworthy than the Baron, and nobody has seriously questioned the veracity of Caulaincourt. As for Metternich, he no doubt had his own ax to grind, but the substance of his crucial interview with Napoleon in Dresden in 1813 went into a state dispatch, so there was hardly any likelihood of exaggeration or fraud. Talleyrand's scant record of Napoleon's meeting with Goethe, though the report of an arch-opportunist, nowhere conflicts with Goethe's own meager notes of the talk. Most authentic of all is indisputably Lady Malcolm's chronicle of Napoleon's verbal skirmish with Sir Hudson Lowe on St. Helena. Admiral Malcolm, who dictated the details of the conversation to his wife the same night, was a man without prejudice or rancor. There was absolutely nothing to gain by falsifying a strictly personal record of a clash between his respected superior and this garrulous but likable captive. Again, there is one word of caution to add. One must not suppose that, however faithful the record of a conversation, the quality of Napoleon's discourse could ever come through completely. These Fleurys and Caulaincourts were after all not recording machines. Inevitably, hundreds of phrases, nuances of inflection and gesture must have slipped through their net. The ebullience of a Napoleon is not easily bottled in the bare dialogue of print. Yet, as one reads, one readily pictures the flashing eyes, the mobile features, the incessant motion of hand and head—in short, Napoleon's utter concentration of self in this fascinating business of talk.

Napoleon

1.

FAMILY REUNION IN THE TUILERIES ON THE EVE OF A CORONATION.

Have you a throne to give me, my dear brother?

THE scene of our opening conversation is the apartment of Josephine in the Tuileries Palace during the night of December 1, 1804. We are in the private chambers of an empress-to-be, for in a few hours, at the Cathedral of Nôtre-Dame, Josephine's husband will place upon his head the imperial crown of France. First Consul Napoleon will thereafter be Emperor Napoleon, and she the Empress Josephine. Only two short years before, the people of France, drugged by the successes of this master-adventurer, had voted him First Consul for life. A second plebiscite has now elevated the Man of Destiny one step higher. The obedient Senate has confirmed the title, and a new Constitution now offers the strange preamble that "The Government of the Republic is confided to an Emperor." Officially, at any rate, we are still among Jacobins, and the Emperor, we are told, is merely the greatest of them. The republic is now embalmed in the empire. Here in Josephine's apartments a dynasty is about to be born. Tomorrow the Pope will solemnize the coronation, and "Napoleon I" will join history's other titles of first magnitude. Naturally, Josephine is exultant. This very evening the Pope has sanctified her civil marriage to Napoleon in the Tuileries chapel. The growing threat of divorce now seems permanently removed. "Never have I seen on any physiognomy such an expression of joy, content, and happiness as that which then animated the countenance of the Empress." So writes her first femme de chambre, Mlle. Avrillion, who witnessed the ceremonies of the following day. Josephine—the childless—will remain Empress exactly five years; to be legally discarded and replaced by Marie Louise of Austria, a woman better qualified by nature to provide Napoleon with an imperial heir. But tomorrow at Nôtre-Dame Josephine's face will be "radiant," and Napoleon, fixing a smaller crown on her forehead, will be proud of his Empress in her dazzling furs and jewels.

Tonight the door of Josephine's room is locked to everyone not in the immediate family circle. One by one the Bonapartes arrive: sister Caroline and her husband Murat, to become King of Naples and later to be shot; sister Elisa and her husband Felix Bacciochi; sister Pauline; brother Joseph, to become King of Spain, and his wife; brother Louis, to become King of Holland, and his wife Hortense, step-daughter of Napoleon; and "Madame-Mère"—Letizia Bonaparte—who will survive to see this new imperial family scattered and in ruins. A special word of introduction is needed for Monseigneur Fesch—step-brother of "Madame-Mère." It is he who as Napoleon's envoy extraordinary to the Vatican has persuaded Pope Pius VII to be present at Nôtre-Dame tomorrow.

As for the dialogue itself, it is offered here as an obvious reconstruction "within the framework of historical fact." How much may be accepted as literal and how much as purely imaginary it is impossible to determine. The Baron de Étienne-Léon Lamothe-Langon who relays it to us was notorious for mixing the genuine with the fanciful in his accounts of the "soirées secrètes" of the Napoleonic period. We are not surprised to learn that he later became a novelist. A prolific writer, the Baron filled countless volumes with Mémoires of this kind, the bulk of them a patchwork of hearsay, known facts, and pilferings from the reminiscent coffers of others; but a great number the record of personal observation. During this period the Baron faithfully served France as auditor, State Councillor, Sub-Prefect, and Prefect. He was on intimate terms with a great many celebrities who had moved within the charmed circle of the Corsican parvenu. He thought highly enough of the record of the family reunion at the Tuileries to use it twice in his published works. It may be found in his L'Empire ou Dix Ans sous Napoléon (Paris, 1836) and in expanded form, in his Napoléon—sa famille, ses amis, ses généraux, ses ministres, et ses contemporains (1840). We have only his word for whatever detailed validity it may have as an approximate account of an established event.

The Baron tells us he obtained the story from a titled lady* who was an intimate friend of an unnamed member of Napoleon's family. This mysterious intermediary wrote it out for the Baron, who "swore for her honesty." Our only comment is that the record is plausible enough and that this power-drunk clan of Corsicans unquestionably spent a few moments that night discussing the imperial prospects ahead. In any case,

---

* "A lady among my friends who was fond of collecting anecdotes about European celebrities some years ago gave me a record of a conversation held in the Tuileries. I do not hesitate to reproduce it here because I know what intimate ties this lady had with Napoleon's family. It is she who wrote it."—Baron de Étienne-Léon Lamothe-Langon (L'Empire ou Dix Ans sous Napoléon, Volume I).

the brief domestic scene, however doctored, is a convenient prologue to the drama that ensues.

The Baron himself sets the scene as follows:

("*Napoleon had fixed December 2, 1804, as the date of the official ceremony which would elevate him from the ranks of ordinary men to a place so high that the only one higher than he would be God in heaven and the Pope on earth as the vicar of Jesus Christ. On the evening of December 1, the door of the Empress Josephine's apartment was carefully closed to everyone not in the immediate family circle. The members now began to enter the imperial chambers. Prince Murat arrived a little late. He looked as handsome as a star, truly magnificent in the costume he was planning to wear on the morrow. Everyone cried out with delight and admiration when they saw him in this splendid attire.*"—Lamothe-Langon)

MURAT: All things considered, tomorrow's ceremony will be quite a beautiful affair!

CAROLINE (*his wife*): Yes, for those who will play the leading roles.

NAPOLEON: And whoever told you, sister, that such a role will not be yours some day?

CAROLINE (*turning pale with joy*): Have you a throne to give me, my dear brother?

JOSEPH: I don't see a single vacant one anywhere in Europe.

HORTENSE (*quoting from* Tancrède): "*Il s'en présentera, gardez-vous d'en douter.*" *

ELISA (*Madame Bacchiochi*): To be perfectly truthful, I think a throne is an excellent *chaise longue*.

JOSEPHINE (*sighing*): In which one never sleeps soundly.

LOUIS: And not for lack of people cradling one to sleep.

PAULINE: A throne! A scepter! All very pretty so long as they are garlanded with prosperity or adorned with the laurels of victory (*turning to Napoleon*)—like yours, brother.

NAPOLEON (*kissing her*): You're very sweet, Paulette, but Josephine is right. Tranquillity is not for crowned heads.

MADAME-MÈRE: I should like to know what the man who calls himself King of France is thinking at this moment. No doubt his mind is also on tomorrow's ceremony.

---

* "It will present itself, have no doubt."

(*A long silence ensues.*)

NAPOLEON: Mother, the Count of Lille is a very sensible man. He will probably spend the night cursing the people who flattered his brother and sister-in-law—cursing all the male and female favorites, the mistresses and court pets, the false measures, the wasteful expenses, the bad ministers, the incompetent councillors and the traitors. He will bewail his grandfather's vices—the weaknesses of Louis XVI, the obstinacy of the queen, the greed and ineptitude of the Polignacs—the idiotic confidence with which the Estates-General were assembled, the cowardice of cringing before them, and to crown it all, the irreparable blunder of the emigration. All these were positive causes of *his* bad luck and *my* good luck. They are the serpents which will gnaw at his heart. He is to be pitied. I could have made it easier for him . . . if he had let me.

CAROLINE: Ah, brother, how was that possible? Who would have so advised him among his followers? And who among us would have done it in his place? In a word, who would voluntarily renounce a crown maintained in the family for centuries? . . . It is far better to die!

MURAT (*in a fateful voice*): I agree with my wife. If I were King I would not relinquish my scepter at any price. There is always a bottle of poison handy, or a friendly bullet, to spare a fallen king the final humiliation of begging a stranger's help. If I ever suffered great reverses, I would die amid the ruins of my throne rather than abandon it.

NAPOLEON: By doing so you would only succeed in sacrificing every chance of ever recovering it. Brother, only madmen and cowards end their careers that way. The true hero patiently awaits the propitious moment, seizes it and makes best use of it. A stroke of good luck will restore him to the place he left.

MURAT (*laughing*): In that case, my luck would restore me to Figeac. But there's hardly a chance of going back there, now that my brother's and my Emperor's kindness, together with my sword and his, are creating a greater opportunity for me. . .

JOSEPHINE (*as if awakening from a reverie*): So tomorrow I shall be crowned Empress?

HORTENSE: And consecrated besides, Mother—something which the proudest queen of France could never boast.

JOSEPHINE: My head is spinning! She was right, that old Negress of Martinique, when she predicted that I would some day become a greater lady than Marie-Antoinette!

NAPOLEON (*gaily*): No one ever predicted anything for me, though in my own way I built magnificent castles in Spain. None of them, however,

compared with the Tuileries. Even when I dreamed that I was brandishing the sword of Roland, I never quite saw myself wearing the
diadem of Charlemagne. (*Gravely*) I must add, however, I never had a
childhood delusion in which I was not somehow concerned with the
welfare and grandeur of France. As an adolescent in 1780 and as a
young man in 1789 I wanted her to be rich and strong. Providence has
seen fit to give reality to my obsession, and for my part, I am resolved
to accomplish the hopes of my youth. My empire will never reproach
me for having failed to bring it glory, just laws, and a wise administration. I have taken an oath to myself to work only and always for my
country, and you may rest assured I shall not break it!

Napoleon

2.

NAPOLEON AND GOETHE: A CONQUEROR OF MEN INTERRUPTS HIS BREAKFAST TO QUESTION A POET.

Sire, I observe that when Your Majesty travels he does not neglect to take notice of even the smallest objects.

Few meetings have fired the imagination of historians as that of Goethe and Napoleon in Erfurt on the morning of October 2, 1808. The situation would seem too rich in ironic contrasts to have been real. One comes to suspect that perhaps after all the encounter was only a fabrication evolved and abetted by generations of historians and biographers. The confrontation is almost unique: on one side Europe's foremost man of action, adventurer par excellence, and unparalleled military genius; on the other side, a giant intellect and poet, blandly remote from the fray, an Olympian in world outlook. And the contrast does not end there. . . .

Goethe, the German, had watched Napoleon, the Frenchman, devastate his land and crush the Prussian army at Jena. Indeed, the Frenchman had come to Erfurt to meet the Tsar Alexander for the purpose of completing the humiliation of Prussia. All the vassal kings and princes of Germany were "persuaded" to attend. One's immediate impression is that of the humbled foe before the conqueror. Yet, the impression is false. For we must remember the character of this German Olympian. In the words of Brandes, Goethe could scarcely regard Napoleon as the destroyer of the fatherland, since he "had never known any German fatherland." Indeed, Goethe for years had been an open admirer of Napoleon, going so far as to describe him in a poem as the all-knowing hero whose "giant mind" had "intuitively" encompassed ideas over which "centuries had brooded." Angrily he had refused to join German patriots in their crusade of liberation from French vassalage. To Goethe Napoleon was the man who had brought some order into the chaos of the German principalities. He even viewed him as a colossal patron of the arts and sciences. There

204

was something else, too, a hint of the same adulation of rank that was to infuriate Beethoven in Vienna. "Never," wrote Goethe to Cotta after the Erfurt meeting, "has another individual of higher rank conducted himself in this way toward me . . . he gave me a place in the world alongside of himself." We begin to suspect there is something of the flunky here, of the employee of the Duke of Weimar suddenly elevated to a position of equality with the most illustrious man of his time. Having been repeatedly snubbed by the King and Queen of Prussia in their visits to Weimar, Goethe now stands face to face with an Emperor and Conqueror who recognizes him as equal. One is scarcely surprised to learn that after the brief encounter, Goethe exclaimed of Napoleon: "His is the greatest mind the world has ever known." For the first time in his life, Goethe "had met his equal in genius." From that high pinnacle the two surveyed one another.

Sly fox that he was, Napoleon knew how to make the best of the situation. He had himself instructed his minister Maret to invite Goethe to the Erfurt palace. He had read The Sorrows of Werther seven times and could best flatter its author by quoting freely from it. Indeed, his criticism of Werther's confused motivation was recognized by Goethe as the shrewdest ever made to him. Cunningly, Napoleon plied him with questions about the drama, about Tacitus, and suggested he could write a play about Caesar superior to Shakespeare's. Finally, he invited Goethe to France to make Paris the center of his world influence. Goethe could not help but be flattered. When he was informed some days later that he had been made a member of the Legion of Honor, it was only the crowning tribute of a master-diplomat. The Olympian responded with a pledge of "complete devotion." Against this one recalls Beethoven's own reaction to the news of Napoleon's self-coronation—an outburst of rage followed by the removal of Napoleon's name from the dedication page of the "Eroica" symphony.

As for the record of the Erfurt meeting, it has come to us only in scraps —three of them, to be exact. Of these the smallest fragment is Goethe's own note, which gives a bare outline of the talk about Werther and is chiefly significant as the source of Napoleon's historic greeting to Goethe: "Vous êtes un homme!" The second version is that of Friedrich Müller, a Weimar state official, who accompanied Goethe to Napoleon's quarters. Müller, who waited in an antechamber till the interview was over, pieced the details together from information supplied by Goethe and others. These he incorporated in his Erinnerungen aus den Kriegszeiten von 1806 bis 1813 (Braunschweig, 1851). Müller reports that the meeting lasted one hour, which would have it end at noon; that Napoleon was seated at a small round table having breakfast when Goethe entered. Among those present, he tells us, were Talleyrand,* who stood to the right of the Emperor, and Daru, the General Intendant and interpreter, who stood to the left. According to Müller, Napoleon motioned Goethe to approach the moment he entered and promptly asked his age; after which followed the famous "Vous êtes un homme!" They soon began discussing Voltaire's play, Mahomet, whereupon Napoleon complained of the way Goethe had weakened Werther by mingling the motives of unrequited love and thwarted ambition. Goethe, Müller tells us, rather liked this and agreed with Napoleon. The talk was momentarily interrupted by the entrance of Marshal Soult, with whom Napoleon exchanged some jests about the Polish situation. Then he returned to Goethe, inquiring about his family and urging him to write a new "Julius Caesar," which would be the crowning achievement of his life. Finally, Napoleon invited Goethe to come to Paris for a "broader outlook" and "material for his poetry." Then the two men parted, and as the door closed behind Goethe, Napoleon observed to Talleyrand and the others, "Voilà un homme!" Such is Müller's account.

A third and more extended version is that of Talleyrand himself. It is woefully scant, to be sure, but it has the charm of being in dialogue form and of having been checked, if we are to trust Talleyrand, with Goethe himself. There are conspicuous omissions, especially of the discussion about Werther and Napoleon's opening and closing remarks about Goethe's being a man. Talleyrand, though deposed as foreign minister, had accompanied Napoleon as a member of the council to this brilliant round-up of emperors and kings, arranged by the French ruler to overawe the Tsar Alexander. Cynical schemer and turncoat. Talleyrand was secretly advising the Tsar Alexander to resist Napoleon's pleas for support against Austria. Talleyrand, who began as a bishop, worked for the Revolution and Napoleon, and ended in the service of the Restoration. Though his Mémoires were first printed late in 1891 in Paris, a version of the Erfurt interview had already appeared in Le Correspondant of Paris on January 23 of that year. What follows is my translation of that version, prefaced by Talleyrand's own scene-setting, and ending with his remarks about the exactness of the report.

("*Faithful to his leisurely system of doing things, Napoleon had so arranged the first few days that there was never any time to discuss*

* Goethe also told Soret that Talleyrand was present (see page 195).

business. *His breakfasts were long: while eating, he received people and talked quite freely. I have seen many of these breakfasts last longer than two hours. It was then that Napoleon admitted the great men of the day who had come to Erfurt to see him. Every morning he contentedly read through the list of people who had just arrived. The day he saw the name of Goethe there, he sent for him."*—Talleyrand)

NAPOLEON: Monsieur Goethe, I am charmed to see you.

GOETHE: Sire, I observe that when Your Majesty travels he does not neglect to take notice of even the smallest objects.

NAPOLEON: I know you are the leading tragic poet of Germany.

GOETHE: Sire, you insult our country. We believe we have our great men: Schiller, Lessing, and Wieland must be known to Your Majesty.

NAPOLEON: I must confess that I scarcely know them. Still, I have read *The Thirty Years' War*. That work, if you will forgive me, only seemed to furnish tragic themes for our boulevards.

GOETHE: Sire, I am not familiar with your boulevards, but I suppose it is there that the big spectacles are given for the people. I am chagrined to hear you judge one of the finest geniuses of modern times so severely.

NAPOLEON: As a rule you live in Weimar—don't you? Isn't that the place where Germany's celebrated men of letters gather?

GOETHE: Sire, they are very well protected there. But at the moment Wieland is the only man residing there who is known all over Europe, for Müller is living in Berlin.

NAPOLEON: I would be very happy to see Monsieur Wieland.

GOETHE: If Your Majesty will permit me to send for him, I am sure he would appear at once.

NAPOLEON: Does he speak French?

GOETHE: He knows it. He has himself edited several translations of his works into French.

NAPOLEON: While you are here, you must come every evening to see our plays. It will do you no harm to see performances of good French tragedies.

GOETHE: Sire, I shall do so with the greatest pleasure, and allow me to inform Your Majesty that that was my intention. I have translated, or, rather, imitated some French plays.

NAPOLEON: Which ones?

GOETHE: *Mahomet* and *Tancrède*.

NAPOLEON: I shall ask Remusat if we have the actors to perform them here. I would be very happy to have you see them performed in our language.

You people are not as rigorous as we are in observing the rules of the theater.

GOETHE: Sire, among us the unities are not essential.

NAPOLEON: How do you find our sojourn here?

GOETHE: Quite brilliant, and I hope it will be useful to our country.

NAPOLEON: Are your people happy?

GOETHE: They have not lost hope.

NAPOLEON: Monsieur, you should stay here for the whole trip and write your impressions of the great spectacle which we are offering you.

GOETHE: Ah, Sire, it would require the pen of a writer of antiquity to undertake such a project.

NAPOLEON: Are you one of those who love Tacitus?

GOETHE: Yes, Sire, very much.

NAPOLEON: Well, not I. But we shall talk of that some other time. Write to Monsieur Wieland to come here. I shall return his visit at Weimar. The Duke has invited me to visit him there. I shall be delighted to see the Duchess. She is a woman of great merit. The Duke was quite ill for some time, but his health has improved.

GOETHE: Sire, if he was ill, the improvement has been quite remarkable. But I am no judge of such matters. He is a patron of the arts and sciences, and we have no reason but to be proud of him.

NAPOLEON: Monsieur Goethe, come tonight to see *Iphigénie*. It is a good play, though not one of my favorites. The French think very highly of it. You will see a great number of sovereigns in my box. Do you know the Prince Primate?

GOETHE: Yes, Sire, almost intimately. He is a prince of great wit, great knowledge, and great generosity.

NAPOLEON: Excellent! Then you shall see him tonight dozing on the shoulder of the King of Württemberg. Have you seen the Emperor of Russia yet?

GOETHE: No, Sire, never, but I hope to be introduced to him.

NAPOLEON: He talks your language well. If you write anything about your Erfurt interview, you must dedicate it to him.

GOETHE: Sire, that is not my practice. From the moment I began to write, I adopted it as a principle never to make dedications, so that I would never have to reproach myself later.

NAPOLEON: The great writers of the century of Louis XIV were not at all like that.

GOETHE: That's true, Sire, but Your Majesty would not assure me that they never felt any regrets.

NAPOLEON: What has become of that bad fellow Kotzebue? *

GOETHE: Sire, they say he has been sent to Siberia and that Your Majesty will ask the Emperor Alexander to pardon him.

NAPOLEON: But do you know that he is not my man?

GOETHE: Sire, he is a wretchedly unhappy man with a great deal of talent.

NAPOLEON: Adieu, Monsieur Goethe.

(*"I followed Goethe out and invited him to come and dine with me. When I returned, I wrote out this first conversation. During dinner, I put many questions to Goethe, and his answers satisfied me that the record I had made was absolutely exact. After dinner Goethe attended the play . . ."*—Talleyrand †)

---

* August Kotzebue, brilliant Weimar playwright, who pamphleteered at various times against France and Russia, after serving them both; promoted German insurrection; was once exiled to Siberia, suffered a change of heart in 1815 by supporting the Holy Alliance, and was assassinated in 1819 at Mannheim.

† Talleyrand assures us that Dazincourt, to whom he entrusted Goethe, found a good seat for him amid the throng of kings, princes, and ministers of state that occupied the best locations.

Napoleon

3.

A FORMER FRENCH AMBASSADOR TO RUSSIA HEARS AN EMPEROR PREPARING FOR WAR AMID PROTESTATIONS OF PEACE.

I repeat, I do not want war.

B Y THE spring of 1811 Napoleon seemed to have entrenched himself solidly as founder of a dynasty. The Bonapartes sat on thrones from one end of Europe to the other. Josephine was conveniently put out of the way through a divorce, and in her place at the Tuileries had followed the 18-year-old Marie Louise of Austria, who now bore Napoleon a son on March 20. "Here is the King of Rome!" Napoleon exclaims to his marshals, proudly exhibiting the infant. The marriage of Marie Louise had followed a fresh defeat of recalcitrant Austria. At long last, except for the fighting in Spain, Napoleon's grip seemed to be on all Europe. The Continental System, a blockade designed to starve England into submission, was functioning satisfactorily but for a few leaks. Then, abruptly, the little Corsican flew into a tantrum. Russia resolved to detach herself from the "System." The reason was a matter of simple self-preservation. Agricultural Russia needed industrial Britain. Napoleon was seized with a great suspicion and a great ambition. Russia, he told himself, was secretly preparing to attack. There was only one way to outsmart her: he would attack first. By early June of 1811 Napoleon, despite repeated avowals of peaceful intentions, had secretly made up his mind to launch an invasion. Yet, however he might mask his maturing designs, there was one man in his entourage who saw through the façade of pretense and dreaded the outcome. This man was the Marquis Armand de Caulaincourt.

An honest and chivalrous soldier and diplomat, Caulaincourt had been Napoleon's ambassador to St. Petersburg. The Tsar Alexander had come to trust and respect him as much as did Napoleon himself. Caulaincourt's one aim had been to preserve the alliance between Russia and France. As a guarantee of peace, he had even tried to promote a marriage between Napoleon and the Tsar's sister. In the words of the British historian

Gooch, "Caulaincourt never ceased to stress the need of co-operation, and
it was not his fault that Napoleon made the greatest mistake of his life."
Caulaincourt's efforts at conciliation soon began to vex Napoleon, and
the man who was to serve his master loyally even through the suicidal
gamble of the Hundred Days found himself contemptuously rebuffed.
Nothing daunted, Caulaincourt continued his efforts to preserve the
peace. On the morning of June 5, we find him hastening to the palace of
Saint-Cloud for an appointment with the Emperor. It is to Caulaincourt
himself that we owe the privilege of being able to overhear their crucial
conversation. For this devoted but despairing agent of Napoleon kept a
faithful record of his experiences. "My notes," he tells us, "were made
everywhere, at my desk and in camp, every day and at all times of day.
They are the work of every moment. I have touched up nothing and
disguised nothing. . . . If these pages should some day be read and severity
imputed to me, I hope that allowance will be made for the happenings
under the influence of which they were penned." In the words of George
Libaire, these jottings "are the findings of a professional soldier, sitting
in judgment upon the foremost soldier of fortune the world has known."
It was not till 1933 that the memoirs of this trusted friend of Napoleon
were first published in Paris, with Jean Hanoteau as editor. The following
excerpts are taken from the translation edited by George Libaire (William
Morrow, N. Y., 1935).

("The Emperor was at Saint-Cloud. By eleven o'clock I was there.
His Majesty received me coldly, and at once began heatedly to enumerate his imaginary grievances against the Tsar Alexander, but without
reproaching me personally. He spoke of the ukase prohibiting foreign
imports, and of the admission of neutral and American ships into Russian ports, which, he said, was an infringement of the Continental System. He went on to say that the Tsar was treacherous, that he was
arming to make war on France. The Emperor repeated all the fantastic
stories which, to please him, were fabricated in Danzig, in the Duchy
of Warsaw, and even in the north of Germany—stories the accuracy of
which had been disproved time and again, sometimes by means of investigations carried out on the spot, sometimes even by the march of
events."—Caulaincourt)

NAPOLEON: The admission of neutral and American ships into Russian
ports is an infringement of the Continental System. The Tsar is treach-

erous. He is arming to make war on France. Admit frankly that it is Alexander who wants to make war on me.

CAULAINCOURT: No, Sire. I would stake my life on his not firing the first shot or being the first to cross his frontiers.

NAPOLEON: We're agreed, then, because I have no intention of going into Russia, nor any wish for a war or the re-establishment of Poland.

CAULAINCOURT: Then, Sire, you ought to explain your intentions, so that everyone may know why Your Majesty's troops are concentrated in Danzig and the north of Prussia.

NAPOLEON (*disregarding the question*): In the event of war, the Russian nobles would fear for their palaces, and, after a good battle, would force the Tsar to conclude a peace.

CAULAINCOURT: Your Majesty is mistaken. Allow me to repeat the words used by the Tsar in the course of the private conversations I had with him after the arrival of M. Lauriston,* when my position no longer had any political significance, words which were merely a more emphatic expression of what he had led me to understand some time before.† "If the Emperor Napoleon makes war on me," the Tsar Alexander said to me, "it is possible, even probable, that we shall be defeated, assuming that we fight. But that will not mean that he can dictate a peace. The Spaniards have often been defeated; and they are not beaten, nor have they submitted. But they are not so far away from Paris as we are, and have neither our climate nor our resources to help them. We shall take no risks. We have plenty of room; and our standing army is well-organized, which means, as the Emperor Napoleon has admitted, that we need never accept a dictated peace, whatever reverses we may suffer. What is more, in such circumstances the victor is forced to accept the terms of the vanquished. The Emperor Napoleon made a remark to this effect to Tchernychev ‡ in Vienna after the battle of Wagram. He would not have made peace then if Austria had not kept an army intact. Results have to keep pace with his thoughts, because, being often absent from France, he is always anxious to return there. This is the teaching of a Master. I shall not be the first to draw my sword, but I shall be the last to sheathe it. The Spaniards have proved that lack of perseverance has been the undoing of all the States

---

* Caulaincourt's successor as French Ambassador to St. Petersburg.

† This sentence appears in indirect discourse in Caulaincourt's narrative. The Tsar's words impressed him so much that he noted them down on returning home. "I quote them here," he continues, "with the certainty that, to the best of my knowledge, my recollection of them was substantially correct."

‡ Alexander's aide-de-camp. He was present at the battle of Wagram, and stood beside Napoleon, who decorated him with the Legion of Honor.

on which your master has made war. The Emperor Napoleon's remark
to Tchernychev, in the latest war with Austria, shows clearly enough
that the Austrians could have obtained better terms if they had been
more persevering. People don't know how to suffer. If the fighting went
against me. I should retire to Kamchatka rather than cede provinces
and sign, in my capital, treaties that were really only truces. Your
Frenchman is brave; but long privations and a bad climate wear him
down and discourage him. Our climate, our winter, will fight on our
side. With you, marvels only take place where the Emperor is in personal attendance; and he cannot be everywhere. He cannot be absent
from Paris year after year."

(*"The Emperor listened to me with the closest attention, even with
some astonishment. He appeared to be greatly preoccupied, and kept
silent for a while. I thought I had made a deep impression on him, since
his face, his whole bearing, which hitherto had manifested only an
extreme severity, became open and friendly. He seemed to wish to encourage me to go on, not only by looks but by the questions he put. He
spoke of society in Russia, of the army, of the administrations, and
even referred to the Tsar Alexander without manifesting his usual ill-
humor at mention of this name. In fact, the Emperor gave every indication at this moment of being kindly disposed toward me, and referred appreciatively to the manner in which I had served him.... After
listening to me attentively, the Emperor began enumerating the troops
and general resources at his disposal. When he reverted to this theme I
realized that all hope of peace was at an end, since it was enumerations
of this kind which, more than anything, intoxicated him. . . ."*—
Caulaincourt)

NAPOLEON: One good battle would knock the bottom out of my friend
Alexander's fine resolutions, not to mention his sand fortifications.[*]

CAULAINCOURT: I assure Your Majesty he is mistaken about the Tsar
Alexander and about Russia. It is of the utmost importance not to base
your conclusions about Russia on what certain persons have told you,
or about the army on what you have seen at Friedland. Having been
threatened for a year, it has been possible for the Russians to take account of all eventualities, particularly to take account of the possibility of our enjoying immediate successes.[†]

NAPOLEON: Alexander is fickle and feeble.

CAULAINCOURT: He is obstinate. His conciliatory nature makes him give

---

[*] "An allusion to the defense works which were being thrown up along the banks of
the Dwina and at Riga."—Caulaincourt's note.

[†] Indirect discourse in original.

way easily when he does not feel the issues at stake to be particularly important. But nonetheless he draws a line beyond which he will not be pushed.

NAPOLEON: He has the Greek character—he is untrustworthy.

CAULAINCOURT: I would not suggest that he has always spoken everything that was in his mind. But whatever he has deigned to say to me has proved correct, and whatever promises he has made to Your Majesty through me he has kept.

NAPOLEON: Alexander is ambitious. There is some hidden purpose which he hopes to achieve through war. He wants war, I tell you. Otherwise, why should he refuse every arrangement I put forward? He has some secret purpose. Can't you see through him? No, he has larger motives than Poland and Oldenburg.

CAULAINCOURT: These motives, and the fact that your army is at Danzig, are in themselves enough to explain the line he has taken; though naturally, like every government in Europe, he is uneasy about the change Your Majesty has made in your policy since Tilsit, and, more particularly, since the Peace of Vienna.

NAPOLEON: What has all that to do with Alexander? It does not affect him. Have I not told him to take Finland, Wallachia, and Moldavia? Have I not suggested that he should partition Turkey? Did I not give him three hundred millions for the Austrian war?

CAULAINCOURT: Yes, Sire; but you would not expect such enticements to blind him to the fact that Your Majesty has since then marked out a quite new policy, whose execution begins in Poland—that is, in Russian territory.

NAPOLEON: Like him, you are simply dreaming! Once more—I do not want to go to war with him. But he must fulfill the commitments which he has undertaken, and enforce an embargo on English trade. What has he to fear from changes in my policy? What do such changes matter to a country like Russia, away at the back of beyond?

CAULAINCOURT: On that point he has never explained himself to me.

NAPOLEON: I don't prevent him from extending his dominions in Asia, or even in Turkey, if he wants to, so long as he does not touch Constantinople. He is vexed that I should hold Holland. That galls him because he needs foreign loans.

CAULAINCOURT: The reunion of the Hanseatic towns, the establishment of the Grand Duchy of Frankfort, which means that Your Majesty intends to keep Italy; the giving of Hanover to Westphalia. All these changes, made in times of peace and simply announced by decree, alienate England and put obstacles in the way of making peace with her.

Therefore they conflict with Russia's best interests. Even so, it will not be on that account that she goes to war.

NAPOLEON: And must I be dictated to by the English and by my brother *
just to please Alexander? Rumiantsof † knows quite well that before taking these steps I did everything in my power to induce England to make peace. Labouchère has been to London several times, even on behalf of the Dutch. Am I to allow the north of Germany to be flooded with English goods?

CAULAINCOURT: Had one merely threatened to put those measures in force, that would have been good policy. The execution of those measures, however, plus the movement of whole armies toward the north—instead of a few battalions to put pressure on the customs officers—has aroused apprehension.

NAPOLEON: You see no further than Alexander, and he is merely frightened. It is these very policies to which you object that are taking all the heart out of the English, and will force them to make peace.

(*"This conversation continued for some time longer. The Emperor jumped from one question to another, and, at long intervals, returned to the same questions, no doubt to see if I kept to the same answers. To judge from his air of preoccupation, and from the long silences which broke up our five hours of conversation, it looked as if he were giving more serious consideration to the matters under discussion than perhaps he had ever given them before...."*—Caulaincourt)

NAPOLEON (*after a long silence*): It is the Austrian marriage which has set us at variance. The Tsar Alexander was angry because I did not marry his sister.

CAULAINCOURT: May I take the liberty of reminding Your Majesty that, as I have formerly reported to you, Russia was not at all eager for such a marriage. Although the Emperor had not been able to refuse outright to lend himself to the project, he would never have given way on the question of religion. In any case, there would have been a year's delay, even if the Tsar had been able to obtain his mother's consent. In short, he had not committed himself in regard to the matter, and Russia was rather pleased than otherwise to learn of the unexpected Austrian marriage having taken place, notwithstanding our somewhat unceremonious manner of going back on the proposals of our own making— proposals which, had they not been accepted, would have made my position decidedly embarrassing.‡

---

* Probably Louis of Holland.
† The Russian Foreign Minister.
‡ Indirect discourse in original.

NAPOLEON: I have forgotten the details of the affair, but Russia was certainly angry about our rapprochement with Austria.

CAULAINCOURT: On the contrary, Sire, the immediate reaction in Petersburg was an agreeable sense of relief at the removal of a very delicate question between the French and Russian governments, and a still more delicate question between the Tsar and his mother and family. This was proved by my conversations with the Emperor and Count Rumiantsof when the first overtures in regard to the matter were made.

NAPOLEON: I desire neither war nor the re-establishment of Poland, but an understanding in the matter of neutral shipping and other differences is essential.

CAULAINCOURT: If Your Majesty really desires an understanding, it will not be hard to bring one about.

NAPOLEON: Are you sure about that?

CAULAINCOURT: Quite sure. But reasonable proposals must be put forward.

NAPOLEON: What proposals? Enumerate them.

CAULAINCOURT: Your Majesty knows as well as I do, and has known for long enough, the causes of the present estrangement. And you know better than I do what you are prepared to do to remedy it.

NAPOLEON: But what? What does he want me to do?

CAULAINCOURT: In regard to trade between the two countries, an arrangement should be made on a basis of reciprocal benefits, and a similar arrangement for merchant shipping in general. The admission of neutral ships into Russian ports should be countenanced, as long as we go on selling licenses and allowing licensed vessels into French ports. The Prince of Oldenburg should be provided for in such a way that he is not, as at Erfurt, entirely dependent on you. An arrangement should be made about Danzig, another about Prussia, and so on . . .

NAPOLEON (*interrupting*): * Monsieur Lauriston has been responsible for the carrying out of this policy. You ought to take a holiday.

CAULINCOURT: I beg Your Majesty to let me say one thing more.

NAPOLEON: Go on.

CAULINCOURT: It is for you, Sire, to decide whether there is to be peace or war. May I beseech Your Majesty, when you make your choice between the certain good of the one and the hazards of the other, to take full account of your own welfare and of the welfare of France.

NAPOLEON: You speak like a Russian.

CAULAINCOURT: On the contrary, like a good Frenchman—like one of Your Majesty's most faithful servants.

---

* "The Emperor saw that I was touching on political matters the discussion of which would force him to commit himself probably more than he wished to."—Caulaincourt

NAPOLEON: I repeat, I do not want war. But I cannot prevent the Poles from wanting me and expecting me. Davout and Rapp report that the Lithuanians are furious with the Russians; and that they are constantly sending delegates to them to urge us on, press us to make up our minds.

CAULAINCOURT: You are being misled, Sire. Of the governments which have partitioned Poland, the Russian government is by its nature best suited to the Polish nobility. They had been well treated by the Tsar Paul, and even better treated by Alexander. I have met many landowners from Polish Russia and have found that, while of course they regretted their lost national independence, they had little stomach for a new venture to recover it which might not, even if it succeeded, involve Poland's being reinstated as an independent power. The example of the Duchy of Warsaw, whose situation, from their point of view, is far from satisfactory, has not turned them in our favour so much as Your Majesty thinks. The rivalries persisting between the great Polish families, no less than the natural instability of the Polish character, would always hinder their common action. Your Majesty ought not to shut his eyes to the fact that it was only too well understood in Europe nowadays that when you concern yourself with the affairs of a country it is to serve your own rather than its interests.

NAPOLEON: You think so, do you?

CAULAINCOURT: Yes, Sire.

NAPOLEON (*jokingly*): You don't believe in spoiling me. It's time to go to dinner.

(*Withdraws.*)

(*"Thus ended a conversation which had lasted five hours and left me with no hope that peace would be maintained in Europe."*—Caulaincourt)

Napoleon

4.

MOSCOW AND THE ROAD BACK.

*Can you picture to yourself, Caulaincourt,
the figure you would cut in an iron cage, in
the main square of London?*

H AD Napoleon listened to his former ambassador, the history of Europe
—as well as his own—might have been different. Not only do Caulaincourt's repeated warnings go unheeded, but Napoleon continues bantering and rebuking him for his advice. "The Tsar's cajoleries have turned
your head," he says to him. "You have become a Russian." When Napoleon launches his massive attack with 600,000 men on June 22, 1812,
Caulaincourt, loyal even in the conviction of certain disaster, is at his
side. Along the route Napoleon chides him on his predictions. "The Tsar
will capitulate soon," he boasts. After Borodino, Caulaincourt finds Napoleon less jocular. Some of the Emperor's confidence vanishes as the
casualties are counted. Finally, Moscow is sighted, and Napoleon jubi-
lantly shouts, "Here is the famous city at last!" There follows the grim,
bleak sojourn in the empty shell of a sinister metropolis. But the weather
is good, almost like that at Fontainebleau, Napoleon observes, ridiculing
Caulaincourt's dire forecasts. Again Caulaincourt warns him: "Winter
will come like a bombshell, Sire!" Ironically, Moscow is suddenly ablaze
in a carnival of incendiarism, and Napoleon looks on in helpless rage.
Still no word of surrender from the Tsar. "This is getting serious," he
tells Caulaincourt gloomily; "I am still defeating the Russians, but that
brings nothing to an end."

Then, on October 13, the first snow falls, and Napoleon, remembering
the earlier winter campaign in Poland, gives the order: "Evacuate Moscow!" And now begins the slow, catastrophic retreat, over an endless white
waste, of a numb and tattered army, the bulk of its forces to litter the
fields of Russia as a macabre warning to all Moscow-bound conquerors
of the future. As the French approach the border, Napoleon, to escape
capture, disguises himself as a Monsieur de Rayvenal, secretary to the
Duc de Vicence, a title which he had earlier conferred on Caulaincourt.

Harold Nicolson* gives us a picture of the two fugitives: "On reaching Kowno, Caulaincourt discovered an old covered sledge—a mere box on runners which had once been painted red. They abandoned the comfort of the travelling carriage; they abandoned the luggage; even Rustam, the mameluke, and the Emperor's dressing case were left behind. Unshaven and alone they pursued their journey day and night across the snow. At Tilsit they entered Prussian territory and the Emperor became afraid lest he might be recognized and seized; he cowered back into the recesses of the sleigh, pulling his fur cap down upon his eyes, muffling himself in the great green velvet bearskin which he wore."

Well might the Emperor conceal his identity. Of his many bête-noirs during the flight, Prussia, a land he had devastated and humiliated, is his most troublesome. Yet, once in the Grand Duchy of Warsaw he regains some of his old confidence, minimizes his losses, pictures to Caulaincourt the great moral effect of his return to Paris. In moments of righteous self-defense, he solemnly explains to Caulaincourt that by invading Russia he had thought only of saving civilization: "One enemy alone must henceforth be visible in Europe. That enemy is the Russian colossus." But now, as the two arrive in Glogau in Lower Silesia, Napoleon's thoughts are mainly on these vengeful and unforgetting Prussians. We yield the chronicle to Caulaincourt, who jotted down the curious conversation with Napoleon the moment the Prussian danger was behind them.

(*December 12, 1812*—"*On our arrival at Glogau that evening the general in command was not a little surprised to discover that the Master of Horse was none other than the Emperor himself. His Majesty went closely into the condition of the country, issued various orders, and barely took time to sup, so anxious was he to be on the way once more. We set off in the carriage offered by the general and accepted by the Emperor, who was very tired from being unable to lie at full length in the sledge. Certain as I was that the snow would prevent us going far on wheels, I took the precaution of having our faithful sledge follow; and it was as well that I did so, for, being unable to proceed in the carriage at more than a walking pace, we had not left Glogau far behind when we transferred into our less comfortable conveyance. Half-frozen in this modest vehicle, which we should have done well not to leave, the Emperor was unable to sleep, and began to talk of the army, of which, owing to the rapidity of our movements, we could have no news.*

* The Congress of Vienna (Harcourt, Brace, 1946, p. 5).

He longed to get into Saxony. He did not like having to cross Prussian territory, and this led to the following conversation. . . ."—Caulaincourt)

NAPOLEON: If we are stopped, Caulaincourt, what will they do to us? Do you think I shall be recognized, that it will be known that I am here? You are popular enough in Germany, Caulaincourt. You speak the language. You protected the postmasters and took all my gendarmes to furnish them with escorts. They would never allow you to be arrested or ill treated.

CAULAINCOURT: I do not suppose they will have very grateful memories of a protection that did not hinder their being pillaged.

NAPOLEON: Bah! They may have suffered for twenty-four hours, but you had their horses given back to them. Berthier never stopped talking of your claims on their behalf. Have you ever been in Silesia?

CAULAINCOURT: Only with Your Majesty.

NAPOLEON: Then you are not known here?

CAULAINCOURT: No, Sire.

NAPOLEON: I did not reach Glogau until after the gates had been closed for the night. Unless the general or the courier have been chattering in front of the postilion, it is impossible that anyone should know I am in Prussia.

CAULAINCOURT: That is true; and no one would imagine that it was the Emperor travelling in this sorry vehicle. As to the Master of Horse, he is not of sufficient importance for the Prussians to compromise themselves by arresting him. Your Majesty's journey has been so speedy that no one on the road so much as knows about it. Some sort of plan would have to be arranged before any attempt could be made on us. Even a spiteful and determined man must get three or four kindred spirits to help him.

NAPOLEON: If the Prussians were to stop us, what would they do to us?

CAULAINCOURT: If it was the result of a definite plan, not knowing what to do with us they would kill us. So we must defend ourselves to the utmost extremity. We may be lucky; there are four of us.

NAPOLEON (*jokingly*): But if they take you alive, what will they do to you, my good Duke of Vicenza?

CAULAINCOURT: If they take me it will be because of my secretary, in which event I shall be in a bad way.

NAPOLEON (*briskly*): If we are stopped, we shall be made prisoners of war, like Francis I. Prussia will get back the millions she has paid, and will ask for millions more.

CAULAINCOURT: If they dared strike such a blow, Sire, we should not get off so cheaply as that.

NAPOLEON: I think you are right. They fear me too much. They would want to keep me.

CAULAINCOURT: That is highly probable.

NAPOLEON: For fear I should escape, or that some terrible reprisals would be undertaken, the Prussians would hand me over to the English.

CAULAINCOURT: Possibly!

NAPOLEON: Can you picture to yourself, Caulaincourt, the figure you would cut in an iron cage, in the main square of London?

CAULAINCOURT: If it meant sharing your fate, Sire, I should not complain.

NAPOLEON (*with a laugh*): It is not a question of complaining, but of something that may happen at any moment, and of the figure you would cut in that cage, shut up like a wretched Negro left to be eaten by flies after being smeared with honey.

("*And there he was for a quarter of an hour, laughing at this foolish notion, and the idea of that man in the cage. Never had I seen the Emperor laugh so heartily, and his gaiety was so infectious that it was some time before we could speak a word without finding some fresh source of amusement. It was with considerable relief that the Emperor reflected that nothing could be known of his departure and that the Prussians, even if they did learn about it, would not dare take any action against him while their troops were in the midst of ours and we were as strong as they imagined us to be.*"—Caulaincourt)

Napoleon

5.

NAPOLEON AND METTERNICH: AN IMPERIAL TANTRUM OVER THE PROSPECT OF AUSTRIAN NEUTRALITY.

I was brought up on the battlefield and a man like me does not concern himself much about the lives of a million men.

IF NAPOLEON felt that in Goethe he had met his equal in genius, he was soon to learn that in Prince Metternich he had met his superior in Machiavellian intrigue. The conversation between these two masters of Europe's destiny in Dresden on June 26, 1813, marks a turning-point in modern history. From it one may date the certainty of Napoleon's ruin and the beginning of what is known as the Age of Metternich, an age of black reaction, that ended only in the widespread revolutionary upheavals of 1848. As foreign minister of Austria, Metternich had been playing a watchful game since Napoleon's ruinous adventure in Russia. In an inflamed Europe divided between France on one side and a coalition of Russia, Prussia, and England on the other, Austria had remained "benevolently neutral." Napoleon was son-in-law to the Emperor Francis, besides which Austria was far from eager to have any member of the coalition strengthened at the expense of France. The historic thesis of the balance of power had already taken shape in Metternich's mind. Still, if Napoleonic France should succumb, Metternich was prepared to see Austria fill the vacuum as the dominant power in Europe.

Meanwhile, the Russian disaster has been followed by Wellington's victories in Spain. Moreover, Napoleon's latest Prussian campaign has brought only Pyrrhic victories. Something like equilibrium prevails between the forces lined up against each other—Napoleon and the three-power coalition. This balance Austria, with her secretly massing troops, can shatter overnight. For a while Napoleon plays his cards cautiously. Suspecting Austria's double game, he agrees to a six weeks' armistice on June 4, thus shifting the conflict from a military to a diplomatic plane.

And now all Europe becomes one whispering coulisse of secret maneuvering. Sensing that the supreme opportunity of ending Napoleon's rule is approaching, the coalition is consolidating its forces. England is pouring in millions of pounds; hundreds of thousands of fresh troops are promised on all sides. Spies bring Napoleon reports of ominous signs all over Europe. Metternich continues to play his ostensible role of mediator; yet on June 24 he confers with the rulers of the coalition at Reichenbach and pledges Austria's support if Napoleon fails to evacuate large areas of Europe. Two days later, this master-schemer is in Dresden assuring the French Emperor that "Austria is free from all engagements." Metternich's main object is to prolong the Armistice to August 10, to enable Austria the better to prepare for the crushing blow. "The whole scene," wrote Walter Alison Phillips, "was on his part a masterpiece of Machiavellian diplomacy."

Thus, it is a sanguine Metternich, unafraid of Napoleon's blustering threats, who takes leave of the Emperor Francis at Gitschin in Bohemia on June 24 to set out for Dresden. Metternich arrives in Dresden the following day at 2 o'clock in the afternoon. An interview with Maret, Napoleon's foreign minister, follows immediately. At 11 A.M. of June 26 an invitation arrives from Napoleon to come at once. At a quarter to twelve Metternich reaches the Marcolini Palace (located in the suburbs and built by the Emperor Frederick Augustus for his friend the Italian Camillo Marcolini). Napoleon is waiting for him in the gallery of the palace. The two men greet each other amicably and a conversation follows which lasts eight and a half hours.

Of this conversation there are at least four records, the standard one being that rendered by Metternich himself and used below. This accepted version began as a dispatch to the Emperor Francis, was expanded for the state documents published many years later, and further amplified in Metternich's autobiography for the section devoted to the "History of the Alliances" (Memoirs, Vol. II, translated by Mrs. Alexander Napier, Scribner's, 1880–82). On the French side there are three versions to counterbalance Metternich's. One is Napoleon's own operatic monologue given to Montholon on St. Helena. Another is that of the Baron Fain, incorporated in his Manuscrit de 1813 (Paris, 1824) and based on Maret's oral reconstruction of the interview. This became the basis of most French histories, notably that of Thiers, who used it as gospel truth at full length.

It is the Baron Fain who reports that Napoleon tauntingly asked Metternich: "How much has England paid you?" The Germans, and Austrians of course, have ridiculed this. Metternich, they protest, would never have tolerated such a shameful accusation. A second French version, unearthed only in recent years, is that of Caulaincourt, who later replaced Maret as Napoleon's foreign minister. Caulaincourt's version was based on Napoleon's own impassioned account of the interview shortly after Metternich left the Marcolini Palace. The French versions all agree that Napoleon not only offered to return the Illyrian provinces to Austria as a gesture of good-will, but that he saw completely through Metternich's double-dealing.

At the moment we are back in the Marcolini Palace, eavesdropping on a garrulous conqueror and his Austrian nemesis. . . .

("*The appearance of the Austrian Minister of Foreign Affairs at Napoleon's headquarters could, under such circumstances, only be regarded by the leaders of the French army as decisive in its results. I was received in Dresden with this feeling. It would be difficult to describe the expression of painful anxiety shown on the faces of the crowd of men in uniform, who were assembled in the waiting-rooms of the Emperor. The Prince of Neufchâtel (Berthier) said to me in a low voice, 'Do not forget that Europe requires peace, and especially France, which will have nothing but peace.' Not seeing myself called upon to answer this, I at once entered the Emperor's reception-room. Napoleon waited for me, standing in the middle of the room, with his sword at his side and his hat under his arm. He came up to me in a studied manner, and inquired after the health of the Emperor. His countenance then soon clouded over 'and he spoke, standing in front of me, as follows:*"— Metternich)

NAPOLEON: So you, too, want war; well, you shall have it. I have annihilated the Prussian army at Lützen; I have beaten the Russians at Bautzen; now you wish your turn to come. Be it so; the rendezvous shall be in Vienna. Men are incorrigible: experience is lost upon you. Three times have I replaced the Emperor Francis on his throne. I have promised always to live in peace with him; I have married his daughter. At the time I said to myself, you are perpetrating a folly; but it was done, and today I repent of it!

("*This introduction doubled my feeling of the strength of my position. I felt myself, at this crisis, the representative of all European society. If I may say so—Napoleon seemed to me small!*"—Metternich)

METTERNICH: Peace and war lie in your Majesty's hands. The Emperor, my master, has duties to fulfill, before which all other considerations fall into the background. The fate of Europe, her future and yours, all lie in your hands. Between Europe and the aims you have hitherto pursued there is absolute contradiction. The world requires peace. In order to secure this peace, you must reduce your power within bounds compatible with the general tranquillity, or you will fall in the contest. To-day you can yet conclude peace; tomorrow it may be too late. The Emperor, my master, in these negotiations is only guided by the voice of conscience; it is for you, Sire, now to take counsel of yours.

NAPOLEON (*sharply*): Well now, what do they want me to do? Do they want me to degrade myself? Never! I shall know how to die; but I shall not yield one handbreadth of soil. Your sovereigns, born to the throne, may be beaten twenty times, and still go back to their palaces; that cannot I—the child of fortune; my reign will not outlast the day when I have ceased to be strong, and therefore to be feared. I have committed one great fault in forgetting what this army has cost me—the most splendid army that ever existed. I may defy man, but not the elements; the cold has ruined me. In one night I lost thirty thousand horses. I have lost everything, except honor and the consciousness of what I owe to a brave people who, after such enormous misfortunes, have given me fresh proofs of their devotion and their conviction that I alone can rule them. I have made up for the losses of the past year; only look at the army, after the battles I have just won! I will hold a review before you!

METTERNICH: And it is that very army which desires peace!

NAPOLEON (*interrupting hastily*): Not the army. No! my generals wish for peace. I have no more generals. The cold of Moscow has demoralized them. I have seen the boldest cry like children. They were physically and morally broken. A fortnight ago I might have concluded peace; to-day I can no longer. I have won two fights; I shall not conclude peace.

METTERNICH: In all that your Majesty has just said to me, I see a fresh proof that Europe and your Majesty cannot come to an understanding. Your peace is never more than a truce. Misfortune, like success, hurries you to war. The moment has arrived when you and Europe both throw down the gauntlet; you will take it up—you and Europe; and it will not be Europe that will be defeated.

NAPOLEON: You think to conquer me by a coalition, then? But how many are there of you Allies—four, five, six, twenty? The more you are, so much the better for me. I take up the challenge. (*With a forced laugh*) But I can assure you, that next October we shall meet in Vienna; then it will be seen what has become of your good friends, the Russians and Prussians. Do you count on Germany? See what it did in the year 1809!

To hold the people there in check, my soldiers are sufficient; and for the faith of the princes, my security is the fear they have of you. Declare your neutrality, and hold to it, then I will consent to the negotiations in Prague. Will you have an armed neutrality? Be it so! Send three hundred thousand men to Bohemia; the word of the Emperor is sufficient that he will not make war against me before the negotiation is ended.

METTERNICH: The Emperor has offered the Powers his mediation, not his neutrality. Russia and Prussia have accepted the mediation: it is for you to declare yourself today. If you will accept what I have just proposed, we will fix a time for the duration of the negotiations. If you refuse it, the Emperor, my gracious master, will consider himself free to make what decisions and take up what attitude he chooses. The situation is critical: the army must live; very soon there will be two hundred and fifty thousand men in Bohemia; they may stay there a few weeks, but they cannot remain for months in quarters.

(*"Here Napoleon again interrupted me, to go into a long digression on the possible strength of our army. According to his calculation, we could at the most send seventy-five thousand men to take the field in Bohemia. He based these calculations on the normal condition of the population of the country, on the supposed losses in the last wars, and on our rules for conscription. I expressed my astonishment at the incorrectness of the information he had obtained, when it would have been so easy for him to obtain fuller and more correct statistics."*—Metternich)

METTERNICH: I will pledge myself to give you an exact list of your battalions; and should your Majesty not be as well informed on the strength of the Austrian army?

NAPOLEON: I am so. I possess most minute information respecting the army, and am certain I do not deceive myself as to its effectiveness. M. de Narbonne sent a number of spies into the field, and his information includes the very drummers of your army—my headquarters have done the same; but I know better than anyone the value to be placed on such information. My calculations rest on mathematical grounds, and are therefore reliable; in fact, no one has more than he can have.

(*"Napoleon took me into his study, and showed me the lists of our forces as they were daily sent to him. We examined this with great particularity, and almost regiment for regiment. Our discussion on this subject lasted more than an hour. On returning into the reception-room, he did not speak again on political subjects, and I might have thought that he wished to draw my attention away from the object of*

*my mission, if a former experience had not taught me that such digres-
sions were natural to him. He spoke of the whole of his operations in
Russia, and expatiated at length and with the pettiest details about his
last return to France. It was clear to me from all this that he was constantly endeavoring to show that his defeat of 1812 was entirely owing
to the time of year, and that his moral position in France had never
been firmer than it was in consequence of this same event. 'It was a
hard test,' he said to me, 'but I have stood it perfectly well.' After I had
listened to him for more than half an hour, I interrupted him with the
remark that in what he had just told me I saw strong proof of the necessity of putting an end to so uncertain a fate."—Metternich)*

METTERNICH: Fortune may play you false a second time, as it did in 1812.
In ordinary times armies are formed of only a small part of the population; today it is the whole people that you have called to arms. Is not
your present army anticipated by a generation? I have seen your soldiers: they are mere children. Your Majesty has the feeling that you are
absolutely necessary to the nation: but is not the nation also necessary
to you? And if this juvenile army that you levied but yesterday should
be swept away, what then?

NAPOLEON (*overcome with rage, pale, and his features distorted*): You are
no soldier, and you do not know what goes on in the mind of a soldier.
I was brought up on the battlefield, and a man like me does not concern
himself much about the lives of a million men.* (*Throws his hat,
which he had been holding in his hand, into a corner of the room.*)

METTERNICH (*leaning against the edge of a console between the two windows*): Why have you chosen to say this to me within these four walls;
open the doors, and let your words sound from one end of France to the
other. The cause which I represent will not lose thereby.

NAPOLEON (*recovering himself, and in a calmer tone*): The French cannot complain of me; to spare them, I have sacrificed the Germans and
the Poles. I have lost in the campaign of Moscow three hundred thousand men, and there were not more than thirty thousand Frenchmen
among them.

METTERNICH: You forget, Sire, that you are speaking to a German.

(*"Napoleon walked up and down the room, and at the second turn
he picked up his hat from the floor. Then he began to speak of his marriage."—Metternich*)

NAPOLEON: So I have perpetrated a very stupid piece of folly in marrying
an Archduchess of Austria.

---

* "I do not dare to make use here of the much worse expressions employed by Napoleon."—Metternich's note.

METTERNICH: Since your Majesty desires to know my opinion, I will candidly say that Napoleon the conquerer made a mistake.

NAPOLEON: The Emperor Francis will then dethrone his daughter?

METTERNICH: The Emperor knows nothing but his duty, and he will fulfill it. Whatever the fate of his daughter may be, the Emperor Francis is in the first place a monarch, and the interests of his people will always take the first place in his calculations.

NAPOLEON (*interrupting*): Well, what you say does not astonish me: everything confirms my idea that I have made an inexcusable mistake. When I married an Archduchess I tried to weld the new with the old, Gothic prejudices with the institutions of my century: I deceived myself, and I, this day, feel the whole extent of my error. It may cost me my throne, but I will bury the world beneath its ruins.

(*"The conversation had lasted till half-past eight o'clock in the evening. It was already quite dark. No one had ventured to come into the room. Not one pause of silence interrupted this animated discussion, in which I can count no less than six moments in which my words had the weight of a formal declaration of war. I have no intention of reproducing here all that Napoleon said during this long interview. I have only dwelt upon the most striking points in it which bear directly on the object of my mission. We wandered far away from it twenty times;* * *those who have known Napoleon, and transacted business with him, will not be surprised at that. When Napoleon dismissed me, his tone had become calm and quiet. I could no longer distinguish his features. He accompanied me to the door of the reception-room."*—Metternich)

NAPOLEON (*holding the handle of the folding-door*): We shall see one another again!

METTERNICH: At your pleasure, Sire, but I have no hope of attaining the object of my mission.

NAPOLEON: Well now (*touching Metternich on the shoulder*), do you know what will happen? You will not make war on me.

METTERNICH (*quickly*): You are lost, Sire. I had the presentiment of it when I came. Now, in going, I have the certainty.

(*"In the anterooms I found the same generals whom I had seen on entering. They crowded round me to read in my face the impression of the nearly nine hours' conversation. I did not stop, and I do not think I satisfied their curiosity. Berthier accompanied me to my carriage. He*

---

* "The account of his campaign of 1812 alone took up several hours of our conversation; many other things quite foreign to the object of my mission occupied his attention for a long time."—Metternich's note.

seized a moment when no one was near to ask me whether I had been satisfied with the Emperor. 'Yes,' I answered, 'he has explained everything to me; it is all over with the man.' I heard afterwards that the same evening, at bedtime, Napoleon said to some one about him, 'I have had a long conversation with Metternich. He held out bravely; thirteen times did I throw him the gauntlet, and thirteen times did he pick it up. But the glove will remain in my hands at last.' "—Metternich)

(As for the famous episode of the hat which Napoleon flung to the ground in a rage, there are again several versions. That Napoleon threw down his hat seems certain. That he himself picked it up after Metternich showed no sign of stooping to do so, is Metternich's story. In the accepted French version Napoleon gives the hat a furious kick when he next strides past it. It was once thought that Napoleon deliberately let fall the hat to force Metternich to stoop to raise it for him. But Metternich himself assured the Earl of Stanford in 1848, "*Non, il ne l'a pas laissé tomber, mais il l'a jeté avec fureur contre le mur.*" * According to the French versions, Metternich's parting remark to the marshals waiting outside Napoleon's private cabinet was: "I declare to you solemnly that your master is out of his mind!" In any case, Metternich, before he rejoined his Emperor at Gitschin, got what he had come for, an extension of the Armistice to August 10. Napoleon, fully conscious of being trapped, but incorrigibly headstrong to the end, refused to budge on Austria's demands. Just before dawn on August 12 soldiers bivouacked in Silesia saw beacon-fires light up along the Riesengebirge. The savage fighting was on again. Austria had joined the coalition that would soon bring the imperial upstart to his knees in a colossal retreat across Europe.)

---

* "No, he did not let it fall, but threw it angrily against the wall."

Napoleon

6.

EPILOGUE TO WATERLOO: A DEFEATED CONQUEROR CONSIDERS THE SHAPE OF THINGS TO COME.

*I shall go to the United States. They will
give me some land. . . . I shall exist on the
products of my fields.*

AFTER the disastrous defeat of the "Battle of the Nations" at Leipzig in October, 1813, Napoleon's hordes retreated swiftly back to France. The vast net of the coalition now closed in on the French Emperor and soon Paris was under siege and finally occupied. The dynasty had crashed about his ears and family and friends deserted him en masse. In despair Napoleon signed an act of abdication on April 11, 1814, surrendering all claim to the throne for himself and his heirs. One night he attempted suicide, but survived through a timely attack of nausea. Then, on April 28, accompanied by a sizable retinue, and still sporting the title of Emperor—by the grace of the coalition powers—the fallen conqueror boarded the H.M.S. "Undaunted" for the island of Elba, landing a week later at Porto Ferrajo.

The Congress of Vienna went on with its work of recharting the torn continent of Europe. Less than a year later the news of Napoleon's escape struck every chancellory in Europe like a bombshell. The Bourbons fled their recovered throne as the cry "Vive l'Empereur!" went up from one end of France to the other. There followed an anxious Hundred Days for all the kings, ministers, and generals of Europe. By the time Napoleon reached Paris, the massive coalition had reformed. The Congress of Vienna reconvened, and once again vast armies were converging on this undiscourageable Soldier of Fortune. What followed scarcely needs repetition:— the decision of Napoleon to prevent the Prussian and British armies from joining; his departure from Paris on June 12, 1815; Waterloo on June 18. France was now irrevocably lost, and a stubborn little ex-corporal, with a mania for warfare and power, fled back to Paris a thoroughly beaten man. There was no one with him when he arrived in

230

Paris, burst into the Tuileries and cried out to his devoted minister Caulaincourt, "You have heard the news? All is lost . . . I am done for! I must have a bath and two hours' sleep, I am choking!" A few days later Napoleon signed a second act of abdication, and on June 25 left the Tuileries for the beautiful Malmaison château just outside Paris, the same Malmaison that had been the favorite residence of the discarded Empress Josephine, who had died a year earlier. There Napoleon remained five days weighing the alternatives that faced him. Capture by the Prussians meant certain execution. Surrender to the British would be humiliating. Suicide had been tried once and had proved disagreeable. At length, the brilliant thought seized him of escaping to America and being joined there by the scattered members of his dethroned family.

It is at this point that a rather genial little man named Fleury de Chaboulon enters the picture. Fleury, a cabinet secretary and auditor of the French Council of State, had visited Elba on February 22 on a self-imposed mission to urge Napoleon to return to France. To Fleury we also owe a vivid eye-witness account of the Battle of Waterloo, printed as part of his Les Cent Jours (in the original French, by J. Murray, London, 1819). The ubiquitous state servitor was then acting as a combined secretary and messenger to Napoleon. We have his word for it that his only concern was Napoleon's safety. "He must leave tonight," he jots down dramatically on June 29; "God knows where we shall go, but I mean to follow him. More than anything else I want to see him out of danger. Anyway, it is far better to run risks with him than to stay here." Then in a final access of despair, Fleury writes: "France is lost! I wish I were dead!"* And now, as passing troops send up cries of "Vive l'Empereur!" from the nearby road from St. Germain, Fleury enters Napoleon's private chambers at Malmaison. The following dialogue I have translated from his French original.

("As soon as I was free to do as I pleased, I rushed to Malmaison. Napoleon, who was grateful to me for this continual messenger service, was always ready to receive me at once. I reported everything that I thought might interest him. I did not omit the fact that the enemy was already master of some of the environs of Paris and that it was important for him to be on his guard."—Fleury de Chaboulon)

---

* It is no dishonor to Fleury to note here that he survived to write his memoirs of the Hundred Days and to prosper in the Restoration as director of one of France's first insurance companies, then as State Councillor, and finally as deputy from the arrondissement of Château-Salins.

NAPOLEON: I shall have no fear tomorrow. I promised Decrès to leave and I shall leave tonight. I am bored with myself, with Paris, and with France. Make your preparations and remain here.

FLEURY: Sire, when I promised Your Majesty to follow you yesterday, I only consulted my devotion to you. But when I informed my mother of my decision, she made me swear on her white hair not to abandon her. Sire, she is seventy-four years old. She is blind. My brothers were all killed on the field of battle. She has only me in the whole world to protect her. Your Majesty, I did not have the strength to resist her pleas.

NAPOLEON: You did well. You belong to your mother. Stay with her. If some day you are free to do so, come to me. You will always be welcome.

FLEURY: So Your Majesty is resolved to leave.

NAPOLEON: What do you want me to do here now?

FLEURY: Your Majesty is right, but. . . .

NAPOLEON: But what? Do you prefer me to stay?

FLEURY: Sire, I must confess that I cannot see you leave without some alarm.

NAPOLEON: To be sure, difficulties lie ahead, but a good wind and luck. . . .

FLEURY: Luck! Ah, Sire, that's not for us! Besides, where will Your Majesty go?

NAPOLEON: I shall go to the United States. They will give me some land, or else I shall purchase it, and we will cultivate it. I shall end the way man began. I shall exist on the products of my fields and my flocks.

FLEURY: That's all very fine, Your Majesty. But will the English leave you in peace to cultivate your fields?

NAPOLEON: Why not? What harm can I do them?

FLEURY: What harm, Sire! Has Your Majesty by any chance forgotten how you made England tremble? As long as you live, Sire, or as long as you remain free, England will fear the consequences of your hatred and your genius. And perhaps you were less dangerous to her on the degraded throne of Louis XVIII than you would be in the United States. The Americans love and admire you. You would exercise a great influence over them. And you might even incite them to adventures that would prove fatal to England.

NAPOLEON: What adventures? The English know very well that the Americans would give their lives in defense of their national soil, but that they dislike fighting a war away from their homes. They have not yet reached the point where they can seriously worry the English. Some day, perhaps, they will be the avengers of the sea, but that day is still far off. The Americans will become great slowly, or not at all.

FLEURY: Granted that the Americans cannot cause England any serious anxiety at the moment, your presence would nevertheless furnish England with an excuse for arousing Europe against them. The Allies will regard their work as unfinished so long as you remain beyond their reach and they will force the Americans, if not to turn you over to them, at least to banish you from their territory.

NAPOLEON: Very well! Then I shall go to Mexico! I shall find patriots there and place myself at their head.

FLEURY: Your Majesty forgets they already have leaders of their own. People make revolutions for themselves, not for others, and the rebel leaders would either sell out Your Majesty or force you to go elsewhere.

NAPOLEON: Good! I would leave them there and go to Caracas. If I don't get on well there, I shall go to Buenos Aires. I might even go to California.* In short, I shall travel from sea to sea until I find refuge from the malevolence and persecution of men.

FLEURY: Supposing Your Majesty *is* serious, do you flatter yourself you can elude the British fleet forever, or escape the traps they will set for you?

NAPOLEON: If I cannot escape the British, I shall have no qualms about being captured. Their government may be worthless, but they are a great, noble, and generous nation. They will treat me as I should be treated. In any case, what would you have me do? Do you take me for a fool to let myself be taken prisoner here by Wellington, and to give him the pleasure of marching me in triumph, like King John, through the streets of London? I have but one course—since my services are not wanted—and that is to leave. Destiny will do the rest.

FLEURY: There is still another course, Your Majesty, and I make bold to submit it for your consideration. . . . Your Majesty is in no position to save himself. . . .

NAPOLEON (*with a proud and angry look*): Wait a moment! Where do you see me trying to save myself?

FLEURY: I implore Your Majesty not to be annoyed at my expression. . . .

NAPOLEON: Continue! Continue!

FLEURY: I think, Sire, that for your own safety and glory you should not leave France in this way. The English have been informed of your designs to go to the United States, and doubtless their cruisers are already

---

* "Caliphornie" in Fleury's French.

swarming along our coasts. That's not all. Your Majesty knows the hatred and treachery of the Duke of Otranto. How do you know that secret orders have not already gone out to prevent your departure by holding up the ships and allowing the British to capture you? I therefore think it impossible for Your Majesty to escape, and if you do escape, sooner or later you will fall into the hands of the British. Such being the dilemma, you should try at least to acknowledge your defeat as honorably as possible.

NAPOLEON (*good-humoredly—thinking that Fleury is proposing suicide as the way out*): I realize that I could shout like Hannibal: "Let us deliver them from the terror which my name arouses in them!" But suicide is only for craven souls and sick brains. Whatever my ultimate destiny may be, I do not propose to anticipate it by a single moment.

FLEURY: That was not what I had in mind, Your Majesty. Since you are disposed to listen, Sire, this is what I would do in your place. I would give up the chimerical hope of finding refuge in any foreign country. And I would say to the Chambers: "I have abdicated to disarm our enemies. I understand they are not satisfied. If they also demand my liberty or my life, I am prepared to give them either. I am ready to submit to their will, happy that at such a price I can save France and my son." Ah, it will be beautiful to see Napoleon the Great, after removing the crown which twenty years of victories had placed on his head, offer himself as sacrifice to redeem the independence of his country!

NAPOLEON: Yes, yes, such self-sacrifice would be beautiful indeed. But a nation of thirty million which allowed it would be disgraced forever. Besides, to whom should I give myself up? To Blücher? To Wellington? They have not the required power to negotiate with me on those conditions. They would begin by making me their prisoner and then they would do to France and to me whatever entered their heads.

FLEURY: I would surrender myself, Sire, to the Emperor Alexander!

NAPOLEON: Alexander! You don't know the Russians! That would cost us both our lives! However, your idea deserves consideration. I shall think about it. Before taking any irrevocable step one should weigh it carefully. It would be nothing for me to give up my life. But it might prove a useless sacrifice for the good of France. One must never trust one's enemy.

Napoleon

7.

FINALE ON ST. HELENA: AN IRATE CAPTIVE LECTURES A BRITISH GOVERNOR ON THE PROPER BEHAVIOR TOWARD A FORMER EMPEROR.

I am an emperor in my own circle, and
will be so as long as I live.

N APOLEON left Malmaison on the night of June 28. What he did during
the next week is conjectural. That he continued to mull over the
plan to escape to America is certain, for we know that Lafayette had
arranged to have an American vessel pick him up. Unluckily the British
tightened their blockade of the coast, so that even a rowboat could not
slip through. Finally Napoleon threw himself on the generosity of the
British. On July 14 we find him writing to the Prince Regent of England:
"I place myself under the protection of the laws of the English people.
This I claim from your Royal Highness as the most powerful, the most
steadfast, and the most generous of my enemies." On July 15 he boarded
the H.M.S. "Bellerophon," commanded by Captain Maitland, and sailed
for Plymouth, arriving there on July 25. For days Britons gathered on the
shore to gape at the "Little Corporal" who had long threatened to invade
their land. The conqueror had finally arrived.

For a time the British thought of interning their imperial captive in
Scotland. The cabinet next considered turning him over to the King of
France as a state prisoner. Finally, it was decided to put the "outlaw"
completely out of reach by banishing him to the desolate island of St.
Helena. "It was thus almost by chance that Great Britain for a hundred
years had to bear the full odium of his captivity," is Harold Nicolson's
wry comment on the decision. The news infuriated Napoleon and his entourage. "I came freely on board the 'Bellerophon,'" protested Napoleon
on August 4. "I am not a prisoner; I am a guest of England . . . I appeal to
history." The appeal fell on deaf ears. Three days later Napoleon and his
suite were transferred to the H.M.S. "Northumberland," and soon the
rotund little Corsican was bound for his last island home. When the

news of Napoleon's banishment reached Goethe at Weimar, the great man who had once interviewed him at Erfurt exclaimed to his young friend Eckermann: "They have chained down another Prometheus. For the sake of a great name he knocked half the world to pieces. All romance, all illusions, all poetry are as nothing before the brute strength of such a character."

Conspicuous in the small group that was permitted to accompany Napoleon into captivity were Generals Bertrand, Montholon, and Gourgaud, and Count Las Cases, who, unlike Napoleon, were allowed to bring their families. (Generals Bertrand and Gourgaud were part of the loyal band of surviving friends who returned to St. Helena in 1840 to escort Napoleon's body back to France.) A surgeon and twelve servants completed the entourage. The "Northumberland" reached St. Helena on October 17.

There now begins a prolonged anticlimax of five and a half years for this "chained Prometheus." Surrounded by his small band of fawning votaries, he becomes a prodigious chatterbox. To Montholon he dictates reams of reminiscences. To these are added further pronouncements on the great battles which had occurred before his own advent on the stage of history. From this unending talk Las Cases also assembled huge tomes of conversation. Nor is the midnight pen of General Gourgaud idle. Unhampered by the duties of Empire, Napoleon gives himself completely to the pleasures of self-revelation. Every action of his past life is carefully scrutinized and justified. From these giant mounds of notes will grow a great legend that no amount of reasoned analysis will dissipate.

And for the great empire-builder and empire-destroyer there is a new role—that of petty squabbler. His enemy now becomes the new Governor of St. Helena, Sir Hudson Lowe, a stern taskmaster who has been sent to replace General Wilks, a man regarded by the British as too easy a mark for Napoleon's insidious charm. Sir Hudson also relieves Admiral Sir George Cockburn, who, besides commanding the naval area about St. Helena, had been given charge of the French Emperor. Like General Wilks, Sir George was also a susceptible victim. At any rate, the new governor becomes the object of Napoleon's last campaign. When they meet in April, 1816, outside the ex-Emperor's island residence at Longwood, Napoleon accuses him and the British government of every conceivable crime—of trying to kill him, of spying on him, of condemning him to slow death in a vile climate; of refusing to call him "Emperor." The man who had resisted five formidable coalitions is now reduced to a bickering battle against one British official. Sir Hudson greets all these grievances with a cool disdain, which only adds to Napoleon's fury. No serious attempt is made at reconciliation till the arrival of Admiral Sir Pulteney Malcolm, designated to succeed Sir George to the naval command of the area.

Sir Pulteney and his wife are introduced to Napoleon on June 20, 1816. The couple soon become very friendly with the captive. Since the Admiral strongly opposes Sir Hudson's rigorous methods, the suspicion grows that he is being craftily worked upon by Napoleon. However, the Admiral is no fool. He soon discovers that spread over the island is a network of petty intrigues and vicious gossip, and he resolves to act as conciliator between Sir Hudson and Napoleon. A meeting is arranged at Lockwood on August 18, 1816.

What happened at that encounter was first divulged in a dispatch of Sir Hudson Lowe's to his government—a report confirmed at the time by Malcolm. Quite humanly, Napoleon's island scribes record the conversation in a manner reflecting glory on their master. Not till 1899 was complete corroboration of the English version obtained. In that year a granddaughter of Sir Pulteney permitted publication in London by the house of Innes of a manuscript that had long been in the family: A Diary of St. Helena; The Journal of Lady Malcolm (1816–1817). The editor, Sir Arthur Wilson, wrote an introduction, which was replaced by one by Muriel Kent, another descendant of the Admiral's, for the subsequent edition of 1929 (G. Allen & Unwin, 1929, London). Lady Malcolm was herself present at most of the conversations recorded in the diary. When she was not, her husband made it a practice to dictate the details of a fresh meeting the same night. This habit of Admiral Malcolm is confirmed by a remark made in an official letter of Sir Hudson's. Of the Diary itself, Miss Kent observes: "A sober, first-hand record of my great-great uncle's conversations with Bonaparte seems at least worth comparison with other more highly colored and partisan literature relating to the ex-Emperor at St. Helena." Napoleonic scholars—particularly the British ones—have endorsed her judgment.

Before we watch Admiral Malcolm bring these two island adversaries together, a glimpse at Napoleon's mode of life at Longwood might be helpful as background. The routine was very regular: "He usually rose early and employed an hour or two either in dictating to one of his generals or in a ride on horseback. He generally took his breakfast about ten o'clock, sometimes in his own room, and sometimes with his suite. He devoted the early part of the day to reading or dictation, until about two or three o'clock, when he was in the habit of receiving visitors. After this he again took an airing, either on horseback or in his carriage, attended by the whole of his suite. On his return he either resumed his book or continued his dictation until dinner-time, which was at eight o'clock. He preferred plain food, of which he ate plentifully and with appetite; his drink was claret, of which he took but little, very rarely more than a pint. After dinner, chess, cards, a play or a romance read aloud, or general conversation, served to pass away the time until ten or eleven o'clock, at which hour he usually went to bed."*

Though Lady Malcolm does not give the hour, the visit of the two British officials obviously occurred during that part of Napoleon's afternoon routine when he relaxed after another stream of dictated self-glorification. Let us keep in mind that the Admiral participates in the talk largely as conciliator between two men who face one another with undisguised contempt. Lady Malcolm begins her diary entry as follows:

("*The Admiral met Sir Hudson at Hutt's Gate, from whence they proceeded to Longwood. On their arrival they saw Bonaparte walking in front of the house with Madame de Montholon and Count Las Cases; he endeavored to avoid them—Count Montholon came to them. Sir Hudson desired him to say to Bonaparte that he wished to speak to him. He returned to say that the Emperor waited for us. On joining, Bonaparte took little notice of Sir Hudson, but received the Admiral in his usual manner, conversed with him for a few minutes on common subjects.*"—Lady Malcolm)

SIR HUDSON (*addressing Napoleon*): I am sorry to importune you on any disagreeable subject, but the very improper conduct of Count Bertrand renders it indispensable. Having received instructions to limit the expenses at Longwood, I mentioned the subject to Counts Bertrand and Montholon. The latter fully met my wishes, but I was desirous to converse with yourself, that I might be enabled to make such arrangements as would be most agreeable to you. I came here for that purpose, but was told that you were in the bath, and that you requested that I would communicate with Count Bertrand. In compliance with this request I waited on the Count, who received me in a very extraordinary manner. Nevertheless, I told him my business and put the necessary papers into his hands. He took them and said he would show them to the Emperor. I proposed to explain, when he abruptly replied: "The less communication you and I have either verbally or in writing the

---

* R. W. Phipps, who edited a revised English edition of Bourrienne's *Mémoires*.

better." I replied the wish was reciprocal, and left him. Now I think the conduct of Count Bertrand to me, as Governor of this island, highly improper, and particularly so as I called on him in compliance with a request of the person he acknowledges his sovereign.

(*Silence for several minutes; they continue to walk to and fro, Bonaparte, apparently, meditating an answer.*)

NAPOLEON (*addressing himself to the Admiral*): Count Bertrand is a man well known and esteemed in Europe. He has been distinguished and has commanded armies. He (*nodding at Sir Hudson*) treats him like a corporal. Madame Bertrand is a lady well born, who has been accustomed to the first place in society; he does not treat her with the regard that is her due. He stops her letters, and prevents her seeing those that wish to visit her, except under restrictions. (*Turning to Sir Hudson*) Since your arrival we have experienced nothing but vexations. Your instructions are the same as Sir George Cockburn's—he told me so—but you execute them with fifty times more rigor. He never vexed us with trifles. I had reason to be displeased with some of his proceedings, but we never conversed that we were not satisfied with each other. But there is no talking to you—you are quite untractable. You suspect everything and everybody. You are a Lieutenant General, but you do your duty like *un consigne*. You never commanded any men but Corsican deserters. You vex us hourly, by your little ways. You do not know how to conduct yourself toward men of honor. Your soul is too low. Why do you not treat us like prisoners of war? You treat us like Botany Bay convicts.

SIR HUDSON (*coolly*): I have every desire to render your situation as agreeable as it is in my power, but you prevent me. General Bertrand has written to me that I render your situation dreadful. He accused me, as you do now, of abuse of power and injustice. I am the subject of a free government. I hold every species of tyranny and despotism in execration, and I will repel every attack upon my character on this point, as a calumny against a man who cannot be attacked with the arms of truth.

NAPOLEON: There are people whom one respects and people whom one disrespects.

SIR HUDSON: I am quite familiar with that tactic—to castigate oneself when one is unable to avail himself of other weapons.

ADMIRAL MALCOLM (*to Napoleon*): I know that Sir Hudson is very desirous of showing you every attention in his power, but you do not understand one another. I am certain there is much misrepresentation by communications coming through a third person.

NAPOLEON (*to Admiral Malcolm*): Do you know, he has had the meanness to keep from me a book, because on its cover I was designated "Emperor," and he has boasted of having done so.

SIR HUDSON: I boast?

NAPOLEON: Yes; Colonel Keating, late Governor of Bourbon, told me so.

SIR HUDSON: Colonel Keating knew the author of that book. I am certain that he would approve of its not being delivered.

ADMIRAL MALCOLM: Permit me to explain to you the story of the book. Sir Hudson showed it to me, and told me the author had desired him to give it or not, as he thought proper. The book itself is of little consequence, but Sir Hudson is forbidden to give you the title of "Emperor." I think he could not with propriety have sent it to you, with the inscription that is on it.

NAPOLEON: He has sent me letters addressed "Emperor."

SIR HUDSON: Yes, but they came through the Secretary of State's Office, and from your own relations, not Englishmen.

NAPOLEON (*to Admiral Malcolm*): He (*again nodding at Sir Hudson*) has also had the meanness to speak of the contents of our letters that came open to him. My old mother, although I forbade her to write to me, wrote to say that she would come to St. Helena and die with me. This was told round the island.

SIR HUDSON: Not by me.

NAPOLEON: Yes, by you! Mr. Balcombe * mentioned it.

SIR MALCOLM: I have never heard the circumstances. I know that Sir Hudson holds sacred the contents of all letters that come open to you.

NAPOLEON: Moreover, I am not permitted to write notes of civility to the people of the island, except through the Governor. For example, suppose I wished to invite Lady Malcolm to dinner, and I put a piece of gallantry into my note, could a gentleman send this open to another for his inspection? Impossible! If I meet an officer of the 53rd regiment and am desirous to ask him to dinner, I cannot without obtaining his (*pointing to Sir Hudson*) permission, for which there is not probably time.

SIR HUDSON (*interrupting*): You have refused to see the officers of the 66th regiment.

NAPOLEON: Yes, because their Colonel had not called on Marshal Bertrand to make the request.

SIR HUDSON: I have written to the Count to say I wished to introduce them.

NAPOLEON (*with warmth*): I am an Emperor in my own circle, and will be

---

* English Purveyor to Napoleon. His daughter, Mrs. Abell, published her *Recollections of Napoleon*.

so as long as I live. You may make my body prisoner, but my soul is free. Europe will hereafter judge of my treatment, and the shame of it will fall on the English nation. Even the poor sentinels of the 53rd regiment weep at my unworthy treatment. You ask me for money to pay for my living. I have none. But I have plenty of friends who would send me whatever sum I required if I could write to them. Put me on rations if you please. I can dine with the officers of the 53rd regiment, and if not with them, with the soldiers.

SIR HUDSON: I did not seek the situation I now hold. It was offered to me. I will do my duty and execute my instructions.

NAPOLEON: If you were ordered to assassinate me, would you do so?

SIR HUDSON: No, I would not. My countrymen do not assassinate.

NAPOLEON: I see by your arrangements that you are afraid I should escape; you take useless precautions. Why do you not tie me hand and foot? And then you will be tranquil. You are not a general; you are only a scribe of office. Tomorrow you will receive a letter from me, which I hope may be known in all Europe.*

SIR HUDSON: I should have no objections if all my proceedings were published in England and in every other country.

NAPOLEON: Sir George Cockburn permitted us to correspond with people in the island on points of civility.

ADMIRAL MALCOLM: I believe the change was made, or at least intended, by Sir George. Improper use had been made of the indulgence.

NAPOLEON (*exclaiming*): The Governor tells you so, but it is false. The English Government has insulted me in sending a man like you to guard me. You are no Englishman!

SIR HUDSON: That makes me laugh.

NAPOLEON (*turning to Sir Hudson with a look of surprise*): What, laugh, sir!

---

* The letter in question was actually written to Sir Hudson Lowe on August 23rd, and not by Napoleon, but by Count Montholon on his orders. The specific occasion was Napoleon's receipt of the Convention of August 2, 1815, which applied to his imprisonment, though it was really prompted by the arrival of the Commissioners of Austria, Russia, and France. Napoleon sharply objected to the conditions and timed his protest to Sir Hudson to coincide with the arrival of the allied delegates, whose only business, according to the sardonic Sir Hudson, was "to ascertain that General Bonaparte was alive." In the letter it was emphasized that Napoleon was "not the prisoner even of England, and in no sense in the power of the other parties" to the convention. He reminded the Emperors of Austria and Russia and the King of Prussia that they were still under obligation to him. Then he listed his other grievances: that the title of Emperor was denied to him and instead he was addressed as "General"; that he was confined on the island of St. Helena; that restrictions were placed on his correspondence and communication with the people of the island. As for Sir Hudson Lowe's conduct as Governor of St. Helena, Napoleon condemned it *in toto*.

SIR HUDSON: Yes, yes. I say what I think. I say it not only makes me laugh but it excites my pity, to see how misinformed you are with respect to my character, and for the rudeness of your manners. I wish you good morning. (*Leaves abruptly, without further ceremony.*)

ADMIRAL MALCOLM: I must also wish you good morning (*bows*).

NAPOLEON (*returning the bow*): My compliments to Lady Malcolm.

(*In entering the conversation in her journal that night, Lady Malcolm further noted: "During this conversation Sir Hudson never for a moment lost his temper; Bonaparte frequently, particularly when he addressed Sir Hudson. They walked to and fro in the garden, and could not fail to be overheard by Count Las Cases, Madame Montholon, and Major Gorresquer [aide-de-camp to Sir Hudson], who continued walking at a little distance. As soon as the Admiral and Sir Hudson were gone, Bonaparte as usual repeated all that he had said to his suite, and they told his speeches again to various people, so that in two days they were circulated amongst a great proportion of the island, whilst the knowledge of Sir Hudson's replies, which did him much credit, were confined to a very small number, who were prevented from circulating them, from the desire of the Governor that every transaction at Longwood should be secret."*)

Shelley-Trelawny

A POET AND AN ADVENTURER EXCHANGE THOUGHTS ON WOMEN, BOOKS, AND CLIPPERS DURING A TRIP TO LEGHORN.

We are indebted to the poets for having transformed women from what they were to what they are.

"I saw Shelley the last year of his life, and Byron the last three years of his life. I was on the most intimate terms with both, and saw them almost every day. . . ."

In so many words Edward John Trelawny advances his major claim to immortality. As a writer he is still remembered for his Adventures of a Younger Son—an exciting chronicle of a swashbuckling career in exotic lands and seas. As a sailor he belongs in the great tradition of England's doughty adventurers of the sea. "His whole appearance," said Fanny Kemble, "gives one an idea of hardship, peril, and wild adventure." In short, he would scarcely seem the man best qualified to become the close friend and chronicler of Percy Bysshe Shelley. Yet this same Trelawny is one of the few witnesses who could truthfully answer in the affirmative to Browning's now proverbial query: "And did you once see Shelley plain?" Trelawny had seen Shelley plain—in moods of dejection and exaltation. He had seen him as the target of his wife's nagging, as the pathetic boy trying to learn how to swim in the Arno. One day he had hunted anxiously for him in a pine forest, only to find him gazing pensively into a pond. Once he had ridden with Shelley to the docks of Leghorn and spent part of an afternoon on an American Clipper with the young dreamer who preferred solitude and books to the noisy affairs of men. "I never lost an opportunity of giving the dreamy bard glimpses of rough life," Trelawny boasts.

Shelley admired this young adventurer with the physique of a Greek god, and in turn Trelawny played the part of big brother, worshipping his genius and coddling his boyish impracticality. And it was Trelawny who grieved like a brother when Shelley drowned in the Gulf of Spezia;

Trelawny who directed the search for the shipwrecked "Ariel" and its tragic cargo; Trelawny who snatched the poet's heart from the flames as they cremated the body on the seashore near Via Reggio. It was again Trelawny who, in a final act of generosity, financed the return of Mrs. Shelley to England.

He had known Byron, too, though never the way he knew Shelley. To the shy and slender Shelley, maligned and hounded by a world of dogma and convention, this powerfully built man of the world could conveniently act as self-appointed protector. Byron, on the other hand, idol of millions, resourceful athlete, swimmer, and boxer, wealthy and titled, needed none. His Lordship must have overawed Trelawny and perhaps aroused some envy, for his record of Byron is by no means that of a fawning idolator. Byron was perhaps too sure of himself to please the completely self-assured rover of distant seas. "I have met men similar to Byron, but never to Shelley," Trelawny significantly remarks.

After four years of wandering in northern Italy, the Shelleys had finally settled in Pisa in January, 1822. With them were their friends Edward and Jane Williams. Both families occupied apartments in the Tre Palazzi di Chiesa on the Lungarno, the poet and his wife having the upper floor. Charming as it was, the Tre Palazzi were humble indeed beside the sumptuous Palazzo Lanfranchi on the opposite side of the Arno. When the affluent Byron, on Shelley's instigation, presently joined the growing English colony at Pisa, it was the Palazzo Lanfranchi which became his residence. Into its manorial grounds His Lordship drove one day, followed by a retinue of servants, horses, monkeys, bulldogs, mastiffs, cats, peafowls, hens and other livestock, to give the sleepy town "a taste of the noisy, bright-colored, pompous comedy that a Byronic entrance on a new scene always provided," to quote Margaret Armstrong, Trelawny's adroit biographer.

Shortly after the Shelleys and Byron established themselves on both banks of the Arno, Trelawny arrived. He put up at an inn, ate dinner, and drove to the Tre Palazzi. The Williamses, who were his friends too, received him cordially. A few moments later Mrs. Williams looked over Trelawny's shoulder into the dark corridor and shouted: "Come in, Shelley!" And a tall, thin stripling, holding out both his hands, entered the room, "blushing like a girl." A six-month friendship, the memory of which was to dominate his whole life, began for Trelawny. Till he was well over eighty, this man whom Swinburne called "sea-king, swordsman, hater of wrong" would still be "thinking and talking and writing about Shelley as if he still saw him as on that evening in Jane's parlor, 'gliding in with outstretched hands.' " The introduction over, Shelley was soon reading and translating passages from Calderon's Magico Prodigioso for the company. There was a sudden silence, and Trelawny looked up. Noiselessly, Shelley had vanished. To the dumbfounded visitor Mrs. Williams explained: "He comes and goes like a spirit. No one knows where or when."

The following afternoon Trelawny and Shelley crossed the Ponte Vecchio and strode along the Lungarno to the Palazzo Lanfranchi. They entered a spacious marble hall, climbed up a broad stone staircase, passed through a huge reception room, and were shown into a smaller apartment where there were books and a billiard-table. "A surly-looking bulldog announced us," Trelawny recounts, "and the Pilgrim instantly advanced from an inner chamber, and stood before us. His halting gait was apparent, but he moved with quickness; and although pale, he looked as fresh, vigorous, and animated as any man I ever saw." The three men chatted amiably about poetry and swimming, and Byron shot some billiards with Trelawny. Neither poet could possibly suspect that in this swarthy English giant with an unquenchable thirst for exotic adventure, they had met the man who would provide generations of readers with the most intimate close-ups of themselves.

For the next few months Trelawny saw his new friends almost every day. He observed and later recorded their daily habits: Byron rose at noon, dawdled till two or three, rode horseback, fired his pop-guns, ate a "frugal dinner" (he dreaded getting fat), visited "an Italian family" (probably his mistress, the Countess Guiccioli, who was discreetly lodged in town), and returned home to "the midnight lamp and the immortal verses." Shelley was up and about at six, breakfasting with a volume of Plato, Sophocles, or Spinoza and a few crumbs of dry bread, joined the Williamses for a sail on the Arno in a flat-bottomed skiff, then slipped off to a pine grove—book in hand at all times; and "when the birds went to roost returned home, and talked and read until midnight."

Scattered through the two volumes of Trelawny's Records of Shelley, Byron, and the Author are fragments of conversation in dialogue form, some sustained, some exasperatingly brief and abruptly cut off. Of those in which Shelley figures I have chosen the one involving the trip to Leghorn. This required some minor transpositions to avoid the flashback involutions of the original.

In any case, let us remember that it is Pisa in the spring, that the Arno lies a few short steps away for those with a taste for sailing, that a nearby pine forest offers secluded retreats for poets with a thirst for the silence

of the great outdoors, that the year is 1822, and only a few months before
a squall will overtake the small schooner "Ariel" sailing in the Gulf of
Spezia with a poet aboard. . . .

*("At 10 a.m. by appointment I drove to Shelley's house and hailed
him; he was always prompt as a seaman in a squall, and, rushing downstairs, was brought to by his wife on the first landing."—Trelawny)*

MRS. SHELLEY: Percy, do change your cap and jacket! You promised Tre to
call on his Yankee girl and Highland beauty at Leghorn. Caterina!
bring down the padrone's coat and hat!

SHELLEY *(submitting reluctantly; muttering)*: Our bones should be outside, or our skins as tough as alligators'; the thing you have put on my
head feels like a crown of thorns, and the ligature round my throat a
halter. I bear what I can, and suffer what I must.

*(Springs down the stairs, and, striding adroitly over a fair fat child
squatting on the doorstep beside its nurse, steps into Trelawny's chaise
at the door. The child cries.)*

SHELLEY: When we are born, we cry that we are come
    To this great stage of fools.

TRELAWNY: Whose child is it?

SHELLEY *(looking at it)*: Don't know.

MRS. SHELLEY *(from an open casement)*: That's too bad, not to know your
own child. Why, you goose, it is Percy!

TRELAWNY: You are not the wise man who knows his own child.

SHELLEY: The wise men have none.

TRELAWNY: Those wise men must be in the moon; there are few such on
earth.

*(As they turn off the Lungarno, a gust of wind blows off Shelley's
hat and sets it rolling. Trelawny stops the horse.)*

SHELLEY: Oh, don't stop! It will get into the river and I shall find it at
Leghorn.

TRELAWNY: That will depend on the wind and current.

*(Two Florentine gentlemen run after the hat. They pick it up, wipe
the dust off and bring it back to Shelley.)*

SHELLEY: They say that beavers are nearly exterminate; if hats go too, I
cannot mourn for them.

*(Outside the Port, on the Leghorn road, some small children are
clustered round a ruined building, tormenting a family of beautiful
bright green-and-gold-colored lizards.)*

SHELLEY: The young demons!

TRELAWNY: You are blaspheming, for is it not said, "Of such is the kingdom of heaven"? Children, until restrained, kill everything that runs from them; but if a beetle or a mouse moves toward them they fly in terror: cruel and cowardly; and that is the nature of man.

SHELLEY: He is in process of training.

TRELAWNY: It is very slow.

SHELLEY: The animals that subsist on herbs are docile, the flesh-eaters are untamable.

TRELAWNY: In the tropics we can live on fruits, not in the north. The Brahmins live on grains and fruit and are docile, the flesh-eaters make serfs of them. Mrs. Shelley says I am as eccentric as you; I wish I were as reasonable.

SHELLEY: Mary is under the dominion of the mythical monster "Everybody." I tell her I am of the "Nobodies." You have been everywhere; have you seen the ubiquitous demon "Everybody"?

TRELAWNY: Yes, in Egypt; a harmless and most useful beast. The loaded camels of a caravan are piloted by a donkey. His head-stall is decorated with bells; he leads the way and the docile animals follow, guided by the jingling. Without him they stray always. So you see the much-abused donkey is not the most stupid of animals. "Everybody" follows him.

SHELLEY: You have solved the mystery. You must tell Mary. Wise men in all ages have declared everything that is, is wrong. Those who stray away find something that is right. A donkey decorated is a guide for those that are as stupid as camels. We stray, we are eccentric.

(*They pass some masons building a chapel and watch some women, acting as bricklayers' helpers, carrying heavy stones and mortar.*)

SHELLEY: See the barbarism that the priests have reduced Italy to.

TRELAWNY: It is the primitive state of things. In the earliest records of the human race the duty of men was as hunters and warriors, and women did all the drudgery—fetched the wood and water. The professor of anatomy at the university of Pisa—and he is a high authority—says that women, though not the strongest, are the toughest. He says the female of all the races of animals are less highly organized than the male; they are not so subject to diseases, and wounds more readily heal with them than with the male. It is the poets, artists, and others of imagination who have reversed the natural order of things, and who have placed women where we should be.

SHELLEY: We are indebted to the poets for having transformed women from what they were to what they are—a solace and delight.

TRELAWNY: No; they have overshot their mark. They tell us that our principal object, aim, and end is to seek in the world for a fair skin, silky hair, and bright eyes; the emptier the mind the better; and that this is all life has to bestow. It is the old story—the sirens luring one to the sea-beach paved with human bones. Nature has lavished all its beauties on the male in the animal races as well as the human. Look at the hen-pheasant and the pea-hen, and the singing birds, it is only the male that sings. Now we search the four corners of the earth to transform a dowdy into a fine lady. Half the world pass their lives in searching for gems and silks and satins to ornament them, and what torments does one suffer when captured by one of these dragonflies! Men have nothing to cover themselves with but the cast-off winter clothing of sheep. The primitive people in the Indian Archipelago and other countries alone preserve the natural order of things. I once put into a bay on the eastern coast of Madagascar for fresh provisions and water. A great chief came down to barter with a retinue of nude followers, he himself being clothed by having a gold-laced cocked hat with feathers, such as worn by generals of division, and hunting boots, otherwise as naked as Adam; his face and body elaborately ornamented by tattooing with colors which I had never seen before.

SHELLEY: In youth I thought the reasoning faculties, if fairly developed, would triumph, but passions overpower all our faculties. The animals are guided by their instincts, we by our cultivated cunning and blind passions.

TRELAWNY: And reason.

SHELLEY: No, that faculty is paralyzed by the priests.

("*Of such stuff was our ordinary talk, to keep him awake from his dreamy reveries, and so we reached Leghorn . . . After we had done our business (which included collecting some scudi at the bank), I called on my Scotch friends and lured my companion in. He abhorred forcing himself on strangers—so I did not mention his name, merely observing, 'As you said you wanted information about Italy, here is a friend of mine can give it you—for I cannot.' The ladies—for there was no man there—were capital specimens of Scotchwomen, fresh from the land of cakes,—frank, fair, intelligent, and of course, pious. After a long and earnest talk we left them, but not without difficulty, so pressing were they for us to stop to dinner . . .*"—Trelawny)

(*Later, before returning home, Trelawny drives Shelley to the docks.*)

TRELAWNY: As we have a spare hour let's see if we can't put a girdle round about the earth in forty minutes. In these docks are living specimens of all the nationalities of the world; thus we can go round it, and visit and examine any particular nation we like, observing their peculiar habits, manners, dress, language, food, productions, arts, and naval architecture. For see how varied are the shapes, build, rigging, and decoration of the different vessels. There lies an English cutter, a French chasse-marée, an American clipper, a Spanish tartan, an Austrian trabarcolo, a Genoese felucca, a Sardinian zebec, a Neapolitan brig, a Sicilian sparanza, a Dutch galleot, a Danish snow, a Russian hermaphrodite brig, a Turkish sackalever, a Greek bombard. I don't see a Persian dhow, an Arab grab, or a Chinese junk; but there are enough for our purpose and to spare. As you have lately written a poem, "Hellas," about the modern Greeks, would it not be as well to take a look at them amidst all the din of the docks? I hear their shrill nasal voices, and should like to know if you can trace in the language or lineaments of these Greeks of the nineteenth century A.D., the faintest resemblance to the lofty and sublime spirits who lived in the fifth century B.C. . . . But here comes the Capitano Zarita; I know him.

(*Trelawny introduces Shelley to the Captain and all three cross the plank from the quay to the deck of the "San Spiridione." The crew are squatting about the deck in small knots, shrieking, gesticulating, smoking, eating, and gambling like savages.*)

TRELAWNY: Does this realize your idea of Hellenism, Shelley?

SHELLEY: No! but it does of Hell.

("*The captain insisted on giving us pipes and coffee in his cabin, so I dragged Shelley down. Over the rudder-head facing us there was a gilt box enshrining a flaming gaudy daub of a saint, with a lamp burning before it; this was Il Padre Santo Spiridione, the ship's godfather. The skipper crossed himself and squatted on the dirty divan. Shelley talked to him about the Greek revolution that was taking place, but from its interrupting trade the captain was opposed to it.*"—Trelawny)

SHELLEY (*to Trelawny*): Come away! There is not a drop of the old Hellenic blood here. These are not the men to rekindle the ancient Greek fire; their souls are extinguished by traffic and superstition. Come away!

(*They leave the "San Spiridione" and return to the quay.*)

TRELAWNY: It is but a step from these ruins of worn-out Greece to the New World; let's board the American clipper.

SHELLEY: I had rather not have any more of my hopes and illusions mocked by sad realities.

TRELAWNY (*pointing*): You must allow that graceful craft was designed by a poet's feeling for things beautiful; let's get a model and build a boat like her.

(*"The idea so pleased the Poet that he followed me on board her. The Americans are a social, free-and-easy people, accustomed to take their own way, and to readily yield the same privilege to all others, so that our coming on board, and examination of the vessel, fore and aft, were not considered as intrusion. The captain was on shore, so I talked to the mate, a smart specimen of a Yankee."*—Trelawny)

TRELAWNY: We were commending the beauty of your ship.

MATE: I do expect, now we have our new copper on, she has a look of the brass sarpent, she has as slick a run, and her bearings are just where they should be. We hoist up to heaven, and shoot home to hell, and cover the ocean with our canvas.

TRELAWNY: We wish to build a boat after her model.

MATE: Then I calculate you must go to Baltimore or Boston to get one; there is no one on this side the water can do the job. We have our freight all ready, and are homeward bound; we have elegant accommodation, and you will be across before your young friend's beard is ripe for a razor. Come down, and take an observation of the state cabin.

(*Trelawny and Shelley follow the mate. The cabin is ten and a half feet by five or six.*)

MATE: Plenty of room to live or die comfortably in. (*Taking out some tobacco and offering it to Trelawny and Shelley*) Have a chaw of real old Virginia cake.

(*"I seduced Shelley into drinking a wine-glass of weak grog, the first and last he ever drank. The Yankee would not let us go until we had drunk, under the Star-Spangled Banner, to the memory of Washington, and the prosperity of the American commonwealth."*—Trelawny)

SHELLEY: As a warrior and statesman he was righteous in all he did, unlike all who lived before or since; he never used his power but for the benefit of his fellow-creatures—

> He fought,
> For truth and wisdom, foremost of the brave;
> Him glory's idle glances dazzle not;
> 'Twas his ambition, generous and great,
> A life to life's great end to consecrate.

MATE: Stranger, truer words were never spoken; there is dry rot in all the main timbers of the Old World, and none of you will do any good till you are docked, refitted, and annexed to the New. You must log that song you sang; there ain't many Britishers that will say as much of the man that whipped them; so just set these lines down in the log, or it won't go for nothing.

(Shelley writes some verses in the book—not those he had quoted. He and Trelawny leave. They take the road back to Pisa.)

TRELAWNY *(while driving)*: You had better dine with me.

SHELLEY *(disturbed)*: What for? When?

TRELAWNY *(producing a basket of fresh fruits)*: Now! The Muses might dine on this food.

SHELLEY: No; they live in the blue regions of the air.

("Notwithstanding his protest, he went on picking the grapes and eating the fruit, unconscious of what he was doing. He invariably read when he was eating. He now had in his hand a monthly review, sent to him from England. He never in such cases laughed, but I saw by his eyes that he was amused."—Trelawny)

TRELAWNY: What is it that amuses you?

SHELLEY: The "Epipsychidion," that you like so much, the reviewer denounces as the rhapsody of a madman. That it may be a rhapsody I won't deny, and a man cannot decide on his own sanity. Your dry, matter-of-fact men denounce all flights of imagination as proofs of insanity, and so did the Greek sect of the Stoics. All the mass of mankind consider everyone eccentric or insane who utters sentiments they do not comprehend.

TRELAWNY: The Persian poet Hafiz would have consoled you by saying, "You are like the shell of ocean that fills with pearls the hand that wounds you." ... What was your object in writing the *Cenci?*

SHELLEY: In writing the *Cenci* my object was to see how I could succeed in describing passions I have never felt, and to tell the most dreadful story in pure and refined language. The image of Beatrice haunted me after seeing her portrait. The story is well authenticated, and the details far more horrible than I have painted them. The *Cenci* is a work of art; it is not colored by my feelings nor obscured by my metaphysics. I don't think much of it. It gave me less trouble than anything I have written of the same length. I am now writing a play for the stage. It is affectation to say we write a play for any other purpose. The subject is from English history; * in style and manner I shall approach as near our great dramatist as my feeble powers will permit. *King Lear* is my model, for that is nearly perfect. I am amazed at my presumption. Poets should be modest. My audacity savors of madness. Considering the labor requisite to excel in composition, I think it would be better to stick to one style. The clamor for novelty is leading us all astray. Yet, at Venice, I urged Byron to come out of the dismal "wood of error" into

---

* Charles the First.

the sun, to write something new and cheerful. *Don Juan* is the result. The poetry is superior to *Childe Harold*, and the plan, or rather want of plan, gives scope to his astonishing natural powers. My friends say my *Prometheus* is too wild, ideal, and perplexed with imagery. It may be so. It has no resemblance to the Greek drama. It is original; and cost me severe mental labor. Authors, like mothers, prefer the children who have given them most trouble. Milton preferred his *Paradise Regained*, Petrarch his *Africa*, and Byron his *Doge of Venice*. I have the vanity to write only for poetical minds, and must be satisfied with few readers. Byron is ambitious; he writes for all, and all read his works.

TRELAWNY: The son of a man of genius has sent me a very silly poem to show Byron. Why are not germs of genius transmitted in a race? Their physical diseases are, but none of their mental qualities.

SHELLEY: It would be a more intolerable wrong of nature than any which man has devised; the sons of foolish parents would have no hope.

TRELAWNY: Then the sins of parents, their diseases, should not be transmitted.

SHELLEY: With regard to the great question, the System of the Universe, I have no curiosity on the subject. I am content to see no farther into futurity than Plato and Bacon. My mind is tranquil; I have no fears and some hopes. In our present gross material state our faculties are clouded. When Death removes our clay coverings the mystery will be solved.

("*During the rest of our drive we had nothing but sea yarns. He regretted having wasted his life in Greek and Latin, instead of learning the useful arts of swimming and sailoring. He resolved to have a good-sized boat forthwith....*"—Trelawny)

TRELAWNY: I propose we form a colony at the Gulf of Spezia. You get Byron to join us, and with your family and the Williamses, and books, horses, and boats, undisturbed by the botherations of the world, we shall have all that reasonable people require.... Well, propose this to Byron tomorrow.

SHELLEY (*enchanted with the scheme*): No! You must do that! Byron is always influenced by his last acquaintance. You are the last man, so do you pop the question.

TRELAWNY: I understand that feeling. When well-known, neither men nor women realize our first conception of them; so we transfer our hopes to the new men or women who make a sign of sympathy only to find them like those who had gone before, or worse. (*Quoting Shelley's own lines*)
Where is the beauty, love, and truth we seek,
But in our minds!

(*"After returning with Shelley from Leghorn, I put up my chaise at the hostelry, and went in to dine with Mrs. Shelley. All fixed rules of feeding the Poet looked upon as ridiculous; he grazed when he was hungry, anywhere, at any time . . . Finding no one about the house, I went into his library; the Poet was untying the bag of scudi that we brought from Leghorn. Standing up he turned out the bag on to the hearth-rug, and the glittering coins bespangled the floor. It was amusing to see him scraping them together with the shovel out of the fireplace; having adroitly got them into a lump, he pressed them as flat as he could with his foot, then skillfully with the shovel divided them as nearly as possible into two equal portions; one of the halves he divided again into two equal portions by guess-work . . ."—*Trelawny*)

SHELLEY (*to Mary*): That half will feed the house and pay the rent. (*Pointing to the smaller portion.*) That will do for you. This is my portion. (*Lowering his voice.*) I will give this to poor Tom Medwin, who wants to go to Naples and has no money.

TRELAWNY (*aside to Mary*): Why, he has left nothing for himself.

MRS. SHELLEY: No, if he wants anything he tells me to get it, and if he wants a *scudo* to give anyone, perhaps I lend it him (*smiling*), but he can't be trusted with money, and he won't have it.

(*"The following morning I told Byron our plan of going to the Gulf of Spezia. Without any suggestion from me he eagerly volunteered to join us, and asked me to get a yacht built for him, and to look out for a house as near the sea as possible. . . . As he grew more urgent I wrote to an old naval friend, Captain Roberts, then staying at Genoa, a man peculiarly fitted to execute the order, and requested him to send plans and estimates of an open boat for Shelley, and a large decked one for Byron. . . ."—*Trelawny*)

Byron-Trelawny

A BITTER EXILE SOUNDS OUT A COUNTRYMAN ON THE SITUATION AT HOME AND TOASTS A "ROYAL PERSONAGE."

*If I met the Devil at your table I should
treat him as a friend of yours.*

(*Trelawny and Byron on horseback.*)

BYRON (*after a long silence*): I have a conscience, although the world gives me no credit for it; I am now repenting, not of the few sins I have committed but of the many I have not committed. There are things, too, we should not do, if they were not forbidden. My *Don Juan* was cast aside and almost forgotten, until I heard that the pharisaic synod in John Murray's back parlor had pronounced it as highly immoral, and unfit for publication. "Dost thou think, because thou art virtuous, there shall be no more cakes and ale?" Now my brain is throbbing, and must have vent. I opined sin was inspiration, but cant is stronger. Today I had another letter warning me against the "Snake"—Shelley. He, alone, in this age of humbug, dares stem the current, as he did today the flooded Arno in his skiff, although I could not observe he made any progress. The attempt is better than being swept along as all the rest are, with the filthy garbage scoured from its banks.

TRELAWNY: You might do him a great service at little cost, by a friendly word or two in your next work, such as you have bestowed on authors of less merit.

BYRON (*assuming a knowing look*): All trades have their mysteries; if we crack up a popular author, he repays us in the same coin, principal and interest. A friend may have repaid money lent—can't say any of mine have; but who ever heard of the interest being added thereto?

TRELAWNY: By your own showing you are indebted to Shelley; some of his best verses are to express his admiration of your genius.

BYRON (*with a significant look*): Ay, who reads them? If we puffed the "Snake," it might not turn out a profitable investment. If he cast off the slough of his mystifying metaphysics, he would want no puffing.

254

(Observing Trelawny is not satisfied.) If we introduced Shelley to our readers, they might draw comparisons, and they are *odorous.*

TRELAWNY: Shelley says the distinguishing quality of the humans is super-stition—Landor that we have the worst of all the animals and the best of none.

BYRON: Man is a two-legged reptile, crafty and venomous. *(After a pause, coming close to Trelawny, and smiling cynically.)* Everybody hates everybody.

TRELAWNY: That's in his way.

(Byron takes no notice of Trelawny's remark, but urges on his horse. They trot a mile or two.)

BYRON: I wrote thirty-five lines of *Don Juan* last night, or rather this morn-ing; was stopped for a rhyme. It was in my head, there it stuck; strong waters could not loosen it, trotting has. I read it in a magazine, an old one, years ago, in a couplet quoted from Swift. He beat all the craft; he could find a rhyme for any word. Tonight I shall write thirty more lines, and that will finish a canto—a thousand guineas. Murray now says pounds: I won't be stinted of my sizings. Murray told Tom Moore he was no judge of the morality; but sermons did not sell, and the "Don" had a "devil of a sale." I must make him a sinner, but he shall reform and end as a saint. . . . Who are your friends that passed us?

TRELAWNY: A captain of the navy and his wife. He paid his ship off, and having nothing to do, spliced himself to a widow.

BYRON: Money?

TRELAWNY: No, worse—two children.

BYRON: Why marry a widow? Could he not catch a mermaid? "Well, God is a good man"; he supplies the widows and orphans with fools.

(Another brisk trot, then a walk.)

BYRON: Mrs. Shelley demurs at my grammar and spelling. I am in good company—Cromwell and Napoleon, they were careless of grammar, but careful of the matter; so am I. *(Reflects a moment, then comes close to Trelawny.)* What would you do when dared to do a thing?

TRELAWNY: Do it.

BYRON: Shelley was so trapped by a canting parson at the Mer de Glace; I am not to be caught by chaff. People talk of their hosts of friends. Can anyone name twelve intimate acquaintances? I don't feel friendship for anyone, not even for Shelley. My London acquaintance I have no sympathy with.

TRELAWNY: Tom Moore and Hobhouse?

BYRON: We have been comrades; we must have allies. Moore is the best convivial companion, Hobhouse is a good man of business, and I am the worst. If we have a good balance at our banker's, we shan't want friends. They make free with our *scudi*; gold is a jealous god.

TRELAWNY: The Tuscans have a humane law; they imprison all beggars except the blind.

BYRON: They should imprison borrowers; they are the worst of beggars. Travelling in Greece, Hobhouse and I wrangled every day. His guide was Mitford's fabulous History. He had a greed for legendary lore, topography, inscriptions; gabbled in *lingua franca* to the Ephori of the villages, goatherds, and our dragoman. He would potter with map and compass at the foot of the Pindus, Parnes, and Parnassus, to ascertain the site of some ancient temple or city. I rode my mule up them. They had haunted my dreams from boyhood; the pines, eagles, vultures, and owls, were descended from those Themistocles and Alexander had seen, and were not degenerated like the humans; the rocks and torrents the same. Hobhouse's dogged perseverance in pursuit of his hobby is to be envied; I have no hobby and no perseverance. I gazed at the stars, and ruminated; took no notes, asked no questions.

TRELAWNY: Your memory did more than his notes. You wrote *Childe Harold*. What have his notes produced?

BYRON: He said nature had intended him for a poet, but chance made him take to politics, and that I wrote prose better than poetry.

TRELAWNY: That proves he has no poetry in him.

BYRON: If I am a poet—Gifford says I am; I doubt it—the air of Greece made me one. (*Smiling ironically.*) I climbed to the haunts of Minerva and the Muses. Hobhouse can plod at books twelve hours a day; one or two hours does for me, excepting Scott's—I read him through. Shelley wants me to read more and write less. My mind is vagrant; I can't do drudgery. . . . Scott and Cobbett are the popular writers now, and their pens are never idle. You must go on; if you lag you are outstripped in the race. When a new book is sent me, I read the last chapter and then the first; if they are good, I may go through it. I like Cobbett's *Register*; if I were Minister, I would make him my Attorney-General. . . . When Sam Rogers has hatched a stanza, he sends it round to his poetical friends for approval. His *Italy* has cost him thousands in illustrations; his brats are stillborn. Why did you prevent his riding my black horse?

TRELAWNY: He is a stumbler.

BYRON (*glancing cynically*): Yes, he fell with me the second time I rode him; he is now reserved for my particular friends. A fall would do old Rogers some good; his blood is stagnant.

TRELAWNY: He has a parboiled look; it's difficult to believe he is a poet.

BYRON: He is a banker and a poetizer. He feeds the needy critics, and they dub him poet. The black horse I bought of a captain of the Pope's guard at Ravenna, warranted. I sent for the captain and demanded my money paid. He refused; I waxed wroth. He blustered, and said he was descended from a noble Roman family, was commander of a troop of his Holiness the Pope's Guard. "Then I'll give you satisfaction." I opened a chest in the hall, and told him to choose his arms. I took a Spanish rapier; he had his sword. I drew my Toledo, an heirloom, and went toward him. He faltered and retreated, and as I neared him, he exclaimed, "I don't fight in the dark, and we are forbidden duelling." * As I lifted my arm to strike he decamped in haste.

TRELAWNY: Should you not, as a Carbonaro, have, as Iago has it, removed him by yerking him under the ribs? Your groom would have sacked him, dropped him in a hole in the yard or in the pine forest.

BYRON: You are a cool hand.

TRELAWNY: At Ravenna they say manslaughter is not considered a heinous offense.

BYRON: It used not to be so, but it is now. Noblemen hired bravos. I am a respecter of the law. When I want to punish a man, I let an attorney loose at him—he tortures him, and so worries him to death . . . A Frenchman visited me this morning. He said he was translating a poem of mine, and wished me to revise it. I told him I could not speak French.

TRELAWNY: Can't you?

BYRON: I would not lower myself by speaking it like a German waiter at a hotel. The Frenchman expressed his astonishment, and then jabbered in vile English; said his wife was English, and she corrected him; asked me to refer to my poem. I told him I had no copy, that after they were sent to the publisher I saw no more of them. I said I had never been in Paris, or any part of France. He was amazed, and asked why. When I left England, Paris was occupied by the allies. Foreigners are told that I write pretty verses, and they think I can do nothing else—that I am a literary grub. I could not endure to witness a country associated in my mind with so many glorious deeds of art and arms so fallen, bullied by certain rascal officers, slaves in authority, the knaves of justice, her eagle chained, and the allied despots crowing over her. English money has done it!

---

* "Byron's great-uncle fought with swords, in a room in London, in the dusk of the evening, killed his opponent, was tried for his life, and doubtless this was in Byron's mind when he challenged the captain to fight in the twilight, with swords, and without witnesses."—Trelawny

TRELAWNY: Shelley says he finds it far more irksome to write prose for publication than poetry.

BYRON: So do I. All this morning I was in labor at a letter to John Murray. It will be made public in his back parlor, where the rooks meet and will caw over it. They complain of my showing letters; mine go a regular circuit.

TRELAWNY: Why do your London friends treat Shelley so cavalierly? They rarely notice him. He is as well born and bred as any of them. What are they afraid of?

BYRON (*leeringly*): He is not a Christian.

TRELAWNY: Are *they*?

BYRON: Ask them!

TRELAWNY: If I met the Devil at your table, I should treat him as a friend of yours.

BYRON (*scanning Trelawny keenly to see if he was jeering*): The Devil is a royal personage.

Byron-Kennedy

AN ERRANT POET DISCUSSES THE STATE OF HIS
SOUL WITH AN ANXIOUS BRITISH
MINISTER.

What, then, you think me in a very bad way?

I N THAT endless procession of men and women who for one reason or
another sought the company of Lord Byron perhaps none stands out
so singularly as Dr. James Kennedy. Writers came to Byron for money
and guidance, expatriates for moral support, women for what the romantic
young exile cared to give. Greek revolutionaries came, and Byron gave
them money, leadership . . . ultimately his life. For his part, Dr. Kennedy
sought something even more precious—he came for His Lordship's soul.
Perhaps, it would be fairer to say he came to save His Lordship's soul.
For this venturesome Scotsman was something of an evangelist. A surgeon
of the British army, he dedicated to mending damaged souls what time
was spared him from mending damaged bodies. The few scant records
of his spiritual work show that it bore considerable fruit. The Europe of
his day was overrun with young Englishmen engaged in sowing their wild
oats, and among them the good doctor found abundant material to work
on.

The summer of 1824 found this roving evangelist on the Greek island of
Cephalonia. There the worthy doctor set to work upon the theological
waverings of a small colony of educated young Scotsmen. Dr. Kennedy
was enjoying some dubious success among his gay compatriots when
presently the chance of an evangelist's lifetime came to him. On August
3 there arrived from Leghorn, Italy, at the harbor of Argostoli a round-
bottomed, 120-ton brig bearing the name "Hercules." From it stepped
Lord Byron and a retinue of servants, medical attendants, and friends,
including the Italian Pietro Gamba and Edward James Trelawny. In the
words of John Drinkwater, Byron had now entered "upon the last stage
of his pilgrimage." A staunch friend of freedom, the rebel English lord
had long espoused the cause of Greek independence. Finally, at the behest
of his Greek friends and the urgings of his own conscience, he had come

to the scene of the fighting. The cause was to give him a martyr's death, make the malarial marshes of Missolonghi a hallowed site, and bring everlasting overtones of liberty to his poetry. The arrival of the "Hercules" gave fresh impetus to what was beginning to look to the despairing Greeks like a suicidal bid for freedom. Byron plunged in with praiseworthy ardor. Despite the intriguing and factionalism that bedevilled the rebel camp, he was resolved to see the thing through. Oral and written instructions poured out from Argostoli, where Byron settled himself and his staff in a house at the nearby town of Metaxata. Quite understandably, the Greek insurgents worried continuously about the state of Byron's health, purse, and political temperature. Only one man on the island of Cephalonia seemed to be worried about the state of His Lordship's soul. . . .

As Lord Byron planned revolutionary strategy in his house at Metaxata, Dr. Kennedy began mapping out a strategy of his own. He was ordinarily a patient man, but time seemed to be short now, for he had learned that Byron would soon set out for the war-torn areas of the mainland. The prospect of so great a man going to his death with so burdened a soul saddened him. Tactfully, reports were allowed to reach Byron of the revivalist work going on in the adjoining port. An incorrigible cynic, Byron became curious when he learned of the prescribed duration of this spiritual treatment. Dr. Kennedy laid it down as "sole condition" that "he should be allowed to speak for twelve hours, at intervals, without interruption." His Lordship at length attended a collective session that lasted but four paltry hours. This first grapple with Byron's soul was scarcely encouraging to Dr. Kennedy. Throughout the meeting the "sole condition" was repeatedly violated by Byron's disturbing queries about the truth of the Bible and the validity of miracles. The good man began to fear for the spiritual welfare of his little flock, and was relieved when political meetings at Metaxata kept the romantic heretic away from the remaining sessions. But Byron's interest had been aroused. It was a jubilant Dr. Kennedy who some days later received an invitation to come to Metaxata. His Lordship was ready to submit to some private evangelism. Arming himself with his faith and an assortment of religious tracts, Dr. Kennedy called on Lord Byron. There now began a series of talks which were published by John Murray in London in 1830, shortly after the doctor's death, with the title of Conversations on Religion with Lord Byron. The following conversation, somewhat condensed from the original, is the first of the series.

Byronic scholarship has been sporadically unkind to Dr. Kennedy, who has been called all things from a pompous fanatic to a pitiful dupe. When the Conversations appeared one magazine dismissed him as "a weak-headed Evangelical though a well-intentioned twaddler." Several critics charged him with being taken in by Byron's hypocritical avowals of spiritual preoccupation. Widely regarded as "a rebel against God and a slanderer of God's creatures," His Lordship was now pictured as a fiendish schemer exploiting Dr. Kennedy to elicit material for a new canto of his satiric epic, Don Juan. Of the same nature was the suspicion that Byron had arranged these private seances on Cephalonia "to master the slang of a religious sect, in order to hit off the character with more verisimilitude"—a judgment that so probing a scholar as Samuel C. Chew is ready to endorse as "quite possibly true." It is hard to say just what effect, if any, Dr. Kennedy's revelations had upon Byron's adoring public. Chew's conclusion was that if it had any influence at all, "it may have been favorable to Byron's reputation among the orthodox." For Dr. Kennedy's evident aim was to give the picture of a skeptic grown weary of his doubting and, unable to return to the bosom of orthodoxy, seeking some way out of his spiritual dilemma. How close Dr. Kennedy came to the truth it is idle to speculate. Byron, of course, may have been baiting and bantering him as an amusing distraction from the pressing realities of war and revolution. Then, Byron had a disputatious turn of mind. Such conversations would thus provide a challenge to his polemical skill. We may be sure, from the doctor's own tactful hints, that Byron was convinced he had impressed his adversary with his own argumentative powers.

As for Dr. Kennedy's effect on Byron, it is certain that he was impressed by one thing—the man's indubitable sincerity. He treated this conscientious proselytizer with the utmost courtesy, and though he freely denounced the sham and hypocrisy of established creeds and questioned the very basis of Dr. Kennedy's belief, he listened carefully and tried to answer every statement, however dogmatic and pretentious, in a spirit of fair play. If Dr. Kennedy was convinced Byron had profited from these communings, he refrained from making such a boast in his manuscript. The impression he leaves with us is that he found His Lordship eager to learn but stubborn to yield. There were annoying excursions into poetry, for which Dr. Kennedy had little sympathy when it distracted from the major issue, and Byron's remark about Dr. Kennedy reminding him of the atheist Shelley was hardly likely to please the humorless evangelist. There and in other places we can only applaud Byron for the courage of his convictions and his unshakable stand on tolerance.

The talks, which continued over several days, sometimes lasted four and five hours, a fact confirmed in the reminiscences of Byron's friend Gamba, who laconically remarked of Dr. Kennedy that he was "rather methodistically inclined." At the final interview Byron accepted some books from Dr. Kennedy, graciously giving his word to read and digest them. It is very likely that Byron never looked at these religious tracts. We know that he gave them to his valet, William Fletcher, the same loyal but naïve Fletcher, incidentally, who indiscreetly allowed Trelawny to view Byron's body at Missolonghi and, in the words of Drinkwater, report to the world "the result of his observations with ghoulish delight." For Byron's part, he, too, regaled Dr. Kennedy with the gift of a book, a posthumous publication, to be sure, but one that gave the good man a modest claim to immortality that neither his surgical nor his spiritual ministrations would have assured him. Admittedly the Conversations on Religion with Lord Byron is a strange book, even an irritating book—by no conceivable standard the work of a literary artist. There is, however, an inescapable air of honesty and sincerity about it, besides a vastly grotesque yet fascinating drama of ironic contrasts. For pitted here against one another, in grave, exalted debate, are on one side a faithful servant of God and the British Crown, and on the other, a moral outcast from England, regarded by organized religion and respectable society as nothing less than a devil's disciple. There was hardly a chance that Dr. James Kennedy would win, yet one can only applaud him for trying, and, having tried, for writing down the record of his attempt to reform the most celebrated sinner of his time.

BYRON: I cannot conceive why people will always mix up my own character and opinions with those of the imaginary beings which, as a poet, I have the right and liberty to draw.

DR. KENNEDY: They certainly do not spare your lordship in that respect; and in *Childe Harold, Lara,* the *Giaour,* and *Don Juan,* they are too much disposed to think that you paint in many instances yourself, and that these characters are only the vehicles for the expression of your own sentiments and feelings.

BYRON: They do me great injustice, and what was never before done to any poet.

DR. KENNEDY: But, although it may be carried too far, is there not, at least, some foundation for the charge? Virtue and piety are qualities of too insipid a nature to excite a vivid interest in the minds of too many readers; and in order to produce effect and impression, beings of high talents and evil dispositions may be drawn by the poet as well as figured by the painter; but unless care is taken in drawing some good qualities, in which a noble and virtuous mind must feel delight, the inference will be against the poet, if he seems unable or unwilling to draw anything but that which is bad, however lofty the qualities and actions. *Don Juan*, as far as I have understood from the extracts in the reviews, has no counterbalancing effect, in bringing forward good and virtuous characters, nor by the punishment of the wicked; but the hero goes on, prosperous and uncontrolled, from one vice to another, unveiling and mocking at the crimes and vices of mankind.

BYRON: Even in this work I have been equally misunderstood. I take a vicious and unprincipled character, and lead him through those ranks of society whose high external accomplishments cover and cloak internal and secret vices, and I paint the natural effects of such characters; and certainly they are not so highly colored as we find them in real life.

DR. KENNEDY: This may be true; but the question is, what are your motives and object for painting nothing but scenes of vice and folly?

BYRON: To remove the cloak which the manners and maxims of society throw over their secret sins, and show them to the world as they really are. You have not been so much in high and noble life as I have been; but if you had fully entered into it, and seen what was going on, you would have felt convinced that it was time to unmask the specious hypocrisy, and show it in its native colors.

DR. KENNEDY: My situation did not naturally lead me into society, yet I believed, before the publication of your book, that the world, especially the lower and middling classes of society, never entertained the opinion that the highest classes exhibited models of piety and virtue; nay, from circumstances we are naturally disposed to believe them worse than they really are.

BYRON: It is impossible you can believe the higher classes of society worse than they are in England, France, and Italy, for no language can sufficiently paint them.

DR. KENNEDY: But still, my lord, granting this, how is your book calculated to improve them, and by what right, and under what title, do you come forward in this undertaking?

BYRON: By the right which everyone has who abhors vice united with hypocrisy.

DR. KENNEDY: Then he that teaches others should be pure himself; and as your lordship belongs to that class, you cannot complain if they examine your own conduct to see if your lordship has a right to become a reformer. From what I have seen of *Don Juan*, I cannot perceive that morality is much inculcated in it, or that vice, united with hypocrisy, is held up to abhorrence. On the contrary, it is a pure, unvarnished display of vice, and in language by no means calculated to render the Don odious, or the subject odious, to any mind unfortified by sound principles.

BYRON: It is the plan to lead him through various ranks of society, and show that wherever you go vice is to be found.

DR. KENNEDY: This is a fact already known, and it has also been known by experience that no satire, however witty, poignant, or just, ever did any good, or converted, as far I have heard, one man from vice to virtue. Neither Horace, nor Juvenal, nor Persius could stop the torrent of vice, and folly, and crime which inundated Rome, and which finally overthrew it, notwithstanding all the declamations of these satirists. Nor have I heard that Donne's or Pope's satires ever effected any good. Your language is not so gross as that of Juvenal or Persius, yet this is owing to the manners of the times; and while your satire is useless, it will call down on your head the exclamations, both of the virtuous and the vicious; of the former, because they do not perceive in you the proper qualifications of a reformer of morals, nor believe that you have adopted the means calculated to promote such an object, but rather the reverse; while the latter will naturally hate him who unmasks those vices—more particularly if he be stained with any himself.

BYRON: But it is strange that I should be attacked on all sides, not only from magazines and reviews but also from the pulpit. They preach against me as an advocate of infidelity and immorality, and I have missed my mark sadly in having succeeded in pleasing nobody. That those whose vices I depicted and unmasked should cry out is natural, but that the friends of religion should do so is surprising; for you know that I am assisting you in my own way as a poet by endeavoring to convince people of their depravity; for it is a doctrine of yours, is it not, that the human heart is corrupted, and therefore, if I show that it is so in those ranks, which assume the external marks of politeness and benevolence,—having had the best opportunities, and better than most poets of observing it,—am I not doing an essential service to your cause, by first convincing them of their sins, and thus enable you to throw in your doctrine with more effect?

DR. KENNEDY: This is a very ingenious turn which your lordship has given to the question, but it will not do. The heart of man is viler than you, with all your talents, can describe, and the vilest actions are often committed in secret by those who maintain a fine character externally. All this is true. But you have not conciliated these unhappy persons to yourself, nor to a new mode of life: you have not shown them what to do. You may have shown them what they are, but you have neither shown them by precept, nor by example, the proper remedy. You are like a surgeon, if I may use a simile from my own profession, who with diabolical delight tears the old rags, ointments, and bandages from the numerous wounds of his ulcerated patients, and, instead of giving fresh remedies, you expose them to the air and disgust of every bystander; laughing, and smiling, and crying out, "How filthy these fellows are."

BYRON: But I shall not be so bad as that. You shall see what a winding up I will give to the story.

DR. KENNEDY: I shall be glad to see any winding up, which can have the effect of remedying the pernicious consequences of the first part of the work. But the best way of remedying this is for your lordship to study Christianity, now that you have time, and the matter is pressed upon you, and then you will know and feel what is right; and when you have exhibited proofs of your conversion, your attempts at reformation will be better received and more successful.

BYRON: But what would you have me to do? I do not reject the doctrines of Christianity; I want only sufficient proofs of it to take up the profession in earnest; and I do not believe myself to be so bad a Christian as many of those who preach against me with the greatest fury, many of whom I have never seen nor injured. They furnish the suspicion of being latent hypocrites themselves, else why not use gentler and more Christian means?

DR. KENNEDY: I do not commend their conduct. It is wrong and imprudent to preach against individuals, either by name or character, and it is inconsistent with the dignity of a minister of the Gospel. It is, besides, calculated to exasperate the offender, rather than to effect a reformation. But you must excuse these zealous preachers, for their very imprudence proceeds from the high idea they have formed of your talents, and that whatever you do or say is of infinite importance to the church. They think your writings promote infidelity and immorality; and corrupt the youth who are disposed to admire your genius, and bow to your authority, and they act as if the church was in danger. I am not of that opinion, though it is desirable for your own sake and that of all those whose conduct and principles you may influence that you should become a Christian.

BYRON: But what excuse will you find for that preacher in London, about whom they have lately raised such infamous calumnies, and who has written against me in the review with which he is connected, as well as preached against me? I do not believe there is the least foundation for the calumny; but how delighted he would have been, had it been raised against me! He would have readily believed it, and many others would have done so too, perhaps; so that I show a greater degree of

Christian charity in believing him innocent, than he would have done toward me.

DR. KENNEDY: We do not know the heart, but we judge from conduct and conversation. The gentleman to whom you allude may consider it his duty to raise his voice against you as long as you continue in your present mode of writing and acting; but change your conduct, and you will be received with joy and open arms by him, and also by thousands who have never seen your face.

BYRON: Of course a convert to any party is received with gratulation and joy, and, especially, a convert like myself, to whom circumstances have given a much greater degree of notoriety, as well by praise as by censure, than I ever expected, or desired.

DR. KENNEDY: Your lordship can remove the one, and increase the other, whenever you please. You have only to examine the causes which prevent you, and you will find that they are futile, and only tend to withhold you from the enjoyment of real happiness; which, at present, it is impossible that you can find.

BYRON: What, then, you think me in a very bad way?

DR. KENNEDY: I certainly think you are, and this I say, not on my own authority, but on that of the Scriptures. No Christian can say that he has been better than your lordship; on the contrary, many will acknowledge their hearts to have been more sinful, and their lives as bad, though their rank and talents never placed them in so conspicuous a point of view. But while they thus acknowledge themselves to have been as bad, or worse than your lordship, they consider themselves entitled to say,—considering you simply as a fellow creature, possessed of an immortal soul, which will either be saved, or damned,—that your lordship must be converted, and must be reformed, before anything can be said of you, except that you are bad, and in a bad way.

BYRON: But I am now in a fairer way. I already believe in predestination, which I know you believe, and in the depravity of the human heart in general, and of my own in particular: thus you see there are two points in which we agree. I shall get at the others by and by; but you cannot expect me to become a perfect Christian at once.

DR. KENNEDY: There is a wide difference between us, and there are more points of variance than you have calculated. Predestination is of no importance in the present state of affairs, whether you believe it or whether you do not. The other is important, and the first step, without which the others would not be useful. But, if you really believe, and feel that you are weak, depraved, and helpless, then you will naturally inquire from whence help may be derived. The Scriptures say,—"Believe in the Lord Jesus Christ, and thou shalt be saved." If you really feel that you are lost, cannot save yourself, and need a Saviour, why not apply to Christ, and seek him as your Saviour?

BYRON: This is going too fast. There are many points and difficulties to clear up; when that is done, I will consider what you say.

DR. KENNEDY: What are your difficulties? If the subject is of importance, why not have them cleared and removed? You do not want time; you can reason, and reflect. The means of clearing up these difficulties are at hand. If it were a question of poetry, or of poetic literature, you would search and examine, and soon form your own judgment: on a point of far greater consequence, why do you linger and delay?

BYRON: This is true, but here I am, the slave of circumstances, surrounded by things and people which distract my attention, with nothing to lead me to the consideration of such subjects.

DR. KENNEDY: Your own judgment, and the consciousness of your own happiness and that you are not fulfilling the ends of your creation, should lead you to the examination of the subject; and besides, there are no circumstances which bind you with such irresistible power that you cannot easily surmount and conquer them. Religion must be sought after; your habits and studies must be subdued and laid aside in part, till you have obtained this, and then we may expect to see fruits worthy the high talents which God, whose revelation you neglect, has given you. I wish more earnestly than before that your lordship would study the subject night and day, till you ascertain its truth and your difficulties vanish. Everyone would help you in your research: small as my abilities and experience are,—they are at your service. And I give you my testimony in the most solemn manner, that if you allow any worldly circumstance to interfere with you, till you have succeeded in the search to which I encourage you, you will have deeply to repent of your neglect.

BYRON: Well, what would you have me to do? How shall I set about it?

DR. KENNEDY: Begin this very night to pray that God would pardon your sins, and grant you understanding to find out the truth, and continue praying on the one hand, and reading your Bible on the other, and do it with an earnest desire and an unbiased mind, and the result will be what we so earnestly wish. I do not mean that you are to take the subject on trust; examine it with the strictest scrutiny; weigh every objection, and hear every answer, and give on each side the fairest play: if you do this with justice and candor, you must believe. Ignorance is the mother of infidelity. High as are your attainments, and contemptible as I am in those gifts in which you excel, yet I am ready to prove to you that on every subject connected with Christianity you are very deficient; and that your difficulties, doubts, and contradictions proceed from a false, erroneous, and mistaken idea of the subject, which a little more knowledge would easily and infallibly remove. Will your lordship bestow on these subjects an earnest and attentive consideration? You will rejoice that you took my advice, when a deathbed arrives; when the tumultuous pleasures of life, and the gay dreams of high ambition, and rank, and fame, pass away, and when the value of life will concentrate in one moment.

BYRON: I shall most certainly study the subject with due attention.

DR. KENNEDY: And will you keep in mind that I requested you not to be discouraged at first, even though your difficulties and doubts increase? and if the light, force, and clearness of the Christian scheme do not at once appear to you, remember that it will, if you persevere; and you must admit, that nothing can be gained, or understood, without time and labor. Keep your mind unbiased, fairly weigh every argument, and continue constant in prayer to God, in whom, at least, you believe,—to give you that light which you at present want.

BYRON: You recommend what is very difficult. For how is it possible for a person acquainted with the history of the Church,—with the writings more or less of the most celebrated Divines,—with the questions which have been discussed, and which have convulsed the whole Christian world,—with the errors, the strange and contradictory opinions, which prevail; and above all, to see Christians at the present day split into so many sects and denominations, each envying, hating, and often reviling, at least writing, against one another,—how is it possible to see all this, and yet not inquire into many of those points which have been so much agitated? We have sentences of one Council against the sentence of another; Pope against Pope; book against book; sects rising up and dying away, and new ones succeeding them;—the Pope against Protestants and Protestants against the Pope, and against each other; Arians, Socinians, Southcotians, Methodists, Quakers, Harmonists, and I do not know where to end. Why do these exist to perplex and puzzle the mind? And does it not seem a fair conclusion—let it alone, and let these people fight among themselves, and when they have settled what religion is, then we can begin to study it.

DR. KENNEDY: I would exclude Arians, Socinians, Swedenborgians, and fanatics of all descriptions, leaving to them not only toleration but perfect liberty of conscience. These people have no right to the name of Christians. The Arians deny that the Son is equal to the Father; although He Himself expressly declares that He is. The Socinians say

He is not a divine character; yet these sects call themselves Christians, while they reject the testimony of Christ. The other fanatics are too absurd in their fancies and imaginations to be reasoned with.

BYRON: You seem to hate the Socinians.

DR. KENNEDY: Not the individuals, but their principles. I believe their system a terrible delusion, and that there is more hope of a deist, than of a Socinian, becoming a real Christian.

BYRON: But is this charitable? Why would you exclude a sincere Socinian from the hope of salvation?

DR. KENNEDY: I do not exclude him, and certainly I am no judge; nor ought we to judge of the ultimate state of anyone; but comparing the Socinian doctrines with those in the Bible, the one or other must be wrong.

BYRON: But they draw their doctrine from the Bible.

DR. KENNEDY: Yes, so do all the fools, enthusiasts, and fanatics; so the Church of Rome founds a system of idolatry, as absurd as ancient or modern paganism, on the Bible. The Socinians reject such parts of the Scripture, as interpolations, or corruptions, which do not suit their scheme; they turn literal things into metaphorical, and metaphorical into literal, until they succeed in representing original sin, the depravity of our nature, the necessity of atonement, and consequently the whole necessity of a revelation, as perfectly useless.

BYRON: Their religion seems to be spreading very much. Lady Byron is a great one among them, and much looked up to. She and I used to have a great many discussions on religion, and some of our differences arose from this point; but on comparing all the points together, I found that her religion was very similar to mine.

DR. KENNEDY: I am exceedingly sorry to hear that her ladyship is among such a sect, and I hope that ere long she will see her errors and danger.* But were thousands more of the great, and the noble, and the learned among them, Christianity will stand and raise its head with ultimate success from amidst the ruins of superstition, ignorance, idolatry, and damnable heresies.

BYRON: I should have been pleased that you had known Shelley. I should like to have seen you argue together. You very much remind me of him, not only in countenance but in your manner of speaking. He was to have been my companion in Greece, poor fellow, had the unfortunate accident which deprived him of life not taken place.

DR. KENNEDY: I should indeed have been pleased, were he here now: not that I might argue with him, but that time might have been given to

---

* Indirect discourse in original.

him to change his sentiments, and amend his life. I never read any of his writings, but I have seen some extracts from them in the *Quarterly Review*, and most certainly it would be no honor to resemble him in his opinions, whatever it might be to do so in other respects. From what he says there, he appears to me to have been a man totally destitute of common sense. His poetry may perhaps be fine and sublime, but to me it is perfectly unintelligble; unless so far as it appeared that the poor man was a virulent hater of Christianity, and ascribed all the evils and miseries of life to its introduction.

BYRON: I do not at all mean to defend his sentiments nor to approve of the mode in which he published them; but Shelley possessed many virtues, and many excellent qualities, and you would have liked him as a companion. He was cool in his manner; yet impassioned, animated, and eloquent in his conversation. I was much amused with him and another gentleman.* One was a Platonist, the other was not; and, after long arguments, they converted each other.

DR. KENNEDY: A proof that the opinions of neither were sound nor well weighed. Such things do very well for schoolboys; but how a man of sense can conscientiously believe in the numbers and ideas of Plato is to me inexplicable. I wish sincerely, however, that Shelley had been alive, that the wanderings of his imagination had subsided, and that he had become a sober, sensible man, a good Christian, and an honest member of society.

BYRON: He possessed one of the first Christian virtues, charity and benevolence. His benevolence was universal, and his charity far beyond his means.

DR. KENNEDY: This is a virtue, and esteemed such among Christians, undoubtedly, but it is not a Christian virtue, unless it proceeds from Christian principles. With Shelley it surely could not be a Christian virtue. I admit that it is a virtue, a heathen or an infidel virtue, if you please; and he has had, and let him have, as much praise from men on account of it as he deserves: but in the sight of God it is nothing, for he has declared that nothing is pleasing to him but what proceeds from a proper motive and principle, the fundamental point of which, belief in and love of Christ, was unfortunately wanting in Shelley. His fate is lamentable. I heard that he came out either to prosecute his inquiries with a view to overturn Christianity, or to write a book with that intent. Poor man! he little knew against whom he was fighting. His time came, and he died; died with his sins unrepented of and

---

* Byron mentioned the name but Dr. Kennedy forgot it.

unanealed,—a striking warning to others, as to the opinions they should form, the mode in which they should live, and the necessity of preparing for death and judgment.

BYRON: I see it is impossible to excite in your mind sympathy, or obtain a proper degree of allowance, for an unfortunate man of fine genius and imagination.

DR. KENNEDY: I have as much sympathy and more than those who may praise and lament him the loudest; at least I ought to have more, not because a fine poet was lost to the world, but because a fellow-creature died so awfully and suddenly; and, in such a career of wild and infidel principles and sentiments, was summoned to the presence of his judge. . . . I must now return to the city, and I trust and pray that your lordship will give the attention to them; for without a belief in these doctrines, you can never be happy here, nor safe hereafter. God has given you a fine understanding, a knowledge to distinguish between right and wrong. Every subject to which you choose to direct your attention you can master; but there is no art or science which you can learn by intuition. Bestow then as much of your time on the examination of religion as you would upon any other subject which may excite your interest, and you will find that it is in every respect most reasonable: and I trust you will become, what I hope one day to see you, an ornament and boast to your country, and an object of joy to every honest and sincere Christian.

BYRON: I intend to study the subject certainly. You must give me time: you see I have begun well; I listen to everything that is said, but you cannot expect me to become a good Christian all at once; you have found me, have you not, approach nearer to your sentiments than you had expected?

DR. KENNEDY: You have indeed done so, and I rejoice at it; and I have no hesitation in saying that I have more hope of your lordship than of the others, for you have shown more candor and patience than I could possibly have expected. . . . As for the others, I do not know what to think or say. They seem so hardened and indifferent that the subject appears only as an exercise of their reason, or a means of amusement and ridicule. It is difficult to keep your attention fixed on the subject. You enter into other studies, amusements, and occupations, and religion does not engage your thoughts; thus, you can never understand it. The accidental circumstance of my being here has excited a transient interest and curiosity, which will vanish probably as soon as we are separated. I shall do what I can among you, and the principal thing which I would urge with you all is your almost perfect ignorance of the subject, consequently the necessity of studying it. . . . One thing is evident, that every one of you must change your sentiments, and mode of life, before you can be safe; and if you reject religion, it must be at your own peril, and not from any defect in the clearness, force, and evidence of its truth.

BYRON: I own the difficulty of fixing and continuing one's attention to such subjects, considering the circumstances in which we are placed, and the strong and urgent calls to other matters. I think, however, that I may say I shall bestow more attention on it than I have hitherto done; but whether I shall reach the standard of orthodoxy, I know not.

DR. KENNEDY: We have no standard of orthodoxy, except the leading principles of Christianity, followed by a pure and pious life. I do not wish you, nor anyone else, to enter into the mazes of theological specu-lation. Christianity is a practical thing: reduce it to practice, believing first in the fundamental doctrines, and we shall all be satisfied. I have very few books with me on religious subjects, and none which present a complete view, or systematic arrangement of Christianity, except one. . . . It is Boston's *Fourfold State*, which describes man as he was in a state of innocence, before the fall; in a state of condemnation after it; in a state of begun recovery, or regeneration and sanctification; and in a state of happiness or misery. It has the merit of being short, and though it is written in a plain, and rather antiquated style, it is bold and energetic in its language: every assertion is supported by reference to Scripture, and it is full of matter and ideas, and some of them strik-ing and original: if you please, I will send it to you; I think that you may read it with great advantage.

BYRON: I shall read it with great pleasure. I have not the least prejudice against the style of our older writers, I am quite accustomed to it, and prefer the force and energy of their language to the soft harmonious periods of the present day, which have more sound than sense.

DR. KENNEDY (*rising*): Although I may perhaps have wearied your lord-ship with so long a lecture, yet, I am so pleased with the attention you have shown, and I have so much hope that it may be useful, at least so far as to induce your lordship to prosecute the study of Christianity, that I should feel great pleasure to have another opportunity of con-versing with you, if agreeable and convenient.

BYRON: I shall be glad to see you at all times, and as often as you can come out. I have no particular engagements. When my friends come from Argostoli, it is on no fixed day.

DR. KENNEDY: Does your lordship intend soon to go to Greece?

BYRON: In about ten days or a fortnight all things will be ready, I believe,

for our departure; but there is nothing that can prevent me from seeing and hearing you at any time; and if you should come when I am
out riding, just sit down, and take a book, and amuse yourself till I
return. You will find (*looking at the books on the side-tables*) something to amuse you, although they are rather upon profane than sacred
things.

("*I then took leave of Lord B., and rode down to see an officer who
lived a mile beyond his house, and on my return I met his lordship
and Count Gamba riding home with great speed, for a heavy shower
had just come on.*"—Dr. Kennedy)

Charles Lamb

SOME LONDON WITS GATHER TO CONSIDER WHICH OF THE CELEBRATED DEAD THEY WOULD MOST HAVE LIKED TO MEET.

*Yet, I would rather have seen Chaucer in company
with the author of the Decameron and have heard
them exchange their best stories together.*

I F, LIKE the man in the play Berkeley Square, one could open a door and find himself in the London of a vanished day, one might do worse than choose the door to a modest little apartment on the third floor of a Mitre Court Building in the Temple in the early years of the nineteenth century. For this door opened on the dwelling of Mary and Charles Lamb, two of the most beloved figures in English literature. In its humble way the flat occupied by this devoted brother and sister was the scene of perhaps the most brilliant literary gatherings of the day. If one tarried long enough, one might watch the door open and admit De Quincey or Coleridge, Wordsworth or Southey. As the evening advanced and the clouds of pipe smoke thickened over this conclave of penmen, more footsteps might be heard climbing heavily up the three flights, and into the room might step William Godwin, Crabb Robinson, or "Barry Cornwall." And if one were lucky enough, at perhaps eleven o'clock, Lamb's most cherished friend, the strange, misunderstood, and passionately sincere William Hazlitt might make a belated appearance.

It is to this same brilliant essayist and fiery dissenter, Hazlitt, that we owe the single sustained record of an evening at the Lambs'. To be sure, it amounts to very little when measured against the fervid testimonials to Lamb's conversational powers. But such is the niggardliness of history. So often we must accept the bald, unillustrated avowal of contemporaries; evidence, such as Boswell gave us of another great talker, is lacking. Talfourd, "Barry Cornwall," and others have testified to Lamb's powers as conversationalist. But even in critical appraisal it is again Hazlitt who has best celebrated his friend's powers. Throughout the essays and reminiscences of the period we find tantalizing tidbits of recovered talk. Yet, it *is only in a reminiscent essay of Hazlitt's*—"Of Persons One Would Wish to Have Seen"—that any serious attempt is made to recapture the actual words and setting of Charles Lamb and his cronies in action.

Now this essay poses a few problems. For one thing, it was first printed anonymously in The New Monthly Magazine of January, 1826. For another, the speakers were long identified only by initials, and the very initials were altered to complete the concealment of the participants' identity. Such was the meticulous prudence of the magazine editors of the day. Most of the speakers recalled by Hazlitt, including Lamb himself, were alive when the essay appeared and probably spotted themselves with little difficulty. A fresh complication set in when Hazlitt's son, several years after his father's death, reprinted the conversation piece and proceeded, with bland confidence, to identify the speakers by name. Unfortunately, the identifications were largely wrong because they were based on the substituted initials of the printed magazine text. This error was repeated by virtually all Hazlitt editors till the arrival on the scene of P. P. Howe, who edited the monumental centenary edition of A. R. Waller and Arnold Glover for publication by J. M. Dent and Sons in 1933. The initials used in the essay "Of Persons One Would Wish to Have Seen" were now made to correspond with those given in the original manuscript then in the possession of A. C. Goodyear. In the following dialogued form of the essay I have filled in the names on the basis of Mr. Howe's identifications; and I have availed myself of many of his scholarly findings in my footnotes.

Who were these friends of the Lambs who dropped in on that Thursday night, so thoughtfully recalled to life by William Hazlitt many years later? One notes their names: William Ayrton, musician, music-critic, and impresario . . . George Dyer, phenomenal classical scholar, slovenly, half-starved from a complete self-forgetfulness in books . . . John Richman, amiable raconteur, "the finest fellow to drop in a'nights," according to Lamb . . . Captain James Burney, who had been with Captain Cook on his famous circumnavigations, and his queer-looking son Martin Burney, lawyer and man of good judgment in literature, whom we overhear in a whispered exchange with Edward Phillips, his partner at piquet . . . And of course the three Lambs: Mary, Charles, and brother John, a bulky, laughter-loving man. John worked as a clerk in the same South Sea House which employed his brother Charles as accountant for thirty-three years. It was in that South Sea House that Charles Lamb produced those three hundred official folios of trade figures which he later referred to as his real "works."

We may now visualize Charles Lamb returning that Thursday from his dismal accountant's office, mounting the stairs of the Mitre Court Building, sharing a simple meal with his sister and then perhaps burying himself in a volume of Elizabethan drama as he waits for the company to arrive. The card tables have been placed about the room. There will be games of piquet and whist tonight. Mary will serve veal pie, potatoes, and porter, and there will be talk, endless, fanciful, unfettered talk. Everyone liked "good talk," Hazlitt tells us. "When a stranger came, it was not asked, has he written anything. We were above that pedantry. If he could take a hand at piquet, he was welcome to sit down. If a person liked anything, if he took snuff heartily, it was sufficient." They all abhorred three things: "Insipidity, affectation, and fine gentlemen."

How much of that "Thursday at Lambs" is literal reporting and how much is Hazlitt's embroidery, it is, of course, impossible to say. Biographers of Lamb have found the reported conversation reliable enough to reproduce as an authentic evocation of one of the regular reunions held in that poorly furnished and low-ceilinged apartment in the Temple. As it happens, Hazlitt was probably second only to Boswell in the lively recollection of talk. Proof of this gift is his volume of conversations with James Northcote. Moreover, we have this own characteristic admission: "I am sometimes, I suspect, a better reporter of the ideas of other people than an expounder of my own." In any case, Hazlitt thought it was Lamb who suggested the subject for conversation that Thursday night, and William Ayrton who started the ball rolling. . . .

AYRTON: I suppose the two first persons you would choose to see would be the two greatest names in English literature, Sir Isaac Newton and Mr. Locke?

(*Everyone bursts out laughing at the expression of Lamb's face, in which impatience is restrained by courtesy.*)

LAMB (*stammering hastily*): Yes, the greatest names, but they are not persons—not persons.

AYRTON (*looking wise and foolish at the same time, afraid his triumph might be premature*): Not persons?

LAMB: That is, not characters, you know. By Mr. Locke and Sir Isaac Newton, you mean the "Essay on the Human Understanding," and the "Principia," which we have to this day. Beyond their contents there is nothing personally interesting in the men. But what we want to see anyone *bodily* for, is when there is something peculiar, striking in the individuals, more than we can learn from their writings, and yet are curious to know. I daresay Locke and Newton were very like Kneller's portraits of them. But who could paint Shakespeare?

AYRTON: Ay, there it is; then I suppose you would prefer seeing him and Milton instead?

LAMB: No, neither. I have seen so much of Shakespeare on the stage and the bookstalls, in frontispieces and on mantelpieces, that I am quite tired of the everlasting repetition. And as to Milton's face, the impressions that have come down to us of it I do not like. It is too starched and puritanical; and I should be afraid of losing some of the manna of his poetry in the leaven of his countenance and the precisian's band and gown.

AYRTON: I shall guess no more. Who is it, then, you would like to see "in his habit as he lived," * if you had your choice of the whole range of English literature?

LAMB: Sir Thomas Brown and Fulke Greville, the friend of Sir Philip Sidney, are the two worthies whom I should feel the greatest pleasure to encounter on the floor of my apartment in their nightgown and slippers, and to exchange friendly greeting with them.

(*At this Ayrton laughs outright, and conceives Lamb is jesting with him; but as no one follows his example, he thinks there might be something in it, and waits for an explanation in a state of whimsical suspense.*) ·

LAMB: The reason why I pitch upon these two authors is, that their writings are riddles, and they themselves the most mysterious of personages. They resemble the soothsayers of old, who dealt in dark hints and doubtful oracles; and I should like to ask them the meaning of what no mortal but themselves, I should suppose, can fathom. There is Dr. Johnson. I have no curiosity, no strange uncertainty about him. He and Boswell together have pretty well let me into the secret of what passed through his mind. He and other writers like him are sufficiently explicit. My friends, whose repose I should be tempted to disturb—were it in my power—are implicit, inextricable, inscrutable.

> And call up him who left half-told
> The story of Cambuscan bold.†

When I look at that obscure but gorgeous prose-composition—the "Urn-Burial"—I seem to myself to look into a deep abyss, at the bottom of which are hid pearls and rich treasures; or it is like a stately labyrinth of doubt and withering speculation, and I would invoke the spirit of

---

* *Hamlet*, Act III, scene 4, line 135.
† "Il Penseroso," lines 109-10.

the author to lead me through it. Besides, who would not be curious to see the lineaments of a man who, having himself been twice married, wished that mankind were propagated like trees! As to Fulke Greville, he is like nothing but one of his own "Prologues spoken by the ghost of an old king of Ormus," a truly formidable and inviting personage; his style is apocalyptical, cabalistical, a knot worthy of such an apparition to untie. And for the unravelling a passage or two, I would stand the brunt of an encounter with so portentous a commentator!

AYRTON: I am afraid in that case that if the mystery were once cleared up, the merit might be lost. (*Turning to Hazlitt, whispers a friendly apprehension, that while Lamb continued to admire these old crabbed authors, he would never become a popular writer.*)

SOMEONE: Of the same period Dr. Donne was a writer with an interesting countenance, whose history was singular, and whose meaning is often quite as uncomeatable, without a personal citation from the dead, as that of any of his contemporaries.*

(*A volume of Donne's poetry is produced.*)

AYRTON: (*while someone expatiates on the exquisite simplicity and beauty of the portrait prefixed to the old edition*): What have we here? (*reads aloud*):

> Here lies a She-Sun and a He-Moon there,
> She gives the best light to his sphere,
> Or each is both and all, and so
> They unto one another nothing owe.

LAMB (*seizing the volume, turns to the beautiful "Lines to his Mistress," dissuading her from accompanying him abroad; reads them "with suffused features and a faltering tongue"*):

> By our first strange and fatal interview,
> By all desires which thereof did ensue,
> By our long starving hopes, by that remorse
> Which my words' masculine persuasive force
> Begot in thee, and by the memory
> Of hurts, which spies and rivals threaten'd me,
> I calmly beg. . . .

SOMEONE (*to Lamb*): Can we not see from the window the Temple-walk in which Chaucer used to take his exercise? †

---

* Indirect discourse in the original.
† Indirect discourse in the original.

(*Chaucer's name is put to a vote, and all agree except Ayrton, who says something about the ruggedness of the meter, and objects to the quaintness of the orthography.*—Hazlitt)

HAZLITT (*vexed at this superficial gloss, pertinaciously reducing everything to its own trite level*): Don't you think it would be worth while to scan the eye that had first greeted the Muse in that dim twilight and early dawn of English literature? To see the head, round which the visions of fancy must have played like gleams of inspiration or a sudden glory? To watch those lips that "lisped in numbers, for the numbers came" *—as by a miracle, or as if the dumb should speak? Nor was it alone that he had been the first to tune his native tongue—however imperfectly to modern ears—but he was himself a noble, manly character, standing before his age and striving to advance it; a pleasant humorist withal, who has not only handed down to us the living manners of his time, but had, no doubt, stores of curious and quaint devices, and would make as hearty a companion as Mine Host of Tabard. His interview with Petrarch is fraught with interest. Yet I would rather have seen Chaucer in company with the author of the *Decameron*, and have heard them exchange their best stories together, the Squire's Tale against the Story of the Falcon, the Wife of Bath's Prologue against the Adventures of Friar Albert. How fine to see the high mysterious brow which learning then wore, relieved by the gay, familiar tone of men of the world, and by the courtesies of genius! Surely, the thoughts and feelings which passed through the minds of these great revivers of learning, these Cadmuses who sowed the teeth of letters, must have stamped an expression on their features as different from the moderns as their books, and well worth the perusal! Dante is as interesting a person as his own Ugolino, one whose lineaments curiosity would as eagerly devour in order to penetrate his spirit, and the only one of the Italian poets I should care much to see. There is a fine portrait of Ariosto by no less a hand than Titian's— light, Moorish, spirited, but not answering our idea. The same artist's large colossal profile of Peter Aretine is the only likeness of the kind that has the effect of conversing with "the mighty dead," † and this is truly spectral, ghastly, necromantic.

LAMB: Would you like to see Spenser as well as Chaucer? ‡

HAZLITT (*without hesitation*): No; for that his beauties were ideal, visionary, not palpable or personal, and therefore connected with less

---

* Pope, "Prologue to the Satires," 128.
† Thomson, *The Seasons*, Winter, 432.
‡ Indirect discourse in original.

curiosity about the man. His poetry was the essence of romance, a very halo round the bright orb of fancy; and the bringing in the individual might dissolve the charm. No tones of voice could come up to the mellifluous cadence of his verse. No form but of a winged angel could vie with the airy shapes he has described. He was—to our apprehension —rather "a creature of the element, that lived in the rainbow and played in the plighted clouds," * than an ordinary mortal. Or if he did appear, I should wish it to be as a mere vision, like one of his own pageants, and that he should pass by unquestioned like a dream or sound—

> —*That was Arion crown'd;*
> *So went he playing on the wat'ry plain!* †

CAPTAIN JAMES BURNEY: Columbus . . . ?

MARTIN CHARLES BURNEY: Or The Wandering Jew . . . ?

(*Both rejected by the company, the first as "made over to the New World," the second as "spurious."*)

MARY LAMB: I should like to have seen Pope talking with Patty Blount; and I *have* seen Goldsmith.

(*Everyone turns round to look at Miss Lamb as if by so doing they too could get a sight of Goldsmith.*)

SOMEONE (*with a harsh croaking voice*): Where was Dr. Johnson in the years 1745-6? He did not write anything that we know of, nor is there any account of him in Boswell during those two years. Was he in Scotland with the Pretender? He seems to have passed through the scenes in the Highlands in company with Boswell many years after with lack-luster eye, yet as if they were familiar to him, or associated in his mind with interests that he durst not explain. If so, it would be an additional reason for my liking him; and I would give something to have seen him seated in the tent with the youthful Majesty of Britain, and penning the Proclamation to all true subjects and adherents of the legitimate Government.

AYRTON (*turning short round upon Lamb*): I thought that you of the Lake School did not like Pope?

LAMB: Not like Pope! My dear sir, you must be under a mistake—I can read him over and over forever!

AYRTON: Why certainly, the "Essay on Man" must be allowed to be a masterpiece.

LAMB: It may be so, but I seldom look into it.

---

* Milton, "Comus," 299-301.
† Spenser, *The Faerie Queene*, IV, xi. 23.

AYRTON: Oh! then it is his Satires you admire?

LAMB: No, not his Satires, but his friendly Epistles and his compliments.

AYRTON: Compliments! I did not know he ever made any!

LAMB: The finest that were ever paid by the wit of man. Each of them is worth an estate for life—nay, is an immortality. There is that superb one to Lord Cornbury:

> *Despise low joys, low gains;*
> *Disdain whatever Cornbury disdains;*
> *Be virtuous, and be happy for your pains.**

Was there ever more artful insinuation of idolatrous praise? And then that noble apotheosis of his friend Lord Mansfield—however little deserved—when, speaking of the House of Lords, he adds—

> *Conspicuous scene! another yet is nigh,*
> *(More silent far) where kings and poets lie;*
> *Where Murray (long enough his country's pride)*
> *Shall be no more than Tully or than Hyde!* †

And with what a fine turn of indignant flattery he addresses Lord Bolingbroke—

> *Why rail they then, if but one wreath of mine,*
> *Oh! all accomplish'd St. John, deck thy shrine?* ‡

Or turn ("*With a slight hectic on his cheek and his eye glistening*") to his list of early friends:—

> *But why then publish? Granville the polite,*
> *And knowing Walsh, would tell me I could write;*
> *Well-natured Garth inflamed with early praise,*
> *And Congreve loved and Swift endured my lays:*
> *The courtly Talbot, Somers, Sheffield read,*
> *Ev'n mitered Rochester would nod the head;*
> *And St. John's self (great Dryden's friend before)*
> *Received with open arms one poet more.*
> *Happy my studies, if by these approved!*
> *Happier their author, if by these beloved!*
> *From these the world will judge of men and books,*
> *Not from the Burnets, Oldmixons, and Cooks.* §

---

* "Imitations of Horace," Epistles, I, vi. 60-2.

† Ibid., 50-3.

‡ "Epilogue to the Satires," II, 138-9.

§ "Prologue to the Satires," 135-46.

(*his voice totally failing him, throws down the book*) Do you think I would not wish to have been friends with such a man as this?

AYRTON: What say you to Dryden?

LAMB: He rather made a show of himself, and courted popularity in that lowest temple of Fame, a coffee-house, so as in some measure to vulgarize one's idea of him. Pope, on the contrary, reached the very *beau ideal* of what a poet's life should be; and his fame while living seemed to be an emanation from that which was to circle his name after death. He was so far enviable—and one would be proud to have witnessed the rare spectacle in him—that he was almost the only poet and man of genius who met with his reward on this side of the tomb, who realized in friends, fortune, the esteem of the world, the most sanguine hopes of a youthful ambition, and who found that sort of patronage from the great during his lifetime which they would be thought anxious to bestow upon him after his death. Read Gay's verses to him on his supposed return from Greece, after his translation of Homer was finished, and say if you would not gladly join the bright procession that welcomed him home, or see it once more land at Whitehallstairs.

MARY LAMB: Still, I would rather have seen him talking with Patty Blount, or riding by in a coronet-coach with Lady Mary Wortley Montagu!

EDWARD PHILLIPS (*deep in a game of piquet at the other end of the room, whispers to Martin Burney*): Would not Junius be a fit person to invoke from the dead? *

LAMB: Yes, provided he would agree to lay aside his mask.

SOMEONE: Fielding . . . ?

(*No one seconds the proposition.*)

SOMEONE: Richardson . . . ?

LAMB: By all means, but only to look at him through the glass door of his back-shop, hard at work upon one of his novels—the most extraordinary contrast that ever was presented between an author and his works. But not to let him come behind his counter lest he should want you to turn customer, nor to go upstairs with him, lest he should offer to read the first manuscript of Sir Charles Grandison, which was originally written in eight and twenty volumes octavo, or get out the letters of his female correspondence, to prove that Joseph Andrews was low.

(*"Of all persons near our own time, Garrick's name was received with the greatest enthusiasm, who was proposed by John Lamb. He*

---

* Indirect discourse in original.

presently superseded both Hogarth and Handel, who had been talked of. . . . We were interrupted in the heyday and mid-career of this fanciful speculation by a grumbler in a corner. . . ."—Hazlitt)

GRUMBLER: * It is a shame to make all this rout about a mere player and farce-writer, to the neglect and exclusion of the fine old dramatists, the contemporaries and rivals of Shakespeare.†

LAMB: I anticipated this objection when I named the author of Mustapha and Alaham and out of caprice insist upon keeping him to represent the set, in preference to the wild hare-brained enthusiast Kit Marlowe; to the sexton of St. Ann's, Webster, with his melancholy yew-trees and death's heads; to Decker, who was but a garrulous proser; to the voluminous Heywood; and even to Beaumont and Fletcher, whom we might offend by complimenting the wrong author on their joint productions. Lord Brook, on the contrary, stood quite by himself, or in Cowley's words, was "a vast species alone."

SOMEBODY: What about the circumstance of his being a Lord? ‡

LAMB (*rather startled*): A ghost would perhaps dispense with strict etiquette, on being regularly addressed by his title.§

("*Ben Jonson divided our suffrages pretty equally. Some were afraid he would begin to traduce Shakespeare, who was not present to defend himself.*"—Hazlitt)

SOMEONE (*"whispering aloud"*): If he grows disagreeable, there is Hazlitt can match him.

("*At length, Jonson's romantic visit to Drummond of Hawthornden was mentioned, and turned the scale in his favor.*")

LAMB: Is there anyone that was hanged that you would choose to mention? ‖

HAZLITT: Eugene Aram. . . . ¶

RICKMAN: Are there any metaphysicians to whom one might be tempted to apply the wizard spell? ☞

HAZLITT: There are only six in modern times deserving the name— Hobbes, Berkeley, Butler, Hartley, Hume, Leibnitz; and perhaps Jonathan Edwards, a Massachusetts man. As to the French, who talk fluently of having *created* this science, there was not a tittle in any of

---

* Not otherwise identified anywhere.
† Indirect discourse in original.
‡ *Ibid.*
§ *Ibid.*
‖ Indirect discourse.
¶ Hanged in 1759 for a murder he committed several years before. Thomas Hood wrote a poem about him, "The Dream of Eugene Aram," and Bulwer-Lytton a novel.
☞ Indirect discourse in original.

their writings that was not to be found literally in the authors I have mentioned.*

("*None of these names seemed to excite much interest, and I did not plead for the reappearance of those who might be thought best fitted by the abstracted nature of their studies for their present spiritual and disembodied state, and who, even while on this living stage, were nearly divested of common flesh and blood.*"—Hazlitt)

MARTIN BURNEY: If Coleridge was here, he would undoubtedly be for having up those profound and redoubted scholiasts, Thomas Aquinas and Duns Scotus.

HAZLITT: This might be fair enough in him who had read or fancied he had read the original works, but I do not see how we could have any right to call up these authors to give an account of themselves in person, till we had looked into their writings.†

LAMB (*at the mention of the early Florentine masters, Giotto, Cimabue, and Ghirlandaio*): Egad! Those are the very fellows I should like to have had some talk with, to know how they could see to paint when all was dark around them.

GEORGE DYER: But shall we have nothing to say to the "Legend of Good Women"? ‡

RICKMAN (*In a boisterous tone of friendly exultation*): Name, name as many as you please, Mr. Dyer, without reserve or molestation!

(*Dyer is perplexed between so many amiable recollections, that the name of the lady of his choice expires in a pensive whiff of his pipe.*)

LAMB (*impatiently*): The Duchess of Newcastle!

SOMEONE: Mrs. Hutchinson . . . ! §

("*Mrs. Hutchinson was no sooner mentioned, than she carried the day from the Duchess. We were the less solicitous of filling up the posthumous lists of Good Women, as there was already one in the room as good, as sensible, and in all respects as exemplary, as the best of them could be for their lives! 'I should like vastly to have seen Ninon de Lenclos,'* || *said that incomparable person (Mary Lamb); and this immediately put us in mind that we had neglected to pay honor due to our friends on the other side of the Channel; Voltaire, the patriarch of levity, and Rousseau, the father of sentiment, Montaigne and Rabelais (great in wisdom and in wit), Molière and that*

---

* Indirect discourse in original.
† *Ibid.*
‡ A reference to an unfinished poem by Chaucer.
§ Lucy Hutchinson, born 1620, wrote a life of her husband, Colonel Hutchinson.
‖ Famous French courtesan, beauty, and salon figure (1615–1705).

illustrious group that are collected round him (in the print of that subject) to hear him read his comedy of the Tartuffe at the house of Ninon; Racine, La Fontaine, La Rochefoucauld, St. Evremont, etc. . . ."—Hazlitt)

HAZLITT (*in a shrill, querulous voice*): There is one person I would rather see than all these—Don Quixote!

RICKMAN: Come, come! I thought we should have no heroes, real or fabulous! What say you, Mr. Lamb? Are you for eking out your shadowy list with such names as Alexander, Julius Caesar, Tamerlane, or Ghengis Khan?

LAMB: Excuse me. On the subject of characters in active life, plotters and disturbers of the world, I have a crotchet of my own, which I beg leave to reserve.

RICKMAN: No, no! Come, out with your worthies!

LAMB: What do you think of Guy Fawkes and Judas Iscariot?

RICKMAN (*turning an eye upon him like a wild Indian, but cordial and full of smothered glee*): Your most exquisite reason! * (*echoed on all sides; and Ayrton thinks that Lamb has now fairly entangled himself.*)

LAMB: Why, I cannot but think that Guy Fawkes, that poor fluttering annual scarecrow of straw and rags, is an ill-used gentleman. I would give something to see him sitting pale and emaciated, surrounded by his matches and his barrels of gunpowder, and expecting the moment that was to transport him to Paradise for his heroic self-devotion; but if I say any more, there is that fellow H——† will make something of it. And as to Judas Iscariot, my reason is different. I would fain see the face of him, who, having dipped his hand in the same dish with the Son of Man, could afterwards betray Him. I have no conception of such a thing; nor have I ever seen any picture—not even Leonardo's very fine one—that gave me the least idea of it.

RICKMAN: You have said enough, Mr. Lamb, to justify your choice.

LAMB: Oh; ever right, Menenius,—ever right! ‡

RICKMAN: There is only one other person I can ever think of after this. If Shakespeare was to come into the room, we should all rise up to meet him. But if *that* person was to come into it, we should all fall down and try to kiss the hem of his garment!

("*As a lady* § *present seemed now to get uneasy at the turn the conversation had taken, we rose up to go. The morning broke with*

---

* Shakespeare, *Twelfth Night*, II, iii. 155.
† Not identified.
‡ Shakespeare, *Coriolanus*, II, i. 209.
§ Mrs. Reynolds.

that dim, dubious light by which Giotto, Cimabue, and Ghirlandaio must have seen to paint their earliest works. And we parted to meet again and renew similar topics at night, the next night, and the night after that, till that night over-spread Europe which saw no dawn. The same event,* in truth, broke up our little Congress that broke up the great one. But that was to meet again: our deliberations have never been resumed."—Hazlitt)

---

* Napoleon's escape from Elba.

Hazlitt-Northcote

1.

AN ESSAYIST AND A PAINTER EXCHANGE THOUGHTS ON PRUDERY AND NUDITY.

I have seen pictures muffled up to the chin that had twenty times as much vice in them.

B UT for William Hazlitt's collection of talks, it is probable that the British painter James Northcote would today be little more than a museum relic. The Conversations of James Northcote, which Hazlitt originally entitled Boswell Redivivus, have preserved the painter's memory as one of the most pungent talkers of all time. Northcote had studied with Reynolds, became a highly revered member of the Academy, and knew most of the celebrities of art, literature, and politics of his day. And his day had been a long one. When Hazlitt began his famous conversations, Northcote was already a man of eighty. He had six more years to live and he filled them with acidulous judgments on many of his contemporaries. In his eighty-fifth year he collaborated with Hazlitt on a Life of Titian. Hazlitt, a man of unabashed candor and passionate conviction, found a kindred soul in this blunt and cynical old man. What more natural than that the two should meet regularly and converse on a whole curriculum of subjects?

And what more natural than that Hazlitt should think of committing these talks to writing? A thought, a book, a personality immediately addressed itself to this chronic writer in terms of a potential magazine article. So, it is not surprising that in time he built James Northcote into a book. The magazine series that had begun in The New Monthly Magazine in 1826, and continued in 1829 in The London Weekly Review and The Atlas, became a handsome little volume published in London in 1830 with a frontispiece portrait showing the patriarchal painter in his eighty-second year.

"Called on Mr. Northcote; had, as usual, an interesting conversation." So begins the first of the printed talks; twenty-two others followed in the

1830 edition. Three further conversations were unearthed from the early London magazines and printed in book form for the first time in the centenary edition edited by P. P. Howe. Hazlitt's personal relations with Northcote were always on a very frank basis. In the second of the conversations reprinted below he permits Northcote to flay the unsociable side of his character. This gives him another occasion to defend himself in print, and as a candid self-portrait it adds one more document to our study of the puzzling and passionate confession, Liber Amoris, that is Hazlitt's own record of a season in hell.

Northcote at first disclaimed any interest in the conversations. Then, when they aroused bitter feelings among the "personalities" discussed, he besought his "Boswell redivivus" to be more discreet. Actually, Northcote enjoyed the notoriety they brought him, and soon he developed what Mr. Howe calls a "proprietary interest in the dialogues, in which no doubt Hazlitt indulged him." In any case, it is impossible to find the dividing line of this curious collaboration. Obviously it was Hazlitt who turned them into literature. Yet, it was Northcote who gave them their special flavor. Hazlitt tried to catch the tone and manner, as well as the substance of Northcote's discourse. Where the exact expression eluded him, he doubtless had a good substitute of his own. The artist in him could not be repressed for very long. "Sometimes," he admitted, "I have allowed an acute or a severe remark to stand without the accompanying softenings or explanations, for the sake of effect." One can see the smile of satisfaction on the face of his octogenarian collaborator as he read: "Mr. Northcote is only answerable for whatever wit, sense and spirit there may be in these papers; I take all the dullness, impertinence, and malice upon myself."

It was William Ernest Henley, a critic of seasoned taste and shrewd discernment, who once asked: "Where outside Boswell is there better talk than in Hazlitt's 'Boswell Redivivus'—his so-called 'Conversations with Northcote'?" That, of course, is a matter of opinion. One might name some sources of sprightlier talk. Yet, these conversations have a wise and literary quality of their own. The hand of the artist may have forfeited some of the spontaneity, but for a few revealing moments there is a ringing poignancy as the old man counsels this troubled spirit that was William Hazlitt.

The first of the two excerpts that follow is from "Conversation the Nineteenth," which first appeared in The Atlas in July and August of 1829. The second is the final section of "Conversation the Twenty-Second," which appeared in The Atlas on November 15, 1829.

HAZLITT: Fashion is gentility running away from vulgarity, and afraid of being overtaken by it. It is a sign the two things are not very far asunder.

NORTHCOTE: Yes. Mr. —— used to say that just before the women in his time left off hoops, they looked like bats. Going on from one affectation to another, they at last wore them close under their arms, so that they resembled wings growing out of their shoulders; and having reached the top of the absurdity, they then threw them aside all at once. If long waists are in the fashion one season, they are exploded the next. As soon as the court adopts any particular mode, the city follows the example, and as soon as the city takes it up, the court lays it down. The whole is caricature and masquerade. *Nature only is left out*; for that is either common, or what is fine in it would not always be found on the fashionable side of the question. It may be the fashion to paint or not to paint; but if it were the fashion to have a fine complexion, many fashionable people must go without one, and many unfashionable ones would be at the height of it. Deformity is as often the fashion as beauty, yet the world in general see no other beauty than fashion, and their vanity or interest or complaisance bribes their understanding to disbelieve even their senses. If cleanliness is the fashion, then cleanliness is admired. If dirt, hair-powder, and pomatum are the fashion, then dirt, hair-powder, and pomatum are admired just as much, if not more, from their being disagreeable.

HAZLITT: The secret is that fashion is imitating in certain things that are in our power and that are nearly indifferent in themselves, those who possess certain other advantages that are not in our power, and which the possessors are as little disposed to part with as they are eager to obtrude them upon the notice of others by every external symbol at their immediate control. We think the cut of a coat fine, because it is worn by a man with ten thousand a year, with a fine house, and a fine carriage: as we cannot get the ten thousand a year, the house, or the carriage, we get what we can—the cut of the fine gentleman's coat, and thus are in the fashion. But as we get it, he gets rid of it, which shows that he cares nothing about it. But he keeps his ten thousand a year, his fine house, and his fine carriage. A rich man wears gold buckles to show that he is rich. A coxcomb gets gilt ones to look like the rich man, and as soon as the gold ones prove nothing, the rich man leaves them off. So it is with all the real advantages that fashionable people possess. Say that they have more grace, good manners, and refinement than the rabble. But these do not change every moment at the nod of fashion. Speaking correctly is not proper to one class more than another. If the fashionable, to distinguish themselves from the vulgar, affect a peculiar tone or set of phrases, this is mere *slang*. The difference between grace and awkwardness is the same one year after another. This is the meaning of *natural politeness*. It is a perception of and attention to the feelings of others, which is the same thing, whether it is neglected by the great or practiced by the vulgar. The barrier between refinement and grossness cannot be arbitrarily effaced. Nothing changes but what depends on the shallow affectation and assumption of superiority. Real excellence can never become vulgar. So Pope says in his elegant way:

> *Virtue may choose the high or low degree,*
> *'Tis just the same to virtue and to me;*
> *Dwell in a monk or light upon a king,*
> *She's still the same belov'd, contented thing.*
> *Vice is undone if she forgets her birth,*
> *And stoops from angels to the dregs of earth.**

Pope's verse is not admired because it was once the fashion. It will be admired, let the fashion change how it will.

NORTHCOTE: When Sir Joshua Reynolds wanted to learn what real grace was, he studied it in the attitudes of children, not in the school of the dancing-master, or in the empty strut or mawkish languor of fashion. A young painter asked me the other day whether I thought that Guido † was not chargeable with affectation. I told him that I thought *not*, or in a very trifling degree. I could not deny that Guido sometimes bordered on and reminded me of it; or that there was that which in anybody else might be really so, but that in him it seemed only an extreme natural gentility. He puts his figures into attitudes that are a little too courtly and studied, but he probably could not help it.

HAZLITT: It was rather the excess of a quality or feeling in his mind, than the aiming to supply the defect of one.

NORTHCOTE: Yes; there is no suspicion of what he is doing. The odious part of affectation is when there is an evident design to impose on you with counterfeit pretensions. So in another point that might be objected to him, the impropriety of his naked figures, no mortal can steer clearer of it than he does. They may be strictly said to be clothed with their own delicacy and beauty. There is the "Venus Attired by the Graces." What other painter durst attempt it? They are to be all beauties, all naked; yet he has escaped as if by a miracle—none but the most vicious can find fault with it. The very beauty, elegance, and grace keep down instead of exciting improper ideas. And then again,

---

* *Epilogue to Satires*, Dialogue I.   † Guido Reni (1575–1642).

the "Andromeda Chained to the Rock." Both are, I believe, in the drawing room at Windsor. But there is no possible offense to be taken at them, nothing to shock the most timid or innocent, because there was no particle of grossness in the painter's mind. I have seen pictures by others muffled up to the chin that had twenty times as much vice in them. It is wonderful how cause is seen in the effect. So we find it in Richardson. *Clarissa* is a story in the midst of temptation; but he comes clear and triumphant out of that ordeal, because his own imagination is not contaminated by it. If there had been the least hint of an immoral tendency, the slightest indication of a wish to inflame the passions, it would have been all over with him. The intention always will peep out. You do not communicate a disease if you are not infected with it yourself. Albani's * nymphs and goddesses seem waiting for admirers. Guido's are protected with a veil of innocence and modesty. Titian would have given them an air of Venetian courtesans. Raphael would have made them look something more than mortal. Neither would have done what Guido has effected, who has conquered the difficulty by the pure force of feminine softness and delicacy.

HAZLITT: I am glad to hear you speak so of Guido. I was beginning, before I went abroad, to have a sneaking contempt for him as insipid and monotonous, from seeing the same everlasting repetitions of Cleopatras and Madonnas. But I returned a convert to his merits. I saw many indifferent pictures attributed to great masters. But wherever I saw a Guido, I found elegance and beauty that answered to the silver sound of his name. The mind lives on a round of names. And it is a great point gained not to have one of these snatched from us by a sight of their works. As to the display of the naked figure in works of art, the case to me seems clear. It is only when there is nothing but the naked figure that it is offensive. In proportion as the beauty or perfection of the imitation rises, the indecency vanishes. You look at it then with an eye to art, just as the anatomist examines the human figure with a view to science. Other ideas are introduced. Jeffrey,† of Edinburgh, had a large sprawling "Danae" hanging over the chimney-piece of his office, where he received Scotch persons and their wives on law-business. He thought it a triumph over Presbyterian prudery and prejudice, and a sort of chivalrous answer to the imputed barbarism of the North. It was certainly a paradox in taste, a breach of manners. He asked me if I objected to it because it was naked. "No," I said, "but because it is ugly. You can only have put it there because it is naked,

---

* Francesco Albani (1578–1660).
† Lord Francis Jeffrey (1773–1850), Scottish judge and literary critic.

and that alone shows a felonious intent. Had there been either beauty or expression, it would have conducted off the objectionable part. As it is, I don't see how you can answer for it to the kirk-sessions."

NORTHCOTE: I remember Sir Watkin Wynn employed Sir Joshua and Dance, who was a very eminent designer, to ornament a music-room which he had built. Sir Joshua on this occasion painted his "Cecelia," which he made very fine at first, but afterwards spoiled it, and Dance chose the subject of "Orpheus." When I asked Miss Reynolds what she thought of it, she said she had no doubt of its being clever and well done, but that it looked "like a naked man." This answer was conclusive against it, for if the inspiration of the character had been given, you would have overlooked the want of clothes. The nakedness only strikes and offends the eye in the barrenness of other matter. It is the same in the drama. Mere grossness or ribaldry is intolerable, but you often find in the old comedy that the wit and ingenuity, as well as custom, carry off what otherwise could not be borne. The laughter prevents the blush. So an expression seems gross in one person's mouth, which in another passes off with perfect innocence. The reason is, there is something in the manner that gives a quite different construction to what is said. Have you seen the *Alcides*, the two foreigners who perform such prodigious feats of strength at the theater, but with very little clothing on? They say the people hardly know what to make of it. They should not be too sure that this is any proof of their taste or virtue.

HAZLITT: I recollect a remark of Coleridge's on the conclusion of the story of *Paul and Virginia* by Bernardin St. Pierre. Just before the shipwreck, and when nothing else can save the heroine from perishing, an athletic figure comes forward stripped, but with perfect respect, and offers to swim with her to the shore. But instead of accepting his proposal, she turns away with affected alarm. This, Coleridge said, was a proof of the prevailing tone of French depravity, and not of virgin innocence. A really modest girl in such circumstances would not have thought of any scruple.

NORTHCOTE: It is the want of imagination or of an insight into nature in ordinary writers. They do not know how to place themselves in the situations they describe. Whatever feeling or passion is uppermost, fills the mind and drives out every other. If you were confined in a vault, and thought you saw a ghost, you would rush out, though a lion was at the entrance. On the other hand, if you were pursued by a lion, you would take refuge in a charnel-house, though it was full of spirits, and would disregard the dead bones and putrid relics about you. Both passions may be equally strong. The question is, which is roused first.

Hazlitt-Northcote

2.

APOLOGIA PRO VITA SUA.

*You certainly have not spared others. Why
should you expect nothing but the milk of
human kindness?*

NORTHCOTE: I ought to cross myself like the Catholics, when I see you.
You terrify me by repeating what I say. But I see you have regulated
yourself. There is nothing personally offensive, except what relates to
Sir Walter.* You make him swear, which he did not do. He would
never use the expression *Egad*. These little things mark the gentleman.
I am afraid, if he sees it, he'll say I am a babbler. That is what they
dread so at court, that the least word should transpire.

HAZLITT: They may have their reasons for caution. At least, they can gain
nothing, and might possibly lose equally by truth or falsehood, as it
must be difficult to convey an adequate idea of royalty. But authors are
glad to be talked about. If Sir Walter Scott has an objection to having
his name mentioned, he is singularly unlucky. Enough was said in his
praise; and I do not believe he is captious. I fancy he takes the rough
with the smooth. I did not well know what to do. You seemed to express a wish that the conversation should proceed, and yet you are startled at particular phrases, or I should have brought you what I had
done to show you. I thought it best to take my chance of the general
impression.

NORTHCOTE: Why, if kept to be published as a diary after my death, they
might do. Nobody could then come to ask me questions about them.
But I cannot say they appear very striking to me. One reason may be,
what I observe myself cannot be very new to me. If others are pleased,
they are the best judges. It seems very odd that you who are acquainted
with some of the greatest authors of the day cannot find anything of
theirs worth setting down.

HAZLITT: That by no means pleases them. I understand Godwin is angry

---

* "Conversation the Sixteenth," appeared April 19 and 26, 1829, *The Atlas*.

at the liberty I take with you. He is quite safe in this respect. I might answer him much in the manner of the fellow in the *Country Girl* * when his friend introduces his mistress and he salutes her, "Why, I suppose if I were to introduce my grandmother to you . . ." "Sir," replies the other, "I should treat her with the utmost respect." So I shall never think of repeating any of Godwin's conversations. My indifference may arise in part, as you say, from their not being very new to me. Godwin might, I dare say, argue very well on the doctrine of philosophical necessity or many other questions; but then I have read all this before in Hume or other writers, and I am very little edified, because I have myself had access to the same sources that he has drawn from. But you, as an artist, have been pushed into an intercourse with the world as well as an observation of natures, and combine a sufficient knowledge of general subjects with living illustrations of them. I do not like the conversation of mere men of the world or anecdote-mongers, for there is nothing to bind it together, and the other sort is pedantic and tiresome from repetition, so that there is nobody but you I can come to.

NORTHCOTE: You do not go enough into society, or you would be cured of what I cannot help regarding as a whim. You would there find many people of sense and information whose names you never heard of. It is not those who had made most noise in the world who are persons of the greatest general capacity. It is the making the most of a little, or the being determined to get before others in some one thing, perhaps for want of other recommendations, that brings men into notice. Individuals gain a reputation as they make a fortune, by application and by having set their minds upon it. But you have set out, like other people brought up among books, with such exclusive notions of authors and literary fame, that if you find the least glimmering of common sense out of this pale, you think it a prodigy, and run into the opposite extreme. I do not say that you have not a perception of character, or have not thought as far as you have observed; but you have not had the opportunities. You turn your back on the world, and fancy that they turn their backs on you. This is a very dangerous principle. You become reckless of consequences. It leads to an abandonment of character. By setting the opinion of others at defiance, you lose your self-respect. It is of no use that you still say you will do what is right; your passions usurp the place of reason, and whisper to you that whatever you are bent upon doing is right. You cannot put this deception on the public, however

---

* A Comedy by David Garrick, based on Wycherley's *The Country Wife.*

false or prejudiced their standard may be. And the opinion of the world, therefore, acts as a seasonable check upon willfulness and eccentricity.

HAZLITT: What you have stated is the best excuse I could make for my own faults or blunders. When one is found fault with for nothing, or for doing one's best, he is apt to give the world their revenge. All the former part of my life I was treated as a cipher, and since I have got into notice, I have been set upon as a wild beast. When this is the case, and you can expect as little justice as candor, you naturally in self-defense take refuge in a sort of misanthropy and cynical contempt for mankind. One is disposed to humor them, and to furnish them with some ground for their idle and malevolent censures.

NORTHCOTE: But you should not. If you do nothing to confirm them in their first prejudices, they will come round in time. They are *slow* to admit claims, because they are not *sure* of their validity. And they thwart and cross-examine you to try what temper you are made of. Without some such ordeal or difficulty thrown in the way, every upstart and pretender must be swallowed whole. That would never do. But if you have patience to stand the test, justice is rendered at last, and you are stamped for as much as you are worth. You certainly have not spared others. Why should you expect nothing but the milk of human kindness? Look to those men behind you. (*Pointing to a collection of portraits on the same frame.*) There is Pope and Dryden. Did they fare better than living authors? Had not Dryden his Shadwell,* and Pope his Dennis,† who fretted him to a shadow, and galled him almost to death? There was Dr. Johnson, who in his writings was a pattern of wisdom and morality. He declared that he had been hunted down as if he had been the great enemy of mankind. But he had strength of mind to look down upon it. Not to do this is either infirmity of temper, or shows a conscious want of any claims that are worth carrying up to a higher tribunal than the cabal and clamor of the moment. Sir Joshua always despised malicious reports. He knew they would blow over. At the same time, he as little regarded exaggerated praise. Nothing you could say had any effect, if he was not satisfied with himself. He had a great game to play, and only looked to the result. He had studied himself thoroughly, and, besides, had great equanimity of temper, which, to be sure, it is difficult to acquire, if it is not natural. You have two faults. One is a *feud* or quarrel with the world, which makes you despair and prevents you taking all the pains you might.

---

* Thomas Shadwell (1642?–1692), dramatist and poet-laureate.
† John Dennis (1657–1743), an inveterate critic of Pope.

The other is a carelessness and mismanagement, which makes you throw away the little you actually do, and brings you into difficulties that way. Sir Joshua used to say it was as wrong for a man to think too little as too much of himself. If the one ran him into extravagance and presumption, the other sank him in sloth and insignificance. You see the same thing in horses. If they cannot stir a load at the first effort, they give it up as a hopeless task, and nothing can rouse them from their sluggish obstinacy but blows and ill-treatment.

HAZLITT: I confess all this, but I hardly know how to remedy it. Nor do I feel any strong inducement. Taking one thing with another, I have no great cause to complain. If I had been a merchant, a bookseller, or the proprietor of a newspaper, instead of what I am, I might have had more money or possessed a town- and country-house, instead of lodging in a first or second floor, as it may happen. But what then? I see how the man of business and fortune passes his time. He is up and in the city by eight, swallows his breakfast in haste, attends a meeting of creditors, must read Lloyd's lists, consult the price of consols, study the markets, look into his accounts, pay his workmen, and superintend his clerks. He has hardly a minute in the day to himself, and perhaps in the four-and-twenty hours does not do a single thing that he would do if he could help it. Surely, this sacrifice of time and inclination requires some compensation, which it meets with. But how am I entitled to make my fortune, which cannot be done without all this anxiety and drudgery, who do hardly anything at all, and never anything but what I like to do? I rise when I please, breakfast at length, write what comes into my head, and after taking a mutton-chop and a dish of strong tea, go to the play, and thus my time passes. Mr. Coutts * has no time to go to the play. It was but the other day that I had to get up a little earlier than usual to go into the city about some money transaction, which appeared to me a prodigious hardship. If so, it was plain that I must lead a tolerably easy life. Nor should I object to passing mine over again. Till I was twenty, I had no idea of anything but books, and thought everything else was worthless and mechanical. The having to study painting about this time, and finding the difficulties and beauties it unfolded, opened a new field to me, and I began to conclude that there might be a number of "other things between heaven and earth that were never thought of in my philosophy." † Ask Godwin, or any other literary man who has never been taken out of the leading-strings of learning, and

---

* Assumed to be Coutts, the millionaire-banker, though the place for the name is left blank in Hazlitt's essay.

† Paraphrase of *Hamlet*, Act I, Scene 5, line 166.

you will perceive that they hold for a settled truth that the universe is built of words. Godwin has no interest but in literary fame, of which he is a worshipper. He cannot believe that anyone is clever, or has even common sense, who has not written a book. If you talk to him of Italian cities, where great poets and patriots lived, he heaves a sigh. And if I were possessed of a fortune, he should go and visit the house where Galileo lived or the tower where Ugolino * was imprisoned. He can see with the eyes of his mind. To all else he is marble. It is like speaking to him of the objects of a *sixth sense*. Every other language seems dumb and inarticulate.

---

* Count Ugolino della Gherardesca, whom Dante, in his vision, meets in the ninth circle of Hell, where traitors are punished. The story of his immurement and starvation, in the company of his four sons, is one of the most terrifying passages of the "Inferno" (Canto XXXIII).

Alexandre Dumas

AN ASPIRING YOUNG WRITER SPURNS A SUGGESTION MADE BY AN OFFICE COLLEAGUE.

DUMAS: *What is France waiting for?*
LASSAGNE: *The historical novel.*
DUMAS: *But the history of France is so boring!*
LASSAGNE: *What!*

THE year 1823 found a rather naïve and cumbersome young man from the small town of Villers-Cotterets settled in Paris in a hall bedroom on the top floor of a house on the Place des Italiens. A bulky, eager-faced youth with a taste for loud raiment, he had already become the object of whispers and giggles as he passed along the street. They did not know it, these Parisians, but the lad had come down from the provinces to conquer their city of magic. For this Alexandre Dumas, son of Napoleon's heroic mulatto general, wanted to be a writer. Just what kind of writer he wasn't quite sure, though at the moment the stage dazzled him most. To move an audience to tears and excite its laughter seemed the rosiest of prospects. Of books young Alexandre knew little, and that little showed abominable taste. Somehow the classics—Homer, Dante, Shakespeare, Goethe, Scott, even Molière—had passed him by. His education had been meager and fitful. Equipped with a tremendous ego and an incredible naïveté, he had supposed that to write, all one needed was pencil and paper. Literature meant little, and history to this untutored fledgling, particularly that of France, even less. If the first conspicuous fact about this young man from Villers-Cotterets was his egregious ignorance, the second was his bland unawareness of it. "The history of France is so boring," he blurts out cockily. Yet in a few years this scantily informed and incredibly unread provincial would make this same history one of the most thrilling chronicles of all time.

From his house on the Place des Italiens young Dumas daily repairs to the Palais-Royal. There he has been provided with a desk, paper, pens, ink, and sealing wax. Has he started on his literary conquest of Paris? Hardly. For Alexandre is in the employ of the Duc d'Orléans, the same man who as Louis-Philippe will presently become citizen-king of France.

298

The duke is possessed of a fabulous fortune, reputed to be in the neighborhood of $40,000,000. This includes vast tracts of land and entails equally vast tracts of negotiation. Letters must be copied in a clear and dignified hand. It is at this that Alexandre Dumas, dreamer of literary empires, is employed; and it is his handwriting, rather than his writing, that has brought him this clerk's desk at 1200 francs a year. In fact, here at the Palais-Royal they frown on any other kind of literary endeavor. In a little cubby-hole of the Palais-Royal, at the side of his friends Ernest and Lassagne, Alexandre copies the Duke's correspondence. With a growing panache he affixes the seal of the house of Orléans on the melted wax.

Yet, it is in this very office, at a humble copyist's desk, that the great awakening comes to Alexandre Dumas. It is here that the horizons of literature and history first open to this aspiring writer; here that he first learns of the mighty penmen of Greece and Rome; of the great poets of the day; of the novelists Cooper and Scott; of the fascinating history of his own land. This great awakening young Alexandre owes to his industrious co-worker Lassagne, who, himself enmeshed in the humdrum routine of copying, is secretly dreaming of another paradise of letters. This Lassagne is a godsend to Dumas. He has a vast knowledge of books which he is eager to share with a willing listener; he has taste, and he has patience. Gently, he twits his uncultured colleague for admiring the cheap and pompous tragedies of his friends, the Arnaults. Adroitly he shatters young Dumas' illusions about the current idols of the literary marketplace. Not once does he coddle the young man's ego. Gradually it dawns on Dumas that he is ignorant indeed, that he has not even begun to know books, and that in order to write one must first read. What is literary France waiting for, he asks Lassagne. "The historical novel," answers his new mentor. "But the history of France is so boring!" exclaims the callow provincial. "What!" flares Lassagne, and the good-natured drubbing is on again.

For the few years that Dumas remains in the service of the Duke, Lassagne is his closest friend; later they are to become collaborators. But today, shortly after assuming his new duties, Lassagne is his guide and adviser, steering the eager young writer into what are for him strange and uncharted seas. Lassagne is a patient counsellor, and Dumas is to prove a conscientious listener. By dint of study and stupendous toil he will write what the whole world will read; he will create Monte Cristo and chronicle the exploits of three musketeers; he will make Thackeray and Stevenson and a host of their peers confess that in the telling of stories they bow to one master—Alexandre Dumas. He will do all this from the plenteous coffers of French history. Yet today, in this tiny office of the Secretariat of the Duc d'Orléans, he has the gall to dismiss this same history as dull! As we overhear his bovine exclamation, we cannot help wondering, in the shrewd words of Herbert Gorman, whether at that very moment the ghosts of d'Artagnan, Athos, Aramis, Porthos, Chicot, Coconnas, Henri Quatre, Bussy d'Ambois, Queen Margot, Ange Pitou, La Mole, the Duc de Beaufort, Fouquet, the Chevalier de Maison-Rouge, Mauleon, Richelieu—the ghosts of these and a hundred more— did not stir uneasily "in the misty cavern of the future." Let us, like the good Lassagne, be tolerant as we listen. Dumas tells us (in Mes Mémoires —Paris, 1863, Vol. 3) that he had just blurted out the great news that the playwright Arnault, author of the current hit Régulus, had invited him to dinner. "Ernest," he tells us, "seemed quite indifferent, and Lassagne appeared only moderately impressed. I asked Lassagne to explain his lack of interest in such celebrities." And the eyes of Alexandre Dumas begin to open.

LASSAGNE: As a political matter, I don't belong to the same party as these gentlemen. As a literary matter, I don't think much of what they are doing.

DUMAS (*stupefied*): Then you haven't read *Germanicus*?

LASSAGNE: I have; but it's very poor stuff.

DUMAS: But you haven't seen *Régulus*?

LASSAGNE: I have seen it; but it's mediocre.

DUMAS (*lowering his head, more stupefied than ever*): But how do you explain the success of these plays?

LASSAGNE: Talma is acting in them.

DUMAS: But the reputation of these men . . . ?

LASSAGNE: They make their reputations themselves—in their own newspapers. Let Monsieur De Jouy or Monsieur Arnault or Monsieur Lemercier give us a play without Talma and you will see the difference. It will have ten performances. (*As Dumas again lowers his head, Lassagne adopts a kindly and paternal tone.*) Look here, my boy—you want to be a writer, don't you?

DUMAS (*eagerly*): Oh, yes!

LASSAGNE (*laughing*): Not so loud! I've already told you never to talk too loudly on that subject, around here, anyway. . . . Well, since you're determined to become a writer, don't take the literature of the Empire as your model. That's my advice.

DUMAS: But which *should* I take?

LASSAGNE: Frankly, I'd find it hard to tell you. Certainly our young playwrights—Soumet, Guiraud, Casimir Delavigne, Ancelot—have talent. Lamartine and Hugo are poets, so I leave them aside. They haven't written for the theater, and I don't know if they ever will. Even if they did, I doubt if they would be successful.

DUMAS: Why is that?

LASSAGNE: Because one is too much of a dreamer and the other too much of a thinker. Neither of them lives in the world of reality. The theater, my boy, is humanity. As I was saying, Soumet, Guiraud, Casimir Delavigne, Ancelot are talented young playwrights. But bear in mind what I'm telling you: they are nothing but transitional figures—mere connecting links in the chain of the past and the future. They are points which lead from what has been to what will be.

DUMAS: And what is your idea of "what will be"?

LASSAGNE: Ah, my dear friend, now you're asking me more than I can tell you. The public itself is undecided. It knows what it *doesn't* want, but not what it *does* want.

DUMAS: In poetry, in drama, or in the novel?

LASSAGNE: There is still a great deal to do in drama and fiction. As for poetry, Lamartine and Hugo are meeting the demands of the moment quite nicely. Let's not look for anything more.

DUMAS: But Casimir Delavigne?

LASSAGNE: Oh, he's something else again! Casimir Delavigne is the poet of the bourgeoisie. He has his clientele. Let him keep it and let's not offer him any competition.

DUMAS: So, whom should I imitate in writing comedies, tragedies, and dramas?

LASSAGNE: To begin with, don't ever imitate at all. You should study, yes. But the man who follows a guide must walk behind. Do you want to walk behind someone?

DUMAS: No.

LASSAGNE: Good! Then, study. Don't sit down to compare comedies, tragedies, and dramas. Take events, characters, passions, let them fuse together in your imagination, and make statues of Corinthian bronze.

DUMAS: What is Corinthian bronze?

LASSAGNE: You don't know?

DUMAS: I haven't the slightest idea.

LASSAGNE: Fortunate man!

DUMAS: Why so?

LASSAGNE: Because in that case you will learn everything by yourself; because you will submit to no standard but that of your own intelligence and no rule but that of your own education. . . . The bronze of Corinth? . . . Do you happen to know that Mummius set fire to Corinth one day?

DUMAS: Yes, I believe I once translated that somewhere . . . in *De Viris*.

LASSAGNE: Then you must know what happened. All the gold, silver, and bronze melted in the intensity of the fire and ran along the streets in streams. Now, the mixing of these three precious metals produced a single metal. This metal was called the bronze of Corinth. So. . . . The man who, out of sheer genius, will do for comedy, tragedy, drama, the same thing that Mummius, out of sheer ignorance and barbarity, did for gold, silver, and bronze; the man, in short, who will fuse in the fire of one imagination an Aeschylus, a Shakespeare, and a Molière, that man, my good friend, will have found a bronze as precious as the bronze of Corinth.

DUMAS (*after a few moments' reflection*): That's very beautiful, what you've just told me. And since it's beautiful it must be true.

LASSAGNE: Do you know Aeschylus?

DUMAS: No.

LASSAGNE: Do you know Shakespeare?

DUMAS: No.

LASSAGNE: Do you know Molière?

DUMAS: Very slightly.

LASSAGNE: Well, begin by reading everything these three men wrote. When you have finished reading them, re-read them. And when you have finished re-reading them, learn them by heart.

DUMAS: And after that?

LASSAGNE: After that . . . you will go on to those who proceeded from them. From Aeschylus you will pass to Sophocles, from Sophocles to Euripides, from Euripides to Seneca, from Seneca to Racine, from Racine to Voltaire, and from Voltaire to Chénier. So much for tragedy. By so doing you will be witnessing the transformation of a race that began as eagles and ended as parrots.

DUMAS: And to whom do I go after Shakespeare?

LASSAGNE: To Schiller.

DUMAS: And after Schiller?

LASSAGNE: To no one.

DUMAS: What about Ducis?

LASSAGNE: Oh, let's not confuse Schiller with Ducis. Schiller is inspired. Ducis imitates. Schiller is always original. Ducis is a copyist, and not even a good copyist.

DUMAS: And now Molière. . . .

LASSAGNE: As for Molière. . . . There it would be best to work backwards.

DUMAS: From Molière to whom?

LASSAGNE: From Molière to Terence, from Terence to Plautus, from Plautus to Aristophanes.

DUMAS: But Corneille . . . ? It seems to me you're forgetting him.

LASSAGNE: I'm not forgetting him. I'm setting him apart.

DUMAS: For what reason?

LASSAGNE: Because he is neither an ancient Greek nor an old Roman.

DUMAS: And what is he, then?

LASSAGNE: He is a Cordovan, like Lucan. You will see, when you compare them, that his verse greatly resembles that of the *Pharsalia.*

DUMAS: Would you let me write down everything you've just told me?

LASSAGNE: Why would you want to do that?

DUMAS: I would use it as a set of rules for my reading.

LASSAGNE: That's not necessary. You'll have me here to consult.

DUMAS: I may not always have you.

LASSAGNE: If you don't have me, you'll have someone else.

DUMAS: That someone else might not know as much as you.

LASSAGNE (*shrugging his shoulders*): My dear boy, what I know the whole world knows. The first person you run into will be able to tell you what I've been telling you now.

DUMAS (*murmuring, and letting his head fall into his hands*): That means I must be terribly ignorant.

LASSAGNE: The fact is you have a great deal to learn. But you're young. You'll learn.

DUMAS: And speaking of the novel—what is there to do?

LASSAGNE: Everything—the same as the theater.

DUMAS: I was under the impression that we had some excellent novels.

LASSAGNE: What novels have you read?

DUMAS: Those of Lesage, Madame Cottin, and Pigault-Lebrun.

LASSAGNE: What effect did they produce on you?

DUMAS: The novels of Lesage amused me. Those of Madame Cottin made me cry, and those of Pigault-Lebrun made me laugh.

LASSAGNE: Then you haven't read Goethe, Walter Scott, or Cooper?

DUMAS: I have not read Goethe, Walter Scott, or Cooper.

LASSAGNE: Well, read them.

DUMAS: And when I've read them, what do I do next?

LASSAGNE: The bronze of Corinth—always; except that you must try to add a little ingredient which none of them has.

DUMAS: Namely?

LASSAGNE: Passion. Goethe will give you poetry. Walter Scott will give you character study. Cooper will give you the mysterious grandeur of prairies, forests, and ocean. But you will look in vain for passion among them.

DUMAS: In other words, the man who can be a poet like Goethe, an observer like Scott, a painter like Cooper, and a man of passion in the bargain . . . ?

LASSAGNE: Exactly . . . that man would be very nearly complete.

DUMAS: Which three outstanding works by these masters should I read?

LASSAGNE: *Wilhelm Meister* by Goethe; *Ivanhoe* by Walter Scott, and *The Spy* by Cooper.

DUMAS: I read right through *Jean Sbogar* last night.

LASSAGNE: Oh, that's something different.

DUMAS: What do you mean?

LASSAGNE: It's a genre novel. That's not what France is waiting for.

DUMAS: What *is* she waiting for?

LASSAGNE: The historical novel.

DUMAS: But the history of France is so boring!

LASSAGNE (*raising his head and staring at Dumas*): What!

DUMAS: The history of France is so boring!

LASSAGNE: How do you know that?

DUMAS (*reddening*): That's what I've been told.

LASSAGNE: Poor child! That's what you've been told! . . . Why don't you read first and then form your own opinion?

DUMAS: What should I read?

LASSAGNE: God, it's a whole world in itself! Joinville, Froissart, Monstrelet, Chatelain, Juvenal des Ursins, Montluc, Saulx-Tavannes, l'Estoile, Cardinal Retz, Saint-Simon, Villars, Madame de la Fayette, Richelieu . . . and I don't know who else!

DUMAS: And how many volumes in all would that make?

LASSAGNE: Two or three hundred, perhaps.

DUMAS: And you've read them all?

LASSAGNE: Certainly.

DUMAS: And you say it's necessary for me to read them?

LASSAGNE: If you want to write historical novels, it's not only necessary for you to read them. You've got to know them by heart, besides.

DUMAS: To be perfectly frank, you frighten me. At that rate, I shouldn't dare write a word for two or three years yet.

LASSAGNE: Even longer than that. . . . Unless you prefer to write without knowing anything.

DUMAS: My God, my God! The time I've lost!

LASSAGNE: You must make up for it.

DUMAS: You'll help me, won't you?

LASSAGNE: At the office?

DUMAS: Oh, I'll read at night; I'll study all night long. During office hours I'll work, and from time to time we'll talk a little.

LASSAGNE: Yes, like today, except that we've talked a great deal.

DUMAS: Just one more word. You've told me what to read in the way of plays?

LASSAGNE: Right.

DUMAS: In the way of fiction?

LASSIGNE: Right.

DUMAS: In the way of history?

LASSIGNE: Right.

DUMAS: Good! Now, in the way of poetry, what should I read?

LASSAGNE: First let me know what you've already read.

DUMAS: Voltaire, Parny, Bertin, Demoustier, Legouvé, Colardeau.

LASSAGNE: Fine—now forget them all!

DUMAS: Really?

LASSAGNE: Of ancient Greece, read Homer; of ancient Rome, read Virgil; of the Middle Ages, read Dante. That's the lion's very marrow I'm giving you there.

DUMAS: And of the módern world?

LASSAGNE: Ronsard, Mathurin Regnier, Milton, Goethe, Uhland, Byron, Lamartine, Victor Hugo, and, most of all, a little volume which Latouche is printing soon.

DUMAS: Namely?

LASSAGNE: André Chénier.

DUMAS: I've read him.

LASSAGNE: You've read Marie-Joseph Chénier. Let's not confuse Marie-Joseph with André.

DUMAS: But to come back to all those foreign authors. How am I going to read them if I don't know Greek, English, or German?

LASSAGNE: Beautifully put, by Jove! You'll make it your business to learn those languages!

DUMAS: But how?

LASSAGNE: I haven't the faintest notion. But bear this in mind: one always learns what one wants to learn. . . . And I think it's time we got back to work. Oh, by the way, let me give you a piece of advice. . . .

DUMAS: Yes?

LASSAGNE: Don't tell a word of your little plan of study to Monsieur Arnault.

DUMAS: Why not?

LASSAGNE: Because you wouldn't remain a friend of his for long.

DUMAS: You think so?

LASSAGNE: I'm positive of it.

DUMAS: Thanks. I won't open my mouth.

LASSAGNE: Good! Now a second piece of advice....

DUMAS: I'm listening.

LASSAGNE: You mustn't tell a word of our conversation to either Monsieur Oudard * or Monsieur de Broval.

DUMAS: Why not?

LASSAGNE: Because if you did, we wouldn't remain long in the same office.

DUMAS: But, damn it, I do want to stay here with you.

LASSAGNE: That depends entirely on you.

DUMAS: Oh, if it depends on me, we'll have each other's company for several years.

LASSAGNE: So be it!

(Lassagne was to find the young provincial a diligent pupil. Dumas applied himself to the classics with enormous energy, reading during office hours and late into the night in his room on the Place des Italiens. He took lessons in physics, chemistry, and physiology, and Lassagne was soon baffled by this boundless avidity for learning of all kinds. One result of the unofficial literary sessions at the Palais-Royal was the production of two "vaudevilles"—"La Chasse et l'Amour" and "La Noce et l'Enterrement." What modest profits accrued from the staging of these sketches Dumas shared with a staff of collaborators, among them Lassagne. Later Lassagne joined Dumas in the struggles of the romantic school headed by Victor Hugo. His name is then lost in the mists of history, for neither Dumas nor anyone else mentions him again. The good Lassagne had played his part in the gathering drama of Alexandre Dumas, and gracefully made his exit. In five years' time Dumas became one of the foremost playwrights of the Parisian theater. Both his plays *Christine* and *Henri III* were triumphs, so much so that the Duc d'Orléans, himself an ardent theater-goer, rewarded his copyist with the post of assistant librarian. The connection with the Palais-Royal ended with the revolution of 1830. Dumas and his former employer remained on friendly terms, but politically their paths had diverged. In 1832 Dumas almost lost his life in a republican uprising that was quickly put down by the king's troops. Warned in time of his impending arrest, Dumas decided that his health required an immediate change of climate. On July 21, 1832, he quietly slipped out of Paris, bound for Switzerland. The history of France was proving anything but "boring" for the future creator of *Monte Cristo*.)

---

* *Chef de bureau* and director-general of the Duc d'Orléans, who had warned the young Dumas about their attitude toward the literary aspirations of the office help.

Stendhal

A FIERY ADVOCATE OF FREE THOUGHT FINDS
HIMSELF IN A LAIR OF ADVERSARIES.

*You see, we have no way of understanding one
another. I am a rat and you are a cat.*

"TUESDAY at Mme. Ancelot's; Wednesday at Baron Gérard's; Saturday at Cuvier's; Sunday afternoon at Delécluze's. . . ." So reads an excerpt from the weekly social calendar of Henri Beyle, better known to the world as Stendhal. The year was 1826. The widely travelled student of human affairs, biographer of Mozart and Rossini, cynical analyst of "L'Amour" and staunch friend of Italian revolutionaries had become the darling of the Parisian salons and coteries. Though they differed with him, cultivated men and women sought his company. They sharply rebuked him for his anti-clericalism, gasped over his esthetic heresies, and invited him to their next soirée. For Stendhal had a ready tongue and an emphatic conviction. And if anyone dismissed him as a charlatan, he was soon undeceived by the publication of La Chartreuse de Parme and Le Rouge et le Noir, novels that revolutionized the whole art of fiction with their probing psychology.

"Sunday afternoon at Delécluze. . . ." That would be Etienne Delécluze, leading art critic of the time, who launched his eagerly awaited judgments from the esteemed Journal des Debats. A versatile man, Delécluze had abandoned painting for criticism and literature, and by 1826 had become the trusted friend and adviser of the literary youth of the Restoration. Stendhal was not long in joining his circle. In his Souvenirs de Soixante Années (1862), Delécluze acidly pictures Stendhal as the kind of talker who would force the conversation his way and then introduce a long tirade against pedantry with "some salty story gathered from the greenrooms of the Paris theaters," to quote Matthew Josephson. Yet it is Stendhal, with his sententious quips on art and life, who gives life and luster to Delécluze's otherwise tedious reminiscences. Nor did Stendhal spare his Sunday host in his own "Souvenirs d'Egotisme." While granting him excellent taste in arranging his literary parties, he ridicules him unsparingly as an art collector, charging him with that most unpardonable of esthetic sins, "the pettiness of a typical bourgeois." Oddly enough, Delécluze is much gentler with Stendhal in several pages of supplementary "Souvenirs" which did not appear till several years after his own death. Published in Paris in 1889 in Volume X of the Revue Retrospective, the posthumous notes reveal Delécluze's secret devotion to Stendhal as a man of unassailable integrity. We find, too, a remarkable understanding of this unrelenting enemy of fraud and orthodoxy who, by some·strange quirk of temperament, studiously rebuffed all offers of personal friendship.

Delécluze occupied an attic apartment on the sixth floor of a house in the old Rue Nôtre-Dame-des-Champs. There Stendhal would mingle with a distinguished assortment of gens de lettres, artists, and scientists, and "sitting before a small fire would begin to function ... as a trumpeter and vanguard leader of the new literary revolution."* In the posthumously printed "Souvenir," which is rendered below as the only available glimpse of Stendhal in sustained conversational action, Delécluze records a meeting which occurred in his mansard chambers on Sunday, February 11, 1827. The talk had turned to the writings of Joseph de Maistre, an uncompromising royalist and ultramontane pamphleteer who preached the gospel of "one world" ruled by the spiritual authority of the Vatican. De Maistre had denounced eighteenth-century rationalism tirelessly. In a book, Soirée de Saint-Petersbourg, he had gone so far as to predict that a man of great faith would presently appear who would explode all the accepted theories of science, including the principles of lunar and solar attraction and the composition of water. A passage containing this bland prophecy had been read out loud that Sunday afternoon, presumably by Delécluze himself. No doubt all eyes turned to the plump, head-shaking Stendhal as the reading concluded with De Maistre's belief that it was the mysterious voice of conscience that was prompting a "revolt against certain theories." As an apostle of science and freethinking, Stendhal accepted the challenge, and the discussion began in that high attic retreat overlooking the roofs of Paris. . . .

STENDHAL: Monsieur de Maistre writes well, but he is a rascal.
CERCLET: † Do you mind telling me why?
STENDHAL (*in an incisive tone*): A man who begins by talking to me about conscience! What is conscience, I beg you? Only a hypocrite address-

---

* Matthew Josephson.
† Later became secretary-editor of the Chamber of Deputies; died in 1849.

ing himself to fools to make worse dupes of them, would today dare to invoke the testimony of conscience. . . . (*Noting a general refusal to take up the challenge on this point.*) If anyone present believes in conscience, let's pretend I said nothing and move on to another point. I have seen water decomposed and recomposed. I have *seen* it, *seen* it with my own eyes, everything that is meant by the word *seen*. Now I'm not the only person in Europe who has *seen* it. Nobody nowadays doubts that phenomenon. What do you want me to think of Monsieur de Maistre, who in the very first pages of his book begins to lie like a coward or a scoundrel? I suspect his purpose is to trick me, therefore he is a scoundrel.

DELÉCLUZE: But in denying that particular phenomenon, de Maistre has but one purpose—to present conscience, in his opinion, as intellectually superior to the combined results of all the sciences.

STENDHAL: Which is precisely what I object to. He does what all the rascally priests do when they substitute vague ideas for facts. Facts, after all, are not as obliging as ideas. Facts have to be appraised, measured, proved!

MEYNIER: * But do you dismiss as of no consequence the unanimous verdict of the. . . .

STENDHAL: Cicero's *consensus omnium gentium* † is utter nonsense to me—a piece of tomfoolery that made a fortune in its day, but which has become so stale that no one would dream of defending it now.

CERCLET: You are quite aware that there are people, and even people of talent like Monsieur de Maistre, who not only defend it, but make it the basis of their reasoning.

STENDHAL: So all such people are scoundrels, when they are not blockheads. It's the history of the priests of all countries and all times—they have either been rogues or fools. There is no middle term. From which I conclude that governments do wrong by paying them.

CERCLET: Let us assume, as you say, that all priests are either rogues or fools. But what if the people want them?

STENDHAL: They don't want them.

DELÉCLUZE: For a man as wedded to facts as you are, you should be careful not to deny those that are true.

STENDHAL: Do you want to know what the priests have been doing since the beginning of the world? They know that we all come into the world with some little complaint. Some have it in an arm, some in a leg, and so on. What does the priest say to himself? "If I leave that fool alone

* A German.
† "General agreement."

with his malady, he will get used to it, forget it, and perhaps even heal it. Let's put a fear into him, and exploit that fear by continually irritating his wound." The priest, under pretext of healing, places his hand on the hurt, touches it, irritates it, keeps coming back to it, endlessly, until the poor fellow really becomes sick and he can no more do without his rogue of a priest than he could, in other cases, do without his rogue of a doctor. From which I conclude that there are only rogues and fools in this world, present company excepted, of course.

DELÉCLUZE: Granting every point of your argument, you still haven't answered Cerclet's question. What if these people want the priests?

STENDHAL: Let everyone pay them as they see fit, so long as it is not the state that pays them and raises taxes to pay them. For it is quite evident that in giving a fixed salary to priests, you employ them to scratch people's wounds and threaten them with the terror of death if they do not turn to them. "Listen to me! Have faith in me! Pay me!" says the priest. "Otherwise I shall curse you, I shall consign you to Hell, and you will be boiled in steaming cauldrons for all eternity!"

DELÉCLUZE: You are shifting the difficulty without resolving it. We agree with you that men are imbeciles, but if in their error these imbeciles are agreed to recognize God and want priests to act as their agents before God, then this is a positive good, for it has been going on since the world began. You who don't want to be led by the priests, would you force people who do want to be led by them to give them up? That would merely be changing the nature of despotism, without ending the tyranny.

STENDHAL: But who believes in God nowadays?

CERCLET: A great number of people.

STENDHAL: Let's not linger on that point. For my part I don't know if there is a God. But assuming there is a God, what reasonable man can believe that this God is good? Do you really expect me to love and worship a God who invented the plague and the itch—who lies in ambush waiting to make me suffer every step of the way—who lets me be born to become the prey of disease and everything else?

MEYNIER: You have just put your finger on the main point. All men, after going through the things you say, arrive at an idea of divine justice, the true laws of which we can only grasp with great difficulty, because of our imperfect nature. At the same time we all have a certain intuition of this divine justice in our intellectual conscience, as Monsieur de Maistre calls it.

STENDHAL: My only answer to that is that I have seen water decomposed and recomposed and I don't think anyone has yet succeeded in decomposing and recomposing the *intellectual conscience*. Now, Monsieur de Maistre is denying a physical fact that has been fully proved and demonstrated. Why hasn't one the right, when he speaks of this intellectual conscience, which no one has heard anything about, to deny its existence? I, for one, flatly deny its existence. De Maistre adds, moreover, that the Catholic religion has constantly protected and propagated the sciences. That is a lie, for the Inquisition condemned Galileo for having proved that Joshua could not have held back the sun. When an author tells a lie in his book—he's finished for me. He may go on saying the most beautiful things in the world after that. I won't believe him any more. It's the same story all over again—Plato, Jesus Christ, Bossuet, and Monsieur de Maistre.

(Enter Monsieur de Guizard.*)

Ah, wait a moment, gentlemen! Here is Monsieur de Guizard, who will now tell us a few good stories about the ladies of the Court. That ought to be more worth while!

GUIZARD: I don't know a single one, but if you like I shall tell you about the latest rumors about the nomination of the forty peers.

STENDHAL: Bravo! Forty peers? † And all bishops, no doubt.

GUIZARD: All bishops, as you say.

CERCLET: But is the minister quite sure that the forty votes he gains for himself that way will not cost him sixty or a hundred others? The existing peers will be offended by the introduction of this episcopal batch. With their vanity hurt, this might even make liberals out of the most rabid *ultras*.‡

STENDHAL: There are many peers who are not rich. The minister is keeping those. As for the blockheads and the scoundrels, the Jesuits will certainly let them go.

(Stendhal leaves.)

MEYNIER: What a strange man, this Beyle!

CERCLET: He's so wrong-headed! He gives me the impression of understanding no one but himself. He seems utterly lacking in the faculty of sympathizing with the rest of the world.

DELÉCLUZE: It's his great pretension. When you discuss anything with him and express an opinion contrary to his own, he usually ends the conversation by saying: "You see, we have no way of understanding one another. I am a *rat* and you are a *cat*."

---

* Louis LeBlanc de Guizard (1797–1879), prefect, deputy editor of the *Globe* and *Revue Française* and director (1850–1852) of the Beaux-Arts.

† *Quarante pairs*—a possible pun, *pères* being pronounced the same as *pairs* in French.

‡ I.e., ultramontane, or for the ultra-Papal party in the Church of Rome.

MEYNIER: That's quite true. He always comes back to his dominant idea: He resists anything that might bring about unanimous agreement.

DELÉCLUZE: Yes, he insists that some see yellow, some see blue and some see green.

CERCLET: There's a certain element of truth in that.

DELÉCLUZE: No doubt. But there is a difference between presenting it as a relative or as an absolute truth.

MEYNIER: That's where all those who share Beyle's opinions go wrong. They discover a partial truth and, without further investigation, immediately erect a ladder of conjectural analogies. Then, without taking the intermediary steps, they proceed to jump from the particular to the general.

(*Cerclet leaves.*)

DELÉCLUZE (*to Meynier*): Well, how do you feel about it?

MEYNIER: I am quite puzzled by the assurance and, if I must say it, the ignorance of this man Beyle.

DELÉCLUZE: Ah, monsieur, for a long time now I have been dismayed by the fact that there are a great many men in France who along with that unhappy disposition possess brilliant faculties of the mind.

MEYNIER: But hasn't this man ever been to England or Germany?

DELÉCLUZE: On the contrary, he has been there several times.

MEYNIER: Then I don't understand it at all.

DELÉCLUZE: Beyle and people like him make it very easy for one to understand why there are Jesuits. I'll go one step further. When I talk to him or anyone like him, I am surprised to find myself rather glad that there is a militia of priests which furnishes its own exaggeration as a counterweight to those of its enemies. To be perfectly honest, I expect no good to come of the continual clash of these two extreme forces. If the Jesuits knew their business, they would let people speaking Beyle's language move freely through the world. There is hardly a chance that such people would win a following.

MEYNIER: After persecution, denunciation is the force that most confirms sectarianism.

DELÉCLUZE: The one good thing about Beyle is that he is not a liar.

MEYNIER: Oh, no! He is quite frank. Besides, there's a certain gaiety in his face and in his talk that is very pleasant.

DELÉCLUZE: Frankly, I have no doubt that he says exactly what he thinks, or, at any rate, what he feels. He avows all the truths that people expound to him, even when they tend to destroy the very system he defends. He is a good enemy and it is a pleasure to fight with him.

MEYNIER: What I can't forgive him, however, is the way he insists that there isn't nor could there ever be an honest priest who is also not a fool.

DELÉCLUZE: There Beyle is actually contradicting himself, for if you were to discuss love with him in any analogous way, his position would be just the opposite. He would agree that a highly intelligent man can be a complete fool in love. Many people would deny this. People who have never experienced love always regard it as an emotional affectation or an access of folly among those who have. Such people use the same language about love that those who, because they have no religious feeling by nature or education, use to deny the existence of religion altogether.

MEYNIER: Does Beyle love poetry?

DELÉCLUZE: Yes.

MEYNIER: I suppose he is insensible to music.

DELÉCLUZE: Quite the contrary. He loves it, and I can assure you that his tastes are natural and sincere. He loves poetry, music, and the arts in general.

MEYNIER: You amaze me!

DELÉCLUZE: I'm telling you the truth. Beyle is an extraordinary man. I'm sure, for example, that I have a better opinion of him than he has of himself.

MEYNIER: How is that? I don't quite follow you there.

DELÉCLUZE: I have travelled with Beyle. I have seen him in foreign countries, and there I have always found him a much completer man than in Paris and in the atmosphere of the salons. That atmosphere doesn't suit him. He breathes it with difficulty. You can see quite easily in his awkward movements, in the nervous assurance of his talk, and in the often brutal bluntness of his remarks, that the *beau monde* is not Beyle's element.

MEYNIER: That's very true. I have watched him change from the crudest frankness to a somewhat affected politeness.

DELÉCLUZE: Quite so. He is completely unnatural in his conversation. Yet his true character is stronger than his habits, and that's what I like in him. He is never more amusing than when he makes it a point to be especially sweet and honeyed and almost mawkish in his manners, only to find himself suddenly stung to the quick by something that shocks him. Then he will talk excitedly, make biting remarks, and even use an improper word.

MEYNIER: That's exactly what sets him apart. He never follows a straight line in his talk. And people always find that captivating in him.

DELÉCLUZE: Yes, and by a singular piece of irony, he has a mania for being regarded as a logician. He aspires to be numbered among the straight-thinkers and mathematicians.

MEYNIER: You don't really mean that! Why, that's not possible!

DELÉCLUZE: It's not only possible but true. In his *History of Painting in Italy* this pretension of his comes through on every page. But where it appears even more clearly is in his book on love—*De l'Amour,* no doubt because the material lends itself well to mathematical demonstration. In the first fifteen or twenty pages Beyle divides his subject into propositions, demonstrations, corollaries, axioms, and so on. And then, all of a sudden, our author discards this scientific apparatus and plunges into the wave, a style which suits his temperament better and which, admittedly, often goes well with the subject.

MEYNIER: Do you know Beyle's family?

DELÉCLUZE: Not at all! He lives alone in a furnished room, here in Paris. I know only that he comes from Grenoble, that his father, who died a long time ago, left him very little. Neither I nor any of those who see him more habitually knows exactly what his means of existence are. He lives among us, but shows no desire to establish any social relations other than conversation. He says he discourages friendship as a tie that can become an obligation. In short, this man seems to arrange his whole life so that in any place, at any time, he may enjoy his full independence. However, I must add in all honesty that I have never felt prompted to accuse him of egotism.

MEYNIER: He is an extraordinary person.

DELÉCLUZE: Quite extraordinary. Without that last reservation which I made to the catalogue of his qualities, I would find that man unbearable. As it is, I'm actually very fond of him. I've often tried to make him know it, but he has always rebuffed my attempts. Far from being hurt, I felt a kind of respect for his independence. I saw only a firm resolution in his pretended coldness. It was a safeguard against forming any dreaded tie of friendship. Have I judged him too favorably? I really don't know.

Victor Hugo

AUTHOR MEETS ACTRESS: A YOUNG PLAYWRIGHT SPARS VERBALLY WITH HIS LEADING LADY OVER THE LINE, "MY SUPERB AND GENEROUS LION."

The fact is that it seems awfully funny to me to be calling Monsieur Firmin "my lion."

IN THE long and turbulent career of Victor Hugo the night of February 25, 1830, stands out as the crucial and unforgettable night of nights. To mention that the following day was his 28th birthday is merely to stress the element of youth. For it was on that night that the Théâtre-Français staged Hernani, a flamboyant poetic drama that struck Paris like a volley from heavy siege guns and raised a romantic young poet to the status of prophet. Men and women forgot the bitter cold as the fiery drama unfolded in the old theater. From the lower balcony came the organized jeers of the bald and scholarly "classicists." From the upper gallery cascaded the choral retorts of Hugo's picturesquely accoutered claqueurs—the already famous "Hernanistes" who had paraded through the streets of Paris in embattled phalanxes, shouting the gospel of Victor Hugo. For long before its historic première Hernani had become a battle-cry, and already friendships had broken over Hugo's sonorous Alexandrines. In its glowing hyperbole the classicists among Hugo's friends had sensed a personal affront and joined the enemy. Hernani, this play of stormy passions, fanatic oaths, and fiendish revenge, was now seized upon as the blazing manifesto of romanticism. Opposing schools of French letters clashed over it rabidly. The fervent rhetoric of the play, its unrestrained emotionalism and ringing bombast seemed to suit the heightened mood of the time, and in a few days Parisians went through the streets chanting or mocking its surging cadences. Thwarted republicans of this bleak age of post-Napoleonic reaction throbbed to its fervid promise of freedom. Even the most tone-deaf of classicists grudgingly admitted the impetuous sweep of Hugo's lines. For this was poetry that rang with a new melody.

As the battle lines formed outside the theater, it was but natural that within the Théâtre-Français itself esthetic skirmishes would echo the fray of the streets. Heading the opposition was the brilliant classical actress, Mlle. Mars—a woman who had garnered three decades of laurels in the great roles of Racine and Corneille. For Hugo's camp-followers it had been an unexpected triumph to persuade Mlle. Mars to accept the role of Doña Sol. And great artist that she was, the woman resolved to master the flaming new style of Hugo and assure the success of Hernani. But in the course of some fifty rehearsals the classicist in Mlle. Mars finally asserted herself. Having surrendered her talents to the service of the enemy, Mlle. Mars now resorted to a campaign of personal ridicule of the young author. Rehearsals would be interrupted while Mlle. Mars advanced to the footlights to address some acid gibes to the playwright. Hugo would rise calmly and reply with the utmost urbanity—and the utmost determination not to surrender a single word of his text.

Alexandre Dumas the elder, who as a struggling playwright had himself felt the lash of Mlle. Mars' mordant candor, was present during a series of rehearsals at which Mlle. Mars and his friend Hugo sparred verbally across the historic stage of the Théâtre-Français. The duelling was witnessed by thirty or forty actors, musicians, stage director, firemen, and stagehands who eagerly greeted any suggestion of a personal feud as a welcome lapse from humdrum routine. We owe the lively record of the daily dialogue between Mlle. Mars and Victor Hugo to Dumas, from whose autobiography* I have made the following translation. . . .

MLLE. MARS (*suddenly stopping in the middle of the rehearsal; turns to Firmin, the Hernani*) : Forgive me, my friend, I must have a word with the author.

(*Firmin nods his consent and remains where he is, silent and motionless. Mlle. Mars steps to the edge of the stage, puts one hand over her eyes, and though she knows exactly where the author is seated, pretends to look for him in the orchestra.*)

MLLE. MARS: Monsieur Hugo, is he there?

HUGO (*rising*) : Here I am, madame.

MLLE. MARS: Ah, very good! Thank you! . . . Tell me, Monsieur Hugo. . . .

HUGO: Madame?

MLLE. MARS: I am supposed to say this line:

"*Vous êtes mon lion superbe et généreux!*" †

---

* *Mes Mémoires*, Vol. V, Paris, 1863.
† "You are my superb and generous lion!"

HUGO: Yes, madame. Hernani tells you:

> *"Hélas! j'aime portant d'une amour bien profonde!*
> *Ne pleure pas.... Mourons plutôt! Que n'ai-je un monde,*
> *Je te le donnerais! Je suis bien malheureux!"* *

And you reply to him:

> *"Vous êtes mon lion superbe et généreux!"*

MLLE. MARS: Do you really like that, Monsieur Hugo?

HUGO: Like what?

MLLE. MARS: *Vous êtes mon lion!* ...

HUGO: I wrote it that way, madame—so I must have thought it was good.

MLLE. MARS: Then you insist on your *lion*?

HUGO: I insist and I do not insist, madame. Find me something better and I'll substitute it for the other.

MLLE. MARS: It's not my job to find it. I'm not the author.

HUGO: In that case, madame, suppose we leave it the way it's written.

MLLE. MARS: The fact is that it seems awfully funny to me to be calling Monsieur Firmin "my lion!"

HUGO: Oh, that's because in playing the role of Doña Sol you prefer to remain Mademoiselle Mars. If you were really the ward of Ruy Gomez de Silva, that is to say a noble Castilian lady of the sixteenth century, you would not see Monsieur Firmin in Hernani. You would see in Hernani one of those terrible bandit leaders who made Charles V tremble even in the security of his capital. You would then understand that such a woman might call such a man her "lion," and that would seem less funny to you.

MLLE. MARS: Very well! Since you insist on your *lion*, we won't discuss it any further. I am here to speak what is written. The manuscript says, "My lion!" I shall say, "My lion!" My God, what difference does it make to me! All right, Firmin, let's go!

> *"Vous êtes mon lion superbe et généreux!"*

(*The rehearsal continues.*)

(*The next day.*)
(*Having reached the same passage, Mlle. Mars stops again and repeats her little scene: she steps up to the edge of the stage, puts one hand over her eyes, and pretends to look for the author.*)

MLLE. MARS (*in her very special dry voice*): Monsieur Hugo, is he there?

HUGO (*with the same placidity*): Here I am, madame.

---

* "And yet, alas, I love you with a love profound!
Weep not, let's rather die! Had I a world,
I'd give it to you! How unhappy am I!"

MLLE. MARS: Ah, so much the better. I am very glad that you are there.

HUGO: I had the honor, madame, of paying you my respects before the rehearsal began.

MLLE. MARS: That's true. . . . Well, have you given it any thought?

HUGO: Have I given what any thought, madame?

MLLE. MARS: What I said to you yesterday.

HUGO: Yesterday you did me the honor of telling me a great many things.

MLLE. MARS: Yes, you're quite right. . . . But I'm referring to that famous hemistich.

HUGO: Which one?

MLLE. MARS: My God, you know very well which one!

HUGO: I swear to you, madame, I don't. You make so many good comments that I confuse some with others.

MLLE. MARS: I'm speaking of the hemistich of the "lion."

HUGO: Oh, yes! "*Vous êtes mon lion!*"—I remember now . . .

MLLE. MARS: Well, then, have you found another hemistich?

HUGO: I must confess I didn't even look.

MLLE. MARS: You don't find that hemistich dangerous?

HUGO: What do you mean by dangerous?

MLLE. MARS: I call anything dangerous that might be hissed.

HUGO: I have never insisted on not being hissed.

MLLE. MARS: Good! But you should be hissed as little as possible.

HUGO: So you think the hemistich of the "lion" will be hissed?

MLLE. MARS: I'm positive of it!

HUGO: If that happens it will mean only one thing—that you have not delivered the line with your customary power.

MLLE. MARS: I shall do my very best with it. . . . However, I should prefer. . . .

HUGO: Prefer what?

MLLE. MARS: Something else—in short!

HUGO: Such as?

MLLE. MARS: Something like (*with the air of groping for a word*) . . . something like this, for example . . .

"*Vous êtes mon seigneur superbe et généreux!*"
Doesn't *mon seigneur* fit the line as well as *mon lion*?

HUGO: As far as it goes, yes, madame. But *mon lion* lifts the line and *mon seigneur* flattens it. I would rather be hissed for a good line than applauded for a bad one.

MLLE. MARS: All right! All right! Let's not quarrel. Your *good line* will be delivered unchanged! Very well, Firmin, my friend, let's go on:
"*Vous êtes mon lion superbe et généreux!*"

("*Further on in the play, Ruy Gomez surprises Hernani and Doña Sol in each other's arms. When the arrival of the King is announced, Gomez hides Hernani in a room, the door of which is concealed by a painting. Now begins the famous 'Scene of the Portraits,' a scene between Don Carlos and Ruy Gomez consisting of seventy-six lines, and a scene in which Doña Sol remains silent and motionless, like a statue, and in which she takes no part until the King is on the point of having the Duke arrested. She then tears off her veil, and flinging herself between the Duke and the King's guardsmen, cries out: 'Roi Don Carlos, vous êtes un mauvais roi!'* . . . This long silence and immobility had always galled Mlle. Mars. The Théâtre-Français, being accustomed to the tragic traditions of Corneille, strongly opposed modern stage direction and understood neither the ardor of motion nor the poetry of immobility. The result was that the poor Doña Sol did not know what to do with her body during those seventy-six lines. One day she resolved to have it out with the author.*"—Dumas)

MLLE. MARS (*approaching the edge of the stage and scanning the orchestra*): Are you there, Monsieur Hugo?

HUGO (*rising*): Yes, madame.

MLLE. MARS: Good! Will you do me a favor?

HUGO: With the greatest pleasure. Name it.

MLLE. MARS: Tell me, then, what I'm supposed to be doing here.

HUGO: Doing where?

MLLE. MARS: Right here on the stage—while Monsieur Michelot and Monsieur Joanny are talking together?

HUGO: You are listening, madame.

MLLE. MARS: Ah, so I am listening! . . . I understand. However, I find that I am listening a little too long.

HUGO: Of course, you know the scene was much longer and that I cut out some twenty lines.

MLLE. MARS: Very good, but couldn't you shorten it another twenty lines?

HUGO: Impossible, madame!

MLLE. MARS: Or at least arrange it so that I have some part in it?

HUGO: But you do take part in it by your very presence. The scene is concerned with the man you love. It is a matter of life or death for him. The situation is dramatic enough for you to be anxiously, but silently, awaiting its outcome.

MLLE. MARS: It's still a long scene!

HUGO: I don't find it so, madame.

---

* "King Charles, you are a bad king!"

MLLE. MARS: Very well, let's not discuss it any further. . . . But, surely, the public will be asking: "What's Mademoiselle Mars doing there with her hand on her breast? It was scarcely worth the bother of giving her a role to keep her standing on her feet, with a veil over her eyes, and saying nothing for half an act."

HUGO: The public will say to itself that under the hand, not of Mlle. Mars but of Doña Sol, a heart is throbbing; that under the veil, not of Mlle. Mars but of Doña Sol, a face is glowing with hope or blanching with terror; that during the silence, not of Mlle. Mars but of Doña Sol, Hernani's beloved, a storm is gathering in her heart which finally bursts out in the words *"Roi Don Carlos, vous êtes un mauvais roi!"*— hardly respectable words coming from a subject of the king! Believe me, madame, that will be quite enough for the public.

MLLE. MARS: As you wish—it's your idea. I'm a fool to worry myself over it. If there's any hissing during the scene, it won't be for me, because I won't be saying a word. . . . Very well, Michelot. . . . Joanny—let's continue. *"Roi Don Carlos, vous êtes un mauvais roi!"* . . . There, you're satisfied, aren't you, Monsieur Hugo?

HUGO: Very much so, madame.

(*Hugo seats himself with imperturbable calm.*)

(*The following day.*)
(*Mlle. Mars stops the rehearsal at the same place and again approaches the edge of the stage.*)

MLLE. MARS (*putting one hand over her eyes, and in the same dry voice as the day before*): Monsieur Hugo—are you there?

HUGO: Here I am, madame.

MLLE. MARS: Good! . . . Did you find something for me to say?

HUGO: To say where?

MLLE. MARS: You know very well. . . . In the famous scene where these two gentlemen exchange one hundred and fifty lines, while I keep quiet and look at them. . . . I know they are charming to look at. . . . But for one hundred and fifty lines—that's too long!

HUGO: In the first place, madame, the scene has only seventy-six lines. I've counted them. In the second place, I did not promise to find something for you to say. On the contrary, I tried to prove to you that your silence and immobility, which end in an awesome outburst, were one of the beauties of this scene.

MLLE. MARS: One of the beauties? . . . I'm afraid the public will not be of the same opinion.

HUGO: We shall see.

MLLE. MARS: That's very fine, but then it will be too late. . . . In any case, you are determined not to have me say a single word during the whole scene?

HUGO: I am determined.

MLLE. MARS: It really doesn't make any difference to me. I shall go to the rear of the stage and leave these gentlemen to discuss their affairs out here in front.

HUGO: You may go to the rear of the stage, madame, if you so wish. However, since the affairs these gentlemen will be discussing are yours as much as theirs, you will merely create an absurd situation. . . . When you're ready, madame, we'll go on with the rehearsal. . . .

(*Hugo, in desperation, finally demanded that Mlle. Mars give up the role. The embattled classicist was on the point of yielding when Hugo slyly hinted that her successor would be her detested rival, Mlle. Despreaux. Stung to the quick, Mlle. Mars now charged Hugo with being Mlle. Despreaux's lover. "I shall keep your role and play it as no other woman could play it!" she announced majestically. Mlle. Mars was a brilliant success as Doña Sol, but she never forgave Hugo for being the one author in her long and brilliant career who refused to crumble before her withering sarcasm.*)

Heinrich Heine

ONE feels presumptuous in offering three short dialogues as a "portrait" of Heinrich Heine. So much is inevitably omitted of this multiple personality who was divine poet and peerless wit—so much of the vast harlequinade and tragedy. Even Houben's massive Gespräche mit Heinrich Heine, published in Frankfurt in 1926, leaves huge gaps to be filled. One would have to add the poetry, the prose works, the letters, and personal memoirs to round out a truly revealing "portrait." And still one might be pardoned for feeling baffled before the final synthesis. This man was so many things that, to paraphrase himself, there never was "a united Heine." He was clown and he was tragedian; he was German and he was French; he was a Jew and he was a Christian; he idolized "pure love" and patronized brothels; he was a monarchist and he was a Communist; he was a sublime lyrist and a coarse rhymester; he loved life and for nine years lay buried in pain in what he called a "mattress-grave." In his fifty-nine years Heinrich Heine overlooked nothing. From the blackest despair he rose to rare ecstasy, and in the clutches of a monstrous anguish of body he fashioned a sweet music of words. This was a man—passionate, witty, confused, the prey of swift shifts of mood, from gaiety to gloom; in a word, a man very much alive. And this was a fighter, too, crusading against smugness and misrule, against stodgy and mildewed thinking, against the Germany he loved but fought pitilessly in a one-man war from exile in Paris. We need neither condemn nor applaud his conversion —in the best sense he was a good Christian and a good Jew. Nor could this born cosmopolite help being a good German and a good Frenchman. The mixture that was Heinrich Heine made the whole world at once the province of his genius and the arena of his pathos and struggle. Except in the fellowship of art, he never belonged anywhere in particular, and, not belonging, he could lash out with unsparing irony at all who deserved it. By never betraying himself, Heinrich Heine never betrayed anyone else.

It was this same German Jew, plagued by censors and Philistines at home, who abandoned Germany to settle in Paris in 1831. For a quarter of a century Heine made it his home and his fortress. From Paris he launched barrages of satire at the brutish officialdom of Prussia, till again the censors clamped down. And in this "New Jerusalem," as he hailed it, he wrote German poetry that became a lasting glory of the harsh mother-land he had left. For the cruel years of abuse and rebuff this Jew had re-paid her with a priceless legacy. In Paris a new world opened to Heine. The very air he breathed smacked of freedom and friendliness. The vast fund of humor that was his found ampler scope in this city that behaved as if life were a song and not a funeral march: "If anyone asks you how I am enjoying myself, say, 'Like a fish in the sea.' Or, better still, say that when one fish asks another how he is enjoying himself, the fish replies, 'Like Heine in Paris!' " He frequented the opera, the concert halls, the theaters, and the salons. Soon he numbered among his friends Meyerbeer and Mendelssohn, de Musset, Gerard de Nerval, Gautier, Hugo, Balzac, Eugène Sue, and Dumas. A man of wit—even one from across the Rhine —bore a passport to the choicest coteries of Paris.

Heine revelled in the enchantment of it all. His flair for ready repartee flourished and sparkled in this new setting. His mots circulated swiftly through Paris—ironic quips like "The aristocracy is composed chiefly of asses—asses that talk about horses"; slashing gibes at literary mediocrity like "All women love him except the Muses." This man had a born gift for the right phrase at the right moment. And when the frightful spinal disease struck with full fury, he could jest even in the teeth of death: "My constitution grows worse—even worse than the Prussian constitution." At the end of that noble martyrdom to art, when blind, paralyzed, a mere bundle of bones, he could still reply to a query about the state of his soul: "Dieu me pardonnera; c'est son métier." * Perhaps even more typical were the two words that broke through the final coma: "Paper! Pencil!" In the words of Louis Untermeyer, "No man ever died more in character."

---

* "God will forgive me; it is his job."

Heinrich Heine

1.

A GERMAN EXPATRIATE PULLS THE LEG OF A REPRESENTATIVE OF THE FRENCH PRESS.

There's nothing so amusing as to mystify your contemporaries, but, taking everything into account, there's nothing so difficult.

IN THE first of these dialogues we meet Heine in one of his many lodgings in Paris. The particular address is unknown. Already an ailing man, Heine, on doctor's orders, had begun that ceaseless change of residence which was to end in the "mattress-grave" of his top-floor apartment at 3 Avenue Matignon, off the Champs Elysées. The date is January 15, 1835. The German expatriate has been four years in Paris, is lionized in the best circles of Paris, and has even acquired a French wife, a shop-girl named Crescentia Eugénie Mirat, whom he renames "Mathilde" because "her real name sticks in my throat." Mathilde does not appear in the dialogue, and perhaps it is just as well. She is lazy, sharp-tongued, and illiterate, is tone-deaf to music and poetry, and is Heine's wife only because, by his own admission, she is sensual as an animal. In a few months Heine, in disgust with himself, will leave her, only to return later—and permanently—to this witless voluptuary.

We owe this brief interview to a newspaper man of the day—Philarète Chasles, who also signed himself Philibert Audebrand. The morsel appears in Chasles' chatty and gossipy Petits Mémoires du XIX Siècle (Paris, Calmann-Lévy, 1892). Chasles, commissioned by a Parisian magazine to get a story from Heine, arrives at the poet's apartment early in the afternoon. He finds Heine lying down on a sofa, almost asleep. Perhaps it is Mathilde who has opened the door, or only the "Joseph" who later brings the tea. In any case, the two are formally introduced and the interview begins. . . .

HEINE (*rising*): *Cher confrère,* you've arrived just in time.
CHASLES: How is that?

HEINE: Because in one more minute I would have been asleep—I was reading a page of Nodier.

CHASLES: What! Nodier has that effect on you! You don't care for this worthy man who is Tacitus and Laurence Sterne rolled into one?

HEINE: On the contrary—I'm passionately fond of this prose that is always charming, *too* charming. I must confess, these pages dazzle me with their glittering diamonds. The effect is so blinding that it ends by inducing sleep. . . . But what good wind brings you here?

CHASLES: Achille Deveria is demanding your head—I'm demanding your life.

HEINE: Seriously?

CHASLES: Quite. I've got to get up at least three hundred lines of biography about you.

HEINE: So it seems I am being taken seriously enough to deserve a biography and to have it written by a man of talent.

CHASLES: Naturally. Why should that astonish you?

HEINE: In the first place, my dear friend, nothing astonishes me. In the second place. . . . Wait, I have a wonderful idea!

CHASLES: What's that?

HEINE: In the guise of literary history you and I together might improvise a little novel with myself as the chief character.

CHASLES: I have no objection.

HEINE: I have come from afar—since I am an escaped Prussian. . . . Ah, the beautiful things I could tell you!

CHASLES: Still, we ought to keep it as close to the truth as possible.

HEINE: What isn't true the moment it is printed? (*As if dictating.*) "Heinrich Heine was born in Düsseldorf in 1800. His father was a very rich merchant. But was Herr Heine really his father? It is said that the famous brigand Schinderhannes, while passing through the city one day, deposited an unknown child in the corridor of the honorable Herr Heine." . . . How is that for a beginning?

CHASLES: That would be very stimulating, but I don't think abandoned children are the fashion any more, not since "Victor, or the Child of the Forest."

HEINE: You're absolutely right. (*Ringing; enter Joseph.*) Joseph, bring some tea and two cups. And don't forget the bread and butter—German style. (*Resuming.*) Let's drop the childhood days. Suppose we go on to my youth? Shall we?

CHASLES: As you wish, *cher confrère.*

HEINE: I must have a stormy youth, tormented and crowded with adventure. Remember, I did not assume the ambitious title of "Byron's cou-

sin" for nothing. Consequently, I must somehow be raised to the stature of that Titan of all the revolts who composed *Manfred*.

CHASLES: That's only fair. (*Takes a notebook from his pocket.*) Go ahead!
Dictate! I'll write it all down.

HEINE: Wait a moment! Let's first have a cup of tea.

(*Joseph enters and serves the tea. There is a moment of silence.*)

CHASLES: Facts, facts, supported by exact dates—that's what the *Revue de
Paris* especially urged me to get from you. Well, then, *cher grand
homme*, are we ready?

HEINE: How you hurry me! Never was the pistol of glory pointed so closely
at anyone!

CHASLES: It's a revival of the Delphic technique, when violence was used
to make the oracle speak.

HEINE: And only a moment ago I was beginning to think how easy it was.
. . . Adventures? . . . A duel? How exciting! How novel! A kidnapping?
No, that would be stealing bread from Monsieur Scribe, who writes all
those one-act sketches. . . . An attempt at suicide? . . . They would laugh
at me, and they would be right. My dear fellow, shall I tell you something? There's nothing so amusing, perhaps, as to mystify your contemporaries, but, taking everything into account, there's nothing so difficult. Besides, I'm not in the mood today.

CHASLES (*smiling*): Forgive my insisting—but I was sent to get some information, and I'll have to make some sort of report.

HEINE: Don't you worry. You'll have your material. (*Gravely.*) It's just occurred to me that for this sort of thing it's best to tell the stupid and
prosaic truth. (*Rings; enter Joseph.*) Joseph—bring me something to
write with. . . . *Mon cher Monsieur Chasles*, while I fill two pages with
my scrawling, amuse yourself by deciphering this manuscript.

CHASLES (*reading*): *William Ratcliff*. What is it?

HEINE: A play by your humble servant—a play which will never be performed.

CHASLES: A play by Heinrich Heine—that ought to be a treat! (*Begins to
read.*)

(*As Chasles reads, Heine concentrates on the task before him. He
writes out the material in the form of a letter to his visitor. It runs to
some hundred lines and bears the date of January 15, 1835. The letter
was printed in the* Revue de Paris *of the following March. . . . Heine
finishes writing the letter just as Chasles finishes reading the manuscript. The men have another cup of tea together and, after a warm
handclasp, Chasles departs.*)

Heinrich Heine

2.

THE BIG THREE: HEINE, BALZAC, AND EUGÈNE SUE
CLASH AT BREAKFAST OVER A SHEAF OF "ISMS,"
PAUSING LONG ENOUGH TO CONSIDER
A MARITAL PROBLEM.

*I can't understand why fidelity is more strongly
demanded of a woman than a man. We lose
nothing by a woman's infidelity.*

To A FORMER Jewish cantor is due a special posthumous citation for
having preserved the record of a breakfast conversation held in his
home at 14 Rue Cadran one summer day in 1847. Certainly there is no
other like it in the annals of recorded conversation. For here we meet
Balzac, Eugène Sue, and Heinrich Heine—three sharply contrasted personalities—locked in a battle of the political "isms" over their coffee cups.
Their host is Heine's close friend, Alexandre Weill, a writer of some distinction, who had sung in synagogues as a youth and whose rendering of
Hebrew chants deeply moved the poet. While these three gens de lettres
consume Weill's food and decide the fate of the world, let us examine the
political setting.

Paris of 1847 was seething with radicalism. A young friend of Heine's,
Karl Marx—a German expatriate like himself—is soon to launch his fiery
"Communist Manifesto." The Revolution of 1848, which is to sweep all
Europe, is one year off. In every salon, boulevard café, and home there is
talk of socialism, republicanism, Bonapartism. The city's atmosphere is
thick with new terms, and the "isms" are in control of the French language. The days of Louis-Philippe as a ruler of France are numbered. In one
short year the Second Republic will be born, only to die, indeed, in the
Napoleonic afterglow of four years later. Everywhere people are taking
sides for the upheavals ahead. Ironically, this same Balzac, whose Comédie
Humaine is the most slashing indictment of the propertied classes, is himself an arch-conservative, a royalist, in politics. If his nightmare is socialism,
his sweetest dream is monarchical legitimacy. Eugène Sue, novelist and

parliamentarian, is the opposite. Socialism has become his avowed creed, the milder socialism of Saint-Simon, Louis Blanc, and Proudhon, to be sure, not the sterner, methodical brand of these young German exiles in Paris. One has only to read Sue's Mysteries of Paris and The Wandering Jew, both prodigiously popular in these troubled years, to know where his sympathies lie.

This man Heine is not so easy to label. In his periodic avowals he has covered most of the political map, from benevolent monarchy to a kind of Christian communism. He has flirted with socialism, espoused revolutionary causes, and dreamed of a German Republic. To Louis Untermeyer he was essentially, irrevocably bourgeois:– "His sympathy was all with the inarticulate, the property-less, and the exploited millions, but he was not one of them; he could not even understand them. He was an uncomfortable, skeptical, often self-divided, but definite member of the middle class." Yet bourgeois and divided as he was, Heine knew that this growing specter—call it socialism, call it communism—could not be exorcised by a wave of the hand. Prophetically, in 1842, he had spoken of communism as the "dark hero of the modern tragedy" biding its time in secret garrets for its entrance upon the world stage. In six years the cue would be given this "dark hero."

The Heine we meet in the following dialogue is scarcely a serious disputant. He is the jester of the breakfast table, a conciliator at times, and it is he who finally breaks the deadlock between his overheated fellow-breakfasters with a typically facetious compromise. Perhaps it is best to have Monsieur Weill himself explain, through the pages of his Souvenirs intimes de Henri Heine (1883), how these three men happen to be breakfasting here at all:

("In 1847 my work, 'Guerre des Paysans' was printed in the magazine Phalange. Shortly afterwards, Eugène Sue, having heard that I could not find a publisher, wrote me, placing a thousand-franc note at my disposal for the expenses of bringing this work out as a book. The letter arrived the day after I sold the book to Père Amyot for 120 francs. When he read Sue's letter, Heinrich Heine marvelled not only that a writer could be so generous, but that he could dispose of a thousand-franc note so freely. Heine urged me to invite Sue to have breakfast with him. These two eminent men did not know one another personally. 'The moment I tell Sue that you want him to breakfast,' I said to Heine, 'he'll come even if he's five hundred miles from Paris.' 'Go also to my friend Balzac,' Heine added, 'and tell him it's a long time since I saw him. Invite him over too. Sue and Balzac are at opposite poles of our intellectual planet. One represents the North, the other the South. Together they will give us a temperate zone.' I went to Balzac, I'm not sure whether it was shortly before his departure for Russia or shortly after his return. Since 1838 he had been extremely cordial to me. When I gave him Heine's message, Balzac made a wry face. He did not care much for Sue and socialists like him. But, being eager to see Heine, he promised to come, and he did. Sue made the same promise, and the breakfast took place at my house on the Rue Cadran, now called the Rue Saint-Sauveur. The street number was then 14; today it is 50. The strangest thing happened when these three first-class writers got together. Not for one minute did the conversation dwell on literature, poetry, journalism, or the Academy! That same day I jotted down all the high-points of the talk, all the remarkable thoughts expressed in a discussion which flew about like a weaver's shuttle along the five-fold threat of republicanism, monarchism, socialism, Fourierism, and communism. Balzac held the center of the stage. He demanded silence and attention, not indulgence."—Weill)

BALZAC: My opinions are known. They are old-fashioned. But the truth does not have to be new. Nor am I blind to the weak points of my own position. In any case, my friend Heine would spot them easily enough. What I want to prove, and what I came here especially to prove, is that the so-called new is false, completely chimerical.

SUE (*interrupting*): Since we're discussing monarchy and republic, I should like to point out that it is the republic which is old and monarchy which is new. Liberty dates from the creation of the world and of man.

BALZAC: I would quite gladly accept a republic. What I refuse to accept are its social consequences, which are inevitable by its very nature. It is my turn to point out that socialism, which believes itself new, is an old matricide. It has always killed its mother, the republic, as well as its sister, liberty. It will always be that way. It is the eternal quarrel between grace and liberty, between Plato and Aristotle, between Saint Augustine and Saint Thomas, between Abélard and Saint Bernard, between Luther and Münzer.

HEINE: Now you're on my territory! There's no need to say "between Luther and Münzer." You can say between Luther and Luther, between Münzer and Münzer. No German ever agreed with himself for more than six months. Every German contains within himself several contradictory systems. There never was and there never will be a "united German." If national unity ever comes to Germany, it will be maintained only by force and violence, never in the name of reason, because as a rule the Germans deny at twelve o'clock the philosophy which they invent at eleven.

BALZAC: Look here— let's be French and clear! What is the essential difference between elective power and hereditary power? Elective power belongs to a nation, monarchical power to a family. At first sight a republic would seem to have indisputable right and a monarchy would seem to be an odious usurpation. But examine it more closely, and the whole complexion of the question changes. What is this elective power actually? Ten million citizens delegate their power for a given time, reserving the right to revoke it if the prescribed program is not carried out. Every Frenchman may accordingly delegate his one-ten-millionth part of this power. And by virtue of what right may he do this? By virtue of his birth on French soil. Very well, then! By the same right the soil itself belongs to him. He may lay claim to his one-ten-millionth part of property and delegate it to anyone he pleases, exactly the way he does his share of power . . . in return for services rendered. It was that very thing that brought about the agrarian laws of Athens and Rome. And yet, the republics of the ancient world used slaves to work the soil. And what about Moses—the greatest democrat of history. After installing the republic and dividing the land among the tribes, he instituted the jubilee, providing for the return of all lands to the same families every fifty years. Solon, when he set up a republic, cancelled all debts. Lycurgus established the equality of poverty. As for Münzer, no sooner did he proclaim the republic at Mulhouse, in Saxony, than he was forced to declare the common ownership of all goods. At Münster the Anabaptists even declared themselves in favor of communizing wives. Babeuf * is the inevitable successor of Danton and Robespierre. . . .

HEINE (*interrupting*): Allow me to make one comment. I've read that Solon and Lycurgus, after establishing their republics, fled to foreign countries. Moses did better. He gave a republican form of government to a land he never set foot on.

BALZAC (*resuming*): I feel certain that my friend Sue has espoused Fourierism in order to escape being a communist. But the public, being frightfully logical, understands nothing of nuances and formulas. The moment power becomes elective, it demands that property be equally elective.

---

* François Noël Babeuf (1760–1797), French revolutionary, who preached communist doctrines, organized secret societies, and was guillotined during the Directory.

SUE: And America?

BALZAC: America has four million slaves who work but do not vote. If ever these slaves are given the right to vote and their numbers afford the majority its needed balance, they will elect a man who will divide the land among them, or at least the profits which are now made by those they work for.

SUE (*shouting*): And why not? No one should have more than he needs when the rest are without the barest necessities.

BALZAC: As much as to say: no one should have genius when so many men don't even have common sense!

HEINE (*interrupting*): That's the first time that my friend Balzac has combined the ideas of genius and superfluity. Ordinarily, the sole purpose of genius is to find ways of dispensing with both what is necessary and what is superfluous. Philosophy, from the creation, is nothing but the eternal glorification of the minimum—even in the spiritual sense. That is why the Jews can never be exterminated. They will last forever, and they will never be supplanted. They have taken their minimum of God —no more than they absolutely needed.

BALZAC (*smiling*): Beauty is also superfluous. So long as a young woman is in good health, no matter how ugly she may be, she suffices for love— provided, of course, that she has what is absolutely essential. Ugly women might well say, "No one shall have beauty till we all have a given minimum."

HEINE (*interrupting again*): The minimum would be a husband *and* a lover. . . . I can't understand why fidelity is more strongly demanded of a woman than a man. We lose nothing by a woman's infidelity. It was Voltaire who said that God has put woman at our disposal at all hours, whereas a woman really loses something whenever her husband is unfaithful. . . . I'm astonished that the French socialists haven't raised that point yet. The Moravian Brothers in Saxony have been far more logical. They make their marriages by lottery and demand absolute fidelity. The young marriage conscripts are examined and given numbers. The girls draw their husbands out of a bag. There are no losing numbers. Bartering husbands is forbidden. The only ground for divorce is adultery. But, then, the guilty party is expelled from the community.

SUE: Are such marriages happy?

HEINE: Captious question! A good marriage is the reward rather than the promise of happiness. I've just told you that the marriage candidates are examined by a doctor before being properly ticketed. There is both a minimum and a maximum age. These marriages are often models of strength, health, and propagation.

SUE: And there has been no instance of a young man or woman rebelling against the "number" drawn?

HEINE: There have been a few cases. They did so and quit the community.

BALZAC: There, you see! Such a communist society is only possible alongside of our civilization. If it existed by itself on a universal scale, it would not last six months. If all men and women were subjected to such a law, it would mean civil war in perpetuity. As among the lions, ten males would lose their lives fighting for one female's virginity.

HEINE: The only thing which it is a pleasure to lose!

SUE: And the only thing, that, once lost, is never recovered!

BALZAC (*placing his napkin around his neck*): Let's not wander away from the subject. Without seeming to, gentlemen, I have made a perfect study of Saint-Simonism, Fourierism and communism. Communism is the logical and inevitable consequence of all the other "isms." The public does not split hairs. It goes straight to the extreme. Now, what is communism? It is a return to a savage state, in which men and women will all eat at the same table without having a single *sou* to spend. For once you introduce a bill of fare some will economize, some will be extravagant, and before long you will have inequality and finally . . . war. For all work and all workers there will be only a minimum, never a maximum of pay. And the planter's whip will coax the lazy and unruly workers. Thus you will have not only servitude and tyranny, but perpetual anarchy. Will you collectivize property, proclaim polygamy and monoandry? Infamies—all of them! Will you maintain compulsory polygamy? That's slavery! It's one vicious circle—an odious circle! It is impossible to admit that even one man of intelligence can be a sincere communist. If the republic returns to France, I predict not one Robespierre against the Babeufs, but a hundred thousand, for a true republican must be a thousand times more severe with communism than a monarchist. Communism is the most direct and violent enemy of democracy. It is the natural auxiliary of absolute monarchy. If you will permit me a metaphor, to make Sue happy I will say that the republic is a state of natural health and that communism is its cancer. It promotes the welfare of the charlatan who represents despotism. Under the pretext of applying a cure he kills one with the other, and inherits everything.

SUE: So be it! And since it makes my honored * friend Balzac happy, I declare that I am not a communist. I am only a socialist. I shall explain this distinction later. But, first, let Balzac answer the following argu-

---

* A pun on Balzac's first name, Honoré.

ment. Granted that neither a republic nor a monarchy is responsible for certain social blunders. Communism has always existed. Social maladies have always existed. What does monarchy do, what has it ever done and what can it ever do to cure those maladies? Isn't monarchy the mother, the first cause, of these evils? Isn't it the source of the infection? The republic, in which every citizen can voice his opinions, will at least propose remedies. It can search out the cause. It can struggle. It has health and strength. But what can the monarchy do against social corrosion? Hasn't it been the chief cause of poverty for a thousand years, of ignorance, of the brutalization of the masses? Isn't it the monarchy that seizes the work of nine-tenths of the population and bestows its products upon the remaining one-tenth—its pretorians, its rhetors, its aristocrats, its priests and its courtiers? What is this Catholic monarchy that is the dream of Monsieur Balzac? Open the history of the last seventeen centuries!—A tissue of iniquities, sufferings, and infamies! What were the people before 1789? A multitude of beasts of burden! The Christian serf was three times as miserable as the slave of ancient Rome. He was fastened to the soil, he was declared a piece of real estate, without soul and without volition. No Christian could free his serfs, like an ancient Roman, without ruining himself. The serf couldn't even become a monk. Communism, they tell me, has always been smothered by monarchism. Were the people any happier as a result? My God! by what right do you demand that one hundred thousand aristocrats and priests be allowed to swim in plenty while ten million Frenchmen, their equals and often far more deserving, languish in poverty? As Voltaire says, "When a tiger flies at my throat, I'm not concerned about whom to put in his place." Let's first abolish privilege, iniquity, unearned wealth—then we can decide what to do! The young herdsman always thinks he sees the sky touching the ground when he looks from a distance. As he comes closer, the horizon broadens. The same is true of all humanity. Through sheer force of going forward the horizon broadens before us!

HEINE (*noting Sue's unusual ardor, pours him a glass of champagne from a bottle he had sent Weill that morning*): You have been pouring out your very best vintage—now try mine.

BALZAC: Sue has only been pouring us the foam. It all sparkles and crackles and bubbles, but it evaporates and volatilizes in the air of criticism. . . . To begin with, humanity requires some sort of minimum, because there is a minimum of peaceful activity. To live in a material way one must work—one must be a sower, a reaper, a spinner, a weaver, a carpenter, a mason, a blacksmith, a wheelwright. Above all one must beget children. It is the stock-in-trade of humanity. The rest is luxury—luxury of the mind, of genius, of reason. The world could not survive a year without the rudimentary occupations for which God has created nine-tenths of the human race. In a monarchy, barring the great calamities of war, elementary life is possible. It is not in a democratic state. If the citizen is compelled to take up arms every eight days against the good-for-nothings who not only prevent him from working but who keep threatening to prevent him from enjoying the fruits of his labor, nothing more is possible and no one will work any more. The result is chaos—a desert. The communist will not take a tithe—a tenth part—as the priest and noble once did; he will take everything. He is like the drone who not only appropriates the honey without working but who destroys the hive because the work-plan of the honeycomb differs from his own. Naturally, the drone has no use for it. He doesn't produce, he doesn't work, he doesn't make any honey. A common hole is all he needs, just as a cave is all a band of brigands needs. Apart from that consideration there is the pivotal question, as the Fourierists say, of human nature itself. I've already pointed out that political issues are completely subsidiary to the ancient and eternal quarrel between grace and liberty. Answer me yes or no. Is it true that some men are born stronger, more beautiful, wiser, more spiritual, more balanced and more virtuous than others? There's a stickler for you—the real question. Aren't most people born for the manual labor which is the basic need of all human society? Let's be honest about it. Aren't some people zeros, and others numbers? Do the zeros ever count except when they come after a number? For their own happiness aren't they compelled to obey, just as the others are born to command? Don't you destroy the numbers by placing the zeros before them? Isn't monarchy better suited to the nature of man than a republic? Far be it from me to force the future into a pattern of the past! Yet, it is a fact that in the history of all nations one finds thousands of years of monarchy against a half century of republic. Let's admit that the republics of the past were only preludes, models, ideals for the future. We always have something to learn. Like the individual, humanity is always going to school. It only remains to determine whether the fundamental truths aren't always the same, if there can ever be anything absolutely new. I've forgotten the name of the philosopher who compared the truths of history to the various layers of onion skin. Every layer which is removed discloses a fresher and younger skin beneath it—but it is always the same onion!

HEINE: And always making us cry! I now understand the onions of Egypt, so much bewailed by the dwellers of the desert. . . .* Moses, the republican, acted exactly like Robespierre, when he said to his Levites, after smashing the tables of the law, "Destroy the offenders!"

BALZAC: The truth is that the great majority of men are not happy and don't know how to be happy except when forced by those with better minds and stronger wills. Absolute freedom never was and never will be anything but absolute anarchy.

SUE (*preparing to rise as it is getting late*): But what is the opinion of our friend Heine?

HEINE: As a German, I have many opinions. To summarize them, this is my position. . . . But I warn you, I shall go back as far as the deluge. Shall I proceed?

BALZAC: Proceed! It shouldn't be hard for you, with Pegasus to carry you!†

HEINE: I have observed that the twenty-four-hour day consists of both day and night. Two contrasting entities. No matter how beautiful, the day alone, without night, would have its disadvantages. The same goes for the night without day. I have also observed—I am now at the deluge— that to beget a child, a man and a woman are needed, particularly a woman. Again two contrasting entities which unite, on occasion, with a certain harmony. I have also observed that for every successful business transaction you must have both a fool and a man of intelligence. Someone told me—I believe it was Berlioz, for Meyerbeer has been cool to me lately—that two dissonances always produce a harmony, and that the perfect chord consists of a third, a fifth and the octave, a mysterious relation which the cabalists have even applied to love. I have even been assured that there is such a thing as a scale of colors. In short, whatever lasts, whatever gives us pleasure is made up of contrasts. My friends, I think we may assume that the same thing is true of republic and monarchy. What we need is not *one or the other*, but *one and the other*, the two combined. Either one alone is a dissonance. Together they produce a perfect chord. *What is needed, therefore, is either a republic governed by monarchists, or a monarchy governed by republicans.* I have more than two hundred and fifty irrefutable arguments to support my thesis, which has only one defect—it smacks of eclecticism. . . . But I really must stop now. I have a wife, or rather my wife has me. She'll

---

* An apparent reference to Numbers, Chap. 11:—"And the people cried unto Moses. . . . Who shall give us flesh to eat? We remember the fish, which we did eat in Egypt freely; the cucumbers, and the melons, and the leeks, and the onions, and the garlic."

† Balzac makes an untranslatable pun here on the word "*remonter*," which means both "to trace back" and "to remount."

never believe that I'm breakfasting out with geniuses. I've got to get back home. I hope to have the pleasure to see you all soon at my house. We shall then proclaim the republic. Balzac will be president. Sue will be secretary-general. As for me, I shall sing your glory in German verses, for the French will never permit a novelist to have political genius. Meyerbeer will set my verses to music, and our little friend Weill, who has a tenor voice, will sing them.

Heinrich Heine

3.

A BRITISH VISITOR HEARS A GLOWING TRIBUTE TO HIS COUNTRYMEN, THE INMATES OF BEDLAM.

I found English madmen infinitely saner than my own Germans or than these Parisians— indeed, much saner than myself.

In the spring of 1852 we find the mad little ménage that consists of the invalided Heinrich Heine and his stupid, shrewish wife Mathilde established on the third floor of a house on the Rue d'Amsterdam. For the dying poet there is to be only one more "mattress-grave," the bedroom of the house off the Champs Elysées, where death will end his prolonged torment on February 17, 1856. . . .

Even in 1852 the suffering of this brave man is incredible. Seizures of twisting, clawing pain are a daily occurrence. Almost complete paralysis of limb has set in, and Heine is already partially blind. There are long spells of insomnia, as a relentless atrophy slowly gnaws away at his spine. Once, from the depths of his agony, he writes, "Blindness is the least of my ills." In this black night of anguish, only opium, in growing dosages, can give him moments of peace; opium and his beloved poetry.

For amid this inhuman distress of body Heine is now dictating a warmer and deeper music, that of the Romanzero. And between these giant spasms of pain, he even contrives to remain the vivacious wit, the nimble juggler of words and ideas. Propped up on a chair, he receives friends and strangers with avid inquiries about the world now forbidden him. Newspaper men still come for stories and continue to find him a refreshing change from routine assignments. There is much that Heinrich Heine can still tell the world, can tell even the England he had once visited as a roving and restless youth of twenty-eight. It is probably with some nostalgic twinges that he receives the editor of The Critic, a London literary journal, one spring day in 1852. This man is presumably John Crockford, the then editor, though he prefers to sign his conversational dispatches from the continent simply "The Critic."

To Crockford—or "The Critic"—go our warmest thanks for turning in
such a handsome report of his visit. We have only his word, of course,
for the accuracy of the transcript. Yet the authentic ring of Heine's vast
gusto is in his part of the dialogue, and, beside it, the Englishman's share
sounds smug and self-righteous. One visualizes Crockford—or "The
Critic"—congratulating himself on the factual rebuttal of this incorrigible cynic and clown. He speaks of the "interesting invalid" and the
"pale intelligence of his countenance," but we have no way of knowing
whether the English editor even guessed the cruel drama of anguish
behind the pallor, a drama of which this interview was perhaps one of
the brief entr'actes of drugged respite from pain.

For the conversation as it was printed in the April 15, 1852, number of
The Critic, the correspondent thoughtfully provided the stage setting
which follows. . . .

SCENE: *A dimly lighted room in Paris, au troisième. At the further end,*
with a writing-table touching his breast, and a chiffonier piled up with
books beside him, Heinrich Heine, in a dressing-gown of voluminous
folds, propped up by, and sunk in pillows, which give his huge arm-chair
the appearance of a miniature bed.

HEINE: Sit down, sir, you are welcome.

CRITIC: I am afraid—this intrusion—your delicate health.

(*Takes a seat near the interesting invalid, admires the pale intelli-*
gence of his countenance, and the fine beard which depends from it.)

HEINE: Come! Come! Be at home. You are an Englishman, and, therefore,
I like you. I like all Englishmen. I was in England once, and I never met
a stranger set of persons than its inhabitants. It was like being among a
nation of animated puppets. About a week after I landed, I heard that
there was a madhouse in London; Bedlam, or some such name, they
called it. It was incredible; mad Englishmen! I hurried off to it, and
found the English madmen infinitely saner than my own Germans, or
than these Parisians, whom I may call my own, for I have lived long
enough among them—indeed, much saner than myself.

CRITIC: Mr. Heine! We are a practical people, and of cold exterior. We do
not speak much, unless after dinner, or in political assemblies, for political objects. But we think a great deal, we feel deeply, and we are the
countrymen of Shakespeare and of Milton.

HEINE: And of Byron. Ah! Byron! It was not as now, propped upon the
pillows of a sick couch, but with the sighing of the German pine forest,

and the torrent's roar for accompaniment, that first I heard thy song! I was young, my friend, young with the life of five-and-twenty, when my bosom echoed the wild melancholy of Childe Harold, when I bounded over the ocean, fierce and free with the Corsair, when I wandered on the beach with Haidee, while the waves softly sang the sun to its rest. Byron is gone, and poetry is going. Type of modern poetry, Heinrich Heine lies sick upon his pillows, drinking the bitter potions of the physician, not the pure waters of the Castilian fount. Poetry and Heine are dying. Have you heard my swan-song? Have you read my *Romanzero*?

CRITIC: Sir,—I am a critic, and an Englishman. The English are a practical people, and English critics seldom read. A notice of your poem, however, from the pen of a talented young friend, has appeared in a journal of which I am editor.

HEINE: So. A journalist! Everybody is a journalist nowadays. The other morning my coiffeur, instead of babbling as usual, kept asking me what I thought of this, that, and the other and listened with wonderful attention to my replies. When his operations were over, my Parisian makes me a bow. "Would Monsieur object if the brilliant and shining remarks which have dropped profusely from Monsieur's mouth, like the pearls and diamonds from the maiden's lips in the fairy tale"—I was amazed at the fellow's exordium—"would Monsieur object if they appeared tomorrow in my journal?" I nearly killed myself with laughter. Old Goethe used to say, "Nobody wants to be a tailor; everybody wants to be a poet"; had he said everybody wants to be a journalist, he would have hit the mark.

CRITIC: Excuse me, Mr. Heine: if Goethe had made such a remark, it would have been an erroneous one, so far at least as England is concerned. The English, as I have already observed, are a practical people; and it is not uncommon among us for a tailor to be also a journalist. I have been in parts of England where the fingers that stitched my small clothes would exchange the needle for the pen and instruct me twice a week through the medium of the press on the deepest points of social economy. That, however, was in the provinces, and the practice has not yet reached London in which *my* journal is published.

HEINE: Tell me, then, what are you, Whig, Tory, Radical? I never meet with one of your countrymen but I draw him into a discussion on English parties, although for the life of me I have not yet been able to make out the difference between them.

CRITIC: Sir,—I have my political sentiments, and those sentiments I am not ashamed to avow, on a proper occasion. But, as an editor, Mr.

Heine, I am of no politics. Mine is a literary journal, the largest, and, I may say, the best in Europe. It numbers amongst its subscribers two thousand of the clergy, many hundreds of the magistracy, the bulk of the aristocracy, and all the most cultivated members of the middle classes of my native country. Sir! the copy of it which I have the honor of offering to you contains a translation of a small poem of your own, and has thus carried the name of Heine to every corner of the British Empire, to Buckingham Palace, to the wilds of Connemara, to the Orkneys, to Australasia, to Hindustan.

HEINE: Ah! *"Nach Frankreich zogen zwei Grenadier."* Almost the first poem I ever wrote—"The Grenadiers!" It was in 1814 that I composed it; I was but fifteen then; I remember singing it low to myself one evening early in summer, on the bank of the Rhine, just when the news had come that the Emperor was to be exiled to Elba. My friend! I have gone through every phase of modern thought and feeling—I have been Werther, René, Lara, Faust, Mephistopheles—I have expanded into a self-deification with that prince of cloud-embracers, Hegel—I have plunged into the dreamy abyss of mystical ecstasy—I have dined with the literature of despair, I have helped to chant the frantic psalm of Young Germany—I have earned a right to be called the Coryphaeus of sensualism—I have sped through the universe and veiled it in a soft mist of irony—but I have never swerved from my faith in the Emperor. I have never ceased to doubt of his advent—My Emperor—the ruler of the people for the people.

CRITIC: Mr. Heine, although I have not been able entirely to follow you, I have gathered enough to produce on my mind a firm conviction that you must have gone through a good deal. Allow me further to express an opinion that a practiced writer like yourself might compose an interesting autobiography. Published in the cheap form which appears to be universal here, it would no doubt have a large circulation in France. Permit me also to remind you that by the terms of the copyright convention recently agreed to between France and England, you are enabled to secure the choice of an English translator, and the profits of the English version. I shall be happy if I can be of any use in forwarding an arrangement between yourself and one of those eminent English literati, whose power and speed of translation are the envy of surrounding nations.

HEINE: Yes; I am writing my memoirs, and in these sheets I have already managed to daguerreotype the colored shadows that flitted before my infancy and boyhood. George Sand is writing hers, Dumas his; what else is there left us to do? We have striven, attained, enjoyed, suffered, lost,—and of the whole there remains with us nothing but reminiscence —let us bequeath that, my friend, to the universe. But what would you English care for my legacy? My life has been one of passion, not of action; of emotion, not of achievement—my autobiography will be pictures of inward moods and dreams—of spiritual joys and sorrows, worship, desperations, angelic peace, gay soarings to the heights that overlook creation! What are these to an Englishman, who reads his autobiography in the banker's book, whose poems are his lucky strokes of speculation, whose highest raptures are the birth of a public meeting? Yes, even the gay, impressionable French are turning practical. The theater languishes; novels are becoming pamphlets; poets, politicians; Béranger is silent; and Heine—Heine is dying! See! here is a book just published by a friend of mine, Lemoinne, one of the writers in the *Journal des Debats*—fugitive essays he has collected on Shakespeare, Goethe, Manon Lescaut, Madame Récamier. Well! he has prefixed an introduction, and what do you think this introduction treats of? Of the laws of art, of the historical development of poetry, of *Hamlet* and *Faust*, of the delicacies of sentiment and the feminine nature? Not at all. It is entitled "Journalism and the Tribune." You remember that passage in Hugo's *Nôtre-Dame*, where Claude Frollo takes into his hands one of those massive volumes which the new-born printing press of Mayence had sent forth, and pointing to the towers of Nôtre-Dame exclaims, "This will annihilate that"—the press will supersede the priest. So Lemoinne says of the newspaper: "The journal will supersede the Parliament." He may be right or he may be wrong, when he says that the framing and discussion of laws—in truth that the whole government of kingdoms—is passing into the hands of newspaper-writers. Strange if it should be so—if the writer should from day to day become the ruler. But if these hopes, even irrationally, are beginning to inspire men of intellect—which of them, do you think, will spend his time stringing rhymes, weaving novels and romances, when he can aspire to rule national masses of men? Your England has been the favored refuge of Parliaments for these two hundred years—Lemoinne talks as if even there Parliamentary government were insecure, and he quotes in corroboration from two of your writers—one of them called Carlyle, who seems an odd fellow, a sort of embittered and concentrated political Jean Paul—

CRITIC: A very eminent man, sir, is Mr. Thomas Carlyle. He published a half-guinea volume lately, not on any subject of temporary interest, and it came to a second edition in a fortnight. As safe an author to publish as we have.

HEINE: And the other is a Mr. Disraeli, who has become a minister. I remember reading his *Contarini Fleming*, many years ago; a strange, wild book, of the kind I might have written myself. A singular phenomenon in England—a novelist becoming a minister.

CRITIC: Sir, Disraeli is a minister, but not because he wrote clever novels, but because he is a clever parliamentary debater and tactician, and a squire in his own way, to boot. As to your M. Lemoinne and his notion, I don't see that there is much in it, as regards England, at least. Our political writers don't seek to originate; they content themselves with repeating the opinions of the leaders of the parties to which they belong. No, Mr. Heine! If there is any extra-parliamentary legislation in England, it is done by the platform, not by the press. You have nothing in France, and are not likely to have, that resembles our "agitations," which you will perhaps allow me to explain to you. First, you get a "cause," it doesn't matter what, so as you can find people to subscribe money to support it, then a "committee," it doesn't matter who, then a secretary, the cleverer and more unscrupulous the better; the best I ever knew had been a Jesuit. Most important of all, you must secure a couple of persons of what we call "respectability," which means possessed of from five hundred to a thousand a year, and, if possible, above the rank of shopkeepers. Sir! if your two respectable persons are fluent with their tongues, and have as much talent as a second-rate barrister, your "cause" is won. You take a large room, placard and advertise, and the English, who are very dull at home, rush to hear what is going on. You set your men a-talking; the people are delighted. Your men perambulate the country, talking, and, if they still delight, the press takes the matter up. Everybody is all of a sudden convinced, and Parliament embodies the "cause" in a law. The press is quite a subordinate matter with us, as yet; and follows or accompanies, but never leads. But I came to listen, Mr. Heine, and not to talk. So French literature, you think, is dying out?

HEINE: How can I tell? I live in the past, and a future not of this earth is within a short distance from me,—how can I interpret the present? Perhaps we others have been the debauchees of thought, and because, as your own Shakespeare says, we have grown virtuous, there shall be no more cakes and ale. The German Bursch settles down into a domestic Housefather; but the beer-jug still passes, and the mist of tobacco smoke still rises in the tavern he has deserted. The dramatist who used to be successful is hissed, and he declares that the theater is going down, because tastes are changing and forms are altering. The man of letters, no longer content with the laurels of his calling, aspires to political power, and he veils his ambition by ascribing the change of his aims to a change in the conditions of things. Can literature, can printed speech ever cease, while the human tongue remains, or pen and paper, ink and type? Will not nature and society, and life, and friends, and loves, and hatreds, kindle ever-new emotions and thoughts in the young soul: where is there the power that can forbid him to cast them into elaborate forms, and keep literature always fresh? But I have talked too much, and you will excuse me, if I ask you to retire. Good-by, my friend! and when you return to London remember me to the Governor of Bedlam. Its inhabitants were the only poets I found in England

Thomas Carlyle

A GLOOMY DEAN OF ENGLISH LETTERS BEMOANS
THE STATE OF ENGLISH MORALS
AND POLITICS.

*I see no hope for these times—they must go
to perdition their own way.*

ANYONE working in the rugged terrain that is Thomas Carlyle and his explosive opinions feels a glow of grateful warmth as he comes upon the name of William Knighton. It is to this obscure Anglo-Indian of the British government service that we owe the truest record of the conversational sputterings of the wrathful nineteenth-century Jeremiah who damned the world about him and the people in it. Other chroniclers, like Sir C. G. Duffy, issued volumes of Conversations with Thomas Carlyle, all rich in irate pontifications. Most of them, however, are endless soliloquies unbroken by the direct discourse of any interlocutor. Knighton not only interposed himself during his talks with Carlyle, but recorded each of his own queries and rejoinders in the play-like sequence of his reported dialogue. He commends himself to this book of recording angels on several other counts as well.

To begin with, Knighton jotted down notes as fast as he could the moment he reached home, and checked his memory of each conversation with that of his wife, who had also been present. Both were highly attentive listeners. Knighton later regretted that his notes were so scant beside the incredible superabundance of Carlyle's talk. The precious hoard of manuscript remained in Knighton's safekeeping for a quarter of a century. Prizing Carlyle's friendship, he refrained from printing the notes till 1881. In June of that year, four months after the death of England's gloomy dean of letters, the "conversations" appeared for the first time in the Contemporary Review. In releasing them for publication Knighton resisted the sternest temptation of all—he printed them completely unaltered. "It was a happy inspiration," commented the great Carlyle scholar, David Alec Wilson. "Perhaps nothing published then was a more undeniable addition to permanent literature." Paradoxically, it was the very fact that Knighton had approached the material in the humble role of amanuensis, rather than that of literary artist, that gave the "conversations" this distinction.

At the time the conversations took place Knighton was on a furlough from government service in India. This Indian experience, incidentally, later materialized into two books—Forest Life in Ceylon and The Private Life of an Eastern King. During the winter of 1856 he and his wife occupied an apartment in Chelsea not far from Cheyne Row, where the Carlyles lived. Another resident of that neighborhood was Geraldine Jewsbury, a novel-writing bluestocking whose name comes up in the course of the conversations. Mrs. Carlyle once referred to this stalwart member of the Cheyne Row circle as "the most intimate friend I have in the world." Part of Miss Jewsbury's function, no doubt, was to bolster the much-harried Mrs. Carlyle against the neurasthenic fulminations of her husband. Characteristically, it was a Rev. J. G. Macvicar, D.D., author of such erudite tomes as A Sketch of a Philosophy and The Economy of Nature, who introduced the Knightons to the Carlyles. The two men got along famously, and Knighton records that "our wives, too, became great friends." For several months the Carlyles and Knightons spent an evening a week together at the house in Cheyne Row. Knighton noted with amusement how Carlyle sharply resented his wife's correcting him on any point of fact. In the first conversation given below we find Mrs. Carlyle gleefully catching the irascible savant in a misquotation from the Bible. Carlyle, Knighton tells us, heard her patiently to the end and later took occasion to repeat his misquotation with defiant emphasis. "His wife," remarks Knighton, "like a prudent woman, did not hear it."

The Carlyles lived simply, almost austerely, in their rooms in Cheyne Row. The great man was then working on the first two volumes of his massive Frederick the Great. One of Jane Carlyle's wifely duties was to barricade her grumpy husband from the outside world during his prolonged seizures of working fury. For if no man could work like Carlyle, neither could any man unleash such tirades of protest over any form of intrusion. The mildest infractions might be greeted with "grotesque explosions." Carlyle worked in an elaborately devised "sound-proof" room on the second floor. Insomnia, dyspepsia, the crowing of "demon-fowls" in adjoining yards only added to his ever-growing stock of grievances against life. For Carlyle existence was often nothing but a fabric of annoyances and irritations. The whole world seemed engaged in a conspiracy to bear out his thesis that all was evil, that some fearful catastrophe would soon overtake this spectacle of sin, decay, sham, and anarchy. Into his writings he had poured the full measure of his wrath.

The world had come to look upon this man as a dour prophet of doom. He had lost faith in both spiritual and materialist creeds, in parties, governments, and people. Reform and progress had become delusions, and all around him he saw moral desolation. What was lacking, he preached, was heroes, the chosen and anointed who molded men's minds and shaped history; heroes one could worship, like Cromwell or this extraordinary Prussian egotist and empire-builder whose voluminous biography he was now writing.

As this giant creative process functioned upstairs in the house on Cheyne Row, downstairs a bitter, frustrated, childless woman recorded in a secret diary: "My most constant and pressing desire is to keep out of Bedlam." But this woman's tragedy is hidden from the outside world, hidden even from the roaring lion of the "sound-proof" room on the floor above. To the poets, preachers, philosophers who come to hear the Oracle of Cheyne Row, Jane Carlyle is the perfect hostess, gracious, lively, attentive. The tragedy that is hers will startle even Carlyle when he comes to read her diary after her death. Meanwhile she is the perfect wife, making things easy for England's most irritable man, and suffering in silence.

In his obsession with the twin themes of moral collapse and political decay Carlyle never changed. As a youth he had discussed the world's disorder with another somber prophet of chaos, the poet Southey. "We sat on the sofa together," Carlyle himself narrates; "our talk was long and earnest; topic ultimately the usual one: steady approach of democracy with revolution, probably explosive, and a finis incomputable to man. Southey's last word was in answer to some tirade of mine against universal mammon-worship, gradual accelerating decay of material humanity, of piety and fidelity, to God or man, in all our relations and performances. To which he answered, not with levity, yet with a cheerful tone in his seriousness, 'It will not and it cannot come to good.' " *

Carlyle might very well have adopted Southey's reply as his lifelong creed. To William Knighton in 1856, and to others in 1881, he was still preaching the same bleak doctrine: "It will not and it cannot come to good."

("Oct 22nd, 1856.—My wife and I spent the evening, 8 to 11, with Mr. and Mrs. Carlyle. Miss Jewsbury there, and an Oxford Commissioner and his wife—'intelligent people,' as Carlyle called them. We

---

* Paraphrase of *Hamlet*, Act I, Scene 2, line 158.

had tea. The Commissioner handed the kettle for Mrs. Carlyle."—
Knighton)

CARLYLE: I had some men to make a room for me on the top of my house.
They used bad timber—did not know their work—came tumbling
through the roof often into the other rooms at the top—workmen complained of the master—the master of the workmen—everything done
in the same way nowadays—an age of shams—shams in religion, in social life, in politics. It was the same two hundred years ago, it was all
sham, and the people that would not have shams, the earnest thinking
men, rose and swore it should not be so any longer—they would cut
each other's throats for it, if need were, but the shams they would not
endure.

KNIGHTON: If everyone thought so now, we should have another revolution.

CARLYLE: That's exactly what we do want—a thorough revolution; but not
a revolution after the French model—a quiet, peaceful, sensible revolution. But I see no help for these times—they must just go to perdition
their own way, and then—

KNIGHTON: And then?

CARLYLE: And then revolutions and misgovernment in cycles—in eternal
cycles, so far as I can see. (*The subject changes to literary men.*) The
most contemptible man of the day is the literary man—the honest shoe-
black is a more respectable and useful citizen. If I knew of any young
man going to devote himself entirely to literature as a profession, I
should say, "For God's sake, sir, stop, don't; be an honest, useful man
any other way. You never will be *that* way." Men write without thinking nowadays. Everyone thinks he can write—that's all the thinking
many do. Even history is written without research. (*The subject
changes. The Oxford Commissioner speaks of the "dogs of Constantinople."*) Strange the bad name the dog has got; yet he is the most respectable of all the animal creation we come in contact with—

KNIGHTON: Except the horse—

CARLYLE: No, not even excepting the horse. "Is thy servant a dead dog that
he should do this thing?"

MRS. CARLYLE: Not a dead dog, Carlyle—"Is thy servant a dog."

CARLYLE: Dead dog occurs somewhere as the vilest of things—very odd—
perhaps because they are scavengers in the East; in some cases, the only
scavengers. (*The quotation introduces the subject of the Hebrew
Scriptures, Carlyle speaking warmly in praise of their sublimity and
beauty.*) Homer comes next—the next book to the Bible for everything
grand and great; and yet how tiresome parts of both are. Take the com-

bats in Homer—one man gets a spear run through him one way, another another way. Men we heard nothing of before, and never shall hear of again—very tiresome. The *Odyssey*, written by a different hand, a younger man, in a more artificial age—a finer poem in many respects than the *Iliad*. Nothing finer than Ulysses bending his bow on those who were eating his substance, and shooting out, a stentor-like, "Ye dogs" (ὦ κύνες)—the dog again, poor fellow! The *Iliad*, evidently a collection of ballads by one hand, with interpolations, etc., of a later age. Robin Hood's Garland similar. The simplicity—the grand simplicity of it! The epithets applied to different men very strange. One fellow has nothing to distinguish him but well-fitting boots (εὔχνημις). Only think of calling a man "the well-booted"—"the well-booted Knighton," for instance, ha! ha! ha! (*Speaks of Thirlwall's "Greece."*) Thirlwall so hedges himself in with qualifications and *ifs* and *buts*. He takes you a little one way, and then says, "Stop, turn back with me so far; perhaps that's the way, but So-and-so thinks differently"; and so on. It spoils a man to make a bishop of him.

COMMISSIONER: Dean ——— would probably have been a bishop had he not spoken of the "extraordinary conduct of Judas Iscariot." *

CARLYLE (*laughing long and loudly*): The "extraordinary conduct!" Very good! "Conduct not to be expected from any gentleman," he might have added. Was it the same man who always spoke of the crucifixion as "the execution of Jesus Christ"? But the "extraordinary conduct of Judas Iscariot" was far better. (*Returns to subject of Greece.*) Plato is too inconclusive for me; his fancy is wonderful and his language polished, but he is the most inconclusive of great writers. I have no patience with him. His *Republic* is the best of his works by far. With what disdain he speaks of the great unwashed and their blatant democracies! It is a pity we have no readable literal translations of Sophocles and Aeschylus. I was looking at an English translation of Aeschylus the other day, and I had to turn to the Greek to see what the man meant.

KNIGHTON: Why not have the works turned neatly into blank verse, without sacrificing the original?

CARLYLE: No, no—no blank verse. I would say to the translator—"Give me Sophocles, give me Aeschylus; I don't want your silly poesy. I want to know what those men, in their wisdom, thought and wrote; not what you, in your folly, think and write." Such works, properly done, ought to be very popular, for England sympathizes with ancient Greece, and the great men of ancient Greece.

---

* Indirect discourse in original.

("Nov. 28, 1856.—Spent the evening with Mr. and Mrs. Carlyle at
5 Cheyne Row, Chelsea. Had tea when we went in. Mrs. Carlyle in
cap and shawl—an invalid. Carlyle in dressing-gown."—Knighton)

KNIGHTON: The magazines and reviews have been very busy with you
lately, sir.

CARLYLE: Ay, have they? I never read them. I have the most utter contempt and abhorrence for the literary *canaille* of the day, with their
Reviews, and Magazines, and *Times* newspaper. They should try and
understand me—that would be more sensible. And what have they
been saying?

KNIGHTON: The *North British Review* had an excellent article, as I thought
it, on "The Religious Tendencies of the Day—Newman, Coleridge, and
Carlyle," endeavoring to point out what they believed to be your influence in religious questions on the world. One of Ainsworth's Magazines—*Bentley* or the *New Monthly*—has an article this month too
about you, but solely as a literary man—a poor article—all about your
style, which is not to their liking.

CARLYLE: Blind leaders of the blind! How shall they understand me with
their devotion to the devil? Give me a God-fearing man and a God-
believing man, and that man will understand me; but your Ainsworth's
Magazines are only a part of that awful system of cant and lying that
sweeps England to perdition in these days. When there is no truth,
there can be no utterance worth listening to. Some of these reviewers
remind me of men accumulating first laboriously a heap of refuse, and
then proceeding diligently to examine it and grope in it for novelties.
That's the work that befits them, believe me. I care nothing what they
say of me, or to me.

MRS. CARLYLE: Some time ago a clergyman sent him an essay—a voluminous essay in MS. We were sitting together when he got it, and he read
the first sentence, something after this manner: "Sir, I have a great respect for you. You are drawing on toward the brink of the grave. Age is
creeping over you. It behooves you to think of another world and of
religion." He read no more, but, getting up, put the whole mass of
writing into the fire there, and watched it consume. I pitied the poor
man who had taken so much trouble in vain—to say that his laborious
composition should not even be read!

CARLYLE: Ha, ha, ha!—ha, ha, ha! O yes, they will send me such things;
but they cannot make me read them. Ha, ha, ha!

MRS. CARLYLE: We have been greatly amused with a book of Mr. Charles
Reade's, *It Is Never Too Late to Mend.* Mr. Reade has evidently
adopted, unconsciously I suppose, Carlyle's style and mannerism—

completely so—and yet the views of the two men are so widely dissimilar—as opposite as possible to each other, in fact. It is a stupid book—a very stupid book: the author sympathizes with criminals and such like, all which Mr. Carlyle and I hold in abhorrence.

CARLYLE: That sympathy with criminals, and convicts, and ticket-of-leave men is just one of the worst symptoms of the age in which we live. But it is not to be wondered at that men, with no sincerity about themselves, should do their best for their brethren, the children of the devil. If they had any real abhorrence of the crime, they would fling their mawkish sympathy to the winds. They don't see, they never will see, that men who act so are like unto those they succor. The one is the liar, with dirty linen, living in a prison—the other is the liar, with clean linen, living in his own house.

KNIGHTON: The ticket-of-leave system sometimes leads to crimes in our very streets. What is the use of prisons, one may ask, if the people that ought to be in them are jostling us at every corner?

CARLYLE: The people that ought to be in them! ha, ha, ha!—(*A loud, hearty, honest laugh.*) They would be large prisons that would hold all that ought to be in them. Had these sympathizers any conscientious abhorrence of crime, they would say to the criminal, "Out of my sight, villain! Go away with you to your father, the devil." They do not see that their sympathy with these wretches only proves they are convinced of the fact that it is accident, as we call it, that prevents them taking the other's place. The result of all this, and of all our hollowness and deceit, and want of faith and godliness, is that we are rushing on to ruin—all our English and American agitations and democracies, notwithstanding. I have no faith in these democracies, or in republics at all. Things may last so for fifty years, perhaps, not longer, certainly.

KNIGHTON: Is there no native energy in the English race to prevent this? Have we not men of genius to lead us in as great abundance as ever?

CARLYLE: Yes, I think we have as many men of genius, as much talent; but that will not save us, as things go. Our talent is all directed to talking and writing, instead of doing.

KNIGHTON: The age of Elizabeth was a heroic age: yet there was much writing then, too, although not quite so much talking.

CARLYLE: No nation was ever saved by writing and talking, only by acting. It was the great ages before Elizabeth, and the great men in those ages, who prepared the way for the achievements of the reign of Elizabeth. England has been held ever since the Norman Conquest, and long before, by a superior race; but for a thousand years they were doers simply, not talkers and writers. Compare *Domesday Book* with our modern blue books and parliamentary committees' reports and such like, that nobody reads or can read. This very Chelsea is described in that *Domesday Book* as a *sylva sexaginta porcorum*.* It could feed just sixty swine, and a fellow in a leathern jerkin, with a horn to look after them, and make puddings of them. Two lines of such a book teach us more than whole volumes of frothy blue books.

KNIGHTON: Yet our Parliament contains some of the cleverest men, and our aristocracy, as a class, is a noble and superior race.

CARLYLE: So far as my experience goes, the best of actual men in England —infinitely better than aristocracy, than the talking and writing lawyers and editors, and unbelieving divines.

KNIGHTON: And yet no hope for England?

CARLYLE: None; for a hundred years we have been going down-hill fast, losing faith and hope. What kind of a boy is this that is to be our King of England next? † The German race we have imported from the Continent has been a heavy, stupid race. Prince Albert is an exception. He looks forward, I think, and is preparing for what he foresees—that those boys of his will live in troublesome times; but he cannot say so, of course.

("*There was a pause, and we talked afterwards of Ceylon and Buddhism. He said there was doubtless much in that old creed if we could get at it; but the men who had translated hitherto were utterly incompetent for their task, giving us, for the most part, words and not ideas. Sir Arthur Buller, one of his old pupils, had told him the Cinghalese were incorrigible liars. I mentioned their belief in transmigration and its effects.*"—Knighton)

KNIGHTON: One man committed suicide to escape the pain of a toothache, another to get rid of a whitlow. All over the East man seems more earnest in religion than in the West.

CARLYLE: True, very true. The only great outburst we have had of true faith within the last two centuries in Europe was Methodism; but, in our own time, it is like the rest, hollow and false—utterly untrue.

KNIGHTON: I have seen some, sir, that were as devoted to their creed—some Methodists—as any devotees of the East.

CARLYLE: Exceptions. I heard one of the best of them at Derby once. He had been a joiner, I believe, and he spoke earnestly. That man saw before him, in the other world, two states of existence—the one that in which he would be roasted everlastingly, the other that in which he would float everlastingly in bliss of some kind. "It is of infinite impor-

---

* A forest of sixty pigs.

† Edward VII, then Prince of Wales; became king in 1901.

tance to me," said he to himself, "that I should not roast everlastingly"; and hence his speeches and his rantings, his violent sayings, and his Methodistical cant. But truly, anything more despicable, anything more unworthy of an honest, noble soul, we could not easily find anywhere than that. It is the rankest flunkyism, yet that is enthusiastic Methodism in these days.

KNIGHTON: I believe it is; I never heard it so put before; but, honestly and candidly, I think it is, and I have seen much of Methodism. I startled one of their preachers once, in Ceylon, by showing him the word μεϑοδεία, a *trick* or *imposture,* in the Greek lexicon, as the derivation of the word "Methodism."

CARLYLE: Good, very good. He was dumbfounded at that, I should think. Ha, ha, ha! But the word doesn't come from that, does it? It looks like it.

KNIGHTON: No, I believe now that it comes from our own word *method*. Wesley, at Oxford, originated both the appellation and the schism with his prayer-meetings.

CARLYLE: I was going to tell you about an Indian poem some one sent me translated, when you led me off to Methodism. I think it is called the "Mahabarat." It describes seven sons as setting off to seek their fortunes. They all go different ways, and six of them land in hell, after many adventures. The seventh is of nobler seed. He perseveres, fights his way manfully through great trials. His faithful dog, an ugly little monster, but very faithful, dies at last. He himself, fainting and well-nigh despairing, meets an old man, Indra, disguised, who offers to open for him the gates of heaven. "But where are my brothers?" he asks; "are they there?" "No; they are all in hell." "Then I will go to hell, too, and stop with them, unless you get them out." So saying, he turns off and trudges away. Indra pities him, and gets his brethren out of hell. The six enter heaven first. The seventh stops. "My poor faithful dog," says he, "I will not leave him." Indra remonstrates, but it is useless; the faithful dog, ugly as he was, is too well remembered, and he will not have paradise without it. He succeeds finally. Indra relents, and lets even the dog in; but, sir, there is more pathos about that dog than in a thousand of our modern novels—pathos enough to make a man sit down and cry almost.

KNIGHTON: The whole story must have been intended to illustrate the efficacy of prayer. It reminds one faintly of Abraham's intercession for Sodom and Gomorrah—a grand old picture, not inferior on the whole, I should think, to yours of the "Mahabarat."

CARLYLE: Lot's intercession, you mean.

KNIGHTON: No, Abraham's. Lot was living in the vale at the time, in Sodom.

CARLYLE: Lot certainly interceded for someone. However, it is a point of little consequence. As I said, sir, there is true pathos about that dog. I have seldom read anything with more.

("18th Feb. 1857.—Spent the evening with Carlyle at his home. We were alone. Mrs. Carlyle ill. I mentioned that I had seen some verses of his written in Sir J. E. Tennant's album, dated Paris, 1824,—subject, a moth and candle."—Knighton)

CARLYLE: I remember that Emerson—he was a poor, sickly-looking, white-haired lad then—going about with a much finer man every way, a Mr. Tennant. They were going out to liberate the Greeks. Tennant spoke with a broad Irish accent. We were to meet Washington Irving at a coffee-house at breakfast. It was in Paris. We went, but Washington Irving did not come. I suppose he thought it wiser to take his refection at home, quietly, instead of going to a coffee-house to be stared at; and he was right. I have seen nothing of Irving since; but I saw Emerson, or Emerson-Tennant, as he calls himself now, five or six years ago, somewhere. I congratulated him on the improvement in the color of his hair—ha, ha, ha!—it turned out to be a wig he wore—ha, ha, ha! He was dreadfully disconcerted—ha, ha, ha!

KNIGHTON: Were you much interested in Paris?

CARLYLE: I was at that time, very much. I was young, and my mind was open to fresh impressions; but I was there since, a year or two before this man made himself Emperor, and I found them all empty, grimacing, going on all day with foolish empty grimacings. There is no hope for Paris. They are on the high-road that is so easily travelled downwards, but the ascending of which is the difficulty. Alas! it is not Paris only that is thus. (*Pause.*) I sat one evening at the foot of the column in the Place Vendôme and smoked my cigar there, watching their grimacing, and superficial, empty, nonsensical mimicry, and hollowness, when a party of soldiers came, with two or three drummers, beating away in earnest, ahead of them—rat-at-tat-ta, rat-at-tat-ta they went —and the Parisians were delighted with them. They could understand that, but anything better they could not. Rat-at-tat-ta, rat-at-tat-ta they went along, waking the echoes, the drummers seemingly delighted with their own performance, the people charmed, and there were the stars and moon above them that night just as there are tonight, as clear and silent and solemn. (*Another pause.*) One Sunday evening I went out to the Champ de Mars and saw a lamentable spectacle. The Champ was covered with people, its dusky half-grass, half-gravelled extent was almost hidden with the multitude. And what, think you, had they to recreate themselves with, that blessed Sabbath evening? A balloon was to go up, and the men were there holding it down by ropes during its inflation in great numbers; but before it was ready a sort of inflated semblance of a man was sent up. It was guided by ropes, I suppose, but the ropes were invisible from where I stood. I saw it go up, to the great delight of the Parisian populace. They shouted, yelled, clapped their necks, opened their eyes and mouths, and gave every evidence of intense satisfaction. It was pulled down afterwards somewhere, and by that time the balloon was ready. That was the amusement of the Parisian populace that blessed Sabbath evening. A spectacle to make one sad.

KNIGHTON: I doubt if you would find any other populace that would not be equally delighted with it. Sabbath or no Sabbath, the poor have not their books and thoughts to fall back upon. They want something to see, or hear, or taste—something palpable.

CARLYLE: They do. But this open-mouthed levity and grimacing is a characteristic not of the poor only in France. Look at their writers. I opened Lamartine's *History of the Girondins*, and found it a foolish romance, yet professing to be a history. The man is a grimacing caricaturist, an empty windbag, and flatulent. History! It's no history at all. And that's the man that thought he was to be the man of the age— the presiding genius of France. A genius worthy of the France of the present day, which is all talk, grimace, and insincerity.

KNIGHTON: Thiers is a profounder historian than Lamartine, but where the glory of France is concerned not over-scrupulous or accurate as to facts.

CARLYLE: Guizot is a cadaverous-looking man, who believes in Louis Philippe. When I conversed with him long ago about Cromwell, he though Cromwell first an enthusiast and afterwards a hypocrite. In his *English Revolution*, however, I find he has adopted my view of him, as far as it was possible for him so to do. But he is an undecided man. He believes in Louis Philippe and the Spanish marriages still. Indeed, I don't know but he may be looking for the resurrection of Louis Philippe and his Second Advent. The second part of his work is a mere political essay on the present state of France, or rather on its state when he wrote, for its state changes every year now. A wretched country! I once thought the Revolution was working itself out to a higher, holier, and better state of things; but I find my mistake now.

France, like England, will have to go through the baptism of fire and blood that awaits us all, before anything better can come out of it. Look at its literature and you will find it all lying and romance—the worst of both.

KNIGHTON: Your hopes for literature center in Germany, I suppose; for I know you don't think much of our current literature in England?

CARLYLE: Our current literature is like our current life—made up of shams, hypocrisies, counterfeits, deceits, lies. I have a profound contempt for it. Lessing did a great deal for Germany in showing them that their French models were no models at all, but falsities, and in preaching up Shakespeare to them; and, since his time, Germany has done more for literature than France and England—a great deal more.

KNIGHTON: I have somewhere seen it remarked—in T. Jouffroy, I think—that Germany gives the raw material of thought; France puts it into shape and makes it clear; whilst England applies it practically.

CARLYLE: Germany has given no raw material, then, for some quarter of a century that I know anything of.

KNIGHTON: Are we making no progress, then, in Western Europe? Is there nothing great and good being done either in Germany, France, or England at the present day?

CARLYLE: Progress! Our progress is in the wrong direction. We move with accelerated velocity downwards. As to Germany, the only thing they do there now is in a philological way; but they do that well. They are men of immense patience, of wonderful plodding perseverance. They can clothe the dry bones of history and ancient literature for us in a perfectly marvellous way; telling us of the pots and pans the Greeks and Romans used, how they walked and talked, and sat, and slept, and rose, and did other things less noble. Heyne did that in a wonderful way for Virgil, and that sort of thing has its use. Heeren told us much, too, of their commerce and politics that we knew not before; but he is tedious, prolix, and dry. In philology, they still dig out new facts, and put them together for us, with wonderful labor; but of anything better than that going on at the present day in Germany, I know nothing.

KNIGHTON: You laugh at our progress. Is there no progress apparent in India and in British colonization—in the opening-up of new countries, peopling waste continents, and founding new empires?

CARLYLE: A Gibeonitish sort of progress truly; all hewing of wood and drawing of water; nothing nobler or better that I can see. The United States were a greater and nobler people eighty years ago, when they were our colonies, than they are now, though they had only three millions of people, then, and thirty now. The whole of the thirty put together wouldn't make one Franklin, or even a Washington.

KNIGHTON: Should we ever have heard of Washington had it not been for the circumstances in which he was placed?

CARLYLE: Perhaps not; but he would not have been the less a great man on that account. I do not rate him very highly, however; certainly not to compare with Franklin.

KNIGHTON: And with the States, the Cape, Australia, New Zealand, India, as they are, you see no progress in the right direction?

CARLYLE: I see terrible calamities impending, a total severing of every tie and bond of the world as it exists—bloodshedding and destruction. As to Australia, what is it doing but upsetting all our economic arrangements here by digging out gold that had much better be left where it was? We didn't want it. The world didn't want it. There was enough before for all practical purposes. No nation ever became great by finding gold, though it were found in tons. Rome was pretty much as we are when it was congratulating itself on being the mistress of the world. Seneca was writing of her greatness, her prosperity, and her wonderful progress, and yet the northern barbarians were even then whetting their swords for slaughter. Death was nigh unto those luxurious Romans, steeped in refinement, and a career of "progress" that promised them, short-sighted as they were, wonderful things. And so with us.

KNIGHTON: Where are these modern barbarians to come from?

CARLYLE: I don't know. History does not exactly reproduce itself, but we want a superior race, to be got somewhere and somehow—a race of God-fearing, honest, sincere men. But it's no use cursing the world as it is. It remains the same after we have expended all the vials of our wrath upon it.

(*"Miss Jewsbury came in at this moment. She had been with Mrs. Carlyle. We walked home with her, and then Carlyle walked home with me. He spoke of preaching and preachers as we went."*—Knighton.)

CARLYLE: If I were a preacher, I would tell them one Sunday what to do, and then, when they came back next Sunday, I would ask them, "Well, have you done that? How much have you done of it? None! Then go home and do it." I would remind them once more, giving them a little at a time, but not a step faster than I thought right. A little at a time. What conceivable use is there in their going over a long rigmarole of the same thing, Sunday after Sunday, that they know well no one intends to practice, they themselves, perhaps, least of all. It is the silent, steady, persevering work that has been of use in all ages, not the windy clamorous work, that can't go on unless people talk about it.

KNIGHTON: The Bishop of St. Asaph went into St. Mark's School one day, and asked one of the boys there, "Who am I?" "A bishop, my lord," said the youngster. They often see bishops there. "Who made me a bishop?" asked his lordship, solemnly. "Lord John Russell, my lord," said the urchin. The bishop said no more to them that day!

(*"Carlyle laughed heartily at the anecdote, and left me laughing, as we shook hands near my door. It was then half-past eleven, the river before us, and the moon shining brightly on it—a beautiful night, cold, bright, and frosty"*—Knighton.)

(*"Spent Tuesday evening, the 25th of March, 1857, with Carlyle at his home. He asked me of my health when in India and Ceylon, and I told him it was excellent, except when I went to Anuradhapura in Ceylon, and got jungle-fever in consequence. This led us to talk of the district through which I passed, the wild animals, the cheetah, and so we settled at last on the cat."*—Knighton)

CARLYLE: Tiger, lion, cheetah—they are all of the feline race.

KNIGHTON: According to naturalists, I believe they are; but there is an important distinction. The tiger and cheetah, like the cat, can sheath their claws; the lion, like the dog, cannot.

CARLYLE: The cat is inferior to the dog in its affections; it becomes attached to places rather than to persons. There are some cats, however, that display strong affections. Mrs. Carlyle tells of one which, when its kitten was drowned, exerted itself perseveringly until it got the kitten out of the water again, and did its best to restore it, poor thing; failing that, it pined away and died for the love of it.

KNIGHTON: I suppose their nature is improved by contact with man, as that of the dog unquestionably is.

CARLYLE: Doubtless the nobler animal influences the baser beneficially; but still the cat will never be equal to the much-abused dog in many things. Did you happen to know, when you were in India, a man of the name of Mackenzie?

KNIGHTON: Brigadier Mackenzie?

CARLYLE: The same.

KNIGHTON: I did not know him, but I know that his wife wrote a book on Indian life, entitled *The Court, the Camp, the Mission*, or something of that kind.

CARLYLE: She did. Her husband was in England some time ago. He is a

Scotchman, and I had some slight acquaintance with him long ago. He gave me a pamphlet giving an account of an extraordinary mutiny which occurred amongst some troops in India at the station to which he was attached, and in which he suffered most severely.

KNIGHTON: I remember only this much of the circumstance—that the newspapers considered him over-zealous in endeavoring to stop some native procession, and that he had brought on the attack by his want of judgment.

CARLYLE: His pamphlet gives what I have no doubt is a very correct account of the transaction. It appears that this Mohammedan procession, with drums playing and flags flying, was marching past his encampment on the public road, consisting almost entirely of soldiers— some sort of irregular corps—they had no right to be there, and he sent them away. They came again in greater force, with more drums, I suppose, and more flags, and he went out to them again, accompanied by another European. They attacked him mercilessly, cut and wounded him in many places, and in fact, left him for dead. The real culprits were allowed by some incompetent magistrate to escape, and a native officer, a Havildar I believe, was about being punished for it—deprived of his office—who was really the only efficient and orderly officer in the regiment. Mackenzie interfered to prevent this injustice. He seems to me to have played quite a heroical part in the business. He appealed to the Governor-General against the decision of the incompetent magistrate, but I suppose the Governor-General wouldn't take the trouble to read his statement, and so he got no redress. The impression is strong in my mind that that man played quite a heroical part in the whole business, and I believe what he says, because I respected him of old as a truth-telling, honest, sincere man. It is quite true, as the papers state, that he is a devout Christian; but how that should be to any man's discredit in a Christian country is not easily explained, except in this way—that unbelief, and cant, and humbug, and insincerity are gaining the day.

KNIGHTON: Is belief—such as belief was before geological and astronomical discoveries—possible nowadays?

CARLYLE: Only possible to those who are ignorant of such discoveries; but when existing, it is a beautiful thing.

KNIGHTON: And what is the position of the clergy in this matter?

CARLYLE: The position of the clergy is one of ignominy and deep degradation. The spectacle of a body of enlightened men solemnly, and in the face of God and man, professing their steadfast faith and belief in that which they know they do not steadfastly believe in, is enough to make any thinking man sick at heart. What enlightened man can conscientiously in these days tie up his reason by formulas and articles drawn up centuries ago, and say, "I believe," whilst the inner soul of him all the time is exclaiming, "I do not believe—it is a lie"?

KNIGHTON: Some men, like Dr. Newman, for instance, first persuade themselves that there is an infallible Church that cannot err, and then, taking refuge therein, are troubled no further about the matter—accepting all its *dicta* as heaven-descended truths, whatever their reason may whisper about the matter.

CARLYLE: And what is that but moral emasculation?—one of the most lamentable religious phases of our times. Even with respect to the clergy of the English Church, they doubtless have persuaded themselves, in most instances, that they did believe before they made their declaration to that effect. For the time being they do not believe, but —believe that they believe. There is little hope for a Church existing under such circumstances. No, no; things cannot go on long in this way. Swift destruction is impending, not on the Church only—mother of dead dogs.

KNIGHTON: The Buddhistic idea of the universe is that it goes on through certain cycles of existence, each cycle terminating in destruction, and reproduction again resulting from that destruction. This rule seems to hold to a certain extent in the moral world.

CARLYLE: Geology seems to favor this Buddhistic idea—there have undoubtedly been certain ages of animal and vegetable life separated from each other by vast changes and world-wide destruction.

KNIGHTON: Humboldt has given a pleasant summary, succinct and agreeable, of these changes in his *Cosmos*.

CARLYLE: I read one volume of that book in German, but could never get further. What does he see in the universe? Nothing but an old marine-store-shop collection of things putrefying and rotting, under certain forces and laws. A most melancholy picture of things! The spiritual world, and all spiritual life, quite ignored. The higher and nobler side of man's existence not even hinted at—a lamentable picture, truly. Long ago I read his account of his travels in South America, and the same impressions struck me; but he was regarded by all men as one of the greatest of modern philosophers, and I did not then venture to say what I really thought. I was a young man then. Even this old marine-store-shop *Cosmos* of his was so highly praised by those whose opinions I revere that I thought it my duty to read it; but I never could get further than the end of the first volume. There is certainly something higher in Nature than rocks and laws, something nobler than mountains, and fossils, and forces, something more sublime than natural scenery, however grand. It is a very big universe, he confesses, it is true—so big that it quite surprises him with its bigness, but nothing more. I saw him in Germany some years ago. He was talking all day about—(*Miss Jewsbury comes in with a message from Mrs. Carlyle.*) I had nearly forgotten. A poor German,* a Slav by descent, brought up at Berlin, who was teaching in a provincial town, wrote to me some time ago, without any introduction, complaining of his position, and asking my advice. He was under a vulgar-minded man acting as an usher. I advised him not to come to London; to carry on in his provincial engagement under all disadvantages rather. He came, however, and I advised him to go back again. He went; but he soon returned once more, finding it impossible, as he said, to continue. I employed him as an amanuensis—he found out places for me, copied some extracts; he was of assistance to me from his excellent knowledge of German and French. He can write creditably in English, although he made nonsense of what I said. My words and style were so peculiar, he maintained. He is a man of gentlemanly manners, and cultivated. I discharged him on Saturday. He has a wife and one or two children. If you can find any work for him, educational or other, I shall be obliged. It is astonishing how all men's eyes turn toward London as the great world-mart for every kind of talent and skill. I was going up the Drachenfels with a friend, and we lay down to rest on the side of the road. There were two German lads trundling barrows up the side of the hill, which was steep. As they went up the barrows were empty. They filled them at the top with flint for the roads, and then, in coming down, they leaned backwards with all their might. It was hard work. They got about a penny for each journey up and down. They could make about sevenpence in the day. Seeing us lying down, one of them came up to us, and I asked him these particulars. He told me his mother wove the stuff for his clothes and made them. He evidently could live well on his sevenpence a day, for he was fresh and plump. He wanted to know if it would be wise for him to come to London. We dissuaded him, telling him there was no hope for him in London. He said he would not come, but I dare say he has for all that.

KNIGHTON: It is a wonderful city, such a city as has never existed in this world before.

CARLYLE: Cities as large and populous have existed, I suspect, before, but never one so badly governed. Think of a fifth of the world being gov-

---

* Frederick Martin, young teacher, who copied manuscript for Carlyle.

erned from this city, and yet we cannot get a glass of clean water in it.

KNIGHTON: Your denunciation is somewhat absolute.

CARLYLE: We cannot get a glass of clean water in it—there is one fact; the river is a huge sewer, filthy and corrupt—there is another. And yet we have thousands of men without work, we have colonies, and idle ships, and overflowing wealth. Nothing but the government of the wise will save us. People ask me how are we to get it? I say it's not my business to show you how. I tell you the fact. It is of importance you should have your breakfast, too, every one of you, I answer. If you are without it long, you will be the worse for it, depend upon it. Is it my business to tell you how you are to get it? I content myself with telling you that you had better get it; see if it be not worse for you if you do not.

KNIGHTON: A thoroughly practical illustration—ha, ha, ha!

CARLYLE: Ha, ha, ha! They all see the force of that. Will the government of the wise ever be got out of the government of the foolish? Will getting five or six hundred fools to talk together ever do it,—these five or six hundred elected by pot-wallopers and other fools? The wise man governing would make the best use of the existing means. He would promote emigration; the idle ships of war would be employed in it. It was no degradation to the Roman soldier to dig and build and hew; the best soldiers now do these things best. Ours should help in the good work. We cannot do without soldiers and ships of war, but we have not yet found out how to make use of them in times of peace. One can advise a fool, but the fool won't take wise advice. What is the wise man to do then? Why simply to say, "Get out of my sight, fool; the more speedily the better for you and me. I have told you what to do. I will hold no further converse with you. You want to advise me; nay, I will not have that." But the men of this generation regard the matter very differently. They have said to Folly, "Be thou my goddess; under thy guidance I will climb heavenward; lead me thou."

KNIGHTON: They will be long getting heavenward under such guidance. (*Rises to depart.*)

CARLYLE: Ha, ha, ha! They will assuredly. In the meantime, if in this folly-led world you can do anything for the poor Slav, it will be well.

Wagner-Rossini

REUNION IN PARIS: A RETIRED COMPOSER OF THE
OLD SCHOOL INVITES A FELLOW EXPATRIATE
TO EXPOUND THE MUSIC OF THE FUTURE.

*Ah! Monsieur Wagner—like a new Orpheus you
have no fear of crossing the redoubtable threshold!*

IT WAS with some misgivings that the French writer E. Michotte resolved in 1906 to publish a conversation between Richard Wagner
and Gioachino Rossini which he had heard and taken down forty-six
years before in Paris on a March afternoon in 1860. The problem for
Michotte was not so much that of recalling as accurately as possible the
detail and substance of the talk. The young journalist of a half century
before had provided for that handsomely. On his promise not to publish
the talk, he had obtained the permission of both men to sit by and jot
down the colloquy for his own personal record. Thus, the risks of a faulty
memory were not his main difficulty. The problem was of another nature.
To begin with, there was the stature and reputation of the speakers. To
have Rossini speak was to invite pitiless scrutiny, for Rossini in 1860 had
been the reigning wit of Paris. The sparkling quips of this Italian expatriate
were the constant delight of Europe. Some of this flavorsome quality
would have to come through Michotte's dialogue to give it an air of
validity. And Wagner! Here was the storm center of a new school of
opera, a man painstakingly, passionately seeking to be understood by way
of an avalanche of words. Wagner speaking for himself would have to
bear comparison with Wagner the voluminous self-apologist. Plainly,
Michotte could make himself absurd by reproducing conversation which
failed to live up to expectations.

What further complicated—and perhaps dramatized—Michotte's decision was that Wagner and Rossini had met only once. That meeting,
moreover, had given rise to vast speculation as to the subjects discussed.
Wagner had to some extent revealed its content in his own autobio-
graphical writings and in a respectful magazine article that appeared in
Augsburg some time after Rossini's death. Final confirmation of the

362

meeting came with the publication of Wagner's Mein Leben, in 1911. To be sure, Michotte is not mentioned as the man who had brought them together. Yet even Wagner's most searching biographer, Ernest Newman, avers that Wagner's own two accounts of the interview "agree in essence with that of Michotte." In fact, the astute Mr. Newman has seen no reason for rejecting Michotte's record as a willful fabrication. "All in all," he concludes in the third volume of his Life of Richard Wagner (Knopf, 1941), "when full allowance has been made for Michotte's mistakes and embroideries, there seems little reason to doubt that he was present at the interview and that the talk was substantially as he represents it to have been."

If we are to take him at his word, Michotte was in an enviable position as regards both composers. He had met them both and admired them equally. While he never wearied of hymning the praises of Wagner's "music of the future," he was no less valiant in expounding the merits of Rossini in the vanguard circles of Paris. It would thus seem that history had chosen an ideal intermediary for the first and last encounter of the two most famous musical exiles of the Paris of 1860. Moreover, the contrast appealed strongly to the journalist Michotte. On the one hand, an Italian whose career as opera composer had long ended and who now dominated the Parisian scene as dean and bon vivant; on the other, a German whose strange new music was whipping up a storm of abuse, yet who was struggling with an unquenchable idealism to make himself heard as the bearer of new operatic tidings. For Rossini creative activity had come to an end. Secure in his fame and finances, he could look back on his succession of triumphs as he might on the work of another man. But Wagner was still fighting, one might say, for his life and his music. Recognition, such as it was, came from embattled little cliques and a few generous-minded celebrities like Franz Liszt. The conquest of the public was still in the future. And the shadow of elementary economic need was always at Wagner's heels. Yet he never doubted that his day was near. Tristan und Isolde was a finished product, the Ring des Nibelungen was by way of completion, and at the moment he was editing a French version of Tannhäuser for the Paris stage.

For Michotte a great obstacle in the way of arranging the meeting was the malicious newspaper campaign raging against Wagner. Many of the most vicious jokes were publicly attributed to Rossini. There was, for example, the anecdote of how Rossini once invited his friend, Carafa, a staunch Wagnerian, to dine with him. Rossini, whose cuisine was the talk of Paris, served his friend fish-sauce without fish. When Carafa protested, Rossini impishly replied, "Sauce without fish is the right thing for any man who likes music without melody." Rossini wrote an angry protest to the newspaper which had attributed this mauvaise blague to him. Actually, the march from Tannhäuser was all that Rossini knew of Wagner's music. And that he happened to like. "For the rest," remarks Newman, "he had too much respect for an artist who was trying to enlarge the scope of his art to permit himself jests at his expense." Michotte's job was to assure Wagner that Rossini was utterly blameless, that he was above such petty tactics, and that he would be enchanted to receive his younger colleague. Wagner was persuaded. Unfortunately, after the meeting the campaign of vilification sharpened in the press. Rossini's name was again affixed to some waspish remarks, and Wagner, despite the intercession of Liszt, refused to see the Italian composer again. "The explanation of it all," ventures Newman, "probably is that in that hotbed of envy, hatred, malice and of uncharitableness he felt it useless to struggle against the powers of evil." Newman imputes the full blame to the work of "journalistic gangsters."

Suppose we follow Michotte on his little journey of preparation for that greatest of all days in his life. He begins by visiting Wagner in his modest quarters at No. 16 Rue Newton, near the Barrière de l'Étoile. Outside, one can see the Bois de Boulogne, where Wagner is in the habit of taking a daily stroll with his little dog. The young Frenchman pays his respects to Minna Wagner, whom he finds very "simple and self-effacing," and then makes his arrangements with her husband. Wagner agrees to come to Michotte's chambers two days later in the morning, and from there the two will continue to Rossini's. Michotte resumes his travels and presently arrives at a fashionable site on the corner of the Chaussée-d'Antin and the Boulevard des Italiens. There Rossini occupies a sumptuous apartment on the first floor of an attractive house. It is here that literary and artistic Paris comes to pay tribute to the aging Italian master and savor his good food, good wine, and good talk. Michotte makes his proposal. "But, of course," Rossini assures him. "I shall receive Monsieur Wagner with the greatest pleasure. . . . You know my hours. Bring him whenever you wish." Rossini pauses thoughtfully; then: "I hope you have told him that I am completely innocent of these stupidities which have been fathered upon me." Two days later Wagner knocks on Michotte's door, and the two walk the short distance to Rossini's house. . . .

(*Michotte and Wagner climb the stairs to Rossini's apartment.*)

MICHOTTE: If Rossini is in the mood, you'll be charmed with his conversation. It will be a real pleasure. Don't be surprised if during your talk with him you see me taking some notes.

WAGNER: For the newspapers?

MICHOTTE: Not at all. Strictly for my own personal souvenirs. If the maestro had the slightest suspicion I was going to give this to the press, he would scarcely open his mouth. In any case, he has complete faith in my discretion. He abominates any kind of publicity about his private life.

(Michotte and Wagner are announced to Rossini, who is having breakfast. They wait a few minutes in the large drawing-room. Wagner's attention is drawn to a portrait of Rossini, life-size, showing him in a large green cloak and red skull-cap.)

WAGNER: That lively face, that ironic mouth—that's the composer of "The Barber," all right. This portrait must date from the time Rossini was composing the opera.

MICHOTTE: Four years later. It was painted by Meyer in Naples in 1820.

WAGNER *(smiling)*: He was a handsome lad, and in that country of Vesuvius where women kindle easily, he must have been quite devastating.

MICHOTTE: Who knows—if, like Don Juan, he had had a good book-keeper like Leporello, he might have even exceeded the number "1003" entered in the notebook.

WAGNER: Now you're exaggerating! A "thousand" I'll concede, but three more besides, that's going too far!

(The butler enters to announce that Rossini is ready to receive them. Michotte and Wagner enter the corner of the apartment that Rossini has reserved for himself. The room is to one side of the dining-room. Four windows overlook the boulevard. There is a bed in one corner, a Pleyel piano in another. A desk and secretary complete the furnishings. It is here that Rossini receives all manner of visitors, from the "lowest beggars to crowned heads," as Michotte observes.)

ROSSINI *(the moment his visitors enter)*: Ah! Monsieur Wagner—like a new Orpheus you have no fear of crossing the redoubtable threshold. *(Without giving Wagner a chance to reply.)* I know that people have been blackening me to you. I am supposedly the author of all kinds of sarcastic gibes about you. I plead innocent. Besides, why should I behave that way? I am no Mozart or Beethoven. I certainly make no pretension of being a learned man. But I do pride myself on being polite and refraining from insulting a composer who I am told is striving to extend the boundaries of our art. These malicious people who take such a keen interest in my affairs should at least give me credit for common sense, if nothing more. As for having any contempt for your music—first, I should make myself acquainted with it. To become acquainted with it, I should hear it at the opera house. For it is only in the opera house—and not from a simple reading of the score —that it is possible to reach any fair conclusion about music that is intended for the theater. The one composition of yours that I know is the march from *Tannhäuser*. I heard it several times at Kissingen when I went there for a cure three years ago. It produced quite an effect, and I must confess quite frankly that for my part I found it very beautiful.

WAGNER (*with great deference*): Allow me to thank you, *maître*, for your kind words. They touch me deeply. They prove how great and noble your character is—something I have never doubted. But please be assured that even if you had uttered some severe judgments about me, I would not have taken offense. I am quite aware that my music is often misunderstood. With the best will in the world, the judges can go wrong in appraising such a vast system of new ideas. That's why I am so anxious to see my operas performed as perfectly as possible. That would be the logical and complete demonstration of my theories.

ROSSINI: That's only fair, for actions speak louder than words.

WAGNER: To begin with, all my efforts are now concentrated on getting a performance of *Tannhäuser*. I had Carvalho listen to it recently. He was quite impressed and seemed prepared to risk producing it. But nothing has been decided yet. Unfortunately, a hostile campaign in the press is now threatening to become a very serious cabal against me. There is always the danger that Carvalho * may yield to this pressure.

ROSSINI (*aroused by the word "cabal"*): What composer hasn't been exposed to cabals, beginning with the great Gluck himself? Believe me, I was by no means spared myself. There was the night of the première of "The Barber," to cite one instance. According to the practice of the time in Italy, whenever *opera buffa* was given, I sat at the clavicembalo accompanying the recitatives. I had to protect myself against the threats of an audience that had gone completely wild. I thought they were going to kill me. Even here in Paris—when I arrived for the first time in 1824 on an invitation from the director of the Italian theater, I was greeted by the nickname of Monsieur Hulla-baloo.† The name stuck. And it certainly was not by pure coincidence that certain circles of the press and music turned their guns on me. They were joined in a common accord—*accord aussi parfait qui*

---

* *Tannhäuser* was finally produced in Paris on March 13, 1861.
† "Monsieur Vacarmini."

majeur.* Nor was it any different in Vienna, when I came there to produce my opera *Zelmira* in 1822. Weber had already been writing some excoriating articles about me. After my opera was produced at the court Italian Theater, he hounded me relentlessly.

WAGNER: Oh, I know how intolerant Weber could be! He was quite intractable from the moment the defense of German art became an issue. It was pardonable. I gather you quite naturally had nothing to do with him while you were in Vienna . . .? A great genius and dying so prematurely! . . .

ROSSINI: A great genius, certainly—and a true one, because as a powerful creator, he imitated no one. . . . You're right, I had no dealings with him in Vienna. But let me tell you how I happened to see him later in Paris, a few days before he left for England. Shortly after he arrived he paid his respects to the composers then in the public eye—Cherubini, Hérold, Boïeldieu. He even called to me. Not having been forewarned of his visit, I must admit that I was prey to much the same emotion I had earlier felt in the presence of Beethoven. He was very pale and panting from climbing up my stairs. He was already a very sick man. The moment he saw me the poor fellow felt it necessary to tell me that he had been very harsh to me in his musical criticism. His embarrassment was only heightened by his struggle with the French language. I did not let him finish. "Look here," I said. "Let's not talk about that. Besides," I added, "I never even saw your reviews. I don't know German. The only words of your devilish language that I as an Italian have been able to retain and pronounce after heroic application are '*Ich bin zufrieden.*'† I was quite proud of them," I said, "and in Vienna I made good use of them, with great impartiality, on any and all occasions, public and private, especially public. They procured me the good will of the Viennese, who pass for the most amiable of the Germanic peoples. And especially among the beautiful ladies of Vienna I earned a reputation for consummate urbanity—." "*Ich bin zufrieden!*" These words made Weber smile and put him immediately at his ease. "Moreover," I continued, "in discussing my operas at all, you really did me a greater honor than I deserved—I who am such a small thing beside the geniuses of your country. So I'm going to ask you to let me embrace you. And, believe me, if my friendship has any value in your eyes, I offer it to you completely and with all my heart." I embraced him warmly and I saw a tear appear in his eyes.

---

* Untranslatable pun: "Accord [or harmony] as perfect as a major chord."
† "I'm satisfied."

WAGNER: I believe he was already afflicted with tuberculosis then and he died of it shortly after.

ROSSINI: That's quite right. He struck me as in a pitiful condition at the time. He was very thin, his complexion was livid, and he had the dry cough of people suffering from lung ailments. Then, he limped. It was painful to see him. A few days later he came to see me again with a request for some recommendations for London, where he was going. I was depressed at the thought of his undertaking such a trip. I tried very hard to dissuade him, telling him he was committing a crime—suicide. It was useless. "I know," he replied. "I shall die there—but I've got to go. I must be there to produce *Oberon*. My contract calls for it. I've just got to go!" I had made some important ties in England during my stay there, and among the letters I gave Weber was one to King George, who happened to be very partial to artists and had been particularly affable with me. With a heavy heart I embraced this great genius once more, with a presentiment that I would never see him again. It was only too true. *Povero* Weber! . . . But we were talking about cabals. This is how I feel about them: There is only one way to fight them—passive silence. It's far more effective, believe me, than a furious rebuttal. Malice is legion. No one who wants to fight this sow ever manages to strike the last blow. I say, the devil take such sneak attacks! The more they rail at me, the more I reply with *roulades*. I rebuff their name-calling with *triolets*. I oppose my pizzicati to their buffooneries. And I swear to you that all the hubbub raised against my music by those who don't like it hasn't made me fire back at them one bass-drum broadside less in my crescendos, nor prevented me, when it suited my purpose, from horrifying them with one *felicità* the more in my finales. If you observe me wearing a wig, please rest assured that it wasn't this scum that caused me to lose a single hair of my head.

WAGNER (*trying not to laugh*): Oh, when it comes to that, Maestro, thanks to what you had in there (*touching his temple*), wasn't your passive silence really a powerful force backed by the public's acclaim? Actually one should pity the fools who dared hurl themselves against this power. . . . Incidentally, didn't you say a moment ago that you knew Beethoven?

ROSSINI: Quite so—in Vienna. It was in 1822, during the time I remarked that my opera *Zelmira* was being produced there. I had already heard some quartets of Beethoven in Milan—I don't have to tell you with what delight! I also knew some of his piano music. In Vienna I heard the "Eroica" Symphony for the first time. That music bowled me over.

From that moment I had only one thought—to meet the great master, to see him, even just once. I consulted Salieri about this. I knew that he was in contact with Beethoven.

WAGNER: Salieri, the composer of *Danaides?*

ROSSINI: The same. He had made quite a name for himself in Vienna as a result of the success of many of his operas at the Italian Theater. He told me that he often saw Beethoven, but assured me that because of his violent and suspicious character, my request was not easy to satisfy. Parenthetically, this same Salieri had also been closely associated with Mozart. After Mozart's death, he was suspected and even seriously accused of having killed him with a slow poison out of professional jealousy.

WAGNER: In my time that rumor still persisted in Vienna.

ROSSINI: I had some fun one day when I told Salieri, in jest of course,— "It is lucky for Beethoven that his instinct for self-preservation prevents his having you to dinner. You might dispatch him to the next world the way you did Mozart." "So I have the air of a poisoner?" replied Salieri. "Oh, no," I answered. "You have the air of an arrant blackguard!" I might add the poor devil seemed very little bothered by being taken for Mozart's murderer. What he could not endure was the remark of a Viennese journalist, a champion of German opera who had little love for Italian opera and Salieri in particular. Said the journalist: "Contrary to the *Danaides* story, Salieri had emptied his cask with very little effort, for there never was anything to speak of in it." This had quite a harrowing effect on Salieri. To return to Beethoven— Salieri, to satisfy my desire, did render me a service. He decided that the best way to approach him would be through the Italian poet Carpani, who was *persona grata* with Beethoven. Carpani agreed and persisted till Beethoven consented to receive me. Need I confess that in mounting the stairs to the modest lodgings of this great man I had some difficulty in controlling my emotions? When the door opened I found myself in a dirty, dingy hovel. The place was in a frightful mess. I especially remember the ceiling, which was right under the roof. It was all lined with huge cracks through which the rain must have poured in torrents. The portraits we know of Beethoven quite faithfully convey the features of his face. But what no painter could express was the indefinable sadness spread over his features. Beneath thick eyebrows his eyes glittered as from the depths of caverns. Though small, they seemed to pierce through you. His voice was sweet and perhaps a little veiled. When we entered, without paying any attention to us, he remained for some moments bent over some music proofs which he had just corrected. Then, raising his head, he said brusquely to me, in fairly good Italian, "Ah, Rossini—so it's you, the composer of *The Barber of Seville*! My congratulations! It's an excellent *opera buffa*. I read it with great pleasure. So long as Italian opera lives, 'The Barber' will be performed. Don't ever try to do anything but *opera buffa*. It would be going against your destiny to attempt to succeed in any other genre." Here Carpani, who was with me, interrupted—in writing and in German, of course—since it was not possible to carry on a conversation with Beethoven in any other way. He said: "Maestro Rossini has already composed numerous serious operas— *Tancredi, Otello, Moïse.* I sent them to you not so long ago, advising you to look them over." "To be sure, I have run through them," replied Beethoven. "Look here, serious opera is not for the Italians. They don't have sufficient musical knowledge to handle true drama. And how could they acquire such knowledge in Italy? . . ."

WAGNER: That blow of the lion's claw would scarcely have assuaged Salieri's *Consternation* if he had been present. . . .

ROSSINI: It certainly would not! I related the whole thing to Salieri later. He bit his lips . . . without hurting himself too much, I suppose. For, as I said before, he was so contemptible that no doubt in the next world the King of Hell, to spare himself the embarrassment of roasting such a worm, must have ordered the job done elsewhere! . . . But let's come back to Beethoven. "Nobody can equal you in *opera buffa*," he continued. "Your language and your temperament have destined you for it. Look at Cimarosa. How far superior to the rest are the comic passages of his operas! The same thing is true of Pergolesi. I know you Italians make a great deal of his religious music. I admit that there's a very touching feeling in the 'stabat.' But the form lacks variety. The effect is monotonous. On the other hand, his *Serva Padrona* . . ."

WAGNER (*interrupting*): Fortunately you did not follow Beethoven's advice, Maestro. . . .

ROSSINI: To tell you the truth, I did feel a greater aptitude for *opera buffa*. I was more eager to handle comic subjects than serious ones. But I scarcely had any choice in my librettos, which were imposed upon me by impresarios. How often it happened that I would receive the libretto piecemeal! Sometimes one act at the time. And I was supposed to write the music without knowing either what followed or how the story ended! Remember, I was obliged to support my mother, father, and grandmother. Roaming about from city to city like a nomad, I wrote three or four operas a year. And let me assure you that my income hardly permitted me to play the *grand seigneur*. I received a flat sum of twelve hundred francs for "The Barber," plus a chestnut-colored suit with gold buttons, which the impresario gave me as a gift to make me look presentable while conducting the opera. It is very possible that suit was worth a hundred francs. Total, thirteen hundred francs. It took me only thirteen days to complete "The Barber." That meant I was being paid a hundred francs a day. So you see (*smiling*) I was actually earning a big salary. It made me feel quite proud to think that my father when he was employed as trumpet-player in Pesaro never earned more than two and a half francs a day.

WAGNER: Thirteen days! That certainly is a unique accomplishment! But I can't help marvelling how under such conditions, forced to live that kind of Bohemian life, you were still able to write such music as *Otello* and *Moïse*, music which bears the mark not of improvisation but of carefully thought-out work and complete concentration of brain power. . . .

ROSSINI: Oh, I had facility . . . and plenty of instinct. Naturally my musical training had not been very profound. Lacking that—and where would I have acquired it in Italy?—the little I learned I found in German scores. A musical amateur in Bologna possessed a few—*The Creation* was one, *The Marriage of Figaro*, *The Magic Flute*. He lent them to me, and since at fifteen I did not have the money to order them from Germany, I copied them avidly. Often I would only transcribe the vocal part, without looking at the orchestral accompaniment. On a loose sheet I would then write in my own accompaniment. This I would compare with Haydn's or Mozart's accompaniment. After which I would finish my copy by adding theirs. This system of study taught me more than all the courses at the Lyceum of Bologna. Ah, if I had only been able to study in your country, I feel I would have produced something better than I have.

WAGNER: Surely not better than the "Darkness Scene" in *Moïse*, the "Conspiracy Scene" in *William Tell*, and of a somewhat different order the *Quando Corpus Movietur*—to cite only a few examples. . . .

ROSSINI: What you cite there I admit frankly are some happy quarters-of-an-hour in my career. But what are they beside the work of a Mozart or Haydn? I couldn't begin to tell you how much I admire the supple science and natural sureness in the writing of these masters. I have always envied them. But that must be mastered on school-benches, and then it takes a Mozart to turn it to account. As for Bach—there's an overwhelming genius! If Beethoven is a miracle of humanity, Bach is a miracle of God! I have subscribed to the great edition of his complete works. Wait a moment, there's the latest volume printed, right there on my table! And I'm not exaggerating when I say that the day the next volume arrives will be a day of incomparable joy for me. How I would like, before leaving this world, to hear a complete performance of his *Passion According to St. Matthew!* Of course here in France there's no point in hoping for one.

WAGNER: It was Mendelssohn who first introduced the *Passion* to the Germans in a magnificent performance which he conducted himself in Berlin.

ROSSINI: Mendelssohn! What a lovable nature that man had! I remember with great pleasure the wonderful hours I spent with him at Frankfort in 1836. I had come to Frankfort to attend a marriage in the Rothschild family. It was Ferdinand Hiller who introduced me to Mendelssohn. What a pleasure it was to hear him play the piano! Among other things he played a few of his own delightful *Songs Without Words*. Then he played some Weber for me, and then I asked him to play Bach, a great deal of Bach! Hiller had told me that nobody played Bach better than Mendelssohn. . . . Mendelssohn was quite taken aback by my request. "How can you, an Italian, love German music that much?" he asked me. "I love only German music," I replied, adding rather unceremoniously, "as for Italian music, I'm fed up with it!" He looked at me, bewildered. Which did not prevent him from playing several fugues and other pieces by the great Bach with admirable grace. Hiller later told me that after I left Mendelssohn recalled my sally to him and asked, "This Rossini, was he really serious? In any case, he certainly is a queer fish!"

WAGNER (*laughing heartily*): I can understand Mendelssohn's bewilderment, Maestro. . . . But may I ask you how your visit to Beethoven ended?

ROSSINI: Oh, it didn't last long. You can understand why, with one side of the conversation being conducted in writing. I made him understand how much I admired his genius and expressed my thanks for having been permitted to convey it in person. He replied with a profound sigh and one short phrase in Italian, "Oh! *un infelice!*"—"Oh —an unfortunate!" He paused a while and then asked me some questions about the opera houses of Italy, who the most celebrated singers were, whether Mozart's operas were frequently performed there, if I was satisfied with the Italian company of Vienna. Then, after wishing me a good performance and success for *Zelmira*, he rose and accompanied us to the door. Once more he said to me, "Above all, write more *Barbers of Seville*." While descending the ramshackle stairs, I was seized with such strong emotion in thinking how this great man was being neglected and abandoned that I could not restrain my tears. "Oh," said Carpani, "he prefers it that way. He's a peevish misanthrope and doesn't know how to keep a friend." That same evening, I attended a gala dinner at the house of Prince Metternich. Upset as I was by my visit to Beethoven and with that mournful *"un infelice"* still ringing in my ears, I could not help feeling confused by the flattering attention given me in this brilliant Viennese gathering. Without any ceremony, I shouted out what I thought of the way the court and aristocracy were behaving toward the greatest genius of our time, a genius about whom few seemed to trouble themselves and who was allowed to live in such distressful circumstances. They all replied the same way Carpani had. Nevertheless, I asked them if Beethoven's deafness shouldn't excite their pity, and if it was really charitable to use his idiosyncrasies as an excuse for not going to his aid. I added that such help would be very simple. A subscription could be raised among all the wealthy families of Vienna that without being very large would at least assure Beethoven enough income to keep him out of hardship. Not one person there agreed to my proposal. After dinner, the evening concluded with a reception which brought together the biggest names of Viennese society in Metternich's salon. There was even a concert. On the program was Beethoven's latest trio—it was always Beethoven, Beethoven everywhere, the way it used to be with Napoleon. The new masterpiece was listened to religiously and applauded with great enthusiasm. As I listened to it in such magnificent surroundings, I thought sadly how at that very moment, isolated in his dismal lodgings, that great man was perhaps working on still another masterpiece, another work of high inspiration destined, like the others, to regale with sublime beauty this same brilliant aristocracy from which he was excluded—an aristocracy enjoying his music but never troubling itself about the wretchedness of the man who had composed it. Despite my failure to procure an annuity for Beethoven, I did not lose heart. I tried next to raise the necessary funds to buy him a house. I managed to get some pledges for contributions. But when I added my own contributions to the others, the total proved too meager. So, it was necessary to give up this second project, too. The usual reaction was this: "You little know Beethoven. The day after he becomes the owner of a house, he will sell it. He can never stay for long in one place. He feels the need to change his apartment every six months and his housekeeper every six weeks. . . . But enough about me and the others, who belong to the Past and even the Dead Past. Let's discuss the Present now, if you don't mind, Monsieur Wagner, and, even better, the future. For I notice that your name is invariably linked to that word in all the talk about you. Please don't suspect me of the slightest malicious intent. Now, first of all, tell me, are you definitely settled in Paris? And about your opera *Tannhäuser*. I feel certain you will succeed in having it performed. There has been so much noise about it that the Parisians are now dying of curiosity to hear it.

WAGNER: It's not quite finished yet. I'm working at it furiously with a collaborator who is not only very capable, but what is more important, very patient, too. For the difficulty is this—to make the musical expression perfectly understandable, it is necessary to identify, so to speak, each French word with the corresponding German word under the same notation. It's a frightful job and difficult of realization.

ROSSINI: But why don't you follow the example of Gluck, Spontini, and Meyerbeer and work from the start with a French libretto? Surely you now know the taste that prevails here and the special temperament of the French for the things of the theater. It is inherent in the French spirit. I went through all this myself when I left Italy and gave up my Italian career to come to live and work in Paris.

WAGNER: In my case, Maestro, that would be out of the question. After *Tannhäuser*, I wrote *Lohengrin* and then *Tristan und Isolde*. From both the literary and musical standpoint, these three operas present a logical evolution in my concept of the absolute and definitive form of lyric drama. My style shows the inevitable effects of this gradation. And if it is true that I still see the possibility of writing other operas in the style of *Tristan*, I must confess myself absolutely incapable of returning to the style of *Tannhäuser*. So, if I decided to compose an opera for Paris on a French libretto, I could not and should not follow any other path than that which led me to write *Tristan*. The result would be that a work like *Tristan*, including such a dramatic disturbance of the usual forms of opera, would unquestionably be misunderstood and, things being what they are, the French would not accept it.

ROSSINI: Now tell me, Monsieur Wagner, what exactly was your point of departure in these reforms?

WAGNER: At the outset they were not developed as a system. I felt very strong doubts after my first attempt. I was not satisfied. Actually it was in the poetic rather than the musical conception that the idea of these reforms first took shape in my mind. In other words, my first efforts had a primarily literary purpose. Then, when I began seeking ways of enriching the meaning through deep musical expression, I found myself in a strange dilemma. I realized now how the freedom of my thought in an ideal domain was restricted when confronted with the formal demands of music drama. I mean those *arie di bravura*, those insipid duets fashioned on the same deadly model, and all those other *hors-d'oeuvres* which interrupted the scenic action for no reason at all. And then those septets! For every respectable opera had to have its solemn septet in which all the main characters of the opera would abandon their roles and step up to the footlights together—all reconciled—and declaim their harmony (and my God, what harmony at times!) in one of those mawkish sermons.

ROSSINI (*interrupting*): Do you know what we used to call that in Italy: "the parade of the artichokes." Yes, I, too, realized how perfectly ridiculous it was. It always made me think of a band of *facchini* * stepping forward to sing for a few coins. But what could you do? It was the custom of the time, a concession made to the public—otherwise they would have thrown baked apples at us, and maybe not even baked.

WAGNER (*continuing, without giving much attention to Rossini's interruption*): And as for the orchestra . . . those routine accompaniments, wholly lacking in color, continually repeating the same formulas without regard to the diversity of character and situation. In a word, all that *musique de concert*, alien to the action, having no excuse for being there except convention—music which often mars even the very best operas. It all seemed to me so contrary to good sense and so incompatible with the high mission of a noble art worthy of the name.

ROSSINI: Among other things you just referred to the *aria di bravura*. You complain! It was my nightmare! Think of satisfying the *prima donna*, the *primo tenore* and the *primo basso* all at the same time! Some of the popinjays even went to the trouble of counting the number of measures in their aria and then coming to tell me that they would not sing because another member of the cast was given an aria that contained more measures than theirs. And when it wasn't the number of measures, it was trills and *grupetti* and so on.

WAGNER (*gaily*): That was taking one's measure with a vengeance! All the composer needed was a meter † to measure his music by!

ROSSINI: Yes, you might say an *ariameter*! Those people were quite ruthless, now that I think of it. It was they and only they that caused me to become bald at an early age—from making my head sweat so much. But let's go on with our discussion. . . . To be sure, there's no reply to the point you raise—provided the only thing to consider is the ra-

---

* Street-porters.
† Untranslatable pun here on "*mètre à musique*"—"*maître de musique*."

tional, rapid, and orderly development of the dramatic action. However, how are you going to maintain this independence of the literary conception, when you join it with musical form, which is all *convention*? You used the word yourself. If you're going to insist on absolute logic, it goes without saying that people don't sing when they talk. An angry man doesn't sing; a conspirator, a jealous man doesn't sing. (*Gaily.*) A single exception may be allowed, perhaps, for lovers, who may be regarded as making cooing sounds. To go still further—does anybody go to his death singing? That's opera for you—*convention* from one end to the other. And how about the orchestration itself? While an orchestra is raging full blast, who can tell precisely whether what is being described is a storm, a riot, or a fire? Again and always —*convention*!

WAGNER: Granted, Maestro, that *convention* does operate on a vast scale —otherwise we would have to abolish lyric drama and even musical comedy. Still, it cannot be disputed that this *convention*, having been raised to the status of artistic form, should be so understood as to prevent its degenerating into excess and absurdity. It is that sort of abuse against which I have rebelled. But people have deliberately distorted my aims. Haven't they represented me as some arrogant upstart who makes disparaging remarks about Mozart?

ROSSINI (*with some humor*): Mozart—*l'angelo della musica*. But who would dare commit the sacrilege of laying a finger on Mozart?

WAGNER: I have been accused of repudiating practically the whole opera repertory, with some scant exceptions like Gluck and Weber. People persist, no doubt from having already committed themselves, in refusing to understand any of my writings. But why? I am far from denying the charm—as pure music—of many admirable pages of the truly great operas. But I am against having this music condemned to playing a servile role in some piece of light entertainment and I am opposed to its becoming the slave of routine or being used for strictly sensuous purposes without regard to the dramatic action. It is against such a role that I have revolted and wish to react. To my thinking, an opera, because of its complex nature, is a kind of organism in which is concentrated the perfect union of all the arts that form part of it—the art of poetry, the art of music, the art of decoration, and *plastique*. Doesn't it debase the mission of the composer to force upon him the role of mere instrumental illustrator of some libretto or other which prescribes in advance the number of arias, duets, ensembles, in a word, of *morceaux*—(which literally means things cut up into little bits)— that he has to translate into so many notes? Indeed, very much like a painter who adds colors to black engravings. To be sure, a great many composers have been inspired by a gripping dramatic scene and written immortal pages. But how many other pages of their score have suffered because of the vicious system I have just described. Thus, no real music drama can exist so long as these bad practices remain, so long as a complete mutual penetration is lacking between the music and the text, and so long as we fail to sense that *double conception* founded on a single thought from the very outset.

ROSSINI: That is to say, if I follow you, the composer should be his own librettist if he is to realize your ideal. That would seem to me, for many reasons, an almost unattainable condition.

WAGNER (*quite excited*): But why should it? What prevents a composer from studying literature, history, and mythology at the same time that he studies counterpoint? Such studies would lead him instinctively to fasten on those themes of poetry and tragedy best suited to his temperament. And even if he should lack the ability or experience to work out the dramatic intrigue himself, he certainly would know better where to find the playwright with whom he could collaborate in close sympathy. Besides, there are very few dramatic composers who have not revealed, at some time or other, a truly remarkable literary and poetic instinct. Often they have gone so far as to make drastic alterations in the text or sequence of scenes, to suit themselves. They instinctively grasped a scene better than their librettist. Not to look any further, let's take the example of the "Conspiracy Scene" in your own *William Tell*. You can't tell me that you followed, word for word, the text furnished you by your collaborators! I wouldn't believe it! Anybody examining it closely would soon discover effects of dynamics and declamation bearing the true imprint of what I might call "the musicality of spontaneous inspiration." I personally refuse to believe that they appeared that way in the sketch of the text which you had before you. A librettist, no matter what his ability, could not possibly know, especially in scenes full of ensemble complications, how to plan a distribution best suited to the composer in his efforts to achieve the musical fresco fashioned in his imagination.

ROSSINI: What you say is very true. As a matter of fact, that particular scene was considerably modified on my instructions, and not without difficulty. I composed *William Tell* at the countryplace of my friend Aquado. I spent a whole summer there, and I was cut off completely from my librettist. As it happened, it was Armand Marvast and Crémieux who came to my aid. Parenthetically, these two men became actual conspirators themselves, against the regime of Louis-Philippe.

Marvast and Crémieux were also vacationing at Aquado's and both helped me make the necessary changes of text and versification to best "hatch the plot" against Gessler of my own conspirators.

WAGNER: Your experience bears out by implication what I have been trying to say. It would only require an extension of the same principle to prove that my ideas are by no means as inconsistent and impossible of realization as they might appear at first sight. I am convinced that through sheer inevitable logic and by a natural and perhaps slow evolution, there will be born not that "music of the future" which people persist in saying that I would pretend to achieve single-handed, but that "future of the music drama," in which the whole trend will play a part and from which a new and fecund orientation will arise in the minds of composers, singers and public.

ROSSINI: In short, a complete revolution! And do you really believe that the singers or the public, dazzled by all the old tricks of the game, would submit meekly to such a transformation of long-accepted practice? Singers who have been accustomed to showing off their virtuosity and who would now be asked to substitute for their brilliant exhibitions a sort of, yes, I can guess pretty well, declamatory chant? I doubt it very much.

WAGNER: I admit that a long period of education would be needed. But that could be done easily enough. As for the public, who does the educating? Does the public educate the composer, or the composer the public? Allow me to state one more thesis, of which I find you a brilliant example. Wasn't it really your thoroughly personal style that made Italy forget all your predecessors and won you an unprecedented popularity in an incredibly short time? And isn't it true that your influence became universal? With regard to the singers, who you say would offer great resistance, I feel they could only gain by submitting to a change which in the last analysis would ennoble them as artists. Once they perceive that lyric drama will no longer offer them a facile means of success through strong lungs or a charming voice, they will come to understand that the art of music has assigned them a higher mission. Forced to give up confining themselves within the strictly personal limits of their role, they will identify themselves with the philosophic and esthetic spirit dominating the work. They will live, if I may so express it, in an atmosphere where, everything being a part of everything else, nothing can be secondary. Moreover, once they have learned to do without the short-lived success of a facile brilliance, once freed from the torture of holding their voices on insipid words and banal rhymes—the singers will readily see the chances of surrounding their names with a more lasting and artistic glory. Think how their psychological mastery of the role will be complete when they once have grasped its *raison d'être* in the dramatic scheme; when they have studied the ideas, customs, and character of the period in which the action unfolds, when they have added a faultless diction to a splendid declamation, noble and true in style.

ROSSINI: From the standpoint of pure art, those are certainly broad views and dazzling perspectives. But from the standpoint of strictly musical form, it is as I said before, a fatal trend toward declamatory chanting —"The funeral oration of the art of melody." Otherwise how could one possibly adjust the emotional pitch, so to speak, of each syllable of the text, to melodic form, which derives its special physiognomy from a precise rhythm and a symmetrical distribution of the units that constitute it?

WAGNER: I admit, Maestro, that a system pushed to such extremes would prove intolerable. But my aim, if you follow me, is not to discard melody, but on the contrary, to restore it in all its fullness. Isn't melody the final flowering of every musical entity? Without melody nothing can exist. However, let's be clear about this. My idea is to restore it beyond the narrow restrictions which force it into symmetrical periods, inflexible rhythms, prefixed harmonies and prescribed cadences. What I seek is a free melody, without shackles, and completely independent. A melody that can adapt itself not only to every special contour of character to the point where no role can be confused with any other, but one that can specify any definite fact or episode in the dramatic fabric. A melody, to be sure, of a certain precision, which by pliant application to the sense of the text can be restrained or extended according to the special effects sought by the composer.

ROSSINI (*interrupting*): A fighting melody!

WAGNER (*disregarding the interruption*): You yourself, Maestro, have given a sublime example of the kind of melody I have in mind. It is in the big scene of *William Tell*, where a sort of free song, accenting every word and sustained by the panting phrases of the 'cellos, reaches the highest summits of lyric expression.

ROSSINI: In other words I was writing the "music of the future" without knowing it!

WAGNER: What you wrote there, Maestro, was the music of all time, and that is the best there is.

ROSSINI: I must confesss to you that the feeling that has most moved me in life has been my love for my mother and father, a love I am happy to say, which they repaid with interest. It was there, I believe, that I found the note needed for the scene of the apple in *William Tell*. But one more question, Monsieur Wagner. How do you reconcile the simultaneous use of two or more voices with your system? To be perfectly logical you would have to prohibit them. . . .

WAGNER: Yes, it would, as a matter of cold logic, be necessary to model the musical dialogue on the spoken dialogue and restrict the characters to singing only in turn. On the other hand, it must be admitted that two different persons, at a given moment, may find themselves in the same emotional state, sharing a common feeling and thus joining their voices to identify themselves in a single thought. So with a large group of people. If they are animated by conflicting feelings, they may quite conceivably express them all at once, though each member of the group will do it his own way. Do you see now, Maestro, what infinite resources this system offers the composer of applying to each character and situation a specific melodic formula, which, while keeping its original character, lends itself freely to the broad currents and developments of the action? And take the ensembles. There each of the characters appears in his own individuality; yet all these different elements combine in a polyphony suited to the action. I repeat: such ensembles will no longer afford us those absurd spectacles in which people gripped by the most antagonistic passions are condemned at some given moment, without rhyme or reason, to unite their voices in a sort of *Largo d'apothéose*, where the patriarchal harmonies remind us that "*One cannot be happier than in the bosom of his family*." * As for the use of choruses—it's a psychological fact that large masses of people respond more energetically to a specific sensation than individuals. Sensations like terror, fury, pity. So it is logical to permit crowds to express these collective states in the language of opera without shocking common sense. Besides, the introduction of the chorus, assuming its logic in the situations of the plot, adds a powerful impact to the general dramatic effect. A hundred examples come to mind. Think of the strong impression of anguish aroused by the fiery chorus in *Idomeneo*—"Corriamo, fuggiamo!" Without forgetting, Maestro, that admirable fresco from your own *Moïse*—"Le choeur est desolé, des ténèbres. . . !"

ROSSINI (*slapping his forehead in mock amazement*): What, again? There is no longer any doubt about it—I, too, had a great propensity for "the music of the future!" You make my mouth water! If I were not so old, I would begin all over again, and then let the *ancien régime* beware!

---

* "*On ne saurait être mieux qu'au sein de sa famille*"—a reference to the final chorus of Grétry's opera, *Lucille*.

WAGNER: Ah, Maestro, if you had only not thrown away your pen after *William Tell!* What a crime, and only thirty-seven! You don't realize yourself what you would have done with that brain of yours. You would have only begun. . . .

ROSSINI (*becoming serious again*): What do you expect? I had no children. If I had had, no doubt I would have gone on working. But to be perfectly honest, after having labored for fifteen years and composed in that so-called "lazy" period forty operas, I felt the need to rest and to go back to Bologna to live a tranquil life. Added to that, the Italian theaters, which already had left much to be desired during my career, had fallen into a state of complete decay. The art of singing had rapidly declined. It was all to be expected.

WAGNER: How do you account for that in a country boasting such a super-abundance of beautiful voices?

ROSSINI: I attribute it to the disappearance of the *castrati*. It is impossible to form any idea of the vocal charm and consummate virtuosity of these bravest of the brave. No doubt these gifts were a charitable compensation for their deficiencies in other matters. Moreover, the *castrati* became incomparable teachers. Instruction was usually entrusted to them in the schools attached to the churches and maintained at their expense. Some of these schools became famous. They were veritable academies of singing. Pupils flocked to them, and many of them frequently deserted the church choirs for a career in opera. But as a consequence of the new political regime installed by my rebellious compatriots, these schools were suppressed and replaced by "conservatories," where as far as the fine tradition of *bel canto* is concerned, they "conserve" nothing at all. As for the *castrati*, they vanished, and the practice of making new ones was abolished. There you have the cause of the irreparable decay of the art of singing. As a consequence, *opera buffa* was set adrift. And serious opera? The public, which in my time was already little disposed to rise to the level of great art, no longer showed any interest in this form of entertainment. The announcement of a serious opera on the billboards merely drew some plethoric spectators whose only desire was to breathe in some cool air away from the mob. So now you understand why I decided that the wisest thing for me to do was to shut up. I shut up, and so *finita la commedia*. (*Rossini rises and warmly squeezes Wagner's hands.*) *Mon cher* Monsieur Wagner, I don't know how to thank you for your visit and particularly for being kind enough to explain your ideas to me in such a clear and interesting way. I who don't compose any more, being instead at an age where one "decomposes" while waiting to be "redecomposed" once and for all, I am too old to turn my gaze toward the new horizons. But your ideas, whatever your detractors may say, are of a kind to make young men think. Of all the arts music is the one that, because of its ideal essence, is destined to undergo transformation. Such changes are limitless. Could one predict Beethoven, after Mozart? Weber, after Gluck? And certainly Beethoven and Weber aren't the end. Everyone should try, if not to go forward, at least to seek something new. Not like a certain Hercules, a great traveller I'm told, who, having arrived at a place from which he could no longer see clearly ahead, planted his column and then retraced his steps.

WAGNER: That might have been intended as a warning of private hunting grounds to prevent others from going any farther.

ROSSINI: *Chi lo sa?* Who knows? You're doubtless right, for history assures us that Hercules showed a gallant preference for lion-hunting. In any case, let's hope that no such erecter of columns will ever place any limits on our art. For my part, I belong to my time. It is up to you others, and especially you, with all your splendid vigor and vision, to make something new and succeed. I wish you that with all my heart.

(*Rossini accompanies Wagner and Michotte through the adjoining dining-room. On the way he stops before an exquisitely inlaid mechanical organ made in Florence in the seventeenth century.*)

ROSSINI (*to Wagner*): Wait a moment! This little organ is going to make you hear some old airs of my country. They may interest you.

(*Rossini releases a spring and immediately the instrument begins to play its whole repertory, with its archaic flageolet sounds. The pieces are all little folk tunes.*)

ROSSINI: What do you say to that? There's the past for you, the truly dead past! It is simple and naïve. Who was its unknown maker? Some fiddler or other, no doubt. It dates far back and it lives forever! Will as much of us survive a hundred years from now?

(*Wagner and Michotte take their leave of Rossini.*)

WAGNER (*while descending the stairs, to Michotte*): I must admit I hardly expected to find in Rossini the simple, natural, and serious-minded man we just met. He seemed inclined to interest himself in every point that came up in our short conversation. Naturally, I couldn't expound in a few words all my ideas about the necessary development of lyric drama toward a new destiny. I confined myself to a few general remarks and some practical details to give him the general drift of my theories. You would have supposed that such a man would have found my statements extravagant, given the systematic spirit that prevailed in his time and of which he necessarily still carries some traces. Like Mozart, he possessed in the highest degree the gift of melodic invention. He had, too, a marvellous instinct for the theater and dramatic expression. What might he not have done if he had received a thorough musical education, and if, had he been less Italian and less skeptical, he had felt the religion of his art within him. There is no doubt that he would have reached the highest peaks. In a word, he is a genius gone astray from lack of good preparation and from not having found the *milieu* for which his high creative faculties had designed him. Still, I must say this much for him: of all the musicians I have met in Paris, Rossini is the only truly great one.

(*Wagner and Michotte separate, Michotte hastening home to "put in order the notes I had taken during the conversation of these two celebrities."*)

Lincoln

A NEW ENGLAND MOTHER PLEADS WITH A PRESIDENT
FOR THE LIFE OF HER SON OVER A WAR
SECRETARY'S PROTEST.

Don't be in such a hurry, Stanton; listen to
any woman speaking for her son's life

O NE OF the grimmest aspects of the Civil War—as it is perhaps of any
war—was desertion. As the war dragged on into the bloody cam-
paigns of 1864, those who deserted the ranks increased in number. Moreover, "bounty-jumping" had grown into a lucrative practice. A clause in
the draft permitted a man to pay someone else to serve his country for
him. The quoted price of such substitutions fluctuated daily in the open
market. Unscrupulous men would join up only to receive the "bounty"
and promptly skip town to pocket a second cash payment elsewhere. In
his epic work on Lincoln,* Carl Sandburg gives the instance of one man
who confessed to having jumped bounty thirty-two times. As a rule such
actions brought penitentiary sentences rather than the firing squad. Yet,
so strong was the stigma that even actual deserters in uniform resented
the charge of "bounty jumping." A special shame evidently attached to
that ubiquitous species. Thus, we can readily sympathize with Mrs. Putnam, the mother pleading for her condemned boy in the following dialogue, when she cries out to War Secretary Stanton: "He is no sneaking
bounty jumper! If so, I would say: 'Execute him, he is not of my blood;
though I bore him, he is not my son!' "

Mrs. Putnam was only one of hundreds of mothers of actual or suspected deserters who hastened to Washington to beg either Stanton or
President Lincoln to intercede for their condemned sons. Mostly they
came to see Lincoln, whose reputation for tempering justice with mercy
was the last hope of the offender's kin. For hours Lincoln would pore
over court transcripts searching for the loophole that would permit one
more pardon. "Let him fight instead of shooting him," he commented

* Abraham Lincoln: The War Years, by Carl Sandburg, Volume III, Harcourt, Brace
& Co., 1939.

after reading one such document. About a certain offender he "doubted if it would make any one man better to shoot him." After scanning three pages of a mound of adverse testimony in the case of another death sentence, Lincoln remarked to a Senator who had just entered his office: "The boy said that when first arrested he was going home to see his mother. I don't think I can allow a boy to be shot who tried to go home to see his mother." When a Congressman awoke him at midnight on the plea that a man to be shot the following morning was an old neighbor of his, Lincoln replied: "Well, I don't think shooting will do him any good. Give me that pen." And once again, "What possible injury can this lad work upon the cause of the great Union?"

Those who came to plead in person naturally had a still better chance. And just as naturally Lincoln, besieged by an inhuman burden of cares, could not see them all. Sandburg has stated that in one year alone army courts-martial were handling 30,000 cases of military offenders. Yet, the mothers and wives who reached Lincoln through the various lines of defense at the White House always found a patient and sympathetic listener. Often they came after a curt rebuff from Secretary Stanton, and in some cases it was a matter of a few days or a few hours before execution. Mothers, sisters, wives, frequently trailing children, beleaguered the care-worn President with their prayers to intercede. Lincoln scarcely relished the ordeal, but his heart went out to all; all, that is, except the obvious frauds. Even less did Secretary Stanton relish what was happening. Again and again this stern disciplinarian found his orders countermanded by a benign President. By one subterfuge or another, Lincoln would out-smart his War Secretary in the grim game of saving another young life. Stanton expressed his own verdict upon all such offenders: "Every man of them when caught or in hiding or asking for relief has some plausible excuse." Over his War Secretary's order of execution Lincoln once stated: "A private soldier has as much right to justice as a major general." The day was indeed a sad one for Lincoln when, despite every temptation to yield to a mother's pleas, he was forced by sheer necessity of discipline to let military law take its course.

As one reads the following account,* one can understand Secretary Stanton's position. This man's relation to Lincoln was curious. Before 1862 he had been his bitter political foe and, a Democrat himself, distrusted Lincoln as a Republican. Yet Lincoln had given him the war

---

* Put in dialogue form from an article by A. R. Cazauran, written in collaboration with Archibald Clavering Gunter for *Gunter's Magazine*, Feb. 1905; reprinted in *Lincoln Talks*, a Biography in Anecdote, collected, collated, and edited by Emanuel Hertz, The Viking Press, New York, 1939.

ministry, believing him the man best fitted in training and honesty for the assignment. Stanton had done a good job of cleaning out graft, galvanizing a staff of laggard generals into action and stepping up the department's efficiency. Lincoln's merciful humanitarianism jarred on his rigorous sense of discipline. Had there been no war, perhaps Stanton would not have minded so much. But the war to Stanton was a matter of iron control and strict adherence to army rule. The tragic desolation of it never weighed on this inflexible martinet as it did on the more sensitive Lincoln. For Stanton absolute severity could alone be counted on to prosecute the war to a successful finish. As we examine the period of Mrs. Putnam's visit to his office, his insistence on drastic observance of the rules seems less harsh.

In one month General Grant had lost 55,000 men in his efforts to take Richmond, and a short time before, on July 12, the fantastic Jubal A. Early and his daredevil army of 20,000 had been flung back at great cost from the very gates of Washington. A dismal defeat and humiliation had been averted at Fort Stevens by the quick arrival of reinforcements. As we learn in the dialogue that follows, Lincoln had himself watched the action from one of the fort's ramparts—his very first view of an actual battle—watched "with grave and passive countenance" as the bullets whizzed by and killed a soldier not three feet from where he stood. It was there, according to this anxious New England mother, that Private Charles Allen Putnam, of the Seventh Vermont, had fought and been wounded. It is even possible that as Private Putnam fell a shudder went through the lank, stooped figure observing the fighting from a high rampart of Fort Stevens.

A summer day in 1864. A. R. Cazauran, Lincoln's private stenographer, accompanies the President to the War Department to make notes on some confidential papers. As they arrive both notice a tall, gaunt woman sitting in the waiting room of Secretary Stanton's office. She is dressed plainly in an unpretentious calico gown and gazes around with frightened, anxious eyes.

LINCOLN (*whispering*): Find out who that woman is and what is the object of her visit.

(*Enters Stanton's office, escorted by Madison, Stanton's Negro attendant.*)

WOMAN (*to a passing orderly, in a whisper*): I must see Mr. Stanton at once.

ORDERLY: You will have to wait your turn, my good woman.

CAZAURAN (*beckoning her to one side, cautiously*): Perhaps, madam, if you will tell me your business, I can transmit it to some of the higher officials and so obtain for you an interview more rapidly than would be possible under other circumstances.

WOMAN (*with a grateful look, stammering*): My son is to—to be shot to-day by sentence of the court martial!"

CAZAURAN: May I have the details, madam?

WOMAN (*rapidly outlining the case, then sighing*): If Mr. Stanton could understand, he would not condemn, he would pardon him. (*Whispering indignantly.*) My boy is no bounty jumper! He risked his life in every engagement of the Army of the Potomac for two long years. (*Muttering piteously.*) He is all that is left to me. Speak to Mr. Stanton for me! Hurry! Executions nearly all take place in the forenoon. Hurry!

CAZAURAN: I will speak to one who may aid you. (*Steps up to Madison.*) Rap upon the door of the Secretary's private office.

MADISON: I dassent, sah.

CAZAURAN: You've got to. Mr. Lincoln directed me to make a report to him immediately of a certain matter. It is vital that he should hear it. The President will protect you from any reprimand for obeying his personal orders.

MADISON: Yas, but after Mass Lincoln has gone away, how 'bout dat?

CAZAURAN: Will you do a favor for Mr. Lincoln?

MADISON: Yas, sah.

CAZAURAN: Then I am sure he will regard your action in this matter as a personal obligation.

(*Madison approaches door to Secretary Stanton's private office. His fingers tremble as they rap on the inner portal.*)

STANTON (*sharply, from within the office*): Damn you, come in!

WOMAN (*rushes through the passageway and enters Stanton's office*): As you love God, give me the life of my son!

STANTON: How dare you interrupt me, madam!

WOMAN: How dare I interrupt! How dare I interrupt! My boy fought through the battles of the Peninsula with McClellan, at Antietam, at Fredericksburg, at Gettysburg. He was wounded twice, enlisted again, and has now been sentenced (*laughing desperately*) as a bounty jumper!

STANTON (*frigidly, precisely*): Ah, Private Charles Allen Putnam of the Seventh Vermont. Madam, I am sorry for you, but I do my duty. Don't distress me by an appeal that is useless.

LINCOLN (*interposing*): Don't be in such a hurry, Stanton. Listen to any woman speaking for her son's life. (*Turning to the woman.*) You say your son, Mrs. Putnam, fought for his country for nearly three years? 'Tis strange he is a deserter now.

MRS. PUTNAM: Not really a deserter. He is simply a boy made foolish by a woman. (*Suddenly looking up and realizing she is speaking to the President.*) God has sent you here, Mr. Lincoln, to hear my prayer! I am a widow up in Vermont. I have given seven sons to death for their country; will you take the eighth, the last—the only—the youngest from me?

LINCOLN (*sadly*): Seven sons? Seven sons? (*Turning to Stanton.*) Stanton —you hear—*seven* sons!

MRS. PUTNAM: Yes, all volunteered from our farm in Vermont. The eldest fell at the First Bull Run; one more died in McClellan's Peninsula Campaign, though they couldn't find his body; one at Antietam; one at Fredericksburg; two were slaughtered at Gettysburg and one at Brandy's Station. And this one—all that is left to me—fought in all those battles, protected by God, and came back on furlough two months ago to our farm in Vermont and there saw the woman who has brought him to this. He was refused leave six days ago. He would see her eyes. He came into Washington and was arrested as a deserter, and you know what a quick court martial means. It was only to get a kiss or two from the fool girl and go back and fight again—listen, please listen to me, Mr. President! Seven sons dead and one to be shot because he— wanted to kiss the girl he loves.

LINCOLN (*huskily, his eyes filled with tears*): Stanton, you must listen to this lady, this patriotic lady who has given up more than either you or I for this country.

STANTON (*glancing quickly at Lincoln, seats himself at his desk, writes a few lines hurriedly, signs them, folds the paper, and addresses the envelope. Steps to the door and hands the note to Madison*): Immediate! Tell the orderly to hurry! (*Turns to the President.*)

LINCOLN: Listen to this lady, Stanton, and see if there isn't virtue in her appeal for some revision, some commutation of her son's sentence.

STANTON: Mr. President, under my duty as Secretary of War I have sworn to myself, for the salvation of the American army, whose effectiveness is now necessary for the preservation of this country, that no convicted deserter shall have pardon or commutation of sentence. It is vital that we stop bounty jumping in the present status of the recruiting service.

MRS. PUTNAM (*imploringly*): But my son only a few days ago fought at Fort Stevens and protected you and the capital. He was slightly wounded there and the scar of the Southern bullet is not yet entirely healed upon his arm. (*Moaning desperately.*) Mercy, Mr. Stanton!

(*Turning to Lincoln.*) Mr. President, as you love your own offspring, listen to me; you have a kinder heart.

LINCOLN (*sadly*): Recite your case to Mr. Stanton. I do not wish to interfere, if possible. Tell me then what he says.

(*Steps out of the office into the passageway, where he finds Cazauran taking note of the scene through the half-closed door; sighing.*) I believe her honest Vermont face. Seven sons! Women like her do not lie. But it's awful hard bucking up against Stanton.

CAZAURAN (*whispering*): Mr. President, if you have any intention of pardoning that man, you have no time to lose.

LINCOLN: What do you mean?

CAZAURAN (*whispering, hurriedly*): I mean, Mr. President, that if you do not act immediately—the sentence will be carried out before executive clemency can reach the condemned. An orderly has just galloped away from this building and turned north toward Fort de Russey, where I believe the prisoner is held awaiting execution. He carried with him the few lines Mr. Stanton wrote at that desk while the woman was appealing to you.

LINCOLN (*growing taller, his eyes flashing*): Well, I'm damned! (*Strides rapidly over to the nearby telegraphic office of the War Department and steps inside. To the head clerk.*) A wire is run to Fort de Russey?

CLERK: Yes, Mr. Lincoln, to every fort in the fortifications of Washington, of course.

LINCOLN: Call up Fort de Russey at once!

CLERK: The wire is at present in use, Mr. President, on very important orders with regard to the movement of the Sixth Corps.

LINCOLN: Hold the dispatch!

CLERK: It is very important, Mr. President. It has Mr. Stanton's personal orders that it be put through immediately.

LINCOLN: Stop the dispatch! I direct it! (*Clerk carries out the order.*) Now! (*Striding behind the rail; in a commanding voice.*) Telegraph to the Provost Marshal having in charge Private Charles Allen Putnam of the Seventh Vermont, sentenced to execution today. Direct him to bring immediately to the War Department his prisoner. Order him under the personal commands of the President of the United States to disregard all other orders whatsoever, as regards the disposition of this prisoner. Inform him that this dispatch is given to you by Abraham Lincoln in person, and ask for the Provost Marshal's personal acknowledgment by telegraph of the receipt of this order. I will wait here till I receive your statement that answer is received to this dispatch.

(*After Lincoln receives the Provost Marshal's acknowledgment, he*

*returns to Secretary Stanton's private office, followed by Cazauran.
Mrs. Putnam is still pleading with the Secretary of War, who remains
inflexible.*)
You have concluded, of course, Stanton, to at least postpone the execution of this man until you can make further investigations?

STANTON: On the contrary, Mr. President, in order to avoid discussion on
this matter, you having promised me yourself, in such cases, to withhold pardoning power and leave it entirely in my hands, I have already
taken such steps that discussion is—

LINCOLN (*interrupting sharply*): Discussion is never useless as long as a
man is *alive!*

MRS. PUTNAM (*screaming*): Ah, you intend to pardon my son, Mr. President!

LINCOLN: If what you have said to me is substantially true, I do, madam.

MRS. PUTNAM: God forever bless you!

LINCOLN: Now, my good woman, I will listen to the details of your story.

MRS. PUTNAM (*repeating the account of how her other sons had died in
battle, and how Charlie, her youngest son, had come back to spend his
furlough with her on the old farm at Stowe, Vermont*): Such a happy
month, and now—now! But I must convince you, Mr. President. There
he met a girl that he took to powerfully, and she—this fool girl who has
brought him death—loved him like an idiot. So after Charlie had come
down to Washington and done his duty here—you saw him, Mr. President, at the battle of Fort Stevens. They all say you were there. . . .

LINCOLN (*with a chuckle*): Why, yes. Bluff old Wright of the Sixth Corps
said, "Come along," and I went to the front and found myself as much
in the fighting line as I was in the Black Hawk War. But when a bullet
killed a surgeon within a foot or two of me, Wright almost on his knees
begged me to get out of the line of battle, remarking that I'd be a loss
to the country. "And what would you be?" said I. "Nothing, only a
soldier doing his duty," replied the veteran. "There are plenty of generals and only one President," and hang me if he didn't threaten, unless
I left the zone of danger, to put me, the President of the United States,
under a guard and move me to the rear.

MRS. PUTNAM (*earnestly*): Then you saw my son fight. You saw the Sixth
Corps drive the Rebels out of Maryland and run them back into Virginia and save this capital. My boy was wounded in the line of battle
beside you. (*Tearfully.*) Have my boy brought here and I will show you
the unhealed wound upon his arm! These records will prove that he was
present at every engagement of his regiment during this whole bloody
war. (*Producing some documents.*) Bring him here, and I will show

you, Mr. Secretary Stanton, that he risked his life not a week ago for his country and his flag. . . . Then, then, that fool country girl to whom my boy had taken such a shine came trolloping down to Washington after him. Charlie couldn't get leave to come into the town to see her, and she, unknowing military law, beguiled him. Fool that he was, cajoled by her pleadings, he left the camp at Fort de Russey and came into the city to have a day of bliss with her. He was captured by Baker's Secret Service without a pass, and then—then I was telegraphed, and I came on and found him sentenced to death. Yesterday I saw him and he gave me his word of honor as a man that he had not intended to desert; that he would have returned to the flag the very day he was seized. My son has never lied to me in his life, Mr. Stanton. He is no sneaking bounty jumper. If so, I would say: "Execute him, he is not of my blood; though I bore him, he is not my son!" But he is and has been true to his country and—he is the only one left to me.

(*The clank of a cavalry escort is heard outside. Madison enters.*)

MADISON (*to Stanton, grinning*): The Provost Marshal from Fort de Russey with a prisoner.

STANTON (*springing up*): How? What? Impossible!

(*Enter cavalry captain, covered with dust.*)

CAPTAIN (*to Stanton, saluting*): I have the President's personal orders by telegraph to present before him in your office the prisoner condemned to execution today, Private Charles Allen Putnam of the Seventh Vermont.

(*Four troopers bring in the manacled prisoner, a young Vermont giant, fair-haired and gray-eyed, like his mother, drawn lines on his haggard face.*)

PUTNAM (*seeing Mrs. Putnam; with a gasp*): Mother!

MRS. PUTNAM (*screaming*): My son! (*Embraces him.*)

(*Turning to Lincoln.*)

Mr. President, you have let my boy come into my arms once more. You have given me hope. See! (*Tears the blue sleeve from her son's arm and shows an unhealed wound inflicted by a Confederate Minie bullet.*) This is proof he risked his life for his country. I have here a certificate from all the officers of the regiment in which he served stating he did his duty gallantly through his first enlistment. I have here the affidavit of the girl that he told her he must leave her to return to his command. You have given him to my arms; you cannot take him from them to murder him.

LINCOLN (*hastily writing, hands Mrs. Putnam a slip of paper*): The free pardon of your son!

STANTON (*while Lincoln is writing, turns to the captain of the provost guard; hoarsely*): You received my commands by orderly?

CAPTAIN: Yes, sir; but not until I had received by direct telegram, attested from the telegraph clerk of this department, directions that the execution be stayed and that I forthwith report with the prisoner here personally to the President of the United States. The orders were attested to have the sign manual of Abraham Lincoln. I had signed for their receipt; I could not disobey them.

LINCOLN (*chuckling*): Stanton, that's where I had a little joke on you. You're not up to the modern telegraph, Mr. Secretary. Electricity beats horse-flesh. (*Turning to Putnam.*) Young man, your sentence to death by court martial acts as a discharge from the Army of the United States. My pardon has made it an honorable discharge. Go home and support and cherish your noble mother who has given you a second life.

(*Tears come to his eyes as he watches Putnam, his manacles removed, carrying his half-fainting mother from the room. Turning to Stanton.*)

I think, Stanton, that we had better burn, *unopened*, this dispatch you sent to the Provost Marshal. (*Lights the dispatch over a blazing taper used for sealing official papers.*)

STANTON (*rising*): Mr. President, this action of yours will produce a thousand deserters in the Army of the Potomac.

LINCOLN: I don't care if it does. It has made one less broken heart in this country—perhaps two. The fool girl who lured that young fellow from his duty loves him also. (*With a sigh.*) Oh, if I could send all my Boys in Blue home to their mothers. Yes, and all the Johnnies, too! (*His voice grows commanding.*) We will discuss the details of the reinforcements to be sent to Grant this afternoon. Good-by, Stanton.

(*Lincoln leaves with Cazauran.*)

(*To Cazauran.*) I had a pretty hard time with the Head of the War Department, didn't I? Stanton makes a bully good Secretary of War. The only trouble with him is, he has no more philoprogenitiveness than an alligator who lays a pile of eggs in the burning sand and thinks it's done its whole duty by its family.

Bismarck

THE IRON CHANCELLOR AT VERSAILLES IS OUTSMARTED
BY A BOGUS SPANISH GRANDEE DURING
THE SIEGE OF PARIS.

*No one will ever make me believe that Paris
is a "heroic" city; but, be that as it may, we
shall soon be in it.*

"NOT BY speeches and majority resolutions are the great questions of
the day to be decided—but by blood and iron." Such was the dictum of Otto von Bismarck, the Prussian absolutist who stamped out what
liberalism was budding in Germany, preached the divine right of kings,
and launched his country on a series of imperialistic adventures that
plunged Europe into bloody struggle for years. In this powerfully built
and rigorously trained foe of democracy, Prussianism found its spokesman
and symbol. Militarism flourished and in the machinations devised by an
enemy of the sovereign rights of states was laid the groundwork of two
world wars.

For our purpose we are now in the autumn of 1870. The Franco-Prussian
war, fiendishly kindled by a master of intrigue and international sabotage,
has been raging since mid-July. By mid-August General Bazaine's French
army was bottled up in the city of Metz, one of the so-called gateways to
Germany. By the second of September General MacMahon's army had
capitulated at Sedan, and Napoleon III, himself a major culprit in the
outbreak of the war, had been taken prisoner. In a few weeks Bazaine's
army had surrendered at beleaguered Metz, and two days after the fall of
Sedan, Paris, having declared itself free of Napoleon III, had proclaimed
the Third Republic. The Emperor was pronounced guilty of the "ruin, invasion, and dismemberment of the country." The provisional government
now strove to drive back Bismarck's armies. Aid was sought for France
from the outside world, but in vain. Virtually alone, Paris undertook to
resist a cruel siege. Outside, the Prussian armies waited, certain that
starvation, disease, panic, and winter would prove their best allies.

Meanwhile the "Iron Chancellor" had taken up residence in nearby

Versailles, hourly awaiting the capitulation of Paris. Emissaries of England and America were admitted daily, and correspondents of the world press came panting with questions. "Will Paris be starved out or cannonaded into submission?" A John L. O'Sullivan, former American minister to Lisbon, dined with the Chancellor one day, proposing mediation, only to find himself turned out of Versailles the next morning. Still the intrigant, Bismarck continued to play off the envoys of Napoleon III against those of the new-born Republic. And all the while the deadly, unrelenting siege of a cold and hungry city went on.

On October 12, Lieutenant von Usslar introduced an important personage to the Chancellor. The passport bore the name and title of "M. Angel de Valleyo, Vice-President of the Spanish Finance Commission in Paris, attaché to the Spanish Embassy." To confirm his claims, Señor Valleyo proudly displayed on his breast the picturesque orders of the Star of Isabella and the Cross of St. John of Jerusalem. Before this Spanish grandee's title and rank Bismarck was all deference. Valleyo was even invited to dinner, the other guests being the Chancellor's nephew, Count Bismarck-Bohlen, and Count Hatzfeldt, afterwards German Ambassador to London. . . .

THE DINNER *

(*The dinner-table is lit by candles stuck into the mouths of empty wine-bottles. Presently the butler appears with several full bottles of wine. Bismarck tries one—a* vin de Nuits—*but it fails to suit his taste. A second bottle is uncorked and found better. Bismarck smacks his lips after sipping the wine and holds up the roseate fluid between him and the candle light.*)

BISMARCK: Ah, this is excellent! It is from Romanée.

VALLEYO: You are a connoisseur of wine, M. le Comte, and so I trust you will have every reason to feel satisfied with the cellar of this house.

BISMARCK: Ah no, you are mistaken, this wine here comes from the "Hôtel des Reservoirs." I buy everything that I want; I don't wish my sons ever to have any cause to blush for me. That will also explain to you why I must content myself with empty bottles for candlesticks.

(*Observing a faint smile of incredulity on Valleyo's face, turns to the butler.*)

---

* Put into dialogue form from *Bismarck's Table-Talk*, selected and edited by Charles Lowe (Grevel, London, 1895).

Tell me, how much do we pay for this Romanée?

BUTLER: Six or eight thalers, Excellency. I think it is eight.

(*Bismarck proceeds to speak of his own cellar in Berlin.*)

BISMARCK: Yes, an excellent cellar, seeing that it all comes from that celebrated dealer, the Marquis de T——, whom you must have met in Paris.
He is the son of a rich landowner, who was called simply Lemarquis.
But after getting himself appointed to the French Legation at Frankfort, he appended to his name that of an estate belonging to his father,
and thus became Lemarquis de T——. After that he gradually reconciled himself to the practice of others who committed the mistake of
writing his name in two parts—till at last he took to the writing of it
himself in this manner. Once he came to Berlin; and perceiving how
very pleased he was (for I knew the story) when addressed as "Marquis," I invited him to a diplomatic dinner, when he found his menu
under his napkin inscribed round and large with his aristocratic title.
The consequence was that next day I received from him the present of
a case of fine Burgundy, which had just reached him from his place in
France; and ever since then he has continued to serve me to my complete satisfaction.

(*The talk now turned to the defenders of the French capital.*)

VALLEYO: The Parisians are firmly, nay fiercely resolved on resistance to
the death.

BISMARCK (*scoffingly*): Their vanity has kept them up so far, their vanity,
which is the chief feature of the French character. But in the face of
real suffering this quality will not hold out. No one will ever make me
believe that Paris is a "heroic" city; but, be that as it may, we shall soon
be in it.

VALLEYO: You will scarcely do it by main force, unless you decide to destroy the city by bombardment, and sacrifice a large portion of your
army in storming it.

BISMARCK: How the thing is to be done is not my affair, but that of our
Generals. For my own part I would never advise recourse to an escalade
—seeing that it would cost more than it is worth. But with a little patience we shall get possession of the place all the same, thanks to the
two allies that we have inside—Famine and the Reds.

VALLEYO: As for the Reds, they seem to be kept pretty well in hand by the
National Guard. And as for Famine—that is still a long way off.

BISMARCK: Oh, well, we can wait for months yet, but enter Paris we shall.

VALLEYO: But if the matter lasts as long as that, are you not afraid of the
approach of a relieving army, or of the intervention of all Europe?

BISMARCK: Where is such an army to come from? From the Loire, where some battalions, more of the character of an armed mob than of regular troops, have just been scattered? From Metz, where the starving garrison are sending out daily flags of truce to treat for capitulation? Pray get rid of your illusions. France has no longer got any army, nor will she have one for years. And as for the neutral Powers, they are at least as friendly to us as to France, whose self-conceit and restless, aggressive policy have been a standing danger to Europe for the last two centuries. Besides, it seems to me that all the other Powers will soon have quite enough to do with their own affairs. In the worst of cases, however, we should know how to cope with any foreign interference with a war into which we entered at our own risk and peril.

VALLEYO: In Paris great hopes were entertained of M. Thiers's mission to the Courts of Europe.

BISMARCK: Bah! Believe me, this mission had much less to do with peace than with the accession of the Prince of Orléans. The French are fools if they don't see that. But perhaps they do see it, . . . and I can quite understand that they should prefer this to the dictatorship of M. Gambetta, this briefless barrister, whose whole political outfit consists of some coffee-house cackle and three Chamber speeches stuffed with liberal phrases.

VALLEYO: I do not think that people in Paris have looked at the mission of M. Thiers in this light. Anyhow, it was said that England and Russia had agreed to intervene.

BISMARCK: Good Heavens! What is the next thing that will be said in Paris? England and Russia going hand in hand? Ha! ha! ha! (*Bursting out into a loud laugh, looking as he does so at Count Hatzfeldt, who merely responds with a discreet smile, as he thinks of the Black Sea comedy now in active preparation.*) And you Spaniards, do you also mean to join this terrible coalition against us? I expected that you would even have become our allies in the present war.

VALLEYO: M. le Comte is pleased to jest. . . .

BISMARCK: Far from it. It is to some extent on your account that we are waging this war, and I should have thought it quite natural of you to join us. Thus it was that, on the day after war was declared, I asked Marshal Prim what was the strength of the contingent he proposed to place in the field. I was very surprised to hear that the Marshal now shrank from the consequences of his policy.

VALLEYO: I beg your pardon, but it is just as little the habit of Spain as of Marshal Prim to retire. Had the Prince of Hohenzollern not withdrawn from his candidature, and if we had had to stand up for our rights, we should have fought France.

BISMARCK (*with a sigh*): Pity that it was not so, for France would then have been taken in front and rear, and by this time we should have been in Paris. What an awakening that would have been for your nation, which has been slumbering so long! (*After a pause.*) But what, then, are Marshal Prim's present intentions?

VALLEYO: Ah, that I know not. The Marshal, it is true, honors me with his confidence, though not to the extent of acquainting me with his political plans.

BISMARCK: Very well, but as you will soon have an opportunity of seeing him, you may tell him from me to think of it. I am not the man to meddle with the affairs of others, and Prussia has not the slightest intention of interfering with the policy of Spain or of any other country. At the same time, it seems to me that your selection of a German prince for your King would have been a guarantee of your regeneration. For look you, the Latin race is now used up. I admit that in its time it has done great things, but its mission is now at an end; it is now fated to dwindle, and possibly even to disappear altogether—as a whole at least. This is a process which far-seeing statesmen in Latin (Romanic) countries should expedite instead of exhausting themselves in fruitless endeavors to thwart the decrees of destiny. Our Hohenzollern Prince on your throne would have infused some German life and energy into the Spaniards, without humiliating them. The German race is young and strong, and possessed of all the virtues and spirit of enterprise which formerly distinguished yours. The future belongs to the northern nations, which will play the glorious part that has been allotted them for the good of humanity.

(*The conversation turns on the course of the war and the prospects of peace.*)

BISMARCK: All I want now is a government to deal with, even one of Robert Macaire. Nor am I at all certain that Napoleon will not after all be re-instated. For what can France reproach me with? Of having incurred defeat while endeavoring to gratify the dearest wish of my nation—the conquest of the Rhine?

VALLEYO: The cession of Alsace-Lorraine does not seem to me to offer the prospect of a lasting peace.

BISMARCK: In any case such is the will of the King. But whatever may be the condition of peace, it will be nothing but an armistice. France is much too vain ever to forgive us for her defeats. Even supposing that we were to agree to quit France tomorrow without demanding compensation of any kind, the national vanity would feel none the less wounded, and the French would force another war upon us as soon as ever they could. Therefore, in the interest of Germany, as well as of all Europe, our policy must aim at enfeebling France as much as possible, and rendering her incapable for a long time of breaking the general peace.

(*An interval of gloomy silence.*)

VALLEYO: You are always, M. le Comte, harping on the will of the King, whereas Europe looks upon you yourself as the supreme arbiter in this war.

BISMARCK: Well, Europe is wrong if it thinks so. But it is only in France, I fancy, that this superficial view prevails. This undisciplined people, which is accustomed to be made the plaything of political adventurers, cannot comprehend our respect for monarchy, our organization, our hierarchical system. With us, sir, there is no sovereign will but that of the King. It is he alone who wills, because he alone has the right to do so. However high my position, I am only the tool of his political will, as the Generals are equally the instruments of his military will. When his Majesty says so-and-so, it is my duty to propose measures for the execution of his ideas, and my reputation consists in this—that I have often succeeded in carrying these ideas out. For the rest, my present activity is completely subordinated to that of the Generals in the army, who are not always of my way of thinking.

(*Valleyo begs leave to retire. Bismarck accompanies him to the door and instructs his nephew, Count Bismarck-Bohlen, to look after his distinguished Spanish visitor.*)

BISMARCK: It is difficult to find quarters in Versailles; but I think we shall be able to put you up, and tomorrow I will do my best to procure you a passport from the military authorities.

(*Stepping into the carriage which is waiting for him, the Spaniard, five minutes later, is deposited by Bismarck's orderly at a house in the Rue Montbauran, where rooms have been ordered "for a personage of distinction."*)

ORDERLY (*to the owner of house*): Do your best for this gentleman, for he is a person of great importance; he has just given me a twenty-franc piece, and his Excellency conversed with him for about three hours.

(At the end of the dinner, after Señor Valleyo was driven safely home, Bismarck began to wonder about his titled guest. The more he wondered the deeper grew his suspicion that something was amiss. Promptly he began inquiries about this "Spanish attaché." And Bismarck was soon cursing himself for the hospitable fool that he was. For it developed that this self-styled "Vice-President of the Spanish Finance Commission" was none other than Angel de Miranda, a political writer on the Paris *Gaulois*. In a recent article this same Miranda had bitterly denounced Prussia and dubbed King William a *caporal mystique*, among other unflattering things. So Miranda, alias Valleyo, was seized before he could slip out of Versailles and placed under arrest. When they searched him they found a carefully drawn-up plan of the German positions around the French capital! After giving his word of honor not to escape, Miranda was interned at Mayence. But he promptly eluded his captors and returned to Paris. The story of how the hated Prussian Chancellor had been hoodwinked caused considerable merriment among the beleaguered Parisians at a time when laughter was rare. As for Valleyo-Miranda's masquerade, it has been properly called "one of the boldest feats of journalism that was ever performed.")

Meanwhile in Paris

ERNEST RENAN PRECIPITATES A LITERARY STORM
BY CALLING THE BESIEGERS "A SUPERIOR RACE."

*The Germans have very few pleasures, and
of these the greatest are hatred, meditation,
and vengeance.*

MEANWHILE, in Paris, horror is closing in on a starved, besieged, but doggedly unyielding population. Men of all ages have been furnished arms. The food supply is dwindling fast, and in the famished hunt for provisions the menagerie is slowly vanishing. Soon diners will be glad when the meat served is feline, canine, or equine, and not worse. Confusion reigns everywhere. But the spirit of the city is resolute, and from street and boulevard the repeated cry goes up, "Vive la République!" It is a time of bold sacrifice and daring exploit—of Gambetta's flight from Paris in a balloon to set up defense headquarters at Tours; of minister Jules Favre's proud boast, "We shall not cede an inch of our territory or a stone of our territories!"

On the very day of Favre's pronouncement an excitable band of book-men gather at Brébant's Restaurant on the Boulevard Poissonnière for a literary chat and whatever the chef can scrape together. They file in alone or in pairs, these scholars, scientists, journalists. Pale and shaken by events, they climb up slowly to the "salon rouge." First to arrive is Ernest Renan, historian, biographer of Christ, agnostic. Edmond Goncourt, who follows, finds him seated disconsolately at the huge round table, reading a newspaper, and "making hopeless gestures with his arms." Next to arrive is Paul Saint-Victor, drama critic of Le Pays, who slumps dejectedly into a chair beside Renan. After him come Antoine DuMesnil, writer and state official; Auguste Nefftzer, editor of Le Temps; Pierre Berthelot, co-founder of organic chemistry, now on the defense committee of the beleaguered city. It is Goncourt, keeper of the most famous literary diary of the century, who invites us to join his dismal cronies chez Brébant on a bleak September evening of 1870. Later, we shall learn more of this midnight diarist Goncourt and his voluminous record of the day's best literary chatter. At the moment books are furthest from the minds of these joyless Parisians. "C'est la guerre," and the "Boche" is at the gate. . . .

SAINT-VICTOR (*exclaiming, as if in the grip of a terrifying vision*): It's the Apocalypse! . . .

("*We proceed to dine in the desolation of one another's words. The talk is about the great defeat, the impossibility of resistance, the incompetence of the men of the National Defense, of their discouraging lack of influence on the diplomatic corps and the neutral governments. Everyone stigmatizes this Prussian savagery which began with Genseric.*"—Goncourt)

RENAN: The Germans have very few pleasures, and of these the greatest are hatred, meditation, and vengeance.

("*Everyone proceeds to recall this great hatred, which has accumulated since Davoat, in Germany, and to which was added the hatred bequeathed by the war of the Palatinate. A hatred the wrathful expression of which survived even in the mouth of the old woman who showed me around a Heidelberg castle many years ago. Someone now told how yesterday—no later than yesterday—a railroad administrator had related the following story. Some years before he was in Karlsruhe paying his respects to the governing official. He heard him say to one of his friends, a man of pronounced partiality to the ladies: 'Here, my dear fellow, you will accomplish nothing. The women happen to be very easy to make, but they don't like Frenchmen.'*"—Goncourt)

SOMEONE: Precision instruments are contrary to the French temperament. Fire quickly, fix bayonets and charge—that's what our soldier wants. If that's not possible, he is paralyzed. The *mechanization* of the individual is not for him. That's the very thing that gives the Prussians their superiority at the moment.

RENAN (*looking up from his plate*): In all the things I have studied I have always been struck by the superior intelligence and workmanship of the Germans. It is not surprising that in the art of war, which, after all, is an inferior but complicated art, they show the same superiority which, I repeat, I have found in everything I have studied and know. Yes, gentlemen, the Germans are a superior race!

ALL: No! No! No!

RENAN (*growing animated*): Yes, very superior to us. Catholicism is a cretinization of the individual. Education by the Jesuits and Christian brothers arrests and restricts all *summative* virtue, while Protestantism develops it.

BERTHELOT (*"in his sweet and sickly voice recalling the gathered intellects from their sophisticated heights to threatening reality"*): Gentlemen, perhaps you do not know that we are surrounded by enormous quantities of petroleum. They are deposited at the gates of Paris and do not enter because of the tariff. The Prussians will seize them and then throw them into the Seine and make a river of fire that will burn both banks. That's how the Greeks set fire to the Arab fleet.

GONCOURT: Why not warn Trochu * about this?

SOMEONE: Do you suppose he has the time to occupy himself with anything at all?

BERTHELOT: If the flood-gates of the Marne canal are not blown up, the Prussians will bring up their heavy siege artillery as if on rollers right under the walls of Paris. But is anyone thinking of blowing them up? I can go on telling things of that kind till tomorrow morning.

GONCOURT: Do you hope to bring forth some engine of destruction from the committee over which you preside? †

BERTHELOT: Hardly a chance! They have given me neither money nor men, and every day I receive two hundred and fifty letters which give me no time to do any experimenting. No doubt we could find something and try it out. But time is lacking for any big experiment. And then there's the problem of having it approved. For example, there's a certain bigwig of the artillery corps. I talked to him about the petroleum. "Yes," he said, "it proved quite useful in the ninth century." "But the Americans in their last war ..." I began to reply. "That's quite true," he remarked, "but it's dangerous stuff to handle, and we don't want to blow ourselves up." So you see how it is!

(*"The whole conversation at the table now turns to the conditions presumably being laid down by the Prussian king—like the surrende of part of the armored fleet and the new set of boundaries, already indicated on a map belonging to Hetzel—boundaries which would deprive France of some departments. . . . Renan, clinging obstinately to his thesis of the superiority of the German people, continues developing it between his two neighbors."*—Goncourt)

DUMESNIL (*interrupting Renan*): As regards that feeling of independence among your German peasants, I can say this much. I did some hunting around Baden once and the usual thing was to give them a few kicks in the pants before sending them off to gather up the game.

---

* General Louis Jules Trochu (1815–1896), governor of Paris, 1870–1871.
† Indirect discourse in the original.

RENAN: Good! I prefer peasants to whom one gives kicks in the pants to peasants like our own, who have become our masters through universal suffrage—these peasants, this inferior element of civilization, that for twenty years has forced us to submit to this government.

(*"Berthelot now continues his dismal revelations."*—Goncourt)

GONCOURT: Then it's all over! Our only hope now is to raise an entire generation for revenge.

RENAN (*rising, his face red all over*): No! No! Not revenge! Let France perish! Yes, let our homeland perish! Higher than France herself is the Kingdom of Duty, of Reason . . . !

ALL (*shouting*): No! No! Nothing stands above one's country!

SAINT-VICTOR (*"in a rage, and clamoring still louder"*): Damn it, let's stop being esthetic and arguing like Byzantines! There's nothing at all above our country!

(*"Renan rises, walks around the table with an unsteady gait, beating the air with his little arms, quoting fragments of Holy Scripture, and saying that everything is written there. Then he goes to the window and watches the carefree going and coming of the Parisians below."*—Goncourt)

RENAN (*to Goncourt*): That's what will save us! The softness of those people down there!

The Goncourt Brothers

RECORDED FRAGMENTS OF INTIMATE COLLOQUIES AMONG FLAUBERT, GAUTIER, DAUDET, ZOLA, TURGENIEFF, AND OTHERS.

I never go near a woman without a feeling of respect and surprise at my good luck.

EDMOND GONCOURT aroused a tempest of shocked protest when he published Volume IV of his famous Journal. Since this volume contained a record of the stormy dinner at Brébant's Restaurant during the siege of Paris, it was Ernest Renan who naturally protested the loudest [See page 400]. The infuriated historian charged Goncourt with violating a gentlemen's agreement that nothing of these sessions would be divulged to the world. A sacred principle of these dinners had been that "everyone could say everything, because nothing would be repeated." And Goncourt, according to Renan, had only added insult to injury by misquoting his former friends, by failing to grasp many issues because of a closed mind, by, in short, being a bad reporter. To the first charge Goncourt replied: "My indiscretions are not revelations of private life, but in every sense revelations of the thoughts and ideas of my contemporaries, documents for the intellectual history of the period." To the second charge of inaccuracy, he retorted: "My ambition was to make the men I portrayed real. For nothing in the world would I have attributed words to them which they did not speak." In all fairness to Renan, it must be admitted that Goncourt, an arch-conservative in thought, was not without malice in his attitude to this brave and impassioned freethinker.

Since it raises the whole question of the validity of recorded conversation, it is worth while examining the background of the Goncourt Journal. To begin with, the first three volumes were the work not of one man but of two, Edmond Goncourt and his younger brother Jules. This collaboration also extended to the writing of several "naturalist" novels and a few fastidious chronicles of eighteenth-century social bric-a-brac. To amuse themselves further, the brothers began to keep a diary of everything they heard during the day that they agreed was worth preserving. This was in 1854. Jules' share of the diary ended with his untimely death on June 20,

1870. Crushed by the blow, Edmond at first thought of abandoning the diary, but then changed his mind. "I was seized by the bitter desire to recount to myself the final months and death of my beloved brother," he explains, "and almost immediately thereafter the tragic occurrences of the Siege of Paris and the Commune impelled me to continue this journal." He carried out his plan to 1895, a year before his death. These Mémoires de la Vie Littéraire thus form "a colossal storehouse of the manners, morals, and conversations of virtually all the celebrities who lived or passed through Paris between 1854 and 1895."*

As for the recording method employed by the two brothers, we have Edmond's own statement: "What we have tried to do is to bring our contemporaries to life for posterity, to paint them in their living, animated resemblances. We have employed to this end the vivid stenography of conversation, the physiological surprise that springs from gesture . . . and finally, a little of that feverishness which is characteristic of the heady life of Paris. . . ." The brothers would return home from some dinner, and, while the material was still fresh in their minds, make their entry in the diary. "The whole manuscript may be said to have been written by my brother at the dictation of us both," Edmond jots down at Schliersee two months after Jules' death. Of the quality of the Journal, Arthur Symonds stressed the "morbidly sensitive noting of the inédit," which was probably the same thing Lewis Galantiere had in mind when he spoke patly of the Goncourts' "taste for the instantaneous." It was this complete lack of restraint in recording everything heard—however scabrous—that has prevented much of the material from being released. The publication of the Journal (Bibliothèque Charpentier, Paris) was begun in 1887 and completed in 1896. In the early 1930's a definitive edition was prepared under the direction of the Goncourt Academy, established through the endowment of Edmond's huge estate. In 1937 a portion of the Journal appeared in an excellent English version rendered and edited by Lewis Galantiere, The Goncourt Journals—1851–1870 (Doubleday, Doran & Co., 1937, New York). Many of the quotations used above and two of the conversations given below—those of August 24, 1860, and June 22, 1863 —are in Mr. Galantiere's translation.

Since each of the conversations reprinted here is introduced by the mention of a dinner in a restaurant or private home, a word may be needed about this so-called "littérature qui mange." It was that deft phrase-maker and literary gourmet, Barbey d'Aurevilly, who first dubbed it "the literature which eats," and René Dumesnil, who remarked that under the

---

* Matthew Josephson.

Second Empire "the fork, no less than the pen, became the symbolic instrument of the literary profession." In the fifties and sixties the literary dinner, held usually in some inconspicuous bistro, became quite the rage. Food and wine were consumed in noble quantities by these gens d'ésprit, and reputations were made and unmade between mouthfuls. The talk was frank and unhampered, and strangers were rarely, if ever, admitted to these inner sancta. Confidences were revealed on the most intimate matters, and everyone felt protected by a protocol of secrecy. Each diner felt at liberty to tear anyone or anything to shreds, and many an absent idol of the day was subjected to the gruelling process. "Some of these dinners were real feasts of cannibals," remarks Dumesnil, "on y mange de l'homme, et à toutes sauces." Most famous of them all was "le dîner Magny," celebrated in the Goncourt Journal and in the correspondence of Flaubert.

"Le dîner Magny" was founded, as a bi-monthly observance, by six friends in November, 1862—the brothers Goncourt, the critic and essayist Sainte-Beuve, the writer and state administrator Philippe Chennevières, the great caricaturist and illustrator Gavarni, and a Dr. Veyne, presented to the other five as "l'ancien médecin de la bohème," a description sufficing to render him "worthy to sit beside these men of letters." Soon the group expanded. One day the Goncourts brought Flaubert with them; someone else introduced Charles-Edmond, editor of the Presse, and he in turn created a stir one evening by presenting the Russian novelist Ivan Turgenieff. The literary historian Hippolyte Taine joined the company at the dinner of March 14, 1863, and two weeks later the dinners grew in animation by the arrival of that little fiery rebel Renan. About that time two others joined the group—the editor Nefftzer and the poet, novelist, and critic Théophile Gautier. The name of Edmond Scherer, critic and essayist, begins to appear in the proceedings some time later, and a few months later Renan introduces the celebrated chemist Berthelot to his fellow-diners. There is some doubt about just when Alexandre Dumas and George Sand first attended the sessions. In any case we have the word of a second female diner, Juliette Lamber, that when Jules Goncourt told "une histoire salée" about Baudelaire, the ladylike Mme. Sand (who often sported trousers and smoked cigars), exploded: "I detest that kind of conversation! It disgusts me!" One evening these valiant souls discovered they were thirteen. A frantic summons brought Monsieur Magny's son to take the fourteenth place at the table.

Magny's Restaurant, which was located on what is now the Rue Mazet, remained the main gathering-place of these bi-monthly banquets of wit and wine, till the death of Sainte-Beuve in 1869. They were then transferred to Brébant's on the Boulevard Poissonière. "Le dîner Brébant" never quite achieved the reputation of "Le dîner Magny." Dumesnil points out that only two years after its founding every writer in Paris was "burning with longing" to be invited. "It is quite clear," he observes, "that a place at Magny's was as difficult to secure as a chair in the French Academy."

In reading the three "conversations" that follow one must bear in mind the Goncourt method of recording only what they remembered. These are largely scraps of dialogue caught sur le vif and put in writing perhaps a few hours later with no attempt to give them sustained dramatic flow. The record breaks off abruptly in the middle of a brisk exchange or an intimate disclosure and then resumes on another track. The Goncourts are trying to recapture anecdotes, sentences, phrases, flashes, and sensations, strung together in the free disorder of the rambling discourse of the dinner-table. There is no thread except their own interest, no attempt to give artistic unity where there is none. The three selections that follow are among the diary entries offering the longest dialogue. Some of the material is petty and dated, some frankly shocking, all of it tantalizing in its sudden silences. They are like a broken phonograph record with some pieces lost. Perhaps for that very reason one feels the breath of life, the very tang of living speech, as nowhere else in the whole body of recorded conversation. The journalist Maynard, struck by this savor of actuality, made the aptest remark of all when he said of the conversations: "Elles suent d'authenticité"—"they sweat authenticity."

(*August 24, 1860*—"*Aubyret gave a dinner this evening for Charles Edmond, Saint-Victor, Flaubert, Ludovic Halévy, Claudin, Théophile Gautier, and ourselves. Fifth story, rue Taitbout, an apartment with which a decorator for kept women has had his way. A drawing room lined with padded pigeon-blood silk and a ceiling by Faustin Besson. A dining room furnished with those odds and ends of porcelain and glass which Arsène Houssaye has made fashionable. We sat down to table and immediately conversation flared up on the subject of Ponsard.*" *— The Goncourts)

SAINT-VICTOR: Have you never seen Ponsard? Imagine a comic policeman writing his own farces. You were good, Theo; you gave him a fearful drubbing.

---

* François Ponsard (1814–1867), successful but shallow playwright whose best drama, in verse, was Lucrèce.

GAUTIER: Oh, me. I am the fellow they always use to beat up the people I admire. I am the ass's cheekbone they use to lay out Hugo.

FLAUBERT (*emphatically*): Well, there's one fellow I abominate even more than Ponsard, and that is that lad Feuillet.* I have read his *Jeune Homme Pauvre*—who has ten thousand francs a year—three times. Do you know how you can recognize that his young man is a gentleman? He can ride a horse. And what's more, in all Feuillet's books there are young men who have albums and sketch landscapes.

A GUEST (*sighing*): Do you fellows know what it took to make a man rich twenty years ago? Read Paul de Kock; it's there: Charles was rich, for he had six thousand francs a year, ate truffled partridge every night, and kept an Opéra dancer—and what is more, it could have been done on that!

(*"Twenty-two-year-old champagne is served. The talk is now of those who had died during the Revolution, of a sort of exhumation of the Madeleine Cemetery and La du Barry's scaffold out of which comes, heaven knows how, a discussion of ancient art between Saint-Victor and Gautier, who declares that Phidias is decadent. Guests now come away from the table."*)

SAINT-VICTOR (*stirring his coffee*): Today is the anniversary of the Massacre of St. Bartholomew's Eve. Voltaire would have been in a fever about it.

FLAUBERT (*theatrically*): Perfectly right!

(*"Both Saint-Victor and Flaubert are off, proclaiming Voltaire the most sincere and guileless of apostles, while we protest with all the strength of our conviction. . . . The room is filled with shouts, outbursts, and vociferations."*)

FIRST GUEST: A martyr!

SECOND GUEST: In exile part of his life!

THIRD GUEST: Yes, but what of his popularity?

FOURTH GUEST: A sensitive nature!

FIFTH GUEST: The Calas Case! †

SIXTH GUEST: On a par with Balzac's Peytel Affair!

FLAUBERT (*roaring*): I say the man was a saint!

---

* Octave Feuillet (1821–1890), popular novelist and dramatist.

† "The Calas Affair was the Dreyfus Case of the eighteenth century, and the part played in it by Voltaire won him the admiration of all Europe. Jean Calas, a Protestant, was a well-to-do merchant in the city of Toulouse. One of his sons desiring to follow the law, and being, as a Protestant, ineligible for the Bar, became a Catholic. Another son had the same ambition but was repelled by the notion of apostasy. That second son 'fell into a sadness then into a fast . . . and by this declension' hanged himself. Foolishly, the family thought to avert scandal by concealing the whole business; but the town got wind of it, the good burghers of Toulouse, like a Tennessee mob, took fire, and the

SOMEBODY: You, who are a physiologist: have you never looked at his mouth?

GAUTIER: As for me, I can't bear the man. To me he is priestish, a sky pilot, the Alderman of Deism. Yes, that's what he is, the Alderman of Deism.

(*"The dispute dies down for a moment and arises again with Horace for subject, some expressing the opinion that he is a kind of Béranger, while Saint-Victor extols the purity of his language, which Gautier thought decidedly inferior to the admirable Latin of Catullus. And with that we reach the question of the immortality of the soul, a subject inescapable by superior minds who have just risen from an excellent dinner."*)

GAUTIER: It won't do. Can you imagine my soul retaining consciousness of my being, remembering that I wrote for Le Moniteur, number 13, Quai Voltaire, and that the owners of my paper were Turgan and Dalloz. . . .

SAINT-VICTOR (*cutting in*): Or can you imagine the soul of our friend the alderman turning up before God in gold spectacles and beginning a speech, "Architect of the universe . . . !"

GAUTIER (*calmly resuming*): We all accept the notion of oblivion before life; why should it be hard to conceive of it after life? The fable of the ancients, the lethal cup—that is the way it should be. The only thing I am afraid of is that particular moment when my ego is about to enter into the night, when I shall lose the consciousness of having lived.

CLAUDIN * (*stammering timidly*): There is, nevertheless, a great Clockmaker.

SOMEONE: Oh, if we are to go into clockmaking! . . . Do you know, Claudin, that matter also is infinite? It is a recent discovery.

SAINT-VICTOR: Yes, yes. Heine said it first. We ask what the stars are, what God is, what life means; and our mouths are stopped with a bit of clay. But is that an answer?

GAUTIER (*continuing, placidly and imperturbably*): Listen, Claudin. Assume the sun was inhabited. A man five feet tall on earth would be

---

father was accused of murdering his son for reasons of religion. On the tenth of March, 1762 Jean Calas was broken on the wheel and his body burned at the stake. His property was confiscated and his family were scattered, some members banished and others locked up in convents. Voltaire heard of this quite by chance, acted with a vigor and a courage for which he was not ordinarily conspicuous, and singlehanded obtained the declaration of Jean Calas's innocence on the ninth of March, 1765, the rehabilitation of his name, and the restoration of his property to his family. David de Breaudrique, one of the overzealous municipal officers responsible for the prosecution, went mad and killed himself."—Galantiere's note.

* Gustav Claudin (1823–1896), journalist and novelist.

seven hundred and fifty leagues high on the sun. That is to say, that the soles of your shoes, assuming you wore heels, would be two leagues long, a length equal to the depth of the ocean at its deepest. Now listen to me, Claudin: and along with your two leagues of boot soles you would possess seventy-five leagues of masculinity in the natural state.

CLAUDIN (*stiffly*): All that is very fine, but still. . . .

SAINT-VICTOR (*breaking in brutally*): Catholicism and Markowski! That is your motto, Claudin.

GAUTIER (*coming over to the others*): You see, the immortality of the soul, free will—it is very pleasant to be concerned with these things before one is twenty-two years old; but afterwards such subjects are no longer seemly. One ought then to be concerned to have a mistress who does not get on one's nerves; to have a decent place to live; to have a few passable pictures on the wall. And most of all, to be writing well. There is what is important: sentences that hang together . . . and a few metaphors. Yes, a few metaphors. They embellish life.

FLAUBERT (*repeating the words in a corner of the room "with the ignorance of a true provincial"*): Markowski? Markowski? What's that?

CLAUDIN: My dear chap. Markowski was a bootmaker. He began to teach himself to play the violin, and also to dance by himself. Pretty soon he was organizing balls, with the aid of a number of tarts. The good Lord blessed his efforts. He escaped with his life from the several drubbings that Adele Courtois arranged to have administered to him, and now he is the proprietor of the house he lives in.

(*The guests begin to depart.*)

GONCOURTS (*to Gautier, as they descend the stairs together*): Does it not disturb you to be no longer living in Paris?

GAUTIER: Oh, it makes no difference to me. This is no longer the Paris I knew. It is Philadelphia, St. Petersburg, anything you like.

(*June 22, 1863—Dinner at Magny's.*)

GAUTIER: The *bourgeoisie!* Strange things are going on in our middle classes. I have been in their houses. It's enough to make a man hide his face in shame. Tribadism is their normal state; incest is permanently installed; and bestiality.

TAINE: I know the middle classes pretty well. I come of a *bourgeois* family myself. For one thing, what do you mean by *bourgeois*?

GAUTIER: People who have fifteen or twenty thousand francs a year and nothing to do.

TAINE: So? Well, I can name thirty *bourgeois* women of my acquaintance, all of them pure.

A VOICE: What do you know about it, Taine? God himself couldn't be sure.

TAINE: Look here. In the town of Angers they keep such a close watch on women that there is no breath of scandal about a single one of them.

SAINT-VICTOR: Angers? But they are all paederasts. There was a case recently. . . .

SAINTE-BEUVE: Madame Sand, gentlemen, is doing a book on a son of Jean Jacques Rousseau during the Revolution. It will be most generously written. She is full of her subject; has written me three letters about it. Wonderful organization, that woman.

SOULIÉ: You know, there is a farce by Théaulon on Rousseau's children.

RENAN: Madame Sand is the greatest artist of our time and the truest talent.

(*General protest.*)

SAINT-VICTOR: Isn't it strange that she writes on notepaper?

RENAN: By true I do not mean realistic.

SAINTE-BEUVE: Let's drink. I am for drinking. Come along, Scherer.

TAINE: Hugo? But Hugo is not sincere.

SAINTE-BEUVE: What! You, Taine, you put Musset higher than Hugo? But Hugo writes books! Under the very nose of the government that exiled him he has snatched the greatest popularity of our time.* His books penetrate everywhere: the women, the common people—everybody reads him. Editions go out of print between eight in the morning and twelve o'clock noon. When I first read his *Odes et ballades* I sought him out immediately with all my verse. The editors of the *Globe* called him a barbarian. Well! Everything that I have done I owe to him; whereas in ten years the people on the *Globe* taught me nothing.

SAINT-VICTOR: We are all his descendants.

TAINE: Allow me. Hugo, in our time, is an immense event; but—

SAINTE-BEUVE (*very animated*): Taine, do not say a word about Hugo. You don't know him. There are only two of us here who know him—Gautier and I. Hugo's work is magnificent!

TAINE: It is what you nowadays, I believe, call poetry; painting a steeple, a sky; making things visible, in short. For me that is not poetry; it is painting.

GAUTIER: Taine, you are talking *bourgeois* idiocy. Poetry is not sentimentalism, far from it. Words that radiate; words of light; and rhythm, and

---

* Hugo was, in politics, an idealizing and courageous ass. Having protested against the coup d'état of December 1851 he escaped to Brussels, thence to Jersey, and finally to Guernsey. From Jersey he published *Napoléon le Petit* and the extravagant but eloquent anti-Napoleon poems contained in *Les Châtiments.*—Galantiere's note.

music—there you have poetry. It doesn't set out to prove anything. Take the opening of *Ratbert*: there is no poetry in the world like it. It is the Himalayas. All of heraldic Italy is in it . . . and it is nothing but words.

NEFFTZER: Come now. If it is beautiful, there must be an idea in it.

GAUTIER: You! Don't talk to me. You made up with the good God in order to get out a newspaper. You are on good terms with the *old chap*.

(*The whole table laughs.*)

TAINE: The Englishwoman, for example.

SAINTE-BEUVE: Oh, there is nothing more charming than the French-woman. One, two, three, four, five women. Delightful. Has our lovely friend returned? And to think that when quarter day comes round, and the rent is due, one can have a crowd of ravishing ones. For nothing. The poor dears! For the wages of woman. . . . There is something that historians like Thiers never think of. There is the place to reform the state. These questions—

SAINT-VICTOR: No, there is no way women can earn a living. Little What's-her-name, at the Gymnase Théâtre, who is paid four thousand francs a year, told me yesterday—

GAUTIER: I have always said that prostitution was woman's normal state.

A VOICE: After all, Malthus—

VEYNE: Malthus is an ignominious book!

TAINE: But it seems to me that one should bring children into the world only if one is certain of being able to ensure them some sort of exist-ence. Those poor girls who go off to be governesses in Russia!

A VOICE: Long live our wives! Long live sterile mistresses!

SAINT-VICTOR: Come, Taine. Nature! The great god Pan!

SAINTE-BEUVE (*whispering to his neighbor*): Every year I sell the rights to a little book. That allows me to make little gifts to women . . . in holiday season. They are so sweet; one cannot really . . .

(*At this point in the dinner Sainte-Beuve, cheered up by his memo-ries, makes himself earrings of clusters of cherries. Tableau!*)

(*Somehow the name of Racine falls into the general talk.*)

NEFFTZER (*to Gautier*): Look here, you committed an infamy this morn-ing. In the *Moniteur* you extolled the talent of Racine and Maubant.*

GAUTIER: True. Maubant has a great deal of talent. But, with my govern-ment paper, you see how it is: my minister is idiotic enough to believe in masterpieces. I was therefore obliged to review Racine's *Andro-*

---

* An actor. Agar, mentioned later, was an actress.

maque. For that matter, Racine wrote swinish verse and I said not a word in praise of the creature.

SCHERER (*horrified and staring at the whole tableful over his glasses*): Gentlemen, it seems to me you are excessively intolerant. You proceed by way of exclusion. After all, what should our task be but to reform, to combat instinctive opinions. Taste is nothing. The only thing that counts is judgment. One should possess judgment before all else.

A VOICE: —on judgment! Taste and nothing else! Only taste!

(*Tumult.*)

SOULIÉ: We can hardly hear one another.

GAVARNI: We hear one another only too well.

(*Exeunt omnes.*)

(*Friday, May 5, 1876—"Our 'society of five' had the wild notion to have a bouillabaisse in the tavern behind the Opéra Comique. Tonight everybody is a fervid talker. . . ."—Goncourt*)

TURGENIEFF: To do any work I need the winter, the sort of frost we have in Russia, an *astringent* cold, with the trees loaded with crystals . . . Ah, then. . . . As it happens, I work still better in autumn; that is, during those days when there's scarcely any wind at all, when the sun is elastic, and when the air tastes of wine. . . . My favorite hideout is a little wooden cottage, with a garden of yellow acacias—we don't have any white ones in Russia. In autumn the ground is all covered with husks which crackle when one steps on them, and the air is crowded with those birds that imitate others . . . There, inside, all alone . . .

(*Turgenieff does not finish the sentence, but his clenched fists, pressed tightly against his breast, convey all the joy and intoxication which he feels in that little corner of old Russia . . .*)

FLAUBERT: . . . Yes, a classical marriage. To be perfectly honest, I was just a child. Eleven years old, in fact. It was I who removed the bride's garter. There was a little girl at the wedding. I returned home in love with her. I wanted to give her my heart, an expression I had heard. At that time there used to arrive at my house every day baskets full of game, of fish, of things to eat. They were sent by sick people whom my father had treated. The baskets would be deposited every morning in the dining-room. At the same time I used to hear a great deal of talk about operations, as if they were normal and regular things. I began to think seriously of asking my father to remove my heart. And I began to see my heart carried in a diligence by a handsomely uniformed coachman and placed on the buffet of the dining-room of my little lady . . . And in the actual gift of my heart there was neither wound nor blood. . . .

ZOLA: As for me. . . .*

TURGENIEFF: I had been called back to Russia, and there I was in Naples with no more than five hundred francs on me. There was no railroad at that time. The journey back was hard and disagreeable, and naturally without romantic compensations. Then one day I found myself at Lucerne, looking down from the bridge. Beside me stood a woman who was resting her elbows on the parapet. Both of us were watching those ducks that have a mark shaped like an almond on their heads. The evening was magnificent. . . . We began to chat, then we took a stroll, and as we strolled we entered the cemetery—Flaubert, do you know that cemetery? . . . In all my life I don't remember ever having been more amorous, more excited, more urgent. . . . The woman lay down on a large tombstone. . . .

FLAUBERT (*pressing his elbow against his breast*): Yet all of that, what is it compared with taking the arm of a woman you love, and holding it against your heart for a second as you lead her to the dinner table.

DAUDET (*twisting about in his chair and waving his hands nervously*): Good God! that's not my style at all!

FLAUBERT (*ingenuously*): But, Daudet, you know I'm a pig!

DAUDET: In short, you are a cynic with men and a sentimentalist with women.

FLAUBERT (*laughing*): Damn it, that's true! I even address a prostitute as "my little angel."

TURGENIEFF (*with almost frightened eyes*): It's curious—I never go near a woman without a feeling of respect and surprise at my good luck . . . Daudet, you haven't known the Russian woman. Too bad . . . You would have found something to interest you there. Let's see, how should I describe her to you?—She is a mixture of simplicity, tenderness, and unconscious depravity. . . .

FLAUBERT: In upper Egypt, on a night as black as an oven, between low houses, with the dogs howling as if they meant to devour you, someone leads you to a hut the height of a boy of sixteen . . . There, deep within, you find lying on the ground a woman in a chemise, whose body is entwined six or seven times with a long golden chain—a woman whose buttocks are as cold as ice . . . Then with this woman who remains motionless in pleasure . . . you experience—do you see?—endless delights . . . and delights. . . .

GONCOURT: Come, come, Flaubert, old man, that smacks of literature, all that!

---

* Thus bowdlerized in Goncourt Academy edition.

Alfred Lord Tennyson

A POET-LAUREATE REMINISCES ABOUT SOME EARLY
LITERARY ENTHUSIASMS AND PUZZLES OVER
THE CASE OF JOHN KEATS.

*He was a livery-stable-keeper's son. I don't know
where he got it from . . . unless from heaven.*

THE following dialogue is admittedly little more than an hors d'oeuvre. We should have liked our chronicler to record more of that late summer conversation at Haslemere in 1880. Think only of the names cropping up in the talk—Coleridge, Byron, Shelley, Keats! There must have been hundreds of touches and phrases that eluded the diarist as he sat down that night to recapture what had been said. For William Allingham was no Boswell. Yet we owe him a generous tribute as a diligent, if minor, preserver of talk. The dialogue entries of his diary may be brief, but they ring true, and one applauds the triumph of the reporter over the artist. Allingham, a poet and artist in his own right, passes on his memories without embellishment. To this Irish bard of delicate gift we owe some of our best, if evanescent, glimpses of Thackeray, Carlyle, Browning, and Tennyson.

Since 1867 the secluded town of Haslemere had been to Tennyson a kind of refuge from the world. As his popularity grew, the shy and nervous poet found himself besieged by battalions of curiosity-seekers. In the words of Edmond Gosse, Tennyson "determined to make for himself a haven of refuge against the invading Philistines." Land was purchased at Blackdown, which was just above Haslemere, and in due course Tennyson and his family installed themselves in a newly constructed house. "Aldworth," as the dwelling was named, now became the meeting-place of a small circle of literary friends. In 1880 Allingham and his wife spent the spring and summer at Haslemere, a short distance away from Tennyson's "haven." As it happened, there was little activity at Aldworth till August, when Tennyson and his son returned from a trip to Italy.

Early in August the Allinghams received an invitation to Blackdown, and made their first visit to the hall on August 5. From the summit of a heath-fringed road on Blackdown, the Irish poet noted: "the vast expanses of light and shadow, golden cornfields, blue distances, from Leith Hill to Chanctonbury Ring." The couple walked through the house: "long hall open at each end" and found tea "on the further lawn, smooth, shut in with shrubs." Tennyson, in a gray suit and sombrero, presently took them to an upper balcony of the house, to show them the panorama of hill and dale spread out below. "I sometimes see a spire out yonder, but I don't know what it is," mused the white-haired poet-laureate. "Field Place is near it . . . Shelley's birthplace. . . ."

In many matters Tennyson has become bigoted, embittered, and sharp-tongued. He has lost faith in social progress. Among friends he berates England as "the most beastly self-satisfied nation in the world." At times he fears some vast catastrophe, comparable to the French Revolution, is gathering, "to swallow up mankind in a chaos of Socialism, Atheism, and Materialism." Mercilessly, he flails the Utopian philosophies of the day and grows impatient over any hint of change. . . . And then he will stand on his balcony and stare raptly in the direction of Shelley's birthplace. For Allingham soon discovers that once Tennyson returns to the subject of Shelley or Keats or Wordsworth he is transformed, carried back to that magic childhood of his when, heavy with grief, he inscribed on a rock: "Byron is dead."

The visits of the Allinghams now become a daily ritual. On September 2; we find the couple driving up to Aldworth in a carriage. The following entry is taken intact from the posthumously printed Diary edited by Mrs. Allingham (Macmillan, London, 1908). Like Allingham, Aubrey de Vere, who also figures in the dialogue, was an Irish poet, more richly gifted, and, in his cultivation of a calm, reflective style, an avowed disciple of Wordsworth. One can understand his resenting Ruskin's dismissal of Wordsworth as "a Westmoreland peasant." Dr. Bradley is the Rev. George G. Bradley, of Marlborough, afterwards Dean of Westminster.

(Sept. 2, 1880—"Drove up to Tennyson's to dinner. Helen and I, Aubrey de Vere, Dr. Bradley, Mrs. and Miss Bradley. Alfred Tennyson and Aubrey de Vere and I talk of poetry. Tennyson and I agree on the odiousness of various readings inserted on a poet's page—and of critical notes. De Vere blames Ruskin for his recent remarks on Wordsworth, —'a Westmoreland peasant, etc.' De Vere wishes Wordsworth had written his magnum opus, of which the Prelude was the beginning."— Allingham)

TENNYSON: His small things are the best. Even his "Tintern Abbey," fine as it is, should have been much compressed.

DE VERE: But if it pleased the artistic sense more, might it not appeal less to the sympathies?

TENNYSON: A great deal might be left out.

ALLINGHAM: One could turn the largest part of the "Excursion" into prose, very seldom altering a word, merely rearranging. Here and there a line or a passage of poetry would be left, like a quotation. It is much easier to write bad blank verse than good prose.

TENNYSON: And it is much easier to write rhyme than good blank verse. I should not be sorry to lose anything from a poet which is not beautiful poetry. One plods over Wordsworth's long dreary plains of prose —one knows there's a mountain somewhere, and now and again you come to astonishing things. In old times, when copying was costly, Catullus, Horace, and the others gave only their best.

DE VERE: Wordsworth ought to have done great and perfect things, one fancies. He lived a poetic life, he devoted himself to poetry . . . How was it?

ALLINGHAM: For many years he never read any poetry but his own. His mind became monotonous.

DE VERE: I believe that is true. And he was continually touching and altering, and sometimes injuring, what he had written.

ALLINGHAM: His experience of real life was neither wide nor various. His material ran short.

DE VERE: And yet, if he gives us a good deal of dullness, might not the same be said of Homer and of Milton?

TENNYSON (*grunting*): No, no!

DE VERE: Well, I find a great deal of Homer very dull—and surely the last six books of *Paradise Lost* are much below the first six?

TENNYSON: Possibly—but there's the charm of Milton's style. He invented his verse—just as Virgil invented his.

DE VERE: I once read to Wordsworth your

> *Of old sat Freedom on the heights,*

and,

> *You ask me, why, tho' ill at ease,*

and he said, "Fine poetry and very stately diction."

TENNYSON (*contentedly*): H'm!

ALLINGHAM: Coleridge was more essentially a poet than Wordsworth.

TENNYSON: I don't know that.

DE VERE: I think so. But how melancholy to think that all his finest poems

were produced in one single year of his life. Then he went to Germany
and took to Metaphysics—such a pity!

TENNYSON: But the man I count greater than them all—Wordsworth,
Coleridge, Byron, Shelley, every one of 'em—is Keats, who died at
twenty-five . . . Thousands of faults! (*Twiddling the fingers of one
hand in the air.*) But he's wonderful!

DE VERE: He doesn't pall upon you?

TENNYSON: No!

DE VERE: Shelley used to be a great idol of yours.

TENNYSON: O, yes. . . . We lived near the most prosaic village in the world
—where they had never heard of anything. One day we went there to
meet my brother Frederick, who was coming back from somewhere,
and as we were driving home he whispered, "I've got a poet who's
much grander than Byron," and repeated one line—

Waterfalls leap among wild islands green,

which I thought delicious. "Alastor" was the first poem of his I read.
I said, "This is what I want!"—and still I like it the best, though one
can't tell how much these first loves are to be trusted. "The Revolt of
Islam" is splendid but gives me a headache. It's fatiguing—all mountain tops and glories.

(*De Vere agrees and names as his favorites "The Ode to the West
Wind," "Ode to Naples," of which he recites some lines, and another
piece.*)

TENNYSON (*also quoting a passage from Shelley*): What can you do with
a man who has such a command of language? But Keats was not
wild and willful. He had always an intention. At the same time he was
daimonisch. He had a touch. . . . He was a livery-stable-keeper's son.
. . . I don't know where he got it from . . . unless from Heaven.
(*Quotes.*)

> *Perhaps the self-same song that found a path*
> *Through the sad heart of Ruth when, sick for home,*
> *She stood in tears amid the alien corn;*
> *The same that oft-times hath*
> *Charm'd magic casements opening on the foam*
> *Of perilous seas, in faery lands forlorn.*

What can be lovelier? (*Repeats the last two lines.*) I once saw it
printed "In fairyland forlorn," which totally ruined it . . . one doesn't
know why.

Leo Tolstoy

AN AMERICAN REFORMER STOUTLY RESISTS THE DOCTRINE OF NON-RESISTANCE IN THE COUNTRY PLACE OF A GREAT PACIFIST.

KENNAN: Suppose that this bleeding, defenseless, half-naked girl had appealed to you for protection and had thrown herself into your arms; suppose it had been your daughter—would you still have refused to interfere by an act of violence?

TOLSTOY (silent for a few moments; his eyes filled with tears): Do you know absolutely that that thing was done?

IN THE early months of 1886 an American traveler and explorer by the name of George Kennan * visited a penal colony in the vast, bleak wilderness of the Trans-Baikal in Eastern Siberia. There he watched political convicts of both sexes slaving away in the salt mines. A great anger rose in him which would one day find expression in a fiery denunciation of the Czarist regime—a two-volume study entitled Siberia and the Exile System. Kennan talked with some of these exiles, and one of them, a woman, entrusted a manuscript to him. "Promise to give this document to Count Tolstoy to read," she pleaded. Kennan gave his word, and quickly hid away in his luggage what proved to be the "ghastly narrative" of a hunger strike by four women at the Irkutsk prison. Among these convicts Kennan found a great hope that in the author of War and Peace they had a friend and advocate who would espouse their cause, a man who would one day rise up in his wrath and urge his people to end their long servitude by revolt. Stirred by their pleas, Kennan tried not to disillusion them. Cut off from the world, these wretched exiles scarcely suspected what this American reformer knew—that Count Tolstoy, having become

---

* Grand-uncle of a member of the U.S. State Department bearing the same name and, like him, a specialist on Russian affairs.

the world's leading apostle of the doctrine of non-resistance to evil, would not raise a finger to help them. Yet, Kennan, as a confirmed believer in the necessity of resisting entrenched wrong, resolved to confront Tolstoy and show him the folly of his doctrine. Early in June, 1886, Kennan set out for Moscow, armed with his "ghastly narrative." Arriving there, he learned that the Count had left the city to spend the summer on his estate near the village of Yasnaya Polyana in the province of Tula. Characteristically, the fifty-eight-year-old Count had walked the whole distance of 130 miles. On June 16 Kennan took the late evening train southward over the Moscow-Kursk railway and reached the town of Tula the following morning. There he arranged to have a droshky convey him the few remaining miles to his destination. . . .

Meanwhile, at Yasnaya Polyana, the world's foremost living writer, garbed in the coarse, homespun raiment of a Russian peasant, was working in the fields. For Tolstoy the novelist and thinker had become Tolstoy the man of the soil. In a great spiritual upheaval he had come to look upon wealth and leisure as deadly sins. A new reading of the gospels had convinced him that hard work, humility, and poverty were the sole bases of a truly Christian life. Thus, we now find the author of *War and Peace* and *Anna Karenina* plowing and hoeing the soil for his impoverished neighbors, distributing his worldly goods, and preaching a life of absolute simplicity. And of all his newly acquired beliefs one dominated Tolstoy's new way of life with an iron rigor—the command of Jesus to refrain from resisting evil. For Tolstoy this had come to mean one thing, pure and simple: whatever the provocation, violence should never be met by violence. Wrongs, brutal and inhuman as they might be, could be redressed only by love. The enemy must be loved and pitied and persuaded; never must he be confronted by force. Any form of coercion was unchristian. Under no circumstances, however "just" and patriotic, should one man take another man's life. No resistance should be offered to invaders of one's country, even when they came to enslave. "If anyone would force you to work for him," Tolstoy admonished, "go and work for him; and if anyone would take away your property, abandon it to him." Such was Tolstoy's reductio ad absurdum—or perhaps exact fulfillment—of Christ's injunction, "Resist not evil."

It was to this uncompromising pacifist that the American reformer George Kennan came on "a bright sunshiny June morning" with a plea for support from a hopeful band of political convicts five thousand miles away. As Kennan approached Tolstoy's house he found it completely in character with the man's teachings. Everything bespoke austerity and simplicity. A plain, white, rectangular, two-story structure of stuccoed brick, the house stood meekly among a cluster of trees that concealed it from the road. "It had neither piazzas nor towers nor architectural ornaments of any kind," wrote Kennan in an account of his visit that appeared in the Century Magazine the following year. "There were no vines to soften its hard rectangular outlines or relieve the staring whiteness of its flat walls."

Against this spare background Count Tolstoy appeared through the door. He wore heavy calfskin shoes, loose, shapeless trousers of coarse linen, and a collarless white cotton undershirt. He looked massive and granitic. And the face, resolute, sunburned, rugged, reminded Kennan of the Tuscan phrase, "molded with the fist and polished with the pickax." What Kennan saw here was "an unconquerable strength." He saw, too, that nothing short of an earthquake could shake this man from any position he had resolved to take. After the two men had greeted one another cordially, Tolstoy momentarily excused himself to slip a coarse gray tunic over his undershirt, belting it around his waist with a wide black strap. He then sat down beside Kennan, who, remembering his mission, presently began telling him of his experiences among the Siberian convicts. The conversation that follows has been extracted from the article in the Century Magazine.

KENNAN: Don't you think that resistance to such oppression is justifiable? *

TOLSTOY: That depends upon what you mean by resistance; if you mean pursuasion, argument, protest, I answer yes. If you mean violence— no. I do not believe that violent resistance to evil is ever justifiable under any circumstances. . . . The revolutionists whom you have seen in Siberia undertook to resist evil by violence, and what has been the result? Bitterness and misery and hatred and bloodshed! The evils against which they took up arms still exist, and to them has been added a mass of previously non-existent human suffering. It is not in that way that the kingdom of God is to be realized on earth.

KENNAN (*relating a case of cruelty and brutality which had come to his knowledge in Siberia*): Count Tolstoy, if you had been there and had witnessed that transaction, would you not have interfered with violence?

TOLSTOY: No.

---

* Indirect discourse in original.

KENNAN: Would you kill a highwayman who was about to murder an innocent traveler, provided there was no other way to save the traveler's life? *

TOLSTOY: If I should see a bear about to kill a peasant in the forest, I should sink an ax in the bear's head. But I would not kill a man who was about to do the same thing.

KENNAN: Count Tolstoy, three or four years ago there was arrested in one of the provinces of European Russia a young, sensitive, cultivated woman named Olga Liubatovitch. I will not relate her whole history. It is enough to say that, inspired by ideas which, even if mistaken, were at least unselfish and heroic, she, with hundreds of other young people of both sexes, undertook to overturn the existing system of government. She was arrested, thrown into prison, and after being kept for a year in solitary confinement she was exiled to Siberia by administrative process. You perhaps know—or if you do not know, I can tell you— what hardships and sufferings and humiliations a young girl must undergo who is sent to Siberia alone with a common criminal party. You can imagine the state of nervous excitement, the abnormal mental and emotional condition, to which she is brought by months of riding in springless *telegas*; † by being compelled to yield to the demands of nature under the eyes of a soldier, and by sleeping for weeks on the hard benches and in the foul air of "étapes" swarming with vermin. In this abnormal mental and emotional condition Olga Liubatovitch reached the town of Krasnoyarsk in Eastern Siberia. She had up to this time been permitted to wear her own dress and her own underclothing; but at Krasnoyarsk the local governor directed that she should put on the dress of a common convict. She refused to do so upon the ground that administrative exiles had the right to wear their own clothing, and that if convict dress had been obligatory she would have been required to put it on before she left Moscow. The local governor insisted upon obedience to his order, and Miss Liubatovitch persisted in refusal. I do not know the reason for her obstinacy, but as convicts are not always supplied with new clothing, and are sometimes compelled to put on garments which have already been worn by others and which are foul and full of vermin, it is not difficult to suggest a number of good reasons for objecting to such a change. The chief of police and the officer of the convoy were finally directed to use force. In their presence, and that of half a dozen other men, three or four soldiers seized the poor girl and attempted to take off her clothes.

---

* Indirect discourse in original.
† Russian for "carts."

She resisted, and there followed a horrible scene of violence and un-availing self-defense. Her lips were cut in the contest and her face covered with blood, but she continued to resist as long as she had strength. In spite of her cries, appeals, and struggles, she was finally overpowered, stripped naked under the eyes of six or eight men, and forcibly reclothed in the coarse convict dress. Now, suppose that all this had occurred in your presence; suppose that this bleeding, de-fenseless, half-naked girl had appealed to you for protection and had thrown herself into your arms; suppose that it had been your daughter —would you still have refused to interfere by an act of violence?

TOLSTOY (*silent for a few moments; his eyes filled with tears*): Do you know absolutely that that thing was done?

KENNAN: No, because I did not see it done. But I have it from two eye-witnesses, one of them a lady in whose statements I put implicit trust, and the other an officer of the exile administration. They saw it and they told me.

TOLSTOY (*after some silence*): Even under such circumstances violence would not be justifiable. Let us analyze that situation carefully. I will grant, for the sake of argument, that the local governor who ordered the act of violence was an ignorant man, a cruel man, a brutal man— what you will; but he probably had an idea that he was doing his duty; he probably believed that he was enforcing a law of the government to which he owed obedience and service. You suddenly appear and set yourself up as a judge in the case; you assume that he is not doing his duty,—that he is committing an act of unjustifiable violence,— and then, with strange inconsistency, you proceed to aggravate and complicate the evil by yourself committing another act of unjustifi-able violence. One wrong added to another wrong does not make a right; it merely extends the area of wrong. Furthermore, your resist-ance, in order to be effective,—in order to accomplish anything,— must be directed against the soldiers who are committing the assault. But those soldiers are not free agents; they are subject to military discipline and are acting under orders which they dare not disobey. To prevent the execution of the orders you must kill or maim two or three of the soldiers—that is, kill or wound the only parties to the transaction who are certainly innocent, who are manifestly acting without malice and without evil intention. Is that just? Is it rational? But go a step further: suppose that you do kill or wound two or three of the soldiers; you may or may not thus succeed in preventing the completion of the act against which your violence is a protest; but one thing you certainly will do, and that is, extend the area of enmity, injustice, and misery. Every one of the soldiers whom you kill or maim has a family, and upon every such family you bring grief and suffering which would not have come to it but for your act. In the hearts of perhaps a score of people you rouse the anti-Christian and anti-social emotions of hatred and revenge, and thus sow broadcast the seeds of further violence and strife. At the time when you interposed there was only one center of evil and suffering. By your violent interference you have created half a dozen such centers. It does not seem to me, Mr. Kennan, that that is the way to bring about the reign of peace and good-will on earth.

(The conversation is interrupted by a summons to lunch, which is served in a large, cheerful, sunny room of the upper floor. Kennan and Tolstoy then return to the little reception room on the first floor. Kennan again raises the question of the treatment of the political convicts in Siberia. As an illustration he hands Tolstoy the manuscript of a detailed account of the voluntary self-starvation of four political convicts, all educated women, in the prison at Irkutsk.)

TOLSTOY *(reading a few pages with a gradually clouding face, then returning the manuscript to Kennan)*: I have no doubt that the courage and fortitude of these people are heroic. But their methods are irrational and I cannot sympathize with them. They resorted to violence, knowing that they rendered themselves liable to violence in return, and they are suffering the natural consequences of their mistaken action. I cannot imagine any darker conception of hell than the state of some of those unfortunate people in Siberia, whose hearts are full of bitterness and hatred, and who, at the same time, are absolutely powerless even to return evil for evil. *(Pauses.)* If they had only changed their views a little . . . if they had adopted the course which seems to me the only right one to pursue in dealing with evil,—what might not such people have done for Russia! Mine is the true revolutionary method. If the people of the empire refuse, as I believe they should refuse, to render military service,—if they decline to pay taxes to support that instrument of violence, an army,—the present system of government cannot stand. The proper way to resist evil is to refuse absolutely to do evil either for one's self or for others.

KENNAN: But the Government *forces* its people to render military service and pay taxes! They *must* serve and pay or go to prison!

TOLSTOY: Then let them go to prison! The Government cannot put the whole population in prison, and if it could it would still be without material for an army and without money for its support.

KENNAN: But you cannot get the whole people to act simultaneously in this way. If you were let alone, you could perhaps convert a few hundred thousand peasants to your views; but do you think that you would be let alone? As soon as your teaching began to be dangerous to the stability of the state it would be suppressed. Suppose, for the sake of argument, that you succeeded in converting a quarter of the population; the Government would draw soldiers enough from the other three quarters to put that one quarter in prison or in Siberia, and there would be an end of your propaganda and your revolution. It seems to me that the first thing to be done is to obtain freedom of action—peaceably if possible, forcibly if necessary. You cannot persuade, or teach, or show people how they ought to live, if some other man holds you by the throat and chokes you every time you open your mouth or raise your hand. How are you ever going to get your propaganda under way?

TOLSTOY: But do you not see that if you claim and exercise the right to resist an act of violence that you regard as evil, every other man will insist upon his right to resist in the same way what he regards as evil, and the world will continue to be filled with violence? It is your duty to show that there is a better way.

KENNAN: But you cannot show anything if somebody smites you on the mouth every time you open it to speak the truth.

TOLSTOY: You can at least refrain from striking back. You can show by your peaceable behavior that you are not governed by the barbarous law of retaliation, and your adversary will not continue to strike a man who neither resists nor tries to defend himself. It is by those who have suffered, not by those who have inflicted suffering, that the world has been advanced.

KENNAN: It seems to me that the advancement of the world has been promoted not a little by the protests—and often the violent and bloody protests—of its inhabitants against wrong and outrage, and that all history goes to show that a people which tamely submits to oppression never acquires either liberty or happiness.*

TOLSTOY: The whole history of the world is a history of violence, and you can of course cite violence in support of violence; but do you not see that there is in human society an endless variety of opinions as to what constitutes wrong and oppression, and that if you once concede the right of any man to resort to violence to resist what he regards as wrong, he being the judge, you authorize every other man to enforce his opinions in the same way, and you have a universal reign of violence?

---

* Indirect discourse in original.

KENNAN: If, on the other hand, oppression is advantageous to the oppressor, and if he finds that he can oppress with impunity and that nobody resists, when is he likely to stop oppressing? It seems to me that the peaceable submission to injustice which you advocate would simply divide society into two classes: tyrants, who find tyranny profitable, and who therefore will continue it indefinitely, and slaves, who regard resistance as wrong, and who will therefore submit indefinitely.

(*Count Tolstoy proposes a walk, and Kennan assents. A short distance from the house they meet the Count's eldest daughter, dressed as a peasant girl. She is on her way home from the fields, where she had been raking hay with the village girls of Yasnaya Polyana. . . .*)

TOLSTOY: I believe that it is everyone's duty to labor for others who need assistance, and to work at least a part of every day with his hands.* It is better to labor for and with the poor in their particular employment than it is to work in your own higher and possibly more remunerative intellectual field and then give the poor the results of your labor. In the one case you not only help the people who need help, but you set the poor and the idle an example; you show them that you do not regard even their prosaic toil as beneath your dignity, and you thus teach them self-respect, industry, and contentment with their lot. If, on the other hand, you work exclusively in your own higher intellectual field and give the poor the results of your labor, as you would give alms to a beggar, you encourage idleness and dependence; you establish a social class distinction between yourself and the recipient of your alms; you break down his self-respect and self-reliance, and you inspire him with a longing to escape from the hard conditions of his own life of daily physical toil, and to share your life, which he thinks is easier than his; to wear your clothes, which seem to him better than his, and to gain admission to your social class, which he regards as higher than his. That is not the way to help the poor or to promote the brotherhood of man.

KENNAN: If I admit that it is man's highest duty to do good to others, and that he owes only a secondary duty to himself and to his family, I cannot dispute the soundness of your reasoning. If I accept your premises I leave myself no ground to stand on in an argument; but, waiving that point, the characteristic of your scheme that strikes me most forcibly is its utter impracticability. Given the present organization of society and the existing traits of human character, it seems to me that a man who practices non-resistance, and who devotes his life to the good of

---

* Tolstoy had spent the morning spreading manure over the land of a poor widow who lived near his estate.

others, simply sacrifices himself and his family without any commensurate gain to the world, because nobody else acts upon the same principles.

TOLSTOY: You say that if you admit my premises you leave yourself no ground to stand on in an argument; but why should you not admit my premises? You *must* admit my premises. If every man should do good to every other man instead of evil, the condition of things would be better than it is now, would it not? The state of society in which every man shall do good instead of evil is a thing to be hoped for and worked for, is it not? Then why do you say that I am impracticable when I hope and work for the realization of a social state which you yourself admit is desirable? If we are ever to reach that desirable social state, somebody must make a beginning, must he not? Somebody must take a step in that direction and show that it is possible to live so. What if the present organization of society and the existing traits of human character do make such a step difficult—that has no bearing on my personal duty. The question is not what is easy, but what is right. There is nothing sacred or necessarily immutable about the present organization of society and the existing traits of human character. They are the results of man's activity, and by man's activity they can be changed. I believe that they ought to be changed, and I am doing what I can to change them.

Walt Whitman

A PATRIARCH OF AMERICAN POETRY CELEBRATES HIS SEVENTY-SECOND BIRTHDAY WITH CHAMPAGNE AND TESTIMONIALS.

> *I must say to my friends further along the table that I am about half blind and I cannot see more than ten feet ahead and hardly that—else I am sure I should specify them.*

THE day is May 31, 1891. On the parlor floor of a simple frame house at 328 Mickle Street in Camden, N. J., some two dozen men and women are waiting for their ailing friend Walt Whitman to come down from his bedroom to help them celebrate his seventy-second birthday. Through a window of the parlor may be seen a clump of lilac-bushes in the back yard. Out in front a large tree casts its protective arms over the modest abode of an aging poet. From the Delaware River nearby come the sounds of ferry-bells and whistles—a haunting, nostalgic music to this minstrel of the teeming cities and rivers. Gathered downstairs are lawyers, doctors, businessmen, and writers, all of them fervid booklovers, but almost all of them obscure men whose only claim to remembrance will be their friendship with Walt Whitman—their friendship, and their staunch support through years of cruel ridicule and calumny. They have come now to renew their allegiance to the poet who has been leader and liberator, whose Leaves of Grass is their bible of a brave new way of life and art; to assure this feeble, pain-racked paralytic upstairs that the good fight has been won on many fronts. They have come, also, to eat and to drink champagne.

While the hubbub of literary chatter grows around the huge parlor table, we might examine some of these birthday celebrants, for soon we shall hear them greet the Good Gray Poet in varying degrees of commemorative fervor. Most conspicuous of all, perhaps, is Dr. Richard M. Bucke, a Canadian alienist, whose searching biography of Whitman was the first of a dozen soon to follow. Next, we observe Thomas Harned, lawyer and book-collector; Thomas Donaldson, a businessman and noted raconteur; Talcott Williams, a Philadelphia journalist; David McKay, the publisher, and several more who have become mere names on the honor-roll of time. Most gratifying of all, from our point of view, is the presence of a young, eager-eyed votary named Horace Traubel. We feel confident that there will be a written record of the proceedings. This faithful Traubel is later to give the world three priceless volumes of Walt Whitman's soliloquies on Mickle Street. These revealing monologues Traubel has been jotting down in his own shorthand while aiding the man he worshipped to bring out a new edition of his poems. And for this birthday occasion Traubel has even contrived to engage a trained stenographer to assure a double accuracy. In 1893, some time after Whitman's death, we shall find this same Traubel collaborating with both Dr. Bucke and Thomas Harned on a memorial volume, now almost completely forgotten, called In Re Walt Whitman, and published in Philadelphia. As his major contribution to that volume Traubel will include a record of this "Round Table with Walt Whitman," reproduced, in his words, "from the direct work of a stenographer and liberal notes kept by the writer."

Meanwhile it is time to mount the stairs to summon the host to his birthday party. We find Walt Whitman ensconced in a capacious chair in the large front room of the second floor. The room is crammed with books, manuscripts, and mounds of letters. A roving glance reveals a huge bed, a stove, several packing boxes, a chest, and a few large wooden chairs. Over the fireplace hangs a portrait of the poet's father, a severe-looking man, and beside it one of his mother. "It was a good prison," remarks Henry Seidel Canby of this bedchamber. In the room with Whitman at the moment is Warren Fritzinger, a young man who serves him as coachman, companion, and nurse. "Warry," as we shall hear him called, has come to assist his master down the steep stairs. A semi-paralytic, Whitman is almost helpless now. This once magnificent body is shattered by a host of ailments that, as an autopsy will shortly reveal, would have killed most people half Whitman's age. . . .

Many have traced Whitman's condition back to the physical and emotional strains of the Civil War period, in which he served as volunteer nurse. The theory advanced is that Whitman's blood was then poisoned while treating gangrenous wounds. The death of his mother proved another great shock, and there is no doubt that, for all Whitman's stamina as rebel and crusader, the constant barrage of defamation from all sides took its toll too. Almost from its beginnings in 1855 Leaves of Grass was rabidly pounced upon as the devil's own work. Whitman was unsparingly denounced as obscene, anarchistic, blasphemous. As the poet of untrammeled freedom and loose form, he was laughed at and lampooned, and as the writer of allegedly pornographic poetry he was discharged from his job in the Department of the Interior. But all through the struggle there were friends at his side. Emerson, for one; Swinburne, for another; that bristling iconoclast Robert Ingersoll; English scholars and critics like Ernest Rhys and the unabashedly inquisitive John Addington Symonds; the fiery Irish-American novelist and pamphleteer, William O'Connor, who had greeted Whitman's dismissal from a government job with a withering brochure that first used the term "The Good Gray Poet." Later, there were others—like Tennyson; the essayists Edward Dowden and George William Curtis; like the American poet Stedman, the fighting editor Dana, the journalist Sidney Morse (brother of the inventor); and most cherished of all, the loyal and valiant John Burroughs, who sharply rebuked those for whom his liberty-loving friend was a kind of combined moral leper and caricature poet. Many of these men will be present at the banquet below, though only in spirit. By their written testimonials they have earned an invisible place at this "Round Table." Our meticulous reporter Traubel does not overlook them in the evening's proceedings at the little house on Mickle Street. . . .

With "Warry" Fritzinger's arm about him, Walt Whitman now descends to the parlor room. He has had a bad day, with frequent attacks of excruciating pain. As he reaches the lower floor, there is a chorus of comradely greeting from all sides. Traubel and "Warry" seat the poet next to Mrs. Harned at the dinner table. Whitman immediately asks for some of the champagne which Traubel has thoughtfully provided, and the obliging lady at his side proceeds to ply him with his favorite beverage—"whereby," we are told, "he was at once built up." Although Dr. Brinton has been designated as official toastmaster, it is this noble, if crippled and disease-ridden wreck of a man, bravely mastering his pain in the sunny warmth of good fellowship, who, again in the words of Traubel, "in effect assumed the head of the table."

WHITMAN: After welcoming you deeply and specifically to my board, dear friends, it seems to me I feel first to say a word for the mighty comrades that have not long ago passed away—Bryant, Emerson, Longfellow; and I drink a reverent honor and memory to them. (*Lifting his glass of champagne to his lips.*) And I feel to add a word to Whittier, who is living with us—a noble old man; and another word to the boss of us all—Tennyson, who is also with us yet. I take this occasion to drink my reverence for those that have passed, and compliments for the two great masters left, and all that they stand for and represent. But I won't keep you any longer from your soup. (*Traubel passes up a copy of Dr. Johnston's* Notes of a Visit to Whitman—*elegantly bound, illustrated.*) Say, you fellows who dabble in the rivulets and bigger streams of literature—there is a splendid lesson that such notes as these of Dr. Johnston teach. It is the same lesson that there is in the play of *The Diplomatic Secret.* At the end of that interesting play, which I have seen, a great fellow who is in pursuit of it comes in crying: "At last I have found it—I have found the great secret! The great secret is that there is no secret at all!" That is the secret. The trick of literary style! I almost wonder if it is not chiefly having no style at all. And Dr. Johnston has struck it here in his notes. A man might give his fame for such a secret. (*To Traubel.*) Is pretty much everybody here? What has become of Stoddard? Who will play his part for him? And Hawthorne—wasn't he expected?

TRAUBEL: The table is about full. Stoddart and Hawthorne have not come. How does the champagne go?

WHITMAN: To the right spot—it goes through me, stirs me all up, gives me a show of strength. Mrs. Harned keeps me round with the notch. And is Anne come? Oh! yes—I see—down there by Clifford. Well—well—this is a good family sure enough.

TRAUBEL: You will stay then—you will not leave when the fifteen minutes are up?

WHITMAN: Did I say fifteen? I feel to show myself—perhaps say a word—let the rest take care of itself.

TRAUBEL: Ingersoll telegraphs he cannot come. He lectures tonight in Chicago.

WHITMAN: Lectures?

TRAUBEL: On Shakespeare.

WHITMAN (*laughing*): Next to Camden, Chicago is the luckiest city on the planet tonight!

TRAUBEL: You flatter the Colonel.

WHITMAN: He should be here. And yet wherever he goes, he is our justification. . . . It is to the credit of our land and time that a man so courageous, unconventional, spontaneous, should be followed about by multitudes. Do I stretch the truth when I say that?

TRAUBEL: I guess not.

WHITMAN: It is quite the right thing to call him useless or flippant, but the stream runs far deeper than all that—far deeper.

TRAUBEL: We can't shake off the giant by a shrug of the shoulders.

WHITMAN: Nor can we. I say to such men, welcome! welcome!—I say to Ingersoll, welcome, welcome! . . . And now that I am here myself I can't get rid of the feeling that John Burroughs, instead of sleeping on his farm tonight, should be right here with us! But no matter. Bucke is here, and you, Brinton (*turning to his left*), and Harry Bonsall—and I see Tom, too, and more'n enough to play out the bill. But here's Brinton on his feet. (*Aloud.*) And what is it now, doctor? (*In a low voice as Brinton starts.*) I'd give a lot to have all the English fellows here this minute!

BRINTON: As we are now supplied with what was necessary earlier in the repast for us to respond appropriately to the toast of our distinguished friend, I now offer the health of Walt Whitman on this, his birthday, with the hope that he may live to meet us here on the recurrence of this anniversary for many years to come.

WHITMAN (*as they drink*): I thank you all, my friends. Don't lay it on too thick. (*Pause—flood of remarks and questions.*) We have a word from Tennyson himself—a very short but wonderfully sweet and affectionate word. And we have a word from Addington Symonds, whom you all know well enough. As for me, I think his word not young enough to be fiery, and not old enough to have lost the pulse. But a wonderful man is Addington Symonds—some ways the most indicative and penetrating and significant man of our times; to me very valuable because he has thoroughly absorbed not only the old Greek cultus —all that it stands for, which is indescribably expensive—but the modern Italianism. And we have a graphic and beautiful letter from Moncure Conway—a very many-sided and a very experienced man—a queer kind of fellow, a thorough Londoner and Europeaner, so to speak; an Asiatier, too, for he went off some years ago to Asia and had two years in Calcutta and other Asiatic cities. And we have others. We have word from a cluster of Englishmen in Lancashire, noble young fellows, wonderfully American, cute, progressive, they who sent us a short cable about two hours ago. ("*Joy, Shipmate, Joy!*") And we have others. And I do not know, Horace,—or you, Professor—that you could do better than give us a taste of these messages—(*laughingly*) Not too long!

BRINTON (*letter in hand*): I begin with the words of him whom our host has referred to as "the boss."

WHITMAN: The boss of us all!

Tennyson: "*All health and happiness to you on your birthday and henceforward!*"

WHITMAN: Very short, very sweet! No flummery, no adjuncts, nothing but the heart and the grip of the matter—good will.* (*Sips his glass to the toast.*) But after all is said, I turn everything over to the emotional, and out of that I myself, the actual personal identity for my own special time, have uttered what I have uttered. To me, as I have said, back of everything that is very grand and very erudite and very scientific and very everything that is splendid in our era, is the simple individual critter, personality, if you please—his emotionality, supreme emotionality. . . . Through that personality I have myself spoken, reiterated. That is behind *Leaves of Grass*. It is the utterance of personality after—carefully remember—after being all surcharged with those other elements. But go on, Professor. I do not know how I have been led to speak so much.

BRINTON: As Mr. Whitman has referred to Symonds, I will read you what he says.

Symonds: "Speaking about Walt Whitman has always seemed to me much the same as talking about the universe. You know what Whitman himself said of that:

" 'I heard what was said of the Universe,
Heard it and heard it for several thousand years;
It is middling well as far as it goes,—But is that all?'

When I read panegyrics or criticisms of Walt Whitman these words always recur to my memory, 'It is middling well as far as it goes,—But is that all?' My own helplessness brings the truth of these words home to me with overpowering effect, whenever I attempt to express what I feel about him. In order to estimate, to interpret, to account for a hero, it is necessary to be the hero's peer, or at least his comrade. But let us not pretend to measure and interpret him. The bow of Ulysses proved too strong for all the suitors of Penelope: not a man of them could bend it. Even so the critique of Whitman lies beyond the scope of any living student. His panegyric—even when poured forth by an Ingersoll—is 'middling good as far as it goes,—But is that all?' "

WHITMAN: I like Symonds. One significant point of all first-class men is *caution*. Let us accept; let us whack away; let us absorb; *but don't let us be carried away.* I like that. It is my own spirit, my own feeling—to accept and try and listen, and don't be too quick to reject, and don't bother about its not agreeing with this, that or the other. But also, don't accept too quickly. Symonds is a curious fellow. He is about

---

* "James Russell Lowell sent his 'felicitations and good wishes' in almost as brief phrase, and sweet also, within the few following days."—Traubel's note.

fifty years of age. He is pretty rich, or was originally; lived in Bristol, England; had consumption; was diseased deeply with consumption. And so the doctors—with his wealth and everything—told him that it was pretty skittish business—that he was liable at any moment to be squelched out; so he, himself, finally, with his ten thousand pounds and so forth, went off to Switzerland, where he settled about twelve years ago. He had some money, as I said—not so dreadful, but still some. He had a wife. He had three or four children—three or four daughters—splendid girls. I have their pictures, they are up there. (*Thrusting his thumb toward the mantelpiece.*) He sent them to me. I have never seen him, of course, for he has never been in this country and I have never been there. He has written me many times—I suppose twenty times. I love him dearly. He is of college breed and education —horribly literary and suspicious, and enjoys things. A great fellow for delving into persons and into the concrete, and even into the physiological, the gastric—and wonderfully cute. And there he lives. He has built himself a handsome house. He has a good wife, I guess; has splendid daughters; and there in Switzerland, in this Davos Platz, he lives—once in a while going to London, to England. About every three months he writes me, O the most beautiful, splendid letters; I dare not show them to any one hardly, they are so like those tête-à-tête interviews with your chum, your mate, your comrade who throws off everything—and that is the kind of fellow Addington Symonds is. (*Warry*—go up and get the picture from my mantelpiece.) He has sent me a good picture taken in Switzerland, and I want to show you what kind of a person he is. I have, I suppose, a dozen photos. I had an idea that we in America made the finest photos on earth, but after seeing those Swiss samples, and some others, I have changed my mind. And it's not the first time I have had to change my mind. . . . I doubt if any one realizes the value and depth and grandeur of first-class photos. I think they penetrate somewhere all art from five hundred years ago down.

BRINTON: Suppose I go on with the letters? We ought to hear Roden Noel.

VOICES: Yes, Noel—Noel!

WHITMAN: Sure enough—no one must be omitted—slighted—all are evened up here!

> *Roden Noel:* "*I seem to have been left out of the list of your English friends. Still, I have always been a friend. I have always said I want to go to America to see Walt Whitman and Niagara.*" (*A slight pause.*)

HARNED: Walt, tell us more about Roden Noel.

WHITMAN: I don't know much about him. I know he is a good friend of mine, and believes (and it is a great feather in his cap!) in *Leaves of Grass*. The beauty of all this business is, that here are a lot of the best fellows away off in Switzerland or somewhere, or London and somewhere, who have not the least idea that they are being talked about, toasted, loved—Noel, for one, and Addington Symonds among the rest. I must always swear to Symonds—he is so noble, so true. (*Symonds' picture found and meanwhile passed around.*) The best thing about Symonds is his splendid aspiration. He wished to do something —he wished to do good. He was quite willing to leap into the gulf. He wished to do something. He wrote and wrote. He was very reticent. He was afraid of saying too much. He was afraid of going into anything too strongly and wanted to hedge. He was always anxious to make conditions and all that kind of thing. But he is essentially the most splendid person that England has produced. He was thoroughly critical, to begin with; very cute; very penetrative; very Greek—thoroughly Greek; thoroughly Italian. We don't realize what that word "Italian," in its best sense, means—but he was Italian and is Italian, and he is now a little blue. He thinks he is on his last legs, and it may possibly be that it is so. But he thinks deeply, like perhaps some others—he thinks almost too much of it, and he thinks he has decrepitude and failure and that the last has arrived. I consider it one of the greatest successes, triumphs, feats I have achieved that for twenty years he has been a student of *Leaves of Grass*—that I have his approbation and good will. The finale is, not details, not reasons why, or what has been, but, as in Tennyson's short sweet letter—in Symonds'—that he can say, God bless you, and good will to you, and success to you, and, I thoroughly endorse you, without detailing reasons why. (*Whitman turns, calls for words from absent friends—"Let them speak!"*)

Dowden: "*Among the many congratulations I hope Walt Whitman will accept mine. I wish you better health, if that may be, but in any case we have the happiness of knowing that you are sane in heart and head, and that you must feel how your best self is abroad in the world and active for good. I give you my reverence!*"

WHITMAN: Always the faithful Dowden! It is a good hand across the sea. We all join hands tonight! In the old world Dowden and Noel have their places—Dowden especially ranking high up. . . . Noel has written a book—essays, what not—and in that he takes up the puzzle of *Leaves of Grass*. Some of my friends do not think it goes very deep into the matter—I don't know that it does—but I myself feel that he has struck a true note, which is the main thing, after all.

Burroughs: "*Walt, I keep your birthday pruning my vineyard and in reading an hour from your poems under my fig tree. I will let you eat your dinner in peace, as I shall want to do if I ever reach my 72d.*"

WHITMAN (*leaning toward Traubel*): The only trouble with John is, he has a bit of a suspicion of us all—thinks I must have fallen in bad company (*laughing*)—the Colonel and you and Bucke, . . . and yet John, of all men, ought to be right here tonight. . . . Well, well, here's love to John forever (*sipping his champagne*).

Dana: "*Health and long life! No man is so happy as he who has more friends today than he had yesterday.*"

WHITMAN: Merry for Dana! His hand, too! . . . and now, don't forget Forman, Horace—there's a *love you* from him, too!

Forman: "*I look toward the sea, and see you sitting calmly over there with your face turned to the light. Be not in haste to climb, dear Walt Whitman. Sit there still, 'calm and supercilious' (your own words), and receive for many years yet the expressions of our love for yourself, our respect for your life, and our deep thankfulness for the solid spiritual aid we have received, and expect still to receive, from the inexhaustible treasury of your Book.*"

WHITMAN: Buxton Forman is a Shelleyite of great repute. How strange that Shelley and *Leaves of Grass* should play upon him together! How is it to be accounted for? But what is this you tell me, Horace—a poem from Ernest Rhys?

> *Rhys:* "*Today, oh poet, at your birthday board*
> *Sit many viewless guests, who cross the seas,*
> *(Their talisman, imagination's spell!)*
> *Ambassadors of many lands and tongues,*
> *Who come to hear your voice, to hold your hand*
> *And wish you health, once more upon the earth,*
> *And break the birthday bread of love once more!*
> *(So viewlessly, across the foreign seas,*
> *Your songs went out erewhile, the welcome guests,*
> *At hearth and board that you have never seen.)*
> *Among your viewless guests, who come today, dear host,*
> *To break the birthday bread, count with them Ernest Rhys.*"

WHITMAN: There is Conway's greeting too: let us have Moncure Conway's!

Conway: "*I am happy to find that Walt Whitman has beside him appreciative friends who mean to celebrate his birthday, and I trust they will have many such occasions in future. In writing the* Life of Thomas Paine, *now nearly completed, I have come across many passages and poems in the writings of that revolutionary Quaker which seem to prophesy the appearance of a poet of democracy, and are fulfilled in Walt Whitman. I believe that democracy has never had so true a democrat since Paine's time, and has never had any poet at all except Walt Whitman."*

TRAUBEL: I have here something from Dr. Johnston which reinforces Conway.

WHITMAN: What is that, Horace? Let us hear—what does the Doctor say?

TRAUBEL: Johnston quotes William Rossetti as writing:

"As posterity to a long distance is certain to be interested in Whitman, so your little book is certain to attain a far more than patriarchal age."

WHITMAN: I see—Rossetti speaks of the Doctor's American reports. Who can doubt those reports, Horace? Even those who doubt me, doubt the "Leaves," ought to see how superbly the Doctor handled his material—or let it handle itself. . . . As to Rossetti, he is always manly and confident, and we will all take his hand tonight. But did Johnston write nothing for himself?

TRAUBEL: O, yes!

WHITMAN: Well—let us have that, too.

Johnston: "I wish a very happy birthday to you, my dear good old Friend! As my contribution to your birthday tokens I send you a little souvenir of my visit to you in July last, which I hope you will like. That visit resulted from accumulated stores of gratitude, reverence and personal love, and was the crowning privilege and glory of my whole life. Oh, how I wish that I could be with you on your birthday; to sit beside you in that dear old room, to hear your loved voice and to feel the warm grasp of your hand again! . . ."

WHITMAN: Very happily put, Doctor. Are there more letters ready?

Garland: "I'm very sorry I live so far away that I can be at your dinner to Walt Whitman only in ink and paper. I don't know what I can add to express my regard and admiration for a man who has dared to be himself native and unaffected. In these days of apparent drift toward centralization of power, his doctrine of the Individual comes to have majesty like that of Ibsen's—surpassing it, indeed, for with equal weight of unswerving resolution Whitman has a more fervent humanity. He is a natural lover of man, and does not forget the wounded and crippled even in his moment of hottest warfare. I need only add that prejudice against our most American of poets is rapidly passing away in Boston. . . ."

WHITMAN: Garland has been here to see me several times. He is cordial, warm-hearted, handsome. O yes! more than all that, too, for he is making a great fame for himself by his stories. . . . They tell me his stories are honest as *Leaves of Grass*, which is to set 'em up high, sartain! (*laughing*) and yet the fight is not all over, as he seems to think. I see many a battle ahead, as I have told my friend Horace Traubel here opposite me often.

Chubb: "My affectionate greetings to Whitman! May he live on among us for many a happy year, to illustrate the majesty and peace of old age, as he has illustrated the splendors of full-blooded manhood! . . . I say the future will be grateful because I think that, like other great souls, Whitman has been 'before his time,' and that his influence upon the world has hardly been felt as yet. It will be felt because the world is going to recover from its stupor of soul; and then it will recognize its liberators. I join with you in wishing joy to our dear friend and helpful elder comrade. Health and happiness to him and to you all!"

WHITMAN: That is one of the chief things—spinal to all the rest, in fact. Yes, we need a new manhood, a fresh start, a voyage to sea again! "Before my time?" Yes and no—no doubt at the right moment, if at all.

Ford (Isabella): "My sister Bessie and I both thank you very warmly for the present you sent us of your book. Edward Carpenter sent it on to us. We offer you our warmest greetings and best wishes for your birthday; we never forget it, and always wish you all good."

WHITMAN: Very sweet and noble, very near the heart! I ask myself more than a little if my best friends have not been women. My friend Mrs. Gilchrist, one of the earliest, a picked woman, profound, noble, sacrificing, saw clearly when almost everybody else was interested in raising the dust—obscuring what was true.

Kennedy: "As before, I write you from the stronghold of Puritanism. The shame of the suppressing here of America's greatest book is still not wiped out of existence. And here before me lies a clipping taken from a Boston paper which describes how a college man was arrested the other day for kissing his wife on the street! The Boston Dogberry locked up both man and wife in jail over night until it was proved that the woman kissed was the man's lawful wife. Did you ever hear anything more laughable? Christian anti-naturalism deeply entrenched, you see, yet, in the popular mind. It will probably take a thousand years or so for the new gospel to supplant the effete one. However, sursum corda!"

WHITMAN: All that will come to pass, Kennedy—all is to be provided for! That is one of the things we are here for—that is why we have Ingersoll, great, magnificent fellow that he is! Every blow he strikes for liberty, against what you call Puritanism, is for us, this human critter, the "Leaves," democracy, love! But you know that as well as I do.

A VOICE: And what will we get from Donaldson?

WHITMAN: Tom Donaldson, cannot we have a word from you?

DONALDSON: Mr. Whitman, I did not deserve to be let in. I got here late. But I had been suffering this winter from the attention of three doctors, and after a while I found that by quitting the doctors I might get well. So I am mending now—shaking off the rheumatism—but pretty slow yet, and late, therefore, getting here tonight. But we won't say more of that. I want to talk to you. I am not much given to personal compliment—

WHITMAN: Where have you been lately? You have been West and in Washington?

DONALDSON: Yes.

WHITMAN: Tell us something about it. Tell us, too, about Blaine. We are curious about Blaine.

DONALDSON: I will talk about a more opportune subject—about Walt Whitman. It seems to me I have never seen a book or newspaper article that conveyed to me the real individuality or personality of Walt Whitman.

A VOICE: How about Dr. Bucke's book?

DONALDSON: Since Dr. Bucke's book was written I think the subject has grown, so that Dr. Bucke might write another—a supplementary—book with profit.

WHITMAN: Is he speaking of Dr. Bucke's book, Horace?

TRAUBEL: Yes.

WHITMAN (*with raised voice*): Tom, Horace says you are speaking of Dr. Bucke's book. Look out! Look out! I myself swear by it. I have had a thousand books and essays, and Dr. Bucke's is about the only one that thoroughly radiates and depicts and describes in the way that I think thoroughly delineates me. I thoroughly accept Dr. Bucke's book.

DONALDSON: So do I. But I would like to know where in Dr. Bucke's book is this incident of your life (I am going to give you one particular instance). Oscar Wilde told me—

WHITMAN (*interrupting*): Take out what I slice in. I think Dr. Bucke has accurately depicted my own preparatory and inauguratory life—say a certain sixteen to thirty years on which everything else rests: New York, Brooklyn, experimentation in strange ways, not such as usually go to make poetry and books and grand things, but the flash of active life—yes, in New York, Brooklyn (to me the greatest cities in the universe), and from there down to New Orleans, and up the Mississippi to the big lakes. I travelled over and stopped on them all. Dr. Bucke has briefly, but thoroughly, grasped, gripped, digested all that I was in those twenty years, better than anybody else. I do not so much dwell upon his criticism of *Leaves of Grass*. I still think—I have always thought—that it escapes me myself, its own author, as to what it means, and what it is after, and what it drifts at. Dr. Bucke, with audacious finger, brain, seems to say, "Here is what it means," and "This is not what it means," and "This is a contrast and a comparison," and "This is one side and that is the other side." Well, I don't know—I accept and consider the book as a study. But behind all that (which is anent of what I said fifteen or twenty minutes ago) remains a subtle and baffling, a mysterious *personality*. My attempt at *Leaves of Grass*— my attempt at my own expression—is after all this: to thoroughly equip, absorb, acquire, from all quarters, despising nothing, nothing being too small—no science, no observation, no detail—west, east, cities, ruins, the army, the war (through which I was)—and after all that consigning everything to the personal critter. And the doctor is almost the only one of my critics who seems to have thoroughly understood and appreciated that very important fact. To me it is the personality of the business; it is the personality of the American man, of the fellow from 1850 to 1890—the forty years, the wonderful forty years, the indescribably wonderful forty years of the recent history of America—in a fellow, in a man, in an individuality, thoroughly absorbed. I suppose I am getting a little foggy and cloudy, but the idea is that Dr. Bucke is one of the few who have thoroughly appreciated and understood and realized all that and has dominated his book with it. Most poets, most writers, who have anything to say, have a splendid theory and scheme, and something they want to put forth. I, on the contrary, have no scheme, no theory, no nothing—in a sense absolutely nothing.

DONALDSON: Just let 'er go, eh?

WHITMAN: Almost that. I have uttered the "Leaves" for the last thirty-five years as an illustration of, as an utterance of, as a radiation from, the personal critter—the fellow, man, individuality, person, American, so to speak. To me, as I have said over and over again, almost tiresomely, there is something curious, indescribably divine, in the compound individuality that is in everyone. It is behind all, everything—his time, his degree of development, his stage of development. These have been the main things, and out of them I have reiterated and reiterated and reiterated. I suppose there are four hundred leaves of grass, one after another, which are contradictory, often contradictory—oh! contradictory as hell—perfectly so, but still held together by that iron band, of whatever it may be—individuality, personality, identity, covering our time, from fifty to ninety. That is me, Tom—that is Dr. Bucke's book.

TRAUBEL: But meantime, Donaldson, what's become of your Oscar Wilde story? You've forgotten all about that.

WHITMAN: True enough, Tom; Oscar Wilde! Have you been standing all this time?

DONALDSON: Yes, I have! Is it left for that young man to get me my rights? I leave it to all here if it was not your fault, Mr. Whitman, that my story didn't even get started.

WHITMAN: I own it, Tom. Go on.

DONALDSON: Well, the incident I wish to recall to your attention, Mr. Whitman, is this: Of course you did not find Oscar Wilde the kind of fellow that some people thought he was. On the contrary, you found him a splendid kind of fellow. And he says that not only are you a good poet, but in that room upstairs, in that front room of yours, over your lamp, you can brew the best milk punch of any man in the United States. I am free to claim that no book has ever developed that fact, and yet it is greatly to your credit. Now, I think the most memorable interview I ever had with you, out of many hundred, I had in that little front room. You had a small stove in the corner that looked very much like a fruit can, and you sat in a small armchair with a white robe about you, and the stove pipe got out of the hole, and there was no draft, and the fire went out, and you said finally, "Don't you think this room is cold?" and I said, "Yes, I do," and so we two—Oscar Wilde and me—fished around together, and discovered the reason of the accident, which is just as I have given it.

WHITMAN: Good for you, Tom! The cat's out of the bag.

DONALDSON: But that is not all. I seem almost to have made a speech, anyway, though I expressly intended to avoid that. But before I sit down let me say I brought with me the regrets of some friends over the river—especially of Horace Howard Furness.

TRAUBEL: And I have a letter from him.

WHITMAN: Let Furness speak for himself.

Furness: "What wouldn't I give to be able to be with you! I can join you only in imagination. Yet what imagination is adequate fairly to picture Walt's majestic presence, and the eternal sunshine settling on his head which illumines us all by its mere reflection? I bid him 'take from my mouth the wish of happy years.'"

WHITMAN: When you see him give him my love.

DONALDSON: And I brought with me from an old gentleman on the Allegheny river a bottle of whiskey which he warrants to be fifty-four years old.

WHITMAN: Oh! noble old man! Hurrah for the old man!

VOICES: Bucke! Bucke!

BUCKE: You all know I am no speaker—

WHITMAN: But you can give a word.

BUCKE: If I could speak at all I could say something this evening on the subject in hand. Perhaps the most significant thing of all is the marvellous diversity of opinion about you, Walt, and your book.

WHITMAN: Expatiate a little on that, Doctor: that is very curious.

BUCKE: Well, some think, for instance, that above all things you stand for the divine passion of love, others that you especially voice friendship, others again that external nature is your central and supreme theme; to still others you represent freedom, liberty, joyous and absolute abandonment; again your religious sense is placed at the head, and we are told that a noble aspiration for perfect spiritual manhood, supreme assurance of immortality, intuitions of the unseen, intense faith in the essential friendliness of the universe to man, is the essence of your life and teaching. But the opposite of all these is in you as well; you are as capable of hate and scorn as of love and compassion; imitation and obedience belong to you as much as their seeming opposites; reckless defiance and contempt are, though subordinated, as inherent in the "Leaves" and in you as are reverence and affection; despondency and despair are as truly component parts of your character as are hope and joy; common and even coarse manhood is as developed in you as are the glorious ecstasy of the poet and the high speculations of the philosopher; while you are good you are also evil; the godlike in you is offset by passions, instincts, tendencies that unrestrained might well be called devilish; if on the whole you have lived well and done well yet none the less you have had in you, though subordinated, the elements of a Cenci or an Attila. This side of you is little realized, and therefore I have said and say that no one has yet understood you. Like a group of mountains passaged by dark ravines your Titanic qualities (good and evil) hide one another, so that we who stand by, beholding and admiring someone—or at most two or three—of the majestic summits, or shuddering on the edge of some precipice, necessarily fail to see or adequately to divine the hidden peaks, and, still less, the dark intervening chasms. I do not believe that I or any of us realize, Walt, what you really are. The main thing is that we love you and hope to have you live long with us.

WHITMAN: I scarcely know whether I do or not.

VOICES: Bonsall! Bonsall!

WHITMAN: Yes, Harry, give us your "views"—give us your report.

BONSALL: On my way here the train stopped at Harleigh Cemetery, and as those who had visited the city of the dead and viewed Walt Whitman's tomb entered the cars, I mused how few will honor the living bard tonight compared with the procession of pilgrims from far and near who will make a Mecca of his grave when he is no more! Camden will be known to the world from the fact of one man living and dying here, as Stratford, Concord, and the few shrines that stand alone and need no Westminster or Pantheon in a proud metropolis. In our unstudied and unstinted, our informal and perhaps too careless, colloquialism this evening the thought has been dropped that, until we revere the Man and greet him on each recurring natal day, we do not understand, and cannot comprehend, the length and breadth and height and depth of the philosophy of the Poet. To this, for one, and in common with most of us, I take exception. It is because we do realize what manner of man we honor that we are here tonight. It is because we have imbibed something of his spirit and can translate the message spoken to us with the Right Voice that this responsive echo is called forth. It is because we know whereof we speak that even in our most florid imagery we know that we speak the words of truth and soberness. It is because we have travelled the Open Road with him here, that when we come to tread the highway of the spheres and step from constellation to constellation we shall know that Walt Whitman will await us on a still higher "lift" and extend, as now, the hand we will grasp in courage and confidence because of the light he shed on the way thither.

WHITMAN: I did not know you were such a speechmaker, Harry! So you object to Bucke's argument? Well, well, you are both right, I guess—though Doctor gets rather nearer the nerve, so to speak. There's a point or two you fellows could argue out together, though as for that I don't suppose argument would settle anything. (*To Traubel.*) Harry has kept his hand on the wheel this many-a-day—never weary, never unsteady!

WILLIAMS (F. H.): It has become, I had almost said, a fashion to say that

Walt Whitman lacks form, and that his method of expressing himself is in great chaos of words. But I do not think that the form in which you have seen fit to express yourself is a mere chaos of words. I do not think that the mere fact that you have refused to be bound by the accepted metrical forms, by the laws of versification as they have been accepted by all time, at all argues that you have disregarded form. As I heard Mr. Richard Watson Gilder say at one of our recent reunions: "I think that Walt Whitman's form is one of the most extraordinary things about him. I believe that his form is inimitable." I believe that anybody who will get away from the idea of scanning line by line and will undertake to comprehend the fundamental thought at the bottom of *Leaves of Grass* and which runs through it—not through its sections but through the book as a whole—will find that the form adopted is the only one in which that thought could possibly have been embodied and expressed. Any writer, any poet, who had sought to express that thought and had bound himself by any of the accepted metrical laws, would have found himself in the position of the Irishman who tried to carry home a quart of the critter in a half-pint mug—the verse would not have held the thought. The people who say that his thought is a chaos have simply come across a cosmos which is beyond their comprehension.

WHITMAN: I hope that is so.

WILLIAMS: Mr. Gabriel Sarrazin has said, sir, that you are not an artist— that you are not an artist because you rise superior to art. I believe that is nothing more than saying that genius is a law unto itself. Art is an interpretation of nature, and when the thing to be expressed transcends the laws of art, we then arrive at a point within which a genius—if there be such a man—exists. I mean without regard to the laws of art. That is exactly the idea found in *Leaves of Grass*.

WHITMAN: It is a comfort to hear that. Bravo! . . . Dr. Bucke is my authoritative expresser and explanator, as far as there can be one.

DONALDSON: What about my hundred pages that I am getting out about you?

WHITMAN: Go on, Tom, go on—and God be with you!

MORRIS: Something has been said about the euphony and harmony of Mr. Whitman's verse. I think if Mr. Donaldson had had the pleasure which I had a couple of weeks ago of going to Long Island and visiting Walt Whitman's birthplace, he could scarcely say, as he has said, that there was no euphony and no harmony in Walt Whitman. The one prevailing feature in all that country is that every door-yard—no matter how humble, how much of a shanty—has a bush of lilac growing.

DONALDSON: Did Whitman plant it?

WHITMAN: That was a smart dab, Tom.

MORRIS: He has celebrated it supremely. Another figure which we find in the two lyrics of Mr. Whitman is the hermit-thrush. It is an indigenous bird in Long Island.

WHITMAN: It is the sweetest, solemnest of all our singing birds.

MORRIS: Being on Long Island I was almost constantly in view of the sea. Now, these three elements—the lilac, the hermit-thrush and the sea— are the prevailing elements of those great lyrics, "Out of the Cradle Endlessly Rocking" and the great Lincoln ode. I consider that if any man was to create so much lyric beauty, euphony and harmony are necessarily a main part of his texture.

WHITMAN: No doubt, Harrison, that is part of the story—but there's a deal more beyond—a deal more!

DONALDSON: The idea I have always had of Walt Whitman's euphony and rhythm and poetry was the idea expressed by Mr. Williams: it is not at all what Mr. Morris undertakes to exhibit. And, by the way, I am twice as old as that boy and he can talk twice as well as I can.

WHITMAN: Don't say that, Tom Donaldson—you stand very well on your own feet.

VOICES: Talcott Williams—Williams!

WHITMAN: Get up, Talcott—show yourself!

WILLIAMS (TALCOTT): Yes, Mr. Whitman, and all—I will, and let me say a word, too. We are here marking the fourth of a long series of celebrations of this birthday. From this point we will go on in the development of those broad principles which will gradually overspread the world, and which today are known to all the English-speaking world, and which in time shall know neither let nor limit. As I remember how lesser forms of verse have disappeared, how the bric-a-brac of verse crumbles under the touch of years, I feel that there are new meanings in yours. As we gather at this table, at which few sit but at which all are peers, in the presence which dignifies us tonight, I feel in some sense a new meaning in the line, "Age shakes Athene's tower but spares gray Marathon." For me the democracy of your verse is only the lesser and smaller part of it. The higher and wider side is its spiritual side. The circumstance that, in an age which not only doubts democracy but doubts itself, and doubts, sometimes, the universe, the universe has been to you a road of many roads—the road of travelling souls.

VOICES: Letters! Letters!

WHITMAN: Yes, Horace, the letters—bits of them, anyway.

Wallace: "*This evening—which till a short time ago was dull, cold and overcast, with dark lowering rain-clouds—is now, at sunset, clear, calm, and radiant with heavenliest hues. May it be an omen of your remaining life!*"

WHITMAN: Good boy! Good boy! And a dozen sign with him—royal Lancashire fellows, all. Read their names—read their names! . . . They call themselves "the College."

Mead: "*All lovers of nature and freedom join in grateful thought of your free and stalwart life.*"

WHITMAN: That is a magazinist, but the magazinists as a rule have rejected us.

Stedman: "*Life, after all, is not like a river—although it is the fashion to say that it is—for that stream flows more slowly as it nears the boundless sea. But if Walt's birthdays seem to succeed one another more rapidly as the years shorten, I take all the more the hope that there may be (to use his own word) a long tally of them yet in store. And Whitman's poetry is like the river: nothing of it more tranquil, nothing broader and deeper, than his songs almost within sound of the infinite surge. Take, for instance, the last chant of his—'To the Sunset Breeze.' It recalls the sense of zest, and of physical harmony, with which Borrow's blind gypsy asked to be placed where he could feel the wind from the heath; over and beyond this, the reach of a noble intellect, the yielding of a strong soul to the vast movement of the universe. To such a bard it is of little moment whether he stays in one world or another. But to us it is much to have him still among us.*"

WHITMAN: We all like Stedman: he is hearty, warm, generous—yes, sticks to his guns, too, though his guns are not always ours. Tonight we all seem to melt and flow together. (*To Traubel.*) It might go hard with us if this was all simply directed to Walt Whitman! But we are here, I as much as any, to pay our respects, not to Walt Whitman, but to democracy! (*Aloud again.*) Whose is the next message?

Morse: "*I must join the chorus. A friend visiting Camden some months ago reported to me: 'I found Whitman calmly sitting in the midst of such utter and appalling literary confusion I wondered for a moment how he breathed—vast heaps of everything piled about him. It seemed as though an earthquake had thrown all the life and literature of the hour—everything, in fact—into ruins, but the old god. He alone remained unperturbed and indestructible.' Perhaps this friend did not go so much amiss, forecasting with a wider significance than intended the fate to men and things some far future will reveal.*"

WHITMAN: That is Sidney—our Sidney. We have his bust of us upstairs, and a noble piece of work it is; some think, the best. (*To Traubel.*) John Burroughs, of all men, should be here tonight. He should not only be here but be at the head of the table—see all the fellows, hear all that is said, throw a strain into the music himself.

Curtis (George William): *"My hearty respect and regard for the sturdy and faithful man whom you honor."*

WHITMAN: How cautious—how non-committal!

Blake: *"My reverential greeting to the venerable poet whose songs will wind men's arms around each other's necks if we will sing them truly after him."*

WHITMAN: Blake—Blake: is that Blake of Chicago? Yes—I know him: he has been here. Thanks! Thanks!

Sanborn: *"My earnest love to you, Walt Whitman, on this memorial occasion. We think of you at Concord as often as we look out over the meadows across the river, which you were so fond of feeding your eyes upon."*

WHITMAN: Sanborn was one of our earliest friends! And now, Tom Harned, you don't intend to slip us altogether? Get up, Tom: say your say.

HARNED: We have heard much about *Leaves of Grass*—about Walt Whitman and his methods. But my mind is animated by other ideas. During the past year I have suffered the dread that perhaps it would not now be long that we would know Walt Whitman here in person. The fact must be stated that during the past few months he has occupied a room above us, unable to leave it, his physical condition becoming weaker day by day. It seems to me that the great, the supreme, lesson of Walt Whitman's life is this: that he has been entirely consistent with himself, that he has not advocated any doctrine that he has not lived. And to me, inexpressibly beyond the hope of giving utterance to the thought, the calmness and deliberation with which Walt Whitman invites the future and looks forward unfearingly to crossing the unknown sea, is one of the most beautiful evidences of this consistency. Whitman, above all others, is the poet of immortality. And when I use the word I mean by it a conviction of the immortality of identity —that our lives do not end here, that death is an essential—ay, as he urges, even to be sung to, praised. Calm, exalted, he awaits death. Here, then, in Walt Whitman's presence, I desire to say that that is the sublime, the supreme, index of his character.

WHITMAN: And now comes your turn, Horace.

TRAUBEL: No, I must be excused. I feel myself in the midst of a battle of which I may some time have something to say. My turn has not come. When the battle is over, then I may write of it.

WHITMAN: You are right, boy—your turn is not yet. Years and years from now, when I am gone—when, as you say, the battle is over—much may depend upon your teaching, and you will set out the exact lines of evidence. You are right, boy—and God bless you!

CLIFFORD: I will put in a word, too, though, like Traubel, I feel to be excused tonight. Everybody knows Emerson's remark: "To be great is to be misunderstood." There is a story that I believe to be authentic to the effect that when someone came to him and asked what he had meant by a certain passage or passages in his essays, he replied in his rather embarrassed manner that he supposed that when he wrote the matter referred to he had meant something clear enough, which now was forgotten or obliterated. So, Mr. Whitman, you are not alone in that particular, if your own account of yourself be correct. But I am not going to make a speech. Let me add an amusing episode. In my not very remote experience, when I happened by accident to be one of a company of persons where the name of Walt Whitman was mentioned and pretty warmly espoused by a majority of those present, a somewhat well-known poetaster of these parts, to whose name it would be cruel if I gave it an immortality by mentioning it here, called a halt by crying out: "Well, if Walt Whitman is a poet, then I am not one." A not inconsiderable world of professionals will one day be tried by that standard, and it is not likely that him we call Whitman—him we honor tonight—will suffer in the decision.

WHITMAN: Why, Clifford, you swing a heavy club! Walt Whitman? Sure enough—no poet at all! That is the way the schools have had it for a long time! But here is Miss Porter, too—what has she to say to all this?

PORTER (MISS): I know we all want to say something tonight, and what I would like to say, or the thought that has particularly occurred to me in what I have read of yours, is that you connect literature more closely with life than anyone has done before. And that is what we praise particularly—we narrow people who have just begun to know you—and that is what we look forward to in the future: that that literature may become more widely spread which is more closely connected with life, as you connect it in your *Democracy* and in your *Leaves of Grass*.

WHITMAN: And Eakins—what of Tom Eakins? He is here. Haven't you something to say to us, Eakins?

EAKINS: I am not a speaker—

WHITMAN: So much the better—you are more likely to say something.

EAKINS: Well, as some of you know, I some years ago—a few—painted a picture of Mr. Whitman. I began in the usual way, but soon found that the ordinary methods wouldn't do—that technique, rules, and traditions would have to be thrown aside; that, before all else, he was to be treated as a man, whatever became of what are commonly called the principles of art.

WHITMAN: What wouldn't he give for O'Connor, Ingersoll, Burroughs, tonight! Dear O'Connor—dear, dead! How we would enter into it all—absorb it—glorify it!

CLARKE (MISS): I would like to add my personal thanks to Walt Whitman for his insistence upon the true principle of democracy, which consists not in bringing down those things which are high but in raising up those things which are low.

WHITMAN: A hit sharp on the head of the nail!

EYRE: Walt, I am one of the boys that you cannot see with your eyes. There are a great many millions outside who cannot see you now, but will see you well by-and-by. I met a man in Philadelphia today to whom I said, "I am going to dine tonight with the greatest man of this century." He asked: "Who is that?" and I answered, "Walt Whitman." He seemed surprised: "You don't mean actually to call him that, do you?" and I assured him that I did with all my heart and soul. And I never said a word more true. You are the greatest man of all this century and of all the world. I will tell you, Walt, why you are so great. It is because you have taught me, everyone, that I, they, are as great as you. There is one thing I want to say. You spoke of woman. It has been to me a constant wonder that the man who has written "I see a mother clasping her child to her breast, and I watch her long and long," has never married.

WHITMAN: That is Ingersoll. That has been explained by Dr. Bucke, who, I think, knows me better than anybody, and has sort of intercalated and found out, partly by his own instigation and partly because he feels it to do. I leave a large—a very, very large—explication of that and all other questions to Dr. Bucke. Somebody says you cannot understand anyone except through a good spirit. Well, it is not alone that—that is not all; but until you appeal, or preach, or explicate the whole thing by a good spirit, I don't think it could be thoroughly explicated anyhow. But I think Dr. Bucke and Horace Traubel are the nearest to the explicators—whatever that may be—of me and the difficulties of that question, and all other questions. The whole thing, my friend, like the Nibelungen, or somebody's cat, has an immensely long, long, long tail to it. And the not being married, and the not and the not and the not, and the this and the this and the this, have a great many explications. At the first view it may not be so creditable to the fellow, to the critter, but go on, explicate still more and still more and still more behind all that. Somebody says, and I think it is a wonderfully profound thing, that there is no life, like Burns', for instance,—like Robert Burns', the poet's—no life thoroughly penetrated, explicated, understood and gone behind, and that gone behind, and that fact gone behind, and that fact gone behind, but after all, after awhile, you see why it must be so in the nature of things. And that is a splendid explication of Robert Burns. You go behind all, and you realize that, no matter what the blame may be to Robert Burns, somehow or other you feel like excusing and saying that that is the reason why, and that is the reason why, and that is the reason why. See?

EYRE (*still on his feet, as when interrupted by Whitman*): This has been the most successful speech of my life, and I could stand on my feet for half an hour and hear some other fellow talk; and of all the fellows in the world whom I should love so to hear talk—like a rivulet, like a brook, like a universal cataract, like some babbling spring, like the fields, like the birds—Walt Whitman stands the first.

WHITMAN (*laughing*): But my speech is not yours. Give us yours.

EYRE: I want to ask a question. I don't know that you like the word *literature*. There is something better than that, don't you think?

WHITMAN: There is something better than that, deeper than that, behind that; like religion, which is not the conventional church, by any means, but rests on something deeper.

EYRE: In one of your poems I have found—but will you let me repeat it?

WHITMAN: Go ahead if it is not too long.

EYRE: I want to call attention to "My Captain," a poem which has in it the element of the dramatic in a sublime and startling degree—marvellous contrasts of color and sound. I want especially to call your attention to the third verse. I shall give it, in order to show what I mean. (*Recites.*)

WHITMAN (*leaning across the table*): Horace, what ails Brinton? Isn't he to speak?

TRAUBEL: Ask him. I hope so.

WHITMAN (*turning to Brinton who sits at his left*): What about that, Doctor? We want to hear from you!

VOICES: Brinton! Brinton!

BRINTON (*half risen*): I do not know—

VOICES: Brinton! Brinton!

WHITMAN: You can't escape us, Doctor!

BRINTON: Well—if I must I must!

WHITMAN (*to Traubel*): Did he suppose we intended that he should be left out of the play?

BRINTON: We all know well enough why we are here tonight, and we all know, therefore, that this dinner and its after-talk become an ascription to Walt Whitman and the great cause his *Leaves of Grass* inaugurates and fortifies. And how can I add anything to the warm and loyal words spoken to this effect in his presence by all the eloquent fellows who have spoken before me—

WHITMAN: Good, Doctor! A good start! You can add enough!

VOICES: Yes! Yes!

BRINTON: Thank you, Mr. Whitman—and thank you all! But I feel somewhat in the position of a man who at the last hour is asked and expected to put the keystone in the arch. I know nobody except Walt Whitman himself who can do that for our arch tonight—

WHITMAN: Give us the word of science, Doctor!

BRINTON: The word of science to Walt Whitman would be—you have done me and the world a service beyond all service hitherto done in literature for reason and the rational insight of man. You have made comrades of men. You have made seekers, discoverers, along lines not previously travelled or known. If we are here about this table in testimony of an acceptance of Walt Whitman's interpretation of comradeship and joy, we are also here to give emphasis to his principles affecting the mental life of the race. Walt Whitman's "Leaves" will never fade and sere, for he has given them a touch of vital blood which will preserve them as long as men read and reason, as long as there are eyes to see and brains to comprehend. And this is the case because in this poetic volume there has been no attempt to elude nature, to get away from the actual—because its author wrote on, without sense of shame or motive of apology; recounting the sights and wonders that everywhere appeared before him. In the highest sense a reflector of truth, he is also in the simplest way a lover of men. On the one side we find his soul reaching out to the largest questions of mind, of civilization; on the other we find his heart throbbing in common with the hopes and horrors of the simplest men. Science sees in Whitman a teacher of evolution—sees in him perhaps so far the finest fruit of evolution and its profoundest explicator and defender.

WHITMAN: Do you say that, Doctor?

BRINTON: Yes, I do. You (*turning to Whitman*) have held high the perpendicular hand, and offered us the most precious gift of the ages— offered us freedom, love, immortality. (*Then addressing those about the table.*) Let us hold up as good a hand as high, in affectionate demonstration of our esteem and loyalty!

WHITMAN: Noble Doctor! It is the best note of the song, almost! And yet all is so good—all so fits, is of one piece!

DONALDSON: If I understand what you have done, it is to make a plea for America and the Americans—it is to make a plea for universality and the brotherhood of man. Now, do I understand you right?

WHITMAN: Oh, that is one thing—the commonhood, brotherhood, democratization, or whatever it may be called. But behind all that something remains. I had a dispute with Thomas Dudley some years ago. His theory was that our main thing in America was to look out for ourselves—for the fellows here. Well, in response, I remember I said, rather incidentally (but I felt it at the bottom of my heart), that the theory of the progress and expansion of the cause of the common bulk of the people is the same in all countries—not only in the British islands, but on the continent of Europe and allwheres—that we are all embarked together like fellows in a ship, bound for good or for bad. What wrecks one wrecks all. What reaches the port of one reaches the port for all. And it is my feeling, and I hope I have in *Leaves of Grass* expressed it, that the bulk of the common people, the torso of the people, the great body of the people all over the civilized world— and any other, too, for that matter—are sailing, sailing together in the same ship. And that which jeopardizes one jeopardizes all. And in my contest with Thomas Dudley, who is a thorough "protectionist" (in which I thoroughly differ from him), my feeling was that the attempt at what they call "protection"—though I am not posted in the protection details and theories and formulations and statistics, and all that goes to boost up and wall up and wall out and protect out (doubtless I tread on the corns of a good many people, but I feel it deeply, and the older I live to be the stronger I feel it)—is wrong, and that one feeling for all, extreme reciprocity and openness and free-tradism, is the policy for me. And I not only think that it is an important item in political economy, but I think it is the essential social groundwork, away down; and to me nothing will do eventually but an understanding of *the solidarity of the common people, of all peoples and all races.* And that is behind *Leaves of Grass.* Well, I have talked and garruloussed and frivolled so terrifically this evening, much to my amazement, that I don't think I have anything left. I am glad to see you all, and I appreciate, thoroughly appreciate, your kindness and complimentary honor of me and everything—but oh! I have not felt up to the occasion of making much of a speech, or, at any rate, any more of a speech than I have been flabbing away at from time to time. I must say to my friends further along the table that I am about half blind and I cannot see more than ten feet ahead and hardly that—else I am sure I should specify them. (*He had greeted one after another by name.*) The main thing, as I told my friend Horace Traubel, is, that we are here, and are jolly, and having a good jolly time. I welcome you —give out my love to every one of you—and to many and many a one not here.

VOICES: Are there no other letters?

TRAUBEL: Yes,—several—but no time to read them: the old man is tired and wishes to withdraw. I have letters still—a whole cluster—from Adler, Gilder, Tucker—from Miss Gilder, too, and Miss Lazarus. But we have given what Walt just called "samples." Now he says that his ears and eyes are about given out.

WHITMAN: What a pity! But it is late—and they will forgive us. I'm afraid I have already overshot the mark. And—Warry—where are you? (*Rising—taking his cane—waving his hands to the risen crowd.*) And now to all, good-night and thanks, and God bless you. (*Retires.*)

Oscar Wilde

THE LAST PHASE: AN EXILE ENTERTAINS
SOME FRIENDS IN A PARIS CAFÉ.

The world will not listen to me now.

IT WAS admittedly as a "monologue d'outre tombe" that Laurence Housman, in 1923,* sat down to reconstruct a conversation with Oscar Wilde that had occurred in Paris in the fall of 1899. Housman had sought his company while passing through Paris on his way back from Italy. Several years earlier he had met the tragic outcast in England and still cherished some kindly remarks he had made about a short story of his. Then, too, he remembered Wilde as "incomparably the most accomplished talker" he had ever met. That would have been attraction enough for any open-minded British writer of the day. Added to that was Housman's frank admiration for the "quiet uncomplaining courage" with which this fallen idol of an adoring public was accepting an "ostracism against which, in his lifetime, there could be no appeal."

Wilde had left England a virtual pariah after serving two years imprisonment at hard labor for moral offenses under the Criminal Law Amendment Act. Yet, despite his spectacular fall from grace, the former wit and dandy was not without friends in his Parisian exile. The French coteries relished his irrepressible humor and air of social defiance. Young British writers paid their respects to the leader who had long fought the battle of art for art's sake. Others doubtless came to see him out of morbid fascination, expecting to find a drunken and abject derelict who stalked English visitors for the few sous to purchase his next absinthe.

There was one other thing that drew Housman—what he himself styled the psychology of human failure. He saw Oscar Wilde as a tragic example of failure that had brought in the whole world as spectator. Success, Housman admitted, had never intrigued him half as much, perhaps because failure seemed to reveal human nature more truly, and "on the whole, more encouragingly than anything else in the world." Housman felt that the meeting with Wilde was a great test of his theory that the way a man

---

* Echo de Paris (Appleton, New York, 1924).

faces failure is the best proof of what he is made of. Thus, "I had sufficient reason for putting on record my last meeting with so conspicuous a failure as Oscar Wilde."

Of Wilde's talk, Housman recalled "the smooth-flowing utterance, sedate and self-possessed, oracular in tone, whimsical in substance, carried on without halt, or hesitation, or change of word, with the quiet zest of a man perfect at the game, and conscious that, for the moment at least, he was back at his old form again." Added to that was Wilde's pleasure, infectious to his listeners, "of finding himself once more in a group of friends whose view of his downfall was not the world's view."

While Housman admittedly took liberties in reconstructing the episode, Hesketh Pearson was convinced that a great deal more of the true Wilde came through the dialogue than Housman was prepared to acknowledge. Prompted by Pearson, who was then writing his brilliant biography of Wilde, Housman vouched for several passages "as being Wilde's in substance, and as nearly as possible his in manner." These are the passages dealing with Gladstone, Burns, Napoleon, Carlyle, and death.

Present at the dinner in Paris on that late September day of 1899, were Wilde's devoted friend Robert Ross; Henri Davray; another friend (identified only as H. A.); and Laurence Housman.

"The scene, as regards its setting—the outside of a Paris restaurant—is true to history," writes Housman. "And if, toward the end, a touch of drama has been introduced, the reader will understand that it is more symbolic than actual. The non-arriving guest, with the unreal name,* did not, on that occasion, even begin to arrive. He was, nevertheless, a very real element in the tragic situation which I have tried to depict; and it is likely enough that there were more of his kind than one knew—that he was generic rather than individual."

Of that conversation itself, with its recurring overtones of pathos and tragedy, its blend of boyish humor and pontifical wisdom, Housman concluded that "Whether it had any intrinsic value or not, it was at least a wonderful expression of that gift which Oscar Wilde had for charming himself and charming others."

("*The echo is from as far back as the year 1899. It is late September. By the entrance of a café, on a street opening into the Place de l'Opéra, three Englishmen sit waiting at a small table, relieved for the moment*

---

* "Harvey Jerrold."

from the solicitations of the garçon *anxious to serve them their* apéritifs. *It is all very well for the café to call itself the "Vieille Rose": no doubt by gaslight it lives charmingly up to its name; but seen in the noonday's glare, its interior upholsterings are unmistakably magenta. From the warm sunshade of its awning the street view is charming; and while one of the trio watches it benevolently with an accustomed eye, the other two, encountering Paris for the first time, find in its brisk movement the attraction of novelty. But it is a reversion to English habit which makes one of them presently look at his watch a little anxiously."*—Housman)

HOUSMAN: Is he generally so late as this?

ROSS: Generally never as early.

HOUSMAN: You are sure you said the Café Vieille Rose?

ROSS (*with a disarming smile*): As well as I could, my dear L.H. I can't say it quite like you.

HOUSMAN: I don't pretend to talk French: hearing it spoken absorbs all my faculties.

ROSS: Oh, but you should! They are so charming about it: they pretend to understand you.

HOUSMAN: Well, I did screw up courage to go to a French barber yesterday.

ROSS: Ah! That explains it. I was wondering.

HOUSMAN: You might well. When I looked in the glass after he had finished me I saw myself no longer English, but Parisian.

ROSS (*enjoying himself*): No, L.H., no! Not Parisian, I assure you!—Alsatian.

HOUSMAN: "No longer English" was all that mattered. "*Tout à fait transformé,*" as I managed to say to the man. And he—magnificently: "*Mais oui, Monsieur, c'était bien nécessaire!*" Is that what you call French politeness?

ROSS: Rather the "*amour propre*" of the artist, I should say.

HOUSMAN: In this nation of artists one gets too much of it.

H.A.: There isn't such a thing as a nation of artists. The French only appear so because they take a more transparent pride in themselves than we do. They haven't yet discovered that modesty is the best vanity.

ROSS: Is that your own, Herbie, or did you get it from Oscar yesterday?

H.A.: No. I didn't see him. I invented it as I got up this morning, meaning to let it occur as an impromptu. Now it's gone.

ROSS: Oh, no. Say it again, my dear boy, say it again! We shall all be charmed: so will he.

HOUSMAN: Look; there he is! Who's with him?

ROSS: Davray. I asked Davray to go and bring him, so as to make sure. You know him, don't you? You like him?

HOUSMAN: A Frenchman who can talk English always goes to my heart.

ROSS: Davray is Anglomaniac: he not only talks it, he thinks it: signs himself "Henry," like an Englishman, and has read more of your books than I have.

HOUSMAN: One?

ROSS: Don't be bitter, L.H. I read them—in the reviews—regularly.

(*While they talk, a fiacre, disentangling itself from the traffic of the main thoroughfare, draws up at the newspaper-kiosk on the farther side of the street, and discharges its occupants: one small, alert, and obviously a Frenchman; the other large and sedate, moving with a ponderous suavity, which gives him an air of importance, almost of dignity. But though he has still a presence, its magnificence has departed. Threading his way indolently across the traffic, his eye adventures toward the waiting group. Met by the studied cordiality of their greetings, his face brightens.*)

ROSS: Oscar, L.H. thinks you are late.

WILDE: Thought I was going to be late, you mean, my dear Robbie. If I were, what matter? What are two minutes in three years of disintegrated lifetime? It is almost three years, is it not, since we missed seeing each other?

(*This studied mention of a tragic lapse of time is not quite as happy as it would like to be, being too deliberate an understatement. The tactful "Robbie" hastens to restore the triviality suitable to the occasion.*)

ROSS: Oscar, when did you learn to cross streets? I have just seen you do it for the first time. In London you used to take a cab.

WILDE: No, Robbie, the cab used to take me. But here the French streets are so polite; one gets to the right side of them without knowing it. (*He turns to Housman.*) How delightfully English of you to think that I was going to be late!

HOUSMAN: I thought you might have done as I am always doing—gone to the wrong place, or lost your way.

WILDE: But that is impossible! In Paris one can lose one's time most delightfully; but one can never lose one's way.

H.A.: With the Eiffel Tower as a guide, you mean?

WILDE: Yes. Turn your back to that—you have all Paris before you. Look at it—Paris vanishes.

ROSS: You might write a story about that, Oscar.

WILDE: In natural history, Robbie, it has already been done. Travellers in

South America tell of a bird which, if seen by you unawares, flies to hide itself. But if it has seen you first, then—by keeping its eye on you—it imagines that it remains invisible, and nothing will induce it to retreat. The bird-trappers catch it quite easily merely by advancing backwards. Now that, surely, is true philosophy. The bird, having once made you the object of its contemplation, has every right to think (as Bishop Berkeley did, I believe) that you have no independent existence. You are what you are—the bird says, and the Bishop says—merely because they have made you a subject of thought; if they did not think of you, you would not exist. And who knows?—they may be right. For, try as we may, we cannot get behind the appearance of things to the reality. And the terrible reason may be that there is no reality in things apart from their appearances.

DAVRAY: You English are always talking what you think is philosophy, when we should only call it theology.

WILDE: How typical of the French mind is that word "only"! But what else, my dear Davray, was the thought of the eighteenth century, so far as it went, but an attempt to bring religion and philosophy together in the bonds of holy matrimony?

ROSS: The misalliance which produced the French Revolution.

WILDE: Robbie, you must not be so brilliant before meals! Or do you wish to divert my appetite? May a guest who was supposed to be late inquire—when, precisely?

ROSS: The situation, my dear Oscar, is of your own making. You insisted upon ortolans; L.H. telegraphed for them; they have only just arrived.

WILDE: If they are still in their feathers, let them fly again! A flight of ortolans across Paris: how romantic, how unexplainable!

H.A.: Oh, no! Let's wait for them, please! I want to taste one: I never have.

WILDE: So young, and already so eager for disappointment! Why give up imagination? "Ortolan," the word, is far more beautiful than when it is made flesh. If you were wise you would learn life only by inexperience. That is what makes it always unexpected and delightful. Never to realize—that is the true ideal.

HOUSMAN: Still, one goes on liking plovers' eggs after eating them: at least, I do.

WILDE: Ah, yes; an egg is always an adventure: it may be different. But you are right; there are a few things—like the Nocturnes of Chopin—which can repeat themselves without repetition. The genius of the artist preserves them from being ever quite realized. But it has to be done carelessly.

(*There is a pause, while Housman, with due inquiry of each, orders the* apéritifs.)

ROSS: Oscar, why did you choose the "Vieille Rose"?

WILDE: Will you believe me, Robbie, when I say—to match my complexion? I have never before seen it by daylight. Is it not a perfect parable of life, that such depravity by gaslight should become charming? Will our host allow us to have white wine as a corrective? An additional red might be dangerous.

(*And with the color-scheme of the approaching meal made safe, he continues to charm the ears of himself and of his listeners.*)

I chose it also for another and a less selfish reason. It is here I once met a woman who was as charming as she was unfortunate, or as she would have been, but for the grace that was in her. To say that she was entirely without beauty is to put it mildly; but she accepted that gift of a blind God with so candid a benevolence, and cultivated it with so delicate an art, that it became a quality of distinction, almost of charm. She was the *belle amie* of a friend of mine, whose pity she had changed to love. He brought me here to meet her, telling me of the rare reputation she had acquired in this city of beautiful misalliances, as being a woman of whom nobody could possibly say that she was merely plain. And here, upon this spot, in the first few moments of our meeting, she challenged me, in the most charming manner possible, for that which a woman so rarely seeks to know—the truth about herself. "Tell me, Monsieur," she said—but no: it can only be told in French: "*Dites moi, Monsieur, si je ne suis pas la femme la plus laide à Paris?*" And for once in my life I was able to please a woman merely by telling her the truth; and I replied, "*Mais, Madame, dans tout le monde!*"

ROSS: A poem in six words! What did she say?

WILDE: What could she say, Robbie? She was delighted. To that impossible question which she had the courage to ask I had given the only impossible answer. Upon that we became friends. How much I have wished since that we could have met again. For the unbeautiful to have so much grace as to become charming is a secret that is worth keeping; and one the keeping of which I should have liked to watch. I would not have asked to know it for myself, for then it would no more be a mystery; but—merely to see her keeping it. In Paris (where almost everything is beautiful), they were very happy together. Now they are gone to America; and in that country, from which all sense of beauty has flown, perhaps she is no longer able to keep, as a secret, that which there would be no eyes to interpret. When I was in America, I did not dare to tell America the truth; but I saw it clearly even then—that the discovery of America was the beginning of the death of Art. But not yet; no, not yet! Whistler left America in order to remain an artist, and Mr. Sargent to become one, I believe. . . . But now, tell me of England: who are the new writers I ought to be reading, but have not?

HOUSMAN: Isn't to be told what you ought to like rather irritating?

WILDE: But I did not say "like"; I said "read." There are many things one ought to read which one is not bound to like: Byron, Wordsworth—even Henry James, if Robbie will allow me to say so. But tell me whom you yourself find interesting. I shall, at least, be interested to know why. I have already had two books—from you and your brother *—which have interested me.

HOUSMAN: Like you, as regards my own, I should be interested to know why?

WILDE: Yours interested me—shall I confess?—partly because a few years ago it would have interested me so much less. For at that time, believing that I had discovered—that, in a way, I represented the symbol of my age—I was only interested in myself. Now, in an age to which I do not belong, I find myself interested in others. Robbie, who is the most sincere of flatterers, would have me believe that in this transfer of interest I am making a poor exchange. I am not sure. Till recently, absorbed in myself, I might have missed that new strange writer of things impossible in life, who writes under the name of Benjamin Swift. Ought I to have done so? His style has the gleam of a frozen fire. He writes like a sea-pirate driven by contrary winds to a vain search for tropical forests at the North Pole. Why does he look at life only in profile, as though, met face to face, it might mean death to him? Is he as mysterious, as unaccountable to himself, as he seems to others?

HOUSMAN: I don't know whether the fact that he is a well-to-do Scotsman, who finished his education at a German university, can be said to account for him. We have met, and I find him interesting. He reminds me, somehow, of a lion turned hermit, wearing a hair-shirt, and roaring into it to frighten out the fleas. In other words, he is full of contradictions, and revels in them even while they torment him.

WILDE: A Scotsman? That explains everything. For a man to be both a genius and a Scotsman is the very stage for tragedy. He apparently perceives it. Generally they are unaware of it.

---

* A. E. Housman.

ROSS: My dear Oscar, why cannot a Scotsman be a genius as comfortably as anyone else?

WILDE: I ought to have said "artist": I meant artist. It is much easier for a Scotsman to be a genius than to be an artist. Mr. Gladstone, I believe, claimed to be a Scotsman whenever he stood for a Scottish constituency or spoke to a Scottish audience. The butter-Scotch flavor of it makes me believe it was true. There was no art in that; and yet how truly typical! It was always so successful . . . Because, Robbie —to return to your question—your Scotsman believes only in success. How can a man, who regards success as the goal of life, be a true artist? God saved the genius of Robert Burns to poetry by driving him through drink to failure. Think what an appalling figure in literature a successful Burns would have been! He was already trying to write poems in polite English, which was about as ludicrous as for a polite Englishman to try to write poetry in the dialect of Burns. Riotous living and dying saved him from that last degradation of smug prosperity which threatened him.

HOUSMAN: But do you mean no artists are successful?

WILDE: Incidentally; never intentionally. If they are, they remain incomplete. The artist's mission is to live the complete life: success, as an episode (which is all it can be); failure, as the real, the final end. Death analyzed to its resultant atoms—what is it but the vindication of failure: the getting rid forever of powers, desires, appetites, which have been a lifelong embarrassment? The poet's noblest verse, the dramatist's greatest scene deal always with death; because the highest function of the artist is to make perceived the beauty of failure.

ROSS: But have Scotsmen of genius been any more successful, in a worldly sense, than others? I seem to remember a few who failed rather handsomely.

WILDE: Possibly. Providence is sometimes kinder to us than we are ourselves. But never was there a Scotsman of genius who survived his youth, who was not fatally compromised by his nationality. To fail and to die young is the only hope for a Scotsman who wishes to remain an artist. When, at the end of the eighteenth century, Scotland produced her second great writer of genius, she inspired him to a terrible betrayal (for which the tradespeople of literature still praise him)— to break his art on the wheel of commercial rectitude, to write books which became worse and worse, in order to satisfy his creditors! In Dante's *Purgatorio* there is nothing to equal the horror of it. But he succeeded; and Scotland, in consequence, is proud of him. I see by your faces that you all know the man I mean: one does not have to name him. Think of unhappy Sir Walter, writing his transcendent pot-boilers for no other reason than to wipe out bankruptcy! Bankruptcy, that beneficent fairy, who presents to all who trust her with their insolvency five, ten, fifteen, sometimes even nineteen shillings in the pound of what they owe to their creditors—to those usurious ones whose extortionate demands, recognized in other branches of the law, here get turned down. How much did she give me, Robbie?

ROSS: An extension of time, Oscar. She hasn't done with you yet.

WILDE: No; she does not dismiss the lover from her embraces while she has any hope of securing the restoration of his balance, or of discovering some deeper stain in his character. What touching devotion! She is the romantic figure of the money-market. But I believe—or at least I tell myself—that fewer Scotsmen go bankrupt than any other nationality. It is not, however, merely monetary success which seduces them; success, in all its aspects, has for them a baleful attraction. They succumb to it intellectually, morally, spiritually. On that Carlyle wrecked his chances of producing a permanent work of art greater than his *French Revolution.*

ALL: Carlyle?

WILDE: I surprise you? Is that because we all know that Carlyle remained poor? So do misers. Carlyle was the greatest intellectual miser of the nineteenth century. In his prime he wrote his greatest work—the history of a failure—the *French Revolution.* The time came when, with all his powers matured, he stood equipped for the writing of his supreme masterpiece. There was no need to look far afield for a subject: it stood obviously awaiting him. After his *French Revolution* he should have written the life of Napoleon—the greatest success, the greatest failure that the world has ever known. He would have done it magnificently. What a spectacle for the world: the Man of Destiny receiving from the son of humble Scottish peasants his right measure of immortality! But because Carlyle was a Scotsman, he would not take for his hero the man whose life ended in failure; he could not bring himself to face the débâcle of Waterloo, the enduring ignominy and defeat of St. Helena. Had he been true to his art, he would have realized that St. Helena was the greatest theme of all—for an artist, the most completely significant in the whole of modern history. But because he had the soul of a Scotsman, because he worshipped success, he looked for his hero, and found him, in that most mean and despicable character, Frederick the Great: a man to whom heaven had given the powers of a supreme genius, and hell the soul of a commercial traveller with that unavailing itch for cultural gentility which Voltaire has exposed for us. On that mean theme he wrote his most voluminous work, and became, in the process, that skeleton in Mrs. Carlyle's cupboard which the world now knows.

You smile at me, Robbie, but believe me, in my own ruin I have found out this truth. The artist must live the complete life, must accept it as it comes and stands like an angel before him, with its drawn and two-edged sword. Great success, great failure—only so shall the artist see himself as he is, and through himself see others; only so shall he learn (as the artist must learn) the true meaning behind the appearance of things material, of life in general, and—more terrible still—the meaning of his own soul.

HOUSMAN: Why is a man's soul more terrible than life in general? Does not the greater include the less?

WILDE: Because an epitome is always more terrible than a generalization. We do not see life in general steadily diminishing in force and vitality, or we do not realize it; the whole bulk is too great. But when a man really sees into himself, the process of diminution that is going on becomes apparent: he meets there a problem he cannot escape—a problem to which religion, and philosophy, and history can give no certain answer, however much they may pretend. As I sit here—with a few friends left to me; friends who, however faithful, their number must needs diminish—for I shall never make a new friend in my life, though perhaps a few after I die—as I sit here and look back, I realize that I have lived the complete life necessary to the artist: I have had great success, I have had great failure. I have learned the value of each; and I know now that failure means more—always must mean more than success. Why, then, should I complain? I do not mean that a certain infirmity of the flesh, or weakness of the will would not make me prefer that this should have happened to one of my friends—to one of you—rather than to myself; but admitting that, I still recognize that I have only at last come to the complete life which every artist must experience in order to join beauty to truth. I have come to see that St. Helena is, for a world which follows Caesar and not Christ, the greatest place on earth next to Calvary. It is more neglected: men do not fight for it, they do not go out to conquer it in weary generations of disastrous crusades, like those which did so much to destroy for Catholic Europe the true significance of Christianity. But it is there; and only when men begin to fight for it as a thing desirable and precious to possess, only then will its spiritual significance change, and its value diminish.

If I could write what I have been saying to you, if I could hope to interest others, as I seem to have interested you, I would; but the world will not listen to me—now. It is strange—I never thought it possible before—to regret that one has too much leisure: leisure which I used so to lack, when I myself was a creator of beautiful things.

HOUSMAN: But you told me, in your last letter, that you were writing something?

WILDE: I told you that I was going to write something. I tell everybody that. It is a thing one can repeat each day, meaning to do it the next. But in my heart—that chamber of leaden echoes—I know that I never shall. It is enough that the stories have been invented, that they actually exist; that I have been able, in my own mind, to give them the form which they demand.

ROSS: If you won't write them, Oscar, you might at least tell them.

WILDE: You have heard them all, Robbie.

ROSS: The others have not.

WILDE: My dear Robbie, you are not nearly artful enough; but you are very kind. I will tell you one of my stories presently. Let us go on talking till the appropriate moment makes it more possible. . . . Is it I, or is it the ortolans that are still keeping us here? I do not mind; I would only like to know.

ROSS: To tell you the truth, Oscar, the ortolans were merely a delicate excuse. We are now waiting for the most perfectly forgetful, and the most regularly unpunctual person that any of us know. Do you mind if I cling for five minutes more to my belief that he really intends to meet us?

WILDE: Not at all; a charming experiment. Forgetfulness is a great gift. While he exercises it, we have more time for being happy where we are than we should otherwise have allowed ourselves. Who is our benefactor?

ROSS: I thought you might like to meet Harvey Jerrold again. I was keeping it behind the ortolans as a surprise for you.

(*The name has evoked a look of eager, almost of startled, pleasure; and response comes with animation.*)

WILDE: My dear Robbie; but how inventive of you! What a finishing touch to a circle which already seemed complete! I did not know that he was here.

ROSS: He only arrived last night. I phoned to his hotel and left a message for him asking him to join us. This morning he sent word that he would come.

WILDE (*with just a shade of doubt in his tone*): Did you tell him who we all were?

ROSS: I only said "friends." He knows all of us.

WILDE: If he has not, in the exercise of his gift, forgotten some of us. That —as I remember him—is possible.

ROSS: He can't have forgotten you, at any rate, considering it was you who published his first plays for him. Or did you only write them?

WILDE: Ah! but he has done so much better since. Suppose he were now ashamed of them. He was one of those—true artists—who make a reputation before they do anything. That is the right way to begin; but few have the courage to persevere. It is so difficult. Yet he, of course, is the most complete artist who is able to remain perfect— doing nothing.

ROSS: I have heard you say that before. But for the sake of the others won't you explain it? Your explanations are so much more illuminating than your statements, you know.

WILDE: I may have said the same thing before, Robbie. (It requires a friend to tell one so!) But my explanation, I am sure, will always be different. And yet the one which comes at this moment seems only too obvious. The greatest work of the imagination, for an artist, is to create first himself, then his public. The writing of my plays and my poems was never difficult: because they belonged to me, they came at call. But to make my own public was a labor of Hercules. That is what I did first. The effort lay in the fact that while one appeared to be doing nothing, one was actually prostrated by the exertion. I have known what it is to come back from a week-end—one of those ordeals by tattle which the stately homes of England provide for the passing guest—almost literally at death's door, from which nothing but hermetic seclusion, until the week-end following, enabled me to escape. One of my doctors called it "heart-strain," the other "brain-fag." It was really both. I remember once, on a Monday morning, missing an unreasonably early train and having to return for four hours to the bosom of a ducal family, when its exhibition hours were over. It was a charnel house; the bones of its skeleton rattled; the ghosts gibbered and moaned. Time remained motionless. I was haunted. I could never go there again. I had seen what man is never meant to see—the sweeping up of the dust on which the footfall of departing pleasure has left its print. There for two days I had been creating my public: the two days given by God to the Jewish and the Christian world for rest; and from that breaking of the sabbath, creator and created were equally exhausted. The breath of life I had so laboriously breathed into their nostrils they were getting rid of again, returning to native clay. And yet how few understand what a life of heroism is that of an artist when he is producing—not his art, but the receptacle which is to contain it.

That, dear friends, is why the world is to the artist so tragic. It is always a struggle. The artist may possibly for a while mold the world; but if the world molds him, he has failed to become an artist, though he may have succeeded in acquiring the Scotch accent.

HOUSMAN: You spoke just now of the artist creating a public for the appreciation of his work; can he not also create other artists? Would not that be the ideal aim?

WILDE: Ideal, but impossible. You cannot create an artist; you can only invent one—and it always remains a fiction. Artists—God's last creation, secret recipients of the Word of Life—continue to create themselves. But invention is often tried as a substitute. I remember, years ago, Hermann Vezin inventing an actress who was to be a second Rachel. For years and years he continued to invent her, telling us what to expect. Then one day he produced her. . . .

ROSS (*after allowing the rhetorical pause its due weight*): What happened? I don't remember.

WILDE: On the day he produced her, she ceased to exist.

ROSS: You mean she didn't arrive?

WILDE: Her arrival was a departure: the stage was her terminus. Engines whistled; the uproar became frightful. She ran to Brighton without stopping; and, I believe, still dies there.

HOUSMAN: Was she so bad, then, after all?

WILDE: She may have been almost a genius; who can tell? The fatal mistake was when Hermann Vezin began inventing her. What would happen to an actress, however great, who came upon the stage bejewelled with the names of Sarah, Rachel, Ristori, Siddons? Probability becomes violated; the sense of the theater is destroyed. When that happens all is over. Hermann Vezin should have held his tongue till the gods themselves applauded. But he lacked faith. The worst thing you can do for a person of genius is to help him: that way lies destruction. I have had many devoted helpers—and you see the result. Only once did I help a man who was also a genius. I have never forgiven myself.

ROSS: Oscar, you are perfectly absurd!

WILDE (*with a glance of genuine affection*): But I have forgiven you, Robbie.

HOUSMAN: What happened?

WILDE: To the man I helped? He never told me; and I would not ask. When we met afterwards, he had so greatly changed that, though I recognized him, he failed to recognize me. He became a Roman Catholic, and died at the age of twenty-three, a great artist—with half the critics and all the moralists still hating him. A charming person!

HOUSMAN: How often one hears that said, as though it were the final summing up of a man's life and character—covering everything.

WILDE: But surely it is so. What is more fundamental, more inalienable from a man's personality, than charm? He may lose his looks; he may lose his character; but in almost every case that I have known—in spite of adverse circumstances—the charm remains, like the gift of a fairy godmother: something which cannot be got rid of. A person who has charm has the secret of life; but does not know what the secret is—he himself being the secret. For in this wonderful turning world we can know other people by their differences—as I know all of you; but we can never know ourselves. Matthew Arnold, a fine but a very mistaken poet, was always trying to do the most impossible thing of all—to know himself. And that is why sometimes, in the middle of his most beautiful poems, he left off being the poet and became the school inspector.

HOUSMAN: I thought you said that the artist must know himself in order to know others.

WILDE: Never! You misunderstood me. "See himself!" is what I said; and, seeing himself naked but not ashamed, learn the terrible meaning of his own soul—how it exists to torment and divide him against himself, but always as a stranger within his gates, remote, inscrutable, unnatural. For this thing, which he can never understand, goes deeper than the consciousness of self—it is something primitive, atavistic, fierce, and savage with a fanatical faith in gods whom this world tries no longer to believe in, but still fears, lest they should become true. When news of Matthew Arnold's death came to Robert Louis Stevenson in Samoa, he said (for he was a Scotsman with a fine sense of humour): "How dreadful! He won't like God." You smile; and yet there was a very real truth in it. The theology of Matthew Arnold was a terrible mistake; it arose out of that insistence on trying to know himself: he wanted also to know God. And just as trying to know yourself savors of social snobbery—being an attempt to know the person you think the most important in the world—so in the other attempt there is a certain spiritual snobbery. It is surely quite sufficient that He should know us, without any pretended recognition on our part, which, in any case, would be futile. For if a man cannot know his own soul with real understanding, still less can he know with real understanding that which directs its ministry of pain—that constant intolerable reminder that we can never, unless we would choose only to be dust, belong separately and entirely to ourselves. Man's destiny is to be haunted; however deserted of his fellows, he is never for a moment alone. Matthew Arnold, in one of his poems, made that beautiful but ridiculous statement which appeals to us, perhaps, as true because we would so much like it to be true:

> *Yes, in this sea of life enisled,*
> *We mortal millions live alone!*

We don't: we live with a familiar who is a stranger, always eating out of our hand, always defrauding us of the joys of life while denying us the reason. And we never know from day to day whether that stranger is going to murder us in cold blood, or make us become saints.

ROSS: Why not both? To me they sound almost synonymous.

WILDE: Robbie, you must not interrupt me, saying clever, sensible things like that: you put me out. People who want to say merely what is sensible should say it to themselves before they come down to breakfast in the morning, never after.

HOUSMAN: That was when Lewis Carroll's "White Queen" used to practice telling herself all the things she knew to be impossible.

ROSS: I always thought that meant saying her prayers.

WILDE: But saying prayers, Robbie, is always possible. It is only the answer to prayer that is impossible. Prayer must never be answered. If it is, it ceases to be prayer, and becomes a correspondence. If we ask for our daily bread and it is given us as manna was given to the Israelites in the wilderness, it is merely an invitation to dinner reversed. How much more devotional the exercise becomes when we know that our food comes to us from quite mundane sources, irrespective of prayer.

DAVRAY: But your prayer then becomes merely a superstition.

WILDE: Not at all: a compliment—a spiritual courtesy which one may surely hope is appreciated in the proper place. I do not say it derisively. There is a proper place for the appreciation of everything. And perhaps it is only in heaven—and in hell—that art, now so generally despised, will receive the appreciation that is due to it.

H.A.: In heaven, yes; but why in hell?

WILDE: Why in hell? I must tell you one of my stories.

(*A grave smile passes from face to face, as the friends lean forward attentively to listen; for they know that this born story-teller only tells them when, for the moment, life contents him.*)

In hell, among all the brave company that is ever to be found there of lovers, and fair ladies, and men of learning, and poets, and astrologers, amid all the ceaseless movement of doomed bodies, tossing and turning to be rid of the torment of their souls, one woman sat alone and smiled. She had the air of a listener, ever with lifted head and eyes raised, as though some voice from above were attracting her.

"Who is that woman?" inquired a newcomer, struck by the strange loveliness of her face, with its look the meaning of which he could not read, "the one with the smooth, ivory limbs, and the long hair falling down over her arms to the hands resting upon her lap. She is the only soul whose eyes are ever looking aloft. What skeleton does she keep in the cupboard of God up yonder?"

He had not finished speaking before one made haste to answer, a man who carried in his hand a wreath of withered leaves. "They say," he said, "that once on earth she was a great singer, with a voice like stars falling from a clear sky. So when doom came for her, God took her voice and cast it forth to the eternal echoes of the spheres, finding it too beautiful a thing to let die. Now she hears it with recognition, and remembering how once it was her own, shares still the pleasure which God takes in it. Do not speak to her, for she believes that she is in heaven."

And when the man bearing the wreath of withered leaves had finished: "No," said another, "that is not her story."

"What then?"

"It is this," he said, as the man with the withered wreath turned away: "On earth a poet made his song of her, so that her name became eternally wedded to his verse, which still rings on the lips of men. Now she lifts her head and can hear his praise of her sounded wherever language is spoken. That is her true story."

"And the poet?" asked the newcomer. "Did she love him well?"

"So little," replied the other, "that here and now she passes him daily and does not recognize his face."

"And he?"

The other laughed, and answered: "It is he who just now told you that tale concerning her voice, continuing here the lies which he used to make about her when they two were together on earth."

But the newcomer said, "If he is able to give happiness in hell, can what he says be a lie?"

(There is an appreciative pause: no one speaks: from those listening faces no word of praise is necessary. Once more the speaker has secured the homage of his fellow men; and so, forgetting for a while the pit that life has dug for him, continues to narrate to his friends the stories which he will never write.)

Since that has appealed to you, I will tell you another. . . . Once there was a young man, so beautiful of mind that all who heard him wished to be of his company; so beautiful of form—

(*In the middle of a sentence he pauses, as he sees advancing— though the others, intent only on him, do not—a young man, graceful in person, indolent in motion, who, with a light nonchalant air, meets and lets go the glances of strangers as they pass. From these, as he draws near, his eye turns toward the group seated at the outdoor table under the sun-bright awning, and becomes fixed and attentive. Glance meets glance, holds for a moment, till that of the younger man is withdrawn. Without any change of countenance he slightly deflects his course and passes on. In the face they are watching, the friends see a quick change: the color goes, the look of quiet expectation ends abruptly, as though sight had stopped dead. But it is with his accustomed deliberation of tone that at last he resumes speaking.*)

Ah, no; that is a story of which I have forgotten the end; or else it has forgotten me. No matter; I will tell you another. This is one that has only just occurred to me; and I am not quite sure yet what the end of it will be. But it is there waiting. You and I will listen to this story together, as I tell it for the first time.

This shall be called "The Story of the Man Who Sold His Soul."

A certain traveller, passing through the streets of a great city, came upon a man whose countenance indicated a grief which he could not fathom. The traveller, being a curious student of the human heart, stopped him and said: "Sir, what is this grief which you carry before the eyes of all men, so grievous that it cannot be hidden, yet so deep that it cannot be read?"

The man answered: "It is not I who grieve so greatly; it is my soul, of which I cannot get rid. And my soul is more sorrowful than death, for it hates me, and I hate it."

The traveller said: "If you will sell your soul to me, you can be well rid of it." The other answered: "Sir, how can I sell you my soul?" "Surely," replied the traveller, "you have but to agree to sell me your soul at its full price; then, when I bid it, it comes to me. But every soul has its true price; and only at that, neither at more nor at less, can it be bought."

Then said the other: "At what price shall I sell you this horrible thing, my soul?"

The traveller answered: "When a man first sells his own soul he is like that other betrayer; therefore its price should be thirty pieces of silver. But after that, if it passes to other hands, its value becomes small; for to others the souls of their fellow men are worth very little."

So for thirty pieces of silver the man sold his soul; and the traveller took it and departed.

Presently the man, having no soul, found that he could do no sin. Though he stretched out his arms to sin, sin would not come to him. "You have no soul," said sin, and passed him by. "Wherefore should I come to you? I have no profit in a man that has no soul."

Then the man without a soul became very miserable, for though his hands touched what was foul, they remained clean, and though his heart longed for wickedness, it remained pure; and when he thirsted to dip his lips in fire, they remained cool.

Therefore a longing to recover his soul took hold of him, and he went through the world searching for the traveller to whom he had sold it, that he might buy it back and again taste sin in his own body.

After a long time the traveller met him; but hearing his request he laughed and said: "After a while your soul wearied me and I sold it for a smaller sum than I paid for it."

"Ah!" cried the man, "if you had come to me I would have paid more." The traveller answered: "You could not have done that; a soul cannot be bought or sold but at its just price. Your soul came to be of small value in my keeping; so to be rid of it I sold it to the first comer for considerably less money than I paid in the beginning."

So parting from him the man continued his quest, wandering over the face of the earth and seeking to recover his lost soul. And one day as he sat in the bazaar of a certain town a woman passed him, and looking at him said: "Sir, why are you so sad? It seems to me there can be no reason for such sadness." The man answered: "I am sad because I have no soul, and am seeking to find it."

The other said: "Only the other night I bought a soul that had passed through so many hands that it had become dirt-cheap; but it is so poor a thing I would gladly be rid of it. Yet I bought it for a mere song; and a soul can only be sold at its just price; how, then, shall I be able to sell it again—for what is worth less than a song? And it was but a light song that I sang over the wine-cup to the man who sold it to me."

When the other heard that, he cried: "It is my own soul! Sell it to me, and I will give you all that I possess!"

The woman said: "Alas, I did but pay for it with a song, and I can but sell it again at its just price. How then can I be rid of it, though it cries and laments to be set free?"

The man without a soul laid his head to the woman's breast, and heard within it the captive soul whimpering to be set free, to return to the body it had lost. "Surely," he said, "it is my own soul! If you will sell it to me I will give you my body, which is worth less than a song from your lips."

So, for his body, the other sold to him the soul that whimpered to be set free to return to its own place. But so soon as he received it he rose up aghast: "What have you done?" he cried, "and what is this foul thing that has possession of me? For this soul that you have given me is not *my* soul!"

The woman laughed and said: "Before you sold your soul into captivity it was a free soul in a free body; can you not recognize it now it comes to you from the traffic of the slave-market? So, then, your soul has the greater charity, since it recognizes and returns to you, though you have sold your body miserably into bondage!"

And thus it was that the man had to buy back, at the cost of his body, the soul which he let go for thirty pieces of silver.

(*With occasional pauses imposed for effect, but without any hesitation or change in the choice of word, the ordered narrative has run its course. But in spite of the decorative form, and the decorative modulations of tone, there is an undercurrent of passion; and his friends, undeceived by that quiet deliberateness of speech, know that the speaker is greatly moved. And so, at the end, there is a pause while nobody speaks. At the kiosk opposite a newsboy arrives, and delivers a bundle of papers to the woman in charge. Over her is an announcement to the Englishman, in his native tongue, that his own papers are there on sale. From the restaurant comes a garçon charged with a message, and wishing to have instructions. The two who have shared in the arrangement exchange glances interrogatively; Ross looks at his watch and nods. Housman signs to the garçon who has served the apéritifs.*)*

ROSS: Let us go in to lunch. Jerrold is not coming; he has forgotten us.

WILDE: Not all of us, Robbie. He came, but he has gone again.

(*They all look at him in astonishment; and, for a moment, nobody speaks. Then:*)

ROSS: Came? Here, do you mean?

WILDE: Looking as young and charming as ever. But as soon as he looked at me, I saw he had entirely forgotten me.

(*There is nothing possible to be said. Housman makes haste to pay for the* apéritifs; *and with the anxiety of an Englishman unpractised in foreign ways, to do what is right for the reputation of his country in a strange land, he puts down an additional* pourboire, *five bronze pieces in all, to correspond to the number who have been served. With grave apologetic politeness his guest lays an arresting hand upon his arm; and (while the* garçon *whisks away the* douceur *with cheerful alacrity) instructs him for future occasions.*)

WILDE: My dear L.H., you should not do that! The Frenchman, for these casual services, gives what you call a penny. The Englishman gives what some of them call "tuppence"; not because he does not know that the Frenchman's penny is sufficient, but because he is an Englishman. If you give more than that the waiter only thinks that you do not know where you are.

HOUSMAN (*who has a weakness for putting himself in the right, even in quite small matters*): Ah, yes, Mr. Wilde, that may be, but here, at St. Helena, one tips the waiters differently.

(*It is touching to see what pleasure that foolish but fortunate little "mot" has given to the man for whom it was designed. They have all now risen; and their next move will be to the tabled interior, where pleasant courses are awaiting them. But the forward movement is delayed; and it is with a curious air of finality, as though already taking his leave, that Wilde speaks.*)

WILDE: My friends, we have had a wonderful hour together. I have been very happy. Excuse me: I am going across to get an English paper. The woman at the kiosk, who sells them, is a charming character: she compliments my accent by pretending to think that I am French. Go in: I beg you not to wait for me.

(*They see him cross the street, with his accustomed air of leisurely deliberation—a little amused to notice how the vehement traffic has to pause and make way for him. At the kiosk he and the woman exchange words and smiles. He lifts his hat and turns away.*)

HOUSMAN (*startled*): He's not coming back?

ROSS: Harvey Jerrold wants kicking. Poor Oscar!

H.A.: Shall I go after him?

ROSS: No, No! Let him go. We understand.

(*And they all stand and watch, as he passes slowly down the street, till he disappears in the crowd.*)

(As a postscript to Housman's account, one may venture to pick up Wilde's trail at this point. One pictures him returning to his dingy quarters at the Hôtel d'Alsace. The windows of Wilde's tawdrily furnished bedroom open on a courtyard that becomes almost his only refuge during the few scant months of life remaining to him. There, undisturbed, he reads his favorite author Balzac for hours on end, with a constantly replenished glass of cognac to add to his comfort. There are, of course, periods of dejection. "Somehow I don't think I shall live to see the new century," he confides to a friend. Such moments become more frequent as Wilde undergoes a siege of severe headaches and earaches. Yet, one notes the inevitable flashes of wit, even in the grip of a growing agony of mind and body. "I am dying, as I have lived, beyond my means," he remarks over a bottle of champagne one day. As the winter of 1900 draws near, Wilde's condition grows worse. The dosages of morphine are increased as the pain makes him delirious. Wilde is dying from cerebral meningitis, "probably complicated by syphilis." * Two days before his death Robert Ross, knowing Wilde's leanings, brings in a Catholic priest, who baptizes the dying man and administers Extreme Unction. Ross is present on November 30, when Wilde gives a final sigh and dies. To this devoted and inseparable companion of his last agony Wilde, in a moment of elfin charm, once pronounced the words that Pearson regarded as a fitting epitaph for the fallen wit and dandy: "When the Last Trumpet sounds, and we are couched in our porphyry tombs, I shall turn and whisper to you, 'Robbie, Robbie, let us pretend we do not hear it.'")

---

* Pearson, *Oscar Wilde*, Harper and Bros., N. Y. and London, 1946; p. 332.

Thomas Hardy

WILLIAM ARCHER FEELS OUT HIS HOST ON THE
CHANCES OF A MIDNIGHT VISITATION
FROM THE SPIRIT WORLD.

*I seriously assure you that I would give ten
years of my life—well, perhaps that offer is
rather beyond my means—to see a ghost.*

WHEN Thomas Hardy decided to build himself a new house in 1883,
he naturally chose a site that lay at the heart of the "Wessex" country
which he had already made famous in four of his novels. "Wessex," of
course, was largely Dorsetshire, the maritime county in the south of
England, romantic in medieval abbeys and castles and strewn with
vestiges of an ancient Roman colony. Hardy found a spot about a mile
outside of Dorchester, not far from his birthplace. In October of that year
the well-diggers were already at work close to the foundation of Hardy's
new home. One day their spades turned up a heap of Roman urns and
skeletons. The foundation-diggers unearthed a further bundle of relics,
and when later they were building the driveway, five Roman soldiers were
"decapitated," to use Hardy's own word. The great fatalist of British fiction had purchased a Roman cemetery for the site of his new home! Far
from being dejected by these grisly exhumings, Hardy, always the hardened materialist and scholar, welcomed the prospect of living, as it were,
in the lap of antiquity. And one notes here, in passing, that this sense of
the dead but palpable past broods desolately over Hardy's grim chronicles
of "Wessex."

It was in this quaint red-brick house on a lonely hill—a house built to
Hardy's own design and baptized "Max Gate"—that Hardy wrote his
last three novels, his dramatic masterpiece The Dynasts, and most of his
lyric poetry. To the second Mrs. Hardy we owe an intimate picture of the
shifting locations of Hardy's place of composition: "To the right of the
front door upon entering is the drawing-room, and to the left the dining-
room. Above the drawing-room is the room which Hardy used as his first
study at "Max Gate," and in this room The Woodlanders was written.
Later he moved his study to the back of the house with a window facing

475

west, where Tess of the d'Urbervilles took shape. *In after years another study was built over a new kitchen, and here The Dynasts and all the later poems were written, with the remaining literary work of Hardy's life. The rather large window of this, the last of all his workrooms, faced east, and the full moon rising over the tops of the dark pines was a familiar sight."* * *It was in the study with "a window facing west" that Hardy also worked on that powerful and tragic novel* Jude the Obscure, *which aroused such a storm of righteous protest that he gave up writing fiction and returned for good to his first love, poetry. In a diary note of September 13, 1893, Hardy gives us a brief glimpse of himself while at work on* Jude the Obscure: *"A striated crimson sunset; opposite it I sit in the study writing by the light of a shaded lamp, which looks primrose against the red."*

It was at this same "Max Gate" that Hardy † received a week-end guest some time late in 1900—the drama critic, playwright, and translator of Ibsen, William Archer. A great admirer of Hardy's fiction, Archer had thoroughly familiarized himself with the landscape and people of "Wessex." Moreover, he had heard of the Roman graveyard upon which "Max Gate" rested, and there had been talk of the further exhumation of a Roman lady. In the London of Archer's day, ghosts had once again become a favorite drawing-room topic. The Society for Psychical Research had been flourishing briskly, and such celebrities as Sir Oliver Lodge and Sir Arthur Conan Doyle had been drawn into the inner circle of confirmed believers in occult phenomena. Telepathy, clairvoyance, ectoplasm, anti-Newtonian levitation and the spontaneous cracking of crockery were common subjects of serious talk in high places. It was at once natural and supernatural that in this congenial atmosphere ghosts too should enjoy a new lease on life. Quite understandably, Archer was eager to sound out this notorious skeptic on the prospects of an afterworld and the chances of communication with its inhabitants. Still another subject that Archer wanted to discuss was criticism, particularly unsigned criticism, for some of the most vicious reviews of Tess *and* Jude the Obscure *had been anonymous. Finally, there were details about Hardy, his Dorset background, the legends and superstitions he had gleaned as a child, the Dorsetshire dialect, that Archer wanted to know. For comedy relief he would twit this arch-fatalist and non-believer about the specter of a certain Roman lady. . . .*

Archer first published his conversation with Hardy in the Pall Mall Magazine of February, 1901, including it later in a collection entitled Real

---

* *The Early Life of Thomas Hardy,* by Florence Emily Hardy, Macmillan, 1928; page 227.
† Hardy was sixty at the time and Archer forty-four.

Conversations (Heinemann, London, 1904). In its original version, the conversation gave the locale as "near Casterbridge" (used in Hardy's The Mayor of Casterbridge), which is, of course, Dorchester. Throughout the dialogue Archer, rather effectively, uses all the substitute place names of Hardy's "Wessex." Possibly, Hardy, a shy and reticent man, insisted on this camouflage. Even the name of the house, "Max Gate," is concealed behind a row of dots. In any case, Thomas Hardy and his London guest are seated before "a smoldering fire of elm logs" in the library at "Max Gate" as the conversation begins:

HARDY: Have you seen anything of C—— lately?

ARCHER: I've scarcely seen him since our famous midnight expedition to Egdon Heath.

HARDY: Ah, yes, when he wrenched his ankle. How many years ago is that?

ARCHER: It must be five or six.

HARDY: And you haven't been there since then, have you?

ARCHER: I had a little walking tour in Wessex a couple of years ago, but you weren't at home. I climbed up to Shaston, in the tracks of Jude and Sue; went on to Sherton Abbas, and met Grace Melbury and Winterborne in Sheep Street; down through the country of the Woodlanders to Casterbridge; on to Budmouth, looking for (but not finding) Overcombe of The Trumpet-Major on the way.

HARDY: You would have had to turn eastward from the main road.

ARCHER: From Budmouth along the Chesil, and up the escarpments of the Isle of Slingers, till we reached the place where Anne Garland watched the "Victory" fading under the sea-line on her way to Plymouth and Trafalgar.

HARDY: She did, you know—that was a true story.

ARCHER: I've often wondered what proportion, so to speak, of fact there is in your books?

HARDY: In several of my stories there is a very large element of fact, or tradition. For instance, the story of Napoleon's landing in person on the Dorsetshire coast—I don't know whether you remember it—is related as a fact.

ARCHER: Do you yourself believe it?

HARDY: I cannot honestly say I do. But the incident in The Trumpet-Major of the people letting the cider run when Bonaparte was reported to have landed is a literal fact. Few of my longer books, how-

ever, are so closely founded on facts as *The Trumpet-Major*. On a single
series of facts, that is to say. In other books, one situation will often be
an amalgam of many real incidents. In that way, it seems to me, one
may hope to get at what is fundamental in them—to present the typical incident. Just as, in character-drawing, several similar individuals
will blend into one type.

ARCHER: A sort of composite photograph, in fact? I wonder if you are
properly grateful to the deities—the tribal gods of the West Saxons,
I suppose—who have given you such stores of knowledge to draw upon,
and have made you the historiographer of their ancient and delectable
domain?

HARDY: I suppose it *is* an advantage, from one point of view, to be thoroughly at home in one region, however narrow. But think of the men
who have been thoroughly at home in all!

ARCHER: I believe if I were an artist, and had my choice as to the form of
equipment I would prefer, I should choose intensive rather than extensive knowledge.

HARDY: It has been said a man ought to know something about everything, and everything about something.

ARCHER: Well, it seems to me that if ever man fulfilled the latter condition, you are that enviable mortal. What you don't know about this
Wessex of yours isn't knowledge. You are as familiar with the Wessex
stars as with the Wessex flowers. I shall never forget the first page of
yours I ever came across—when I picked up an odd number of *The
Cornhill*, five-and-twenty years ago, and read the passage in *Far from
the Madding Crowd* where you describe Gabriel Oak standing at midnight on the brow of a hill, and actually seeing the revolution of the
earth as the constellations wheel under the horizon. It seems to me
there isn't a contour of the country, from Exonbury to Christminster,
that isn't mapped in your mind. You appear to know every copse and
common, every elbow of every lane, every "church-hay," every water-
mead, every "eweal-eaze." You have history, local tradition, folk-lore,
village gossip, all at your finger-ends. You—

HARDY (*laughing*): Oh, I'm not such an encyclopedia as all that! Perhaps
some of what you take for my knowledge may be "only my artfulness."
But it's true that my feeling for this country is that of the countryman
born and bred. Have you ever noticed the different relation to nature
of the town child and the country child? The town-bred boy will often
appreciate nature more than the country boy, but he does not know it
in the same sense. He will rush to pick a flower which the country boy
does not seem to notice. But it is part of the country boy's life. It grows

in his soul—he does not want it in his buttonhole. Then I lived, too,
in close contact with the people—

ARCHER: Haven't I heard you say that you used to write love-letters for
the village girls?

HARDY: Yes, to their soldier sweethearts in India,—the East Indies, as it
was called then.

ARCHER: That was part of Samuel Richardson's apprenticeship, too. He
trained for Clarissa, you for Tess.

HARDY: But I think you will find that Richardson's case was different. He
was employed to compose the letters; I was only the amanuensis. Indeed, I was chosen on account of my tender years,—because I could
write, and read the replies, yet couldn't understand. They looked upon
me as a mere writing machine, or a sort of phonograph to be talked
into. And as a matter of fact I undertook very little, and took very
little interest in what I wrote and read; though I remember to this day
one lover's address, as given in his letter: "Calcutta, *or Elsewear.*"

ARCHER: I fancy many of those letters remained written in your mind in
sympathetic ink, only waiting for the heat of creation to bring them
out.

HARDY: Possibly, in a subconscious way. The human mind is a sort of
palimpsest, I suppose; and it's hard to say what records may not lurk
in it.

ARCHER: Well, I can see that your village life goes far to account for your
insight into rustic character. But how did you get your surface knowledge—your topographical mastery—of so large a region?

HARDY: I don't know that my surface knowledge of the country is so intimate as you think. But, for one thing, when I was quite a young man,
an architect's pupil, I used to be sent round to sketch village churches
as a preliminary to their restoration—which mostly meant destruction.
I feel very remorseful now; but after all it wasn't my fault—I was only
obeying orders.

ARCHER: Ah, I had forgotten that you looked at the country not only with
the novelist's but with the draughtsman's eye. That accounts for much.
And these sketch-book wanderings must have brought you into many
quaint nooks and corners. I suppose, now, you can yourself remember
many of the old customs—the relics of paganism—that you have described?

HARDY: Oh, yes. They survived well into my time. I have seen with my
own eyes things that many people believe to have been extinct for
centuries. For instance, the maypole was familiar to me in my child-

hood—the flower-wreathed pole, with what they called the garland at the top (that is to say, two intersecting hoops of flowers) round which the people danced. More than that, I have seen men in the stocks.

ARCHER: Is it possible!

HARDY: I remember one perfectly—when I was very young. It was in the village I have called Weatherbury. I can see him now, sitting in the blazing sunshine, with not another human being near except me. I can see his blue worsted stockings projecting through the leg-holes, and the shining nails in his boots. He was quite a hero in my eyes. I sidled up to him and said good-day to him, and felt mightily honored when he nodded to me.

ARCHER: Do you know what his offense was?

HARDY: "Drunk and disorderly," no doubt.

ARCHER: Then by what authority—by what legal process—was he put in the stocks?

HARDY: I can't say exactly. It used to be understood that the constable could put a man in the stocks, but that only a magistrate could lock them. But perhaps that was only a village superstition. Then, again, the Christmas Mummers flourished well into my recollection—indeed, they have not so long died out.

ARCHER: I can remember a sort of mummers in Scotland whom we called "guisers"; but they were simply boys wearing masks and begging for half-pence.

HARDY: Oh, our mummers hereabouts gave a regular performance—"The Play of St. George," it was called. It contained quite a number of traditional characters: the Valiant Soldier, the Turkish Knight, St. George himself, the Saracen, Father Christmas, the Fair Sabra, and so on. Rude as it was, the thing used to impress me very much—I can clearly recall the odd sort of thrill it would give. The performers used to carry a long staff in one hand and a wooden sword in the other, and pace monotonously round, intoning their parts on one note, and punctuating them by nicking the sword against the staff—something like this:—"Here come I, the Valiant Soldier (*nick*), Slasher is my name (*nick*)."

ARCHER: The pacing and rhythmic sing-song suggest kinship with the Chinese acting I have seen in San Francisco and New York. And what was the action of the play?

HARDY: I really don't know, except that it ended in a series of mortal combats in which all the characters but St. George were killed. And then the curious thing was that they were invariably brought to life again. A personage was introduced for the purpose,—the Doctor of Physic, wearing a cloak and a broad-brimmed beaver.

ARCHER: How many actors would there be in a company?

HARDY: Twelve to fifteen, I should think. Sometimes a large village would furnish forth two sets of mummers. They would go to the farmhouses round, between Christmas and Twelfth Night, doing some four or five performances each evening, and getting ale and money at every house. Sometimes the mummers of one village would encroach on the traditional "sphere of influence" of another village, and then there would be a battle in good earnest.

ARCHER: Did women take part in the performances?

HARDY: I think not—the Fair Sabra was always played by a boy. But the character was often omitted.

ARCHER: And when did the mumming go out?

HARDY: It went on in some neighborhoods till 1880, or thereabouts. I have heard of a person here and there trying to revive it; but of course that isn't at all the same thing—the spontaneity is gone.

ARCHER: Now tell me, as to rural superstitions,—belief in witchcraft, and so forth,—are they dying out?

HARDY: On the surface, yes; in reality, no. People smile and say, "Of course we don't believe in these things"—but their skepticism is only skin deep. You will find women to this day who will make an image of some enemy and either melt it before the fire or stick pins into it. The belief in the evil eye subsists in full force; also such ideas as that which I have introduced into one of my stories—that if you can draw blood from a witch, you render her powerless.

ARCHER: Well, who knows? Perhaps the superstition of Wessex is one day going to have the laugh of the skepticism of Middlesex. It really looks as though the whirligig of time were cogitating—if a whirligig can cogitate—some such revenge.

HARDY: You don't really think so?

ARCHER: I find it very hard in these latter days to draw a line and say, "Beyond this the potentialities of Nature do not go." If I disbelieve in the supernatural, it is only because I am willing to give indefinite extension to the boundaries of the natural. Not "willing"—that is the wrong word—I am most unwilling to believe that there are more things in heaven and earth than were dreamt of in the philosophy of the placid eighteen-fifties. I heartily wish there were no intangible, imponderable, incalculable forces in the world. If I had made the universe, I should have omitted them. But unfortunately I did not make the universe—nor John Stuart Mill or Mr. Herbert Spencer. And it seems to me that science itself, nowadays, is rapidly driving the words "credulity" and "incredible" out of the language.

HARDY: Well, now, in this matter my position is just the reverse of yours. I am most anxious to believe in what, roughly speaking, we may call the supernatural—but I find no evidence for it! People accuse me of skepticism, materialism, and so forth; but, if the accusation is just at all, it is quite against my will. For instance, I seriously assure you that I would give ten years of my life—well, perhaps that offer is rather beyond my means—but when I was a younger man, I would cheerfully have given ten years of my life to see a ghost,—an authentic, indubitable specter.

ARCHER: And you have never seen one?

HARDY: Never the ghost of a ghost. Yet I should think I am cut out by nature for a ghost-seer. My nerves vibrate very readily; people say I am almost morbidly imaginative; my will to believe is perfect. If ever ghost wanted to manifest himself, I am the very man he should apply to. But no—the spirits don't seem to see it!

ARCHER: Yet you live in a graveyard, too, don't you?

HARDY: A Roman graveyard,—yes. We decapitated a row of five Roman soldiers or colonists in moving the earth to make the drive there.

ARCHER: And wasn't there a lady as well?

HARDY: Yes. I think I showed you the little bronze-gilt fibula that had fastened the fillet across her brow. I took it from her skull with my own hands, and it lies in the corner cupboard yonder.

ARCHER: Yet she hasn't haunted you? Well, that certainly establishes a very strong presumption against the spooks. I can only suggest that they don't think it worth while to appear to you, knowing that, if you recorded their visits, people would think you were romancing. "What the novelist says is not evidence."

HARDY: My mother believed that she once saw an apparition. A relative of hers, who had a young child, was ill and told my mother that she thought she was dying. My mother laughed at the idea; and as a matter of fact she apparently recovered, and went away to her home at some distance. Then one night—lying broad-awake as she declared—my mother saw this lady enter her room and hold out the child to her imploringly. It afterwards appeared (I need scarcely tell you) that she died at that very time; but the odd thing was that, while she was sinking, she continually expressed a wish that my mother should take charge of the child.

ARCHER: That seems to me a simple case of a very natural dream happening to coincide with a far from improbable event. But indeed I find it much easier to conceive the possibility of apparitions of the living—and the dying are of course living up to the last pulse-beat—than to conceive an apparition of the dead which should be other than a mere hallucination.

HARDY: Why should the one be more credible than the other?

ARCHER: Simply because there seems to be ample evidence for the existence of forms of cerebral energy not as yet measured and catalogued; whereas in death, so far as we can see, cerebral energy ceases altogether. It may be hard to believe that even an active brain, fifty miles away, can instantaneously impress an idea or an image upon mine as I sit here; but if the brain has, to all appearance, ceased to act—nay, has moldered into dust—the difficulty becomes infinitely greater. It is conceivable that, through some hitherto unrecognized property of matter, you, in Casterbridge, might be able to hear my watch ticking in London; but when my watch stops—when the mainspring is run down—you won't hear it ticking even if you hold it close to your ear.

HARDY: The spiritualist would maintain that the human watch, at the moment of its stoppage here below, is wound up afresh on another plane of being. But that, as I say, is precisely what, with the best will in the world, I can find no evidence for.

ARCHER: On the other hand, don't you think there is very fair evidence for the possibility of thought-transference, whether in the shape of words or of images?

HARDY: No. In all the researches of the Psychical Society, I find nothing that carries conviction. I cannot get past the famous principle of Hume—wait a minute—I will get the book. . . . Here it is, in the essay "Of Miracles": the principle "that no testimony is sufficient to establish a miracle, unless the testimony be of such a kind that its falsehood would be more miraculous than the fact which it endeavors to establish." Like Hume, I am compelled to "weigh one miracle against the other, and reject the greater."

ARCHER: Don't you think that the word "miracle" rather confuses the issue? You admit the reality of Roentgen-ray images?

HARDY: Yes.

ARCHER: Well, do they not prove certain forms of matter to be permeable to certain—what shall I call them?—vibrations?—in a way that, twenty years ago, would have been regarded as simply miraculous? You admit the genuineness of wireless telegraphy?

HARDY: Yes.

ARCHER: Well, is it inconceivable that the human brain may prove to be a more powerful transmitter and a more sensitive receiver than any invented by Marconi or Tesla, operating through some medium as much subtler than electricity as electricity is subtler than atmospheric air?

HARDY: Oh, I quite admit that all this is conceivable—that there is nothing in it which contradicts the very laws of thought, like the conception of a triangle in which any two sides should be less than the third side. I merely repeat my demand for evidence! Have you known, in your own experience, an instance of thought-transference?

ARCHER: Divil a wan, as Mr. Dooley would say.

HARDY: Well now, to be candid, I myself would not say that quite so emphatically. For example, the thoughts of a relation of mine used to "jump with" mine in a way not easily to be explained by mere coincidence. It would often happen that, after a long silence, both of us, in the same breath, would speak of some person or thing apparently quite absent from the thoughts of either five minutes before.

ARCHER: Don't you think it probable that some external object or incident, too trivial to be consciously noted, may have started in each of you the same train of association?

HARDY: That might be so in some cases; but the thing used to occur (or so I thought) too frequently to be always accounted for in that way. However, I admit—or rather this is my very point—that the instance is too trifling, and too uncertain, to have the smallest evidential value, yet no nearer approach to thought-transference has ever come within my ken.

ARCHER: Well now, let me give you one or two instances of things that I am inclined, till further notice, to put down to thought-transference, or telepathy, or whatever you like to call it.

HARDY: Hearsay instances?

ARCHER: Yes, but coming from people I know well and trust implicitly.

HARDY: H'm!

ARCHER: In the first case I think I may, without indiscretion, name my authority. It was Mark Twain.

HARDY: "What the humorist said—"

ARCHER: "—is not evidence," you think? I can only assure you that in this case Mr. Clemens was absolutely serious; and indeed if he had invented the story it would have been a much better one. Mr. Clemens and Mr. Cable were giving readings from their own works, and, among other places, visited Montreal. Here, one afternoon, a reception was given in their honor at one of the big hotels. According to the American fashion, they stood at one end of a suite of rooms, and people filed up the the rooms in a long stream, shook hands with the guests of honor, and passed down the rooms again. Mark Twain happened at one moment to look toward the entrance door, and saw, coming in, a lady whom he had known in Nevada twenty-five years before, but whom he had never seen, and seldom thought of, in the interval. He saw her gradually advancing with the stream of people, sometimes hidden for a moment, sometimes emerging again. She did not come up to him or shake hands, but in the bustle of the reception he scarcely noticed this. The same evening he called at the house of some friends. "We're so glad you have come," they said: "there's someone in the next room that's very anxious to see you." "I know," said Mr. Clemens: "it's Mrs. So-and-So." At that moment the lady herself came in, and Mark Twain's first words to her were, "I saw you at the reception this afternoon." "But I wasn't there," she replied. "Oh, yes," he said: "I watched you for some time—and you were wearing the very dress you have on now." "I assure you I haven't been an hour in Montreal," she answered. And he found that beyond all doubt she had only just come in by train from a distant town, and must have been many miles from Montreal when he thought he saw her in the reception-room.

HARDY: A chance resemblance and a coincidence, I should say—nothing more.

ARCHER: Well, my second case, I own, may be accounted for in the same way. A friend of mine was arriving at the London Docks from Australia. He half expected that an aunt of his would come to meet him; and, scanning the crowd of people on the wharf, he saw not his aunt but a girl whom he knew to be a close friend of hers. He lost sight of the girl in the crowd, and did not see her again. He drove straight to his aunt's house, and said, "I saw Miss Blank on the wharf today: I wonder whom she was meeting?" He noticed that his aunt was surprised and rather perturbed by this, and found on inquiry that Miss Blank had been staying with her parents at a Welsh watering-place, but had unaccountably disappeared some days before, and had not been heard of since. A few days afterwards, they learned that her body had been found in the sea, close to the place where her parents were staying.

HARDY: That may of course be a case of resemblance and coincidence, or it may be that your friend saw the living girl—that she came to meet someone who did not arrive—and that she then returned to Wales, and found her way into the sea. In short, there are half a dozen hypotheses less miraculous than the supposition either that her ghost was there objectively, so to speak, or that her image was impressed upon your friend's visual nerves by some mysterious emanation from her still living brain.

ARCHER: Well, listen to my third case; it is of a rather different kind. This was told me by an eminent professor in a leading American university

—an absolute skeptic on all "occult" subjects. He was asked to go and test a celebrated medium—well known to the Psychical Society, by the way. Now, he had had a mortal enemy who had been some years dead —a man of great mental power, but of coarse, overbearing, intolerable character. On one occasion, some particularly notable word had been used between them, under such circumstances that neither of them could possibly forget it "while memory held its seat." The Professor asked the medium—who was, of course, in a trance—to tell him this word. She did *not* tell him the word, but she burst forth into a torrent of abusive rage, exactly reproducing the character of the dead man. The Professor assured me that if her outpouring had been taken down in shorthand, and shown to anyone who had known the dear departed, he would have said, without a moment's hesitation, "That is So-and-So speaking." Curious, isn't it?

HARDY: Did the medium know the Professor?

ARCHER: He said he was sure she didn't, and that it was absolutely impossible that she could ever have known the dead man.

HARDY: Then what is your theory? That the Professor, in putting the question, conjured up and unconsciously dramatized the dead man, and that the medium, in some occult way, overheard, so to speak, the Professor's silent dramatization?

ARCHER: If we take the facts for granted, does not something like that seem the least miraculous explanation?

HARDY: I confess that if belief were a matter of choice, I should prefer to accept the spiritual hypothesis.

ARCHER: And believe that the abusive gentleman's ghost went blaspheming, to all eternity, up and down the Fourth Dimension?

HARDY: Even so. I quite admit the pitiful ineffectualness, even grotesqueness, of all the alleged manifestations of the spirit world, and the eerieness of spirits, to our seeming—

ARCHER (*interrupting*): They add a new terror to death.

HARDY (*continuing*): But for my part I say in all sincerity, "Better to be inconvenienced by visitants from beyond the grave than to see none at all." The material world is so uninteresting, human life is so miserably bounded circumscribed, cabined, cribbed, confined. I want another domain for the imagination to expatiate in.

ARCHER: But the imagination can, and does, expatiate as much as it pleases; else where would the ghost-stories come from?

HARDY: Ah, yes; but the fact that I can't believe them to be true destroys them for me. A ghost-story that should convince me would make me a happier man. And if you come to that, I don't know that the grotesqueness, the incompleteness of the manifestations is at all conclusive against their genuineness. Is not this incompleteness a characteristic of all phenomena, of the universe at large? It often seems to me like a half-expressed, an ill-expressed idea. Do you know Hartmann's philosophy of the Unconscious? It suggested to me what seems almost like a workable theory of the great problem of the origin of evil,—though this, of course, is not Hartmann's own theory,—that there may be a consciousness, infinitely far off, at the other end of the chain of phenomena, always striving to express itself, and always baffled and blundering, just as the spirits seem to be.

ARCHER: Is not that simply the good old Manichaean heresy, with Matter playing the part of the evil principle,—Satan, Ahriman, whatever you choose to call it?

HARDY: John Stuart Mill somewhere expresses surprise that Manichaeanism was not more widely accepted. But is not all popular religion in essence Manichaean? Does not it always postulate a struggle between a principle of good and an independent, if not equally powerful, principle of evil?

ARCHER: And the pessimist holds, I take it, that the principle of evil is the stronger.

HARDY: No, I should not put it precisely in that way. For instance, people call me a pessimist; and if it is pessimism to think, with Sophocles, that "not to have been born is best," then I do not reject the designation. I never could understand why the word "pessimism" should be such a red rag to many worthy people; and I believe, indeed, that a good deal of the robustious, swaggering optimism of recent literature is at bottom cowardly and insincere. I do not see that we are likely to improve the world by asseverating, however loudly, that black is white, or at least that black is but a necessary contrast and foil, without which white would be white no longer. That is mere juggling with a metaphor. But my pessimism, if pessimism it be, does not involve the assumption that the world is going to the dogs, and that Ahriman is winning all along the line. On the contrary, my practical philosophy is distinctly meliorist. What are my books but one plea against "man's inhumanity to man"—to woman—and to the lower animals? (By the way, my opposition to "sport" is the one point on which I am at all in conflict with my neighbors hereabouts.) Whatever may be the inherent good or evil of life, it is certain that men make it much worse than it need be. When we have got rid of a thousand remediable ills, it will be time enough to determine whether the ill that is irremediable outweighs the good.

ARCHER: And you think that we *are* getting rid of the remediable ills?

HARDY: Slowly but surely—yes.

ARCHER: War, for instance?

HARDY: Oh yes, war is doomed. It is doomed by the gradual growth of the introspective faculty in mankind—of their power of putting themselves in another's place, and taking a point of view that is not their own. In another aspect, this may be called the growth of a sense of humor. Not today, nor tomorrow, but in the fullness of time, war will come to an end, not for moral reasons, but because of its absurdity.

ARCHER: It seems to me that the Press, with its thirst for alarmist news, and its gigantic exaggeration and reverberation of every international jealousy, suspicion, and rancor, is one of the great agents for keeping war alive.

HARDY: I noticed that several people who answered that American editor's query as to the chief danger of the twentieth century named the Press as the influence most to be feared—and I'm not sure that I didn't agree with them.

ARCHER: Yet don't you think that on the intellectual, as opposed to the newsmongering side of journalism, there has been a marked advance during the past fifty years? For instance, don't you approve of the way in which signed criticism is gradually crushing the old anonymous review?

HARDY: I think the rule ought to be that favorable criticisms may be unsigned, but that the critic should be bound to take the responsibility of an unfavorable judgment. There should be no stabbing in the dark. Not that I, personally, have any wish to complain of criticism, signed or unsigned.

ARCHER: It seems to me that reviewing, as a whole, is becoming more conscientious, if not more competent.

HARDY: I remember a case in which a critic seemed to me to carry conscientiousness to an inconvenient pitch. Writing of my *Wessex Poems*, this gentleman said that when he first read the book he thought it rather good, but, being determined not to be taken in, and to be conscientious at all hazards, he made a point of getting up to reread it on a wet morning before breakfast, and then found that it was worth very little. That seemed to me an excessive devotion to critical duty.

ARCHER: On that principle, the best criticisms in the language ought to have been produced by the dwellers in Grub Street of old, who seldom breakfasted at all.

HARDY: Other critics seemed to me to take unnecessary objection to my use of local Wessex words, which they declared to be obsolete. But they are not obsolete here; they are understood and used by educated people.

And if they supply a want in the language—if they express an idea which cannot otherwise be so accurately or so briefly expressed—why may not one attempt to preserve them?

ARCHER: It is a beneficent act; but, like so many other beneficent acts, it is apt to be met with ingratitude.

HARDY: I have no sympathy with the criticism which would treat English as a dead language,—a thing crystallized at an arbitrarily selected stage of its existence, and bidden to forget that it has a past and deny that it has a future. Purism, whether in grammar or vocabulary, almost always means ignorance. Language was made before grammar, not grammar before language. And as for the people who make it their business to insist on the utmost possible impoverishment of our English vocabulary, they seem to me to ignore the lessons of history, science, and common sense.

ARCHER: I have been struck, in reading your books, with the large survival of pure Saxon in the Wessex speech.

HARDY: Where else should you go for pure Saxon? It has often seemed to me a pity, from many points of view—and from the point of view of language among the rest,—that Winchester did not remain, as it once was, the royal, political, and social capital of England, leaving London to be the commercial capital. The relation between them might have been something like that between Paris and Marseilles or Havre; and perhaps, in that case, neither of them would have been so monstrously overgrown as London is today. We should then have had a metropolis free from the fogs of the Thames valley, situated not on clammy clay but on chalk hills, the best soil in the world for habitation; and we might have preserved in our literary language a large proportion of the racy Saxon of the West-country. Don't you think there is something in this?

ARCHER: I am inclined to answer, with Robert Bruce in John Davidson's play:

> A *subtle question, soldier;*
> But *profitless, requiring fate unwound.*

And now I fancy it must be bedtime. That clock of yours seems to have been chiming the quarters at intervals of five minutes for a couple of hours past.

HARDY: Well, it is close upon the witching time when churchyards, in my experience, omit to yawn. Here are our candles.

ARCHER: If I should see the ghost of that Roman lady, I will direct her to your room.

HARDY: Thank you. I shall be pleased to meet her. Good night!

Anatole France-Auguste Rodin

REUNION AT VILLA SAÏD: A BROKEN FRIENDSHIP IS REPAIRED AT THE SHRINE OF AN ANCIENT STATUE OF APHRODITE.

A Greek girl with a body like a flower.

ANATOLE FRANCE was sixty-six years old when Madame de Caillavet, the cultivated French Jewess who had inspired, encouraged, and loved him for thirty years, died on January 12, 1910. The blow almost killed this gifted writer who had fought fearlessly against persecution and injustice. For days he refused to touch any food, and vague talk of suicide began to alarm his doctors. When all other remedies had failed, an unusual offer of help arrived from distant Hungary. This was the proposal of the lovely Mme. Georges Bölöni, a writer herself, to become the inseparable companion of the bereaved novelist. Friends and physicians prevailed upon France to undergo the proposed treatment. So this literary angel of mercy, whose pen-name was Sandor Kemeri, installed herself in the life of the aging writer. Mme. Bölöni's aim was to combine the roles of nurse, secretary, guardian angel . . . and listener. Thus attended to, France promptly began to rally. His interest in life about him soon returned, and the lively talker and wit long silenced by grief was again making pointed pronouncements on life and art.

Indeed, so complete was his recovery in the capable hands of Mme. Bölöni that before long France was even prepared to renew friendly ties with Auguste Rodin, from whom he had been estranged for many years. The two had been close friends at one time, and the same love of art and idolatry of woman had strengthened their friendship. Often the artist in words and the artist in stone had passed several reminiscent hours over bottles of choice wine. Then in the nineties the two had drifted apart over the same cause célèbre that was to break many friendships. In the late nineties the Dreyfus Case had reached a stage bordering on civil war. All literary and artistic France had joined in taking sides. Spurred by Jean Jaurès, Anatole France soon entered the battle to rescue from prison and disgrace a French Jew falsely convicted of treason. Like Emile Zola, France saw that this shameful frame-up against Captain Dreyfus, if uncontested, would merely be the first blow struck by anti-Semitic reaction in its war on French liberalism. By plunging into the fight with an unsparing pen, he knew that, like Zola, he risked imprisonment, and he knew, too, that he would lose many close friends, friends like Lemaître, Coppée, Bourget, and Maurras.

What he did not count on was Rodin's refusal to join the struggle. Angrily the sculptor had refused to sign a petition to free Captain Dreyfus. Earlier, when a committee of writers and artists was formed to raise funds to outbid a private offer for Rodin's statue of Balzac, the sculptor had withheld his consent, giving as his reason that only Dreyfusards were on the committee. It was not that Rodin himself was against Dreyfus; it was his apathy that alienated his more zealous friend. Having become himself a man of action at a moment of crisis, France would not grant Rodin the right to be neutral. Doggedly Rodin refused to become involved. "How can I possibly undertake anything more?" he defended himself. "My fight for sculpture uses up all my time and strength, and even then I lose!" But for Anatole France, in the heat of a quarrel that threatened civil war, this was betrayal of the ideals of justice and patriotism they had both long shared.

Some fifteen years had now passed since the break. The smoke of battle had cleared, and the writers and artists had long returned to the calm of their studies and studios. France was back at his beautiful Villa Saïd outside Paris; and the ministering Mme. Bölöni was wondering whether the time had not come for the two friends to meet again. France responded eagerly to the proposal: "I have no objection to our meeting," he told Mme. Bölöni. "It is too dark now in our lives to find many faults with each other."

Rodin proved equally happy at the prospect of reunion with his old friend. "Yes, I'd like to see him," he said to Mme. Bölöni, and then, as if reminded of the long separation, "I'd like to see what life has done to France's features and what it has written on his face." For the incorrigible sculptor a still more alluring bait dangled before him. Word of the fabulous collection of statues at the Villa Saïd had reached even this celebrated recluse. There was one statue in particular the very mention of which was enough to quicken his pulse. This was the famous little Aphrodite which France had unearthed during his travels in Greece. Merely to gaze upon this precious memento of Greek art would alone have persuaded Rodin that it was time to forget the past and pay his old friend and co-artist a visit. We are indebted to Mme. Bölöni for the record* of the words exchanged by these two masters of French art on their tour of inspection through the museum-like rooms of the Villa Saïd.

(*Before Rodin arrives at the villa, France scurries about the house selecting his choicest specimens of Italian porcelain and majolica for the table. For the water glasses he chooses rare Bohemian crystal; for the white wine thin goblets; for the red wine Italian glasses, and French ones for the champagne.*)

FRANCE (*touching one of the French glasses with a quill*): These glasses which give such a clear sound have survived many kings. I wonder whether Marie Antoinette took one of these to her lips? Perhaps that one from which Rodin will drink his champagne. It's the best I have.

MME. BÖLÖNI: Rodin likes simplicity. Why this luxurious repast?

FRANCE: Who knows how often we can eat together? I'd like to give him the best as a compensation for not having offered him anything for so long.

(*Strews violets on the tablecloth. Rodin is announced. France and Mme. Bölöni hasten to meet him.*)

RODIN (*gaily, as he comes up the stairs*): The air is as invigorating here as if you were living in a forest. (*Scanning the long salon; then blurting.*) There is no statue here!

FRANCE (*smiling*): Not one.

RODIN: Where do you hide your Aphrodite, which, I was told, is so beautiful? I hope you will show it to me.

FRANCE: It's in my studio. After you've rested you can see it. You come from your studio, where you've seen plenty of marble. First we can take a glance at my pictures and the Gobelins.

RODIN (*vehemently*): I'm not tired. Let's see that Greek goddess first!

FRANCE (*laughing heartily*): I'll show it to you, although I must confess I don't like to show it to sculptors.

(*All ascend the stairs, Rodin without even glancing at the pictures on the walls.*)

FRANCE: He's like a bridegroom hurrying to his bride.

(*Lifts the heavy curtain of the studio, and his pale small hands for a moment look like marble.*)

---

* Rendered here in dialogue form from the conversation reported by Sandor Kemeri (Mme. Georges Bölöni) in *Rambles with Anatole France*, translated from the Hungarian by Emil Lengyel, J. B. Lippincott Company, Philadelphia and London, 1926.

RODIN: What an interesting hand you have!

(*Mme. Bölöni closes the door of the studio. Rodin takes two hurried steps and comes to a sudden stop on the blood-colored Afghan carpet. The statue of Aphrodite is in a niche of the window. The lines of her delicate body are sharply drawn against the background of the dark blue curtain. All three stand speechless for some moments.*)

RODIN (*mumbling*): The artist must have been either Phidias or one of his great contemporaries. (*Wipes the perspiration on his forehead.*) This statue makes me dizzy. It's more beautiful than the Venus de Milo.

FRANCE (*grasping Rodin's hand*): This is how we render homage to the goddess of Youth and Beauty. I'm of your opinion that this statue is the work either of Phidias or one of his most talented pupils. In order to ascertain its origin I went to Athens. I'm glad I did, because the Minerva of the Parthenon confirmed my supposition. My Aphrodite is like the twin sister of the great Minerva.

RODIN (*musing*): The goddess is hewn in Pentelikon marble, rose-colored with a golden tint. It's as vivid as if it were real flesh. Phidias used only Pentelikon marble.

(*Looks at the statue from all sides, passing his thumb over its round body. Scarcely touching the marble, he feels instinctively its elevations and depressions.*)

FRANCE: A Greek girl with a body like a flower must have inspired the artist to create this Aphrodite.

RODIN (*warmly*): This fragile body is built like a cathedral. The proportions are perfect; every line is well balanced. I'm inclined to call it the product of geometric poetry, a hymn in mathematics. An artist always learns without being conscious of it. He learns from his material, his observations and his own thoughts. A sculptor has to learn very much. Phidias must have been a great scientist.

FRANCE (*bidding the others to be seated*): Phidias had a perfect knowledge of anatomy, geometry, and architecture. He was familiar with all the qualities of his material and with the influence of light and shadow on the marble. As a scientist he knew how to check his ardor when it was more prudent to refrain from exaggeration. He was willing to make sacrifices if the harmony of his work so desired. When carving his giants he was always thinking of the whole. Michelangelo himself learned from him.

RODIN: There is no real art without a long line of ancestry. I don't hesitate to admit that I've learned much from the ancients and Michelangelo. I had learned very much before I dared model my Balzac. My teachers were, besides the great sculptors, the architects of great cathedrals. Consciously and unconsciously I'm learning even now. Aphrodite's stone-carved beauty, as fresh as it was thousands of years ago, is one of my lessons. Everything about it is as simple as truth.

FRANCE: What we call truth would bear much discussion. (*Steps up to his Tanagra box.*) Let's look at these now.

(*Takes a statuette, scarcely larger than his thumb, and gives it to Rodin, who places it on his palm.*)

RODIN: This is the ancestor of impressionism. This burnt clay is almost hot, not from the flames of the oven, but from the fast work of the modelling fingers perpetuating in clay the graceful movements of a dancer. Every sculptor of exuberant temperament likes the clay which makes his finger tips hot. These seemingly calm Tanagras are full of fervor and warmth.

(*Rodin's thumb passes over the bodies of most of the tiny clay figures. The bell rings.*)

Is someone else coming? (*His voice shows disappointment.*) I should have liked to look at all your things: the gladiator, the head of the Medusa, the little Minerva, and the heads of the Greek and Roman savants on the mantelpiece. All your statues are exposed to light in the most advantageous position. A moment ago I should have liked to take down from the mantelpiece that Greek torso but I didn't dare touch it. She was so beautiful as the sun's rays fell on her chest and legs. Women's chests on Greek statues are like pears, while on Roman pieces they're more like apples. The Greek head was oval, the Roman round.

(*Enter housekeeper.*)

HOUSEKEEPER: Monsieur Pierre sent back the books.

RODIN (*rejoicing*): It's very fortunate no one came. (*Stands on tiptoes, and with his short arms takes down the head of a haughty Roman.*) The construction of the skull is similar to that of my Balzac.

FRANCE: There was once in Rome a sculptor who saw the head of a Roman in the same way as Rodin saw the head of a French writer.

(*Both Rodin and France laugh. Rodin puts the Roman head back and takes down a Greek head furrowed by innumerable wrinkles.*)

RODIN (*exclaiming*): In spite of their immobility, the wrinkles are full of movement. When modelling this head the artist must have been thinking of the breeze curling up the water. From nature the Greek sculptors took ornamental motives. In that respect we haven't reached their level even today. The wrinkled skin of the Greek is merely the surface which hides unfathomable depths. Wisdom and age change the skull. The upper part of old men's foreheads broadens out. Thinkers have a Moses forehead, exceedingly well-developed and strong.

FRANCE (*exclaiming*): Look at the deep furrow of this Zeno. It stretches from his nose to the corner of his mouth. His tired eyes are sunk into their hollow. He defies life by defying death.

RODIN: I see first the form and then the expression. The writer first looks for the expression and then finds the form. You say that this piece represents Zeno. Who was he? ...

(*He takes the gladiator from the bookshelf and puts it on the desk. France and Mme. Bölöni watch him with amazement. A ray of light falls on Rodin's powerful chest and the back of the statue.*)

FRANCE: Your strength is enviable.

RODIN: I've become strong wrestling with my blocks of marble. What a powerful back and what splendid muscles this gladiator has! He could hold the globe high, like Atlas, and could fight until he dropped dead with exhaustion. His body is full of explosive forms. Yet, how dignified are his forms, how harmonious the whole. It reflects the balanced unity of the world.

(*The sound of mowing reaches them from the garden.*)

RODIN (*opening the window and leaning out*): It's a young man who cuts the grass. I like to see mowing. There is rhythm in it and much force.

FRANCE: Let's go downstairs. I want to show you something before the other two guests arrive.

RODIN: We can look at the pictures when they are here.

FRANCE: It isn't pictures I want to show you.

RODIN: What is it then? Art is like love; one mustn't have too much of it. I cannot, in half a day, look at all the things that you've collected in many, many years.

FRANCE: You'll have to come to see me very often.

MME. BÖLÖNI (*seeing signs of fatigue on their faces*): Let's look at the ceramics.

FRANCE (*nodding*): We can do that. The only trouble is that Josephine, who doesn't understand and, hence, doesn't respect art, exposed them to the whims of the chickens and the cocks. And they respect my beautiful Hindu and Persian ceramics even less.

RODIN (*laughing loudly*): That doesn't matter. You know that I keep a couple of doves to help develop patina on my bronzes.

(*All three walk to the terrace. On their way they meet the housekeeper.*)

HOUSEKEEPER (*mumbling morosely*): I thought you would come down. Hurry up, Marie, clean up the terrace!

RODIN (*to the maid, with feigned indignation*): Stop! Don't touch the sacred treasures of kings with your lovely broom. That one which you've already touched must have belonged to the great Darius himself.

MARIE (*laughing*): There's no trace left of that king. This thing now belongs to us. A dead king doesn't count, anyway. (*Leaves the terrace.*)

FRANCE: This village girl is quoting Shakespeare, although it isn't likely she ever read him. Primitive souls have their own wisdom and they teach us many things.

RODIN (*looking around among the bright-hued ceramics*): This is an old Persian piece, such as I saw the other day in a German book. The colors are exuberant, Oriental.

FRANCE: One can easily understand how delighted the sleepy Persians were to look at this symphony of blue and green, which reminded them of the ever-changing sea. It dates, as you say, from the time of Darius I, who is also known as Daryavus, the son of Hystaspes, the conqueror of India. I got this piece at Marathon, from the relatives of our friend Jean Moreas, who are, as you know, Greeks of noble blood. When they gave it to me they told me a tale. The three Dariuses, when their death was near, wanted to take leave of life in a room ornamented with these ceramics of surpassing beauty. It had some magic force, they thought, which facilitated their entering the kingdom of shadows with less pain. Loyal Persians have preserved this piece on which the dying glances of three kings had fallen. Legends have the faculty of embellishing beautiful things and I never investigate what's the truth in a legend. It's so difficult to distinguish truth from the creations of imagination.

RODIN: I rely upon intuition to find out the truth. (*Joins the others in examining the Indian ceramics.*) Indian art was nearest to the old Egyptian.

FRANCE: Let's not forget that they had gone back to the same source. The old Persian was the ancestor of both Egyptian and Indian art. We can go now to the Greeks. I'd like to show you my *stèle funéraire*, the tomb of a Greek poet.

(*Pulls down a window curtain and opens the door facing the garden, exposing to the best light the bas-relief of the antique Greek tomb which had been found on the highway leading to Athens. The* stèle funéraire *represents a Muse standing at the grave of the poet.*)

RODIN (*exploding, unable to control his nerves*): Where is it?

FRANCE (*pointing*): It's here. I've hidden it in the shadow of the stairs. My idea was that I should have to pass it on every occasion when I was entering or leaving the house. On the Athens road, too, it was so situated that every traveller bound for the capital of Attica had to see it. It reminded them that every road led to the same end.

RODIN (*rushes to the* stèle, *draws back, then approaches it again; his face is purple-red and his eyes are rolling; he is breathing heavily*): This tomb is glorious! (*Excitedly.*) It makes me intoxicated! This is more beautiful than any of the antique tombs of the Museum of Naples. The Muse breathes. She has just stepped on the fresh grave. I fear she may hurt herself falling on the ground. It's majestic, overawing!

FRANCE: One seldom finds an artistic creation in our cemeteries. Most of them are vulgar slabs, which commemorate the lack of esthetical feeling in the contemporary man. I shudder at the thought that they will place a monstrosity over my dust. I do not want them to mark my grave. There isn't much art in the memorial stones of our Pantheon, either. What little art there is lacks congenial surroundings among the mementoes of conventionalized sham beauty.

RODIN (*grumbling*): They put one marble slab on top of the other. That's what I call the match-box system. Their chief concern is to crowd as many dead under the dome of the Pantheon as possible. We cannot even die esthetically.

FRANCE: We who so love art should have a mark like this over our dead body.

(*Marie enters.*)

MARIE: Dinner is served.

RODIN (*his face lighting up*): Since dinner is served, let's enjoy it thoroughly!

Shaw-Chesterton

TWO MASTERS OF WIT AND PARADOX BREAK A LANCE OVER THE ABSORPTION OF ALCOHOL.

*There is only one form of drunkenness I
acknowledge—the drunkenness of sobriety.*

A T FIRST blush it would seem superfluous to present George Bernard
Shaw in person within the framework of a dialogue. We have his own
word for it that the "character of G.B.S." may be found with very little
effort in every one of his innumerable plays. Besides, his public life has
been one ceaseless dialogue with a blundering, imperfect world. One
would, perhaps, more truthfully call it a monologue, except that Shaw,
no Jove launching thunderbolts without fear of reply, from the beginning
challenged the world he flouted to a frank debate of the issues. As an early
lecturer and pamphleteer for socialism and free-thought, Shaw gave blows
and received them. As a young Fabian idealist he learned to give hecklers
a taste of their own effrontery. Always, he believed in the fair play of
argumentative give and take. Unperturbed by the excoriations of press
and pulpit, Shaw always invited his adversaries to a gentlemanly bout in
the arena of platform polemics. There he invariably observed the rules of
the game, perhaps taking unfair advantage in only one respect—in the
possession of an inexhaustible irony and a devastating flair for the cutting
phrase and epithet. But Shaw has never been the slave of his vast sense
of humor. Always it has been at the service of a great conviction. Behind
the buffoon has towered the thinker and humanitarian. As the world's
jester, he has made three generations laugh with his huge pleasantries, but
the joke has been on the world, for Shaw has lived to see the England
whose sacred institutions he had so sternly lampooned drift more and
more to his way of thinking. The insolence of Empire which he had so
witheringly unmasked was fast becoming a thing of the past. Many of his
Fabian prophecies were materializing in the work of a Labor regime, and
the social rigidities and cleavages he had battled to abolish now promised
to go in the foreseeable future. The rebel prophet was by way of being
honored in his own land.

In this one-man crusade Shaw has remained the brilliant polemicist, awed by none of the sanctities—whether of religion, politics, or diet. And for this exigent role of combined jester and Jeremiah nature and training gave him a ready pen and a readier tongue. He has been the talker extraordinary of our time. Even his most rabid foes have relished the biting waggishness and adroit ingenuity of phrase. After a few hours of his company men have carried away a life-long impression of prodigious mental alertness. For this has been a mind forever awake, steadily pitched at a white-heat focus and reflection. It sparkled through the slightest comment, the most commonplace salutation of the day; it romped nimbly through the scantest communications to publisher or producer or creditor. In company Shaw has relished talk as other men relish the meat and beverages he has never shared. He has made up for his various abstensions by an unhampered indulgence of the spoken and written word. He belongs in the company of the great swordsmen of words. Ever the talker, Shaw has made a debating platform of his plays and a soap-box of his prefaces.

It is this great master of mental sword-play whom we meet in the dialogue which follows. First printed in The Adelphi of London in September 1923, it is one of those rare strokes of good fortune in conversational history—the chance encounter of two magnificent disputants in the presence of a Boswell-like spectator endowed with a fine sense of the dramatic potentialities of the occasion and a pencil and pad to do it verbatim justice. The intensity and gravity of the discourse are often lost in the coruscating play of wit and paradox. This is superb badinage, the more exciting for its spontaneity. Yet badinage would seem a flippant word for the life-and-death issues lurking behind the crisp dexterities of the word battle. The pace here is fast and feverish. Again we have the ideal circumstance of conversation recorded on the spot. Moreover, the amanuensis of the moment in time became an authorized biographer of Shaw. We have thus a combination of the Boswellian adoration and the Boswellian thoroughness. The chronicler has set the scene so well that the mechanics of the staging are best left to his own deft pen. The show is his and the actors' in it.

The brilliant quarrel between George Bernard Shaw and Gilbert Keith Chesterton was, of course, nothing new in their lives. We have Chesterton's own statement that he began arguing with this Irish firebrand "almost as early as I began doing anything." Continually they found themselves on opposing sides of every major conflict in British politics. Religion, of course, brought them into constant friction, especially after Chesterton became a fighting convert to Catholicism. In his posthumously printed autobiography (Sheed & Ward, 1936) Chesterton speaks of having argued with Shaw "on almost every subject in the world . . . without affectation or animosity." Master of paradox to the end, he concludes: "I might say that he is seen at his best when he is wrong, or, rather, everything is wrong about him but himself." This was at least an accolade of warm friendship. Chesterton prided himself on taking the eminently sane side of every issue in which he found himself at loggerheads with his friendly foe. "I have defended the institution of the family against his Platonist fancies about the state," he declared. "I have defended the institutions of beef and beer against his hygienic severity of vegetarianism and total abstinence. I have defended the old liberal notion of nationalism against the new Socialist notion of internationalism." Yet, this inveterate challenger of the Shavian way of life could end with a handsome salute, again paradoxical, to a fellow duellist: "It is necessary to disagree with him as much as I do in order to admire him as much as I do. And I am proud of him as a foe even more than as a friend."

In his estimate of this embattled champion of dogma and tradition Shaw was equally generous. The two had fought out their philosophical battles on many platforms. Shaw might grow impatient with his friend's doctrinaire appeals to churchly authority and his excessive fondness for squeezing out the life of a fact between the two jaws of a paradox. Yet he even greeted Chesterton's book about himself with good grace, making the characteristic reservation that "of course it had little to do with me." Shaw's ultimate appraisal of his intellectual enemy of twenty years is worth quoting: "He might be trusted anywhere without a policeman. He might knock at a door and run away—perhaps even lie down across the threshold to trip up the emergent householder; but his crimes would be hyperbolic crimes of imagination and humor, not of malice. He is friendly, easy-going, unaffected, gentle, magnanimous, and genuinely democratic." So perhaps we should not be too alarmed as we follow the brisk exchange of brickbats in the skirmish reported by Mr. Hesketh Pearson, who will now take over. . . .

("I had for years longed to be present at a word-war between intellectual giants. And at last, most unexpectedly, my desire was gratified. It was at the house of a friend in Chelsea. Mr. Bernard Shaw had been there for at least an hour and was just on the point of leaving when Mr. G. K. Chesterton was announced. They instantly started a debate, as naturally as a cat and dog start a fight, and the rest of us grouped ourselves round them, as naturally as street-loiterers surround the cat *and dog. Consider my position. It was both fortunate and difficult. To begin with, my wildest dream had been realized. Here were, beyond comparison, the two greatest word-jugglers of the century. One of them was a greater man than Socrates—yet I knew he had no Plato. The other was a greater wit than Johnson—yet I knew he had no Boswell. Could I, then, enjoy myself to the full and take no thought for the morrow? Did I not rather owe a duty to posterity, and was I not bound to preserve, at any rate, ten minutes of that feast of reason and that flow of soul which, but for me, would be lost to the world forever? I only had about half a minute to make a decision. Well, I was not conscious of making a decision at all. I simply know that my hand went to my pocket book—posterity no doubt guiding it there in spite of myself—and before Mr. Shaw had got the first sentence off his tongue my pencil was busy. Here, therefore, is that remarkable discourse, given just as it came, in the raw, hot from the brains of the mighty disputants."—* Hesketh Pearson)

SHAW: Have you any adequate excuse to make us for not being drunk?

CHESTERTON: I am desperately drunk. There is only one form of drunkenness I acknowledge—the drunkenness of sobriety. As a consequence of not having tasted a drop of wine or ale today, I am suffering from *delirium tremens.*

SHAW: In that case perhaps you will please tell us why you are sober.

CHESTERTON: That, I fear, is quite impossible. I can explain nothing when I am sober. Sobriety clouds the mind; drink clears it. I would explain anything, at any length, under the calming, clarifying influence of drink. If only you would take my advice, your own style, to say nothing of your mind, would improve beyond imagination. At present your writing is too parenthetical; you wander, lost in a maze of speculation, in a pool of prudery. Compare with your straggling sentences my crisp phrases. I dip my nib in the pot of Bacchus.

SHAW: I don't believe it for a moment. Your pretended love of wine is a snare and a delusion. It is skillfully paraded and exploited by yourself in order to catch all the brainless bairns who look to romance to lead them back into the Garden of Eden. Of course you are superlatively clever; no one denies that. And the cleverest thing you ever did in your life was to hang out the signboard of medievalism. You suddenly realized with a shock that there was no room for a second Shaw among the modern intellectuals. Were you daunted? Not you! You instantly proclaimed to the whole world that you had examined Socialism and found it wanting. Actually you had examined nothing except the state of the book-market, a very cursory glance at which revealed to you that the camp of reaction lacked a brain to give its ideals—or want of them—expression. At the same time you had to admit, even to yourself, that you were a democrat at heart, and your great difficulty was to reconcile your modernism with the exigency of the situation. So what did you do? You talked about Guilds, about Peasant Proprietorship, for all the world as if Henry V were occupying the throne of Edward VII, and by carefully evading every knotty point in the Socialist case and riding roughshod over the unanswerable, annihilating logic of the Fabians which cropped up at every turn, you managed to rally all the wild, romantic idiots in the country round your banner. Then, in order to increase your following and grapple the converts to you with hoops of steel, you professed yourself a High Churchman and a deep drinker. Your slogan became: Back to the land, back to the priest, back to the bottle. Up to a certain point I am willing to believe that all this paradox-prancing, all this intellectual hunt-the-slipper and anachronistic nursery-nonsense, appealed to you. Whether you ever seriously believed in it, whether you have ever seriously believed in anything, I am quite incapable of deciding, since you don't really know what you believe or disbelieve yourself. But there dawned a day—a terrible day for you—when Hilaire Belloc came into your life. Then indeed you were lost forever. He made you dignify your monstrosities with the name of Faith. For you, at any rate, he turned your pranks into prayers, your somersaults into sacraments, your oddities into oblations. By degrees, under his influence, your fun turned to fury. Because the Roman Church says that the indiscriminate breeding of babies is the first duty of civilized man—meaning, of course, babies born for the Church of Rome—you turned and rent the Eugenists, whose sole crime is that they prefer healthy babies to diseased ones. You even suggested that Sir Francis Galton, a charming old gentleman of unblemished moral character, must have been a prurient blackguard whose loathsome lewdness was fitly camouflaged by the imposition of this obscene science upon the world. With viperish violence, and under the same influence, you then fell upon the Jews. Forgetting, with characteristic absence of mind, that Jesus Christ was distinctly Hebraic, you implied that all the dark and dirty dealings in the world were directly traceable to the malign activities of that race. You whipped yourself into a frenzy on the subject; you even paid one thousand pounds for the pleasure of saying in print that a certain Jewish gentleman—who naturally sued you for libel—was a scoundrel . . . And yet we all know perfectly well that you aren't half as bad as you paint yourself. I asked you just now why you weren't drunk. The reason I did this was because in all your writings you glorify inebriation to such an extent that anyone who doesn't know you must assume that you spend the whole of your time in staggering from pub to pub and scribbling your books and articles against the various lamp-posts en route. I, of course, know it's all bunkum. I know that everything you say is bunkum, though a fair amount of it is inspired bunkum. I realize that the only reason you ever go near a pub is to placate your own admirers, who may have come from Kamchatka in order to see you and who would be scandalized almost to the verge of suicide if you didn't stand up and soak your quart like a man.

CHESTERTON: All of which merely goes to prove that you prefer potatoes to potations. Your natural love of truth has been undermined by an acquired love of turnips. The real battle of your life has not been Socialism *versus* Capitalism, but Vegetables *versus* Veracity. Your case is extraordinarily interesting, and I think I can state it in about half the time you took to manufacture a purely fictitious case against me. Elsewhere I have made it perfectly clear that you are a spiritual descendant of Bunyan, that you are, in fact, an out-and-out Puritan.

SHAW: As I have spent the greater part of my life in telling the world that Bunyan is better than Shakespeare, it did not require a superman to point out that I have more in common with Oliver Cromwell than Charles the First. But to call me a Puritan in the old-fashioned sense of the word is sheer folly. All this nonsense about my spiritual ancestry, though an excellent family joke, is frightfully misleading. You must really switch on to something else. It is my firm opinion that nearly all the Puritans in history who were not born fools were unmitigated scoundrels. I must therefore ask you to be good enough in future to qualify the epithet. You can do this in the following manner: "When I call Mr. Shaw a Puritan, I merely mean to imply (1) that he doesn't spend his nights under a table, a victim to mixed drinks, (2) that he doesn't write his books under the influence of opium, cocaine, or morphia, and (3) that he doesn't keep a harem."

CHESTERTON: Your objections to being called a Puritan are puritanical and beside the point. I have written a book proving up to the hilt that your Puritanism is fundamental. You have been unable to answer it.

SHAW: I have spent my life answering it both before and since the appearance of your book—which, by the way, might just as well have been entitled: *Gilbert Keith Chesterton by Himself.*

CHESTERTON: I don't doubt your *belief* that you are not a Puritan. I simply state it as an indisputable fact that you *are* one. For the sake of argument I will grant that you may not be a Puritan with a capital "P," but you are certainly a puritan with a small "p." That, however, is a meta-

physical quibble. The real case against you is not that you prefer Bunyan to Shakespeare or John Knox to Mary Stuart or Shelley to Byron or
Ibsen to Pinero—but that you are constitutionally incapable of understanding the Catholic standpoint, which is, I need scarcely say, my own
standpoint.

SHAW: How in thunder can I understand a point of view that doesn't exist?
Your standpoint is that there is no standpoint. Has anyone on this
planet yet discovered what opinions you really hold? Has anyone even
discovered whether you hold opinions? There is not a single principle
in the universe that you have ever seriously attacked or seriously defended. No one knows anything about you. You have never told a soul
what you believe, why you believe it, or whether you believe that there
is a Belief. Your whole life has been spent in obfuscating issues. You
fight the good fight with all your might—not in order to win, because
that would mean the end of your fight, but for the mere pleasure of
fighting. You pitch on some opponent, whom in your heart of hearts
you secretly admire for the ruthlessness and sincerity with which he
holds his convictions, and then you proceed to graft the most preposterous opinions and inconceivable legends on him for the sole purpose of launching a terrific crusade against him. You are just like Don
Quixote; and though your lunacy on some occasions makes his seem
pale by comparison, you yet contrive in some mysterious manner to be
your own Sancho Panza.

CHESTERTON: Exactly; and anybody but you could see that the combination of these two extremes forms the Catholic standpoint. You might
almost have been quoting me when you said that the Catholic standpoint is that there is no standpoint. The only man who can conscientiously take up a definite standpoint in religious matters is the atheist.
The atheist states as a positive fact that there is no God. Thereafter he
is able, by a perfectly logical process, to prove this and to prove that to
his own complete satisfaction. The Catholic is not so pragmatical as
the atheist or the Puritan. His Faith is built on Belief, not on Knowledge—falsely so-called. He is consequently able to appreciate and sympathize with every form of human activity. He takes the whole world
to his heart. He loves because it is human to love, hates because it is
human to hate, eats, drinks, and is merry because it is human to eat,
drink, and be merry. He leads a crusade not because it is right but because it is glorious to do so. He is neither positive nor constructive. He
is not even consistent. Every book I write, every article I pen, every argument I use, contradicts some other book, some other article, some
other argument of my own. What does it matter? Life is contradictious,

and we are Life. We accept Life as a gift from God; we do not accept God as a gift from Life. You Puritans—

SHAW: I have already told you that I am not a Puritan!

CHESTERTON: You Puritans, I say, fashion God in your own image. You conceive the truth to lie in yourselves. You would not be content merely to remold the world nearer to the heart's desire; you would recast it entirely to the highbrow's dream. The magnificence of uncertainty, the splendor of ignorance, the sublime impossibility of Nature, the marvel and mystery of this miraculous and ridiculous thing called Life—all this is lost on you. It is lost on you because yours is a world of rush, not rolic, where the station hotel has usurped the wayside tavern, where the draught of beer has given place to the sip of bovril, and where Shakespeare and Homer have been run to earth by Sherlock Holmes. . . . We Catholics do not pretend to a knowledge we have not got. We see a thing that we believe to be harmful and we fight it. We see a thing that we believe to be good and we love it. We would not take it upon ourselves to say that this is altogether wrong, or that altogether right, because we think that the wrong may be created by God for a purpose, which it would be presumptuous in us to divine. When you Puritans can explain, conclusively and convincingly, how the daisies grow, we will be willing to believe that you can teach us something. Until then you can hardly expect us to accept your verdict that beer was not made for man but for watering cauliflowers, that Jews were not made for Jerusalem but for the financial control of Christendom, that babies were not born for the home but for the laboratory, and that man was not made to enjoy himself but to read Fabian tracts and listen to University Extension lectures.

SHAW: I think I catch your drift. If a manure-heap close to your front door were fouling the neighborhood, you wouldn't remove it because God might have placed it there in order to test your sense of smell.

CHESTERTON: I couldn't overlook the possibility that my next-door neighbor might be a Socialist; in which case the manure-heap would have its uses.

SHAW: You are evading the point.

CHESTERTON: Points are made to evade. Consider the history of the rapier.

SHAW: There is no getting at you. You are as bad as Dr. Johnson. When your pistol misses fire, which it usually does, you knock your opponent down with the butt end. Why will you never come to grips?

CHESTERTON: The art of argument lies in the ingenuity with which one can hide and seek simultaneously.

SHAW: But what becomes of your philosophy?

CHESTERTON: My philosophy is in the thrust, not the parry.

SHAW: I don't see that. You must be able to hold your own field while you are advancing on the enemy's territory.

CHESTERTON: Not necessarily. If my attack is strenuous enough, the enemy will require all his strength to hold his own fortifications.

SHAW: And if he succeeds in holding them?

CHESTERTON: Then I retire, bring up my reserves, and attack him again in a totally unexpected place.

SHAW: But if he attacks you while you are retiring?

CHESTERTON: I go to ground.

SHAW: I see. Heads you win, tails he loses, all the way.

CHESTERTON: Precisely.

SHAW: Thank you. I am wasting my time. Good evening.

(*Rapid exit of Shaw.*)

Thomas Masaryk

1.

HOW AN AMIABLE ACADEMIC RECLUSE BECAME A
REVOLUTIONARY AND FOUNDED A COUNTRY.

It was no use; I had to bring about the
necessary reform by revolutionary means.

A LARGE part of the heroic history of Czechoslovakia coincides with the
story of Thomas Garrigue Masaryk, who died in 1937. Founder and
first president of the little land that was born in the throes of the First
World War, Masaryk is permanently enshrined in every Czech heart.
In the four bloody years of 1914–18 this man planned and plotted ceaselessly for the liberation of his homeland from Hapsburg rule. His fiery
eloquence won friends the world over. Thousands of émigré Czechs
rallied to his call to arms. From Switzerland, France, Italy, England,
Russia, and the United States this tireless patriot launched his tirades
against the corrupt and outmoded Austrian dynasty that had kept his
land in chains. In Russia the revolutionary authorities permitted him to
round up escaped Slav subjects of the enemy countries into an army of
92,000 that soon began an epic march to Vladivostok, many ultimately
to join the Allies on the Western Front. Later Masaryk came to America,
and before long the Allies recognized the Czech government-in-exile as
the de facto government of the future state of Czechoslovakia. With the
collapse of the Central powers, Masaryk was elected first president of the
new republic by acclamation. That post he held through repeated re-
election till December 14, 1935, when he resigned, to be succeeded by
Eduard Beneš, a close and loyal associate during the war period of preparation.

In all his laborious projects for the seizure of power one seems to
discern the hand of the professional revolutionary. Nothing, of course,
could be further from the truth. For this patriot who showed so sure a
hand at the game of conspiracy had been the most peaceable of political
reformers till 1914 transformed him into a rebel and an activist. For
years he had been a tutor and sociologist, and had lectured on the abstract

verities of philosophy. In the pre-War parliament he had risked reprisal
by lashing out against Hapsburg diplomacy and unmasking its intrigues,
yet he had stoutly resisted appeals to revolutionary action. Once he had
even written that "revolution is gross political primitivism." And within
academic walls he had consistently preached persuasion rather than force
as the civilized approach to social change. Overnight this bespectacled
pedagogue and parliamentarian, now in his sixty-fourth year, became a
rebel and conspirator. Assured that there was little for Czechoslovakia to
gain from an Austrian victory, he fled Vienna and opened the stealthy,
underground battle for his country's freedom. The confirmed pacifist
had turned man of action in the most dangerous game of all.

This unique transformation of philosopher into revolutionary was certainly dramatic, so dramatic, indeed, that in 1933 Emil Ludwig, ever in
pursuit of a good story, resolved to go to Prague to interview Masaryk
about it. A series of meetings were arranged at the Château of Lany, on the
outskirts of the capital. There the biographer of great men of action questioned the eighty-three-year-old statesman-philosopher over a period of
several days. The conversation was conducted in German. When the
written text was submitted for approval, Masaryk made some slight revi-
sions and expanded a few theoretical remarks. "As is usual with me,"
Ludwig explains in a prefatory note, "I was not interested so much in
describing the attitude of the statesman toward the various questions
which he has to solve in his everyday work, but rather in giving a sketch
of his character." This, Ludwig was convinced, could best be done by
direct oral expression. One understands, however much one may regret,
Ludwig's decision to confine his role almost entirely to that of inquiring
reporter. Inevitably, perhaps, the conversation is weighted one way. After
all, it was Masaryk's story; besides which, Ludwig found himself in such
agreement with this "defender of democracy" that he was able "to retire
into the background" during the course of their conversations. Remarkable humility for the biographer of Napoleon, Bismarck, and Goethe!
Ludwig's book about Masaryk was first issued in German and brought
out in America in 1936 by Robert M. McBride & Co. The following is
extracted from that translation:

("I knew that shortly before the War Masaryk had written a book
on Russia wherein he formulated some conditions under which revolution would be permissible and morally justified as 'defense against oppression.' But has there ever been a revolt that did not display just that

motive on its banner? 'It must be proved to be in the true interests of the people.' And ultimately what is it that determines the moral right of a revolution except success? And when it comes off successfully, it is forgiven, said Wallenstein. With these thoughts in my mind I began our conversation. . . . "—Ludwig)

LUDWIG: You have sketched the revolutionary as part gambler and part play actor, superstitious, absolutist and tyrant. Yet that certainly does not apply to yourself, who may be considered as the founder of the Czech Revolution and certainly the leader who carried it through. And shortly before the War we saw you take the part of a mediator. As late as 1912 you preferred to work for peace among the various peoples of the Austrian Empire rather than to support an uncertain struggle for the liberation of the Czechs. And even in May, 1913, you stated in the Imperial Parliament at Vienna that as a pacifist you would not allow yourself to be entrammeled in visions of the dismemberment of Austria. Would you like to tell me when the decisive change in your ideas and career took place?

MASARYK (*nodding*): I have written against revolution and I have even called the revolutionary a *Spiessbürger.** In the Czech language that is a very strong term. I have been constantly occupying myself with the problem, from the ethical and practical standpoints. There are unnecessary and foolhardy revolutions: less foolhardy, well organized, prepared and unprepared, chance successes and chance failures. I spoke against revolution because with us the radicals were children politically. I am not a radical—it is difficult to say, but certainly I am not a radical. As a rule, in politics men take up a position either to the left or to the right. Then the wiseacre comes along and combs his beard with his hand and says: "Children, neither to the right nor to the left: the golden middle way." This man with the beard has no outlook of his own. The right and the left have their definite opinions; the tactical goldseeker slips in or creeps in between them. He needs the radical oppositions so that he can skip to and fro. A man of conviction, provided he has the gift of political insight, acts in conformity with the program that he has constructed independently from the historical situation which he finds before him. We had the Taborites and the Brothers, both radicals, of the left and the right, but the Hussite Archbishop of Prague said: "We must take the golden middle way!"

LUDWIG: Then is the ideal revolutionary a man with a careful reasoning mind or one who is guided more by passion?

---

* Petty bourgeois.

MASARYK: A careful thinker, a calculator, a mathematician. Democracy means self-rule. Autonomy begins with the self. How can I govern others if I do not govern myself? Revolution is the supreme right of self-determination, whereby I take the initiative into my own hands. One must speak to the public at meetings and in parliament, through the newspapers and books; for it is necessary to have explored all peaceful and constitutional ways of bringing about the necessary reform. At last the moment comes when I say to myself: "It is no use, I must bring about the necessary reform by revolutionary means." To a certain extent I may be to blame, in that I did not have sufficient patience. Revolution is not a *Putsch*. The English make a distinction between rebellion and revolution, and the anarchical deed of the individual is quite another thing too. The attempt on the life of a ruler is frequently murder, not mere manslaughter. We ourselves had a case of it in the nineties. At that time I came out in public against the culprits. After they had been sentenced I sent books to the prison for these young fellows, so that they might learn. I studied the problem of revolution in Russian literature. I leave it to the psychologists to say why I have busied myself so much with the problem of revolution. Revolution as a political adventure? No. Serious revolution? Yes, when necessary.

LUDWIG: When do you think that revolution is a moral act?

MASARYK: When it is the only means left for the defense of liberty and justice. Before it is adopted all efforts to achieve that end in a peaceful way must have been made. Schiller says that very well in *William Tell*. Following this line of thought and making all efforts accordingly, I must decide what is necessary to be accomplished. For example, must the king come to terms or must he abdicate, and his whole band with him? They will not agree and they shoot. Then we shoot also. Revolution is not morally justified by success alone but, as in the case of every other deed, it will be judged according to the motives; and not merely as a whole, for each single act is subject to the same moral verdict. In a revolution single acts may be entirely reprehensible. They must be branded as crimes, as the murderous act of the anarchist. Every revolution unchains anarchical elements.

LUDWIG: Do you include the Hussite revolution also in what you have said?

MASARYK: Each revolution is *sui generis*. Austria had broken up internally. In October, 1918, the German and Hungarian regiments were first withdrawn from the Italian front, and after them the Czech regiments. Reformation had an intellectual and moral and religious foundation. We were all Hussites, said Luther. Engels said that Luther and Cromwell had prepared the way for the French Revolution. First came the great ecclesiastical revolution, for that period the Church was the principal power ruling over human society. Once ecclesiastical authority had been overthrown, the struggles against political authority followed of necessity. I myself have always championed natural right, side by side with historical right, which is cherished so much among us—always with the thought: The time may come when you will have to follow natural right, and that means revolution, and without regard for historical antecedents, if that should be necessary.

LUDWIG: And yet you write that at the beginning you feared to make the decision, whether you should demonstrate your renouncement of Austria by a physical act. "I wished that this cup would pass from me," you stated clearly. Why? Because it was not you who sent the ultimatum to Serbia in 1914, but your enemy had played into your hands.

MASARYK (*firmly*): Jesus prayed to God for the same. It was a bitter cup that I had to drink. If I must, so must it be. I knew that I should have to leave my family. All right. That's part of the business. Sacrifices? All right. I must go. Having spoken against Austria all my life, I was ashamed to remain quietly at home when I saw that Austria must now fall because of her own guilty act. I read that Czech soldiers were being shot for high treason and I thought: That is a worthier man than you. He stands up for the one thing you have always demanded. For long years I have spoken against the government and the dynasty, for long years I have demanded our rights. All at once came the opportunity to fight for these rights. Through the amicable way, in Parliament, it had not succeeded. Then I turned revolutionary.

("*As he spoke this man of eighty-three years looked as if he were only fifty. He uttered the above sentences in a firmer tone of voice than any he had used before or afterwards. On this point, which the moralist in him may have sifted and tested through all those years, he was sure of his own absolution. Here he stood before God and History absolutely unarmed. From here, where the psychological climax of the problem lay, I passed on to the single events connected with the beginning of the War and asked first about Count Berchtold, so that I might have an eyewitness' confirmation of my own account of Berchtold, which has been published to the world and thereby given rise to some controversy.*"—Ludwig)

MASARYK: Fine shoes, ironed creases, immaculate ties and wonderfully confident about everything. To the fine Count there comes a deputy who brings proposals from Pasic as to how a lasting peace could be made between Austria-Hungary and Serbia. What the Serbian demanded was not much. Berchtold should have invited him to Vienna. The beau ideal of the superficial and frivolous Vienna aristocrat. It is told that he said of me, after I had visited him: "There was a professor here who wanted to earn a commission."

LUDWIG: Before your departure in the autumn of 1914, you visited Koerber. Because he was the only one of the Vienna War Ministry whom I judged to be a man of worth, may I ask about these final conversations that you had with Austrian officialdom?

MASARYK: I did not tell Koerber what plans I had, so that he should not be forced to imprison me. "I am a politician," I said to him. "I have been making observations in Prague. We fear riots. Tell me honestly what you expect from the War. You must know whether the army chiefs and the armies are efficient, what the spirit of the army will be, how the Archdukes will behave. You are at the source and must know. Also what we Czechs have to hope for if the Central Powers should prove victorious." "We are not well prepared," Koerber answered, "and if we should win together with Germany, Austria will not turn back on its path, it will not grant freedom to its peoples; on the contrary, it will become domineering and create new difficulties." This judgment was very important for me. At the same time, through this and a similar visit to the *Statthalter,* Thun, I got the impression that I had to be careful of the radical hotheads in Prague.

LUDWIG: Were you at that time able to know what were the causes of the War?

MASARYK: I believe today, as I believed then, that all were guilty. There are so many historians in Germany and therewith a kind of thinking that is unhistorical. Germany's tragic fault lies in the fact that for two hundred years she preached militarism through the professors as a scientific accomplishment and in fact the officer was the beau ideal of society. For that reason Germany has to bear a proportionately greater blame. Similarly Russian Czarism and the Russian Church are chiefly to blame. The English have a kind of naval militarism. The internal political situation in Austria was untenable: the German and Hungarian minorities could not permanently shackle and oppress the majority. Before the War, I often formulated the case thus: Austria-Hungary ought to be a peaceful Europe on a small scale, it ought to be a prototype for the conciliation of the peoples; but it could not abandon the traditions of the old regime. Austria-Hungary has been punished for its crime and Germany also has had to examine its conscience. Politically speaking, the national and political past has to be

revised. Unimaginable, how the innumerable historians and political
leaders have treated the war-guilt problem in a purely mechanical way,
without examining the individual conscience. The priests and parsons
preach God, His omniscience and righteousness. Did God sleep
throughout the World War? Germany was militarily prepared but
politically shortsighted. Its great political error was that it did not
recognize the weakness of Austria-Hungary. And the Germans also
did not have a correct estimation of England and America, nor even
of Italy.

LUDWIG: So it appears *post bellum*. But then in the August of 1914, in
perfect ignorance of the origin, did you not have the sense of a great
adventure as you departed?

MASARYK: Of course. Revolution too is always an adventure. But the important thing is the whole motivation of the action. I placed my life
and my family in jeopardy. My son died in the war, of typhus which
he caught from Galician refugees. As an American my wife was protected somewhat. As a matter of fact, the women of America hindered
her imprisonment. I did not think that they would imprison my
daughter instead of her. I never disclosed to my wife a word about my
plans, because she could not lie if she were cross-examined; nor did
I tell my children. My son, an Austrian officer, knew nothing of it.
Naturally, they could soon guess what my plans were. I only said: "I
am now going to Italy," after I had been in Holland twice already. I
wanted to come back again from Italy, and also from Switzerland, but
it was too late. I shall now answer you. I considered the step I was
taking very carefully and conscientiously. It was daring, probably I was
foolhardy, but then I did not act in an adventurous way. In an essay
on the prognosis of the War—naturally and carefully written—I
counted in, as it were, the victory of the Entente Powers.

LUDWIG: And how much did your friends know? How did you arrange
to have a sort of mandate given you for abroad?

MASARYK: I did not explain my plans fully to anyone, only indicated them,
and said: "I go away and I shall fight for our cause." I did not call them
together. I spoke with them individually more or less according to
their political leanings and abilities. When I went abroad I had the
confidence of the political leaders of all parties.

LUDWIG: Why was it that they were not suspicious of you abroad? Why
did they believe you?

MASARYK (*laughing*): I was known, and Austrian stupidity did the rest
for me. That they openly pursued me was quite sufficient for my

prestige abroad. When they imprisoned my daughter, that was worth millions. Assemblies in New York and other states sanctioned me. Remember that my daughter was well known in America as a social worker. I was also known there.

LUDWIG: But after a life of such bourgeois morality, so completely removed from the subterranean career of the professional revolutionary, and in your middle sixties, how did you find yourself for the first time in all those illegal intrigues?

MASARYK (*"assuming a contented expression, that of the peasant who will maintain his point to the end; then, with sparkling eyes"*): From Rome and Geneva I had to keep in touch with Prague. And so the contact had to be established. There was a technician who had discovered something of which the police knew nothing as yet. For example, did you ever think how a piece of lead can be taken out of a lead-pencil—out of this one here—and replaced by a miniature letter written in cipher? (*Opens the double lid of his watch and points to the little wheel.*) No policeman thinks of investigating to find whether or not a little piece of paper may be stuck under these wheels. (*Bends forward and comes near to Ludwig as if he has to speak confidentially, in an undertone—all in mock-play.*) We had a barrel of oil sent to Prague. Hung on a thin wire from the plug, a letter floated on the oil. Our technician knew his job. He had also patented a naval engine. For me the inventing of such a correspondence was a rest for the restless brain. And sometimes also a bit of fun.

LUDWIG: Besides these intrigues numerous conflicts must have arisen within yourself; for your mind was against war as such, and completely against a long war.

MASARYK (*nodding affirmatively*): There was the struggle. As a man, I naturally wanted to shorten the duration of the War as much as possible. As a politician, I knew that if Austria and Germany were quickly defeated we could not achieve what we actually have achieved. We needed a long war. Our cause was little known; for our propaganda we needed a long war. In the training of the legions my preoccupation was to avoid as far as possible the sacrifice of lives. Blood is a precious liquid. At home there were two political Utopias, the Russian and the French. Of Czarist Russia I knew that it offered nothing worth while on which we could build. The French were friendly toward us, but they had to be won over to my ideas. They also, in conjunction with the other Great Powers, wanted to have Austria maintained, beside and against Germany, as we had wanted it with our Palacky. The most that was hoped for there abroad was a revolution in Austria, which

would shorten the duration of the War. I knew that no such event
would happen, and I stuck to my work against Austria. Just think of
this grotesque situation! A foreign politician arrives in a belligerent
country, a professor, a civilian, he is for war—he is well received and
he is believed.

Thomas Masaryk

2.

KAREL CAPEK SOUNDS OUT THE FATHER OF HIS COUNTRY ON HIS RELIGIOUS AND PHILOSOPHICAL BELIEFS.

> They told me that this year the nightingales were
> singing because they had plenty of mosquitoes.
> And a thought passed through my mind: do
> those nightingales sing their praises to the Good
> Lord for those mosquitoes? And those mos-
> quitoes—that buzzing of theirs, is that also a
> song of praise because the nightingales are swal-
> lowing them as they fly?

IN LISTENING to Masaryk, the Philosopher, after eavesdropping on Masaryk, the Revolutionary, we are in another world—in the company, it would seem, of another man. To be sure, true political action is not without its philosophical implications. That philosophy is barren indeed which shies away completely from the immediate scene. Ideally, politics and philosophy complete and interact on one another. And Masaryk hand-somely fulfills Plato's prophecy of the philosopher become—if not king—then president. But we have seen how Masaryk found it feasible to abandon a philosophically held position against revolutionary action. We have seen him compromise with moral abstractions before an expedient situation, and we have heard him reconcile his philosophy to practical necessity. Good sense and patriotic fervor had triumphed over metaphysical scruples.

Very little of the world's din echoes through the following discourse with Karel Capek. For the most part the atmosphere is rare and supramundane; the talk is of monism, pantheism, determinism, of the eternities—and God. At times our groping and pitiful world recedes to a remote speck in the distance. And yet these preoccupations are common to all men; in simpler terms, perhaps, but none the less pressing and sobering. Just what school-label to place on Masaryk's personal philosophy it is hard to decide. That he accepts God is clear, and that he finds evidence of purpose—teleology—in the universe, he makes equally emphatic. Materialism, moral and metaphysical, he seems to reject entirely, a conclusion one would have gathered in any case from a treatise on Karl Marx which Masaryk published as a young teacher of philosophy. There again one finds compromise: Masaryk, the scientist, cannot reject the determinism and causality of natural law, yet he accepts not only freedom of will but the active role of Providence. At moments he would seem to be a deist, asserting the claims of reason but keeping God in the universe; at others, an out-and-out realist. Even Capek remarks at one point, "You talk like a pure spiritualist." Masaryk calls the soul and God "the dual problem of our thinking and striving—the true task of life." Yet he rejects the nebulous, imageless soul of ordinary belief. "I want to be myself after death," he cries; "I don't want to dissolve into some metaphysical jelly."

Masaryk's early espousal of philosophical realism was largely a reaction to excessive German idealism; yet idealist wraiths hover about his metaphysical position as expounded here. Quite frankly he even calls himself a Platonist, and, then, in the next breath, parts company with the Greek thinker by refusing to regard matter as "something lower and less pure than the spirit." Plato blundered badly there, he avows, as did the "theologians and philosophers" after him, because they turned away in contempt "from matter, nature, and the world." A humanitarian piety is at the bottom of this valiant Czech's creed, and one senses the all-consuming love of freedom in the injunction: "Not to be a fatalist, or a slave, a slave of oneself, or a slave of one's surroundings."

It was during the twilight calm of Masaryk's last years that the late Czech playwright and novelist, Karel Capek, spent long days with his great compatriot. One would have preferred a more combative spirit in the interlocutor, though the clever Capek does manage at times to steer Masaryk's discourse into perilous waters. One detects a note of skepticism in the way certain questions and problems are posed. As a rule, however, Capek gives his assent and offers some innocuous remarks of his own that only strengthen Masaryk's position. In an arena designed for speculative combat the author of R.U.R. chose not to dispute. This need not detract from the worth of the dialogue. To those with a taste for metaphysical disquisition, a fascinating realm of thought opens here. And Capek, artist that he is, admits us deftly into the innermost recesses of the mind and soul of this great Czech who fought the good fight for human decency to the end.

The conversation is given in the translation of M. R. Weatherall (Macmillan, 1938).

MASARYK: I am not a materialist, I am not a monist, I am not a pantheist or panentheist, I am not a dualist. I am a pluralist; the all is for me a harmonious system. In this way I have poured out to you the whole of my metaphysics at one go.

CAPEK: A theist then; you accept theism—through what? Through feeling? Reason? Faith?

MASARYK: Through reason; what role faith has in it, that already is one of the problems of religion. I accept theism through experience and reason. The reasons and proofs of theism give me reason.

CAPEK: What proofs?

MASARYK: Mainly the teleological proof. The purposiveness of the world, of life, of historical happenings, of our knowledge, and of moral endeavor lead me to acknowledge a creator, and director of all, a personal being, spiritual, and infinitely perfect. God himself is reason, is νοῦς λόγος. The Greeks understood this when they freed themselves from mythological polytheism and fetishism. "Reason," said Anaxagoras, "is an organizer of the cosmos," and Aristotle praised him for that because "he came like one sober among the drunk."

CAPEK: And how would you demonstrate that purposiveness?

MASARYK: By experience and reason. True, most people only half-believe in purposiveness, and rather unconsciously. A man who would completely deny the order in the world, with its consequences, and the purpose of everything, even of his own life—I ask you, how could he exist with such an idea? Reason, after all, itself ascertains, and to a certain extent it also constructs, an intelligent order in everything it conceives. Reason from its nature seeks for order and purpose; it itself formulates aims. To speak of chance, and aimlessness in the world is contrary to reason; reason itself is the agent of order and of teleology. A purposeful order in the world is provided by reason; our knowledge itself is teleological.

CAPEK: And how do you explain whence, why, and what for is all evil, pain, and misery, wars, and catastrophes?

MASARYK: I shall not explain that, I cannot explain it. But neither can monism, nor pantheism, nor dualism, nor materialism; no one can explain it any better; I stick to it because of all the possible hypotheses concerning the substance and the origin of the world it is the simplest. Tell me, why should the bad, painful, nonsensical—what life gives to us—count for more than what is healthy, cheerful, and pleasant? There is more good in the order of the world; but man feels that evil is stronger. I cannot honestly explain what is served by imperfection, suffering and so on; but I see that man and mankind can and should face the imperfections. Without the overcoming of obstacles, without pressing and sometimes even painful occasions for action, life would not be a full life. I think that philosophy need not refute pessimism and justify God. God has no need of an advocate. And to refute pessimism? Illness, misery, crime, and so on cannot be refuted with words. Don't think that I should close my eyes to physical and spiritual incongruities and misery. When recently I visited Zidichovice in Moravia I heard the nightingales singing there, well, beautifully! They told me that this year the nightingales were singing because they had plenty of mosquitoes. And a thought passed through my mind: do those nightingales sing their praises to the Good Lord for those mosquitoes? And those mosquitoes—that buzzing of theirs, is that also a song of praise because the nightingales are swallowing them as they fly? Teleology —a hard nut, but even if you can't crack it, it is more likely to get into the palm of your hand than a theory of aimlessness, chance, and chaos.

The second argument of theism, here we have the so-called cosmological proof: without a first cause, without a first creator and mover, we cannot understand the origin, motion, and development of the universe. From the causal point of view we must put some beginning to that chain of causes; it does not suffice for us, I think, to accept secondary causes *ad infinitum*. And the positivistic *ignoramus*, the teaching of the impossibility of knowing the first causes, agnosticism in general, I do not regard as any explanation of the world and of life.

CAPEK: Even psychologically it is strange: not to allow oneself to inquire about first causes. It is like the fairy tale of the ten chambers. You are allowed to go into all the chambers except the tenth. Then one thinks that in those nine chambers there is nothing special, and that only the tenth is worth anything.

MASARYK: That's about it; and there's nothing more than that in it, nothing, perhaps. Hume and Comte made a mistake when they rejected *a limine* all inquiry into causes—Comte prohibited it almost as the police might do; also it turned out with him as one would expect, he fell into myth up to his ears.

I think that modern natural science in its teaching of entropy confirms Aristotle's postulate of the first cause: if according to the mechanical theory of heat the universe ends with the same temperature in all its parts, and so with a heat death, then the world is not eternal but it had a beginning in time, and in time it also will have its end. I know that this explanation is not accepted by some physicists.

CAPEK: You deduce the existence of God by these two arguments alone?

MASARYK: Yes. More accurately speaking, the hypothesis of the existence of God; for science theism is a hypothesis which according to the demand of logic is simpler, and therefore more justifiable than other hypotheses, such as materialism and so on. I would go further; as a theist, as a pluralist, I also accept the existence of the soul and its immortality, I am certain of the soul, and of souls; but to prove that by intellectual arguments which would silence everybody—that I can't do. After all, there are scientists who defend materialism, pantheism, monism, and so on—I don't regard myself as infallible, and as knowing everything better. I think that the hypothesis of an immortal soul is not in conflict with biology and psychology, it is not with science. At one time when I was young, it upset me that I had no proofs that were absolutely invincible. Today I say to myself: must we, can we know everything, and have it down in legal black and white? What a world would it be if it had no secret for us! If we believed that we knew everything, we should grow much too fat. When I was a schoolmaster and taught philosophy, the boys used to come to me and ask about this and that; they could not understand when I used to say, "I don't know." They were astonished at the kind of philosopher I was who had not an answer for everything.

CAPEK: But even if you can't prove the immortality of the soul, at least you must have reasons why you are certain of it.

MASARYK: That, yes! I cannot imagine that such a beautiful and fine feeling as thought, knowledge, piety, moral endeavor, perception of beauty, all culture, that it could be lost, that it could not be for something. The physicists say energy is indestructible; and what about the energy in us? The soul moves the matter, reason gives form to the matter, determines the aim, and comprehends the whole of this world: can that matter last—and not the soul? It would be strange.

CAPEK: And then: life itself is an argument against death. It is true, all living things die; but all living things have a tremendous urge to live, to outlive themselves, to survive without change. A plant lives again in its offspring, hands on everything further, and loses nothing of its qualities. The soul alone would not inherit itself; the soul alone would have no continuation. That would be unnatural.

MASARYK: You might say—our deeds outlive us. But how many people are lucky enough to hand over any real achievement to the coming generations? Some die young; others are not given any opportunity for making use of their talents. I can't believe that that potential work in them can be lost just anyhow. It would be unjust.

CAPEK: We cannot prove the immortality of the soul; but on the other hand—we cannot really imagine not-being and not-life; we can only imagine the end of life in a negative sense: that we do not see, do not hear, do not know. Our concept of death is as empty as the concept of not-tree, or not-grass. Perhaps on account of that emptiness we fear death like a dark abyss.

MASARYK: It depends: I am not afraid of it, many people are not. Primitive races have no knowledge of the fear of death. People in the Middle Ages were not afraid of it—it is only modern man who is frightened of it. Above all things he is more afraid of pain than the men of old—

CAPEK: As the dying Wolker wrote: "I do not fear death; death is not bad; it is but the end of a hard life. It is dying that I fear."

MASARYK: And secondly—many a modern man is afraid of death because he is too self-indulgent—life is not for him a big drama, all he wants from it is food and pleasure; he is an unbeliever, he has not sufficient faith and trust. Modern suicide and fear of death—these two are connected together in the same way as fear and flight are connected. But that would be a problem in itself. When I think of immortality, I don't think so much of death, and what will come after, but rather of life and its content. For me, immortality follows from the richness and value of human life, of the human soul. Man to himself, man to man is most valuable as a spiritual being. And the immortality of the soul follows also from the acknowledgment of God, from faith in universal order and justice. There would be no justice, there would be no perfect equality without the eternity of the soul. And lastly—immortality is already experienced now, in this life; we have no experience of life after death, but we have, we can already have experience now, that the real and fully human life we live is only *sub specie aeternitatis*. This experience ultimately depends upon us, on how we live, on what we are concerned with, and on what we try to make of our present lives. Only as souls among eternal souls do we live a full and true life. The existence of the soul is the real basis of democracy: the eternal to the eternal cannot be indifferent; one immortal is in equality with another immortal. This is where love of one's neighbor derives its special—it is usually called metaphysical—significance.

True, I cannot say what the soul is like and what it is; I ascribe spiritual activities to the soul and partly also to the body, the brain, the senses; but how the soul and the body act on each other, that I don't know—after all, no explanation, whether it be materialism or psychological parallelism can explain that satisfactorily. And what will it be like, what will life be like after death—that I know still less. I don't know how to believe that after death we shall pass into some divine primary substance as monism, pantheism teach: I want to be myself after death; I don't want to dissolve into some metaphysical jelly. I am a metaphysical individualist, if you like to call me that. Perhaps after death we shall be given fuller and more complete knowledge, also knowledge of God; it may be that life after death is an asymptote approaching to God: always and always nearer, eternally nearer—well yes, this also is a continuation of life upon earth, because God is the chief and foremost object of our thinking, knowing, and striving. God and the soul. One is connected with the other. The soul and God, that is the dual problem of our thinking and striving—I should say, the true task of life.

CAPEK: You talk like a pure spiritualist; and yet all your life you have been taking on other tasks, actual, practical, real ones—it is not for nothing that they called you a realist.

MASARYK: Of course, sir; but even in the actual and material, a spiritual and eternal process is taking place. Only today I found in my papers the Oriental aphorism: "A man should act as if everything mattered, but in his inner self a small Buddha sits for whom nothing matters." Nothing, that is, expressed and felt in the Oriental way; in our way, it would be. For behind all that is temporal and material, what is eternal and spiritual matters. Faith in the spiritual, the accent on the spiritual, does not mean that we ought to, and are allowed to, disregard matter and the body. After all, in a philosophical sense we do not know what the substance of matter is. It is given us like the soul; it is given to us only by way of the soul, through our perception and thinking: what right have we got to undervalue it? All knowledge of matter is only the expansion of our spiritual activities; soul and matter are not in opposition to each other. The soul, body, and matter, all reality is given to us for our knowledge, and development; our souls and our material surroundings we ought to develop to greater perfection. The idea that matter is something lower and less pure than the spirit is wrong. In this Plato went wrong, and after him the theologians and philosophers because with contempt they turned away from matter, nature, and the world.

CAPEK: And yet you call yourself a Platonist.

MASARYK: Yes. But that does not mean that I accept all Plato's views. I am a Platonist in so far as I seek ideas in the cosmos, that in what is transitory I seek what is enduring and eternal. I cannot be interested solely in movement, but in *what* is moving, *what* is changing. In natural development I seek purpose and order, sense in historical progress; I inquire for what purpose it all happened, and where it is leading to. Against Darwinism, against one-sided evolutionism, and historicism, I accentuate the static side: that which is permanent and eternal. Not simply the παντα ξει of Heraclitus, not simply continual change, but the substance of the things that change; in addition to dynamics, and with it statics, the great architecture of all being. In man, therefore, I also seek that which endures: his immortal soul.

CAPEK: To look for a purpose and meaning in events, and in history, that is almost like believing in Providence.

MASARYK: Of course. I do believe, I must believe in Providence which governs the development of the world, and of humanity, and of any one of us. Once I acknowledge God the creator, and director, I must see in everything some order, plan, and reasonable aim.

CAPEK: Or determinism.

MASARYK: Yes, that's understood. Determinism means a fixed order in Nature, in man, in society, and in its development: everywhere exact law. We find it in matter, we discover the beautiful order of the atoms; more and more we shall be able to see this obedience to law in the life of the man, in the history of states, nations, and of humanity, sir, and we shall be able to collaborate with it consciously! The more knowledge we shall acquire the clearer will the aim and purpose of everything be revealed to us; knowledge itself is the ascertainment of laws, and the bringing of facts into lawful order; and that is only the beginning.

CAPEK: When you say determinism you raise with it the old problem: what then happens with the freedom of the will. If our actions are directed, whether by Providence or by natural causation, is not our supposed will and moral freedom only an illusion?

MASARYK: It is not. We can choose—after all, experience itself guarantees us this. Only in the causal world can we anticipate, act with forethought, prepare for the future, consistently, with real will. Determinism excludes not freedom, but caprice, fancy, and instability. It leads to perseverance and consistency—without determinism, without the exact concatenation of cause and effect there would be no responsibility. There would be mere fortuity; we should not be responsible for our deeds, and the motives for our actions would rise up in us without reason by mere chance.

CAPEK: I think that freedom of the will is not an infringement of causality; it is only the possibility of putting new causes into the causal process.

MASARYK: I should say it like this: the freedom and predestination of man is given by his relation to God, omnipotent, and omniscient, knowing the past and the future, determining this future. Man is after the divine image, God could not create man except after the likeness of his own image; from this follows for man a conscious synergism, collaboration with the divine will. In acquiring knowledge of Nature and of man, in revealing the natural laws, spiritual and historical, in accepting and fulfilling those laws, we participate in the divine creation and direction of the world. God lets us do His work, He wants us to work, and so collaborate. Every co-operation, among men too, includes freedom and subjection, initiative and constraint. Synergism with the divine will gives man his measure of freedom and of determinism; the stronger and the more conscious he is, the more of both.

Determinism—yes: people think that it deprives man of responsibility. But God does not command me to lift now my right hand, or now the left: *minima non curat praetor*. Along with God, and under God, we are autonomous beings; we have the right of initiative, and we bear also the burden of responsibility. Hence the duty of activism, and of striving, of resoluteness, and of courage. Freedom, sir, is just as hard as duty. We feel that to will hurts. To will is labor; to decide tires; it is the creation of something new. During the War I envied the soldiers. They were ordered about, but they could only obey and did not need to decide. I had to decide, to command even, all the time, not only to think, but to will terribly—I know, then, what it is.

Determinism does not mean the absence of freedom. On the contrary. An immature man who does not understand the order of the world and its grandeur, a man in his primeval weakness and lack of judgment, sees in the world and also in his own life a kaleidoscope of single unconnected phenomena. Everywhere he sees the unreasonable caprice of spirits, gods, of chance, and of blind fate.

CAPEK: That can also be seen today: the superstitious most likely are those dependent on chance: gamblers, hunters, people from the theater, and such like.

MASARYK: Naturally: those who believe in chance, believe also in idols, and in miracles. Superstition is indeterminist. A primitive man is a metaphysical indeterminist; he succumbs blindly to impulses, he lets himself be led by his own whims—he is a metaphysical anarchist.

CAPEK: I should not say that. As with savages, with natural races, the life of an individual is mainly bound by tradition, the prescriptions of ritual, and social customs.

MASARYK: So you see, an indeterminist is a slave: he is bound blindly by customs and superstitions, he is subject to instincts, he has no free will. There are also primitives like that among us. A man has only as much reasonable freedom, as much determinism, as he can understand in himself and in the order of the world.

Those controversies over determinism and indeterminism—a curious history, as old as philosophical thought. Already with the Greeks the expression was used: θεὸς κνκίτιος, God without blame. The minds of people in the Middle Ages were racked by predestination: if God knows and determines everything, he knows already and predestines who is going to be good, who evil, who will be saved, and who damned. St. Paul, Augustine, Thomas Aquinas, and later Luther, Zwingli, and Calvin had strange views on predestination; they tried partly to alleviate the harshness of predestination by the doctrine of divine grace. Modern theologians also often invent only words, not concepts, how to reconcile the freedom of the human will with divine omnipotence —it leads nowhere, it seems to me; I am not astonished that one pope simply banned all controversies about the freedom of the will and predestination. It is a hard nut.

To me determinism is a consequence of theism, of the acknowledgment of the teleological order in the world. We also are fulfilling universal laws and are acting causally.

CAPEK: Even in our mistakes?

MASARYK: Of course; but we have the possibility of choosing amidst the plurality of causes, it is possible for us to judge. All education, and re-education, moral responsibility, and punishment, is based on determinism. We hope that through education we may inculcate into children motives of good behavior; and for what would punishment be if it did not deter, if it were not the cause and the motive of reform?

CAPEK: And what about capital punishment?

MASARYK: That is a chapter to itself. The right to punish by death is dreadful, and judging from its history and development, it will be abolished in future. Don't you ask me how I felt when I signed the order for carrying out capital punishment. Capital punishment for me is not mainly requittal or deterrent. It is no safeguard against a dangerous criminal; if it has any sense and justification then it is only as expiation. Nothing but death compensates for and redeems such a terrible thing as the brutal and mercenary murder of a man; a criminal like that has committed an offense against the whole of mankind. But this also is only valid for the existing state of culture—future ages will have greater possibilities of prevention, correction, and re-education —and a better knowledge of criminal responsibility.

In these and other problems progress will have to be by empirical methods; to try to explain how man really does act in particular circumstances; to what extent he can control himself, and his actions, and educate himself; how far he is free and responsible for his actions. I confess that I prefer conscientious statistics, of accidents, say, to a few chapters of Leibniz's *Theodicea*; from statistics I learn what generally is the cause of accidents, and how to deal with them accordingly. If the driver does not drink, mishaps do not happen so easily—ergo, don't drink, and that's the end of it, and don't you try to blame or justify the Good Lord. Illness—for that there are doctors, and science, so that they learn how to face them. Misery—we are all here to remove that. And so on.

This then is determinism: to learn to understand the causes of evil, so that we may induce the causes of reform. Not to be a fatalist, or a slave, a slave of oneself, or a slave of one's surroundings. Wherever we are, not to act and work blindly, but freely and consciously, to anticipate and plan like a worker and collaborator of God. In this I also differ from stoicism. Stoicism makes a virtue out of weakness. It is, if I may call it, a metaphysical shrugging of the shoulders; in it there is a suspicion of titanic dissimulation; theistic resignation is hopeful modesty.

Clemenceau

AN AGING TIGER BEWAILS THE SOFTNESS OF HIS CONTEMPORARIES AND NOSTALGICALLY SURVEYS HIS OWN CAREER.

The truth is that all of you are just waiting for an excuse to twiddle your thumbs.

O NE DAY in August, 1928, Georges Clemenceau pointed out his father's grave at Mouilleron to his friend Jean Martet. "Mine is beside it," he remarked; "it is already dug. . . . Take a look at it. There in a nutshell is all that you can say about me—a hole in the ground and a great deal of noise about nothing." It is this eighty-seven-year-old Clemenceau, blandly resigned to death and garrulously reminiscent about a long past, that we meet in the conversation below. We leave it to history to decide whether that long and agitated career was "a great deal of noise about nothing."

A belligerent and fiery patriot, endowed with a sharp tongue and a flailing wit, he was known as "The Tiger" to Frenchmen of two generations. He had fought splendidly for the freedom of Captain Dreyfus. And as the vigorous, embattled old man of seventy-six who was called in as premier in 1917 to lead a despairing France to victory, Georges Clemenceau became what he had always dreamed of being, "Père de la Victoire." How tigerish and vengeful this father of victory could be, the Germans were to learn at Versailles. For this was the vehement prophet who, Cassandra-like, had long warned his countrymen: "Germany has but one aim—to wipe out France." This man had watched the Germans bombard Paris in 1870, and he neither forgot nor forgave. For four and a half decades after that shame he had warned Frenchmen that it would come again. Passionately, he had argued for preparedness. In editorials and speeches he urged them to face the brute facts of German militarism and imperial expansion. Only skepticism and apathy had greeted him in the press and government alike, and the ministry of which he was premier finally collapsed under the combined assault of his foes. Yet when the enemy struck again, the country remembered this impassioned patriot. Frenchmen now

527

listened to his ringing appeals and nodded assent over his wrathful blasts at a blundering government. This was a man to heed and to follow. Thus, despite his own dislike and distrust of the relentless fighter, President Poincaré called Georges Clemenceau to the helm in France's sorest hour of need. He was called a Cincinnatus brought back from retirement to save his land from a new peril.

But Clemenceau had never really withdrawn from the fray. In the senate or in the columns of his papers he had pounded away at the one theme of "furor teutonicus." In the opinion of this restless man, to be silent was to betray France and to be inactive was to be dead. Yet, for a premier who had been unseated in 1909 to be called back to his post at seventy-six was unique. No greater glory could come to any man in his lifetime. But once the danger had passed and the stern treaty was signed, the mood of the country again changed. The need for a bellicose policy was felt to have passed. The war ministry fell, and a head-shaking old man of seventy-nine went back to what, always excepting France, had been his first love—books. He had read avidly in all languages, and written voluminously—newspaper articles, criticism, books on religion, travel, philosophy, plays, novels, a history of "American Reconstruction," even a study of anatomy. Somehow, this incredible Frenchman who had been doctor, mayor, fearless comrade-in-arms of Zola in the fight to save Dreyfus, deputy, senator, premier, and proud "father of victory" had found time to be man of letters, too. Now, when the country no longer needed him, Clemenceau was back in his study on the Rue Franklin in Passy, barricaded by walls of books. At times he would raise his eyes from a volume of Aeschylus and gaze fondly through a window at the small garden he had planted with rose-bushes and Japanese dwarf-trees. The urge to write was as strong as ever. Newspaper articles poured from his pen, and soon a formidable two-volume treatise on the cosmic postulates, "Au Soir de la Pensée," would be given to the world. In the end we find him, typically, tirelessly, pursuing researches for a book about his old friend, the painter Claude Monet. There was no end to Clemenceau's interests.

Amid his literary preoccupations on the Rue Franklin "The Tiger" faced another appalling task—that of bringing some order into a mountain of personal and political papers. These had accumulated over the years, and much might need suppression or clarification before the final darkness set in. Those who visited Clemenceau during this period found him cheerfully flippant on the subject of death. He would talk of his demise as if the date had been entered in a calendar of personal appointments. Often, with a humorous fussiness, he seemed to be making last-minute preparations for a long journey. His detachment and resignation were complete, except for one thing—he wanted to be absolutely certain that he was leaving nothing behind that might tarnish his memory. To assist him in this there was only one man Clemenceau felt he could trust —his former secretary, Jean Martet.

It is to this faithful and diligent Jean Martet that we owe the liveliest conversational record of "The Tiger" in the twilight of his long life. Martet had first served Clemenceau in 1915 while he was senator and member of the Military Commission. When Clemenceau became premier, Martet was made head of his private secretariat, remaining till the ministry fell in 1920. For two or three years more Clemenceau retained him as private secretary. Martet then gave up the job but remained a trusted friend and literary consultant to the very end. One day in July, 1927, Clemenceau fell dangerously ill, and Martet spent several anxious hours at the house on the Rue Franklin. That night, in the belief that the world would want them, he feverishly wrote down what he feared were Clemenceau's last words. But Clemenceau fooled his doctors. He lived on for two more years, sharp-witted, ironic, and endlessly reminiscent to the last. And that memo made by Martet on that anxious July night was to prove a happy inspiration. Thereafter every conversation held with the patriarch of the Rue Franklin was duly recorded the moment Martet returned to his own rooms. As he listened, the former secretary's love and admiration for the old man grew still stronger. Each day he caught unsuspected facets of this powerful intellect. Clemenceau's erudition was boundless, and so was his unflagging eagerness to know more. The glory that was Greece obsessed him as it never had before, and this obsession found vivid expression in a stirring biography of Demosthenes. Increasingly, the aging "Tiger" seemed himself like someone out of the Age of Pericles, oracular in years and wisdom. And time only sharpened Clemenceau's vast sense of humor. The world outside had become one huge jest for this arch-ironist who looked back nostalgically to his great days of public wrangling. Yet there were poignant moments when he felt alone and beaten. Less than ten years after his great triumph he found himself a forgotten man in the France he had saved; "thrust into a loneliness," observed the devoted Martet, "for which I fervently hope France will one day blush."

Martet's record begins on July 11, 1927, and ends on August 15, 1928. Short of mechanical or stenographic notation on the spot, his method of recapturing the day's talk was perfect. "When I returned home," he tells us, "I set down as faithfully as I could all that I had been listening to, including not only the general substance but also the turns of phrase, the color, intonation, the fire that he had given it. I shall probably be charged with having put in Clemenceau's mouth words which he never uttered

... *Everything that I have written was spoken, and nearly always to the exact word, to the comma, almost. I may have made mistakes in names or dates, may have heard incorrectly or remembered imperfectly, but if so I should be surprised. My hearing and my memory are both quite good. ... No pen could have conjured him up so well as these modest little gramophone records, which I trust will show him to us as he was, in his ardent, impetuous, reckless youth, in his victories and defeats, in the snares and treacheries he encountered in his life. I may presume to utter this eulogy of the following pages—for I only wrote them to dictation."* One is prepared to agree with Milton Waldman, Martet's adroit translator who read the manuscript through three times and was "struck anew each time with the fact that here was a work of art which partook of the nature, though it did not perhaps attain the degree, of Boswell's portrait of Johnson or Plato's of Socrates." Like Boswell, Martet sought to make his idol as real to the reader as he had been to him; to present him as he had revealed himself, in three dimensions—or, in Mr. Waldman's words: "speaking, breathing, scolding, eating, philosophizing, haggling, and musing over the sculpture and pictures which he so deeply and passionately loved."

The three dialogues reprinted here were chosen as giving varied aspects of this amazing personality. There is no central theme in any of them, no single link other than the shrewd and seasoned wisdom, mellowed by life and art and the Greek classics, of an old man hourly awaiting death, yet fiercely alive in mind and body. Together with the accompanying footnotes, they are taken from Mr. Waldman's translation of Jean Martet's Georges Clemenceau (Longmans, Green and Co., New York, 1930).

18th December 1927

(*In Clemenceau's room. He is correcting certain typewritten papers —Martet.*)

CLEMENCEAU (*looking up*): What can I do for you, Monsieur Martet?

MARTET: Sir, the other day you said that you liked me, but that I didn't really deserve your friendship. Well, that annoys me.

CLEMENCEAU: I said that?

MARTET: Perhaps not in those words, but that was the gist of your remarks.

CLEMENCEAU: If that isn't exactly what I said, it isn't exactly what I meant. Don't be a silly fool, Martet. Anyone who ... but first there is that story of Saint-Germain. You promised to show it to me; you should have done so. A promise is a promise. You promised . . . and . . .

MARTET: The trouble is I have too vivid an imagination. Once I've promised to do a thing, I think of it as already accomplished—it's already
ancient history.

CLEMENCEAU: That is a terrible admission to make, for today all Frenchmen think and act just as you do. As soon as an idea has taken form in
their minds they immediately tire of it. They dreamed of the "Victory." But when it came they were no longer interested. The only time
they're capable of positive action is when they haven't had time to
think beforehand. In the second place, Martet—oh, don't think this
is another sermon . . . after all, what's the difference—there is this to
consider: after all, you are not really a fool.

MARTET: I wouldn't go that far, sir. Yes, I mean it. I am a fool! You've
absolutely no idea how little interest I have in intellectual matters.

CLEMENCEAU: Martet, you are not without brains! Now and then you
manage to say things which are . . . well, true. Of course you understand I say they are "true" because they agree with my own beliefs.
After all, I can't tell whether your ideas would appeal to Briand or
Poincaré. And in addition, you have several good points: you're unselfish.

MARTET: I, sir? Why, I'm worried to death because I'm not a millionaire!

CLEMENCEAU: If you're worried to death because you aren't one you will
be one. There's nothing so silly as making money. But you are . . . well,
what else are you? You have a certain appreciation of the beautiful—
for instance, you don't get Phidias mixed up with Bartholomé, or the
Madeleine with the Parthenon. And yet you have a weakness, Martet,
a very stupid weakness—you're lazy.

MARTET: I? Good heavens! I'm restless and can hardly live unless I have
a pencil in my hand.

CLEMENCEAU: Martet, you haven't got enough will power to stick in your
eye.

MARTET: What a pleasant description of me.

CLEMENCEAU: As a member of the present generation you're perfectly
normal. It doesn't do any good to . . .

MARTET: Sir, I think that I understand myself and that I . . .

CLEMENCEAU: Don't talk such nonsense! How can you possibly understand yourself? You've never studied science.

MARTET: And yet I can tell pretty well when machinery isn't functioning
well. My trouble isn't any lack of will power—it's my lack of confidence
in the efficacy of action.

CLEMENCEAU: I realize that, dear fellow. A man who has to be convinced to act before he acts is what you describe—he's *not* a man of action. It's as if a tennis player before returning the ball began to question himself as to the physical and moral value of tennis. You must act just as you breathe.* How old are you?

MARTET: I'm forty.

CLEMENCEAU: Sapristi, when you're forty it's time to be doing something.

MARTET: I'm writing a novel.

CLEMENCEAU: What! a novel! Confound all novels. You should be doing serious work. What? Oh, anything!

MARTET: For whom?

CLEMENCEAU: For yourself! Just tell me why it is that having seen what you have seen you've never written anything? Not one line! Don't you have anything to say of the period we're going through and of the men who are living in it?

MARTET: Why speak of that? What difference would it make? All effort is futile—you know it as well as I do. You've no more confidence than I have in the possibility of changing one fact into another.

CLEMENCEAU: Hold on, there! I'll give you proof that I believe in the usefulness of certain acts and words: I'm in the midst of writing this paper for the Americans. I've got plenty to say—I've said it! You see, I still preserve a certain faith.

MARTET: Well, I congratulate you. After all, your entire life and all your activities prove conclusively that nothing matters.

CLEMENCEAU: Nothing matters because all Frenchmen share your attitude, and because everyone shirks by saying: "I still have sixty or eighty years to live. I'll try to while away the time in the most pleasant fashion possible sitting in my own little corner . . ." Do you have a conscience, Martet? Doesn't it make some demands upon you? Doesn't it make you want to move and strike out a bit? Or does it say to you: "There you are, sitting on the ground, your tail in the dust—You're well off, stay where you are?" Martet, you're not an encouraging type.

MARTET: Yet what can I do, sir? I've already told you—ideas, ideas . . .

CLEMENCEAU: Nothing matters but ideas! Granting that you don't have a brain in your head, you still can use your eyes. Put down what you see. Images are valuable. Moreover, aren't images ideas? Speak, Martet, write, work!

---

* "Pan rules us all. We must act. Action is the beginning, the means, the end. Determined action on the part of each man for the benefit of all, disinterested action (above childish vanity or dreams of reward in eternity or despair in lost battles or the fear of death), action leading toward an ideal—the moving force, the complete virtue. . . ."
This is an extract from Clemenceau's *Grand Pan*.

MARTET: Sir, if I made a book out of what I have seen and heard, you would say: "Surely, you're not going to publish that?"

CLEMENCEAU: Oh, I don't know. And at least, you would have done some writing. You mustn't confine yourself to what I think. It's annoying to find that you are dilatory.

MARTET: But I'm not! I look, I listen . . .

CLEMENCEAU: That's not enough. Read a conclusion.

MARTET: All right. I'll try.

CLEMENCEAU: Don't try—do things! . . . You'll probably be lucky enough to have me with you for a few more months; bring me your observations and I'll tell you what I think of them. Are you willing?

MARTET: Agreed!

CLEMENCEAU: Splendid! Monsieur Martet, I'd like to ask you a question. A man has written to me saying that my style in *Démosthène* and in *Au Soir de la Pensée* is so obscure that it's necessary to read twice to get the meaning. Is that true?

MARTET: Yes, in certain passages. But I feel that if there is any justification to such criticism it's the fact that you wrote those books more for yourself than for others.

CLEMENCEAU: I agree. What a shame that I don't have three or four more years to live—I might have rewritten those books for my cook! Nevertheless, I ought not to have been obscure. I never correct or rewrite sentences. When something isn't satisfactory, I begin the chapter afresh. In my opinion—I don't know whether you feel the same way—the question of style is an arabesque; what difference do one, two, or ten words make? It's merely a matter of the cumulative effect and the general construction. Once you've erected the framework of your building you cannot make additions without overweighting it, cannot withdraw anything without tumbling it to the ground. Looking at it from this point of view, I have perhaps put too much detail into the *Au Soir de la Pensée.*

MARTET: Oh, Monsieur, do not run down the *Au Soir de la Pensée.* What life it has—and vigor and honesty!

CLEMENCEAU: Do you really think so? I thank you. And yet I was eighty-five when I wrote it, racked by diabetes and scarcely able to stand up.

MARTET: Ah, that was a real achievement of will power. I wonder if it can be paralleled in all the history of the world.

CLEMENCEAU: The trouble is, people have wrong ideas about old age. In the first place there is no such thing as old age—one is old only when he begins to act the part of an old man.

MARTET: Sir, you speak like a young man.

CLEMENCEAU: I speak as a man who does not anticipate fate. In business you see persons retiring at sixty. At sixty! What a shame! And what happens to them? They rot away. Of course they do—it's a law of nature. A man who's no longer good for anything must rot away. The truth is that all of you are just waiting for an excuse to twiddle your thumbs. And old age is one of the excuses—and nothing more.

The other day a man suggested that I start life over again.

I answered: "I beg your pardon, but there is no need for me to recommence life—I have only to continue it." Then he said, "Well, I can have you named Deputy from Colmar." I stared at him aghast: "Deputy?" I asked. "Can you picture me in the Chamber? Why not in an asylum?"

MARTET: Then do you feel, sir, that . . .

CLEMENCEAU: I feel that in my day things could still be accomplished in the Chamber; one could fight for some kind of ideal. Now that's all ended. Like everything else, it's had its day. It's no place for a young man.

MARTET: And yet the Chamber in 1914 was never considered brilliant.

CLEMENCEAU: Damn it, no! It wasn't brilliant! I used to meet people there who . . . Oh, well, one wondered how a thousand or ten thousand persons could have voted for those freaks. But the present Chamber is even worse than the 1914 one. I said to that fellow: "Can you show me what outlet there would be for my activity in the Chamber?" He shrugged his shoulders. Ask that same question of any of those men who are standing for election to the Chamber. They'll look at you in amazement. Not one of them has the slightest idea of going to the Chamber to defend anything or fight for anything. One is a deputy today just as one might be a registrar: it is one way to make a living.

MARTET: And yet there are some persons of independent means who enter the Chamber.

CLEMENCEAU: So as to put it on their calling-card—although the word "deputy" hasn't the prestige it used to have. If you're in a room and a deputy enters, there's a sudden constraint. Martet, I'm not going to be deputy from Colmar. I intend to remain young and active. The only thing that annoys me is that I can scarcely move. After walking twenty yards I'm exhausted. I loved to travel—I'll have to give it up.

MARTET: I'm planning this summer to make a little trip—most inexpensively—around the Mediterranean—Cairo, Smyrna, Athens.

CLEMENCEAU: Lucky devil! Above all, see Greece. Ah, Greece—Greece, Martet! Greece is a glorious place. I remember one day in an out-of-the-way corner of the Peloponnesos called Phigalia I had nothing to eat—

oh, yes, I had two bits of chocolate. I saw a hen tied by its leg to a gate. I untied it and put it over a fire. Well, I couldn't dent it either with a knife or my teeth. It was like stone. But the temple is splendid. You know that it was built by Ictinus, the architect of the Parthenon? There are three temples that a man must see before he dies: the Parthenon, Phigalia, and Paestum. You're going to Naples?

MARTET: Yes.

CLEMENCEAU: Then see Paestum. It's magnificent!

MARTET: I'll try to see Paestum. But I don't know whether I'll have enough money to see very much; I expect they'll treat me like an immigrant.

CLEMENCEAU: You're travelling on foot? That's the way! They now have steamboat companies and railways which allow you to see the Pyramids without getting out of bed. They bring them to you in the morning on a platter along with the mail.

MARTET: Money is a terrible plague.

CLEMENCEAU: You can't mean that seriously. Look at my grandson Georges. He married a rather impressive collection of millions. Well, his father-in-law wanted him to become a jeweller, to sell diamonds. The other day he showed Georges a stone and said: "What do you think of that stone?" The youngster answered: "Oh, what a beautiful emerald!" "No," replied Roseneau, "it's the worst ruby I ever saw." So you see what indignities fortune can impose. The youngster likes reading—which is a legitimate, even admirable occupation. Do you know what the father-in-law did? He went to the Hotel des Ventes and bought a complete library for him. Would you want to read books under such conditions?

MARTET: You've just been reading, Monsieur?

CLEMENCEAU: Yes, I'm reading a very amusing book—an old book of Alfred de Vigny's. Do you like de Vigny? He's laborious and conscientious, which after all is something. But actually, if you examine carefully and look behind the words, you won't find much. He's a schoolboy philosopher. His love affair with the actress Dorval was stupid. He weeps and that's all there is to it. And yet about the same Dorval, in the case of a certain Gustavem who was later to become the famous actor Mélingue, the author says: "He became her lover without having uttered one word." Let that be a lesson, Martet. One always talks too much.

(*Albert enters.*)

ALBERT: M. Chichet * is here.

---

* Former editor of *L'Homme Libre.*

CLEMENCEAU: Oh pshaw, what does he want? (*To Martet.*) Come with me. I'll say a couple of words to him and then you're to take him away.

MARTET: How has he offended you? Chichet is very pleasant.

CLEMENCEAU: He reminds me of Napoleon III. (*To Albert.*) Show him into the study.

(*Albert leaves.*)

MARTET: There's a sculptor who without even having seen you has made a bust that's a perfect likeness.

CLEMENCEAU: What's his name?

MARTET: Cogné.

CLEMENCEAU: I've never had any luck with sculptors. Either they have genius and can't make a likeness, or else aren't geniuses but do make a likeness. I don't know why it is but they make me look like an old fool.

(*Albert re-enters.*)

ALBERT: Mme. Bensa is here.

CLEMENCEAU: Into the dining-room. I'm much sought after this morning. I've always told you that I have lost none of my popularity.

(*They go into the study. Chichet is there—very tall, with immense arms and legs.*)

CHICHET (*cordially*): How do you do, Mr. President. Well, is your health good? I've been thinking of you constantly.

CLEMENCEAU: Thank you, my friend.

CHICHET: I must tell you something. I am writing for two papers—the *Courrier du Centre* and the *Nouveliste d'Alsace-Lorraine*—and every time that I can slip in a word about you and what you're doing, I do it. Yes, on my word of honor.

CLEMENCEAU: That's very, very kind of you.

CHICHET: I've also interviewed Mordacq *—just the other day; you'll hear of it soon . . . a rather curious incident. And I was speaking of you to Albert Sarraut,† and Sarraut said: "I'll certainly write to the President."

CLEMENCEAU (*starting*): The devil! And why?

CHICHET: Oh, well, just to assure you of his regard. I mentioned the matter because you notice that to Sarraut you are still "the President." It's an interesting point.

CLEMENCEAU (*drily*): Do you think so?

CHICHET: Don't you? (*A pause.*) And also I want to express to you my sincerest good wishes.

---

* General Jean-Jules-Henri Mordacq, appointed head of Clemenceau's military staff in 1917.

† Minister of the Interior.

CLEMENCEAU: What good are they?

CHICHET: Oh, not much. It's, uh, the thing to say . . . uh, like, oh well . . . I trust I shall have the pleasure of seeing you again.

CLEMENCEAU: Good-by, my friend.

(*Chichet departs.*)

CLEMENCEAU: He looks more and more like Badinguet.*

19th February 1928

CLEMENCEAU (*noticing the portfolio which Martet is carrying under his arm*): Ah, at last! (*Martet takes the papers out of the portfolio and hands them to him.*)

MARTET: I ask you only to look at them after I'm gone.

CLEMENCEAU: Oh! Why?

MARTET: Because I say things which you will perhaps think I oughtn't to have said. But I shall be pleased to have your opinion of it all the same.

CLEMENCEAU: You'll have it all right. (*He begins to turn over the leaves.*) What's this? M. Clemenceau? You speak of M. Clemenceau? What's he ever done to you, that M. Clemenceau?

MARTET: I can only speak of what I've seen, and amongst the things I've seen the one which struck me most strongly was yourself. But don't read it, sir, don't read it.

CLEMENCEAU (*putting the manuscript down*): What can you say about M. Clemenceau? What indeed *is* there to say?

MARTET: How are you today, sir?

CLEMENCEAU: I'm tired.

MARTET: Spiritually?

CLEMENCEAU: You put questions like Victor Cousin.† Physically, spiritually, it all comes from the same shop. Nevertheless, I'm busy writing an article on the Debts. The trouble about writing is that you can never write all that you're thinking—you must use shifts and evasions . . . And you? Have you had a visit from the King of Afghanistan?

MARTET: No. I don't associate with kings very much.

CLEMENCEAU: You're wrong—get firmly hold of the idea that most of the time kings think about exactly the same things as your tailor or your dentist. I've never known a king who had the soul of a king.

MARTET: Did you meet the King?

CLEMENCEAU: Yes, at the Guimet Museum. They asked me if I wanted to

---

* One of Napoleon III's surnames.

† French philosopher, 1792–1867.

go to the reception they were planning for him. I said yes. So I turned up, and it all went off very pleasantly. They put me next to the Queen, who wanted to know who the old gentleman was whom they had seated next to her. She asked the King, who replied vaguely that it was some sort of fossil, now extinct. So, in order to fix this solemn moment in her memory, she took out her watch and looked at the time. I noticed that her watch was something quite extraordinary—like a crabapple cut in two. In the center of this instrument was a diamond—or thirty-six diamonds—I don't know the exact number. It seemed magical.

MARTET: What did they show the King at the Guimet Museum?

CLEMENCEAU: Well, fancy, they had the extremely bright idea of showing him photographs of Afghanistan. It was hardly worth the trouble to have him come so far for that.

MARTET: What impression did he make on you?

CLEMENCEAU: He came out of it not too badly.

MARTET: Are you leaving for the Vendée soon?

CLEMENCEAU: I don't dare to in this vile weather. And you—what are you doing?

MARTET: Preparing my trip to Athens. I'm absorbed in the history of Greece. What a frightful thing it was, that catalogue of atrocities!

CLEMENCEAU: It had its great moments too, Martet!

MARTET: The treacheries, the stupidities. When one thinks that the same people who fought at Marathon and Salamis . . .

CLEMENCEAU: Martet, I shall stop you right there! In the first place, don't take Marathon, Salamis, Thermopylae too seriously. All those yarns . . . I've visited the battlefield of Marathon. They pointed out to me the hillock where were buried the Athenians who died during the conflict. They totalled sixty-three. A battle in which the losses number sixty-three, some of whom probably died of sunstroke—we've seen better since then . . . After all, we only know Greek history through the Greek historians, and Herodotus is like a Marseillais. In speaking of Xerxes' army he says that they dried up the rivers by drinking them. The rest is in keeping. It's all been puffed out and distorted by people who write history like an exchange of fish-stories on the terrace of a café. Greek history is simply the history of three dozen individuals. But, Martet, amongst those three dozen—and that's my second point—were some who did supremely great things.

MARTET: Ah, but there isn't one of them who isn't under suspicion. Themistocles, Pausanias—all takers of bribes, perjurers . . .

CLEMENCEAU: There are others . . . Phocion. Don't you love Phocion? Ah, there's a man I adore. I'd like to have been the friend of that fellow. The derider of the mob—"What asininity could I have uttered that they applaud me thus?" He read the future, that man. And Socrates, Martet?

MARTET: Yes. There was Socrates.

CLEMENCEAU: Ah, Socrates! Isn't he colossal, that man, against whom no reproach can be brought, who lived free, died free, pursued his way with that smile of his? How many such do you find amongst us?

MARTET: But Plato, Plato, sir?

CLEMENCEAU: What about him?

MARTET: Plato writing the *Symposium* when Greek strength and Greek thought were already being engulfed by catastrophe. Don't you find that joy in living and that serenity overwhelming?

CLEMENCEAU: Yes, but—well, I'm not struck by Plato's philosophy. There is no man who has talked more nonsense and reasoned more absurdly —but when you've written the *Symposium*, Martet, and those paragraphs about the death of Socrates, you've well fulfilled your destiny. You're given a meaning to the prodigious adventure which is the history of the race. Another one I like very much is Xenophon. He isn't very shrewd, now and then. He narrates events without quite understanding them. But he is so decent, so balanced. What a splendid specimen of a man! One day I happened to be in the village where he was born, at—oh! this elusive memory of mine. In the morning I opened my window—I saw nothing but a swallow flying past (*he traces the curve of its flight with his hand*)—that was all that remained of Xenophon.

MARTET: But the expedition to Sicily; Alcibiades.

CLEMENCEAU: Yes. Frightful. But . . .

MARTET: And that avalanche which from year to year was on the point of falling—there never was a people who drew so little profit from experience. The Persians had outflanked them the first time at Thermopylae by crossing the Oeta pass. Thermopylae was flanked a second time, and by the same pass. The pass was no more guarded the second time than the first.

CLEMENCEAU: Quite so. But that's not the story of Greece only. Look at all those countries who are throwing themselves into the arms of the Boches just as if there had been no war, no Belgium violated, no ships torpedoed. It would seem that nothing can teach anything to anybody; people seem to grow new minds daily. They imagine that their age is exceptional because they live in it, that it's quite different from all others; they believe that they will live to see the beginning of a new era—then they forget to guard the pass . . . As if there ever were new eras.

MARTET: And Greece in the hands of Rome!

CLEMENCEAU: I give you Rome. It's a degeneration. But Greece! There's a book on Greece by a man named Jardet which you should read. Jardet was a professor at the University of Lyons, and he conceived this history from the most enlightened point of view. He wrote his book, and died, after an illness of two or three months. Then it was learned that he hadn't left enough for his burial, and that his illness had exhausted all of his meager savings. Not a penny was left for his wife. A collection was taken up—I contributed a trifle—and that, Martet, that's how you end up if you write a book on Greece.

MARTET: I'm reading Aeschylus at the moment.

CLEMENCEAU: It's beautiful, isn't it? What heights of grandeur!

MARTET: It's beautiful because he believed in what he was doing. There is no more belief—one no longer even believes in the pen which one is holding.

CLEMENCEAU: That's it exactly. They opened their eyes wide on the world —they discovered it. The world was the world for them and not what it's become for us—words . . .

MARTET: And Aristophanes.

CLEMENCEAU: That fellow—no. I can't see him in the picture—he spoils the composition. He understood nothing about anything whatever, took the great for the small, the small for the great, threw his venom, his rancor about promiscuously, broke everything, soiled everything. It's people like that who corrupt a country.

MARTET: And Sparta.

CLEMENCEAU: When I arrived in Sparta I said, "Show me Sparta." There wasn't any. The Eurotas rolled by, a pretty, limpid stream, but about as wide as this piece of furniture. In the museum, which is about as large as this room, there are a statue and a vase, both Attic. They're all that Sparta has left. I expected to find a countryside as dour as themselves, but no—great fertility, vines bearing enormous grapes. And I crossed the Taigeta, which is something of a mountain, I assure you, and arrived at a place called something like "Coryza"—the women crossed themselves when they saw me and drunken priests kissed me on the mouth.

MARTET: Did you go to Olympus?

CLEMENCEAU: Twenty times! Ah, Olympus. The Circus . . . you still have that before you. And if, on scraping away the earth with your foot and noticing the white line where the runners finished, you experience no sensation, it's because you're made of wood.

MARTET: And the ancient cities—Argos, Mycenae?

CLEMENCEAU: Magnificent! All those huge piles—there's not one of those stone blocks which isn't too large to fit into this garden. They haven't the look of having been made for people like us. You begin to understand the buskin of the Tragedians ...

MARTET: I learned with surprise that the Asclepeion of Athena was quite small ...

CLEMENCEAU: It is. But the temples of the Golden Age are minuscules, and the Asclepeion must be practically contemporary with the Acropolis. That's what constitutes the triumph of those people; they guessed that the key to the problem wasn't size but harmony. They were the only race who understood that. The Egyptians with their pyramids— what were they seeking? They may pile stone upon stone, yet even by breaking their backs they cannot hope to scale the Heavens. The Greeks did not look for their solution in space but in the mind.

And after the Asclepeion, which is so lovely in the evening by moonlight, with the children playing all round it, after the Parthenon, which has been so mistreated, which has inspired so much literature, you will see the Pnyx, Martet. The Pnyx reveals things. An old altar to Apollo— yes, that's all—made with artificial soil, so that the Athenian cobblers might determine the fate of Demosthenes.

MARTET: And Crete?

CLEMENCEAU: Crete! Now and then, in the night, when I'm unable to sleep, I see Phaistos again. It's something that's fixed in my memory.

Ah, Greece, Martet. You must travel by way of Greece to get anywhere you're going. I believe that humanity reached its highest point there, easily, joyously. At Rheims, amongst all those Gothic sculptures, which are very fine and which one can't help admiring, there are two statues—copies of Roman things, probably, badly conceived, badly executed. Well, when you notice the folds of the draperies, which fall in that rhythm which the Romans stole from the Greeks, you're numbed, you can't see anything else—nothing but those two statues which are there as if in exile.

There's nothing beyond Aeschylus, nothing beyond Plato, nothing beyond Socrates. It all ended in bloodshed and domesticity. Well, perhaps it's the history of all peoples, in all times. Baber, my friend Baber, the conqueror of Persia, used to have a pile of heads brought to him every morning, and when the pile was a little smaller than usual, he would say, "It's pretty small, this pile. My men are getting slack." Nevertheless, it was the same Baber who said, "There are sighs which arouse the world to action." Men are like that. And one may even wonder if all that blood and all that brutality were not necessary for the making of an Aeschylus and the building of an Erechtheion. Gentle and kindly men are pleasant to have about, but in general they don't create masterpieces. Soak yourself in Greece, Martet. It's something that's sustained me in trouble. When I was weary of all the imbecilities and the futilities of which politics is composed, I turned my spirit toward Greece. Others went fishing. To each his own way.

1st June 1928

(Albert shows Martet into the study. He waits for some time, perhaps ten minutes, amusing himself as best he can. He scans the books on the shelves—works on sociology, geography, philosophy. There are photographs on the table, of pictures by Monet—"Vétheuil," the "Two Women with the Parasol," etc. Finally Clemenceau enters.)

CLEMENCEAU: Ah, Monsieur Martet. Forgive me for having kept you waiting. I was engaged in making up my accounts with my valet. Do you realize something terrible is happening—the price of everything is double?

MARTET: I know. I know what I'm paying in rent.

CLEMENCEAU: But listen! What's one to do? There's no longer any way to . . .

MARTET: I think the best thing is to get one's share of it.

CLEMENCEAU: That's all very well. Nevertheless, we must pay. And pay and pay. There are limits. Isn't anything being done to meet the situation? I thought that commissions had been appointed to fight the high cost of living. Aren't you and everybody else tired of being throttled?

MARTET: But what would you suggest doing about it?

CLEMENCEAU: Take a dozen individuals and hang them.

MARTET: Yes, if that would lower the price of cauliflower . . .

CLEMENCEAU: Not a doubt of it. In twenty-four hours. But instead of doing that, people—I know what they do; they see that the cost of living is double, so they double their incomes. By stealing. They turn into thieves.

MARTET: I haven't even that resource . . .

CLEMENCEAU: Then you're beyond forgiveness. In my time nothing more was necessary than to go out into the streets. *(He sits down.)* Sit down, Martet. *(Martet sits down and looks at him. He looks at Martet.)* I'm bored.

MARTET: Oh! Why?

CLEMENCEAU: I'm coughing. For two days I've been coughing like a horse. I'm tired. I've had enough of it. All this going back and forth—I've seen him doing it for eighty years. It isn't right. Poincaré—is there anything that looks more like Poincaré than Poincaré? (*He yawns. After an interval.*) By the way, you must give me back the memorandum I wrote on my relations with Foch. I must look it over. I wrote it quickly, and there are probably some things to change.

MARTET: I'll bring it back to you. I haven't read it yet. I'm sorting out your papers on the Commune.

CLEMENCEAU: Are you finding anything in them?

MARTET: Some very interesting things.

CLEMENCEAU: What madness! It is one of the maddest madnesses in all history. No one even knew what the Commune was about. Those people killed, burned, got themselves killed, at times magnificently, but they never knew why! Did you go away for Whitsun?

MARTET: Yes, I went as far as the mouth of the Loire. I discovered a country called la Brière, which is heavenly. Marshes extending as far as you can see, with frogs.

CLEMENCEAU: Don't know it. I went to Giverney the other day.

MARTET: Are you working on your book on Monet?

CLEMENCEAU: I'm doing odd bits. You know, about Monet—I think that I can say quite a good deal about him. For forty years I had him at the other end of a wire. Monet took life as a struggle. I remember seeing him one day in his poppy field, with four canvases set up in front of him. He was going from one to the other, according to the position of the sun. Well, that's it, isn't it? What's fine in Monet is that seriousness, that intensity. There are two self-portraits of Monet—the one I gave to the Louvre and the one that was at Giverney. In the latter he shows his quality—a look that pierces you; there's something cruel, savage about it. He is looking at his ricks. That was Monet; he threw himself into everything like a man possessed.

I don't like everything Monet did. Some of his things are mediocre—his "Cathedrals of Rouen." They're anything you like but stone.*

MARTET: He didn't want to reconstruct them architecturally. He only tried to reproduce the play of light and shade.

CLEMENCEAU: Nevertheless, they're bad. His impressions of Venice are bad. The light is depressing. I've seen Venice and I know what she is.

---

* There was a time, however, when Clemenceau loved Monet's Cathedrals. "I see rising," he says somewhere, "the monolith in its powerful unity, in its supreme authority—a flower in stone, vibrant, inundated with light . . ."

I know that sun and that water—his are silly. But you still have his hay-fields—which are prodigious. And his water-lilies. One should remove one's hat before those water-lilies.

MARTET: Don't you find it odd that he was limited in that way and never tried to pierce through to the soul?

CLEMENCEAU: To the what?

MARTET: The soul. He never attempted to portray human expressions . . .

CLEMENCEAU: Don't take the soul too seriously, Martet. Do you really believe that men have souls? Do you believe that there is more of a soul in Gustave Hervé * than in a blade of grass? No, Martet, he didn't seek that—although in his two portraits, on that day, or rather on those two days, he did penetrate to the soul. But, as you say, he was limited. Do you hold it against him? Not I. It is one of the forms of courage and power. Your first duty is to know yourself, and to limit your field of operations. He selected light—it wasn't a bad choice.

MARTET: What did you go to Giverney for on Sunday?

CLEMENCEAU: I wanted to see the studies he made when he was living on the banks of the stream. They are very odd. They've nothing to do with any of the rest. He only wanted his effect. They're rough, wild, often melancholy. I was given two or three hundred letters, all those written to Monet by Mirbeau, Renoir, and myself. I'm engaged in looking through them now. Mirbeau was—yes, he was a man all the same. There was, naturally, a good deal of pose about him. He was a gentleman who adopted an air and stuck to it through thick and thin. One feels that he would have referred in the same terms to a bowl of strawberries and cream or the murder of an entire family. But after all, his inspiration can only be praised. Do you like Mirbeau?

MARTET: Yes, I consider him one of our greatest writers.

CLEMENCEAU: I'm of the same opinion. An odd fellow, rather tiresome, but with a splendid pen. His "628–E8" is a marvellous stunt. And his breeding, his courage, his generosity! Renoir's letters are also interesting. I don't like Renoir; Monet used to reproach me for it.

MARTET: Renoir and Monet have many points of contact.

CLEMENCEAU: Not in their work.

MARTET: No, but in spirit.

CLEMENCEAU: You know, I can't forgive him for having made woman a sort of monster. It's enough to disgust you with love forever after.

MARTET: Are you in favor of love, sir?

CLEMENCEAU: Aren't you? Or do you prefer spontaneous generation? Have

---

* A journalist who, after having spoken of "erecting the flag on a dung-hill," became a passionate patriot.

you seen the buttocks he gives those poor wretches? It oughtn't to be allowed. Where did he ever see buttocks like that? I've travelled quite a bit, but I've never run into them. But I realize—if it gives you any pleasure—that he was somebody. He sought.

MARTET: And your letters to Monet?

CLEMENCEAU: I don't know what they contain. Friendship and scolding, probably. That's what my life's been made up of. I can't like anyone without scolding him. I've always had great respect for Monet. In the first place, we lived on two different planes—we never collided, never fought. There was never any jealousy or rivalry between us. In the second place, he painted exactly as I should like to have done had I been a painter—stubborn, obstinate painting.* It's stupid to say that genius is merely long-drawn-out patience. Because in the first place patience itself doesn't mean anything—it requires more than patience to get what you want—you must go straight for it. And secondly, there is one kind of genius, perhaps the best and most precious, into which not a grain of patience enters. But there is another kind which is due to effort, a fierce application, and to that, for my part, I pay respect.

MARTET: What is going to happen to the Giverney canvases?

CLEMENCEAU: He left everything to his son Michel.

MARTET: And his daughter-in-law, his son Jean's wife?

CLEMENCEAU: Well, he left her without a penny.

MARTET: Impossible.

CLEMENCEAU: Yes, it's true. I've told you before, Monet was afraid. He was afraid of physical pain, afraid of death. The operation I wanted him to have would have allowed him to use his sight to the end. He funked it. His courage left him at the thought of death—he didn't want to think about it. So he died without doing anything for his daughter-in-law.

MARTET: Extraordinary. And she was so exceedingly good to him.

CLEMENCEAU: She was admirable, in every way. She took care of him, pampered him. She watched over him as if he had been her child. She helped him prepare his canvases; she took care of his investments.

MARTET: I know.

CLEMENCEAU: Well, there you are! He leaves everything to Michel's dis-

---

* Clemenceau once wrote in reference to the quays of the Seine: "The panting crane, with the grating sound of iron, describes a large circle in the air. The great hampers dip suddenly and pour out the ocher-colored sand or tawny slag in a sparkling golden shower. Huge slabs of Burgundy stone rear themselves into white walls, wooden planks are piled up in a homely sort of building construction, and the rose or amber of the pale bricks brighten the river with a caress of colors . . . That's a Monet!"

cretion, which means that I shall have the business on my hands. I said to Michel, "What are you going to do for her? Obviously you must repair your father's oversight." Michel replied, "Well, yes, I'm going to fix all that up." I said, "It isn't a question of fixing it up in the more or less distant future; you must do it right away!" I know that he'll do it. He's not a bad sort and his needs aren't great. He's having a little house built for himself on the banks of the Eure. He's living there. On behalf of the Louvre I said to him, "You ought to set aside the 'Two Women with the Parasol' for the Louvre." He has done so. I also said to him, "You ought to give a canvas to the architect who fitted up the Orangery—he didn't overcharge for it." He did that too. He really does what he ought. Unfortunately there he is, in his car, running about the country—he'll break his neck one of these days and the little sister-in-law will be left without a penny. So there you are. That's how I'm diverting myself for the moment. A man's life is interesting primarily when he has failed—I well know. For it's a sign that he tried to surpass himself. Monet succeeded in his. He found fame, money. Nevertheless, I shall enjoy seeing him again in these letters, reconstructing him, finding an idea where he probably had only an instinct. I shall take the letters away with me to the Vendée. I shan't be bored with them. I prefer that past to your present. Have you read about the Colmar trial?" *

MARTET: Yes.

CLEMENCEAU: What do you think about it?

MARTET: It's very sad.

CLEMENCEAU: That Berthou † carried in triumph by the priests! There's proof for you of the disorientation of everything! And Fachot ‡ insulted by a band of hoodlums who threw stones at him. And that lawyer from Quimper who declared, "France must not be judged by the abominable verdict which has just been rendered." What do you expect to do after that? I have received a letter from a former deputy from that region who says, "When you were young I followed and supported you. During the war I disagreed with you. In memory of your youth and the ideas which you formerly upheld, what do you intend to do by way of protest against the degrading spectacle at Colmar?" That shows you where we are.

MARTET: What's the solution?

---

* The autonomists' trial of Colmar, Alsace. The verdict was returned on the 24th May, 1928.
† Communist deputy, lawyer for the autonomists.
‡ The Public Prosecutor. Some time later he was shot by a fanatic and wounded.

CLEMENCEAU: For myself I see only one—to die. I no longer care to hear those things discussed. France frightens me. People laugh, amuse themselves, understand nothing, or if they do understand, they don't care a hang. The future no longer counts. Where shall we find ourselves one of these days, when we wake up? As for myself, I shall be amongst the dead. I don't ask anything more.

MARTET: When do you leave for the Vendée?

CLEMENCEAU: At the beginning of July. If my book on Monet is good, I shall publish it; if it's bad, I'll toss it into the fire. Have you seen those photographs over there? I don't know where they come from; they're interesting, although they're in black and white. You feel the seeking after color—the pencil trying to drag it out . . . There's a struggle going on there. He has the secret of the convexity of the earth—have you noticed? You feel that it goes on beyond the line of the horizon. the sky loses itself, it doesn't stop.

I'm going to an exhibition of Bourdelle's in the Rue de la Boéthie. Do you know Bourdelle?

MARTET: I know his work.

CLEMENCEAU: What do you think of it?

MARTET: Good Lord!

CLEMENCEAU: That's exactly my opinion. He does Greek sculpture according to the German. He does Gothic, Peruvian, Mycenian. Only there's one thing that bores me about him—he never does anything Bourdellian.

MARTET: Perhaps because there has been a Peru, a Mycene . . .

CLEMENCEAU: And there's never been a Bourdelle? It's quite possible.

In any case he has queer flights of fancy. Do you know what he nearly did for my *Démosthène?* The publisher had ordered some bas-reliefs, from which engravings were to be made. Whereupon my Bourdelle had the idea of doing my portrait in the guise of Demosthenes, dressed in a toga, passing the dead in review in the Champs-Elysées. Do you get the picture?

MARTET: It's a pretty idea, as they say.

CLEMENCEAU: Can you see me in the Champs-Elysées, holding a review of Poincaré, Jules Ferry, Franklin-Bouillon, François Albert? I said to the publisher, "Oh, no, I won't have that." Bourdelle executed another most extraordinary thing. It represents Xerxes on horseback, turning his mount round and saying, "Don't let's go any further. The ground is dangerous." The trouble is (I'll show you the thing presently) that Xerxes is on his horse and his feet are dragging along the ground. Personally I have never seen that happen. When I was young I now and then had occasion to ride a horse, and I always took care to select one tall enough so that my feet wouldn't drag in the mud.

MARTET: Did Xerxes travel on horseback, then? I always imagined him carried in a litter.

CLEMENCEAU: No, he must have been on horseback. Don't you remember how in Herodotus they decided to take for their king the one whose horse neighed the first? It's an idea like another—as good as a plebiscite, at any rate. And it was Darius's mare who emitted the first neigh. Bourdelle is a fantasist. He models his clay in such a way that it gives, at first sight, the impression of power, and at bottom . . . you feel what he'd like to do, what he's seeking, trying to do and can't do. But now and then he pulls it off. He performs a stroke of genius, with an air of swank—and it's serious craftsmanship. However, since I couldn't have Phidias they tossed me Bourdelle.

MARTET: There aren't many French sculptors.

CLEMENCEAU: In return there aren't any foreign sculptors at all. Foreigners can carve cherry-stones or mountains, but as sculpture it simply doesn't exist. They do much better to leave the poor stone in peace or make roads of it. Amongst us, at one time or another, there have been sculptors who knew how to turn out an occasional good piece. There was Houdon—there's going to be a Houdon exhibition. I shall go to see that. There was Rude . . .

MARTET: And Carpeaux.

CLEMENCEAU: He's a little too Second Empire. His grace is languid, a bit stupid. He gave lightness to stone, but it's a question whether stone was made to be light. I don't like Rodin.

MARTET: Nevertheless . . .

CLEMENCEAU: Well, yes, I grant that you must say "nevertheless"—perhaps it's because I knew the man. He was stupid, vain, and cared too much about money. That's quite a bit against him, isn't it? When I returned from South America with the order for a bust I went to see Rodin, who said to me, "They must be made to pay as dearly as possible." It was his first thought.

MARTET: There is the "St. John the Baptist"—and the "Man Walking," tense, nervous . . .

CLEMENCEAU: Yes, yes—there is also the "Balzac."

MARTET: Well, don't you like the "Balzac," sir? It's an admirable effort. It has probably nothing to do with the real Balzac . . .

CLEMENCEAU: Probably—and it's ridiculous.

MARTET: But those two great eye-sockets—the carriage of the body—there's something rather magnificent in it.

CLEMENCEAU: Yes, yes . . .

MARTET: When you compare the "Balzac" of Rodin with the "Balzac" of the Boulevard Haussmann . . .

CLEMENCEAU: The man sitting in his dressing-gown? What a dreadful thing it is!

MARTET: Have you seen Cogné again?

CLEMENCEAU: Cogné? Oh, yes—he came to see me the other day and photographed me again. He had forgotten to light his apparatus.

(*Enter Michel Clemenceau—tall, thin, dressed in gray, his temples delicately silvered and his bearing young. He bears an extraordinary resemblance to his father—a gentler, smiling version.*)

MICHEL CLEMENCEAU: How do you do, Father?

CLEMENCEAU: Oh, there you are!

MICHEL CLEMENCEAU: I've just come from Holland. I went to convey your good wishes to the Burgomaster Six.

CLEMENCEAU: He's not very remarkable, is he?

MICHEL CLEMENCEAU: Remarkable! And the Draper's Guild! That's beyond words, too. And this.

(*"He indicates a yellowing photograph on the mantelpiece: five middle-class women in small white head-dresses, their lips pinched and their eyes dull or fierce. They are the Committee of an almshouse, captured, appraised, and fixed on canvas by Rembrandt. What faces!"*
—Martet)

CLEMENCEAU: What frightful faces! Philanthropy in all its horror!

MICHEL CLEMENCEAU: I like the "Night Watch" even less. There's an effect of light and shade . . .

CLEMENCEAU: Yes. It's easier. But the man putting on his gloves! He did that in two hours.

MICHEL CLEMENCEAU: On my way back to Paris I went to see my granddaughter.

MARTET: Your granddaughter? Are you really a grandfather?

MICHEL CLEMENCEAU: Yes, George has a daughter.

CLEMENCEAU: She's a funny little thing. (*He gets up.*) Come along and see Xerxes.

(*"They pass into the bedroom. Clemenceau takes Bourdelle's bas-relief from a drawer and shows it to the others. It is a Xerxes with huge arms and legs, gesticulating violently. Bourdelle was embarrassed by the necessity of getting horse and man into so small a frame. He seems to have folded them up like lobsters being packed for shipment in the bottom of a basket. In addition Xerxes has the air of pointing out the way to his horse by saying to him, 'Come along. This way.' "*—Martet)

CLEMENCEAU: What do you think of it?

MARTET: ? ? ?

CLEMENCEAU: Hold on—in return look this over for me. (*He shows Martet the catalogue of Bourdelle's exhibition. On the cover is a photograph of Bourdelle—spectacles behind which thoughts are soaring; hair through which the breath of inspiration is blowing.*) He missed his Xerxes, perhaps, but he succeeded with his Bourdelle, eh, what? (*Martet notices the cast of the Samos stele fastened on the wall.*) You're looking at that? You can look at it all your life without getting tired of it. When you are in Athens don't forget to stop in front of it; stop a bit also before the woman who's tying up her sandal. There's a movement of her shoulders . . . Ah, Martet, the man who did that! (*Showing Martet out.*) So I ought to write Monet? He's a man I loved . . .

H. G. Wells-Joseph Stalin

LIBERALISM VERSUS MARXISM.

*It seems to me that I am more to the
left than you, Mr. Stalin.*

"COME back and see us in ten years," Lenin had said to H. G. Wells at
the end of their conversation in the Kremlin in 1920. And now
fourteen years later Wells was back in the Kremlin. His host was no longer
the overworked and ailing founder of the Soviet State, but the man who
had succeeded him to power, Joseph Stalin. On July 23, 1934, Liberalism
and Marxism once more confronted each other across a table in the Kremlin study. On one side sat a staunch British apostle of the sane and scientific way of life, the advocate of progressive reform. Facing him was the
head of the first Workers' State in history, a hardened Marxist in theory
and practice. One preached all reasonable change short of revolution; the
other was a confirmed believer in the need for more drastic remedies and
in the role of the proletariat to remove all remaining obstacles in the path
to world betterment.

Fourteen years before, Wells had visited Moscow to interview the
Nicolai Lenin who was widely regarded as the greatest Marxist teacher
and philosopher after Karl Marx. The intense and animated little man
had then impressed Wells deeply. In Lenin he had found a man of lucid
vision and a dominant personality. In rendering final judgment he had
said: "If we are going to talk at all of greatness among our species, then I
must admit that Lenin at least was a very great man." On his first visit
Wells had found Moscow shabby, shattered, and apprehensive, but "un-
tidily and hopefully renascent." A new Moscow greeted him in 1934, a
city risen from the ruins and branching out in all directions. Yet, significantly, he remarked that one might observe such vigorous expansion "in
the most individualistic of cities."

And in the new incumbent of the Kremlin, Wells now faced a man who
had long aroused his suspicion and prejudice. Quite candidly he later
revealed that a picture had formed in his mind of a "very reserved and
self-centered fanatic, a despot without vices, a jealous monopolizer of
power"—worst suspicion of all, perhaps, of "a Georgian highlander whose
spirit had never completely emerged from its native mountain glen." Such

were Wells' own words in the book he subsequently wrote about himself. And now, as the conversation began on that afternoon of July 23, 1934, he found himself experiencing a shock of surprise. Instead of reserve and fanaticism, he observed a frank directness and in place of the "dour high-lander" he was prepared to confront, he found "an exceptionally unsubtle Georgian."

Of course, the liberal in Wells soon recoiled at what he sensed was iron dogma in Stalin's unyielding outlook. Whereas in Lenin he had found a subtle adaptability, especially in the use of Marxist terminology, in Stalin he felt a doctrinaire fixity of view, an inflexible literalness of Marxist phrase. In Stalin, moreover, Wells missed the "quick uptake" of Franklin Delano Roosevelt, whom he had interviewed in the White House before setting out for Russia. Throughout the talk Wells and Stalin showed a keen interest in one another, and the scheduled forty-minute audience was prolonged on Stalin's own insistence.

Fresh from a close study of the then infant New Deal, Wells was posi-tive that Stalin would agree to a basic similarity in the current programs of the two countries. Yet, by his own written admission later, the one fact that impressed him most in the whole discussion was Stalin's refusal "to see any sort of parallelism in the processes and methods and aims of Wash-ington and Moscow." To Wells in 1934 Franklin Delano Roosevelt and Joseph Stalin between them pointed to the human future "as no other two men could do." Hence the readiness of this restless oracle of the shape of things to come to cross ideological swords with the ruling brain of the Kremlin.

The conversation lasted almost three hours, continuing from 4 p.m. to 6:50 p.m. The talk was naturally bilingual, since Wells spoke no Russian and Stalin spoke no English nor any other language in which the late British writer might be at his ease. Acting as combined interpreter and stenographer was the gifted young linguist Constantine Oumansky, later to become Soviet Ambassador to the United States and subsequently to crash to his death in a plane while serving as envoy to Mexico. At the time of the interview Oumansky was head of the Press Bureau of the Com-missariat of Foreign Affairs. We owe the preservation of this conversation to his faithfully transcribed record, a record, incidentally, later approved by Wells himself.

In taking the discussion down, Oumansky made rapid notes in Russian of what Wells and Stalin said to one another. He would read out Wells' remarks to Stalin in facile Russian and just as readily read Stalin's back to Wells in English. Then, according to Wells, he would sit "alert-eyed over his glasses" waiting for the next statement. In all fairness to Wells,

it should be stated that though he fully sanctioned the text as printed be-
low, he did feel that some of his phraseology was inevitably lost in the
two-way process of translation.

WELLS: I am very much obliged to you, Mr. Stalin, for agreeing to see me.
I was in the United States recently. I had a long conversation with
President Roosevelt and tried to ascertain what his leading ideas were.
Now I have come to you to ask you what you are doing to change the
world. . . .

STALIN: Not so very much. . . .

WELLS: I wander around the world as a common man and, as a common
man, observe what is going on around me.

STALIN: Important public men like yourself are not "common men." Of
course, history alone can show how important this or that public man
has been; at all events you do not look at the world as a "common
man."

WELLS: I am not pretending humility. What I mean is that I try to see
the world through the eyes of the common man, and not as a party
politician or a responsible administrator. My visit to the United States
excited my mind. The old financial world is collapsing; the economic
life of the country is being reorganized on new lines. Lenin said: "We
must learn to do business," learn this from the capitalists. Today the
capitalists have to learn from you, to grasp the spirit of socialism. It
seems to me that what is taking place in the United States is a profound reorganization, the creation of planned, that is, socialist, economy. You and Roosevelt begin from two different starting points. But
is there not a relation in ideas, a kinship of ideas, between Washington
and Moscow? In Washington I was struck by the same thing I see
going on here; they are building offices, they are creating a number of
new state regulation bodies, they are organizing a long-needed Civil
Service. Their need, like yours, is directive ability.

STALIN: The United States is pursuing a different aim from that which
we are pursuing in the U.S.S.R. The aim which the Americans are
pursuing arose out of the economic troubles, out of the economic
crisis. The Americans want to rid themselves of the crisis on the basis
of private capitalist activity without changing the economic basis.
They are trying to reduce to a minimum the ruin, the losses caused
by the existing economic system. Here, however, as you know, in place
of the old destroyed economic basis an entirely different, a new eco-

nomic basis has been created. Even if the Americans you mention partly achieve their aim, i.e., reduce these losses to a minimum, they will not destroy the roots of the anarchy which is inherent in the existing capitalist system. They are preserving the economic system which must inevitably lead, and cannot but lead, to anarchy in production. Thus, at best, it will be a matter, not of the reorganization of society, not of abolishing the old social system which gives rise to anarchy and crises, but of restricting certain of its bad features, restricting certain of its excesses. Subjectively, perhaps, these Americans think they are reorganizing society; objectively, however, they are preserving the present basis of society. That is why, objectively, there will be no reorganization of society.

Nor will there be planned economy. What is planned economy? What are some of its attributes? Planned economy tries to abolish unemployment. Let us suppose it is possible, while preserving the capitalist system, to reduce unemployment to a certain minimum. But surely, no capitalist would ever agree to the complete abolition of unemployment, to the abolition of the reserve army of unemployed, the purpose of which is to bring pressure on the labor market, to insure a supply of cheap labor. Here you have one of the rents in the "planned economy" of bourgeois society. Furthermore, planned economy presupposes increased output in those branches of industry which produce goods that the masses of the people need particularly. But you know that the expansion of production under capitalism takes place for entirely different motives, that capital flows into those branches of economy in which the rate of profit is highest. You will never compel a capitalist to incur loss to himself and agree to a lower rate of profit for the sake of satisfying the needs of the people. Without getting rid of the capitalists, without abolishing the principle of private property in the means of production, it is impossible to create planned economy.

WELLS: I agree with much of what you have said. But I would like to stress the point that if a country as a whole adopts the principle of planned economy, if the government, gradually, step by step, begins consistently to apply this principle, the financial oligarchy will at last be abolished and socialism, in the Anglo-Saxon meaning of the word, will be brought about. The effect of the ideas of Roosevelt's "New Deal" is most powerful, and in my opinion they are socialist ideas. It seems to me that instead of stressing the antagonism between the two worlds, we should, in the present circumstances, strive to establish a common tongue for all the constructive forces.

STALIN: In speaking of the impossibility of realizing the principles of planned economy while preserving the economic basis of capitalism, I do not in the least desire to belittle the outstanding personal qualities of Roosevelt, his initiative, courage and determination. Undoubtedly Roosevelt stands out as one of the strongest figures among all the captains of the contemporary capitalist world. That is why I would like once again to emphasize the point that my conviction that planned economy is impossible under the conditions of capitalism does not mean that I have any doubts about the personal abilities, talent and courage of President Roosevelt. But if the circumstances are unfavorable, the most talented captain cannot reach the goal you refer to. Theoretically, of course, the possibility of marching gradually, step by step, under the conditions of capitalism, toward the goal which you call socialism in the Anglo-Saxon meaning of the word, is not precluded. But what will this "socialism" be? At best, bridling to some extent the most unbridled of individual representatives of capitalist profit, some increase in the application of the principle of regulation in national economy. That is all very well. But as soon as Roosevelt, or any other captain in the contemporary bourgeois world, proceeds to undertake something serious against the foundation of capitalism, he will inevitably suffer utter defeat. The banks, the industries, the large enterprises, the large farms are not in Roosevelt's hands. All these are private property. The railroads, the mercantile fleet, all these belong to private owners. And finally, the army of skilled workers, the engineers, the technicians, these too are not at Roosevelt's command, they are at the command of the private owners; they all work for the private owners. We must not forget the functions of the State in the bourgeois world. The State is an institution that organizes the defense of the country, organizes the maintenance of "order"; it is an apparatus for collecting taxes. The capitalist State does not deal much with economy in the strict sense of the word; the latter is not in the hands of the State. On the contrary, the State is in the hands of capitalist economy. That is why I fear that, in spite of all his energy and abilities, Roosevelt will not achieve the goal you mention, if indeed that is his goal. Perhaps in the course of several generations it will be possible to approach this goal somewhat; but I personally think that even this is not very probable.

WELLS: Perhaps, I believe more strongly in the economic interpretation of politics than you do. Huge forces driving toward better organization, for the better functioning of the community, that is, for socialism, have been brought into action by invention and modern science. Organization, and the regulation of individual action, have become mechanical necessities, irrespective of social theories. If we begin with the State control of the banks and then follow with the control of transport, of the heavy industries, of industry in general, of commerce, etc., such an all-embracing control will be equivalent to the State ownership of all branches of national economy. This will be the process of socialization. Socialism and individualism are not opposites like black and white. There are many intermediate stages between them. There is individualism that borders on brigandage, and there is discipline and organization that are the equivalent of socialism. The introduction of planned economy depends, to a large degree, upon the organizers of economy, upon the skilled technical intelligentsia, who, step by step, can be converted to the socialist principles of organization. And this is the most important thing. Because organization comes before socialism. It is the more important fact. Without organization the socialist idea is a mere idea.

STALIN: There is no, nor should there be, irreconcilable contrast between the individual and the collective, between the interests of the individual person and the interests of the collective. There should be no such contrast, because collectivism, socialism, does not deny, but combines individual interests with the interests of the collective. Socialism cannot abstract itself from individual interests. Socialist society alone can most fully satisfy these personal interests. More than that; socialist society alone can firmly safeguard the interests of the individual. In this sense there is no irreconcilable contrast between "individualism" and socialism. But can we deny the contrast between classes, between the propertied class, the capitalist class, and the toiling class, the proletarian class? On the one hand we have the propertied class which owns the banks, the factories, the mines, transport, the plantations in colonies. These people see nothing but their own interests, their striving after profits. They do not submit to the will of the collective; they strive to subordinate every collective to their will. On the other hand we have the class of the poor, the exploited class, which owns neither factories nor works, nor banks, which is compelled to live by selling its labor power to the capitalists and which lacks the opportunity to satisfy its most elementary requirements. How can such opposite interests and strivings be reconciled? As far as I know, Roosevelt has not succeeded in finding the path of conciliation between these interests. And it is impossible, as experience has shown. Incidentally, you know the situation in the United States better than I do as I have never been there and I watch American affairs mainly from literature. But I have some experience in fighting for socialism, and this experience tells me that if Roosevelt makes a real attempt to satisfy the interests of the proletarian class at the expense of the capitalist class, the latter will put another president in his place. The capitalists will say: Presidents come and presidents go, but we go on forever; if this or that president does not protect our interests, we shall find another. What can the president oppose to the will of the capitalist class?

WELLS: I object to this simplified classification of mankind into poor and rich. Of course there is a category of people which strives only for profit. But are not these people regarded as nuisances in the West just as much as here? Are there not plenty of people in the West for whom profit is not an end, who own a certain amount of wealth, who want to invest and obtain a profit from this investment, but who do not regard this as the main object? They regard investment as an inconvenient necessity. Are there not plenty of capable and devoted engineers, organizers of economy, whose activities are stimulated by something other than profit? In my opinion there is a numerous class of capable people who admit that the present system is unsatisfactory and who are destined to play a great role in future socialist society. During the past few years I have been much engaged in and have thought of the need for conducting propaganda in favor of socialism and cosmopolitanism among wide circles of engineers, airmen, military-technical people, etc. It is useless approaching these circles with two-track class-war propaganda. These people understand the condition of the world. They understand that it is a bloody muddle, but they regard your simple class-war antagonism as nonsense.

STALIN: You object to the simplified classification of mankind into rich and poor. Of course there is a middle stratum, there is the technical intelligentsia that you have mentioned and among which there are very good and very honest people. Among them there are also dishonest and wicked people, there are all sorts of people among them. But first of all mankind is divided into rich and poor, into property owners and exploited; and to abstract oneself from this fundamental division and from the antagonism between poor and rich means abstracting oneself from the fundamental fact. I do not deny the existence of intermediate, middle strata, which either take the side of one or other of these two conflicting classes, or else take up a neutral or semi-neutral position in this struggle. But, I repeat, to abstract oneself from this fundamental division in society and from the fundamental struggle between the two main classes means ignoring facts. This struggle is going on and will continue. The outcome of the struggle will be determined by the proletarian class, the working class.

WELLS: But are there not many people who are not poor, but who work and work productively?

STALIN: Of course, there are small landowners, artisans, small traders, but it is not these people who decide the fate of a country, but the toiling masses, who produce all the things society requires.

WELLS: But there are very different kinds of capitalists. There are capitalists who only think about profit, about getting rich, but there are also those who are prepared to make sacrifices. Take old Morgan, for example. He only thought about profit; he was a parasite on society, simply, he merely accumulated wealth. But take Rockefeller. He is a brilliant organizer; he has set an example of how to organize the delivery of oil that is worthy of emulation. Or take Ford. Of course Ford is selfish. But is he not a passionate organizer of rationalized production from whom you take lessons? I would like to emphasize the fact that recently an important change in opinion toward the U.S.S.R. has taken place in English-speaking countries. The reason for this, first of all, is the position of Japan and the events in Germany. But there are other reasons besides those arising from international politics. There is a more profound reason, namely, the recognition by many people of the fact that the system based on private profit is breaking down. Under these circumstances, it seems to me, we must not bring to the forefront the antagonism between the two worlds, but should strive to combine all the constructive movements, all the constructive forces in one line as much as possible. It seems to me that I am more to the Left than you, Mr. Stalin; I think the old system is nearer to its end than you think.

STALIN: In speaking of the capitalists who strive only for profit, only to get rich, I do not want to say that these are the most worthless people, capable of nothing else. Many of them undoubtedly possess great organizing talent, which I do not dream of denying. We Soviet people learn a great deal from the capitalists. And Morgan, whom you characterize so unfavorably, was undoubtedly a good, capable organizer. But if you mean people who are prepared to reconstruct the world, of course, you will not be able to find them in the ranks of those who faithfully serve the cause of profit. We and they stand at opposite poles. You mentioned Ford. Of course, he is a capable organizer of production. But don't you know his attitude toward the working class? Don't you know how many workers he throws on the street? The capitalist is riveted to profit; and no power on earth can tear him away from it. Capitalism will be abolished not by "organizers" of production, not by the technical intelligentsia, but by the working class, because the aforementioned strata do not play an independent role. The engineer, the organizer of production, does not work as he would like to, but as he is ordered, in such a way as to serve the interests of his employers. There are exceptions of course; there are people in this stratum who have awakened from the intoxication of capitalism. The technical intelligentsia can, under certain conditions, perform miracles and greatly benefit mankind. But it can also cause great harm. We Soviet people have not a little experience of the technical intelligentsia. After the October Revolution, a certain section of the technical intelligentsia refused to take part in the work of constructing the new society; they opposed this work of construction and sabotaged it. We did all we possibly could to bring the technical intelligentsia into this work of construction; we tried this way and that. Not a little time passed before our technical intelligentsia agreed actively to assist the new system. Today the best section of the technical intelligentsia are in the front ranks of the builders of socialist society. Having this experience, we are far from underestimating the good and the bad sides of the technical intelligentsia and we know that on the one hand it can do harm, and on the other hand, it can perform "miracles." Of course, things would be different if it were possible, at one stroke, spiritually to tear the technical intelligentsia away from the capitalist world. But that is utopia. Are there many of the technical intelligentsia who would dare break away from the bourgeois world and set to work to reconstruct society? Do you think there are many people of this kind, say, in England or in France? No, there are few who would be willing to break away from their employers and begin reconstructing the world.

Besides, can we lose the sight of the fact that in order to transform the world it is necessary to have *political power?* It seems to me, Mr. Wells, that you greatly underestimate the question of political power, that it entirely drops out of your conception. What can those, even with the best intentions in the world, do if they are unable to raise the question of seizing power, and do not possess power? At best they can help the class which takes power, but they cannot change the world themselves. This can only be done by a great class which will take the place of the capitalist class and become the sovereign master as the latter was before. This class is the working class. Of course, the assistance of the technical intelligentsia must be accepted; and the latter, in turn, must be assisted. But it must not be thought that the technical intelligentsia can play an independent historical role. The transformation of the world is a great, complicated and painful process. For this great task a great class is required. *Big* ships go on long voyages.

WELLS: Yes, but for long voyages a captain and a navigator are required.

STALIN: That is true; but what is first required for a long voyage is a big ship. What is a navigator without a ship? An idle man.

WELLS: The big ship is humanity, not a class.

STALIN: You, Mr. Wells, evidently start out with the assumption that all men are good. I, however, do not forget that there are many wicked men. I do not believe in the goodness of the bourgeoisie.

WELLS: I remember the situation with regard to the technical intelligentsia several decades ago. At that time the technical intelligentsia was numerically small, but there was much to do and every engineer, technician and intellectual found his opportunity. That is why the technical intelligentsia was the least revolutionary class. Now, however, there is a superabundance of technical intellectuals, and their mentality has changed very sharply. The skilled man, who would formerly never listen to revolutionary talk, is now greatly interested in it. Recently I was dining with the Royal Society, our great English scientific society. The President's speech was a speech for social planning and scientific control. Thirty years ago, they would not have listened to what I say to them now. Today, the man at the head of the Royal Society holds revolutionary views and insists on the scientific reorganization of human society. Mentality changes. Your class-war propaganda has not kept pace with these facts.

STALIN: Yes, I know this, and this is to be explained by the fact that capitalist society is now in a *cul de sac*. The capitalists are seeking, but cannot find, a way out of this *cul de sac* that would be compatible with the dignity of this class, compatible with the interests of this class. They could, to some extent, crawl out of the crisis on their hands and knees, but they cannot find an exit that would enable them to walk out of it with head raised high, a way out that would not fundamentally disturb the interests of capitalism. This, of course, is realized by wide circles of the technical intelligentsia. A large section of it is beginning to realize the community of its interests with those of the class which is capable of pointing the way out of the *cul de sac*.

WELLS: You of all people know something about revolutions, Mr. Stalin, from the practical side. Do the masses ever rise? Is it not an established truth that all revolutions are made by a minority?

STALIN: To bring about a revolution a leading revolutionary minority is required; but the most talented, devoted and energetic minority would be helpless if it did not rely upon the at least passive support of millions.

WELLS: At least passive? Perhaps subconscious?

STALIN: Partly also the semi-instinctive and semiconscious, but without the support of millions, the best minority is impotent.

WELLS: I watch communist propaganda in the West and it seems to me that in modern conditions this propaganda sounds very old-fashioned, because it is insurrectionary propaganda. Propaganda in favor of the violent overthrow of the social system was all very well when it was directed against tyranny. But under modern conditions, when the system is collapsing anyhow, stress should be laid on efficiency, on competence, on productiveness, and not on insurrection. It seems to me that the insurrectionary note is obsolete. The communist propaganda in the West is a nuisance to constructive-minded people.

STALIN: Of course the old system is breaking down, decaying. That is true. But it is also true that new efforts are being made by other methods, by every means, to protect, to save this dying system. You draw a wrong conclusion from a correct postulate. You rightly state that the old world is breaking down. But you are wrong in thinking that it is breaking down of its own accord. No, the substitution of one social system for another is a complicated and long revolutionary process. It is not simply a spontaneous process, but a struggle, it is a process connected with the clash of classes. Capitalism is decaying, but it must not be compared simply with a tree which has decayed to such an extent that it must fall to the ground of its own accord. No, revolution, the substitution of one social system for another, has always been a struggle, a painful and a cruel struggle, a life and death struggle. And every time the people of the new world came into power, they had to defend themselves against the attempts of the old world to restore the old order by force; these people of the new world always had to be on the alert, always had to be ready to repel the attacks of the old world upon the new system.

Yes, you are right when you say that the old social system is breaking down; but it is not breaking down of its own accord. Take Fascism, for example. Fascism is a reactionary force which is trying to preserve the old world by means of violence. What will you do with the fascists? Argue with them? Try to convince them? But this will have no effect upon them at all. Communists do not in the least idealize the methods of violence. But they, the Communists, do not want to be taken by surprise, they cannot count on the old world voluntarily departing from the stage, they see that the old system is violently defending itself, and that is why the Communists say to the working class: Answer violence with violence; do all you can to prevent the old dying order from crushing you, do not permit it to put manacles on your hands, on the hands with which you will overthrow the old system. As you see, the Communists regard the substitution of one social system for another not simply as a spontaneous and peaceful process but as a complicated, long and violent process. Communists cannot ignore facts.

WELLS: But look at what is now going on in the capitalist world. The collapse is not a simple one; it is the outbreak of reactionary violence which is degenerating to gangsterism. And it seems to me that when it comes to a conflict with reactionary and unintelligent violence, socialists can appeal to the law, and instead of regarding the police as the enemy they should support them in the fight against the reactionaries. I think that it is useless operating with the methods of the old rigid insurrectionary socialism.

STALIN: The Communists base themselves on rich historical experience which teaches that obsolete classes do not voluntarily abandon the stage of history. Recall the history of England in the seventeenth century. Did not many say that the old social system had decayed? But did it not, nevertheless, require a Cromwell to crush it by force?

WELLS: Cromwell operated on the basis of the constitution and in the name of constitutional order.

STALIN: In the name of the constitution he resorted to violence, beheaded the king, dispersed Parliament, arrested some and beheaded others!

Or take an example from our history. Was it not clear for a long time that the tsarist system was decaying, was breaking down? But how much blood had to be shed in order to overthrow it?

And what about the October Revolution? Were there not plenty of people who knew that we alone, the Bolsheviks, were indicating the only correct way out? Was it not clear that Russian capitalism had decayed? But you know how great was the resistance, how much blood had to be shed in order to defend the October Revolution from all its enemies, internal and external.

Or take France at the end of the eighteenth century. Long before 1789 it was clear to many how rotten the royal power, the feudal system was. But a popular insurrection, a clash of classes was not, could not, be avoided. Why? Because the classes which must abandon the stage of history are the last to become convinced that their role is ended. It is impossible to convince them of this. They think that the fissures in the decaying edifice of the old order can be mended, that the tottering edifice of the old order can be repaired and saved. That is why dying classes take to arms and resort to every means to save their existence as a ruling class.

WELLS: But there were not a few lawyers at the head of the Great French Revolution.

STALIN: Do you deny the role of the intelligentsia in revolutionary movements? Was the Great French Revolution a lawyers' revolution and not a popular revolution, which achieved victory by rousing vast masses of the people against feudalism and championed the interests of the Third Estate? And did the lawyers among the leaders of the Great French Revolution act in accordance with the laws of the old order? Did they not introduce new, bourgeois-revolutionary laws?

The rich experience of history teaches that up to now not a single class has voluntarily made way for another class. There is no such precedent in world history. The Communists have learned this lesson of history. Communists would welcome the voluntary departure of the bourgeoisie. But such a turn of affairs is improbable; that is what experience teaches. That is why the Communists want to be prepared for the worst and call upon the working class to be vigilant, to be prepared for battle. Who wants a captain who lulls the vigilance of his army, a captain who does not understand that the enemy will not surrender, that he must be crushed? To be such a captain means deceiving, betraying the working class. That is why I think that what seems to you to be old-fashioned is in fact a measure of revolutionary expediency for the working class.

WELLS: I do not deny that force has to be used, but I think the forms of the struggle should fit as closely as possible to the opportunities presented by the existing laws, which must be defended against reactionary attacks. There is no need to disorganize the old system because it is disorganizing itself enough as it is. That is why it seems to me insurrection against the old order, against the law, is obsolete, old-fashioned. Incidentally, I deliberately exaggerate in order to bring the truth out more clearly. I can formulate my point of view in the following way: first, I am for order; second, I attack the present system in so far as it cannot assure order; third, I think that class-war propaganda may detach from socialism just those educated people whom socialism needs.

STALIN: In order to achieve a great object, an important social object, there must be a main force, a bulwark, a revolutionary class. Next it is necessary to organize the assistance of an auxiliary force for this main force; in this case this auxiliary force is the Party, to which the best forces of the intelligentsia belong. Just now you spoke about "educated people." But what educated people did you have in mind? Were there not plenty of educated people on the side of the old order in England in the seventeenth century, in France at the end of the eighteenth century, and in Russia in the epoch of the October Revolution? The old order had in its service many highly educated people who defended the old order, who opposed the new order. Education is a weapon the effect of which is determined by the hands which wield it, by who is to be struck down. Of course, the proletariat, socialism, need highly educated people. Clearly, simpletons cannot help the proletariat to fight for socialism, to build a new society. I do not underestimate the role of the intelligentsia; on the contrary, I emphasize it. The question is, however, which intelligentsia are we discussing? Because there are different kinds of intelligentsia.

WELLS: There can be revolution without a radical change in the educational system. It is sufficient to quote two examples: The example of the German Republic, which did not touch the old educational system, and therefore never became a republic; and the example of the British Labor Party, which lacks the determination to insist on a radical change in the educational system.

STALIN: That is a correct observation.

Permit me now to reply to your three points.

First, the main thing for the revolution is the existence of a social bulwark. This bulwark of the revolution is the working class.

Second, an auxiliary force is required, that which the Communists call a Party. To the Party belong the intelligent workers and those elements of the technical intelligentsia which are closely connected with the working class. The intelligentsia can be strong only if it combines with the working class. If it opposes the working class it becomes a cipher.

Third, political power is required as a lever for change. The new political power creates the new laws, the new order, which is revolutionary order.

I do not stand for any kind of order. I stand for order that corresponds to the interests of the working class. If, however, any of the laws of the old order can be utilized in the interests of the struggle for the new order, the old laws should be utilized. I cannot object to your postulate that the present system should be attacked in so far as it does not insure the necessary order for the people.

And, finally, you are wrong if you think that the Communists are enamored with violence. They would be very pleased to drop violent methods if the ruling class agreed to give way to the working class.

But the experience of history speaks against such an assumption.

WELLS: There was a case in the history of England, however, of a class voluntarily handing over power to another class. In the period between 1830 and 1870, the aristocracy, whose influence was still very considerable at the end of the eighteenth century, voluntarily, without a severe struggle, surrendered power to the bourgeoisie, which serves as a sentimental support of the monarchy. Subsequently, this transference of power led to the establishment of the rule of the financial oligarchy.

STALIN: But you have imperceptibly passed from questions of revolution to questions of reform. This is not the same thing. Don't you think that the Chartist movement played a great role in the Reforms in England in the nineteenth century?

WELLS: The Chartists did little and disappeared without leaving a trace.

STALIN: I do not agree with you. The Chartists, and the strike movement which they organized, played a great role; they compelled the ruling classes to make a number of concessions in regard to the franchise, in regard to abolishing the so-called "rotten boroughs," and in regard to some of the points of the "Charter." Chartism played a not unimportant historical role and compelled a section of the ruling classes to make certain concessions, reforms, in order to avert great shocks. Generally speaking, it must be said that of all the ruling classes, the ruling classes of England, both the aristocracy and the bourgeoisie, proved to be the cleverest, most flexible from the point of view of their class interests, from the point of view of maintaining their power. Take as an example, say, from modern history, the general strike in England in 1926. The first thing any other bourgeoisie would have done in the face of such an event, when the General Council of Trade Unions called for a strike, would have been to arrest the trade union leaders. The British bourgeoisie did not do that, and it acted cleverly from the point of view of its own interests. I cannot conceive of such a flexible strategy being employed by the bourgeoisie in the United States, Germany or France. In order to maintain their rule, the ruling classes of Great Britain have never forsworn small concessions, reforms. But it would be a mistake to think that these reforms were revolutionary.

WELLS: You have a higher opinion of the ruling classes of my country than I have. But is there a great difference between a small revolution and a great reform? Is not a reform a small revolution?

STALIN: Owing to pressure from below, the pressure of the masses, the bourgeoisie may sometimes concede certain partial reforms while remaining on the basis of the existing social-economic system. Acting in this way, it calculates that these concessions are necessary in order to preserve its class rule. This is the essence of reform. Revolution, however, means the transference of power from one class to another. That is why it is impossible to describe any reform as revolution. That is why we cannot count on the change of social systems taking place as an imperceptible transition from one system to another by means of reforms, by the ruling class making concessions.

WELLS: I am very grateful to you for this talk, which has meant a great deal to me. In explaining things to me you probably called to mind how you had to explain the fundamentals of socialism in the illegal circles before the revolution. At the present time there are in the world only two persons to whose opinion, to whose every word, millions are listening: you and Roosevelt. Others may preach as much as they like; what they say will never be printed or heeded. I cannot yet appreciate what has been done in your country; I only arrived yesterday. But I have already seen the happy faces of healthy men and women and I know that something very considerable is being done here. The contrast with 1920 is astounding.

STALIN: Much more could have been done had we Bolsheviks been cleverer.

WELLS: No, if human beings were cleverer. It would be a good thing to invent a five-year plan for the reconstruction of the human brain, which obviously lacks many things needed for a perfect social order. (*Laughter.*)

STALIN: Don't you intend to stay for the Congress of the Soviet Writers' Union?

WELLS: Unfortunately, I have various engagements to fulfill and I can stay in the U.S.S.R. only for a week. I came to see you and I am very satisfied by our talk. But I intend to discuss with such Soviet writers as I can meet the possibility of their affiliating to the P.E.N. club. This is an international organization of writers founded by Galsworthy; after his death I became president. The organization is still weak, but it has branches in many countries, and what is more important, the speeches of its members are widely reported in the press. It insists upon this free expression of opinion—even of opposition opinion. I hope to discuss this point with Gorky. I do not know if you are prepared yet for that much freedom here.

STALIN: We Bolsheviks call it "self-criticism." It is widely used in the U.S.S.R. If there is anything I can do to help you I shall be glad to do so.

WELLS: (*Expresses thanks.*)

STALIN: (*Expresses thanks for the visit.*)

INDEX

Abélard, Pierre, 329
Abraham, 352-53
Addison, Joseph, ix, 97, 124
Aeschylus, 302, 348, 528, 540, 541
Agrippa, 20
Albani, Francesco, 291
Albert, François, 547
Albert, Prince, 351
Alcibiades, 124, 539
Alembert, Jean le Rond d', 45, 83
Alexander (the Great), 20, 256, 285
Alexander, Tsar, 204, 206, 208-18,
   234
Algarotti, Count Francesco, 85, 86
Allingham, E. G., 45, 51
Allingham, Helen, 415, 416
Allingham, William, 415-17
Ambrogio, Fra, 10-13
Amyot, Père, 328-29
Anaxagoras, 518
Ancelot, Jacques Arsène, 301
Ancelot, Madame, 307
Angiolini, Carlo, 83
Antisthenes, 4
Apelles, 15
Apollodorus, 4, 7
Aquinas, Thomas, 284, 525
Aram, Eugene, 283
Archer, William, 475
Archesilas, 15
Aretine, Peter, 279
Ariosto, Ludovico, 84, 87-90, 279
Aristophanes, 540
Aristotle, 329, 518, 519
Armstrong, Margaret, 244
Arnault, Antoine, 299, 300, 305
Arnold, Matthew, 467-68
Asclepius, 7
Aubyret, 407
Audebrand, Philibert, see Chasles,
   Philarète
Augustine, Saint, 329, 525
Aurelius, Marcus, 20
Aurevilly, Barbey d', 405

Ayrton, William, 275-82

Baber, 541-42
Babeuf, François, Noël, 330, 332
Bacciochi, Felix, 200
Bach, Johann Sebastian, 371
Bacon, Francis, 252
Balcombe, Mr. (Purveyor to Na-
   poleon), 240
Balzac, Honoré de, 323, 327-36,
   408, 473, 491, 493-94, 548-49
Barrett, Charlotte Frances, 138
Bartholomé, Paul Albert, 531
Baudelaire, Pierre Charles, 406
Baxter, Richard, 122
Bazaine, François Achille, 393
Beaconsfield, Earl of, see Disraeli,
   Benjamin
Beaumont, Francis, 141, 283
Beauvau, Prince de, 46, 48-51
Beethoven, Ludwig van, 205, 365-
   70, 372, 382
Bell, Aubrey F. G., xxviii, 11
Belloc, Hilaire, 502
Benes, Eduard, 507
Bentham, Jeremy, 191, 192
Béranger, Pierre Jean de, 341
Berchtold, Count, 511, 512
Berkeley, Bishop George, xxix, 283,
   458
Berlioz, Louis Hector, 335
Bernard, Saint, 329
Bernard, Sir Francis, 101
Bernhardt, Sarah, 466
Berthelot, Pierre, 400, 402
Berthier, Prince of Neufchâtel, 224,
   228
Bertin, Louis, 305
Bertrand, General, 236, 238-40
Bertrand, Madame, 239
Besson, Faustin, 407
Beyle, Marie Henri, see Stendhal
Bianchi (Milan banker), 85
Biedermann, Flodoard von, 157,
   159, 163, 164, 177, 187

Bismarck, Otto Eduard Leopold, Prince von, xxii, 393-99
Bismarck-Bohlen, Count, 394, 398
Blaine, James G., 439
Blanc, Louis, 328
Blessington, Marguerite, Countess of, xxiv
Blount, Patty, 280, 282
Blücher, Gebhard Leberecht von, 234
Boccaccio, Giovanni, 84
Boïeldieu, François Adrian, 367
Boileau-Despréaux, Nicolas, 88, 89
Bolingbroke, Lord, 281
Bölöni, Mme. Georges, xxi, **xxiii,** 490-93, 495
Bonaparte, Caroline, 200-02
Bonaparte, Eliza, 200-01
Bonaparte, Hortense, 200-02
Bonaparte, Joseph, 200, 201
Bonaparte, Josephine, 196-202, 210, 231
Bonaparte, Letzia ("Mme.-Mère"), 200, 201
Bonaparte, Louis, 200, 201
Bonaparte, Napoleon, xxii, xxiv, xxvi, xxix, 156, 157, 163, 175, 195, 196-242, 255, 298, 455, 462, 477
Bonaparte, Pauline, 200-01
Boniface, Saint, 160
Bonsall, Harry, 432, 443
Bossuet, Jacques Bénigne, 311
Boston, Thomas, 272
Boswell, James, xxi, xxiii, xxviii-xxix, 33, 67-80, 83, 106-08, 110, 112-19, 121-25, 127-36, 138, 140, 152, 157, 181, 274, 276, 277, 280, 288, 501
Bourbon, family, 230
Bourdelle, Emile Antoine, 545, 550
Bourget, Paul, 491
Bourrienne, Louis Antoine Fauvelet, xxiv
Boyd, Ernest, 83, 84
Brackel, Baron de, 80
Brackel, Mme. de, 80
Bradley, George C., 416

Brandes, Georg, 180, 181, 204
Breaudrique, David de, 409
Briand, Aristide, 531
Brinton, Daniel Garrison, 430, 432, 433, 450-51
Bristol, Lord, 190, 194, 195
Brook, Lord, 283
Brown, Sir Thomas, 277
Browning, Robert, 243, 415
Brutus, 23, 24, 26-31
Bryant, William Cullen, 430
Bucke, Richard M., 428, 429, 439, 440-42, 444, 449
Buller, Sir Arthur, 351
Bulwer-Lytton, Edward George, 283
Bunyan, John, 503, 504
Burke, Edmund, 100, 122, 124, 137, 143, 145, 146
Burney, Captain James, 275
Burney, Dr. Charles, 139, 146, 148
Burney, Fanny, xxiii, 108, 137-39, 141-51
Burney, J., 280
Burney, Martin Charles, 275, 280, 284
Burns, Robert, 450, 455, 461
Burroughs, John, 432, 436, 447
Burton, Robert, vii
Butler, Joseph, 283
Byron, George Gordon, Lord, xxii, xxiv, 34, 188, 189, 243-45, 251-73, 325, 338-39, 415, 416, 418, 460, 504

Cable, George Washington, 484
Caesar, Augustus, 20
Caesar, Julius, xxii, 20, 23, 24, 26-31, 205
Caillavet, Mme. de, 490
Calas, Jean, 408, 409
Calderon de la Barca, Pedro, 245
Caligula, 20
Campis, Gerhard de, 160
Campos, Deoclecio de, 24
Canby, Henry Seidel, 429
Capacelli, Marquis Albergati, 93, 94
Capek, Karel, 516-25
Capitolinus, Julius, 20

Carafa, Michele, 363
Carlyle, Jane, 345-47, 349-50, 353, 356, 357, 360, 462
Carlyle, Thomas, 341, 344-61, 415, 455, 462
Carmichael, Miss, 143
Carpani, Giuseppe, 369, 370, 373
Carpeau, Jean Baptiste, 548
Carpenter, Edward, 438
Carroll, Lewis, 468
Carvalho, Léon, 366
Casanova, Giacomo, 81-99
Cassius, 23, 24, 26-31
Cato, 28
Catt, Henri de, xxi, xxiii, xxvii, 33-43
Catullus, 417
Caulaincourt, Armand Augustin Louis de, xxiv, 210-21, 224, 231
Caylus, Comte de, 46
Cazauran, A. R., 385-87, 389, 390
Cebes, 5
Cenci, Beatrice, 251
Chaboulon, Fleury de, xxix, 231-34
Chapelain, Jean, 95
Charlemagne, 203
Charles I, King, 251, 503
Charles III, King, 122
Charles Alexander, Crown Prince, 187
Charles Augustus, Duke, 158, 159
Charles-Edmond, 406, 407
Chasles, Philarète, 324-26
Chatelain, Georges, 304
Chatêlet, Gabrielle du, 186
Chaucer, Geoffrey, 278-79
Chaulieu, Guillaume Amfrye de, 39
Chavigny, M. de, 81, 82
Chénier, André, 305
Chennevières, Philippe, 406
Cherubini, Maria Luigi, 367
Chesterton, Gilbert Keith, 499-506
Chew, Samuel C., 261
Christopher, Saint, 160
Chubb, Percival, 438
Cicero, 309
Cimabue, Giovanni, 284, 286
Cimarosa, Domenico, 370
Clarke, Helen, 449

Claudin, Gustave, 407, 409
Claudius, 20
Clemenceau, Georges, 527-550
Clemenceau, Michel, 549
Clemens, Samuel, see Twain, Mark
Cobbett, William, 256
Coccaius, Merlin, 92, 95
Cockburn, Admiral Sir George, 236, 239, 241
Coleridge, Samuel Taylor, 273, 274, 284, 292, 349, 415, 417-18
Colman, George, 140
Colonna, Vittoria, xxvii-viii, 9-16, 19-22
Colvin, Sidney, 9
Comte, Auguste, 519
Condillac, Étienne Bonnot de, 45
Congreve, Sir William, 187
Constantine, Emperor, 90
Conti, Abbé, 86
Conway, Moncure, 432, 436
Cook, Captain James, 275
Cooper, James Fenimore, 299, 303-04
Cooper, Samuel, 101
Copernicus, Nikolaus, 91
Coppée, François, 491
Cornbury, Lord, 281
Corneille, Pierre, xxii, 303, 316
Cornwall, Barry, 274
Cotta, Johann Friedrich, 205
Cottin, Marie, 303
Courtin, Abbé, 39
Courtois, Adele, 410
Cousin, Victor, 537
Coutts, Thomas, 296
Cowley, Abraham, 283
Crébillon, Prosper Jolyot de, 95, 96
Crémieux, Adolphe, 377
Crito, 4-7
Critobulus, 4
Crockford, John, 337-42
Cromwell, Oliver, 255, 346, 354, 503, 510-11, 562
Curtis, George William, 430, 447
Cuvier, Baron Georges, 307

Dana, Charles A., 430, 436

Dance, George, 292

Daniell, John Frederic, 187, 188

Dante Alighieri, 23, 24, 26-31, 91, 279, 297, 298, 305, 461

Danton, Georges Jacques, 330

Darius, 548

Dartmouth, Lord, 104

Daru, Pierre Antoine, Count, 206

Daudet, Alphonse, 414

Davidson, John, 489

Davout, Louis Nicolas, 217

Davray, Henri, 455, 457, 458, 468

Decker, Thomas, 283

Delavigne, Casimir, 301

Delécluze, Etienne, 307-14

Demetrius, 20

Demosthenes, 529, 541

Denis, Mademoiselle (niece of Voltaire), 83, 88-90, 93, 99

Dennis, John, 295

De Quincey, Thomas, 273

Deveria, Achille, 325

Dick, Sir Alexander, 134

Diderot, Denis, 44, 45, 54, 57, 64-66

Dietmar, 160-62, 164

Dilly, Charles, 109, 110, 113, 114, 119, 121, 122

Dilly, Edward, 109, 110, 113, 114, 119, 121, 122

Diogenitus, 20

Dion (the Greek), 20

Disraeli, Benjamin, vii, 341

Dobson, Austin, 138

Donaldson, Thomas, 439-42, 452

Donne, John, 264, 278

Doren, Carl Van, 101

Dowden, Edward, 430, 435

Doyle, Sir Arthur Conan, 476

Dreyfus, Alfred, 490, 527-28

Drinkwater, John, 259, 262

Drummond, William, 283

Dryden, John, 281, 282, 295

Duclos, Charle Pinot, 45-51

Dudley, Thomas, 452

Duffy, Sir C. G., 344

Dumas, Alexandre (père), 298-306, 316, 323, 340, 406

Du Mesnil, Antoine, 400, 402

Dumesnil, René, 405, 406, 407

Duns Scotus, Johannes, 284

Dürer, Albrecht, 17

Dyer, George, 275, 284

Eakins, Thomas, 448, 449

Eckermann, Johann Peter, xxi, xxiii, xxvi, xxviii, 34, 157, 180, 187, 190, 191, 326

Edman, Irwin, 4

Edward VII, King, 351, 502

Elizabeth, Queen, 350

Ellis, Havelock, 83, 181, 190

Emerson, Ralph Waldo, vii, ix, 353, 430, 448

Engel, Friedrich, 510

Épinay, Louise Florence Pétronille d', xxi, 45-49, 51

Este, family, 90

Euclid, 4

Fawkes, Guy, 285

Fayette, Mme. de la, 304

Ferry, Jules, 547

Fesch, Monseigneur, 200

Feuillet, Octave, 408

Fichte, Johann Gottlieb, 170

Fielding, Henry, viii, 147, 282

Flaubert, Gustave, 406-08, 410, 413, 414

Fletcher, John, 140, 283

Fletcher, William, 262

Flint, F. S., 34

Foch, Ferdinand, 543

Folengo, Teofilo, 93

Fontenelle, Bernard le Bovier, 85

Ford, Bessie, 438

Ford, Henry, 558

Ford, Isabella, 438

Fordyce, George, 124

Forman, Buxton, 436

Fox, Charles James, 83

France, Anatole, xxii, 490-97

Francis I, Emperor, 220

Francis II, Emperor, 222-26, 228, 229

Franklin, Benjamin, 100-05, 356

Franklin-Bouillon, Henry, 547

Frederick II (the Great), xxii, 32-43, 44, 67, 462
Frederick Augustus, Emperor, 223
Frederick William I, 42, 43
Fréron, Elie Catherine, 82
Fritzinger, Warren, 429, 453
Froissart, Jean, 304
Furness, Horace Howard, 441

Galantiere, Lewis, 405, 409, 411
Galilei, Galileo, 297, 311
Galsworthy, John, 566
Galton, Francis, 502
Gamba, Pietro, 259, 261, 273
Gambetta, Léon, 396, 400
Garland, Hamlin, 437, 438
Garrick, David, 108, 122, 123, 137, 140, 141, 152-54, 282, 294
Gautier, Théophile, 323, 406-12
Gavarni, S. G. C., 406
Gay, John, 282
Genseric, 401
George III, King, 101, 104, 121, 122
George, Saint, 480
Gérard, Baron, 307
Gessler, 378
Ghengis Khan, 285
Gherardesca, Count Ugolino della, 297
Gherardi, Marchese, 130
Ghirlandaio, Il, 284, 286
Giannotti, Donato, 11, 23-31
Gibbon, Edward, 67, 83, 122, 124
Gilchrist, Anne, 438
Gilder, Richard Watson, 444, 453
Giotto di Bondone, 284, 286
Gladstone, William Ewart, 455, 461
Glover, Arnold, 275
Gluck, C. W. von, 366, 374, 376, 382
Godwin, William, 274, 293-94, 297
Goethe, Johann Wolfgang von, xxii, xxix, 33, 156-96, 204-09, 222, 236, 298, 303-05, 339, 341
Goldoni, Carlo, 93, 94
Goldsmith, Oliver, 119, 120, 122, 123, 182, 280
Goncourt, Edmond de, x, xxix, 400-14

Goncourt, Jules de, 404-14
Gooch, George Peabody, 211
Goodyear, A. C., 275
Gorky, Maxim, 566
Gorman, Herbert, 300
Gosse, Edmond, 415
Gourgaud, Gaspard, 236
Grant, Ulysses S., 386, 392
Grétry, A. E. M., 380
Greville, Sir Fulke, 277, 278
Grimm, Baron von, 46, 53, 54, 64, 65
Guiccioli, Countess, 245
Guido, Reni, 52, 290, 291
Guizard, Louis LeBlanc de, 311
Guizot, François P. G., 354
Gunter, Archibald Clavering, 385

Hadrian, 20
Hafiz, 251
Halévy, Ludovic, 407
Haller, Albert de, 82, 98
Handel, G. F., 283
Hannibal, 234
Hanoteau, Jean, 211
Hardy, Florence Emily, 475, 476
Hardy, Thomas, 475-89
Harned, Mrs. Thomas, 430, 431
Harned, Thomas, 428, 429, 447
Harry, Jenny, 109-113
Hartley, David, 283
Hartmann, Karl von, 487
Hatzfeldt, Count, 394, 396
Hawkins, Sir John, 140, 141
Hawkins, Laetitia Matilda, 108, 152
Haydn, Franz Josef, 179, 371
Hazlitt, William, 274, 275, 278-79, 283-97
Heeren, Arnold, 355
Hegel, G. W. F., 340
Heine, Heinrich, xxix, 181, 322-43, 409
Heine, Mathilde, 324, 335, 337
Henley, William Ernest, 288
Heraclitus, 523
Herodotus, 538, 548
Hérold, Louis Joseph, 367
Hertz, Emanuel, 385
Hervé, Gustave, 544

Heyne, Christian Gottlob, 355
Hillsborough, Earl of, 100-05
Hobbes, Thomas, 97, 283
Hobhouse, John Cam, 255, 256
Hogarth, William, 283
Hollanda, Francesco de, xxviii
Homer, 91, 95, 282, 298, 305, 347-48, 417, 505
Hood, Thomas, 283
Horace, 86, 88, 89, 96, 97, 127, 131, 264, 417
Houben, Heinrich, 322
Houdetot, Comtesse d', 54, 55, 64
Houdon, Jean Antoine, 548
Housman, A. E., 460
Housman, Laurence, xxv-vi, 454-61, 463-64, 466-69, 472, 473
Houssaye, Arsène, 407
Howe, P. P., 275, 288
Hugo, Victor, 301, 306, 315-21, 323, 341, 408, 411
Humboldt, Alexander von, 359
Hume, David, vii, 283, 294, 483, 519
Huret, Jules, x
Hutchinson, Governor Thomas, 102, 103

Ibsen, Henrik, 437, 476, 504
Ictinus, 535
Ingersoll, Robert, 430-33, 439
Irving, Washington, 353
Iscariot, Judas, 29, 285
Isham, Lt. Col. Ralph H., 69

James, Henry, 460
Jefferson, Thomas, xxii
Jeffrey, Lord Francis, 291
Jerrold, Harvey, 455, 464, 472, 473
Jesus Christ, 193, 267, 269, 311, 420, 502, 511
Jewsbury, Geraldine, 345, 346, 356, 360
Joan of Arc, xxvii
John, Saint, 87
Johnston, Dr. J., 431, 437
Johnson, Samuel, viii, xxii, xxiii, xxvi, 33, 68, 69, 74, 75, 78, 106-55, 277, 280, 295, 530

Joinville, Jean Sire de, 304
Jonson, Ben, 283
Josephson, Matthew, 64, 69, 307, 308, 405
Jouffroy, T., 355
Jouy, Victor Joseph de, 300
Jowett, Benjamin, 4
Junius, 282
Juvenal, 264

Keats, John, 415, 416, 418
Keith, Lord-Marshall George, 67, 68
Kemeri, Sander, see Bölöni, Mme. Georges
Kennan, George, 420-26
Kennedy, James, xxiv, 259-73
Kennedy, William Sloane, 438, 439
Kent, Muriel, 237
Knowles, Mrs. ("The Quaker Lady"), 109-17
Knebel, Karl Ludwig von, 164
Kneller, Sir Godfrey, 128
Knighton, Mrs. William, 344, 346
Knighton, William, 344-61
Knox, John, 504
Kock, Paul de, 408
Koerber, Ernst von, 512
Kotzebue, August, 209
Kronenberger, Louis, 69, 106

Ladd, Lady, 145
Lafayette, Marie Joseph, Marquis de, 235
La Fontaine, 285
La Forgue, Jean, 84
Lamartine, Alphonse Marie Louis de, xxvii, 301, 305, 354
Lamb, Charles, 274-85
Lamb, John, 275
Lamb, Mary, 274-76, 280, 282
Lamber, Juliette, 406
Lamothe-Langon, Baron de Étienne-Léon, 200, 201
Lampridius, Helius, 20
Landor, Walter Savage, xxviii, 156, 255
Langon, Baron, xxvi, xxix
Langton, Bennett, 119, 122, 131, 136

Langton, Mrs. Bennett, 130
La Rochefoucault, François de, 285
Las Cases, Emmanuel Augustin
  Dieudonné de, xxiv, 236, 238,
  242
Lauriston, Jacques, 212, 216
Lavater, Johann Kaspar, 160
Lazarus, Emma, 453
Lazzarini, Abbé, 86
Lee, Dr. Arthur, 102
Legouvé, Gabriel, 305
Leibnitz, G. W. von, 283, 526
Lemercier, Louis Jean, 300
Lemoinne, J. M. E., 341, 342
Lenclos, Ninon de, 284, 285
Lengyel, Emil, 492
Lenin, Nikolay, 552, 553
Leo X, Pope, 90
Lesage, Alain René, 303
Lescaut, Manon, 341
Lessing, G. E., 207, 355
Levasseur, Thérèse, 67, 68, 70, 75,
  78-80
Levett, Robert, 143
Levetzow, Ulrike von, 180
Libaire, George, 211
Lille, Count of, 202
Lincoln, Abraham, 384-95
Linguet, S. N. H., 146
Liszt, Franz, 363, 364
Liubatovitch, Olga, 422
Livy, 86
Lobe, Johann Christian, 176-79
Lodge, Sir Oliver, 476
Longfellow, Henry Wadsworth, vii,
  430
Lot, 352-53
Louis XIV, King, 208
Louis XV, King, 45
Louis XVI, King, 202
Louis XVIII, King, 232
Louis-Philippe, Duc d'Orléans, 298-
  99, 300, 306, 327, 354
Lowe, Charles, 394
Lowe, Sir Hudson, 236-42
Lowell, James Russell, 433
Lucan, 303
Lucian, xxviii

Luden, Heinrich, xxix, 156, 157,
  163-75
Ludwig, Emil, 508-14
Luis, Infante Dom, 19
Luther, Martin, 160, 329, 510, 525
Lycurgus, 330

Macaire, Robert, 397
Macaulay, Thomas Babington, ix
Machen, Arthur, 83
MacMahon, Marie Edme, Count,
  393
MacVicar, J. G., 345
Maistre, Joseph de, 308-11
Malahide, Lord Talbot de, 69
Malcolm, Admiral Sir Polteney,
  237-42
Malcolm, Lady, xxii, xxiii, 238, 240,
  242
Malherbe, François de, 36
Malthus, Thomas Robert, 412
Mansfield, Lord, 281
Marcolini, Camillo, 223
Marconi, Guglielmo, 484
Maret, Hughes, 205, 223, 224
Marie-Antoinette, Empress, 202,
  492
Marie Louise, Empress, 210
Marlowe, Christopher, 283
Mars, Anne François Boutet, 316-21
Martelli, Pierre-Jacques, 95-96
Martet, Jean, 529-50
Martial, 181
Martin, Frederick, 360
Marvast, Armand, 377-78
Marx, Karl, 327, 516
Mary, Queen of Scots, xxvii
Masaryk, Thomas Garrigue, 507-26
Matthews, William, ix
Maurras, Charles, 491
Maximilian, Emperor, 16
McClellan, George B., 387, 388
McKay, David, 429
Medici, family, 90
Medwin, Tom, 253
Mendelssohn-Bartholdy, Felix, 176-
  79, 323, 372

Metellus, family, 20
Metternich, Clemens Wenzel, Prince von, xxiv, 196, 222-29, 373
Meyer, Hans Heinrich, 365
Meyerbeer, Giacomo, 323, 335, 374
Michelangelo Buonarroti, xxvii-xxix, 8-19, 21-31, 179, 493
Michelet, Jules, xxvii
Michotte, E., xxi, xxiii, xxvi, 362-65
Mill, John Stuart, 481, 487
Milton, John, 188, 252, 280, 305, 338, 417
Miranda, Angel de, 399
Mirat, Crescentia Eugenie, see Heine, Mathilde
Mirbeau, Octave, 544
Mitford, William, 256
Molière, 94, 284, 298, 302, 303
Monet, Claude, 542-45, 547
Monet, Mme. Jean, 545
Monet, Michel, 545-46
Monstrelet, Enguerrand de, 304
Montagu, Elizabeth, 138, 139, 144, 146-49
Montagu, Lady Mary Wortley, 282
Montaigne, Michel Eyquem, vii, 284
Montholon, Charles Tristan de, xxiv, 223, 236, 238, 241
Montholon, Mme. Charles Tristan de, 238, 242
Montluc, Blaise de, 304
Moore, Tom, 255
Mordacq, Jean-Jules-Henri, 536
Moreas, Jean, 496
Morgan, J. P., 558
Morris, Harrison, 444-45
Morse, Sidney, 446
Moses, 330, 335
Mozart, Wolfgang Amadeus, 178, 179, 307, 365, 369, 371, 372, 376, 382, 383
Müller, Friedrich, 205, 206
Müller, Johannes, 168, 174
Mummius, 302
Münzer, Thomas, 329-30

Murat, Prince, 200-02
Muratori, Ludovico, 91
Murray, John, 254, 255, 258, 260
Musäus, Johann Karl, 159, 161
Musset, Alfred de, 323, 411

Napier, Mrs. Alexander, 223
Napoleon III, Emperor, 393, 394, 536
Nefftzer, Auguste, 400, 406
Nero, 13, 20
Nerval, Gerard de, 323
Newcastle, Duchess of, 284
Newman, Ernest, 363
Newman, John Henry, Cardinal, 349, 359
Newton, Sir Isaac, 85, 86, 115, 276
Nicolson, Harold, 235
Nodier, Charles, 325
Noel, Roden, 434, 435
Northcote, James, 276, 287-96

O'Connor, William, 430
Oldenburg, Prince of, 216
Ollanda, Francesco d', 10-14, 17-19, 21-22
O'Sullivan, John L., 394
Otranto, Duke of, 234
Oumansky, Constantine, 552
Oxenford, John, 190

Paine, Thomas, 437
Paoli, Pasquale, 130
Paradisi, Count, 93
Parma, Duke of, 94
Parny, Évariste de, 305
Pascal, Blaise, vii
Pasic, Nikola, 511
Paul, Saint, 10-12, 77, 117, 525
Paul, Tsar, 217
Paul III, Pope, 8, 9, 13-15
Pausanias, 538
Pearson, Hesketh, xxvi, 455, 474, 500-01
Pepys, Samuel, xxiv
Pergolesi, Giovanni Battista, 370
Pericles, 529

Persius, 264
Pescara, Marquis of, 9
Petrarch, Francesco, 91, 252
Petreo, Antonio, 23-25, 31
Phaedo, 4, 7
Phidias, 408, 493, 531, 548
Phillips, Edward, 275, 282
Phillips, Walter Alison, 223
Phipps, R. W., 238
Phocion, 538
Pigault-Lebrun, C. A. G., 303
Pinero, Arthur Wing, 504
Piozzi, Gabriele, 138-39
Piozzi, Mrs. Gabriele, see Thrale, Hester
Pius VII, Pope, 200
Plato, xxv, xxviii, 4, 245, 252, 270, 311, 329, 501, 516, 517, 522, 541
Plautus, 303
Pliny, 21
Plutarch, 20
Polignac, family, 202
Poincaré, Raymond, 528, 531, 543, 547
Pompadour, Jeanne Antoinette Marquise de, 45
Pompey, 20
Ponsard, François, 408
Pope, Alexander, 264, 279-82, 290, 295
Poquelin, Jean Baptiste, see Molière
Pottle, Frederick A., 69, 107
Poussin, Nicolas, 52
Pownall, John, 101-04
Prim, Marshal Juan, 396
Priscianese, Francesco, 23, 24
Proudhon, Pierre Joseph, 328
Ptolemy, 20
Putnam, Charles Allen, 386, 387, 390-92
Putnam, Mrs., 384, 386-91

Quantz, Johann Joachim, 32, 41, 43
Quinault, Mme., 44, 46-52, 53, 54, 62

Rabelais, François, 284
Rachel, Élisa Félix, 466
Racine, Jean Baptiste, xxii, 32, 33, 36, 43, 285, 316, 413
Raczynski, Count A., xxviii
Raleigh, Sir Walter, 169-70
Raphael, Santi, 52, 179, 291
Rapp, Jean, 217
Reade, Charles, 349
Récamier, Madame Jeanne, 341
Regnier, Henri de, 84
Regnier, Mathurin, 305
Renan, Ernest, x, 400-04, 406
Renoir, Pierre Auguste, 544, 545
Retz, Cardinal, 304
Reynolds, Sir Joshua, xxvi, 108, 122, 124, 130-33, 137, 143, 146, 152-55, 287, 290, 292, 295, 296
Rhys, Ernest, 430, 436
Riccio, Luigi del, 23-25, 31
Richardson, Samuel, 282, 291, 479
Richelieu, Cardinal, 304
Ridolfii, Cardinal, 24
Riemer, Friedrich Wilhelm, 191, 193
Ristori, Adelaide, 466
Robespierre, Maximilien, 330, 335
Rockefeller, John D., 558
Rodin, Auguste, xxii, 490-97, 548-49
Ronsard, Pierre de, 305
Roosevelt, Franklin Delano, 552-57, 566
Roseberry, Lord, 33
Ross, Robert, 455-59, 461-62, 464-66, 468, 472-74
Rossetti, William, 437
Rossini, Gioachino Antonio, xxvi, xxix, 307, 362-83
Rothschild, family, 372
Rousseau, Jean Jacques, viii, xxiii, xxv, 35, 44, 46, 53-80, 284, 411
Rude, François, 548
Rumiants of, Count, 215, 216
Ruskin, John, 416
Russell, Lord John, 357

St. Evremont, Charles de, 285
Saint-Lambert, Marquis de, 45-52, 54, 58
St. Pierre, Bernardin de, 292

Saint-Simon, Claude Henri de, 304, 328
Saint-Simon, Louis de R., xxiv
Saint-Victor, Paul, 400-03
Sainte-Beuve, Charles Augustin, 406, 411-12
Salieri, Antonio, 368, 370
Sallust, 86
Salzmann, C. G., 160
Sanborn, Franklin B., 447
Sand, George, 340, 406, 411
Sandburg, Carl, 384
Sargent, John Singer, 460
Sarraut, Albert, 536
Sarrazin, Gabriel, 444
Scherer, Edmond, 411, 413
Schiller, J. C. F. von, 158, 181, 182, 191, 207
Schopenhauer, Arthur, viii
Scipio, Africanus, 21
Scott, Geoffrey, 69
Scott, Sir Walter, 110, 188, 256, 293, 298, 299, 303-04, 462
Scribe, Augustin Eugène, 326
Seingalt, Jacques Casanova, *see* Casanova, Giacomo
Seneca, 356
Severus, Emperor Alexander, 20
Seward, Anna, xxiii, 108, 110, 112, 113, 117, 140
Seward, William, 140
Shadwell, Thomas, 295
Shakespeare, William, 114, 182, 205, 283, 285, 298, 302, 338, 341, 342, 355, 496, 503-05
Shaw, George Bernard, 498-506
Shelley, Mary, 243, 244, 246, 247, 253, 255
Shelley, Percy Bysshe, xxiv, 243-53, 255-56, 258, 261, 269, 270, 415, 416, 418, 436, 504
Sheridan, Robert Brinsley, 124
Siddons, Sarah, 466
Sidney, Sir Philip, 277
Silvester, Saint, 90
Simmias, 4, 5
Sinzendorff, Count de, 35
Smith, Sydney, ix

Socrates, xxv, 3-7, 501, 530, 539, 541
Solon, 330
Sophocles, 245, 348, 487
Soret, Frédéric, 187-89, 190-93, 195
Soult, Nicolas Jean de Dieu, 206
Soumet, Alexandre, 301
Spencer, Herbert, 481
Spenser, Edmund, 279, 280
Spinoza, Baruch, 245
Spontini, Gasparo, 374
Spottiswoode, John, 130
Staël-Holstein, Anne Louise Germaine, viii
Stalin, Joseph, xxvii, 551-66
Stanford, Earl of, 229
Stanton, Edwin McM., 384, 386-92
Stedman, Edmund C., 430, 446
Stein, Charlotte von, 159
Stendhal, xxix, 307-14
Sterne, Laurence, 182, 325
Stevenson, Robert Louis, 299, 467
Stoddard, Richard Henry, 431
Strachey, Lytton, 33, 34
Stuart, Mary, 504
Sue, Eugène, 323, 327-36
Sulla, 30
Swift, Benjamin, 460
Swift, Jonathan, 255
Swinburne, Algernon Charles, 244, 430
Symonds, John Addington, 31, 430, 433-35
Symons, Arthur, 83
Syrus, Publilius, vii

Tacitus, 134, 174, 205, 208, 325
Taine, Hippolyte, 406, 410-12
Talfourd, Thomas Noon, 274
Talleyrand-Périgord, Charles de, 157, 195, 206, 207
Talma, François Joseph, 300
Tamerlane, 285
Tasso, Torquato, 87
Tassoni, Alessandro, 91
Tchernychev, 212, 213
Temple, Sir William, 133
Tennant, Sir J. E., 353

Tennyson, Alfred Lord, 415-18, 430, 432
Tennyson, Frederick, 418
Terpsion, 4
Tesla, Nikola, 484
Thackeray, William Makepeace, 299, 415
Themistocles, 256, 538
Thibaut, B. F., 168
Thiers, Louis Adolphe, 223, 354, 396, 412
Thirlwall, Connop, 348
Thomas, Saint, 91, 329
Thomson, James, viii, 279
Thrale, Henry, 138, 142, 143, 151, 154, 155
Thrale, Hester Lynch, xxiii, 108, 118, 137-40, 142-53
Titian, 279, 291
Titus, 20
Tolomei, Lattantio, 10-13, 15-16, 19, 21, 22
Tolstoy, Leo, 419-27
Traherne, Thomas, vii
Trajan, 20
Traubel, Horace, xxiv-xv, 429, 431, 436, 437, 438, 441, 445, 446, 448, 449, 451, 453
Trelawny, Edward John, xxiv, 243, 254-58, 259
Trochu, Louis Jules, 402
Trollope, Thomas Adolphus, xxvii, xxviii
Turgenieff, Ivan, 406, 413, 414
Twain, Mark, 484

Uhland, Johann Ludwig, 305
Untermeyer, Louis, 323, 328
Urbino (color-grinder), 11, 13
Ursins, Juvenal des, 304
Usslar, Lieutenant von, 394

Valleyo, Angel de, 394-99
Vere, Aubrey de, 416, 417-18
Vezin, Hermann, 466
Vigny, Alfred de, 535
Villars, C. L. H. de, 304
Vinci, Leonardo da, 182, 183, 285
Virgil, 305, 355, 417

Voltaire, François Marie Arouet de, 33, 44, 46, 51, 52, 68, 78, 81-99, 180, 185, 186, 284, 305, 408, 409, 462

Wagner, Gottlieb Heinrich Adolf, 166
Wagner, Minna, 364
Wagner, Richard, xxii, xxiii, xxix, 362-83
Waldman, Milton, 530
Waldstein, Count, 83
Wallenstein, A. E. W. von, 509
Waller, A. R., 275
Walpole, Horace, xxiv
Washington, George, xxii, 250, 356
Weber, Karl Maria von, 367, 368, 372, 376, 382
Webster, Daniel, vii
Webster, John, 283
Weill, Alexandre, 327, 328, 336
Weimar, Duchess of, 208
Weimar, Duke of, 205, 208
Wellington, Duke of, 222, 233, 234
Wells, H. G., xxvii, 551-66
Wesley, John, 352
Whistler, James, 460
Whitman, Walt, xxiv-xv, 428-53
Whittier, John Greenleaf, 430
Wieland, Christoph Martin, 159, 207, 208
Wilde, Oscar, xxvi, 439, 441, 454-74
Wilkes, John, 140
William I, King, 399
Williams, Edward, 244, 245, 252
Williams, F. H., 443
Williams, Jane, 244, 245, 252
Williams, Talcott, 429, 445
Wilson, Sir Arthur, 237
Wordsworth, 416-18, 460
Württemberg, King of, 208
Wycherley, William, 294
Wynn, Sir Watkin, 292

Xenophon, 539
Xerxes, 538, 547-50

Zelter, Carl Friedrich, 176-79
Zola, Emile, 491, 528
Zwingli, Ulrich, 525

About the Editor

HERETOFORE Louis Biancolli has been known to the public primarily as a music critic. For twenty years he has been on the musical staff of the *New York World-Telegram,* and for the past seven years has been co-annotator of the New York Philharmonic-Symphony programs. He has presented several series of radio programs, is co-author of *The Concert Companion,* published in 1947 by Whittlesey House, and, with Robert Bagar, has completely revised *The Victor Book of the Opera* to be published shortly by Simon and Schuster. In addition, he has contributed articles to many magazines. An inveterate student of language and literature, he received his training at New York University and Columbia University, is master of seven languages, ancient and modern, and one of the most widely read men in the country. Of Italian extraction, he is a New Yorker born and bred, and lives outside the city with his wife, daughter, and a huge library.